Religion and Politics
in the United States

Religion and Politics in the United States

Seventh Edition

Kenneth D. Wald and Allison Calhoun-Brown

ROWMAN & LITTLEFIELD
Lanham • Boulder • New York • Toronto • Plymouth, UK

Published by Rowman & Littlefield
4501 Forbes Boulevard, Suite 200, Lanham, Maryland 20706
www.rowman.com

10 Thornbury Road, Plymouth PL6 7PP, United Kingdom

British Library Cataloguing in Publication Information Available

Library of Congress Cataloging-in-Publication Data

Wald, Kenneth D.
  Religion and politics in the United States / Kenneth D. Wald and Allison Calhoun-Brown. — Seventh edition.
     pages cm
  Includes bibliographical references and index.
  ISBN 978-1-4422-2553-4 (cloth : alk. paper) — ISBN 978-1-4422-2554-1 (pbk. : alk. paper) — ISBN 978-1-4422-2555-8 (electronic) 1. Religion and politics—United States—History—21st century. 2. United States—Religion—1960–
3. United States—Politics and government—2001–2009. I. Calhoun-Brown, Allison, 1966– II. Title.
  BL2525.W35 2014
  322'.1097309051—dc23   2013047667

Printed in the United States of America

Contents

Figures and Tables

FIGURES

Preface

On Florida State Road 207 outside the small town of Hastings, there hangs a large banner fastened to a ranch fence. In bright red capital letters, it proclaims "Work Hard, Trust in God, Vote Republican." The sign, with its audacious claim that the GOP owns hard work and God, brought to mind an encounter some years earlier during a lecture tour in China. Following a talk about the importance of religion in American politics, a young woman approached Ken Wald with a question phrased as a statement. "Surely," she said, "all this superstition can't be a good thing in American life."

Although she probably didn't realize it, the Chinese student was in good company. For many observers, including some of our students, professional colleagues, many citizens, and foreign commentators, religious influence in American politics is a problem to be solved. These critics would seize on the arrogance of the ranch banner as a perfect indication of why religion is a toxic political force. Yet we have also encountered others who see the spiritual dimension as a resource with the capacity to improve the quality of American political life. Although we will devote attention to the impact of religion on the quality of democratic politics, our principal concern in this book is to sustain what was not so long ago an unfashionable claim that religion matters significantly in American public life.

Since its first edition, the central argument of this book remains that religion is more important in American politics than most people realize but in different ways than they imagine. That is, religious influences are visible in all aspects of political life—the ideas about politics we entertain, the behavior of political elites and ordinary citizens, the interpretation of public laws, and the development of government programs. The perspective of this volume also follows earlier editions in embracing a social-scientific approach to religion, explaining religion not in terms of supernatural forces but as an enterprise governed by normal patterns of human behavior. Like most social scientists, we also resist the opposite tendency to reduce religion to a biological or genetic trait. Supernaturalists may explain the survival of religion as God's will, while some natural scientists might attribute the persistence of religion in society to the sound dietary principles and healthy lifestyles of believers (see Koenig, McCullough, and Larson 2001). Although both explanations may be useful, the social scientist prefers to emphasize the operation of human consciousness and choice. Thus, chapter 1 invokes neither the hand of God nor the principles of evolution to explain why religion prospers in America. Instead, consistent with the social-scientific outlook, it calls attention to cognitive factors—humanity's apparent need to reduce uncertainty about its place in the universe—and elements of the social and political structure that encourage religious observance. The rest of the book follows suit.

This edition has been brought up to date by covering recent American elections and by incorporating material from the many new scholarly studies that have been published since the previous edition. We have also emphasized new trends that have emerged in the dynamic relationship between religion and politics. To name but a few, these include the religious dimensions of the debate over the Affordable Care Act, growing tensions between economic and religious conservatives in the Republican Party, the contribution of religion to political polarization, signs of change in the political priorities of the Catholic hierarchy, the political mobilization of the Religious Left, the boundaries of morality politics, growing religious tolerance for gay rights, how religious culture is changed by political dynamics, the complicated politics of Latino evangelicals, and the challenges to political inclusion for religious minorities. We have also devoted more attention to the Obama administration's efforts to institutionalize the social justice values of religious liberals, to contemporary policy issues involving religion and politics such as the right to abortion and the civil rights of gay Americans, to the challenges that religious pluralism and minority faith traditions present to American electoral politics, to the limits of the culture war, and to how the Democratic Party was finally able to counterbalance the mobilization of religious conservatives.

We begin with two chapters that establish a framework for studying the relationship between religion and politics in the United States. Chapter 1 demonstrates the continuing significance of religion in American life, and chapter 2 identifies the salient features of religion as they appear in American life. By the end of chapter 2, the reader has been introduced to the three central aspects of religion—creed, institution, and subculture—that recur throughout the book. The ensuing chapters examine the potential political impact of religion on various dimensions of political life: core American beliefs about politics and governance (chapter 3) and views about church-state relations (chapter 4). We then explore the factors that equip religion with the capacity to affect the policymaking process (chapter 5) and the political means through which such influence is deployed (chapter 6). Chapter 7 considers religion as an influence on the political attitudes and behavior of the American public. The next two chapters profile the political behavior of major religious groups in the United States, theologically conservative Protestant churches in chapter 8 and the Catholic, mainline Protestant, and Jewish traditions in chapter 9. Chapters 10 and 11 devote major attention, respectively, to the rich variety of religious, racial, and ethnic minorities active in public life and to the impact of religion on women and sexual minorities. The book concludes in chapter 12 with a discussion of the positive and negative contributions of religion to politics and governance in the United States.

As with previous editions, this book would not be possible without scholars in many disciplines and our own students, who continue to help us understand the nature of religious influence on politics. Allison Calhoun-Brown is grateful to Ken Wald for writing the first edition of *Religion and Politics in the United States* more than twenty years ago. For a generation of scholars, this book has been a foundational introduction to issues and research in this area. As a graduate student, it was the first book she ever read on the topic. She is happy to continue her contribution to the text and hopes with Ken that it will stimulate in others the passion and interest in religion and politics that they both share.

For this edition, we both owe particular thanks to Jon Sisk, Benjamin Verdi, Patricia Stevenson, and Linda Cramer at Rowman & Littlefield. We are pleased by our continuing association with the publisher of one of the best lists in religion and politics.

Ken Wald is pleased to renew the dedication to his wife, Robin Lea West, and to his daughters, Dara and Jaina, who managed to escape the book as required reading during their college experience. Allison Calhoun-Brown dedicates this book to her children, Braxton and Aleah, who are all a mother could wish for, and to her husband, Paul, and her parents, William and Ann Calhoun, for their steadfast love and support. Each of you is a reminder that faith is a factor in more than just politics.

1

A Secular Society?

Religion and politics are necessarily related.

—President Ronald W. Reagan, *Church & State*, October 1984

The last time we mixed religion and politics, people got burned at the stake.

—Bumper sticker spotted by one of the authors

Everyone knows that it is impolite to argue religion or politics with strangers and dangerous to do so with friends. These topics are treated with such delicacy because they evoke strong passions; men and women have been known to debate, argue, organize, demonstrate, resist, fight, and kill—or be killed—on behalf of their religious or political beliefs. What, then, could possibly justify violating both taboos by writing a book about religion and politics?

To answer simply, religion remains an important political factor in the United States. The election of a Catholic president by a predominantly Protestant electorate in 1960 was widely celebrated as marking the end of religious appeals in American politics. As subsequent elections have shown, that conclusion was premature. In 2008, the high volume of "God talk" in the presidential campaign prompted one minister to protest that "candidates for the White House seem to aspire more to the position of pastor-in-chief than commander-in-chief." Although the two major party candidates in 2012 were relatively muted in their use of religious language, their reticence did not stop others from injecting religious themes into the campaign.[1] The religion of the candidates themselves was an

issue, as evidenced by a sign on one church that described the presidential contest as a choice between "the Mormon and the Muslim."[2] The Affordable Health Care Act, the major domestic achievement of the Obama
administration, became a religious issue when the Catholic bishops and
some evangelical Protestants denounced the provision requiring employers to pay for insurance coverage of contraceptive care. It was, they said,
an attack on religious freedom because it ignored religious and moral
objections to birth control.

The president's endorsement of gay marriage raised concern among
some Protestant leaders in the black community. During the long and
bitter campaign for the Republican presidential nomination in the first
half of the year, candidates spoke ferociously about what they claimed
was the Obama administration's "war on religion" (Newt Gingrich) and
charged the president with holding a "phony theology" that put man's
needs above God (Rick Santorum). During his brief moment of fame as
a candidate for the Republican nomination, Herman Cain asserted that
American communities have a right to ban Muslim mosques, a practice
that in fact violates federal law. Even when the election was over, religious issues did not disappear. An Atlanta minister who had been invited
to give the benediction at the presidential inauguration withdrew once it
was learned he had previously condemned homosexuality as contrary to
God's will and seemingly endorsed therapy as a "cure" for the condition.
In a clever play on words, a leading conservative Christian organization
described the withdrawal as inaugurating not the president but rather
"a new era of religious intolerance."[3] In America's single most important
political ritual, the selection of a president, the religious emphasis has
been plain to see.

In recent years, moreover, the national agenda has included a host of
controversial domestic questions that touch on deeply held religious beliefs and outlooks—issues such as abortion, women's role in society, pornography, homosexuality, stem cell research, and euthanasia. These disputes recall the passions aroused by the temperance movement and the
teaching of evolution in the 1920s. In fact, the issue of evolution, which
the scientific community thought was settled decades ago, emerged once
again in the form of calls for teaching "intelligent design" in high school
biology classes. This religiously based creation theory, thinly disguised
as science, became a favorite cause of social conservatives in the United
States. Contemporary controversies about prayer, religious displays on
public property, and the limits of government aid to religious organizations exemplify the continuing debate over church-state relations. Even
economic questions of taxing and spending, traditionally deemed beyond the sphere of religion, are increasingly discussed from a "moral"
perspective (Walsh 2000). President Obama himself defended his plan to

raise taxes on the highest-income Americans by citing the biblical principle of the Gospel of Luke: "for unto whom much is given, much shall be required."

The 2012 election results did nothing to diminish the intense partisan polarization that has fueled gridlock in Washington, D.C. The difficulty of achieving compromise, the recurring story of contemporary American politics, may also have a strong religious connection. In the past, the religious profiles of congressional Democrats and Republicans were quite similar, although some religious groups tended to favor one party more than the other. But over the last forty years or so, the religious differences between the Democratic and Republican Party caucuses in Congress have sharpened. Growing evidence suggests that a religious "sorting" of parties may underlie polarization on both "cultural issues" with overt religious connections (think abortion, homosexuality) and broader disagreement about the role of government in the economy (Asmussen 2011; McTague and Pearson-Merkowitz 2013). As evangelical Protestants have moved almost entirely into the Republican caucus and Jewish representatives and senators have intensified their presence among Democrats, the party coalitions have become more ideological across a wide range of issues. Growing partisan polarization thus reflects the cultural and ideological differences that divide parties with different religious centers of gravity.

As a look at the State Department organizational chart will reveal, religious issues are not limited to domestic politics. The State Department maintains two separate units, the Office of International Religious Freedom and a new agency charged with "outreach to the global faith community and religious leaders," as well as a program in religious peacemaking and interfaith dialogue at the free-standing U.S. Institute of Peace.[4] These initiatives are responses to the growing importance of religion as a factor in foreign policy.

The collapse of European Communism in the 1990s, often stimulated by the uprisings of religious groups, left a number of dangerous ethnic and religious conflicts that developed into vicious ethno-religious civil wars. In cases like Bosnia, where the conflict among Orthodox Serbs, Muslims, and Catholic Croats took on the ferocity of a holy war, some U.S. church leaders demanded American intervention to stop the slaughter. U.S. policymakers were often slow to grasp the religious dimension of these global conflicts (Johnston and Sampson 1994; B. Rubin 1994). For their part, American churches that used to cooperate in overseas humanitarian relief found themselves increasingly divided by political issues. While many churches developed a preoccupation with human rights abuses—pressing the government to negotiate reductions in nuclear weapons, to admit more political refugees from Central America, and to cut economic ties with governments that engage in religious persecution—other, more conservative churches raised funds to combat left-wing movements in Latin America and elsewhere (Buss and Herman 2003). The 1991 Gulf War and the American invasion of Iraq in 2003 produced deep splits in the American religious community.

Some commentators now warn about a "conflict of civilizations" between the West and the Middle East that rests, at base, on religious differences (Huntington 1996). The facts tell a more complex story. In response to the powerful political resurgence of Islam during the 1980s, the United States was held hostage in Iran, tried unsuccessfully to act as peacekeeper in Lebanon, and supplied weapons to Muslim rebels in Afghanistan (Crile 2003). In two of these three cases, as well as the intervention on behalf of the Kuwaiti government in the 1991 Gulf War, the United States was allied with Muslim regimes or movements.

The terrorist attacks on September 11, 2001, justified by the perpetrators in explicitly religious terms, dramatically changed the balance. In short order, the United States fought one war against a fundamentalist Islamic regime in Afghanistan and another even larger conflict with the predominantly Muslim state of Iraq. U.S. military forces advanced quickly in Iraq but stumbled badly during the postwar occupation in the face of ongoing resistance movements calling for Islamic struggle against the "Crusader" West. Although President George W. Bush emphasized that the United States was not at war with Islam, reports of religiously insensitive or insulting behavior by American forces, some true, some false, further inflamed tensions between the Muslim world and the United States. So did comments from official spokesmen, such as the audacious claim by a U.S. general that the Iraqi conflict would be won because the Christian God is "bigger" than Allah, the Muslim "idol."[5]

We may applaud it, deplore it, be repelled or fascinated by it—but our first imperative is to understand how and why religion so animates American politics. Despite evidence of the persistence of religious vitality in the United States, scholars and citizens alike were slow to recognize the political impact of religion in the United States. This underestimation stemmed in large part from a mistaken belief in the inevitable "secularization" of modern life. As the next section shows, the widespread belief that religion was destined to recede from the mind of humankind prepared observers to discount religious influences in the political realm.

THE PUZZLE OF RELIGIOUS VITALITY

Textbooks on American government send a message that "religion is not and never has been a significant factor either in the development of our political institutions or in their operations" (Carey 1982, 7).[6] Critics blame this "secular" prejudice on authors' supposed indifference or outright hostility toward religion. For the most part, however, the neglect of religion as a political force stems from widespread acceptance of certain social theories that guide academic research away from religion. A novelist who wrote that "a man's eyes can only see what they're learnt to see" understood well that expectations can become blinders, prompting us to overlook important information and developments. In the case of religion, most scholars "learnt to see" secularization, broadly understood as the decline of religious influence in advanced industrial societies, and that expectation drew their attention away from the presence of religion in the political realm.

The concept of secularization, what scholars have called "a virtually unchallenged truth of twentieth-century social science" (Katznelson and Jones 2010, i), encompasses a variety of processes as complex as the phenomenon of religion itself (Wallis and Bruce 1992; Gorski and Altinordu 2008). In its most neutral sense, *secularization* refers only to changes in religion as society develops. One process, *differentiation*, means the development of religion as a specialized institution with its own sphere of competence. When religion is differentiated, it surrenders to government responsibility for such fields as law, education, and medicine. The state then manages these realms without regard to religious values. This transformation encourages the *privatization* of religion. That term refers to the evolution of religion into a matter of personal judgment and choice that exerts its profoundest impact on individuals, what some have called "internal secularization." A privatized faith is reluctant to tell society how it ought to behave. A third process associated with secularization, *desacralization*, refers to changes in thought rather than to the transformation of religious organizations. Desacralization is the tendency to explain the universe in terms of material reality rather than supernatural forces, what one influential scholar calls the "disenchantment of the world" (Gauchet 1997). Modern societies often treat as ordinary what more traditional civilizations may imbue with a divine character. Finally, in the religious world itself, secularization is often equated with *liberalization* of religious doctrine, the lowering of barriers between religious groups, and the relaxation of orthodoxy. Together, these processes constitute a neutral definition of secularization.

If secularization is understood simply as religious change, it leaves room for religion—modified, adapted, and adjusted to new circumstances—as a significant force in contemporary society. None of the trends described here would necessarily remove religion from the political universe, and some might even strengthen its relevance to political conflict. But many scholars have made secularization into an iron-clad law that boldly predicts the virtual extinction of organized religion and points to the consequent elimination of religious influences in contemporary culture (Gorski and Altinordu 2008, 56). This particular understanding of secularization, the "naive" version that predicts diminishing significance for religion in politics, is associated with two of the most influential theories of social change: the modernization approach and the class-conflict model.

The modernization approach predicts transformations in life and thought because of the rapid growth of cities; the rise of factory production; the spread of education, communication, and technology; and the emergence of vast administrative apparatuses, or bureaucracies. Sociological observers of the late nineteenth and early twentieth centuries believed these developments, which define what we mean by "modern," had wrought massive changes in the place of religion in society. Before the onset of modernization, most people lived in small, geographically isolated settlements and were preoccupied by the daily task of producing life's necessities. With limited exposure to external influences, people living in the settlements shared a stable set of beliefs, customs, and traditions. Subject to forces beyond their control, particularly weather and disease, people were receptive to supernatural outlooks. The myths and folk religions of primitive cultures are commonly thought to have originated in fear of the unknown, in dread and awe (Goodenough 1972). This description may conjure up images of a Stone Age pygmy tribe in a rain forest, but the portrait would be just as appropriate for the Irish villages, Norwegian communes, and East European shtetls whose migrants eventually populated much of the United States.

According to modernization theory, the forces of modernity shatter such cultures. Migration to a city in search of work removes the villagers from traditional influences and brings them into regular contact with persons from different backgrounds. Traditional values, particularly the emphasis on fate and the supernatural, are undermined by the doctrine of scientific cause and effect taught in school, factory, and mass media (Inkeles 1983). When held up to scientific standards of proof and evidence, religious claims, and therefore religious faith, may falter. The discovery that other people worship different gods may further reduce unshakable confidence in the "one true faith" to a weaker "religious preference." The institutions that arise in modernity—large societies, complex enterprises, extensive governments—treat people impersonally, without regard for their religious identities. Accordingly, behavior formerly governed by deference and obedience, perhaps even as sacred obligation, gives way to exchange, bargaining, and negotiation.[7] As a consequence, people come to define their personal identity and political interests not in terms of religion but as a function of their standing in the marketplace—as owners, workers, proprietors of small businesses, and so forth.

While it is tempting to speak of modernization in terms of such grand historical processes, we should not lose sight of what is sometimes called "agency" in the accompanying loss of authority by religion. Specifically, modernization in early twentieth-century America came to mean the narrowing of religion's social sphere because of purposeful activity by certain elites (C. Smith 2003). In fields as diverse as education, law, science, psychology, sociology, journalism, and social reform, modernizers actively worked to exclude religious perspectives as inconsistent with science, which was sometimes called the religion of the modern age. Though not necessarily irreligious, these professionals simply believed that religion had nothing useful to say about their fields and wanted to claim legitimate authority for themselves. Each field was accordingly recast as a purely secular endeavor with formal education the requirement for admission to leadership roles.

According to the predictions of modernization theory, societies that have been fully exposed to the currents of modern life will accord religion a minor role. Except among the elderly, raised in a more devout age, and the residents of cultural backwaters, the practice of religion will diminish. The institutions of religion will suffer a similar fate unless they are transformed into agencies of social welfare and service centers—and even then churches must compete with the state to perform these tasks. An even more telling sign of religious decay is the erosion of religious thought:

> Men act less and less in response to religious motivation: they assess the world in empirical and rational terms, and find themselves involved in rational organizations and rationally determined roles which allow small scope for such religious predilections as they might privately entertain. Even if . . . non-logical behaviour continues in unabated measure in human society, then at least the terms of non-rationality have changed. It is no longer the dogmas of the Christian Church which dictate behaviour, but other quite irrational and arbitrary assumptions about life, society and the laws which govern the physical universe. (B. Wilson 1966, 10)

The change in the terms of thought, from a God-centered to a human-centered world, is the most dramatic testament to the victory of secularization in the modern world. This understanding of modern society leaves little room for religion as a social or political factor.

The forecast of religious decline in the modern world has been reinforced by another influential theory of social change—Marxism. Like modernization theorists, Karl Marx and Friedrich Engels believed religious sentiments reflected a human response to forces that defied understanding and that faith in the supernatural was likely to be a casualty of economic development (Aptheker 1968). Writing in the mid-nineteenth century, Marx began with the paradox that the human conquest of nature, which ought to have put an end to hunger and oppression, seemed instead to have intensified them. Marx believed the sources of wealth had always been monopolized by and used to enrich the few at the expense of the many. But the coming of industrialization and factory-based economies intensified the process of exploitation. Once subordinate to the forces of nature, workers now found themselves subordinate to economic power. Unemployment replaced natural calamity as the scourge of human existence.

In this setting, Marx suggested, religion appealed most strongly to the oppressed who desperately needed some explanation for their plight. Christianity found its pioneers among slave populations because it promised them the solace of a better life to come; psychologically, the Christian religion was a balm, a salve for despair. Subsequently, the growth of Christianity was encouraged by the dominant groups in society because it might teach the "lower orders"—be they slaves, serfs, or industrial workers—to accept their condition as God's will and to look for solace in the afterlife. In this way, Marx argued in a famous passage, religion became the "opiate" of the people.

In Marx's view, a society built on exploitation could not long endure because the oppressed majority would eventually recognize its exploitation. As conditions worsened, the working class would realize the inequity of prevailing economic arrangements and their source in man-made doctrines and practices. When this occurred, Marx expected an uprising, the seizure of power on behalf of the previously oppressed majority and the creation of a new, more just and humane social order. In this new world, humankind would reclaim its proper place as the maker of its own destiny, and all the artificial doctrines developed to support the dethroned system—including religion—would be consigned to the "dustbin of history." Religion, which had persisted because of intolerable social conditions, would simply evaporate with these social transformations.

Bolstered by theories that confidently forecast the demise of religion, many students of politics predicted that religious controversy would eventually disappear from the political agenda. Although it would still be available as a basis for defending traditional cultures threatened by social change, religion was likely to lose its political relevance, displaced by disputes rooted primarily in economics. Students of political behavior similarly anticipated a shift in the basis of political loyalty from "premodern" factors such as religion, ethnicity, and region to more modern factors such as social class, occupational standing, and socioeconomic status (Epstein 1967, 88). In "mature" political systems, it was said, political campaigns would no longer resemble emotional religious crusades but instead take on the flavor of slick exercises in public relations; sober appeals to self-interest would replace passionate calls for national salvatio͏ͅ political observers never expected to find was an advanc͏ͅ society in which religion exercised a tenacious hold on the public m͏ͅ and strongly influenced the conduct of political life. Yet that is precisely what we find in the contemporary United States.

THE PERSISTENCE OF RELIGION

By most conventional yardsticks, the United States was one of the first nations to have undergone modernization, and it continues to lead the way in many aspects of social development. If modernization leads inevitably to the decline of religious institutions, practices, and feelings—what we have called the "naive" understanding of secularization—then the erosion of religion ought to show up first in such a mobile, affluent, urban, and expansive society. Yet American religion, like Mark Twain, has obstinately refused to comply with reports of its demise.

American religion has certainly experienced the processes associated with the neutral definition of secularization. Religion is a specialized institution with a constitutionally limited public role, and religious affiliation is a matter of personal choice of no interest to government. Religious organizations are treated under the law no differently from other voluntary, nonprofit societies; they are autonomous in their internal operation, entitled to government services but also subject to the rule of public law. Most major social institutions operate on the basis of professional norms rather than religious considerations. Consistent with the experience of desacralization, Americans generally interpret events from a scientific and naturalist perspective. Many orthodox doctrines and forms of devotion have been abandoned or modified by church authorities.

But these changes do not add up to the decline in faith predicted by naive secularization theory. It cannot be denied that some religions have lost intensity, esteem, and membership or that many Americans are indifferent or antagonistic toward religion. Yet even these elements of decline have been offset by spectacular growth in some religions, the flowering of new faiths, periodic revivals of religious enthusiasm, and the spread of religious sentiment to some of the most "secularized" segments of the population (Hastings and Hoge 1986; Hadden 1987b). The naive model of secularization cannot withstand the facts.

Just how poorly modernization and Marxist theories of religion fit the United States is demonstrated in figure 1.1, which reflects information from a diverse set of countries around the world. The diagonal line shows the underlying relationship between each country's level of economic development (per capita gross national income, or GNI) and the proportion

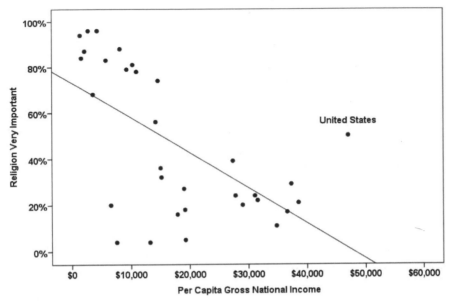

Figure 1.1.   Importance of Religion and Economic Development. *Source:* **See note 8.**

of the population who told interviewers that religion was "very impor-tant" in their lives.[8] The downward slope of the line as the level of "mod-ernization" increases generally confirms that economic development goes hand in hand with a decline in traditional religious sentiment. The United States is a conspicuous exception, however, to the generalization. With the second-highest per capita GNI, it was by far the most "religious" of the affluent countries included in the survey. To highlight the magnitude of American exceptionalism, Americans were more than twice as likely as Australians to report that religion was salient, despite the economic simi-larity between the two countries, and were similar in religious intensity to Lebanon, a country with less than a third of the American per capita GNI.[9]

By all the normal yardsticks of religious commitment—the strength of religious institutions, practices, and belief—the United States has resisted the pressures toward secularity. Institutionally, churches are probably the most vital voluntary organization in a country that puts a premium on "joining up." The best sources estimate that the United States is home to between 255,000 and 345,000 churches (congregations) with more than 150 million adherents (Grammich 2012; Hodgkinson, Weitzman, and Kirsch 1988; Hadaway and Marler 2005). Depending on how "member-ship" is defined, the church members amount to somewhere between three-fifths and three-fourths of the adult population. Despite all the talk about "decline," the proportion of church members among persons aged fifteen and older is virtually the same today as it was in 1950 and, with due allowance for the raggedness of historical data, actually seems to be higher now than throughout most of American history (Finke and Stark 1992). The full extent of American religious consciousness emerges from evidence that nine out of ten Americans identify with some religious group or tradition (Dougherty, Johnson, and Polson 2007).

Support for organized religion shows up in other ways. In annual surveys about confidence in major institutions, churches and organized religion are consistently ranked ahead of many government institutions, medicine, the public schools, the mass media, business, and labor unions.[10] Along the same lines, despite continuing reports of sexual abuse by Catholic priests, the public continues to regard clergy as more honest and ethical than business leaders, government officials, journalists, and lawyers.[11] This vote of confidence has been backed up by perhaps the ultimate expression of commitment—the pocketbook. In 2011, Americans contributed almost $100 billion to religious institutions, making churches by far the most favored recipient of private philanthropy (American Association of Fundraising Counsel 2011). Congregations devoted a significant share of that income to education, human service, health and hospitals, community development, the arts, and environmental protection (Hodgkinson, Weitzman, and Kirsch 1988). With its $4.6 billion annual revenues, Catholic Charities is second only to the U.S. government in welfare activities, and the number of Americans working abroad for Christian organizations dwarfs the number of civilian U.S. government employees stationed abroad (Nichols 1988, 21).[12]

Surveys of church practice, another presumed casualty of the modern age, show an equally high level of attachment to religion. What anthropologists call "rites of passage" (formal celebrations of an individual's progress through life, such as naming ceremonies, attainment of adulthood, marriage, and funerals) are still monopolized by religious organizations in the United States, as they are in many other cultures. But as national data reveal, devotion is hardly limited to such occasions (see figure 1.2).

At one extreme, about four of ten Americans report that they never attend religious services or attend at most once or twice a year. This includes people who consider themselves irreligious as well as those who have some sort of religious identity but are essentially passive about worship. Roughly a third of Americans are intensely involved in religious life, claiming to attend worship at least once a week or more. That leaves approximately one-fourth of the population that reports going to a place of worship a few times a year to a few times a month. Participation in collective public worship—the traditional measure of religious attachment—remains widespread in the United States.

Churchgoing is but one form of religious behavior; Americans engage in a wide range of other public and private devotional acts (see figure 1.3).

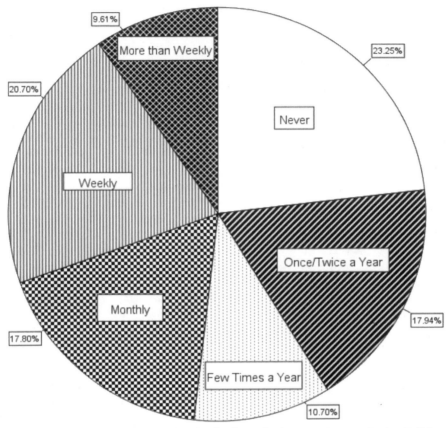

9.61%

More than Weekly

23.25%

20.70%

Never

Weekly

Once/Twice a Year

Monthly

17.94%

17.80%

Few Times a Year

10.70%

Figure 1.2. Frequency of Churchgoing in the United States. *Source:* **Baylor Religion Survey, 2006.**

Clear majorities of the adult population testify that they have no doubts about the existence of a deity, believe in life after death, and belong to a church-related group of some kind. Sizable proportions similarly report that they pray daily, have tried to convert somebody else to their Christian faith, and have experienced a religious turning point in their lives. Curiously, only one out of six consider themselves very religious and barely one-fourth strongly agreed that they tried hard to bring their religious values into daily life. Although churchgoing is reported at relatively high levels (see figure 1.2 above), only a quarter of the American public participate in church activities other than worship each month. Based on questions from other surveys, religious involvement appears far more widespread than many forms of political participation. More Americans identify with a denomination than a political party, and the typical citizen is much more likely to attend church than a political meeting. The

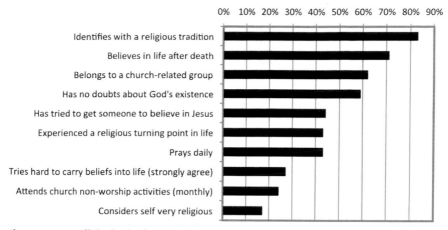

Figure 1.3.   **Religiosity in the United States.** *Source:* Baylor Religion Survey, 2006.

proportion of citizens who claim to evangelize on behalf of their faith on a regular basis exceeds the percentage who report trying to influence another person's vote. The level of religious activity in the United States also stands out when compared with Western Europe, where the population has been described as "believing without behaving" (Davie 1994).

When we enter the realm of belief, detailed findings from a host of surveys emphasize the continuity of religious ideas in the United States. By overwhelming majorities, Americans have continued to endorse the core assumptions of Christianity—the existence of God, the divinity of Jesus, the reality of an afterlife—and to insist on the importance of these values in their own lives (Gallup and Castelli 1989; Greeley 1989). Most Americans believe in the divine origins of humankind, and nearly a majority accepts a literal interpretation of the Genesis story (Newport 1993). When Americans think about God, they imagine a creator and healer; the image of heaven carried in the minds of modern Americans depicts a place of union with God and reunion with loved ones (Harley and Firebaugh 1993). "Two centuries after the intellectual world has said that these kinds of things do not happen," reported a scholar who interviewed two thousand small-town midwesterners, "many people reported mystical experiences such as visions, prophetic dreams, voices from heaven, and visits from spirits."[13] Despite all the publicity accorded the New Age movement, Americans are much more likely to perceive a spirit world of angels and devils than to believe in crystals and channeling (Gallup and Castelli 1989, 75–76) and may in fact be less disposed today to believe in magic and astrology than they were centuries ago (Butler 1990).

To the extent that such things can be measured, religious belief, like religious institutions and practices, has survived intact in probably the most "modern" society known in history. Statistics have been used to make the point because numbers are the currency of argument in a scientific culture. But because national statistics often have a numbing effect, they should be supplemented with a local example. The stability of a religious texture in American life has been demonstrated forcefully by a continuing study of a small industrial town in eastern Indiana. In the 1920s a pair of gifted social observers decided to put "Middletown," a pseudonym for Muncie, under the microscope of social analysis (Lynd and Lynd 1929). Curious about the changes wrought by the passage of fifty years, a team of social scientists set out in the 1970s to repeat the study of Muncie (Caplow, Bahr, and Chadwick 1983). In the half century since the first study, Muncie had experienced all the changes that are supposed to encourage secularization—rapid population growth, relentless technological advance, the spread of education, increasing bureau-·cracy, the penetration of mass media, and expanded governmental presence. Could the vibrant religious tradition of the town possibly survive the corrosive effects of these changes?

Despite the odds against it, traditional religion was found to be doing quite nicely in modern Muncie. In the words of the most recent study of the town, "the Reverend Rip Van Winkle, Methodist minister, awakening in Middletown after a 60-year sleep, would hardly know he had been away" (Caplow, Bahr, and Chadwick 1983, 280). He might have been surprised by the growth of tolerance among religious groups, but little else had changed since the 1920s. The "Middletown" residents of the 1970s seemed every bit as pious as their grandparents and great-grandparents. Most people still subscribed to the core beliefs of Christianity, and—whether measured by the numbers of clergy and buildings, by financial contributions, or by attendance at worship—the churches flourished. But surely, it may be argued, the survival of religion was purchased at a high price—by sacrificing the traditional emphasis on the emotional and spiritual for a more modern style stressing reason and social reform. This plausible suggestion collapses under the evidence of growth in the most theologically conservative churches, a renewed emphasis on emotional forms of worship in all denominations, and the continuing priority placed by the clergies on the spiritual well-being of their flocks. Against all expectations, the most recent study of Muncie uncovered a community with reverence for the sacred and faith in religion as a source of strength and guidance.

STABILITY OR CHANGE?

By claiming that American religious institutions, behavior, and belief have been stable, we are taking on two durable stereotypes in popular thinking. Many people are convinced that American religion has declined while others hold the polar opposite belief that religion has become even more powerful. Critics of the stability hypothesis, who know in their bones that religion is losing influence in society, dismiss the data in the previous section as little more than a superficial tribute to habit and conformity. If we look at "deeper" aspects of religious life, they tell us, such as the capacity of religion to keep people's minds focused on questions of ultimate value, heaven, hell, right, wrong, judgment, and justice, there is compelling evidence that religion was much more important in the past. At the other extreme, we often hear from commentators about a religious revival in the late twentieth- and early twenty-first-century United States. These observers report that Americans have been swept up in a religious awakening similar to previous cycles of American history (Fogel 1999). They are struck by the degree to which religion still influences how Americans think about the world and their own lives.

We think both claims miss the essential stability demonstrated by religious forces in American life. This is a hard argument to make because so much of the debate revolves around religious feeling, something that is extremely difficult to measure or assess. Nonetheless, we should try to address the various arguments made by both sides in the debate.

Those who sense religious decline maintain (1) that contemporary religious commitment is exaggerated—being wide but not deep, (2) that some degree of religious decline has in fact occurred, especially among the young, and (3) that American religion has purchased its longevity by selling its soul to secular culture. There is some truth to each of these claims. In the same way that Americans exaggerate their level of voting, giving charity, or performing other good deeds, they appear massively to inflate their church attendance. Perhaps only half the people who tell pollsters they were in church actually do attend in any given week (Brenner 2011; Hadaway, Marler, and Chaves 1993; Hadaway and Marler 2005; Presser and Stinson 1998), although some of the slippage between self-report and observation appears due to oversampling of religious people in surveys (Woodberry 1998). Presumptuous though it is to assume we can determine when religious commitment is superficial as opposed to authentic, it is striking how little Americans know about the essentials of their declared faiths and how readily they switch from one denomination to another (see Pew Forum on Religion and Public Life 2008, 2010). The critics can also score points by pointing to evidence of decline in religious belief among the best-educated segment of the population and the tenacity of "old-time" religion among people with the least exposure to modernization: housewives, the elderly, inhabitants of rural areas and small towns, southerners, and persons with low levels of education. People deeply embedded in such major institutions of modernization as the marketplace, cities, industry, and schools are less likely to have maintained religious orthodoxy.

The claim of religious continuity is most seriously challenged by the argument that American religion has become much more "secular" than sacred (Wolfe 2003). Consider the way God has been recast in the church advertisement reproduced as figure 1.4. Although the church considers itself traditional and evangelical, there is precious little hell and damnation in the ad. The forbidding and wrathful deity from the Hebrew Bible comes across instead as a therapist, economic adviser, athletic trainer, and friend, the source of stable families, financial prosperity, mental and physical health, and sexual satisfaction (Hunter 1983, chaps. 4, 6). Contemporary sermons talk more about God's forgiving nature and much less about divine punishment or demands for repentance (Witten 1993). As an institution, religion also seems to be grasped less for its truth than its usefulness.

Congregations evolve from holy assemblies to community centers that provide good opportunities for networking and recreation. As the tools of marketing research are brought into the quest for church growth, church planners emphasize comfortable surroundings rather than divine truth as the key to attracting "seekers" (Sergeant 2000). If the critics are to be believed, the quest for religious revival is transformed under modern conditions from a crusade for souls to a battle for market share.

So too, it is argued, secularization has changed what we understand as religion. In place of organized religious worship in a formal denomi-

Not your typical Sunday morning church ...

Common Ground is a church where people can come as they are, with no pressure to be someone or something they are not. You will find great music, relevant messages, high-quality childcare and real people. Check us out this Sunday and see the difference!!

web: www.theground.org
phone: 352.372.4032

GRAND OPENING
Sunday, March 17th - 10:30am
Gator Cinemas AMC 4
Oaks Mall Plaza

What you'll see the next four weeks:

"Living a Different Life"
March 17 - Finding a place that is real.
March 24 - Finding friends that are real.
March 31 - Finding hope that is real.
April 7 - Finding a truth that is real.

Pastor Matthew Mitchell and his wife Lisa.

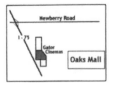

Figure 1.4.   Example of Contemporary Church Advertisement

nation, many people now emphasize a highly individualized personal spirituality that may or may not follow any recognized religious tradition. This personal quest may take the idiosyncratic form of "Sheilahism," an approach that removes faith from the world of institutional religion and reduces doctrine to little more than "a small voice within" the imagination of the individual (Bellah et al. 1985). While many people claim to practice "spirituality" rather than religion, closer inspection of this phenomenon often reveals a shallow and undisciplined self-expression masquerading as a meaningful encounter with the divine (Wuthnow 1998).

It is one thing to acknowledge these changes, quite another to over-interpret them as signs of the imminent extinction of religious sentiment in American life. Religion has certainly been touched and influenced by the modern world, but it is more accurate to speak of secularization as adjustment and adaptation than to employ the image of decline and fall. Many of the trends cited as evidence of changes are actually long-standing traits of American religious life. It is not at all clear that Americans are any less pious or serious about faith today than they were in some distant past (Butler 1990). In 1837, Harriet Martineau (quoted in Powell 1967, 118–27) had already discovered that most clergy soft-pedaled their religious message for fear of offending congregants. Nor is the "selling" of religion as a product something new even if modern techniques are more sophisticated and visible (Moore 1994). Transplanted to the American religious environment, world religions have often been adapted to the rampant individualism of our culture. Indeed, the United States has long been a major incubator of new religions and a pioneer in religious individualism. In sum, the case for "decline" ignores history and tradition.

The case for revival is equally weak. Many advocates of this approach simply overlook evidence of the growth of secularism among various sectors of the population. They also tend to confuse changes in *patterns* of religious affiliation with changes in the overall *level* of religious commitment. For more than thirty years now, scholars have documented a shift in the kinds of religious traditions that Americans prefer. Apart from the growth in the unchurched, the major change involves shifts between different wings of Protestantism. Specifically, the mainline or mainstream denominations have been overtaken by churches from the evangelical wing. (See chapter 2 for a discussion of the differences in these forms of Protestantism.) Because evangelicals put greater emphasis on public professions of faith and have come to dominate the world of religious broadcasting, it may well seem as if there has been a growth in religious intensity in American society. But a growth in the size of one Protestant wing, offset by declines in another, still indicates underlying stability more than revival. The facts of American religious behavior sustain our emphasis on stability.

POSSIBLE EXPLANATIONS

Where did modernization theorists and Marxists go wrong in predicting that religion would disappear from the highly developed United States? These social theories appear to have underestimated both the need for religion, even in the most advanced societies, and, even more important, the capacity of American religious institutions to adapt to changing circumstances.

Some students of religion cite the durability of religious beliefs as proof that religion meets a basic human need, much like food and shelter (Stark and Bainbridge 1985; Barrett 2004). Alone among creatures on Earth, human beings possess the ability to think in a sophisticated way about their place in the universe. They wonder about the meaning of life, the reality of death, the basis of ethical behavior and human cooperation. They ask, among other questions, why some people commit evil; why the good and innocent should suffer from it; and how, apart from instinct, they can even think to know what is good and what is evil. To answer these questions about life—to give meaning to human existence—they develop systems of belief that include religion. So long as the world requires some explanation, it is argued, human beings will create faiths to live by. Nothing about this notion would bother most modernization theorists or Marxists. They would argue merely that the need for a system of meaning will eventually be satisfied fully by science or by a comprehensive body of political ideas, making religion unnecessary.

Science seems inadequate, however, as a religious substitute. The assumption that scientific understanding eliminates a need for religious explanation falters because of persistent questions about life on this planet that no scientific advance can ever settle. It is hard to see how familiarity with, for example, the third law of thermodynamics could ever comfort troubled or grieving individuals or improve on religious faith in enabling them to cope with their inevitable mortality.[14] Science is simply irrelevant to such questions. In other cases, the progress of science may reinforce concern for spirituality. The more Albert Einstein learned about the beauty and symmetry of nature, the more he appreciated what he saw as God's hidden hand; he is not the only scientist to have been so moved (Tracy 1973). Finally, science may actually intensify concern about questions of value. The spectacular growth of medical technology has raised agonizing moral dilemmas about the nature and conditions of life, dilemmas that appear on the political agenda in the form of issues such as abortion, euthanasia, organ transplantation, in vitro fertilization, genetic engineering, embryo experimentation, life extension, and living wills. Progress in weapons development has underlined dramatically the problem of human evil and the necessity for cooperation. To the extent that science liberates us from misery and economic insecurity, it gives us freedom to ponder questions of ultimate value.

In advanced technological societies, paradoxically, there has been a striking loss of faith in reason as a solution to all human problems. Consider this assessment of the current mood: "These are gloomy times. People are fatalistic and death possessed. There is a conviction that we have been collectively asleep at the wheel, that the path of so-called reason has taken us far along the road to hell, probably past the point of no return. More and more, the feeling is taking hold that we are on the edge of a volcano that is about to explode" (Frankel 1984, 162).

This comment, all the more remarkable because its author is "a business consultant who specializes in information and telecommunications technologies," illustrates how a society built on science may generate profound discontent with the consequences of scientific activity. For some people, the reaction to a technological society apparently run amok is a renewed respect for the religious values that science once seemed to render unnecessary. The loss of confidence in modernity also breeds more extreme social reactions, such as the militia movement, which justifies acts of violence against society in the name of "higher" spiritual values.

Ironically, modernizing trends that may challenge traditional religion also equip those traditions with important political resources. Those who subscribe to traditionalist faiths may learn how to use the instruments of modernity—advances in communication technology, larger amounts of disposable time, advanced education—in service of those traditional values. Indeed, evangelical activists who boast what could be called establishment credentials have founded various social movements to promote their conservative values and have increasingly become a key element within the Republican Party (Lindsay 2007). If modernity challenges religious traditionalism in some respects, it reinforces its political relevance in others. In the United States, political faith has not yet managed to supplant religious commitment. While some political activists discard their religious faith as an impediment to social change, others see no need to choose between them. When religious and political loyalties do appear to collide, the choice may actually favor the former. During the turbulent late 1960s and early 1970s, the extremes of the American political spectrum were represented by Eldridge Cleaver, an eloquent and angry spokesman for black nationalism, and his opposite number, a conservative political operative named Charles Colson, who once boasted that he would have sacrificed his own grandmother to gain political advantage. In the 1980s, disillusioned with the consequences of their political activism, these two firebrands shared public platforms to preach for a return to biblical Christianity. With less publicity, other intellectuals have traveled the same path from political activism to religious commitment (Schumer

1984). A few conversions may not indicate a social trend, but they do illustrate that politics may prove to be an ineffective alternative to religion.

WHY THE UNITED STATES?

The inadequacy of science and politics to address basic human needs only partly explains the persistence of religion in the United States. Theories about intrinsic human needs and failed alternatives are global concepts that do not resolve questions about why the United States, in particular, has remained so much more deeply tied to religion than other modern societies. American exceptionalism in religion (see figure 1.1) has usually been attributed to cultural compatibility, a need for social identity, the independence of religion from the state, and a competitive religious environment.

Early American churches emphasized self-government for congregations and voluntary affiliation for individuals, thus encouraging Americans to value their autonomy and to distrust hierarchy (Lipset 1967, 180–92). To this day, Americans find religion "comfortable" because it fits in well with deep-seated cultural values about freedom of choice and individual initiative.

Religion may also reinforce the larger culture by supplying what individuals find lacking in society. Robert Booth Fowler (1989) argues that churches thrive in the United States because they provide an antidote to the extremes of individualism and relativism. People join churches, he argues, because they want a sense of community—a sense that is absent from other parts of their lives. They also turn to religion for rules and guidelines, something sorely missing from a society that makes every individual the arbiter of right and wrong.

Religion has also flourished because it meets a continuing need for social identity that is particularly important in the United States. Physical mobility, economic change, and immigration have constantly threatened people with a loss of roots—the loss of a sense that they belong to any meaningful group or tradition. Confronted with chaos, individuals find much-needed stability in religion. In what John F. Kennedy called "a nation of immigrants," the church helped newcomers adjust to life in a new and confusing environment. Churches still fill that role for newcomers who migrate from abroad or simply move around frequently from place to place.

Visiting the United States in 1831, Alexis de Tocqueville was surprised by the prominence of religion in American life (Bryant 2005). Like most Europeans, he had simply assumed that denial of public funding to religious institutions would inevitably drive the nation into irreligion. The practicing French Catholic was even more shocked when all the American priests he consulted "assigned primary credit for the peaceful ascendancy of religion in their country to the complete separation of church and state." Based on this experience, Tocqueville came to believe that religion could best "win the affection of the human race" by remaining a purely voluntary undertaking. Religion that depended on allocations from government leaders would inevitably incur guilt by association. As he put it, "Religion cannot share the material might of those who govern without incurring some of the hatred they inspire." Tocqueville's insight appears to have been borne out by history and scholarship (Caplow 1985; Tong 1992). In countries where state religions have defended corrupt governments in order to maintain a privileged position, the legacy is often a style of political conflict pitting a "secular" left against a "religious" right (Heath, Taylor, and Toka 1993; McDonough, Barnes, and Pina 1984, 661–63).

American religion appears to have escaped this trap, in part, because religion never stayed in one corner. Slave owners found support for servitude in the Bible, but the slaves could and did read the Old Testament as a call to resistance and revolt. The religious impulse that justified the worst abuses of capitalism as God's will also stimulated countermovements against the oppression of industrial workers. Even today, when many Roman Catholics have joined the ranks of the wealthy and powerful, their church continues to speak out against poverty and to remind Americans about the plight of the oppressed. In light of these trends, it is not surprising to find among Americans a weak relationship between personal religious attachment, on the one hand, and self-described ideology or presidential vote choice, on the other.[15] While religious people may differ in degree from the nonreligious in their political loyalties, devout Americans are spread across the political spectrum.

The separation of religion and state may have contributed further to religious vitality by promoting religious diversity in the United States. The uniformity hoped for by some of the first settlers did not even survive the colonial period. Since then, the religious landscape has been further diversified by the founding of many new faiths (Marty 1984) and the importation of world religions via immigration to America (Eck 2001). As a result, no single denomination today comprises more than about 40 percent of the church membership; thus, it is correct to say that all Americans belong to minority religions. This conclusion holds at the local level: nearly half the U.S. population resides in counties in which no single denomination has majority status (Salisbury, Sprague, and Weiher 1984).

How did the separation of religion and state encourage religious pluralism? Some scholars argue that the absence of state support for religious faiths bequeathed to the United States an unregulated economic market.

Like economic enterprises that are shielded from competition by state favoritism, these observers argue, churches that rely on state support and patronage develop into lazy monopolies. Unwilling to adapt to new realities or engage in innovation, state churches remain attached to symbols, rituals, and patterns of behavior that cannot withstand the social forces that promote secularity (North and Gwin 2004). By contrast, a society that denies official support to religious institutions forces them to compete for members on a voluntary basis. The "start-up" costs for forming a new religion, planting a church, or building a religious community are relatively low in the American market. Much as in politics and economics, competition in an open market has stimulated church leaders to bid for support with all manner of incentives. Denominations have had to master the very latest techniques in persuasion and recruitment as they reach out to potential "consumers"—hence, the churches' use of sophisticated means of communication, marketing skills, and information technology (S. McDaniel 1989; Stewart 1989). The emphasis on attracting members from the religious marketplace has also prompted the churches to offer attractive benefit packages and services that in other countries might be provided by government. This environment makes American religion more vibrant and open than a system that favors certain religions and thus discourages innovation and adaptation.

We have gone to such lengths to stress the staying power of religion for a reason. Religious conflict in politics is commonly treated as a throwback, an interesting diversion from the "real" issues of the modern era. But if religion remains a vital force in this day and age, then one cannot claim to understand the contemporary era without appreciating the role played by religion, especially in the realm of politics. The remainder of the book delineates the many ways religion intersects political life in the United States.

2

Religion in the American Context

When she visited the United States in the 1830s, the British writer Harriet Martineau found little religious seriousness. Disappointed by the gap between noble aspirations and coarse behavior, she denounced American Christianity as a "monstrous superstition" that provided the people "little molestation to their vices, little rectification to their errors" (quoted in Powell 1967, 12). Unlike Martineau, who thought Americans wore their religion lightly, her countryman G. K. Chesterton later characterized the United States as "a nation with the soul of a church" (Chesterton 1922, 12). We hear the same mixed verdicts today.

Such contrasting views may arise because the United States is a confusing mix of both religious and secular, a point we made in the previous chapter. These contradictory conclusions also testify that people understand "religion" very differently. What makes a person religious? Is it faithful attendance at worship services throughout the year, righteous personal conduct, generous financial support of religious institutions, devotion to the needs of others, or some combination of these traits? Is religion something that only happens under the auspices of institutions that we label as "churches" or something that each individual carries inside? These questions are not easy to answer because religion falls among what are sometimes called *contested concepts*, ideas that generate competing and sometimes conflicting definitions.

In this chapter, we discuss what we mean by "religion" in the American context. After distinguishing among types of religion, we emphasize the three "faces" of religion that may take on political relevance. This discussion is followed by an overview of the major religious "families" in the

23

United States today, with particular attention to the issues and perspectives that divide the dominant Christian population into four distinct camps. The chapter concludes by sketching out the basic political tendencies of the major religious families that will play such a large role in the remainder of the book.

UNDERSTANDING RELIGION

In its essence, religion is a feeling of sacredness that was brilliantly captured by Karen Armstrong (1996, xvi):

> When they have contemplated the world, human beings have always experienced a transcendence and mystery at the heart of existence. They have felt that it is deeply connected with themselves and with the natural world, but that it also goes beyond. However we choose to define it—it has been called God, Brahma, or Nirvana—this transcendence has been a fact of human life. We have all experienced something similar, whatever our theological opinions, when we listen to a great piece of music or hear a beautiful poem and feel touched within and lifted, momentarily, beyond ourselves.

Because this sense of spirituality is so internal and personal, scholars seldom try to examine it directly. Rather, we tend to look at the outcropping of that impulse, examining the "manner and form in which religious phenomena appear in human experience" (Capps 1972, 135).

Scholars commonly distinguish between two types of religion: formal and informal. At its simplest, this approach recognizes both the religion of the churches—with "church" standing for all religious institutions of whatever faith—and the religion of the people. While the two forms of religion should not be treated as polar opposites, they do emphasize different domains. Formal religion—variously described as official, institutional, or organized—comprises official religious doctrines that are determined by specialized religious organizations and implemented by trained religious professionals. The doctrines are conveyed to believers through liturgy and other rituals. This is sometimes known as religion from above. By "popular" religion, also known as common or folk religion, scholars instead refer to the way in which individuals understand and work out their own faiths. What do people think and do when they are being religious (Lippy 1994)? This kind of approach emphasizes not just the formal creed of the church but also religious holidays, public displays, inspirational literature, folklore, hymnals, revivals, and other manifestations of grassroots religiosity (Orsi 2004). Some scholars think of informal religion as the "layer" beneath official religion (J. Wilson 1978, 26). As A. E. Kim (2005, 284) puts it, formal religion concerns itself with sacred objectives (i.e., holiness, salvation, and spiritual blessings), "while popular religion is the realm of religion associated with the 'profane'—i.e., paying attention to people's pragmatic needs such as counseling, healing, emotional security, protection from misfortune, and realization of material wishes."[1]

There may be tension between the two realms because religious leaders often consider popular religion as nothing less than "superstition" that will lead followers away from the true faith. For their part, ordinary worshippers may consider church leaders too distant from their concerns. This feeling sometimes fuels the sharp distinction that people make between "organized religion" and intensely personal "spirituality." But even in formal religious institutions, individuals often develop different ways of understanding religious teachings. Messages from the pulpit are not necessarily interpreted as clergy intend, and individual believers may assert the right to put their own understanding on a par with church teachings.

We need a way of approaching religion that recognizes both formal and informal religion. Accordingly, we focus on three human aspects or "faces" of religion throughout this book: creed, institution, and social/cultural group (Wald 1983, chap. 5). Although these three elements may not capture all the things we mean when we use the term *religion*, they provide the qualities that encourage and facilitate political involvement by religious groups.[2] As used here, *creed* refers to the fundamental beliefs, ideas, ethical codes, and symbols associated with a religious tradition, including what others call a theology or belief system. The emphasis is on the content of religious teachings and the values that the tradition encourages. These may well differ between religious leaders who defend the traditional church teaching and the members who filter church messages through their own experience and perceptions.

Religious communities are represented in concrete form by specialized *institutions*, the second face of religion pertinent to political activism. In the United States, religion has traditionally taken the form of a denomination, which is made up of member churches, synagogues, mosques, and temples. Apart from denominational life, there are many specialized religious groups organized around particular issues or activities. Some are connected to specific religious traditions; others draw support from across the religious spectrum. There are also social movements that draw inspiration from popular religious ideas rather than official doctrine.

Finally, religion denotes a *social group*, a subculture or community of believers. The members of a congregation may share regular social interaction, a common status, and a distinctive way of life. Out of these experiences, a common culture may emerge. Adherents may come to develop a similar way of looking at the world, what is sometimes called a "group mind." The views of the church as community may not always coincide with doctrine. Of course, churches differ in the demands they place on members and in the degree to which they constitute genuine communities, as opposed to casual associations. As we see later, the three faces of religion may help draw religious institutions into politics and may equip them with the ability to compete effectively.

PATTERNS OF RELIGIOUS AFFILIATION

Before we can explore the nature of political attitudes among American religious groups, we must first impose some order on the concept of religious group membership. The task is challenging because of the staggering diversity of American religious identity and the fluidity of individual loyalties.[3] While no classification system could possibly represent all varieties of religious expression, scholars have developed several methods that capture the major religious divisions among the American population.

Table 2.1 presents the logic of the four-step religious classification that we will utilize for the discussion of religion and political behavior. To make it more tangible, it includes three hypothetical examples of individuals from the senior author's city. As the first step, we determine whether individuals identify psychologically with a religion, whether they think of themselves as connected in some way to a religious group. At this topmost level, we define religious groups using terms like "tradition" or "religious family" to denote long-standing communities with common histories, similar belief systems, and distinctive racial and ethnic composition (Kellstedt and Green 1993). As the term is meant to imply, these are not formal organizations but something more akin to virtual communities or psychological entities. As noted in chapter 1, roughly four out of five Americans claim such a connection, which may be purely nominal, a residue of childhood experience that does not currently matter beyond the cognitive identification. At the next level down, the organizational dimension, we determine whether individuals who claim a religious identity affiliate formally with a religious community. By "religious community" in this context, we mean a more specific organization like a religious denomination.[4] As collective bodies, denominations often sponsor seminaries to train religious professionals and provide member congregations with religious publications, youth groups, Washington offices, educational curricula, and other services. There are hundreds of such denominations in the United States although the American religious landscape is lush with congregations that are themselves independent of any larger denomination or only loosely networked with like-minded congregations. Sometimes known as *nondenominational* or *independent*, these

Table 2.1. **Examples of Four-Step Religious Classification**

Steps		Religious Affiliation	
Individual:	Jewish	Baptist	Congregationalist
Congregation:	B'nai Israel	Countryside Baptist	United Church
Denomination:	United Synagogue of Conservative Judaism	Southern Baptist Convention	United Church of Christ
Tradition/Family:	Judaism	Evangelical Protestant	Mainline Protestant

congregations have assumed a larger role in American religious life since the 1960s. Not surprisingly, the third level of attachment refers to what scholars typically call congregations, a term that in everyday language may comprise a church, mosque, synagogue, parish, or similar institution. As noted, these congregations may be components of specific religious denominations or, increasingly, free-standing bodies. It might help to think about congregations, respectively, as either franchises of a larger "brand" or "locally owned" enterprises. The final form of affiliation, which brings us down to the individual, is the popular label that the individual employs to describe his or her personal religious identity. Sometimes, this can be as general as "Baptist," a phenomenon that encompasses more than forty denominations claiming the title, or as specific as "Quaker," once a term of abuse that was eventually claimed by adherents of what is formally known as the "Society of Friends." Although we will use the results of this system throughout the book, it is important to recognize the slipperiness of any such classification scheme. When asked about their religious affiliation in surveys, participants may answer with something as specific as the name of their place of worship (congregations such as St. Matthew's or Fourth Street Christian Church) or as general as "Christian" or "Protestant," responses that leave few clues about denomination. Many members of religious congregations seem cheerfully unaware of the denomination to which they belong. Apportioning denominations to families is also fraught with error because individuals may find themselves in particular churches for reasons having nothing to do with the historic creed of the church. Taken together, then, these sources of error warn us against treating the results of religious classification as anything more than good estimates.

Figure 2.1 arrays the adult population of the United States into the six religious traditions that provide the basis for analysis in this chapter. The data come from the 2008 American National Election Study (ANES), an opinion survey of a representative national sample of the adult population that contains a broad range of data about social and political attitudes.[5] Because the surveys also identify the religious preferences of the participants, they make it possible to compare religious groups with one another.

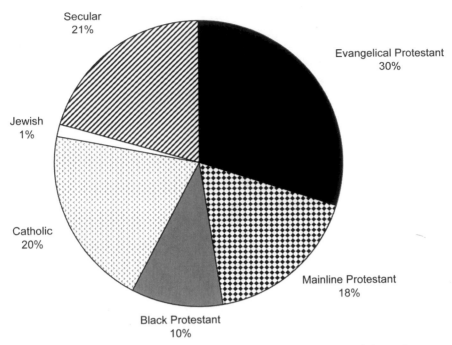

Secular
21%

Evangelical Protestant
30%

Jewish
1%

Catholic
20%

Mainline Protestant
18%

Black Protestant
10%

Figure 2.1. Size of Major Religious Traditions. *Source:* **Calculated from the 2008 American National Election Studies (www.electionstudies.org).**

Even after we exclude some of the smaller religious groups that add variety to the mix of religious commitment, the size of the slices confirms the extent of religious pluralism in the United States. No single religious group comes close to claiming a majority of the population; were the groups to be subdivided to reflect their internal diversity on issues of theology, worship, and church organization, the religious fragmentation would be reinforced. Nonetheless, three groups together account for more than two-thirds of the American religious universe: evangelical Protestants, Roman Catholics (the single largest denomination), and mainline Protestants. The remainder of the adult population is divided among African American Protestants (10 percent of the total), persons for whom no religious tradition could be determined (21 percent), and Jews (roughly 1.5 percent). These figures exclude about 5 percent of the population, people who belong to faiths that run the gamut from such old denominations as Mennonites and Amish through non-Judeo-Christian traditions (Islam, Buddhism) to New Agers or Wiccans, as well as those who refused to answer questions about their religious background and attachment. The differences and small size of these small groups make it impossible to calculate reliable estimates from the ANES. Some of these groups will be discussed at greater length in chapter 10.

The initial distinction between Protestants, Catholics, and Jews is the starting point for any such classification. *Roman Catholics* and *Jews* form distinctive religious and political communities, so their separation from Protestants should come as no surprise. In a society that values religion, those who swim against the tide by disclaiming a religious identity might also exhibit unconventional behavior in the political realm. We thus carved out a separate category for *seculars*, people who neither adopt a religious label nor have any involvement with a recognizable religion. Describing people as "secular" may suggest that they are antireligious. In fact, many Americans who do not identify with a religious faith are nonetheless attached in some way to a religious perspective (Baker and Smith 2009). Samuel Reimer (1995) discovered that the religiously unaffiliated in the United States do not differ much in their fundamental religious values from those who are committed to a religious tradition. Approximately one-quarter of the seculars in the 2008 ANES survey reported that religion was important in their lives, and fully 60 percent indicated that they prayed. Apparently, many people who are best described as "unchurched believers" still consider themselves highly spiritual but do not feel the need for or feel able to find a religious community in which to share their faith.

That leaves us with a majority, a small one, that considers itself part of the Protestant religious family. That percentage that may startle readers accustomed to thinking of the United States as a Protestant nation (Smith and Kim 2005), and they may be even more astonished to learn that the projected Protestant share of the population will drop below 40 percent in thirty years due largely to demographics (Skirbekk, Kaufmann, and Goujon 2010). To those who consider Protestantism a unified faith with minor denominational differences—"sixty sauces with one flavor," in the sarcastic phrase of a Frenchman—it will be surprising to find the Protestant majority apportioned among three distinct families.[6] We created a separate category for *African American Protestants*. By virtue of its historical situation, social role, and organizational independence, black Protestantism demands separate treatment. For the remaining white Protestants, the principal dividing line runs between the *mainline* and *evangelical* camps.

In terms of theology, mainline and evangelical Protestants differ primarily over what Hempel and Bartkowski (2008) describe as the three *S*'s: scripture, sin, and salvation. R. Stephen Warner (1988, chap. 2) argues that this "two-party system" is animated primarily by different understandings of Jesus. Mainline groups regard him predominantly "as a moral teacher who told disciples that they could best honor him by helping those in need"—sometimes known as saving society—while evangelicals treat Jesus principally "as one who offers [personal] salvation to anyone who confesses his name" (33–34). This polarization has led to important variations in religious and social practice. Stressing Jesus's role as a prophet of social justice, the mainline tradition sanctifies altruism and regards selfishness as the cardinal sin.[7] In this tradition, which extends membership to all and understands religious duty in terms of sharing abundance, the Bible is treated as a book with deep truths that have to be discerned amid myth and archaic stories. Consistent with their view of Jesus as personal savior, evangelicals "are obligated above all to share their creed" by bringing others to salvation through a personal embrace of God. The church, a limited community open to those who have attained salvation, sees its principal task as sustaining and extending belief. "Because the Bible is the source of revelation about Jesus," Warner (1988, 34) explains, evangelicals treasure it and credit even its implausible stories. Unlike mainline Protestants, who accept many different sources of religious truth, the evangelicals assign religious authority to the Bible alone. The gap between these two perspectives was captured nicely by two *Newsweek* readers who responded to a cover story on April 19, 1996, about the resurrection of Jesus. In language that no evangelical would ever use, one reader dismissed the debate over whether there was a bodily resurrection: "If he was not the Son of God, then Jesus certainly was the greatest social reformer ever to walk the earth. . . . In the end, it doesn't really matter what happened after he died. It is enough to know that his life, not his death, altered the course of history." But to a reader steeped in the evangelical worldview about the risen Christ, any "attempt to reduce the Son of God to social reformer should be labeled for what it is—blasphemy." Subsequent research by Haskell (2012) suggests that these differences in style of biblical interpretation strongly differentiate the mainline and evangelicals.

Applying these subtle and complex outlooks to individuals who participate in attitude surveys is a daunting task. In practice, the evangelical/mainline cleavage often runs through denominations and churches—and even the minds of individual Protestants (Alwin et al. 2006). Other Protestants, particularly in the African American denominations, manage to combine the evangelical emphasis on salvation with the mainline commitment to social action. To further confuse the picture, some Catholics have adopted aspects of the evangelical approach, and self-described "Messianic Jews" regard Jesus as the messiah promised in the Hebrew Bible. Nonetheless, there is general consensus among scholars that the evangelical label should be reserved for Protestants who share core beliefs in the unique authority of the Bible, the divinity of Jesus, and the relevance of his life, death, and resurrection to salvation of the soul (Hunter 1983, 7). Such views are widespread among Protestants variously described as conservative, traditional, fundamentalist, Pentecostal, holiness, charismatic, free church, Adventist, and reformed. Indeed, those categories are best understood as subgroups under the broad umbrella of evangelicalism which should be understood as a family name rather than a proper noun.

In terms of denominations, most white evangelicals may be found among Baptists and the southern wings of Methodism and Presbyterianism. By contrast, the *mainline* adjective is sometimes used synonymously with labels such as liberal, moderate, historic, and mainstream. As such, it encompasses most Congregationalists, Methodists, Presbyterians, Episcopalians, and Lutherans. We have largely followed this denominational strategy in assigning white Protestants to either the evangelical or the mainline category.

As you can see from table 2.2, the three groups of Protestants differ substantially in their theological vision. Evangelical and African American Protestants mostly subscribe to a literal interpretation of scripture, while members of mainline denominations (and all other religious families) are much less likely to treat the Bible the same way. Similarly, compared both to mainline Protestants and members of other traditions, white and black evangelicals alike are much more likely to draw a great deal of guidance from religion, to attend religious services every week, and to pray on a daily basis. While this may seem to indicate that evangelicals are more religious than members of other faith traditions,

Table 2.2. Religious Beliefs and Behavior of Major Traditions in the United States (%)

Religious Family	Biblical Literalism[a]	Religion Provides "Great Deal" of Guidance in Life	Prays Daily or More	Tries to Be a Good Christian by Helping Others
Catholic	29	35	57	64
Evangelical Protestant[b]	56	43	67	44
Mainline Protestant[b]	30	32	46	57
Secular	14	11	35	na
Black Protestant	68	63	74	46
Jewish	7	3	24	na
Total population	38	34	54	52
N	2,164	2,204	2,200	1,563

Source: Calculated from the 2008 American National Election Studies (www.electionstudies.org) using the classification proposed by Steensland et al. (2000).
[a]Percentage who picked the option "The Bible is the actual word of God and is to be taken literally, word for word," as the best expression of their belief about the Bible.
[b]Excludes African Americans.
na = not ascertained.

it is equally possible that they are simply religious in a different way. The 2008 ANES asked Christians whether they expressed their religious values more by avoiding sinful behavior or helping people in need. A majority of white and black evangelicals picked the first option while larger majorities of mainline Protestants and Catholics said that being a Christian meant helping other people.

BASIC POLITICAL TENDENCIES

Americans are not very enthusiastic about the mixing of religion and politics. When asked whether churches should speak to public issues or remain on the sidelines, a clear majority of the public answers negatively, as demonstrated in table 2.3. More than two-thirds believe that congregations should not endorse candidates for public office and that religious leaders should not try to imitate lobbyists by influencing public policy. One might reasonably ask, then, whether religion matters in American political behavior. This book would not have been written if the answer were negative.

Table 2.3. American Attitudes about Religion in Politics

In your opinion, should the churches keep out of political matters, or should they express their views on day-to-day social and political questions?

Should keep out	54%
Should express views	40%
No opinion	6%
	100%

During political elections, should churches and other houses of worship come out in favor of one candidate over another, or shouldn't they do this?

Yes	24%
No	70%
Don't know/refused	6%
	100%

Do you agree or disagree with the following statement: Religious leaders should not try to influence government decisions.

Strongly agree/agree	66%
Neither agree nor disagree	15%
Strongly disagree/disagree	18%
	99%[a]

Sources: Pew Research Center for the People and the Press (2010, 2012), National Opinion Research Center (2008).
[a]Does not equal 100 percent due to rounding error.

We start by asking whether the six religious families constitute political communities or voting blocs. That is, do we find evidence that groups have characteristic political values that prevail among most members? Previous research has certainly suggested such basic political norms among these religious groups. American Jews, like their coreligionists in other countries, have long been identified with left-wing political causes. Black Protestants have usually supported the same liberal policies and candidates as Jews. Since the 1960s, some commentators have professed to see (and others have hoped for) a movement toward more conservative positions in both groups and the uncoupling of their political alliance. Even with these purported changes, most experts still find African American Protestants and Jews to the left of the political spectrum (Greenberg and Wald 2001). Although seculars have not been subject to much research, one clue about their general direction in politics has been the finding that such people tend to be young, mobile, well educated, and affluent and to live in urban or metropolitan areas and on the West Coast (Edmondson 1995). Because such characteristics are usually associated with unconventional thinking, it has been thought that the nonaffiliated tend to share the liberal political outlook of Jews and African American Protestants.

The white mainline Protestants have been strongly affected by the political and social traumas of recent years. Historically associated with the Republican Party and conservative positions on many issues, the mainline Protestants faced growing liberal sentiment from clergy and denominational leaders in the 1960s (Hadden 1969; Quinley 1974). About a decade later, the evangelicals were encouraged to move in a conservative direction by some of their most vocal pastors. It cannot be assumed that ordinary members of these camps shifted in accordance with their leaders. Many mainline Protestants have strongly resisted the liberalizing tendencies emanating from the pulpit and church officials. And reports of evangelical leaders urging their flocks to embrace conservative political causes have diverted public attention from other evangelical voices calling for social justice and world peace through cooperative disarmament (Wallis 1997). The opinion data will reveal how mainline and evangelical white Protestants have responded to these conflicting messages.

Like Jews and African American Protestants, Catholics coalesced around the Democratic Party in the 1930s; the Catholic commitment to the party was reinforced in 1960 when the Democrats conferred their presidential nomination on a Catholic candidate (Baggaley 1962). Some observers have doubted the depth of this commitment, arguing that attachment to the more liberal political party was a transient stage, reflecting the immigrant and working-class background of Catholics. Under conditions of economic parity with Protestants, they believed, Catholics would embrace the political conservatism that appears to be a more natural outgrowth of church doctrine (Phillips 1969, 140–75). Although many Catholics have moved into the economic mainstream and the Republicans have courted them aggressively (using the abortion controversy and other issues), it remains open to debate whether the Catholic masses have moved to the right side of the political spectrum (Leege 1996a). Except on the issue of abortion, members of the American Catholic religious elite—priests, bishops, and lay leaders—appear to have moved in just the opposite direction (Hanna 1984).

How well do these inherited expectations fit contemporary members of the basic religious families? In table 2.4, we look at three broad types of political disposition: preference for a political party, choice of presidential candidates, and liberal versus conservative self-image.

The most basic component of political identity is preference for a political party. Despite a decline of formal party membership, a rise in the proportion of citizens declaring themselves independent of the parties, and a greater willingness to cross party lines in voting, most Americans still classify themselves, in greater or lesser degree, as supporters of one or the other major political party. The selection of a particular partisan label (including "independent") remains a useful predictor of basic political attitudes, electoral choice, and a wide array of related attitudes. Though finer distinctions are possible, we divided the ANES participants simply into Democrats (51 percent), Republicans (38 percent), and independents (11 percent).[8]

Table 2.4 reveals pronounced partisan differences among the major religious groups. The three most strongly Democratic groups were African American Protestants, Jews, and seculars. Catholics were not quite so Democratic but still favored Democrats over Republicans, mimicking almost exactly the partisan distribution of the entire population. Mainline and evangelical Protestants, however, both reported a majority of Republican identifiers.

Another important element of political identity, ideological self-image, can be measured by asking individuals to characterize their political views on a scale from "liberal" to "conservative," with "moderate" as the neutral midpoint. In the public as a whole, there is a strong majority of self-identified conservatives (58 percent), a smaller group of liberals (37 percent), and the remaining 5 percent in the moderate category. The patterns among religious families in table 2.4 are similar but not identical to the findings for partisanship. Jewish respondents, who were overwhelmingly Democratic, were also the most willing of the six groups to embrace the liberal label. In fact, Jews were the only group with a strong majority in the liberal column. Seculars were more likely to pick the liberal than

Table 2.4. Basic Political Identity of Religious Families

	Catholic	Evangelical Protestant	Mainline Protestant	Secular	Black Protestant	Jewish	Total Population
Party (n = 2,190)							
Democrat	51	36	42	59	88	81	51
Independent	11	13	9	15	7	0	11
Republican	39	51	50	26	5	19	38
	101%[a]	101%[a]	101%[a]	100%	100%	100%	100%
Ideology (n = 2,013)							
Liberal	35	24	32	53	48	70	37
Moderate	8	3	7	3	5	7	5
Conservative	57	73	61	44	47	23	58
	100%	100%	100%	100%	100%	100%	100%
Vote in 2012 (n = 1,512)							
Obama (D)	51	20	45	73	95	70	51
Romney (R)	49	80	55	27	5	30	49
	100%	100%	100%	100%	100%	100%	100%

Source: Calculated from the 2008 American National Election Studies (www.electionstudies.org) using the classification proposed by Steensland et al. (2000). The 2012 voting data come from the National Exit Pool as reported in "How the Faithful Voted: 2012 Preliminary Analysis," Religion and Public Life Project, http://www.pewforum.org/2012/11/07/how-the-faithful-voted-2012-preliminary-exit-poll-analysis/#comp (2012).
[a]Total exceeds 100 percent due to rounding error.

the conservative label but by a smaller margin than Jewish respondents. At the other end of the scale, large majorities of the two white Protestant families and Catholics were prone to embrace the conservative label. That left black Protestants, who were equally divided between conservatives and liberals. For many groups, there was considerable slippage between partisanship and ideology. Despite their preference for the Democrats over the Republicans, minorities of African American Protestants and Roman Catholics selected the "liberal" label. These patterns should warn against inferring policy preferences solely from partisan loyalties or from assuming that ideological labels alone drive voting decisions.

Presidential elections give citizens an opportunity to act on their abstract political leanings. When asked for whom they voted in the 2012 presidential election, the respondents split their vote 51 to 49 percent between Democrat Barack Obama and the Republican candidate, Mitt Romney. The breakdown by religious groups in table 2.4 shows that President Obama had overwhelming support from blacks, Jews, and seculars, while Governor Romney had clear appeal to evangelical and, to a lesser degree, mainline Protestants. Catholics favored Obama over Romney by the same margin as the electorate as a whole in 2012. In general, the group patterns of 2012 were remarkably similar to those recorded in the immediate past. Jews and African American Protestants have been disproportionately Democratic for decades and evangelical Protestants overwhelmingly Republican since the late 1980s. Roman Catholics also showed continuity in their centrist location. Seculars have increasingly moved in a Democratic direction since 2000. As they had in the previous three presidential elections, mainline Protestant Republicans continued to favor the GOP nominee, but at much lower rates than in the past.

Looking over the three measures of basic political identity in table 2.4, then, Jews were consistent in their Democratic partisan identification, self-definition as liberals, and preference for Democratic presidential nominees. African American Protestants and seculars were similar to Jews, with the former showing less tendency to identify themselves as liberals and the latter to vote for the Democratic presidential candidate. Nonetheless, their centers of gravity were on the same side of the political spectrum. White evangelical Protestants constituted their opposite number—conservative in self-definition, Republican in both partisan identification and presidential vote choice in 2012. Mainline Protestants fit the same pattern but were a step behind evangelicals in each dimension. That leaves Catholics with a profile intermediate between the left- and right-wing camps: they were fairly evenly divided in partisanship and vote choice but more likely to identify themselves as conservative on the ideological scale. On questions of political identity, Roman Catholics define the midpoint of the American political spectrum.

These data suggest that Americans do not hermetically seal off their religious identities from their political attitudes and behavior. Throughout the book, we will explore the factors that account for the linkage and trace changes in the intersection of religion and politics in the American context.

CONCLUSION

This chapter has attempted to impose some order on the confusing religious landscape of the United States. We have emphasized the gaps that sometimes divide ordinary people in the pews and the formal creeds of their religious tradition. Nonetheless, we believe that three aspects of religious life—belief, organization, and subcommunity—help explain how religion becomes relevant to political life. The chapter also provided a basic way to divide up the population into six religious families and demonstrated that each tradition has some distinctive political features. Throughout the book, we will refer to these groups and emphasize how their creeds, structures, and social formations come to exert political influence.

3

Religion and American Political Culture

People act politically, economically, and socially in keeping with their ultimate beliefs. Their values, mores, and actions, whether in the polling booth, on the job, or at home, are an outgrowth of the god or gods they hold at the center of their being.

—Robert Swierenga

In hunting for evidence of religious influence in American political life, most observers examine church-state controversies or search for indications that religious groups vote in solid blocs. Another kind of religious influence is not quite so apparent. As William Lee Miller (1961) recognized, religion may contribute to the basic political values of a society:

> There is also a still more important, if less measurable, indirect and long-term effect of the religious tradition upon the nation's politics. This is the impact of ways of thinking, believing, and acting in religious matters upon the shape of the mind, which . . . affects the way other fields, like politics, are understood. Such effects, seeping down into the national character, may be discernible not only in clergymen and church people but in members of the society at large. (83)

By forming an important strand in American culture, religious creeds, institutions, and communities exerted a major impact on colonial life and work. As they spilled over into politics, religious forces helped to define the context of American political life. This chapter will trace connections between the religious ideas and practices prevalent in the American colonies and in subsequent American thought about important political questions.

Because the contribution of religion to American political culture covers such important beliefs as obedience, the design of government, and the national mission, the religious roots of American political culture merit close investigation. Recognizing that religious factors were not the sole influence on the national political creed, we will also consider the contribution of secular thought and material interests of many kinds.

Although we focus closely on history, this topic continues to resonate in contemporary political life. In each of his inaugural addresses, President George W. Bush repeatedly invoked the blessings of God on the United States and emphasized what he understood as a divine mandate behind America's global role. Many European observers, who had a much less charitable perspective on American actions in world politics, found the heavy religious imprint on Bush's rhetoric both peculiar and inappropriate. Whether that is so or not, the use of overt religious language by the forty-third president testifies to the continuing power of such thinking in American public life.

THE PURITAN IMPRINT ON COLONIAL THOUGHT

Although Americans often think of their country as a "new nation," its history and development largely untouched by the rest of the world, much that appears unique about American culture can be traced to the European heritage of the colonial settlers. For American political thought, the critical element of that heritage was the commitment of the settlers and their descendants to the particular form of Christianity that emerged from the Protestant Reformation (Bercovitch 1975; Niebuhr 1959).

Throughout sixteenth- and seventeenth-century Europe, dissatisfaction with the established churches fueled revolts against ecclesiastical authorities and the civil officials who sustained them. The leaders of the revolt in England—recognized today as the inspiration for American Protestantism—regarded themselves as nothing less than God's agents, engaged in a desperate struggle to liberate the church from "centuries of superstition and error" (Simpson 1955, 17). For its part, the Church of England regarded its Puritan critics as dangerous heretics, to be suppressed by any means necessary, including torture and execution. Eventually convinced that they could not reform or replace the state church, many Dissenters (as critics of the Church of England became known) chose to separate themselves from "an unregenerate government which persisted in maintaining a corrupt church" (Simpson 1955, 14–15), leaving England for places where they could practice a religion consistent with their faith. Driven by the impulse to create societies that would honor God in what they saw as the one true Christian fashion, the Puritan settlers crossed the Atlantic to found the American colonies. In America, they were free to build a culture in which the Protestant images of God, humanity, and the church became the core assumptions of everyday thought.

The influence of the Puritan outlook on American thought did not depend solely on the weight of numbers. The denominations most closely identified with the Puritan wing of the Protestant Reformation, the Congregationalists and Presbyterians, were dominant only in New England. The Church of England, though a minority faith in most of the settlements, enjoyed official status at one time or another in the southern colonies of Virginia, Georgia, and North and South Carolina. Roman Catholicism was a force to be reckoned with in Maryland. The Middle Atlantic colonies were settled principally by members of the Dutch Reformed Church, the Quakers, and adherents of several German Protestant traditions. Even in New England, the dominance of Puritan congregations was soon challenged by the strength of newer sects like the Baptists and the Methodists and weakened by internal conflicts over questions of theology and politics. Despite this religious diversity, few modern historians would contest the early nineteenth-century judgment of Alexis de Tocqueville (1945, 32) that the Puritan vision suffused the colonies.

As difficult as it may be for the twenty-first-century mind to comprehend a contemporary, the challenge is compounded many times over when the task involves understanding a seventeenth-century mind. Yet the task is essential if one is to understand the perspectives that shaped the early American political thought. In the century and a half that elapsed between the establishment of the first permanent English settlements on the North American continent and the founding of the republic, the theology of the Reformation was continually adapted to the American situation. The specifically religious impulse may have waned over time—its preeminence challenged by new intellectual currents and commercial considerations—but periodic revivals kept it very much alive in the American mind.

Early American politics bore the imprint of this religiosity. For example, the Puritans were voracious readers of scripture. Under the doctrine that ordinary people needed no intermediary between themselves and the word of God, and indeed God himself, Puritanism encouraged individuals to look for divine guidance in the scriptures. Up to the time of the revolution and perhaps for some time thereafter, the Bible was the book most familiar to the typical inhabitant of America. A study by Donald Lutz (1984) suggests that the biblical tradition seems also to have greatly influenced those who led the American Revolution and wrote the Constitution. In an intensive study of nearly one thousand political documents issued to the public from 1760 through 1805, Lutz found that the Bible was the single most frequently cited work in these documents. Though this hardly supports Thornton's claim that the Bible was "the textbook of the fathers of the Republic" (quoted in Sandoz 1990, 142), it at least suggests an environment of intense scriptural literacy and consciousness and explains why political argument was usually couched in biblical language and why biblical analogies were employed to explain the political situation (Dreisbach 2011).

Further illustrating the impact of religion, preaching and worship styles were quickly transplanted to the political realm. Political campaigning adopted the techniques of mass persuasion seen during the "Great Awakenings," those periodic outbursts of intense religious enthusiasm that swept across the continent. Candidates rallied supporters with torchlight parades, tent meetings, door-to-door canvassing, and public declarations of faith, the same methods pioneered by evangelists seeking religious converts (Jensen 1980). Campaigns appropriated religious hymns for political use or else commissioned campaign songs that drew on sacred music. Daniel Walker Howe (1990, 124–25) traces a prominent American political innovation, the national nominating convention, to the national meetings pioneered by religious associations.

In addition to its impact on the language and techniques of politics, the religious environment was also an important factor in developing national unity among the colonists. In response to the outbreak of hostilities in 1776, an astonished Englishman reported, "From one end of North America to the other, they are FASTING and PRAYING" (quoted in Sandoz 1990, 141). Throughout the Revolutionary War, the Protestant clergy built support for the cause by emphasizing the religious nature of the conflict. In a typical sermon preached in 1777, the Rev. Nicholas Street (Cherry 1972) reminded congregants that the people of Israel had grown restive and fearful when led from the security of Egyptian slavery into the unpredictable freedom of the wilderness. In the same manner, he argued, the colonists had thrown off a tyrant only to find themselves apprehensive about the future. They must confront their fears, he said, by recognizing that "God frequently brings his own people into a state of peculiar trials, to discover to them and others what there is in their hearts." In the case at hand, the minister said, God was looking for signs of genuine piety and repentance before delivering the colonies from the hands of their enemies. In addition to providing aid and comfort to the colonial army, the minister advised his audience that it would render a signal duty to the war effort by confessing its wickedness and endeavoring to avoid sin. Some ministers went well beyond this measured tone to equate Britain with the Antichrist and to treat the republican cause as the pure expression of Christian values (Bloch 1990, 49–52; Noll 1988, chap. 3). Popular support for the Revolutionary War owed something to the way the revolution was "preached to the masses as a religious revival" (Perry Miller quoted in Sandoz 1990, 135).

The imprint of Protestant Christianity on the era of the Founders and, through time, on contemporary U.S. political life is apparent in several respects. From the body of Puritan thought come three elements that proved especially important for subsequent American political practice: covenant theology, the emphasis on the total depravity of humankind, and the concept of a chosen people. Each of these doctrines was applied by the Puritan thinkers and their successors to the earthly realm of politics. Covenant theology helped Americans decide under what conditions governments required obedience. The Puritan image of human sinfulness provided clues about the best design for maintaining stable government. And the idea of "chosenness" encouraged Americans to think about their nation in missionary terms. Despite the passage of centuries, these ideas continue to cast a long shadow over the conduct of American political life.

COVENANT THEOLOGY AND THE RIGHT TO REVOLT

Most Americans take it for granted that citizens owe allegiance to governments that respect their "inalienable" rights and liberties; they also seem to accept without question the assertion in the Declaration of Independence that citizens have a right to revolt against governments that deny fundamental freedoms. The idea of conditional allegiance, of a "contract" between citizens and rulers that can be voided when the government misbehaves, is a cornerstone of American political thought.

This concept of government as a covenant gained such ready acceptance among colonial Americans because it bore a close resemblance to a central element in Puritan theology, the covenant. Puritan thinkers gave considerable warrant to this model of association, which appears at several different points in the Bible (Elazar 1980, 12–20). In the most influential of the biblical covenants, Abraham and God were joined together by bonds of mutual obligation as Abraham accepted the promise of God's blessing for himself; his heirs, the people of Israel, in turn pledged to do God's work in the wilderness (Gen. 12:3). This obligation was imposed on Abraham not by fiat but by a "conscious contract with God" whereby Abraham "promised to do certain things for God in return for which God pledged Himself to recompense Abraham" (P. Miller 1956, 119). As the Puritans understood it, the defining characteristic of a covenant was that of a voluntary agreement, sanctified by God, in which individuals freely surrendered autonomy in exchange for something of greater value. God hovered over covenants either as a partner or, in the case of contracts among individuals, as the sanctifier and guarantor in whose name the agreement was forged.

This model of social organization was applied by the Puritans to all manner of human associations. Under the image of the covenant, the "church" was redefined: rather than an institution with authority in a particular geographic area, it was seen as a community of the elect, a gathering of those who received the promise of eternal salvation in exchange for accepting a mission to act as God's agents in this world. Extended to civil societies, the covenant provided a basis for human governance. In crossing the Atlantic, the Puritans envisioned themselves as a latter-day people of Israel, re-creating the Hebrew covenant in their pilgrimage to the New World. The most famous reenactment of the covenant ritual was the Mayflower Compact, in which the Pilgrims (a Puritan congregation) aboard the ship pledged to create a holy, Bible-based commonwealth in the wilderness in exchange for God's blessing. This ceremony was repeated after landfall in the famous Plymouth Compact. The settlements that spread throughout the New England colonies during the seventeenth century were founded on similar compacts (Lutz 1994).

The political implications of the covenant idea became especially important when Americans sought to justify their decision to cut all legal ties with Great Britain. The crucial link was forged when the idea of a covenant was extended to encompass an entire nation. If the relationship between colonist and king was a contract sealed by the authority of God—in other words, a covenant—then the terms of that contract bore divine authority. The citizens owed allegiance to the ruler, and the ruler, in turn, was committed to honor the contract by acting within its limits. In the view of the colonists, "rulers who violate the agreed-upon forms are usurpers and so are to be legitimately resisted" (P. Miller 1967, 98).

The implications of this type of reasoning were revolutionary. Whereas others interpreted the Bible as saying that God ordained obedience to government, a view that promoted absolutist rule, the Puritans understood the relationship between people and government as one of mutual obligation.

The basis for this revised interpretation was the model of the biblical covenants. Through agreements with Adam, Noah, Abraham, and others, God had entered into binding contracts with human beings. Though surely not the equal of the mortals in these partnerships, God nonetheless promised to behave in accordance with the terms of the contract, acting as a kind of constitutional monarch in the universe. If God had agreed to be bound in this manner, how could any earthly monarch presume to be exempt from limits or obligations?

Fortified by biblical precedent, the colonists insisted that the monarch respect their universal rights as creations of God, along with the specific rights due to them as citizens of the British Empire.[1] Because obedience was conditioned on the ruler behaving in conformity with agreed-upon standards, it could justly be withdrawn whenever the standards were violated. Thus, when King George III clearly abridged the rights to which the colonists felt entitled, they claimed that the colonies no longer owed him loyalty. Resistance to a government that violated God's law could even be seen as a religious obligation.

The colonists repeatedly invoked the covenant tradition to justify the breaking of their bonds with Great Britain. Almost a year to the day before the Declaration of Independence was made public, the Continental Congress called on Americans to observe a day of national confession, marked by "publick humiliation, fasting, and prayer." After promising this confession and pledging repentance, the colonists asked God for help in persuading the British to respect the terms of the compact that bound the colonies to the mother country (P. Miller 1967, 90–91). When the British proved resistant to these prayers, the colonists once again stressed that a broken covenant justified revolt. The Declaration of Independence begins with the assertion that the colonists deserved independence under "the Laws of Nature and Nature's God." Consistent with covenant theory, the colonists asserted that the bond between rulers and ruled was dependent on the ruler's respect for those rights that God granted to men. Once the terms of the compact had been violated by a despotic King George (as the colonists sought to demonstrate in great detail), the people of America could claim a divine mandate to dissolve their ties. The declaration concludes with the submission of the purity of the rebels' claim to "the Supreme Judge of the World."

The breaking of the covenant not only entitled the people to withdraw authority from a corrupt government but also, as the Declaration of Independence emphasizes, authorized them to form a new system of rule. Once independence was secured, the colonists went about the task of building a new state on the promise that a new covenant was required. After a false start, they settled on what is sometimes called the American national covenant—the Constitution of the United States. Although the Constitution does not explicitly recognize God as a partner or invoke divine blessing— a sign of its secular purpose—the document bears the mark of covenant thinking in a number of important respects (Hughey 1984).

Following the original Hebrew concept of covenant as a voluntary undertaking, the Constitution was a contract freely entered into by the people of the thirteen states. It was presented to them as a document that they were free to accept or reject. The biblical covenant created a "people" who, if they accepted the agreement, were promised God's blessings; similarly, the Constitution was presented in the name of the "People of the United States" to achieve for them such beneficent ends as justice, order, welfare, and liberty. Covenants, as the Puritans understood them, routinely set limits on the power of authorities. The privileges of power were legitimate only insofar as they were carried out with respect for the God-given rights of the contracting parties. Commentators have called attention to the corresponding emphasis on limits in the U.S. Constitution. The document is replete with provisions spelling out what government may not do and holding government subject to strict rules and standards in the performance of its duties.

Americans continue to live under the Constitution, of course, but do they ascribe any religious significance to it? Some commentators suggest that the Constitution is enveloped in a virtual aura of holiness. The document enjoys the status of a holy relic, encased in a shrine to which citizens make pilgrimages, its authors revered as saints or demigods, and its meaning entrusted to an elite group of judges (i.e., Supreme Court justices) that strikingly resembles "a priesthood which sits in a temple" (Rountree 1990, 204). If not a full-fledged religion, the Constitution supplies U.S. citizens with a national identity, sacred civic values, and comforting rituals (Levinson 1988; Rountree 1990, 204–7). If they need reminding of the covenantal roots of American political thought, the American people often receive it from their presidents. Bill Clinton (1992) offered the American people a "New Covenant that balanced the government's responsibility to promote opportunity with citizens' obligation to act responsibly" (Barnes 1992). After 9/11, George W. Bush similarly asked Americans, especially the younger generation, to recommit themselves to the nation by supporting the war on terror, deepening their faith, and performing community service (Bostdorff 2003).

PURITANISM AND DEMOCRACY: A QUALIFICATION

Associating Puritanism with democracy sounds strange in an age that views Puritans as "insufferable, self-righteous precisionists with narrow minds and blue noses, authoritarian, clericalist, intolerant, and antidemocratic" (Ahlstrom 1965, 95). Historians remind us that Puritan settlements were motivated not by an abstract commitment to religious liberty, which they routinely denied to dissenters in their midst, but rather by the desire to protect their own religious practices. They succeeded magnificently in this objective, imposing on the colonies "a narrower band of religious choices than fellow subjects enjoyed in England" (Murrin 1990, 21). Reflecting "a narrow, sectarian spirit" (Tocqueville 1945, 41), their legal codes mandated church attendance, forbade worship in alien faiths, and "constantly invaded the domain of conscience" by exacting criminal penalties for every imaginable sin. How could such people possibly lay the foundations of a democracy?

Tocqueville supplied one answer when he credited Puritanism with a "spirit of democracy" that sustained freedom and liberty as cultural values (Kessler 1992). This spirit came first from the egalitarian New Testament vision of the church as an association open to all humanity. It was reinforced by the distinctly Protestant view of individuals as capable of discovering religious truth through their own efforts. Both arguments, deployed against the territorial and hierarchical Church of England, mandated that individuals be granted religious choice. Choice was not to be construed, however, as freedom to run riot, but rather as a divine gift of "liberty for that only which is just and good" (Tocqueville 1945, 44). Paradoxically, Puritan citizens used freedom to impose on themselves "fantastic and oppressive laws" supposedly in accord with God's plan for humankind. But the potent ideal of liberty, once proclaimed, could not be effectively restricted to the narrow channel approved by Puritan orthodoxy. It eventually challenged the very idea of an "official" religion and undermined any special claims to authority by a religious elite. In the political sphere, the assumption that individuals will discover truth by exercising liberty imparted sacredness to majority opinion. If the Puritans neither embraced nor practiced democracy as we know it, they nonetheless paved the way for it.

The democratic elements in the Puritan creed were reinforced by institutional interest and the social practices of Protestant Christianity in the New World. The "interest" that first drew Puritans to the New World, a desire to escape the entrenched Church of England, was increasingly threatened by the efforts of the British government to assert greater control over the colonies. Even the transplanted Anglican establishments in the southern colonies had grown accustomed to remarkable autonomy from the mother church in England (Mead 1976, 25–27). In the 1760s, colonists were particularly agitated by plans to appoint Anglican bishops in America. To persons steeped in a tradition of congregational autonomy and religious pluralism, a system in which religious leaders enjoyed minimal civil authority, the prospect of a centralized system of church government seemed to be the opening wedge in a campaign to undo the legacy of their Puritan forebears. Amid the continuing conflict between the Church of England and the colonies, fear of losing religious liberty played a major role in the development of American nationalism and helped stimulate the drive for independence from Britain (Bridenbaugh 1962).

Viewed as a social force, religion taught the colonists themselves much about the actual practice of democracy. In most of Europe, local churches were held accountable to centralized national hierarchies that prescribed a code of belief, determined acceptable forms of worship, and provided ministers to ensure that local practice conformed to national standards. Membership in the church, determined solely by place of residence, was essentially a matter of passive acceptance rather than active involvement. Colonial religious life, in contrast, developed on the principles of voluntary affiliation and congregational independence. After "planting" a church in the wilderness, the founders could prescribe conditions of membership, formulate their own code of belief and practice, and select a minister who served at the pleasure of the congregants. Membership in a church was an option, rather than an automatic status, and carried with it an obligation to participate actively in the running of the congregation.

The tradition of self-rule that developed in the churches before and after the revolution encouraged the corresponding growth of a vigorous democratic spirit in the political realm (Hatch 1990). These habits and attitudes eventually spread far beyond New England and the Puritans, encompassing most of the religious traditions that claimed the loyalties of colonists (Bonomi 1994; Calhoon 1994). In the judgment of the historian Sydney Ahlstrom (1975, 424), membership in self-governing churches "prepared men to regard the social compact as the proper basis of government." Modern research supports this logic by demonstrating that democratic experience in the home, school, and workplace "spills over" into politics, promoting democratic dispositions (Lipsitz 1964; Renshon 1975). Ahlstrom's conclusion gains further support from the simultaneous development in New England of the congregational principle in church governance and democratic practices in civil life. To a degree unparalleled at that time (though restricted by today's standards), the New England colonies achieved high levels of suffrage, powerful representative institutions, respect for the rule of law, and social policies that encouraged the spread of education, science, culture, and charitable activity (Shipton 1947).

The link between democracy and religion thus turned on all three dimensions of religion. If the creed of Protestant Christianity was ambiguous about democracy as a system of government, the fear of English assaults on the reformed churches and the training in self-government provided by autonomous congregations tipped the scales in favor of the revolutionary cause. For these institutional and social contributions, as much as covenantal theology, the heirs of the Protestant Reformation deserve recognition as precursors of the democratic spirit in America.[2]

"TOTAL DEPRAVITY" AND INSTITUTIONAL RESTRAINT

Another aspect of Puritanism shaped the political system adopted after the American Revolution. The Puritan emphasis on the inherent sinfulness of humankind (a strong theme in Protestant thought) provided principles of governance that the Founders observed in constructing their constitutional alternative to the colonial framework. Though we are apt to think of their creation, the Constitution, as a neutral set of institutional arrangements, the system they fashioned is infused with a moral architecture that still guides the conduct of American political life.

The American governmental system was designed by political architects who assumed that human beings could not be trusted with power. To keep government safely under control, they divided authority among three separate branches, giving each leverage to use against the others, and they added additional safeguards such as powerful territorial governments (the states). As a consequence of that framework, the great challenge to any U.S. political leader is to overcome the inherent division of authority by mobilizing all institutions and levels of government on behalf of a common purpose. Compromise, delay, and deadlock are the characteristics of normal political life, to the frustration of advocates of rapid change.

The ultimate explanation for this aspect of U.S. political life lies in the concept of humanity that guided some of the Founders in their deliberations at Philadelphia. Far from adoring "the people," many of the Founders appraised them with a cold eye and found more to say about the defects of popular will than about its virtues. In emphasizing their suspicions about humanity, the Founders repeated a theme found in Reformation theology. For the Puritans, the fate of mortals was symbolized by the story of Adam. In sinning against God, Adam forfeited eternal happiness for a life of toil and sorrow that would end in death. Puritans saw this story as illustrative of the inherent depravity of human beings, who, given a choice between good and evil, would often choose the latter. Unlike Catholic doctrine, which taught that the church could offer believers an escape from damnation, or the religions that held out some hope for redemption through good behavior, Puritan theology grimly promised that only a few (the "elect") would enjoy the light of God's grace and that the rest would know only sinfulness on Earth and eternal torment thereafter.

This perspective led to two important political conclusions. First, because governments were the creations of fallible mortals, no government could be expected to act with rectitude. Quite the contrary—a government that reflected the sinfulness of its human creators would be prone to exceed its rightful authority. Under those circumstances, prudence dictated that the power of government be limited, or, in the words of one Protestant clergyman, that "we should leave nothing to human virtue that can be provided for by law or constitution" (Strout 1974, 61). Second, because God was the only source of redemption, it was not the task of governments to make people good. The highest aspiration for government should be merely to subdue the most blatant excesses of human behavior. Puritan thought acknowledged that these rules could be softened if those who constructed and ran the government happened to be members of God's elect. But even then, it would be wise to put restraints on government lest it fall into the hands of the unregenerate. And even a government of saints, unlikely as that would be, could do no more than promote the conditions under which men and women might have the opportunity to live righteously.

These assumptions weighed heavily in the deliberations of the Constitutional Convention and were offered to justify the document that emerged from that conclave. Although revered as the foundation of a democratic republic, the Constitution was crafted by politicians who made no secret of their faith in the Puritan doctrine of human sinfulness (Wright 1949). In a series of newspaper articles written to encourage ratification by the states and now regarded as the authoritative reflection of the Founders' intentions, Alexander Hamilton, John Jay, and James Madison outdid one another in trumpeting their belief that human beings should not be trusted with unlimited power. The authors of what came to be known as the *Federalist Papers* presented countless historical examples to show that people were inherently prone to choose evil over good, self-interest over the public good, and immediate gratification over prudent delay. Previous attempts at republican government had foundered because organized groups destroyed the institutions of representation in their single-minded pursuit of power and wealth. With its wealth of examples of past failures, the *Federalist Papers* reads like a catalog of human imperfections. This jaundiced (or, to some, realistic) assessment of humankind was accepted as a basic condition, rooted in human nature, revealed in history, and impervious to changing social conditions.

Like the early Puritan settlers, the Founders identified the innate corruption of humankind as the root problem of government and the great challenge to stable democracy. The task of the Constitution they crafted was to permit republican government in spite of human tendencies to destroy liberty. To accomplish this, the Founders broke with traditional political thought by viewing human depravity both as a barrier to liberty and, under the right circumstances, as a republican asset. The problem, they agreed, was to secure a government capable of providing order, yet limited enough to maintain a large degree of freedom. In practical terms, this meant that the national or central government must be given greater power than it had been allowed in the aftermath of the American Revolution. The question was how to harness and control the power a strong central government would require.

The Founders' principal solution to this problem was to partition the major powers of government by embedding them in distinct and separate institutions. Given an independent base of power, the Founders thought, the three branches of government could be expected to resist encroachments by each other. They would pool their authority to achieve a common goal only when it was clearly in the national interest. By dividing power in this way, John Adams had written earlier, "the efforts in human nature toward tyranny can alone be checked and restrained, and any freedom preserved in the Constitution" (quoted in Wright 1949, 9). In dividing government roles among different institutions and embracing such doctrines as election of public officials, fixed terms of office, geographic decentralization, and strict limits on government authority, the Founders of the late eighteenth century appropriated the very methods that Puritans of the early seventeenth century had developed to restrict local religious and government officials (Witte 1990).

Paradoxically, then, the weaknesses of humankind were called on to fuel the engine of free government. The human shortcomings that other theorists had perceived as the stumbling block to any plan for durable republican government were enlisted by the Founders as the bulwark against tyranny. What would keep the branches independent of one another, the framers predicted, were precisely those less-than-noble qualities that reposed in typical human beings: ambition, envy, greed, lust for power, and so on. Jealous to preserve its own power and status, Congress would never cede to the president the absolute authority of a monarch. Recognizing that their perpetuation depended on preserving the Constitution, the state governments would use the veto power over amendments to retain their role. Judges and executive branch officials would be restrained by the recognition that they could lose their exalted status by impeachment. All in all, as one scholar has written (Diggins 1984, 53), the Founders believed "that the Republic would be preserved by the 'machinery of government,' not the morality of men."

Considering that the Constitution had to be submitted to the people for their evaluation, it may seem remarkable that the Founders were so explicit in denouncing the trustworthiness of human behavior. In one of the most important letters of the *Federalist Papers*, number 51, James Madison did little to flatter the citizens whose votes he sought. To control the government, he wrote, it was not enough to rely on the best instincts of the people; it required "auxiliary provisions" such as the various limiting mechanisms of the Constitution. The great hope for the preservation of liberty was to equip each branch of the new government with "the necessary constitutional means and personal motives to resist encroachments of the others." Then, in a phrase that nicely encapsulated the Federalist philosophy of humankind, he reiterated the principal rationale for the various devices that controlled the exercise of governmental authority: "It may be a reflection on human nature that such devices should be necessary to control the abuses of government. But what is government itself but the greatest of all reflections on human nature? If men were angels, no government would be necessary. If angels were to govern men, neither external nor internal controls on government would be necessary" (Rossiter 1961, 322). Precisely because mortals fell short of angelic standards and angels did not deign to rule, prudence demanded that government be restrained from acting on its worst impulses.

That the framers felt free to defend the Constitution in those terms suggests that their understanding of human depravity was widely shared by the American people. In the fight over ratification, the most effective opposition came from critics who accepted the Puritan diagnosis but doubted that the proposed remedies for it were strong enough to control the weaknesses of human nature (Kenyon 1955). The Antifederalists, for example, believed that the framers of the Constitution were naive to imagine that any strong, centralized government could withstand the depredation of the greedy and ambitious. Whatever the differences between the proponents and the enemies of the new governmental framework, however, the important point is that the entire debate was conducted within the bounds defined by the Puritan vision of human sinfulness.

Skepticism, rooted in the Puritan worldview, also led the Founders to a negative view of government that is still widely shared by U.S. citizens. For all their veneration of the American way of life, Americans are quite cynical about politics and tend to hold its practitioners in low regard. There is a pronounced distrust of the motivations of politicians and an enduring yearning to purify politics by bestowing leadership on persons who have achieved eminence in other fields—astronauts, generals, business leaders, soldiers, engineers, farmers, and the like. These people, untainted by contact with a corrupting system, must be prevailed on to relinquish the pleasures of life and to enter the sordid world of political combat. There they are supposed to save the citizenry from "politics" by restoring a measure of sanity and common sense to political life.

The traditional American view of politics as a sordid endeavor derives in part from the Founders. As we have just seen, they perceived government as a necessary evil, an institution that had to exist to preserve order but not a good thing in itself. By embracing so wholeheartedly the Puritan concept of humanity, emphasizing human bellicosity as the constant threat to liberty, they essentially reduced government to the status of a night watchman. Believing that government could just as easily threaten liberty as safeguard it, they called for as little governmental authority as was necessary to prevent society from collapsing into disarray. As for the higher task of cultivating human virtue, that was to be left to private institutions, such as the church, and did not belong in the government's sphere of responsibility (Diamond 1977).

The Founders' concept of government would have astounded the ancient political thinkers, to whom politics, which Aristotle called "the master science," was the highest expression of human capacity. To the ancients, the state was a moral tutor, whose task was to promote certain virtues among its citizens. According to this conception, politics was the realm in which people could overcome narrow self-interest by searching for the best interests of the community. Citizenship was not a term denoting a dry legal status, but rather a title of honor reserved for those who cared deeply about the community and cultivated the public good. A republican form of government could not survive unless it inculcated such virtuous qualities in its inhabitants. According to classical republican thought, the very maintenance of the state depended on its commitment to elevate, to ennoble, and to advance the interests of the community by promoting exemplary behavior. To accomplish those ambitious goals, the state had to possess substantial means, even the ability to coerce recalcitrant people to conform to what the community defined as acceptable conduct. Participation in that enterprise was seen as important and honorable.

Nothing could be further from the American conception, which equates good government with limited government. Most Americans assume that the inherent rights of individual citizens normally take precedence over the claims of the state or those of any broader social purpose. Because such individual rights can be threatened by an overbearing government, Americans put a premium on protecting individuals from the heavy hand of the state. Following the Founders, Americans have routinely denied government the right or authority to regulate belief or to limit most forms of conduct. Outside a very limited sphere, "personal virtue" is simply not seen as the proper concern of government.

Such a negative view of authority has affected the image of politicians. Those who are most deeply involved in conducting the business of the state, it has commonly been assumed, do so in pursuit of nothing more than self-interest. The vocation of politics, perceived in the classical tradition as the pursuit of public welfare, appears to the modern age as merely a struggle for power and personal advantage. Indeed, there is a widespread suspicion that politics attracts people because, as careers go, it is a fairly good way to make a living.

Limitations on government power can certainly be defended by reference to the terrible damages inflicted by governments that saw themselves as agents of God or history, charged with remaking humanity in a new image. Just as certainly, it presents problems when government tries to persuade the citizenry to undertake actions that contribute in the long run to the public good but run against immediate self-interest. As Robert Horwitz (1977, 333) asked, "How can a republic based solely on the principle of individual self-interest continue to defend itself against its external enemies if its citizenry has not an iota of patriotism, public spirit, or any element of that sense of duty that leads men to make sacrifices in defense of their country?" By teaching that government is a threat to the liberty of freeborn citizens, that it is a necessity born of human imperfection, the Founders unwittingly made it difficult for their successors to motivate behavior in the public interest.

ONE NATION UNDER GOD: A CIVIL RELIGION

Yet another aspect of American political life, a pronounced tendency to approach political issues in moral terms, owes much to the Puritan legacy. Commentators have long noted that American political rhetoric is infused with religious symbols and references and that debates about contending policy choices are frequently couched in terms of competing moral values. According to some scholars, this constant recourse to religious images and symbols in American political culture provides evidence of the existence of what has variously been called a public theology, a political religion, a religion of democracy, a public philosophy, or, most commonly today, a civil religion.

At the core of the rich and subtle concept of civil religion is the idea that a nation tries to understand its historical experience and national purpose in religious terms (Bellah 1975; Bellah and Hammond 1980; Richey and Jones 1974). In the same way that religion may endow the life of an individual with a greater meaning than mere existence, so a civil religion reflects an attempt by citizens to imbue their nation with transcendent value.[3] The nation is recognized as a secular institution, yet one that is somehow touched by the hand of God.

The term *civil religion* does not refer to any formal code of beliefs that is fully developed and authoritatively encapsulated by a single written document. Because there is no formal statement of it, the content of a civil religion has to be inferred from the speeches and writings of political leaders. It lacks the status of a state religion, so citizens are not obliged to assent to it. A civil religion is neither the religion of a particular church nor, at the other extreme, a fully articulated religion that competes with existing denominations. Rather, it is a code subscribed to, in varying degrees, by all religions in the nation. Accordingly, it closely resembles one anthropologist's definition of a creed: "A constellation of ideas and standards that gives people a sense of belonging together and of being different from those of other nations and cultures" (cited in Mead 1974, 45–46). By imparting a sacred character to the nation, civil religion enables people of diverse faiths to harmonize their religious and political beliefs.

In thinking about the transcendent purpose of their nation, Americans have traditionally been drawn to the biblical metaphor of the "chosen people" (Cherry 1972). The Puritan colonists were prone to interpret their passage to the New World as a reenactment of God's covenant with Abraham and his descendants. Like the ancient Jews, the Puritans felt they had been selected by God for the purpose of bringing redemption to humankind. If they succeeded in establishing Christian communities in the wilderness, creating "God's New Israel," the rest of the world would see how the faithful were rewarded with good fortune. Although the settlements themselves strayed far from the Christian models that motivated their founding, the Puritans were constantly reminded that their success or failure had implications for all humankind. That the existence of the United States is still viewed as part of a divine plan shows up in the Pledge of Allegiance in the phrase "one nation under God"—language that was added only in the 1950s.

Ever since the concept of a civil religion was first suggested, in the late 1960s, its existence has been the subject of a sustained debate among scholars of American society (see Gehrig 1979 for a good summary). Some observers have discounted civil religion as nothing more than religious nationalism, the common tendency among nations to endow themselves with divine favor.[4] Robert Bellah (1975), the sociologist who did more than anyone else to popularize the concept, argued that the national traumas of the 1960s and 1970s largely eroded American faith in the nation's higher purpose. Against this backdrop, social scientists have tested for the existence of civil religious sentiments with a variety of research tools. Although the findings have not been entirely consistent, most studies have detected in public attitudes something very much like civil religion.

Civil religion often emerges in studies of political rhetoric (Hart 1977). In a systematic content analysis of inaugural addresses delivered from George Washington to Ronald Reagan, Cynthia Toolin (1983) found the speeches replete with reference to the nation's divine origin and its corresponding moral obligation to light the way for the remainder of the earth. A content analysis of the national magazine published by the Masonic fraternal organization identified a large number of statements emphasizing the nation's divine purpose (Joliceur and Knowles 1978). Using questions listed in figure 3.1, Ronald Wimberley and his colleagues have been able to demonstrate a high level of public assent to statements that seem consistent with the civil religion theme (Christenson and Wimberley 1978; Wimberley 1976, 1979). Responses to these questions, which have been asked of divergent audiences, do not simply reflect commitment to general religious values or any other background factors. Rather, just as predicted by the scholars who first called attention to an American civil

The existence of an American civil religion has been inferred from re-sponses to the following statements:

1. It is a mistake to think that America is God's chosen nation today.
2. I consider holidays like the Fourth of July religious as well as patri-otic.
3. We need more laws on morals.
4. We should respect a president's authority since his authority is from God.
5. National leaders should affirm their belief in God.
6. *Good* patriots are not necessarily religious people.
7. Social justice cannot be based on laws; it must also come from reli-gion.
8. To me, the flag of the United States is sacred.
9. God can be known through the experience of the American people.
10. If the American government does not support religion, the govern-ment cannot uphold morality. (Wimberly 1976)

Figure 3.1. Civil Religious Sentiment in the United States

religion, civil religious feelings have been widely diffused among the per-sons interviewed in the polls. A similar survey among elementary school children in the Midwest yielded comparable support for the civil religion hypothesis (Smidt 1980). These findings are not surprising in view of the many ways that public schools inculcate the beliefs, display the symbols, and act out the rituals associated with the creed of Americanism (Gamo-ran 1990). On the basis of these studies, it does appear that Americans expect their nation to fill a spiritual purpose.[5] Although there is no data to test the proposition, many observers believe that civil religion was re-charged by the trauma of 9/11 (McClay 2004).

The presidency appears to play a crucial symbolic role in American civil religion, an observation brought home in an unexpected way by public reaction to the assassination of John F. Kennedy in 1963. Sociologi-cal investigators noted a marked increase in prayer, worship, and other forms of religious activity. Despite the formal secularization of the gov-ernmental system and President Kennedy's membership in a minority faith (Roman Catholicism), many Americans reacted to the assassination by expressing intense religious commitment. To the political scientist Sid-ney Verba (1965, 354), the public response revealed that "political com-mitment in the United States contains a prime component of primordial religious commitment." In mourning the slain president, Americans were honoring a sacred symbol. The discovery that a political leader could take on a religious significance for the public provided further evidence that the nation is viewed in transcendent terms.

Civil religion has also reinforced the "deep-rooted belief in American culture that political and personal virtue should be inseparable" (Sennett 1987, 42). In the 1988 presidential campaign, southern voters told pollsters they believed a candidate's moral behavior in private life foretold success in office and cited previous drug use, extramarital affairs, and lying as behavior they would weigh against a candidate.[6] Accordingly, one candidate was driven from the race for the nomination by allegations of marital infidelity, another was forced out in response to charges of plagiarism, and two had to endure criticism when they admitted having smoked marijuana in their youth. This was neither the first nor the last example of such moral transgressions affecting political standing. Evidence that he had lied about his knowledge of the Watergate burglary drove Richard Nixon from the White House in 1974. By admitting past use of marijuana, a 1987 nominee for the Supreme Court raised grave questions about his fitness for the post. Questions about Bill Clinton's marital fidelity, drug use, and personal honesty were prominent features of the 1992 presidential campaign. Divorce, once seen as a moral failing, was a major handicap to presidential aspirants before it became so widespread in recent years. There is less room for leeway when a public official is also a religious symbol (Fairbanks 1981).

The concept of civil religion stimulates two contrasting impulses, each of which can be discerned in Puritan rhetoric (Marty 1974). When they described themselves as embarking on an "errand into the wilderness," the first settlers seemingly accepted the responsibility of spreading the Puritan model to the rest of humanity. The alternative description of their settlement as a "city on a hill" implied the task of building a just society worthy of emulation. The first metaphor suggests an active mission to impose a system whose virtue is assumed, while the latter image assigns more priority to setting an example. In much the same way, the civil religion of the United States has encouraged citizens both to celebrate the glory of the nation and to hold it to account.

In what social scientists call "legitimation" or its "priestly" aspect, civil religion helps cement loyalty to the nation. God blesses the nation because it serves a sacred purpose. So long as the nation conducts its affairs according to some higher purpose, it warrants allegiance from its citizens on grounds other than mere self-interest. By giving the nation a mission to which citizens are emotionally attached, civil religion may thus counter the tendencies to elevate self-interest into the only basis for loyalty and obedience. The legitimation function of civil religion has been evident in the attitudes of children who link a religious or spiritual view of the nation with very positive images of political authority (Smidt 1982; Funderburk 1986).

While there is much to be said for the priestly aspect of civil religion in building support for and commitment to the nation, it can easily degenerate into mere religious nationalism, an "ideology that fuses God, country, and flag" as a club to beat down anybody who criticizes the United States or acts differently (Bellah 1966, 16). In some religious traditions, equating any nation with the will of God is considered a form of blasphemy that demeans God.

To balance the priestly effect, civil religion also provides standards by which to judge a nation's behavior. It suggests that there are things higher than the nation and that it is permissible to criticize the nation for its departures from moral codes. As the New Testament taught, a nation "under God" is deemed responsible to God and will be held to a high standard of behavior. Because transgressors suffer severe punishment from a just God, citizens have an incentive to keep the nation firmly on the path of righteousness. This is the "prophetic" function of civil religion, a role often filled by social critics such as the Rev. Martin Luther King Jr. When he admonished American Christians to challenge racial segregation, Dr. King (1963) imagined what St. Paul would have said to them:

> You have a dual citizenry. You live both in time and eternity. Your highest loyalty is to God, and not to the mores or the folkways, the state or the nation, or any man-made institution. If any earthly institution or custom conflicts with God's will, it is your Christian duty to oppose it. You must never allow the transitory, evanescent demands of man-made institutions to take precedence over the eternal demands of the Almighty God. (128)

The deep hold this prophetic concept has had on the American mind is evidenced by its recurrence among those who have resisted the changes sought by King. In their indictment of American policies, conservative critics have stressed that God's blessing on the United States is contingent on the country's adherence to biblical morality. Although they are more prone than King to cite biblical passages that appear to anoint the political system with divine sanction, right-wing leaders have reserved the right to disobedience when they see human law in conflict with divine law.

No American politician expressed the priestly and prophetic themes of civil religion more eloquently than Abraham Lincoln (Morgenthau and Hein 1983). Although relatively untouched by "church religion," Lincoln saw the United States as a nation with a divine purpose that had been most clearly revealed in the noble principles of the Declaration of Independence. For Lincoln, the commitment to secure free government, which had been sanctified by the sacrifices of the revolutionary generation, was the higher purpose that the United States represented. He told Congress in 1862 that, by adhering to the principles of the Declaration of Independence, the nation was nothing less than "the last, best hope of earth." Because the Union was the concrete embodiment of that continuing commitment to liberty, Lincoln made its maintenance and eventual restoration his highest priority. At Gettysburg, he interpreted the deaths of Union soldiers in transcendent terms, saying their sacrifice in the cause of liberty had reaffirmed the sacredness of the American mission. He then asked Americans to respond with "increased devotion" to the cause for which the soldiers had given the "last full measure of devotion" (Kirwin 1959).

If Lincoln enunciated civil religious themes to sanctify the Union, he was equally willing to call down the wrath of God on the nation when he thought it had strayed from the path of righteousness. Although favoring moderate solutions to slavery, he clearly regarded the maintenance of the institution as a great national sin—perhaps the American equivalent of Adam's fall from God's grace. In his second inaugural address, delivered only a month before his assassination, Lincoln (Kirwin 1959) chided Northerners and Southerners alike who claimed God's support for their cause. Quoting from scripture, he noted that God punished those who committed offenses in the world. Those responsible for the "offense" of American slavery included all Americans, both the Southerners who kept slaves and the Northerners who had acquiesced in slavery's continued existence. He saw the bloodshed and violence of the war as God's retribution: "He gives to both North and South this terrible war as the woe due to those by whom the offense came." Unlike many of the clergy and soldiers who were certain that God was on their side and hated the enemy (Woodworth 2001), Lincoln believed that God had little use for either. Rejecting complacency and self-righteousness, Lincoln called on the nation to accept its punishment and then to rededicate itself to the principles of the Declaration of Independence.

To judge from the utterances of the two most recent occupants of the office, the priestly and prophetic strains of civil religion have retained potency but are not always given equal prominence by presidents (Roof 2009). Although George W. Bush and Barack Obama often invoked American exceptionalism, they emphasized two different aspects of this sense of national mission. Obama's "prophetic exceptionalism," according to recent observers (Gorski and McMillan [2012, 41]), "defines America in terms of certain founding ideals—ideals of potentially universal significance which the nation tries, but often fails, to live up to. It is more reflective in tone and more apt to repent of America's excesses." Chosenness, it is implied, confers an obligation on citizens to live up to noble moral values in the conduct of our public life. Such conduct, rather than the force of arms, will create a powerful model that helps spread freedom across the globe.

In the priestly rhetoric of George W. Bush, by contrast, there was much stronger tendency to suggest that "America's way is God's way" (Weaver

2008) and a much greater willingness to utilize military power as the means to realize God's vision on earth. That rhetoric, much closer to Christian nationalism, seems to take for granted that the United States deserves to be the model for other nations because it has been chosen by God. The more prophetic rhetoric of President Obama challenged Americans to build a society that others would want to imitate of their own free will.

CIVIL RELIGION AS A DOUBLE-EDGED SWORD

To be a constructive force in political life, civil religion must balance the priestly and prophetic impulses. In that condition, it can ennoble a people by prompting generous instincts and a resolute commitment to the nation's principles. Yet the two streams of civil religion—legitimation and prophecy—can also be vulgarized. Attributing a sacred purpose to the nation can degenerate all too easily into idolatrous worship of the state. Such priestly civil religion "can provide divine warrant to unscrupulous acts, cheapen religious language, [and] turn clergy into robed flunkies of the state" (McClay 2004, 14). The belief that a nation embodies God's will can inhibit the skepticism and self-criticism that is so important to democratic politics (Lipsitz 1968). Similarly, in holding the nation to high standards of conduct, the civil religious tradition may produce a frame of mind that disdains the kind of compromises necessary for an orderly political life. If the standards are rigid and unbending, the system one of moral absolutes, then all deviations are equally reprehensible—a view that does not encourage a sense of proportion.

The dangers of imbalance have been most visible in American interactions with the rest of the world (Tiryakian 1982; Cobb 1998). Barely concealing his irritation, a Canadian described American foreign policy as "a determined ideological and evangelical offensive to redeem the rest of the world from its backward, sinful self" (Rawlyk 1990, 254).[7] Such critics contend that Americans are so certain of their nation's virtue that they view international politics as a clash of moral opposites, assuming without thought that God has blessed their endeavors. In the lead-up to the Spanish-American War of 1898, when the United States joined the ranks of colonial powers in the Caribbean, the argument for intervention was framed in terms of the moral responsibility of an enlightened, Christian society like the United States to combat the corrupt Spanish civilization (McCartney 2012). Similar sentiment was very much in evidence during World War I, when many clergymen embraced the Allied cause so fervently that their sense of prophecy was altogether lost (Gamble 2003). This sense of righteousness is often blamed for distorting the U.S. government's behavior toward international Communism in the tense period following World War II. When the wartime alliance between the United States and the Soviet Union broke down in the aftermath of victory, American policy reverted to a position of unrelenting hostility. Whatever the real and considerable provocations in Soviet behavior, the U.S. foreign policy leadership was prone to treat the Soviet Union as a moral leper that had to be isolated from the world community (Inboden 2008). Many thoughtful critics who harbored no illusions about Soviet intentions have noted that the moralistic approach prevented American policymakers from recognizing and exploiting the split in the late 1950s between the Soviet Union and the People's Republic of China and may have prompted the United States to enter military conflicts that could have been avoided. As George Kennan (1951) charged, stigmatizing opponents as the embodiment of evil breeds a "total war" mentality, impedes compromise, and thus exacerbates international tension.[8]

The alternative, perceiving the United States solely in terms of its failings, is no more constructive than viewing the country as the embodiment of virtue. Nations do have interests and those interests may occasionally, tragically, require a resort to force. Critics of Allied behavior during World War I helped leave the nation ill equipped for combat when the next global war broke out just two decades later. A loss of faith in America's mission, the product of the Vietnam War experience, left many citizens persuaded that their country could not be trusted to act righteously in foreign policy. Short of providing humanitarian assistance to poor countries, these critics essentially advised the United States to withdraw from world affairs. By undermining confidence in the nation's legitimacy and purpose, the prophetic impulse may simply paralyze national will.

The sociologist Robert Wuthnow (1988, chap. 10) fears that large sections of the American religious community have succumbed to these extreme manifestations of civil religion. He notes the emergence of a "conservative" version of civil religion that endows the nation with holiness and puts the government (at least when under a Republican president) and economic system beyond the reach of criticism. It resembles the religious nationalism that Robert Bellah warned against. Some theologians maintain that President George W. Bush took precisely this position by equating the United States with God's purpose and its critics with evil, overlooking the less savory features of American life (Northcott 2004). This may account for the greater hawkishness displayed by religious conservatives in U.S. military engagements from Korea to the Iraq War (Hero 1973; Wald 1994; Jelen 1994; Froese and Mencken 2009).

Wuthnow also detects a "liberal" version of civil religion that casts doubt on the moral legitimacy of the nation-state itself. Many liberal church leaders in the grip of this critical stance, finding "no conceivable circumstances in which United States military force could ever be justified," automatically condemned U.S. actions in the 1991 Gulf War (Hertzke 1991, 60). Instead of imparting an independent perspective to foreign policy deliberations, religious conservatives invariably sanctify American behavior and religious liberals predictably denounce it. The loss of balance between the priestly and prophetic roles has robbed religion of a distinctive voice and made it a source of conflict rather than consensus (Coles 2002).

The politicizing of civil religion may account for the patterns observed by Chapp (2012) in his analysis of a 2010 national survey about the phenomenon. Using a set of questions that bear a family resemblance to those listed in figure 3.1, Chapp found a civil religious orientation much like that reported by Wimberley (1976) forty years ago but with a crucial difference: Civil religious beliefs in 2010 were much more strongly accepted by individuals from politically conservative religious groups (white Protestants and Mormons) than by politically liberal groups such as Jews, atheists, agnostics and those without a specific religious identity (Chapp 2012, 111).[9] As Chapp notes, this finding calls into question the idea of civil religion as a unifying force that binds Americans of diverse religious traditions.

ONE OF MANY INFLUENCES

It would surely be an exaggeration to state flatly that religion alone caused important political attitudes—including the social contract, limited government, and American destiny—to take hold of the American imagination. The path connecting sixteenth-century religious thinkers and eighteenth-century political activists is tangled and meandering. Religion, in its various guises, should be recognized as only one of the forces operating in the development of American political culture.

At least two other influences shaped the American political system in its formative period—a new intellectual force and the lure of economic advantage. The foremost intellectual rival to the ideology of the Protestant Reformation was the Enlightenment, a body of thought developed in seventeenth- and eighteenth-century Europe (May 1976).[10] This movement, characterized above all by a belief in human progress through the systematic application of reason, supplied a heavy dose of optimism to counterbalance the Puritans' stern view of humanity. Without some sense that humans could engage in reasonable conduct under the proper institutional arrangements, the Founders could not have contemplated constructing a democratic political system. Their attempt to create a written constitution alone bespeaks a tremendous confidence in human ability to discover eternal truths by reflection and debate. The influence of the Age of Reason, as the Enlightenment era has been called, was apparent in the thought and behavior of political activists throughout the revolutionary period and during the early history of the nation.

In addition to the sway of intellectual currents from Europe, the colonists were also moved by material forces. Indeed, many of the early settlements were founded not by religious enthusiasts but by entrepreneurs motivated by the prospect of economic gain and funded by some of the earliest capitalist enterprises. Clearly key elements of the political culture they developed served to advance the economic interests of powerful groups in early American society. As generations of schoolchildren have learned, a major incentive to break with Great Britain was economic: the colonists had serious grievances about taxation and other matters. The Founders' commitment to the idea of limited government may have also been the product of economic self-interest, for a government with limited authority was a government incapable of redistributing income from the wealthy to the poor. The Founders generally came from the more affluent stratum of colonial society, and material interests may well have disposed them to want governmental authority tightly reined in. Similarly, the missionary impulse in American political culture permitted the nation to fuel its economic expansion by the constant acquisition of new land, raw materials, sources of labor, and markets.

Given the many factors at work in forming the American political culture, the more appropriate conclusion is that certain patterns of religious thought, habitual ways of reasoning about God and humankind, made it easier for some political ideas to take root in American society. Accustomed to thinking about God and mortals in contractual terms, Americans were receptive to a political theory that treated government in a similar fashion. The widespread belief that humans behave sinfully disposed the colonists to accept the doctrine of limited government. Trained by their religion to see God at work in the daily lives of men and women, Americans could easily imagine a divine hand guiding the destiny of their country. In this view, religion was one of the factors that facilitated the development of a common political outlook.

Recognizing religion as one among several sources of the founding of America should provide a perspective on the debate about the nation's path since the American Revolution. Among some intellectual heirs of the Puritans, recent American history is often described in terms of decline and fall. Such historical treatments begin with the assumption that the United States "emerged from the generally Christian actions of generally Christian people [who] . . . bequeathed Christian values, and a Christian heritage, to later American history" (Noll, Hatch, and Marsden 1983). By loosening legal constraints on items as diverse as abortion, school discipline, sexual behavior, drug use, and sex roles, it is charged, the government has betrayed its heritage and abandoned its Christian foundations (Murphy 2008). But if Christianity certainly played a prominent role in the American founding, the evidence presented herein does not sustain the claim that colonial America was exclusively influenced by Christian values.[11] Whether early America was morally superior to present-day society will continue to be debated, but presupposing a golden age, a one-time "Christian America," is a dubious starting point (Hughes 2009).

The political concepts of social contract, limited government, and American destiny remain integral elements of American political culture even if they have lost most of their religious grounding. The next chapter explores the formal role of religion in the American system of government. For many foreign observers of the United States in its formative period, the most original and arresting feature of the young nation was the revolutionary divorce of religion and government. While most Americans continue to believe in the wisdom of that principle, there is no such harmony on how to apply that philosophy to many practical issues of church and state.

4

Religion and the State

When Caesar, having exacted what is Caesar's, demands still more insistently that we render unto him what is God's—that is a sacrifice we dare not make.

—Alexander Solzhenitsyn

It may not be easy, in every possible case, to trace the line of separation between the rights of religion and the Civil authority with such distinctiveness as to avoid collisions and doubts on unessential points.

—James Madison

The subject of the previous chapter, the religious sources of early American political thought, leads naturally to questions about the official role of religion in the United States. Some Americans believe that religion contributed so profoundly to the early republic that the Constitution should be understood as the fusion of the "precepts of Christianity, civil government and Christ."[1] To people who subscribe to this way of thinking, the Founders of the United States intended to give Christianity a privileged place in the new nation, and subsequent generations have departed from that plan by artificially separating religion from government.[2] With equal fervor, other commentators acknowledge the importance of religious thinking at the time of the nation's founding but draw radically different conclusions about the intended role of religion. In this perspective, the framers are frequently described as deists and free thinkers who were highly skeptical about traditional forms of religion and who therefore wrote a Constitution to create an impeccably secular state.

Only by imposing a high and impregnable "wall of separation" between church and state, argue those who hold this point of view, does the Supreme Court faithfully implement the mandate of the Founders.

This chapter explores the interactions between government and religion that often come to mind with the phrase "church and state." We explore the reasons for church-state tension, the conflicting claims about "the intentions of the Founders," and how the Supreme Court has interpreted the Constitution on this subject. Because government policy on church and state is not etched in stone, we also examine how the legal relationship between religion and government responds to social and political changes.

THE GENESIS OF CHURCH-STATE CONFLICT

The relationship between church and state presents two sets of problems for democratic governments. On the most fundamental level, governments must decide what legal status to grant to religious forces. Should government take account of religious sentiments, treat churches as just another type of institution, or try to regulate and control religious activity? The problem is particularly severe when, as in the United States, many types of churches compete for the loyalty of the citizens. In such a situation, "taking account" of the public's religious sentiment may inflame members of religious minorities and persons who are not religious. Yet by ignoring religion or limiting its public role in the interest of preserving harmony, the government runs the risk of alienating citizens for whom religion is an important source of personal identity.

The second type of church-state problem stems from possible conflicts between religious motivation and behavior in the secular realm. Religions provide guidance about how people should live their lives. In some cases, religious beliefs may counsel individuals to undertake actions that violate the duly established laws of the state. Government may demand behavior that a church forbids or may prohibit actions that the church requires. In either case, the citizen is forced to choose between loyalty to the public law and loyalty to religious faith. What should be done when church and state provide conflicting guidance about appropriate or permissible behavior?

Because it involves the rights and privileges of two different institutions, the question of the legal status granted to churches is known as the "boundary" problem or, from the phrase made famous by Thomas Jefferson, that of the "wall of separation" between church and state.[3] The second type of church-state problem, collision between the teachings of church and state, is usually described as the "free-exercise" controversy—

a label that recognizes that the free exercise of religious belief may run afoul of limits established by secular law. Both types of problems have repeatedly found their way onto the American political agenda. From any number of possible examples, two incidents will be used to illustrate each type of church-state problem.

The case of a Massachusetts religious community exemplifies in the starkest possible way the religious basis of disobedience to secular law.[4] In February 2002, a judge ordered Rebecca Corneau to jail for refusing to disclose the location of her infant. Just a year or so earlier, Corneau's husband had led authorities to an unmarked grave in a Maine forest that contained her stillborn infant, Jeremiah, and the body of a one-year-old child who had died of starvation in 1999. According to an autopsy, the infant would have survived had the birth been attended by a qualified doctor or midwife. Although the Corneaus were not prosecuted, their three surviving children were taken away from the family, and Mrs. Corneau, who was pregnant when the grave was discovered, was forced into hospital confinement for the duration of the pregnancy. Once safely born, the baby girl was delivered to foster care. State authorities noticed in the fall of 2001 that Rebecca Corneau was again pregnant but subsequently appeared to have given birth. When she reported that she had suffered a miscarriage, the judge plainly did not believe her and insisted she produce the child or evidence of its death. Her refusal to comply led to her jailing. The Massachusetts State Appeals Court eventually upheld the removal of the Corneaus' children.[5]

This case illustrates, in extreme form, the free-exercise basis of church-state conflict. Government and religion came into conflict because each claimed the authority to set standards for human behavior. The authority of government is recognized in codes of law that state the types of behavior that are unacceptable and define the penalties for disobedience. Based on the widespread belief that government should protect children, who cannot defend themselves, most states insist that parents seek timely medical care for sick children and punish those who do not comply. Religions also take positions on what behavior is permissible, and their beliefs are spelled out in sacred documents and religious codes. Recognizing the authority of government in most spheres, churches frequently urge the state to make religious morality the basis for determining what behavior is to be encouraged or forbidden. But when the laws do not agree with church doctrine, the religious may claim the right to follow what they see as God's "higher law." That was the premise of Martin Luther King Jr. when he openly defied laws on racial segregation as incompatible with Christianity. On that same basis, the Corneaus refused to follow a law considered reasonable behavior by the state but denounced as a form of blasphemy by their faith.

The Corneaus belong to "The Body," a small religious commune in Attleboro. An offshoot of the Worldwide Church of God, the Massachusetts group subscribes to a theology that rejects the "World System," its phrase for "seven intricate, self-perpetuating, man-glorifying, unholy organizations: government, commerce, education, science, the arts, medicine and religion" (Balizet 1999, 19). Consistent with their understanding of life as a divine gift dependent on intense spiritual devotion, group members avoid hospitals, reject medical devices such as eyeglasses and hearing aids, refuse immunizations, and do not maintain life insurance or use seat belts. The hostility to medicine takes the form of insisting on the sanctity of a "Zion birth," wholly unattended by trained professionals, and refusing medical care for children. Samuel Robidoux, the baby boy who died of starvation, was denied food for two months after a member of the group received a vision from God that ordered the parents to provide only milk to what had been a healthy and robust infant. In all of these cases, from avoiding medicine to denying nourishment to refusing to cooperate with authorities, members of the group insist they are doing what God ordered.

Though extreme, these cases are not uncommon. Similar charges are frequently filed against Christian Scientists, who may refuse on religious grounds to obtain conventional medical treatment for children, and a variety of religious groups with different doctrinal views that elevate faith healing over conventional medicine (Bullis 1991). All but five states exempt parents with such beliefs from the obligation to obtain medical care for their children. In the period from 1975 to 1995, medical researchers identified 158 children with survivable conditions who nevertheless died when their parents withheld medical care on religious grounds (Asser and Swan 1998; Hughes 2004).

The boundary problem does not usually appear in so dramatic a form, but it probably occurs more frequently than the free-exercise cases. During an in-class party in 1998, Daniel Walz handed out pencils to his fellow kindergartners in the public elementary school of Egg Harbor Township, New Jersey. Because the pencils bore the statement "Jesus loves the little children," his teacher confiscated the pencils and returned them to Daniel. Some months later, Daniel tried to hand out candy canes that came with an attached story attesting to "the Wonder of Jesus" as "the ultimate and dominant force in the Universe today." Once again, school officials refused permission, but told the boy's mother he could distribute the material freely outside class or instructional periods. To do so during class, the school board argued, was effectively to endorse a particular religion in a captive audience of six- and seven-year-olds—something forbidden by the Constitution's ban on government actions to "establish" religion. Unhappy with this policy, Daniel's defenders filed a lawsuit arguing that he was being discriminated against on the basis of his religious beliefs. A federal judge sided with the school board.[6]

In focusing on these two major types of church-state conflict, we do not mean to suggest that the two institutions are permanently locked in a battle for supremacy. Though conflicts occur, not all church-state interaction is marked by hostility. In fact, most such contact is benign. Churches may receive various types of public aid when they perform social services. As corporate institutions, churches are entitled to the protection of government in matters of property and security. Government may also be asked to help individuals secure religious liberty from threats posed by other, nongovernmental institutions. For example, the federal courts have been petitioned to require businesses to recognize the conscience of employees whose faith does not permit them to work on certain days of the week or to perform certain responsibilities. But in most cases, and particularly in those that draw headlines, controversies arise over where to draw the proper line between the institutions (boundary) and the moral authority (free exercise) of church and state. The sources of controversy may be as seemingly trivial as a children's school party or as significant as a parent's decision to withhold medical care from a critically ill child.

OVERVIEW OF CHURCH-STATE RELATIONS

The American approach to the boundary and free-exercise problems is governed by a sentence from the First Amendment to the Constitution: "Congress shall make no law respecting an establishment of religion, or prohibiting the free exercise thereof." These two clauses and a prohibition on "religious tests" for holding public office in Article VI are the only formal references to religion in the Constitution. This brevity has inspired continuing debate over what kinds of government action toward religion are permitted and how far individuals may go in claiming religion as justification for violating secular law. The constitutional language on religion, like that on so many other subjects, has been interpreted differently from one generation to the next. The debate over the precise meaning of the words in different circumstances, a source of passionate controversy and fierce argument, is examined in later sections. Despite its intensity, however, that debate should not disguise what has been a strong American consensus on the role of religion in the state.

The American pattern rejects the two extreme options embraced in totalitarian political systems, subordinating the government to the authority of the church through a *theocracy* as in Afghanistan under the Taliban or, conversely, adopting the *Erastian* model that treats churches as departments under government authority and control, a policy pursued in the former Soviet Union (Francis 1992). Rather, the United States has pursued what might best be described as a "partial" separation of church and state. There has been virtually unanimous agreement that the establishment clause ("Congress shall make no law respecting an establishment of religion") forbids the government to grant preference to any particular religion. Together with the corresponding free-exercise clause ("or prohibiting the free exercise thereof"), it also seems clearly to rule out the possibility of the government imposing one religion as the official faith or prosecuting members of another because their beliefs are repugnant. But if "separation of church and state" is interpreted to mean that government should make no allowances for religion or belief, then the United States is a long way from complete separationism. In numerous ways, the government has recognized the strong religious beliefs held by many citizens and made it clear that separation does not require state hostility to religious influence. The United States is a secular state that has no official religious identity but, unlike other secular states, it remains generally friendly to religion (Kuru 2007).

The currency, national seal, Pledge of Allegiance, national anthem, legislative prayers, and oaths sworn in federal courts all make explicit reference to belief in God. Most of these practices have been upheld in court challenges. In such political events as a presidential inauguration, the religious motif is readily apparent through the Bible on which the oath is sworn and the prominent participation of clergy in the ceremony. On occasion, clergy may be consulted informally to review public policies that raise moral issues.

To appreciate the American solution to the boundary and free-exercise problems, it is essential to examine the circumstances under which it evolved. Most of the American Founders recognized religion as a force with the potential both to enhance and to undermine political stability. Hence, the particular arrangement of church-state relations in the United States constitutes neither a wholehearted endorsement of religious influence on government nor unremitting hostility to it.

When the Founders prohibited "religious tests" for holding federal office in Article VI of the Constitution, they were reacting against their understanding of British history as well as common practices in the colonies. From the Reformation, which had inspired the settlement of America, they acquired the belief that alliances between a powerful church and an absolute state would corrupt both institutions. More immediately, they observed how some of the North American colonies appeared to court that same danger by providing religion with the sanction of government in the form of religious requirements for public office, the establishment of an official faith, and denial of religious freedom to members of minority religions.

Before the adoption of the Constitution, most colonies limited public office to persons who could pass some test of acceptable faith (Wilson 1990). Even where a relatively wide range of religions was recognized, as a rule, Christianity was the basis for these religious tests. Pennsylvania reserved public office for persons who would swear to "acknowledge the Scriptures of the old and New testament [*sic*] to be given by divine inspiration" (Schappes 1971, 68). Belief in God was not sufficient in Maryland; although one of the most tolerant colonies, it further demanded that officeholders accept the concept of the Holy Trinity (Kirwin 1959, 24–29). North Carolina also went one step further than Pennsylvania, excluding not only Jews but also Catholics from holding executive or judicial office (Schappes 1971, 598).

In addition to such religious tests, most of the colonies formally endowed certain religions with official status—what was known as the "establishment" of religion. Under this system, citizens could be obliged to attend church services by law and were taxed to provide for religious organizations. Besides enjoying material support from the government, clergy were often granted legal privileges such as exemption from certain types of civil laws. Competing faiths were put at a further disadvantage by laws making worship the privilege of the established church. For example, the charter for New York colony limited the right of public worship to all "who profess faith in God by Jesus Christ" (cited in Schappes 1971, 18–19).

The degree to which legal support of one church hampered the free exercise of other faiths was apparent in several restrictive features of colonial law. In some colonies, conformity to the official faith was a condition of residence and dissent the grounds for expulsion or worse. The "worse" in Massachusetts was death. According to that colony's charter of 1641 (cited in Dunn 1984, 22), "if any man after legal conviction shall have or worship any other god, but the lord god, he shall be put to death." What it meant to "have any other god" was spelled out by another law that warranted the death penalty for anyone who cursed or blasphemed "the name of God, the father, Son or Holy ghost." This law was invoked in 1660 to hang a Quaker woman who had refused repeated orders to stay out of Massachusetts. For denying the divinity of Jesus, the doctrine of the resurrection, and the occurrence of miracles, a Jewish resident of Maryland faced the possibility of death and the loss of property (Schappes 1971, 13–15). More typically, basic rights of residence, land owning, jury service, and voting were often denied to religious minorities (D'Antonio and Hoge 2006, 346). Under these conditions, the free exercise of religion applied only to the established religions of the colony.

The men who most influenced the Constitution and operated the new system of government in its first years were virtually unanimous in rejecting state support for a national faith (Waldman 2008). Such support was deemed bad for the state because it promoted false values, undermined respect for the law, and introduced an unhealthy fanaticism to public affairs. As men of strong faith, the Founders also shared a belief that establishment of a national religion or government support for religions would do religion more harm than good. Because each of these objections is relevant to current debate over church-state relationships in the United States, the Founders' logic demands careful review.

For some of the Founders, notably Thomas Jefferson and John Adams, organized religion deserved no government support because, among other reasons, it was thought to pervert the true meaning of religion. Both, like most of their contemporaries, were adherents of what was called "enlightened religion," an approach that emphasized reason rather than dogma in determining religious values (Wills 2007). Their extended correspondence shows that the architects of the Declaration of Independence and Washington's successors to the presidency agreed that true religion consisted of benevolent conduct toward one's fellow human beings. They outdid one another in denouncing the "irrelevance" and "superstition" of dogma that obscured the simplicity and beauty of religion's moral content (Cousins 1958, 85, 139, 283; see also the comments of Ben Franklin cited in Cousins on 25–26). All that was important in Christianity and the other religions, Adams wrote (81, 281), could be found in the Sermon on the Mount and the Ten Commandments. Jefferson agreed heartily: years before, he had rewritten the scriptures by pruning away all the doctrines he saw as unnecessary—including the divinity of Jesus, the Holy Trinity, and the structure of the church (173–216). Precisely because formal religion appeared to give more attention to such mystical concepts than to the essential truths of the Golden Rule, it evoked little enthusiasm from Adams and Jefferson. Hence, they believed organized religion would not contribute to the public good if it enjoyed the patronage of government. Government needed protection from such religion.

Establishment was also considered unwise by some of the Founders, especially James Madison (Loconte 2003), because it seemed likely to bring the law into low esteem. As deeply held matters of personal belief, religious views could move people to take extreme actions in defense of conscience. History seemed to demonstrate that government attempts to impose a uniform faith would inevitably unleash passion and violence. With so many different religious groups in the colonies, each offering its own distinct version of the truth, any national establishment would be certain to offend many citizens who subscribed to different faiths. Under these circumstances, a law commanding support for an established church could not realistically be enforced. According to Madison, an unenforceable law would result in a striking demonstration of the government's impotence and a reproach to its authority (Cousins 1958, 108). In the absence of consensus, he thought, it would be better to pass no law at all than one certain to elicit widespread disobedience.

The final political problem connected with establishment was the Founders' firm belief that a state church would inevitably degenerate into a system of religious tyranny. The experience of the colonies suggested to them that although establishment might begin as a benign preference for one church or multiple denominations, the privileges of governmental support would almost certainly encourage attempts to suppress alternate views. In his famous "Memorial and Remonstrance" against Virginia legislation that would tax citizens to pay for churches, Madison pointed out the danger of a slippery slope. He warned that "the same authority which can force a citizen to contribute three pence only" to an established church "may force him to conform to any other establishment." John Adams, whose skepticism of the churches earned him an unwarranted reputation for irreligion, asked rhetorically, "When or where had existed a Protestant or dissenting sect who would tolerate a free inquiry?" Answering his own question, he noted that the clergy would accept all manner of brutality and ignorance in the name of preserving the one true faith. "But," he wrote from personal experience, "touch a solemn truth in collision with a dogma of a sect, though capable of the clearest proof, and you will soon find you have disturbed a nest, and the hornets will swarm about your legs and hands and fly into your face and eyes." Having experienced similar condemnation for his attempt to reduce all religions to a common core of moral commands, Jefferson echoed Adams's appraisal of the tendency of churches to persecute those who did not fully accept their doctrines. To give such an institution access to the full powers of the state, they agreed, would create a powerful engine of oppression.

The harmful political consequences of a national religion were not the only reasons the Founders rejected establishment. They also argued that political support would make for bad religion. Hence, religion needed protection from government. As Jefferson observed, a government that compelled religious exercises could dictate other terms to a church, reducing it to a servant of power (Cousins 1958, 137). More fundamentally, the Founders concurred that religion was meaningful only when it was a sincere expression from the heart and mind of a free people. Second to none in his admiration of religion as a spur to upright conduct, George Washington repeatedly emphasized the need to keep religion a matter of personal conscience, free of government intervention. To do otherwise, Washington argued, was to put human beings in God's role as the judge of other people's conscience (49). Jefferson advised his nephew to "question with boldness" even the existence of God because, if a Supreme Being existed "he must more approve of the homage of reason than that of blindfolded fear"

(128–29). Although the government could force people to swear loyalty to a public faith, it could not make their hearts pure or their behavior any better. From this evidence, it is clear that resistance to establishment did not grow out of hostility to faith. Even Tom Paine, the Founder most widely regarded as an enemy of Christianity, believed the practice of true religion would improve if churches were separated from the state.

All of these supposed defects of establishment would be turned into benefits if government refrained from endorsing a religion or from trying in any way to regulate acceptable belief. Freed from state support, political leaders in the early republic predicted, the false churches would collapse as humanity returned to the essentials of religion (Cousins 1958, 320). Instead of undermining respect for the law by insulting the conscience of dissenters, a government that respected religious freedom would enjoy widespread popular support and obedience in the legitimate exercise of its power. In fact, citizens watchful of their religious freedom would be equally sensitive to safeguard their other fundamental and natural liberties. Finally, in the absence of attempts to enforce a single faith, the Founders expected an even greater number and diversity of churches. In religion, as in politics, they thought that diversity would make tyranny less likely, and so they welcomed the prospect of the growth in the number of denominations. On top of these political benefits, of course, rested a firm belief that religion would be purified as its practice was freed from compulsion and hypocrisy.

The constitutional framework governing church-state relations is thus the product, in part, of the Founders' Enlightenment perspective. So long as it was "universal, noninstitutional, and uncoerced" (Diggins 1984, 80), religion could contribute to good government by teaching restraint and instilling a commitment to good works. It was that kind of faith that was endorsed when, for example, Washington in his Farewell Address referred to the importance of religion to morality. In that sense, religion was a factor with the potential to stabilize republican government. Yet the Founders remained aware that religion in a particular, institutional, and coerced form could do enormous damage to the stability and reputation of republican government (Cousins 1958, 67; Sandoz 1994). Beyond simply forbidding the state from aiding churches or giving them legal privileges, those Founders influenced by the Enlightenment insisted that government "could give no symbolic endorsement, expression, or acknowledgment of religion" and should not "pass laws or policies on religious grounds or religious arguments" (Witte 1991, 495). This perspective inspires contemporary separationism.

The First Amendment religion clauses would not have passed without an alliance between this elite group of Founders and the "free churches" that grew so explosively in the Great Awakening of the prerevolutionary period. Baptists, Methodists, and other new religious movements, offering "palatable spiritual food for the hungry souls of the common folk," challenged the dominance of legally established churches (Mead 1976, 29). These "evangelical separatists" shared the goal of liberating religion from the state, wanting the freedom to perform their religious mission without facing restrictions imposed by established churches (Lambert 2003). Together with the Founders, the Protestant advocates of religious liberty helped persuade the first Congress to adopt the religion clauses of the First Amendment and, in a campaign that lasted until the 1830s, to disestablish the churches in every state of the union. Their support for disestablishment, conditioned on a level playing field, did not extend to the goal of keeping the state free from all religious influence. Unlike the Enlightenment separatists, these Protestant separationists wanted government "to accommodate and aid all churches without conditions or controls and to foster a climate conducive to the cultivation of a plurality of religions" (Witte 1991, 494).

After more than two centuries, it's easy to overlook the boldness of this experiment in cutting the tie between the state and religious institutions. Despite predictions that the Constitution would set religions adrift and undermine the moral foundations of the Republic, chapter 1 recounted the astonishing religious vitality that resulted from institutional separation of the two spheres. By decoupling citizenship from religion, furthermore, the United States became the first society to embrace diversity as a positive outcome.

HOW FAR CAN GOVERNMENT GO?

For different reasons, the Founders and the numerous Protestant sects that soon dominated the religious landscape agreed that the national government created by the Constitution should not prefer any one religion or faith over another. Beyond that central postulate, there is considerable disagreement today about what the government is or is not allowed to do regarding religious values and institutions. This is a seemingly inevitable result of the dual heritage of the First Amendment's religion clauses. The Founders, moved primarily by Enlightenment separationism, acted fairly consistently to limit organized religious influence on the state, while the Protestants influenced by the Great Awakening saw government as a legitimate instrument for spreading a religious message. When we look at the actions taken by individuals and governments during the early republic, we see that the law bears traces of both impulses.

None of the Founders appeared to believe government must ignore religious feeling in its official actions. Thinking God's blessings would be important in the outcome of the Revolutionary War, Washington ordered officers and soldiers in the Continental Army to maintain "punctual attendance" at worship services (Cousins 1958, 50). Samuel Adams, the least reluctant of the founding generation to limit religious expression, used his position as governor of Massachusetts to issue religious proclamations (355–56); Washington did the same when he called for the first day of "thanksgiving" by the new nation (71–72). Even Jefferson, who provided the momentous interpretation of the First Amendment as building "a wall of separation" between church and state, had no objection to the use of municipal buildings for worship by the different congregations in his village (163). Though he steadfastly recommended against paying for religious instruction at the state university he founded in Charlottesville, Jefferson advised the Virginia legislature to encourage the denominations to fund professorships of their own (164). By accommodating the claims of different churches in this manner, he thought the university could counter the false impression that it stood "against all religion."

Does this mean, as some contemporary critics assert, that the Founders understood the Constitution to permit nondiscriminatory support for religion in general? There are several reasons to doubt this claim of nonpreferentialism. First, in the congressional debates over the wording of the First Amendment, Congress failed to pass such language on at least five occasions (Davis 2004, 731). The author of the text first submitted to Congress, James Madison, wrote language that left little doubt he intended to deny any government support for religion. As the bill passed through the legislative process in both houses, critics offered several amended versions that explicitly allowed for aid to churches in a nondiscriminatory manner. Because no transcript of the deliberations exists, we cannot know for certain why these amendments were not adopted, but Congress certainly had the chance to call explicitly for nondiscriminatory aid had it so intended. Second, according to Leonard Levy (1989), the First Amendment language that was finally adopted had a contemporary meaning that expressly prohibited any form of government assistance to any and all churches. He points out that the colonial establishments, the model confronting the Founders, deviated from the European pattern of a single official religious faith. When the First Amendment was framed, "all state establishments that existed in America were general or multiple establishments of all the churches of each state, something unknown in the Europe familiar to Americans" (9). If "establishment" meant that all churches were eligible to be supported by tax revenue, as Levy argues, then the First Amendment's prohibition against establishment must be read as a mandate against any government support for religion—even if that support is neutral vis-à-vis competing denominations.

If we look at the evolution of law and practice during the postrevolution period, there is additional evidence for doubting revisionist claims that the First Amendment was meant to permit nondiscriminatory government aid to religion. Mark Douglas McGarvie (2004) has argued that the early republic experienced an ideological revolution in its conception of law, replacing the communal notion of law as a means of inspiring human virtue with the classic liberal understanding of law as a means of freeing individuals from artificial restraints. This legal transformation sharply divided the public realm from the private sphere, consigning religion to the latter. Religion became a matter of government indifference—meaning individuals were not officially judged or treated on the basis of their personal religious convictions—and religious institutions were stripped of their public functions as the state gradually took responsibility for activities such as education and welfare (see Munoz 2003). Churches thus became strictly private organizations without public privilege but protected from government interference through the contract clause of the Constitution.

Consider an instructive controversy that began in the early years of the nineteenth century (Blakeley 1970; John 1990; Verhoeven 2013). Since the founding of the nation, the post office transported mail between communities on Sunday, the Christian Sabbath. In 1810, Congress enacted a law requiring post offices that received Sunday mail to stay open on that day and directing postmasters to make deliveries the same day they received shipments. Despite numerous protests from Christian organizations over defamation of the Lord's Day, Congress not only repeatedly refused requests to repeal the law but also extended it on several occasions. Early reports from the House committee with jurisdiction over the post office stressed that suspension of Sunday mail would impede the efficient performance of a major and legitimate government function. But as the protests mounted, the committee increasingly cited separationist considerations as the basis for refusal to end Sunday delivery of mail.

The language of a report issued in 1830 made the case for continued Sunday delivery in terms that would probably have pleased the founding generation. By acceding to requests to end mail delivery on Sunday, it was argued, Congress would effectively grant official recognition to the Christian Sabbath. Withholding the mail on Sunday would force non-Christians to respect a holiday that they did not recognize in their hearts. In strong language, the House committee reminded the petitioners that the Constitution gave religious equality to all people by denying privileges to any—even if the faith in question was shared by the vast majority of the population. Echoing the fear of the Founders that even slight concessions to one faith might open up a wedge for greater government regulation in the future, they wrote:

The conclusion is inevitable, that the line cannot be too strongly drawn between Church and State. If a solemn act of legislation shall, in one point, define the law of God, or point out to the citizen one religious duty, it may, with equal propriety, proceed to define every part of divine revelation; and enforce every religious obligation, even to the forms and ceremonies of worship, the endowment of the church, and the support of the clergy. (Committee on Post Offices and Post Roads 1830, 1)

Rather than coerce individuals by using the authority of government, the committee recommended that petitioners try to "instruct the public mind" on the evils of the practice that they condemned. If all men and women truly came to believe in the evil of Sunday mail, the practice would wither instantly; so long as people did not unanimously share the views enunciated by critics of Sunday mail, governmental intervention could only inflame religious passions. Although this view was not unanimously accepted, as indicated by dissents from the 1830 report and by language in earlier committee documents, the ideas of the Founders were interpreted as supporting the "wall of separation" that Thomas Jefferson sought between the institutions of government and the churches.

Many Founders appeared to have doubts about the very idea of governmental aid to religion, even if it were to be allocated on a nondiscriminatory basis by state governments. Washington objected on principle to a bill introduced in the Virginia legislature to pay religious teachers from tax revenue, the same legislation that prompted Madison's famous protest. Rather than rankle the consciences of dissenters and so "convulse the State" with religious conflict, Washington much preferred a scheme like Jefferson's compromise on religious instruction at the state university. In a letter to a political friend, Washington expressed himself as favoring the obligation of all religions—Christianity no less than Islam or Judaism—to pay for their own religious instruction (Cousins 1958, 64–65). "I wish an assessment had never been agitated," he wrote, "and . . . that the Bill could die an early death." Madison, the most relentless critic of public aid to religion, responded with vehemence the same year to a proposal in Congress that would set aside a section of the Northwest Territories to support the church favored by a majority of the inhabitants. He denounced the proposal as "unjust" and "hurtful," a bill "smelling so strongly of an antiquated Bigotry" that it would reduce international respect for the country (306–7). Although neither Washington nor Madison might have considered such proposals as unconstitutional under the terms of the First Amendment, they did declare them to be unwise.

The strongest evidence that the Founders did not favor even nondiscriminatory aid or noncoercive state recognition lay in their expressed sensitivity to the feelings of religious minorities. Their apparent awareness of how state recognition might injure the feelings of religious minorities can be interpreted to support preference for governmental aloofness to any religious expression, however bland and noncontroversial. Madison argued that religious matters, unlike most public disputes, should not be decided by the will of the majority because majorities were indifferent to minority rights. Every benign expression of religious sentiment by the state, he noted, "naturally terminates in a conformity to the creed of the majority" (quoted in Wills 2007, 240). A deeply religious man who served several terms as president of the American Bible Society, John Jay of New York objected to opening the sessions of the Continental Congress with a prayer. Citing the diversity of belief and custom among the delegates, he doubted that a prayer could be found that would not offend some member of the assembly (Cousins 1958, 360). The tendency of that same Continental Congress to invoke religion repeatedly, calling for national fast days and a national Bible, apparently prompted many Founders to push for a separation of religion from politics at the Constitutional Convention (Davis 2000), a conclave in which no group prayers were offered.

As president, George Washington showed the same sympathy to the religious groups that suffered the brunt of exclusion under state laws of establishment. He told a general meeting of Quakers that he believed that "the conscientious scruples of all men should be treated with great delicacy and tenderness" and wrote to the Jewish community in Newport, Rhode Island, of his belief that religious freedom was a "natural right," not a mere "indulgence" of toleration to minority faiths that the majority could grant or withdraw at will (Davis 2000, 60–61). Jefferson provided the clearest display of sensitivity to the implications of state recognition of religion when, as president, he was asked to proclaim a religious holiday (Davis 2000, 136–37). Reluctant to assume an authority that was, if it existed at all, reserved for state governments, he refused to issue a watered-down proclamation encouraging national prayer with nothing more than the force of public opinion behind it. Challenging the proponent of such a plan, he asked, "Does the change in the nature of the penalty make the recommendation less a *law* of conduct for those to whom it is directed?" Jefferson doubted that the Constitution gave the president "the authority to direct the religious exercises of his constituents" even if such "direction" was nothing more than bland verbal encouragement.

The government should avoid recognizing any denomination, even something as broad as Christianity, lest it offend the sentiments of members of other traditions or nonbelievers. The religious authority of the government extended solely to prohibiting conduct that impelled believers to "disturb the peace, the happiness, or safety of Society" (Davis 2000, 301). In his *Notes on the State of Virginia*, Jefferson made the point very clearly:

The legitimate powers of government extend to such acts only as are injurious to others. But it does me no injury for my neighbor to say there are twenty Gods, or no God. It neither picks my pocket nor breaks my leg. If it be said his testimony in a court of law cannot be relied on, reject it then, and be the stigma on him. Constraint may make him worse by making him a hypocrite, but it will never make him a truer man. It may fix him obstinately in his errors, but will not cure them. (Davis 2000, 123)

On this reading, the Founders appear to have been as eager to keep the state from limiting individual religious expression as they were to keep the government from promoting it.

Whatever their philosophical views about the relationship of church and state, the political leaders who dominated the early Republic did not object to numerous provisions that incorporated Protestant values in the operation of government (Witte 1991). From government chaplains, official prayers and proclamations, the institution of religious holidays, and religious symbols on government documents, it was clear that government acknowledged the religious heritage of the United States. In various ways, governmental agencies channeled direct assistance to religious enterprises. Even more fundamentally, many of the laws and institutions created by government were animated by religious values. By attaching criminal penalties to conduct like prostitution, gambling, blasphemy, and sacrilege, the social values of Protestantism were given the force of law. These efforts were most common at the state level, where the First Amendment did not apply, but were not unknown at the national level. To some scholars, the pervasiveness of religiously inspired laws and practices proved that the United States had in fact established a "proxy" religious establishment that enforced a "theolegal" system of Protestant morality rather than a truly secular state (Sehat 2011; Walker and Greenlee 2011).

THE JUDICIAL RECORD

Neither the boundary problem nor the free-exercise concept excited much national attention in the first 150 years under the Constitution. Over that span of time, the controversy over Sunday delivery of mail was one of the few church-state items to engage Congress. At the state level, fierce battles were fought over proposals to drop establishment and to soften other forms of official support for religion. Although denominational competition and conflict remained important elements of political controversy, the constitutional status of religious institutions and belief was simply not a pressing item on the national agenda.

The relatively small volume of "religious" cases decided during the first century and a half of American history set some broad outlines for the relationship between religion and government. In *Reynolds v. United States* (1878), the Supreme Court put an important limit on the free exercise of religion by upholding a congressional ban on the practice of plural marriage. By making polygamy a crime in the Utah Territory, Congress had seemingly intruded on the religious values of the Mormon population, which accepted polygamy as a religious duty. Nonetheless, the Court argued, Congress could restrict *behavior* motivated by religion provided it did not prescribe or proscribe certain religious *beliefs*. Mormons were free to believe that God intended plural marriages, but they could be prohibited from acting on the belief because the government had a legitimate reason to regulate marriage.

If the *Reynolds* decision gave the government authority to limit certain religious practices, the *Pierce v. Society of Sisters* decision in 1925 limited the reach of such authority. The Court struck down an Oregon statute forbidding students from attending private schools. In practice, this law was aimed at Catholic schools, and the Supreme Court concluded that Oregon had usurped the rightful authority of churches to operate schools and of parents to educate children according to their own religious beliefs (Abrams 2009).

From one of the least-litigated provisions of the Constitution, the First Amendment's religion clauses became one of the most frequent topics of federal jurisprudence in the 1940s and after (see table 4.1). The transformation, largely a byproduct of the Supreme Court's decision to apply the Bill of Rights beyond the national government, meant an end to the traditional distinction between national and state action toward churches. Whatever the First Amendment forbade or required the national government to do about religion, the Court now held, also applied to the state and local levels of government. Hence, a wide range of policies and practices that had once been left up to the states now became a subject for judicial review by federal courts.

In the process, the courts inaugurated a perennial debate over how to understand the meaning of the Constitution's references to religion. In resolving what Madison described as "collisions and doubts" vis-à-vis church and state issues, judges have chosen among two major, competing interpretations of the Constitution's religious language: separationism and accommodationism. Favoring Jefferson's "high wall," advocates of *separationism* believe "government and religion will better achieve their ends if they remain independent of each other" (Adams 1986, 69). This doctrine takes a dim view of any government aid or support for religion but is generally sympathetic when individuals seek exemption from laws

Table 4.1. Significant Supreme Court Decisions on Church and State Questions

Case	Year	Issue	Outcome
West Virginia Board of Education v. Barnette	1943	Flag salute	Separationist
Everson v. Board of Education	1947	School transportation	Accommodationist
McCollum v. Board of Education	1948	School time-release program	Separationist
Zorach v. Clausen	1952	School time-release program	Accommodationist
McGowan v. Maryland	1961	Sunday closing law	Accommodationist
Torcaso v. Watson	1961	Religious oaths	Separationist
Engel v. Vitale	1962	School prayer	Separationist
Abington School District v. Schempp	1962	School prayer	Separationist
Sherbert v. Verner	1963	Unemployment benefits	Separationist
United States v. Seeger	1965	Draft exemption	Separationist
Epperson v. Arkansas	1968	Teaching evolution	Separationist
Board of Education v. Allen	1968	Textbook loans to parochial schools	Accommodationist
Waltz v. Tax Commissioner of New York	1970	Tax exemptions for church lands	Accommodationist
Lemon v. Kurtzman	1971	State aid to parochial schools	Separationist
Tilton v. Richardson	1971	State aid to sectarian colleges	Accommodationist
Wisconsin v. Yoder	1972	Compulsory education	Separationist
Committee for Public Education v. Nyquist	1973	State aid to parochial schools	Separationist
Meek v. Pittinger	1975	State aid to parochial schools	Mixed
Roemer v. Maryland	1976	State grants to sectarian colleges	Accommodationist
Wolman v. Walter	1977	State aid to parochial schools	Mixed
McDaniel v. Paty	1978	Religious tests for public office	Separationist
CPERL v. Regan	1980	Money for education	Accommodationist
Stone v. Graham	1980	School prayer	Separationist
Widmar v. Vincent	1981	Religious meetings in college	Accommodationist
Valley Forge Christian College v. Americans United	1982	Money for college	Accommodationist
Larson v. Valente	1982	Regulating solicitation	Separationist
United States v. Lee	1982	Social security tax exemption	Accommodationist

Case	Year	Issue	Classification
Larkin v. Grendel's Den	1982	Zoning around churches	Separationist
Bob Jones University v. United States	1983	Tax exemption for sectarian colleges	Accommodationist
Mueller v. Allen	1983	Tax credit for parochial schools	Accommodationist
Marsh v. Chambers	1983	Legislative chaplains	Accommodationist
Lynch v. Donnelly	1984	Christmas displays on public land	Accommodationist
Alamo Federation v. Secretary of Labor	1985	Minimum wage	Accommodationist
Wallace v. Jaffree	1985	School prayer	Separationist
Thorton v. Caldor	1985	Sabbath exemption	Separationist
Grand Rapids v. Ball	1985	Funding for parochial schools	Separationist
Aguilar v. Felton	1985	Funding for parochial schools	Separationist
Witters v. Washington	1986	Funding for sectarian colleges	Accommodationist
Bowen v. Roy	1986	Social security numbers	Accommodationist
Goldman v. Weinberger	1986	Military dress codes	Accommodationist
Edwards v. Aguillard	1987	School prayer	Separationist
Corp. of Presiding Bishop v. Amos	1988	Employment discrimination	Accommodationist
Bowen v. Kendrick	1988	Birth control	Accommodationist
Texas Monthly v. Bullock	1989	Tax on religious publications	Separationist
Employment Division of Oregon v. Smith	1989	Drug use	Accommodationist
Hernandez v. Commissioner of IRS	1989	Taxes	Accommodationist
Heffron v. International Society for Krishna Consciousness	1989	Religious activity on public land	Separationist
County of Allegheny v. ACLU	1989	Religious symbols on public land	Mixed
Swaggart Ministries v. California	1990	Sales tax exemption for religious items	Accommodationist
Board of Education v. Mergens	1990	School prayer	Accommodationist
Lee v. Weisman	1992	School prayer	Separationist
Lambs Chapel v. Center Moriches Union Free School District	1993	Access to school buildings	Accommodationist
Zobrest v. Catalina Foothills School District	1993	Services for parochial school students	Accommodationist
Church of the Lukumi Babalu Aye v. Hialeah	1993	Prohibition of animal sacrifice	Separationist
Kiryas Joel School District v. Grumet	1994	Separate school board for religious group	Separationist

(continued)

Table 4.1. *(continued)*

Case	Year	Issue	Outcome
Rosenberger v. University of Virginia	1995	State funding for religious publications	Accommodationist
Capitol Square Review Bd. v. Pinette	1995	Religious symbols on public land	Accommodationist
Agostini v. Felton	1997	Funding for parochial schools	Accommodationist
Boerne v. Flores	1997	Reverse *Smith* (1989)	Accommodationist
Mitchell et al. v. Helms et al.	2000	Funding for parochial schools	Accommodationist
Santa Fe Independent School District v. Doe	2000	School prayer	Separationist
Board of Regents of the University of Wisconsin v. Southworth	2000	Student fees	Separationist
Good News Club et al. v. Milford Central School	2001	Access to school buildings	Accommodationist
Zelman v. Simmons-Harris	2002	Funding for parochial schools	Accommodationist
Watchtower Bible & Tract Society of New York, Inc., et al. v. Village of Stratton et al.	2002	Regulating solicitation	Separationist
Davey v. Locke	2004	State college scholarship	Separationist
McCreary County v. ACLU	2005	Ten Commandments posting	Separationist
Van Orden v. Perry	2005	Ten Commandments posting	Accommodationist
Cutter et al. v. Wilkinson	2005	Prisoner religious rights	Separationist
Pleasant Grove v. Summum	2009	Religious display in public park	Accommodationist
Christian Legal Society v. Martinez	2010	Discrimination by student organization	Separationist
Salazar v. Bueno	2010	Religious displays on public land	Accommodationist
Arizona Christian School Tuition Organization v. Winn	2011	Tuition tax credits	Accommodationist
Hosanna-Tabor Evang. Lutheran Church v. EEOC	2012	Church hiring	Unclear

on religious grounds. The separationist viewpoint was most forcefully expressed by Justice Hugo Black in a 1947 Supreme Court decision:

> The "establishment of religion" clause of the First Amendment means at least this: Neither a state nor the Federal Government can set up a church. Neither can pass laws which aid one religion, aid all religions, or prefer one religion over another. Neither can force nor influence a person to go to or to remain away from church against his will or force him to profess a belief or disbelief in any religion. No person can be punished for entertaining or professing religious beliefs or disbeliefs, for church attendance or non-attendance. No tax in any amount, large or small, can be levied to support any religious activities or institutions, whatever they may be called, or whatever form they may adopt to teach or practice religion. Neither a state nor the Federal Government can, openly or secretly, participate in the affairs of any religious organizations or groups and vice versa. (Reports, 330 U.S. 15 [1947])[7]

In sharp distinction, the doctrine of *accommodationism*, sometimes known as benevolent neutrality or nonpreferentialism, urges government to protect the nation's Judeo-Christian heritage. Accommodationists believe government may both recognize and extend benefits to religion in a nondiscriminatory manner. The clarion call for accommodation was sounded by Justice William O. Douglas in 1952:

> We are a religious people whose institutions presuppose a Supreme Being. We guarantee the freedom to worship as one chooses. We make room for as wide a variety of beliefs and creeds as the spiritual needs of man deem necessary. We sponsor an attitude on the part of government that shows no partiality to any one group and that lets each flourish according to the zeal of its adherents and the appeal of its dogma. When the state encourages religious instruction and cooperates with religious authorities by adjusting the schedule of public events to sectarian needs, it follows the best of our traditions. For it then respects the religious nature of our people and accommodates the public service to their spiritual needs. (Reports, 343 U.S. 310 [1952])

The doctrines of accommodationism and separationism pit "those who think that government should accommodate and encourage the sort of religion that they see as a foundation of our culture" against "those who think that the government should not extend aid or support to religion in any way" (Wilson and Drakeman 1987, xviii). What does this mean in practice? Table 4.2 summarizes the implicit logic of the two doctrines in terms of the core problems of church and state, the boundary question (otherwise known as establishment) and the authority issue (which we equate with free exercise). Separationists make a sharp distinction between religious organizations and individual members of religious communities. The former have no rights to government benefits (beyond

Table 4.2. The Logic of Constitutional Positions on Church-State Relations

	Separationism	*Accommodationism*
Establishment	Deny most benefits to religious organizations	Permit most benefits to religious organizations
Free Exercise	Permit most exemptions to individuals	Deny most exemptions to individuals

what other private organizations possess), whereas the latter are granted considerable leeway and protection from government action. Because they perceive religion as essentially a private matter, separationists believe it should be beyond the state's reach or patronage. Following the same logic, individuals should thus enjoy substantial autonomy of free exercise. While accommodationists similarly distinguish between religion in the collective and individual modes, they reverse the pattern by allowing the government to grant benefits to religious organizations but severely restricting the legal basis for religious exemptions to secular law.

As this may seem like a very abstract way of understanding legal scholarship about the religion clauses, it is important to recognize the political dynamic beneath it. The separationist position, recognizing religion as one of those fundamental freedoms that no majority should be able to restrict, tends to favor religious minorities. In any political system driven by majority rule, any benefits granted to religion are likely to favor dominant religious traditions and marginalize minority faiths. Restrictions on religious freedom will most likely operate against outsider faiths. Hence, separationism prevents minority faiths from being rendered second class by state recognition of majority faith or government-imposed restrictions on unpopular religious activities. Accommodationists are more attuned to majority faith, granting benefits that will cement the status of numerically dominant faiths while exposing minority traditions to limitations in religious expression that do not similarly hamper the faiths favored by the majority. There are exceptions and nuances to these generalizations, but they largely hold in specific cases.

Where does the American public stand on this debate? Americans partake to some degree of both separationist and accommodationist doctrines (see figure 4.1). When asked whether government should provide no support to any religion or should support all religions equally, a narrow majority opts for the accommodationist perspective by selecting the latter option. But when the issue is phrased another way, the majority shifts to something closer to the separationist perspective. In the second question, individuals were asked whether government should take special steps to protect the Judeo-Christian heritage of the United States, or, rather, whether there should be a "high wall" of separation between church and state. The majority supports Jefferson's wall.[8]

Should government provide support for religion?

Should government protect America's religious heritage or maintain "high wall" of separation?

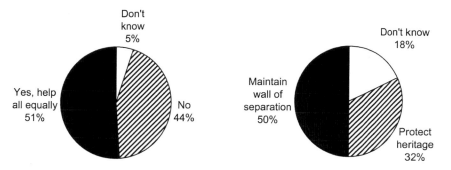

Figure 4.1. General Views on Church-State Separation. *Source: Williamsburg Charter Survey,* 1988.

Public reaction to specific church-state relationships is equally varied (see figure 4.2). Accommodationists could point to majority support for several types of government recognition of religion—practices such as military chaplains, religious displays on public property, voluntary student religious groups in high schools, and prayers at the beginning of high school sporting events. To prove that public opinion demands a high wall between church and state, separationists could seize on the emphatic rejection of aid to religious schools and the requirement that public schools emphasize Judeo-Christian values. On some questions, such as "moment of silence" laws allowing private prayers in school, the public

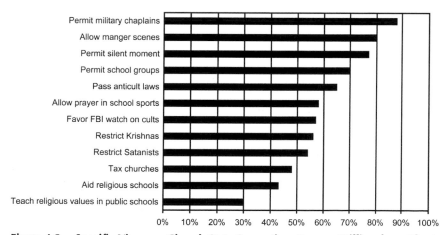

Figure 4.2. Specific Views on Church-State Separation. *Source: Williamsburg Charter Survey,* 1988.

appears to take a strong stand in favor of free exercise rights. Yet, to judge from the number of individuals favoring legal restrictions on religious cults and minority faiths, the public does not want to extend such rights in a nondiscriminatory manner.

The courts have been active in adjudicating religion cases for almost seventy years. The principle that the religion clauses apply to all governments, one part of the change in jurisprudence that began in the 1940s, is now largely settled. The direction of Supreme Court doctrine is much less settled. From roughly the 1940s through the 1970s, the Court usually moved within a strong separationist current. These tendencies prompt us to describe the period from the 1940s through the 1970s as a separationist era. In the 1980s, the Court moved in much more of an accommodationist direction, lowering the wall of separation between religion and state and simultaneously scaling back free exercise when it conflicted with the law.

THE SEPARATIONIST ERA (1940s–1970s)

Establishment Clause

In its separationist phase, the Supreme Court attempted to fortify the boundary between church and state by broadening the list of government actions that constituted an impermissible establishment of religion. Formerly understood to forbid only actions that treated religious groups unequally, establishment was now seen to encompass many activities that appeared to favor religion in general. As part of the separationist trend, the Court became much more sensitive to claims that government rules and regulations unconstitutionally interfered with the free exercise of religion. Before this period, the justices had tended to strike down only those practices that seemed to force individuals to endorse religious beliefs that might be contrary to their own. Now, however, they began to identify a wide range of actions that produced the same effect and either prohibited their enforcement or required government to exempt persons from certain practices on grounds of conscience.

The separationist line from the 1950s through the 1970s was most evident in cases involving religious expression in public schools. The Court was particularly concerned about religious exercises in the public school because children are thought to be especially impressionable, are required by law to attend school, and do so mostly in educational institutions paid for by tax revenue. Under these circumstances, the Court wanted to avoid favoritism and the appearance that government endorsed religion. The threat of endorsement seems less severe in schools for older students who attend voluntarily, persuading the Court to grant much freer rein to religious expression and assistance in institutions of higher learning.

In 1947 the Court decided a case that was to herald a flood of
about the modern meaning of First Amendment prohibitions
ing an establishment of religion." In *Everson v. Board of Education,* the
justices ruled that New Jersey could constitutionally compensate the
parents of all children, including those attending religious schools, for
the expenses of bus transportation to and from school. Defraying the
cost the parents incurred for sending their children to religious schools,
the Court held, did not involve an excessive degree of state support for
religion. Even though this ruling appeared on the surface as a victory
for advocates of government aid to religious education, the language of
the majority opinion made it clear that breaches of the wall of separation
would be tolerated only under the narrowest of circumstances, prompting a Catholic leader to observe, "*We* have *won* on *busing but lost* on the
First Amendment" (quoted in Formicola 1997, 86). Consistent with that
warning, in *McCollum v. Board of Education* (1948), the Court said that the
school board in Champaign, Illinois, could not allow students in public
schools to receive religious instruction on the premises even though attendance at such classes was voluntary and paid for privately. Opening
up the school building to religious training while other classes were in
session struck the Court as virtual endorsement of religion by government, an action prohibited by the establishment clause. But suppose that
instead of inviting religious teachers to offer voluntary instruction in the
school building, the state simply allowed students to travel off-campus
for that purpose during the school day? In a 1952 decision, *Zorach v.
Clausen,* the justices ruled that a New York City law releasing students
from normal classes to attend religious classes somewhere else did not
offend the establishment clause.

Rulings about how far the state could go in helping students receive religious training did not settle the issue of what the public schools could do
about religious ideas. Two decisions that spoke clearly to that issue rank
among the most unpopular rulings in the history of the Supreme Court.
The 1962 case of *Engel v. Vitale* challenged the prayer that New York State
required teachers to read at the beginning of the day. Because a government agency composed the prayer and insisted it be read aloud by state
employees as part of the daily routine, six justices declared that the New
York practice illustrated precisely the type of action that the First Amendment forbids as an establishment of religion. A year later, in *Abington
School District v. Schempp,* the Court extended the ban on state-mandated
religious ceremonies to cover a Pennsylvania law requiring the reading
of Bible verses and recitation of the Lord's Prayer at the beginning of the
school day. In these two decisions, the Court seemed to say that "establishment" included any celebration of religion conducted or promoted by
an agency of the government.

Despite its general turn away from separationism after the 1970s, the Court has consistently struck down laws that, in its view, use the power of the public schools, a governmental institution, to promote religion or religious ideas. One such initiative, state laws permitting a "moment of silence" at the beginning of the school day, was declared unconstitutional in 1985 because it was intended to encourage student prayer (*Wallace v. Jaffree*). In 1992 in *Lee v. Weisman*, the Court cited the *Engel* and *Schempp* precedents to prohibit collective prayers at high school graduation ceremonies. In 2000, the ban was extended to prayers led by students at athletic events in the much-anticipated Texas case, *Santa Fe Independent School District v. Doe*. The Court has been equally vigilant in guarding against efforts to teach religious doctrine through the curriculum. Thus, it rejected as unconstitutional infringements of the establishment clause an Arkansas law that prohibited the teaching of evolution in public schools (*Epperson v. Arkansas*, 1968), Kentucky's requirement that the Ten Commandments be posted in every public school classroom (*Stone v. Graham*, 1980), and a Louisiana law that mandated teaching the religiously inspired theory of divine origin (*Edwards v. Aguillard*, 1987). These precedents suggest that efforts to promote biblically inspired "creation science" in biology classes are not likely to survive a Supreme Court hearing. Lower courts have been vigilant in striking down religious instruction thinly disguised as Bible history courses, a growing movement over the past decade, and some of the "abstinence only" sex education curricula that are clearly grounded in specific religious assumptions.[9]

To some critics, it seemed that these decisions went beyond the goal of making public schools neutral toward religion—the professed goal of the Supreme Court—and created an atmosphere of outright hostility to traditional religious values. In fact, the Court repeatedly emphasized that neutrality did not mean that students were prohibited from religious activity, only that the public school itself could not promote or endorse such actions. The Court actually encouraged schools to offer courses in religious studies that educated rather than preached. To clarify that public schools need not be "religion-free zones," the U.S. Department of Education and several private groups have provided guidelines to emphasize that students are free to pray individually or in groups, discuss their religious beliefs with others, read and distribute religious literature, express religious beliefs through schoolwork and slogans on clothing, and form religious clubs (Riley 1995; First Amendment Center 1999).[10] School authorities may neither encourage these activities nor discourage participation. School officials are not allowed to participate in student religious events and may regulate them only as necessary to ensure order and without putting special restrictions on religious activity. As with many other judicial mandates, these policies are imperfectly implemented at the local level (Brown and Bowling 2003).

The debate over the church-state boundary in education als government action vis-à-vis private religious schools. Precisely such schools exist to inculcate religious values, the Court worried about the degree to which state support would amount to endorsing religion in violation of the establishment clause. From the 1940s through the 1970s, following a no-aid principle, the Court prohibited many forms of state assistance to religious schools. In a string of cases decided during the 1970s, the Court ruled that the boundary was violated if states contributed to the salary of parochial school teachers to cover their "nonreligious" responsibilities (*Lemon v. Kurtzman*, 1971), allowed church schools to finance the upkeep of their buildings with tax money (*Committee for Public Education v. Nyquist*, 1973), reimbursed parents for the costs of private school tuition (same case), paid religious schools for the cost of educational testing required by state law (*Levitt v. Committee for Public Education*, 1973), or lent instructional materials other than textbooks to schools supported by religious institutions (*Meek v. Pittenger*, 1975). Continuing the restrictive trend in two 1985 decisions (*Grand Rapids v. Ball*; *Aguilar v. Felton*), the Court forbade public funding of even part-time or remedial teaching in religious schools.

The Court tempered its separationism by leaving some room for the state to further secular educational goals by working through parochial schools. As we saw in *Everson*, states may help transport pupils to private schools. In *Board of Education v. Allen* (1968), the Court decided that New York State could lend parochial school students the same textbooks provided free of charge to students in the public schools. In subsequent decisions, governments have also been permitted to administer standardized tests to private school students, provide them with diagnostic services, and allow parochial students to participate in therapy offered on "neutral sites" outside private schools (Flowers 2005, 72–74). Most states took advantage of these rulings to provide the permitted services (and other forms of assistance that are probably not allowed) to private religious schools (Abraham 1987, 18).

In deciding these cases during the separationist era, the Court usually drew on a general rule stated most fully by Chief Justice Warren Burger in the 1971 *Lemon v. Kurtzman* decision (Miller and Flowers 1996, 440–56). The *Lemon* test, as it was known, required that a law pass three tests before it could be deemed compatible with the antiestablishment language of the First Amendment: a primarily secular purpose, primarily secular consequences, and no excessive entanglement of church and state. The Court could find no compelling secular purpose in teaching the "creationist" view of human origins in public school, thus striking down the practice as an establishment, but it accepted the New Jersey bus transportation plan because the state had the valid purpose of getting children safely to and from school. On similar grounds, the major effect of lending textbooks was to expand knowledge of secular subjects, but giving parents tax credits for private school tuition, the Court ruled, had the primary effect of supporting instruction for religious purposes. Hence, the Court upheld a New York law on textbook lending but killed a Minnesota tax plan. The entanglement test, the third prong of *Lemon*, led the Court to approve a New York law exempting churches and church-related institutions from property tax (*Walz v. Tax Commissioner of the City of New York*, 1971). Keeping religious property and the holdings of other nonprofit institutions off the tax rolls spared the state having to assign a monetary value to church property and foreclosing if taxes were not paid.

With such a demanding set of conditions, it was hardly surprising that the advocates of a high wall of separation won most of the critical Supreme Court cases and generally succeeded in church-state litigation when cases were decided by lower courts (see Sorauf 1976). Many of these cases had nothing to do with the public schools, attesting to the power of the *Lemon* precedent for any litigation involving the establishment clause.

Free Exercise during the Separationist Era

Even as it broadened the meaning of establishment and restricted the scope of state action to encourage religion during the separationist phase, the Supreme Court grew markedly more receptive to individuals who challenged governmental actions as barriers to the practice of their faith (Evans 1998). The same justices who demonstrated a concern to prevent the state from imposing religious pressure on individuals also defended worship and other forms of religious activity from interference by public authorities. The Court's concern was particularly likely to surface in cases in which the faith was unconventional and the restrictive government regulation reflected hostility to the religion by better-established religious groups, a situation known as the *tyranny of the majority*.

The Court first ensured that religious groups enjoyed full freedom to practice their faith and to undertake activities related to it. As early as 1938, the Court cited freedom of the press in allowing Jehovah's Witnesses to sell literature door-to-door without first having to obtain a municipal permit. The same rationale was cited in a 1943 ruling that exempted Jehovah's Witnesses from a Pennsylvania municipal license fee required of all door-to-door commercial solicitors. The free speech clause of the First Amendment provided the basis for a 1948 decision upholding the right of a preacher from the same sect to broadcast his sermons in a public park. In a Maryland case decided in 1951, the justices overturned the conviction of some Witnesses who had preached in a public park in defiance of municipal ordinances prohibiting such activity. Noting that the ordinance was enforced against the Witnesses but had not been used when mainstream religious groups held prayer services in the same location, the Court decided that the law was enforced unequally—a violation of the Fourteenth Amendment's requirement that all must enjoy the equal protection of the laws.

In time, the Supreme Court moved to defend religious freedom by explicit reference to the free-exercise clause. The majority opinion in *Cantwell v. Connecticut* (1940) was the first to enshrine the principle of free exercise on its own terms and became a powerful precedent. The case arose when three Jehovah's Witnesses ministers were convicted of several offenses against municipal ordinances in New Haven, Connecticut. The key conviction of soliciting without a license was overturned on the grounds that the law unconstitutionally allowed the state government to determine whether the ministers' actions were motivated by genuinely religious convictions. For the government to screen religions in this manner, Justice Robert Jackson wrote, would "lay a forbidden burden upon the exercise of [religious] liberty protected by the Constitution" (Miller and Flowers 1996, 601). In subsequent cases, the Court struck down a number of laws, regulations, ordinances, and administrative practices for interfering with religious exercise or preaching. Even when respect for free-exercise rights might prove burdensome in some way, the Supreme Court generally insisted it take precedence. For example, prison authorities have been required to extend a number of privileges to inmates who practice Muslim, Buddhist, and Native American religions.

The Jehovah's Witnesses also figured in the pivotal case that covered exemptions to secular law under the free-exercise clause (Manwaring 1962). Inspired by the wartime atmosphere, West Virginia's Board of Education had demanded that public-school students salute the American flag or face punishment for insubordination. The state claimed that forcing students to honor the flag was justified as a way to promote the patriotism and national unity essential for preserving liberty. Members of the Jehovah's Witnesses had sued on the grounds that salutes conflicted with the biblical injunction against worshiping a "graven image," a practice forbidden by the denomination's literal reading of passages from the Book of Exodus (20:4–5). The Supreme Court's ruling in *West Virginia State Board of Education v. Barnette* (1943) sided with the Witnesses against the state. The flag was a symbol of state, comparable to the banner of a fraternal organization or the cross of a church, and the salute meant nothing more than a gesture of respect. As such, it was an expression of opinion that could not be forced on a person who was unwilling, for any reason, to endorse the sentiment. As the majority opinion stated, the constitutional provision that "guards the individual's right to speak his own mind" did not give government the authority "to compel him to utter what is not in his mind" (Miller and Flowers 1996, 626). Ever since that landmark decision, the courts have generally supported religious minorities seeking the protection of the First Amendment against different types of required patriotic expression, such as reciting the Pledge of Allegiance, standing during the national anthem, or displaying mottos on license plates.

Beyond simply enlarging the scope of actions covered by the free-exercise clause, the Court also broadened its definition of "religion" to permit other types of belief systems to enjoy First Amendment protection. In essence, the Court has recognized faith motivated by "conscience" rather than just traditional religion (Hammond and Mazur 1995). The principal case in this realm, the 1965 decision in *United States v. Seeger*, ordered local boards that classify men for military service to treat applicants for conscientious objector status with the same respect whether the individual cited nontraditional forms of belief in a Supreme Being or orthodox ideas of God as the basis for exemption.

In the same way that *Lemon* provided the fullest rationale for establishment clause interpretation, the 1963 case of *Sherbert v. Verner* (Miller and Flowers 1996, 687–93) provided the covering rule for free-exercise cases during the separationist era. When confronted with charges that a law unconstitutionally burdened the right of free exercise, the Supreme Court asked whether the law's purpose was sufficiently compelling to warrant the intrusion and whether the state had first tried to achieve the goal without hindering religious observance. This "strict scrutiny" requirement put the burden on the state to show that "only those interests of the highest order not otherwise served can overbalance legitimate claims to the free exercise of religion" (Miller and Flowers 1996, 789). What could survive such a daunting set of legal hurdles? Recognizing the state's interest in protecting public health and safety, the Court approved compulsory vaccination and other medical procedures, especially those involving children, and permitted government to ban religious practices that might endanger the participants. In the interests of public safety and employee health, the Supreme Court also upheld the constitutionality of so-called blue laws, state statutes that compel businesses to close on Sunday. Similarly, when employees claimed that employers infringed their religious rights in various ways, the Court declared that employers need only make a reasonable effort to accommodate the religious beliefs of their workers; there is no legal obligation to incur financial hardship. Even armed with *Sherbert*, plaintiffs claiming free-exercise rights could lose their cases.

During the separationist era, the Court's support for religious objections to secular law inspired a substantial growth in the filing of such cases and a dramatic increase in the success of such suits. A study by Way and Burt (1983) illustrates the magnitude of the trend away from the presumption favoring government. During the first decade covered by their study, 1946–1956, the state and federal courts decided thirty-four cases in which minority religions—groups outside the Protestant, Catholic, and Jewish faiths—claimed free-exercise rights. Although the courts sustained the claims in only 20 percent of the cases, the significance of the decisions apparently stimulated more litigation. Between 1970 and 1980, the number of such cases more than quadrupled to 145. Over that period, "marginal" religious groups won slightly more than half of the cases they brought; in contrast, victories resulted in only about one-third of the lawsuits involving mainstream religions. The minority religious groups were more likely to succeed in legal challenges to laws or practices that limited efforts to spread the faith and in suits brought to extend rights of practice to prisoners. They broke even in cases related to employment and taxation and lost more attempts to gain exemptions from secular laws governing schools or to refuse medical care for minors.

THE ACCOMMODATIONIST ERA

Establishment Clause

Looking back, it is clear that the separationist era gave way after the 1970s to a period dominated by the accommodationist perspective. Although the Supreme Court may still issue the occasional decision with separationist results, it has largely abandoned the *Lemon* test for judging establishment clause violations. During the period 1953–1969, the average Supreme Court justice cast a separationist vote in two-thirds of the cases with church-state issues. After the appointment of Chief Justice Rehnquist in 1986, that average dropped to 45 percent (Hammond 2001). Under the sway of accommodationist judges who believe the state can recognize religion providing it remains neutral among religions, the Court has made it much harder to sustain claims that laws violate the establishment clause. The change registered in several areas, including education. Although the Court did not retreat much on separationism in school prayer decisions, it otherwise allowed much broader state support for religion in the schools. This included action in several high-profile areas:

Equal Access

Although it has never repudiated decisions restricting state-supported religion in public schools, Congress has given tangible support to religious observance in the schools by passing "equal access" laws. Under a 1984 act, high schools that allow noncurricular student groups to meet on campus before or after classes must extend the same privileges to students who want to form religious associations. This apparent concession to the advocates of school prayer was qualified by limiting it to high school students and prohibiting teachers or other school personnel from participating actively or supervising worship. The Court subsequently broadened the principle by insisting that schools and other public facilities that allow community groups to use or rent the facilities may not deny that privilege to religiously affiliated organizations.

State Aid

Perhaps the most dramatic change associated with the accommodationist era involves state support for private religious education. From the strict no-aid stance that dominated the separationist era, the Court has moved to support various forms of what is called indirect governmental funding for religious schools. In a number of cases, the Court has explicitly reversed some of the precedents announced during the separationist era. As a rule, the Court now approves nondiscriminatory aid delivered through a mechanism that allows individuals to use such aid to purchase services from religiously based providers (Millar 2008; Laycock 2008). The most important such case, *Zelman v. Simmons-Harris* (2002), approved a Cleveland school voucher plan. Parents who removed their children from "failing" public schools were given funds that could be used to pay tuition at private schools. Even though virtually all such schools were religiously affiliated and the funds were generally insufficient to pay tuition at nonreligious private schools, the Court upheld the policy. Under the same principle, the University of Virginia's policy of denying student fee money to organizations that engaged in religious proselytizing was struck down as discrimination against religious viewpoints. Outside of education, the new principle governing state aid will probably lead to similar endorsement of publicly funded social service programs run by religious organizations provided that individuals have secular alternatives to choose from.

Public Display

As part of their belief that government should not use the power of the state to promote religion, separationists look askance at the displays of religious documents and symbols in public spaces. During the accommodationist phase that began in the mid-1980s, the Court has been more open to religion in the public square, albeit with conditions. In the 1984 case of *Lynch v. Donnelly*, a divided Court ruled that the city of Pawtucket, Rhode Island, could constitutionally erect a Christmas nativity display without violating the establishment clause (Swanson 1990). Acknowledging the Christian origin of the crèche, the Court nonetheless found that it was a "passive" endorsement of religion. Placed among holiday symbols such as Christmas trees, carolers, candy-striped poles, and a Santa Claus sleigh pulled by reindeer, the crèche was adjudged as primarily a cultural and historical symbol, part of a legitimate government effo~~t~~ "a friendly community spirit of good will in keeping with the ~~s~~ (Miller and Flowers 1996, 182). Five years later, in *County of Allegheny v. ACLU*, the Court followed this somewhat tortuous logic by upholding the constitutionality of a large Chanukah menorah placed outside one government building in Pittsburgh while simultaneously ruling against a Christmas crèche displayed on a staircase in a nearby courthouse. The menorah was acceptable, despite its religious significance in Judaism, because it was deemed to include cultural and historical references and because it was placed among other holiday symbols. By standing alone as an unadorned symbol of Christianity, a seeming endorsement of a particular faith, the crèche violated the establishment clause. These decisions appear to permit government to host religious displays in public space providing the display is not monopolized by a single religious tradition and is open to nonreligious displays. By this logic, the Court ruled in a 1995 case from Ohio that the Ku Klux Klan could not be forbidden from erecting a large cross on a state-owned plaza that had been festooned with a Christmas tree and a menorah.

Standing

When hearing lawsuits challenging government action, the American judicial system requires plaintiffs to show they have suffered harm, often monetary or personal injury, as a result of the policy. Merely objecting to a government action because one is a taxpayer is not enough to demonstrate what is called "standing to sue." In cases involving challenges to government actions that implicate the establishment clause, however, the Supreme Court made an exception during the separationist era. To claim standing, plaintiffs in such cases usually have to show only that government has undertaken actions to promote or favor religion, activities expressly forbidden by the First Amendment. Without that exception, it would be very difficult to win such challenges.

During the accommodationist era, that principle has been narrowed appreciably. In the case of *Elk Grove Unified School District v. Newdow*, a father's challenge to the constitutionality of the "under God" phrase in the Pledge of Allegiance recited by his daughter at school was dismissed because he was not the custodial parent. Similarly, the Court rejected a suit against the Faith-Based Initiative (FBI) developed by the Bush administration in 2001. The case challenged federally funded workshops to help religiously affiliated service providers submit applications for federal contracts. The plaintiff lacked standing, the Court's majority ruled, because there was no specific congressional appropriation for the conferences, which were funded by money set aside for routine department operations (Lupu and Tuttle 2008). The same issue was argued in the closely watched 2009 Supreme Court case of *Buono v. Salazar*, which challenged the placement of a large cross on a federal preserve in the Mojave Desert. The government argued that the plaintiff, a former park official, could not show the display injured him. However, the Court did not deny standing, leaving open the door for more establishment cases in the future.

Many of the cases in the accommodationist era seem to have been decided in direct defiance of the *Lemon* test. While some justices did in fact call on the Court to drop it altogether, *Lemon* has not yet been formally repudiated. Most often, the Court simply ignores it. Two alternatives have been proposed, a coercion test and an endorsement test. The coercion test would hold an action unconstitutional only if it forced a person to engage in religious exercises or make religious professions. Very little state action would be threatened by such an interpretation. The endorsement test prohibits government from actions that appear to favor a particular faith and thus consign members of other faiths to outsider status. Although more stringent than coercion, it too would allow a much broader range of permissible religious activity by government.

Free Exercise

Free exercise was also dramatically altered during the accommodationist era by the Court's startling decision in the 1990 case *Employment Division v. Smith*. The verdict was startling because it overturned the well-established *Sherbert* precedent but even more so because the Court went well beyond what the State of Oregon requested. Oregon had fired two state workers in a drug treatment program because they ingested peyote, a hallucinogenic drug prohibited by federal law. Although the drug was consumed as part of Native American religious rituals, Oregon believed that drug treatment laws demanded drug-free employees. Under the *Sherbert* standard, Oregon asked the Court to rule that it had a compelling purpose in prohibiting illegal drug use by drug counselors and could find no less intrusive way of accomplishing that purpose. Instead of ruling under *Sherbert*, the majority opinion abandoned the compelling-interest test and the strict scrutiny standard altogether. In future free exercise cases, the government only had to show that it had some rational basis for passing the law—not compelling but simply reasonable—and that the law did not expressly target a religion for hardship. If those conditions were satisfied, no group could claim its free-exercise rights were abridged. The requirement of neutrality in the law left some room for free-exercise claims, as the Court showed in 1993 when it struck down a Florida municipal statute that banned the animal sacrifice practiced by the Santeria religion on the grounds that the town permitted the killing of animals by hunters, slaughtering plants, and veterinarians.

Thus the law was not neutral but aimed specifically at Santeria. Beyond insisting on neutrality, *Smith* left it up to governments to choose whether to exempt religious behavior from laws of general application. If this meant that practitioners of Native American religions might have to give up peyote in deference to Oregon's general campaign against drugs, that was the consequence of democracy (Long 2000).

Smith put at risk virtually every exemption that the Court had previously granted on religious grounds and made it much more difficult to sustain free-exercise claims at all. Compared to the era when *Sherbert* mandated strict scrutiny, Smith cut in half the probability that courts would favor plaintiffs, a group dominated by minority religions and sects, or that free-exercise claims would be made (Wybraniec and Finke 2001; Adamczyk, Wybraniec, and Finke 2004). *Smith* thus put the fate of minority religious practices in the hands of political authorities responsive to a public willing to limit religious practices for unorthodox and unpopular religious movements.[11] In the past, governmental agencies, often abetted by courts, have shown no reluctance to impose serious burdens on unorthodox or unpopular religions (Cookson 1997, 2001; Mazur 1999; McLaren and Coward 1998; Morgan 2001; Newton 1995). Because of the unique qualities of Native American religion, for example, governmental authorities have frequently transgressed on sacred beliefs and inhibited hallowed rituals (Deloria 1992; Brown 1999). Hostility rather than ignorance explains the extraordinary persecutions visited on unconventional religious movements labeled as "cults"—the free-exercise rights of adult members have been forcibly violated through "deprogramming" and the collective rights of the churches imperiled by assessments of damages or government investigations of financial practices (Boothby 1986).[12] In deciding cases about child custody, judges have routinely considered the religious beliefs of the contending parties, usually to the disadvantage of parents who practice minority or unconventional faiths (Drobac 1998). *Smith* made it much less likely that religious groups could successfully contest such policies that enjoyed majority support.

Whatever their divisions on other issues, virtually all religious traditions and secular civil libertarians condemned the decision and worked to restore the pre-*Smith* standard.[13] Congress eventually passed the Religious Freedom Restoration Act (RFRA), restoring the *Sherbert* standard of strict scrutiny in cases alleging violations of free exercise. When this statute was challenged in *Boerne v. Flores* (1997), the Court accepted it for federal government actions but not for state and local laws, in which, the Court said, it had not been proven to be necessary. Ironically, given the origins of the *Smith* case in the use of peyote by Native Americans, the Court used RFRA in 2006 to reject the prosecution of another small religious group for the sacramental use of a different hallucinogen (Goldberg 2008, 104–6).

Still concerned about abuses of free exercise in the states, Congress subsequently enacted a strangely titled statute, the Religious Land Use and Institutionalized Persons Act (Waltman 2011). Applied only to cases in which religious organizations faced restrictions on the use of their property and prisoners claimed denial of religious freedom, the land use provisions of RLUIPA were upheld unanimously by the Court in 2005. The force of *Smith* was further blunted by the adoption of state RFRAs. Apart from these exceptions, *Smith* remains the current standard in free-exercise cases.

THE POLITICS OF CHURCH-STATE RELATIONS

Transformations in Supreme Court doctrines—the rise of separationism in the 1940s and its displacement by accommodationism in the 1970s—do not just happen. While the majesty of their surroundings and the dignity of their procedures may seem to exclude the courts from the political process, that is not the case in reality. The behavior of the judiciary is permeated by the same types of political influences that affect other arenas of government. Any discussion of church-state relationships must therefore take into account the larger political context in which the judicial decisions are made. An investigation of the politics of church-state interaction is necessary to understand why the issue became so important when it did and how the religious community reacted to the crucial court decisions.

The Supreme Court's radical transformation of church-state doctrine in the 1940s did not occur in isolation. As noted earlier, one source of revision was the general tendency of the justices to extend the First Amendment to cover the actions of state and local governments. But beyond this general shift in the constitutional interpretation, the consciousness of the Court was shaped by intensive grassroots political activity that raised the church-state issue to a high place on the national agenda (Sorauf 1976; Henderson 2004; Dierenfield 2007). Throughout the era of judicial activism on the church-state question, the churches, allied groups of laypersons, and interfaith organizations functioned much as classic interest groups—designing legislation, raising public support in well-orchestrated campaigns for public opinion, lobbying legislatures and courts, and bringing and defending lawsuits. This description fits both the coalition that supported the Court's separationist stance and those who sought a more accommodationist perspective.

Many of the state aid laws evaluated by the Supreme Court in the decades after World War II were inspired by religious groups as a means of supporting church-affiliated schools. As most of these schools were Roman Catholic, the principal groups defending aid schools were Catholic organizations, such as the Education the United States Catholic Conference, the National Catholic Association, the Catholic League for Religious and Civil Rights, and the Knights of Columbus. Ranged on the other side were liberal Protestant groups in the National Council of Churches; those conservative Christian denominations that feared state aid as the opening wedge in a government drive to take over the schools (e.g., the Baptist Joint Committee on Public Affairs); secular groups such as the American Civil Liberties Union, American Association of Humanists, and Americans United for Separation of Church and State; and the major umbrella organizations for the American Jewish community. The lineup was similar but not identical on questions involving religious expression in the public schools. Because they believed that any such public religion would invariably reflect the values of the predominantly Christian population, Jewish groups were the most consistent separationists (Ivers 1995). Protestants who opposed state aid as a Catholic subsidy generally allied with Catholic organizations in pressing for greater religious content in public schools. Although some of the opponents of state aid and religious expression may have been motivated by hostility to religion in general, the debate split many religious communities internally and is better described as a civil war among religious groups rather than a "war on religion" as it was labeled in a 2012 Republican campaign ad.

Even though separationists won most of the court cases in the 1940s through 1970s, limiting both state aid and public religious expressions, the Court's decisions were unpopular with the majority of Americans— possibly as many as two-thirds of the population—who favored some sort of organized prayer in public schools (Elifson and Hadaway 1985). Not surprisingly, opponents of these decisions tried any number of ways to get the federal courts to change the decisions but were decidedly unsuccessful (Hays 2012). Nonetheless, the apparent public support for restoration of school prayer made it politically appealing to undermine the *Engel* and *Schempp* rulings by the tried and true practice of evasion (Sweet 2010).

Rather than petition the courts for an allowable practice short of organized prayer, some authorities simply ignored the rulings. Because control over school religious practices effectively rests with thousands of local school districts and tens of thousands of classroom teachers, the prayer and Bible-reading decisions offered great opportunities for noncompliance (Patric 1957; Katz 1965; Sorauf 1959). Studying Tennessee's reaction to the prohibition of Bible reading, Robert Birkby (1966) discovered that all but one school district had allowed the forbidden practice to continue, leaving the question of religious ceremonies in the classroom to the discretion of the teacher. Even though the Court had ruled that voluntary religious activity in the classroom was no more constitutional than coerced worship, many local school boards adopted it unless they were faced with legal challenges. Thirty years after the Court issued its blanket prohibition on state-directed school prayer, some school districts continued to promote compulsory religious observance until ordered to cease and desist by federal courts.[14]

Despite this resistance, the Court's decision eventually led to a substantial decline in formal religious observance in the classroom. A nationwide survey of public school teachers during the 1964–1965 school year found that the incidence of morning prayers declined from 60 percent before the *Engel* decision to 28 percent afterward, and that Bible reading, a regular practice in the classrooms of 48 percent of the teachers before *Schempp*, survived in only 22 percent after the case was decided (Way 1968, 191; see also Dierenfeld 1967). Reported compliance was lowest in the southern states, where nearly three-fifths of the teachers continued reading the Bible and just under two-thirds maintained the practice of morning prayers. Studies of compliance patterns in local communities by Muir (1967), Johnson (1967), and Dolbeare and Hammond (1977) have suggested that the degree of conformity to the Court decision depended on a variety of factors—the religious composition of the area, the prestige of the Supreme Court, the willingness of individuals to demand implementation, and the position taken by political elites. In the long run, however, the practices of teacher-led prayer and Bible reading have become rare (McGuire 2009) while compliance with more recent decisions, particularly the ban on organized prayer at school athletic events and graduation, is much less widespread.

Some critics attacked the Court's rulings with a constitutional amendment to overturn *Engel* and *Schempp*. The so-called Amen Amendment failed repeatedly to obtain the required two-thirds majority in the House and Senate (Dierenfield 1997). In 1984, a proposed constitutional amendment to permit vocal prayer by individuals or groups in public institutions, schools included, fell short of the required two-thirds vote in the U.S. Senate. Even with the election of sympathetic Republican majorities in both houses of Congress in 1994, a similar amendment to restore many practices that the Supreme Court had expressly forbidden on establishment clause grounds—prayers at high school graduation and religious displays on public property—repeatedly failed to pass.

Why did the separationist decisions stand, in education and other domains, despite intense criticism from accommodationist critics (Cord 1982; R. Morgan 1984) and determined attempts to get around them? On school prayer, it seems, the explanation was resources. Supporters of the legislation are on average less educated and affluent than supporters of the current policy (Elifson and Hadaway 1985; Woodrum and Hoban

1994), giving accommodationist advocates a constituency with few political resources. More broadly, respect for the judiciary, especi̇͟͟͟, the Supreme Court, gave the separationist decisions sufficient legitimacy to offset attempts to change them. Although many Americans dislike restrictions on prayer in school or other forms of government advocacy of religion (see figure 4.2), they also accept the authority of the Court in this domain. A variety of studies suggest that disagreement with the specific separationist decisions produced only a modest spillover onto the general image of the Court (Kessel 1966; Dolbeare 1967; Caldeira and Gibson 1992; Gibson, Caldeira, and Spence 2003). In a 1966 poll of nearly 1,300 voting-age American citizens, only about five hundred made any response when asked whether there were *anything* they liked or disliked about the recent work of the Supreme Court (Murphy, Tanenhaus, and Kastner 1973). If less than 40 percent of the sample felt the need to volunteer any praise or condemnation of the Court just four years after the first decision on school prayer observance, the salience of the issue for the general public must be questioned. Moreover, 70 percent of the critical remarks about the Court were directed at decisions other than *Engel* and *Schempp*. To the extent that public opinion polls can gauge such matters, the broadening of the establishment clause was not the object of widespread enthusiasm, particularly insofar as it prohibited religious observance as an official part of the school day, but the hostility it engendered should not be overstated either.

So in the absence of a mandate from disgruntled citizens, why did the Court change its orientation from separationism to accommodationism in the 1980s? The transformation in church-state jurisprudence resulted from political changes. From 1968 through 2008, Republicans controlled the White House for more than twice as many years as Democrats, a dominance made possible largely by a movement toward the GOP by southern evangelical Protestants and, to a lesser extent, Roman Catholics (see chapters 8–9). This tilted the party toward groups who favored accommodation. This new dominant coalition handed the major voice in Supreme Court nominations to Republican presidents who accordingly appointed a more accommodationist Court less sensitive about incursions on the establishment clause or sympathetic to free-exercise claims by religious minorities. Although it took some time to materialize (Kobylka 1995) and did not radically change school prayer doctrine, the new era of judicial accommodation became apparent by the mid-1980s. Beyond the judiciary, the dominant coalition also impressed its preferences on the executive and legislative branches, changing policies governing civil rights enforcement, earmarks (special appropriations) for religious organizations, and encouragement of religious groups to compete for government contracts and grants.[15]

THE CONSTITUTIONAL REVOLUTION IN PERSPECTIVE

During its heyday, separationism was subjected to a steady critique by scholars who blistered the Court for its apparent inconsistencies. How, they wondered aloud, could the Court possibly find it acceptable for the government to pay for textbooks loaned to private schools but unconstitutional for that same government to supply those same schools with educational materials like maps, globes, and film projectors? The contrasting decisions about holiday displays, which turned on subtle differences in content and object placement, prompted one federal judge to describe the justices as a bunch of interior decorators. The central problem, according to many observers, was the lack of a coherent theory underpinning the approach to church-state cases. The separationist court split the two religion clauses into mutually exclusive categories and developed a unique approach in each domain. The *Lemon* and *Sherbert* standards provided rules for each of the two religion clauses but no real principles that would guide judges in seeing them as a single entity. The two clauses are plainly about religious freedom, but the Court never articulated a clear vision of what religious freedom meant.

When they rose to majority status in the 1980s, the accommodationists tried to displace the separationists with a unifying principle of religious freedom under labels like *positive neutrality, equal treatment,* or *nondiscrimination*. This approach was pioneered in the political realm by the Christian Coalition, the foremost evangelical interest group of the 1990s. Ralph Reed, the Coalition's director, recognized that the public did not want to give access to public schools or public money to groups that would use the opportunity to proselytize on behalf of traditionalist Christianity. To reframe the policy in terms more acceptable to the public, Reed likened his constituents, "people of faith," to other minority groups that had long faced hostility from government (Watson 1997). Framing the issue in these terms, Reed contended that limits on school prayer or religious displays on public property denied basic freedoms to the religious. Picking up on this language, the law firms that argued accommodationist claims urged the Court to think in terms of individual freedom that was only incidentally religious. If secular groups could erect displays on public property, religious groups were entitled to the same option. If public schools allowed noncurricular student groups to meet in public schools, religious groups should not be singled out for exclusion. A program that funded student publications from fees could not exempt only religious groups and still meet the equality standard. The Ohio voucher program was similarly approved on the grounds that equal treatment forbade excluding religious schools from the pool of institutions eligible to host voucher students. These arguments proved crucial in justifying the Court's accommodationist tack.

As critics have observed, this amounts to trumping the religious clauses with the other parts of the First Amendment (Brown 2002; Blake 2013). That is, it reduces religious freedom to generic speech and lodges its protected status in the First Amendment's free speech guarantees. Apart from its dubious historical claims, this approach comes with costs. "By insisting on equal treatment for religious speech," Derek Davis (2004, 720) has noted, accommodationists "give up the special status that religion is otherwise granted under the Constitution." Under the doctrine of equal treatment, how can religion claim protection that the state does not otherwise allocate to private groups?[16] The evisceration of religious exemption under *Smith*, which evangelical groups protested, was justified precisely under this neutrality principle, that religious groups should not be exempted from laws that bind every other group. Giving religious groups access to public funds that will enhance their capacity to proselytize, another consequence of this doctrine, may well tempt religious groups to participate in programs that are not consistent with their doctrine.

As a plausible example, Davis mentions the evangelical doctrine that opposes mothers working outside the home. If the federal program expanded child-care aid by providing subsidies, evangelical churches might be pressured by members to participate on purely financial grounds. Similarly, the protection against government interference in church affairs under the old *Lemon* precedent would be hard to justify under equal protection doctrine. Churches have no right to special immunity if religious speech and behavior is no different from the speech and behavior enjoyed by nonreligious organizations. The corrosive effect of neutrality also became apparent when the Court ruled in 1995 that the Ku Klux Klan had the right to put up its cross in a public religious display in Columbus, Ohio. How many religious communities would want their success to facilitate such public expression of bigotry? The same logic that permits religious groups to sponsor school clubs can be used to provide constitutional protection for Satanists or gays, surely not the outcome that evangelical Protestants fought for. Surrendering the establishment and free-exercise claims to the free-speech clause may eventually be seen by religious traditionalists as a deal with the devil.

THE CUTTING EDGE

Since the defining cases that gave the accommodationist era its name— *Smith* for free exercise, *Zelman-Harris* for establishment—the Supreme Court has appeared to consolidate its position rather than break new ground. The court has recently decided fewer cases regarding the First Amendment religion clauses and most of those cases have merely clarified earlier rulings rather than indicated sharp departures from previous precedents.

Alexis de Tocqueville once famously observed that in the United States, every political issue sooner or later becomes a legal issue. Partisans increasingly appeal to the courts to overturn policies passed by Congress through the normal legislative process. In an era of intense partisan polarization like the present, that has been the case for many issues with religious implications. No issue has been more controversial than the 2010 health care reform law, known officially as the Patient Protection and Affordable Care Act, passed by a narrow congressional majority. Although the U.S. Supreme Court upheld the general constitutionality of what is popularly known as "Obamacare," the Court has already agreed to hear several cases with religious overtones growing out of the momentous act.

The act mandates that employers who provide health insurance to their employees must cover contraception. The law formally exempts houses of worship from this provision on the grounds that private religious organizations should be free to decide whether they want to extend such coverage. This decision did not go far enough for two categories of claimants—religiously affiliated institutions such as hospitals and social services that serve members of the public and do not exclusively employ members of their own faith, and private employers of for-profit institutions who assert they have religious objections to contraception. The plaintiffs insist their religious liberty is compromised because they are forced to pay for services they consider morally objectionable. The defenders of the new law insist that making religious institutions and private employers exempt from the mandate "imposes faith on unwilling employees" (Stern 2012, 19). Both sides thus claim that the act itself or the broadening of the exemption compromises their religious freedom.[17]

One of the great ironies of this case is that the old *Sherbert* standard of free exercise established by liberal courts during the separationist era would probably have enabled the plaintiffs challenging the contraceptive mandate to win exemption. When that standard was narrowed by the conservative majority in the *Smith* decision, it made any claim for exemption much more difficult to sustain and helped produce the very legal ammunition reinforcing the mandate for contraceptive coverage. A lot of time, money, and legal ingenuity will be spent to argue in favor of and against the contraceptive mandate on free exercise grounds; the Court will ultimately have its say.

We sometimes pity the poor reader who tries to determine how the First Amendment's religion clauses should be interpreted. Although many have called for a more coherent jurisprudence to overcome the current "doctrinal morass," nothing approaching a consensus has emerged. In the last few years alone, highly respected academic presses have published an array of books by distinguished scholars from many academic disciplines offering widely discrepant interpretations. The reader will learn that the religion clauses of the First Amendment were meant only to prohibit a national church (Drakeman 2009), that they left all questions about government/religious interactions to the jurisdiction of the states (S. Smith 1995), that the clauses were intended to secure individual's religious liberty from any agent at any level of government (Bowlby 2011; West 2011), that the founders intended to "express support for religion while keeping the religious and governmental spheres distinct, and without threatening national unity" (Meyerson 2012, 250), that they hoped to encourage religion as a means of instilling virtue in the citizens of the new republic without granting churches a shred of governmental authority (Frazer 2012; Kidd 2010). Not surprisingly, these divergent interpretations often come with equally divergent prescriptions to well-meaning judges on how to bring their rulings in line with the true meaning of the Constitution. About the only common view shared by these authors is the firm belief that the federal courts have gotten the Constitution wrong on religion. We thus see no end to the continuing debate on the legal status of religion in many forms.

Most of the "religious" issues on the national political agenda do not involve the legal standing of religion. Debates about abortion, gay rights, the state of the family, and "obscene" art have little to do with the types of legal disputes examined in this chapter. We now shift our attention from religion itself as a source and subject of political controversy to examine the ways that religious sentiment is drawn into larger debates over the formation and execution of public policy.

5

Mobilizing Religious Interests

Those who say religion has nothing to do with politics do not know what religion is.

—Mohandas Gandhi

The idea that religion and politics don't mix was invented by the Devil to keep Christians from running their own country.

—Jerry Falwell

Man is a religious animal. He is the only religious animal. He is the only animal that has the True Religion—several of them. He is the only animal that loves his neighbor as himself and cuts his throat, if his theology isn't straight. He has made a graveyard of the globe in trying his honest best to smooth his brother's path to happiness and heaven.

—Mark Twain

In September 2012, media outlets all over the nation reported that the sole reference to God had been "removed" from the Democratic Party platform. Though their 2008 platform had cited "God-given talents," the 2012 platform spoke only to being "able to go as far as [our] talent and drive take us." The change was big news. Presidential candidate Governor Mitt Romney concluded that the omission suggested "a party out of touch with the mainstream of American people." His Republican running mate, Paul Ryan, asserted that the change was "not in keeping" with American traditions. Needled by Republicans, President Obama called for "God" to be reinstated and wondered why the reference had been removed in the first place.

That this issue was noteworthy at all seemed to suggest the possibility of gaining the very endorsement or condemnation of God by writing references in or out of a political document. If it were possible to gain favor with references, the twelve references to God in the Republican Party platform put the GOP in a much better position. Questioned about the disparity, Senator Dick Durbin defensively rebutted the implication that "Democrats are godless" and passionately asserted that "God is not a franchise of the Republican party."[1]

All the drama was curious because in the end, political party platforms are expressions by the party elite of the positions for which the party would stand and the policies that it would pursue . . . in an ideal world . . . when conditions are favorable . . . and it has complete control. In other words, in a world that does not exist. In the real world of American democracy, political conditions are rarely "right" and factionalism and compromise are embedded in the very constitutional fibers that hold the states united. Why then did the platform language take on such significance? Why was it important (or not important) to reference "God"? Why did the number of references matter?

The simple answer is that platforms are significant because they communicate a message to the voters that this party comes closest to and will best represent "our views." The tacit understanding behind the platform is that the party and by extension the presidential candidate will work to advance "our interests." Some Americans who favor strong separation between church and state might be uncomfortable with the Republican platform and its generous, otherworldly acknowledgments. For other religious citizens who think God should have a major role in the public discourse, a platform with no references to a deity might signal a party that will not respect or incorporate their religious values very well. The day after Barack Obama was reelected, one evangelical leader called the election "a disaster."[2] Obviously there was deep sense of loss for his perceived interests. Meanwhile, others greeted the outcome with shouts of "Hallelujah! God has again blessed us!"[3]

So what exactly are religious interests? When do they become politically salient? Why do these interests vary so much even among religious people? How do religious grievances arise and become politically relevant? What are the sources of religious group views on politics, and what are the factors that help the religious to formulate political agendas? These questions are the focus of this chapter.

We have all read a good crime novel or at least seen a legal thriller at the movies or on television. Even with only the legal training received from whodunits, everybody knows that a crime involves three crucial elements: motive, means, and opportunity. Motive explains why the crime was committed, means reveals how the crime was committed, and opportunity divulges where and when the crime was perpetrated. While religious mobilization is not a crime, the basic elements of crime theory provide a useful framework to help us understand the ways that religion interacts with politics (Wald, Silverman, and Fridy 2005). A close examination of American history reveals a persistent linkage between religion and politics, a linkage visible among most theological traditions and religious groups. Asking about the motive, means, and opportunity for religiously based political action will help us understand this linkage whether we examine the framers, the abolitionists, or contemporary controversies about stem cell research and gay marriage.

STUDYING RELIGIOUS INTERESTS

The political intervention of churches and religious groups has been often condemned as overly divisive, ideologically biased, and politically induced (Wallis 2005). Indeed, a recent poll by the Pew Forum on Religion and Public Life showed Americans are unsure about the propriety of mixing religion in politics. Two-thirds of respondents (66 percent) believe that churches should not come out in favor of one candidate over another.[4]

Despite voter wariness about the role of religion in politics, it can be a particularly potent resource for political mobilization and participation. This is why politicians and activists continue to seek the support and endorsement of religious figures and organizations. However atypical and peculiar such religious activity may be, the tools and theories that political scientists use to understand politics can be meaningfully applied to it. Religion has been a remarkably reliable indicator of partisan preference, and religious alliances in American politics have been notably stable over time.

Religious interests, like other interests in the political realm, must begin the policy process with articulation and aggregation. Somebody has to say what is wrong and what the group thinks should be done. Expressed more formally, the processes of articulation and aggregation describe how individuals and groups express their needs and preferences to the government and how these needs and desires are combined and formulated into policy programs (Almond et al. 2004). Collective action lies at the heart of both processes. Collective action occurs when individuals work in concert to address what they perceive to be a common problem. There are many forms of collective action—voting, protesting, striking, boycotting, and lobbying, as well as the full range of other types of political participation. The hundreds of thousands of people who marched on Washington in August 1963 demanding civil rights legislation were engaged in collective action. So were the Latter-Day Saints who, encouraged by their religious leaders, actively worked to oppose marriage equality in California and other states in the opening decades of this century (Gordon and Gillespie 2012).[5]

Several well-developed literatures examine the logic of collective action. The expansive research on interest groups explains how formal membership organizations articulate and aggregate the concerns of their members (see, e.g., Olson 1965; Wilson and Bagley 1973; Ostrom 1990; Lichbach 1996; Baumgartner and Leech 1998). Organized religious interests include membership groups such as the Family Research Council or the Interfaith Alliance, denominations such as the U.S. Catholic Conference or the Union of American Hebrew Congregations, representatives of religious institutions such as the Catholic Charities or the American Friends Service Committee, and coalitions of denominations such as the National Council of Churches or the National Association of Evangelicals. Paul Weber and Landis Jones (1994) identified 120 nonprofit organizations that seek to influence policy formulations from a religious perspective, and the number continues to grow. These types of religious groups act much like other secular interest groups attempting to influence the policy process. They decide whether to focus on the local, state, or national level and must determine how to apply political pressure through political campaigning, lobbying, or direct action.

Of course, although many important groups exist in public life, many people do not participate through these formal organizations. Certainly not all evangelical Christians are members or even supporters of the National Association of Evangelicals—although evangelicals today are a politically significant social group. In the 1950s and 1960s, all those working for civil rights were not directly affiliated with Martin Luther King's Southern Christian Leadership Conference. Yet masses of these people participated demonstratively in order to obtain civil rights. Religiously inspired political action among "regular people" is better characterized as a "social movement" than an interest group activity. Social identities based on commonalities in religion or other poles of self-definition such as race, ethnicity, kinship, or occupation can serve as powerful bases for collective activity even without the associational ties of formal organizations. Because social movement groups are less centralized than interest groups they frequently must rely on political mobilization and the power of their numbers to influence policymakers. While groups organized on these bases may well seek tangible benefits—things such as equal pay, nondiscrimination policies, and so forth—their campaigns are also motivated by a drive for self-respect and social honor. The well-established literature on social movements provides us a useful way to identify the motive, means, and opportunity for religiously inspired political action. Contemporary social movement theory looks to culture to understand where religious interests come from, examines resources to describe the means that enable them to participate effectively, and focuses on the importance of the state and political conditions in identifying the opportunities groups have to influence the political system (Tarrow 1998, 2011, 2012; Wald, Silverman, and Fridy 2005; see also Zald and McCarthy 1979, 1987; Oberschall 1992; Johnston and Klandermans 1995). Utilizing a social movement framework, this chapter focuses on unraveling the motives and exploring the means religious groups have to participate in politics, while chapter 6 will focus on opportunity.

ESTABLISHING MOTIVE

Religious Interests and Culture

Religious interests are grounded in religious culture. According to Wildavsky (1987), culture performs three primary functions: (1) it offers identity, (2) it prescribes norms, and (3) it defines boundaries for relationships. Religion is a particularly potent communicator of culture because, as Leege and his colleagues (2002, 45) explain, it "adds both a transcendent and immanent supernatural dimension to identity, norms and boundaries." Wuthnow (1987) describes this as the "moral order." When religion and culture are joined, people come to understand right and wrong not only because of a standard shared by the community but also because that which is "Most High" has revealed its necessity. What better rationale can there be than "God says so"? The intersection of religion, culture, and politics often explains the intensity that accompanies some issues. For instance, Webster and Leib (2002) explain that much of the virulent opposition expressed by white southerners to removing the Confederate flag arose because the banner had come to represent southern religious culture. Religion has so much political potential because it both prescribes how we as individuals should live and suggests the nature of the just society. According to Geertz (1973, 90), it provides an "order for existence." For many, it compels a responsibility to help bring this order about. As Leege (1993, 9–10) has argued elsewhere, "People become something more than ordinary mortals when they share a sacred community. People become empowered, they develop the capacity to act in concert. Religions specify what actions to take, and religious beliefs create the obligation to act." Religious culture provides a framework for understanding how people interpret the world as well as how they respond politically because of that perspective (Olson 2011).

In its most basic form religion is an encompassing and transformative experience (Mitchell 2007). However, the transformation is by no means automatic. Religious leaders and religious communities help people understand the meaning and at times the political relevance of the ecstatic experiences (Wilcox, Wald, and Jelen 2008). Regardless of the content of their theological beliefs, it is important to remember religious groups vary in their willingness to engage the political world. Interests are not always clearly defined, well articulated, or embraced by the faithful. The same grievances that produce mobilization in one religious context may not produce political action in another. Scholars have long understood that both prophetic and otherworldly orientations can exist even in the same religious tradition (Harris 1994; Marx 1967). For example, even though black churches were often characterized as political during the height of the civil rights movement, one critic lamented, "No one will ever be able to organize the black community for united action as long as black preachers stand up on Sunday morning and take people to heaven one by one" (Cleague 1971, 11–12). From this perspective, a concern with the "by and by" leads to a neglect of the here and now. Karl Marx said religion was the "opiate of the masses," and many scholars treated it as such, rarely recognizing the remarkable ability of religion to be the catalyst for tremendous societal change.

Sources of Motivation

Group Identity

The first potential source of religiopolitical motivation is the collective identity that religion can construct. Collective identities can serve as powerful motivations for political participation because group identifications provide cognitive structures through which the world can be viewed. Group-based patterns of political judgments have been repeatedly found among citizens (Berelson, Lazarsfeld, and McPhee 1954; Campbell et al. 1960; Conover 1984; Wilcox 1992; Kellstedt and Green 1993). They often underlie intense and violent political conflicts of the type that abound in Israel/Palestine, Syria, Pakistan, Indonesia, Tibet, India, China, Sudan, Afghanistan, Chechnya, Lebanon, Bosnia, Somalia, Uganda, Ethiopia, North Korea, Nigeria, Iran, Iraq, and other places.

Thankfully, religiously based political violence is rare in the United States. Still, political affiliation in America does reflect religious group tradition and influence. In elections religious groups exhibit distinctive political priorities, attitudes, and positions on issues (Guth et al. 2006). After reviewing numerous studies of voting patterns in different countries, one leading expert on mass political attitudes concluded that "religious differentiation intrudes on partisan political alignments in [an] unexpectedly powerful degree wherever it conceivably can" (Converse 1974, 734). The use of the word *unexpectedly* reveals the bias of modern observers surprised that contemporary political differences might be tied to "primordial" religious cleavages. While such cleavages may surprise academics, politicians and political strategists readily recognize them. Former Democratic Party chair Howard Dean was most certainly overstating in the summer of 2005 when he characterized the Republicans as "pretty much a white Christian party." However, the pronounced differences among religious groups in partisan affiliation is an undeniable fact in American politics (Leege 1996b; Wald 1989). As we saw in chapter 2 (table 2.4), religious groups differ in partisan preference, presidential vote, and ideological self-image.

Group Status

Partisan attachments are not the only way religious identities can become politicized. A second set of motivations for the political involvement of religious groups may come from a perception on the part of the group that it is not being fully valued by society. Class distinctions remain relevant in contemporary religious life (McCloud 2007; Pyle 2006). Group members may feel that the prestige of their group or its way of life is under attack and thus may be motivated to act in an attempt to protect their status and societal influence. Certainly this theory offers an explanation for the religious activism of African American churches. During times of segregation and discrimination, when basic social, legal, and political rights were denied, black churches stood as institutional barriers against further degradation (Wilmore 1998).

In trying to understand how status may motivate political involvement by religious groups, it is important to recognize the striking and persistent inequalities that exist among religious traditions. Scholars have found that denominational groups vary significantly in class, culture, ethnic and racial composition, geographic distribution, and social and economic achievement (Smith and Farris 2005; Coreno 2002; Park and Reimer 2002; Kosmin and Lachman 1993; Roof and McKinney 1987). The religious groups can be ranked according to educational achievement, a major influence on social status and political outlook in the United States (see figure 5.1). Jewish respondents possessed the highest levels of formal education in the population, followed at some distance by Latter-Day Saints, mainline Protestants, Roman Catholics, and the participants who reported no religious affiliation—findings consistent with many other studies. Then, clustered at the lowest level of educational achievement come white evangelicals, black Protestants, and Hispanic Protestants and

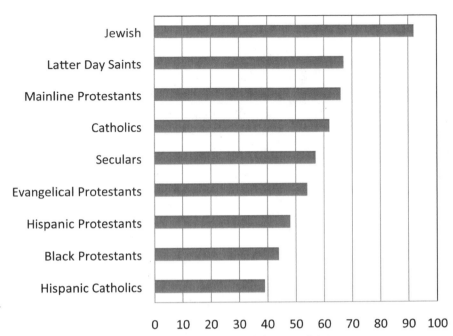

Figure 5.1. Post–High School Education by Religious Tradition

Catholics.[6] Analyses of religious group differences on related indicators of social standing such as income and occupational attainment have disclosed very similar patterns.

Because socioeconomic factors such as education are themselves related to political attitudes and behavior, those skeptical of the influence of religion on politics contend that differences in political orientations among religious groups can be reduced to social characteristics that happen to be associated with membership in different denominational families (Allinsmith and Allinsmith 1948). The claim that political differences among religious groups reflect only the social composition of denominations can be tested by a comparison of religious group attitudes with social standing held constant. Using party identification as an example of political difference, one would try to discover whether, for example, Jews of high education reported the same level of attachment to the Democratic Party as did persons with similar educational levels but different religious preferences. If religious group differences were shown to narrow at each level of education, then education apparently could contribute to political variations. But if the political differences were shown to persist—if, sticking with the same example, college-educated Jews were still more strongly attached to the Democratic Party than college-educated Catholics, evangelical Protestants, or other groups—then religious differences in politics could not be attributed wholly to a factor such as education.

The test results for the religious groups appear in figure 5.2. Members in each group were subdivided by education into those with a high school diploma and no further education and those who possessed additional education beyond the high school diploma. For each group, we calculated the percentage of participants who identified with the Republican Party. The figure shows social status (in the form of education) to be an important but not altogether complete explanation for denominational differences in partisanship. For evangelicals, Latter-Day Saints, mainline Protestants, Catholics, and Hispanic Protestants, gains in education were clearly associated with movement toward the Republican Party. Put another way, the level of Republican identification increased steadily as members of these groups moved from the least- to the most-educated categories.

However, a different pattern emerges for Hispanic Catholics, Jews, and seculars. Regardless of educational level, nearly identical numbers in both religious groups identified themselves as Republican. Moreover, the pattern for black Protestants is entirely different. Regardless of education level, they do not identify with the Republican Party.

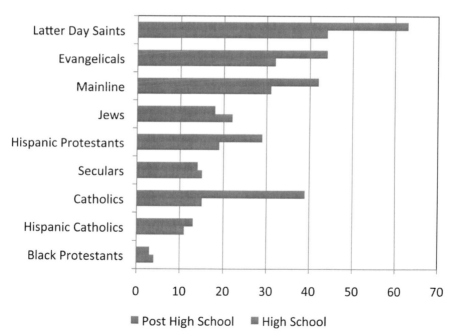

Figure 5.2.   **Republican Partisanship by Educational Attainment for Religious Tradition**

Even if social status influences party loyalties for some denominations, it does not eliminate the full measure of religious group differences. If education were all that mattered, partisanship would be identical among persons from different religious groups but with the same level of formal education. In fact, the general level of partisanship differed considerably among denominations even with educational level held constant. Even taking education into account, there remain distinctive patterns of political affiliation among these religious groups. Something apparently happens in religious groups to foster distinctive political identities among persons who otherwise differ on many politically relevant characteristics.

Of course, this represents only a partial test of the influence of social characteristics. When more rigorous controls have been applied for additional social traits that might distinguish religious groups from one another, differences in political identity have remained significant (Wald 1989; Leege and Kellstedt 1993). Many scholars, studying a variety of political orientations and outlooks, have reported that controls for social conditions may narrow intergroup differences in various political orientations but do not eliminate them altogether (Cohen and Kapsis 1977; Laumann and Segal 1971; Maddox 1979; Miller 1974). That conclusion has stood whether the social status indicator has been education, income, urbanization, ethnicity, or occupational status. There are studies that point to diversity within groups. For example, recent research questions the link between conservative Protestantism and conservative economic positions among less educated Protestants (Felson and Kindell 2007) and the salience of politicized Christianity among highly educated ones (Schwadel 2005). Still, most studies indicate that even when socioeconomic factors are taken into account, political differences between groups remain.

The differences among religious traditions may be all the more significant if religious values are an important determinant of such status distinctions. The concern that political differences based on religion simply reflect societal socioeconomic realities loses credibility if religion itself is the source of the differences. Religion in this case does not just mirror socioeconomic distinctions—it also causes them. If religion is not only related to socioeconomic status but actually confers socioeconomic benefits, then it is linked directly to societal advantages and disadvantages. This form of stratification structures the community and is thus a powerful influence on political perspectives. Moreover, it can be framed to produce the group-based discontent that social movement theorists suggest politicizes identity and facilitates collective action.

The argument that religious values were related to societal position was set forth by German sociologist Max Weber (1920/1958) in his famous—and still controversial—book *The Protestant Ethic and the Spirit of Capitalism*. According to Weber, economic status is partially a function of religion. Since the beginning of capitalism in Europe, Protestants have been more successful than Catholics economically because Protestants embraced religious values that transformed work from drudgery into a calling through which to glorify God. While Catholics were viewing poverty as a sign of grace, Protestants understood material gain to be an indication of salvation and favor with God.

Although the contemporary relevance of Weber's arguments is undermined somewhat by findings that Protestant societies no longer have the strongest "work ethic" (Norris and Inglehart 2004), scholars continue to demonstrate a relationship between the Protestant ethic and what it takes to be successful in society (Harrison 1992; Keysar and Kosmin 1995).[7] Scholars also keep finding religious belief and affiliation as meaningful predictors of core political values. For example, Barker and Carman (2000) show that the individualistic theology of fundamentalists, evangelicals, and charismatics may engender political preferences for individualistic economic policies and opposition to taxation, spending, and governmental activism in economic affairs.

Religious groups may enter politics not only in response to objective socioeconomic changes in their status but also in response to perceived affronts to their way of life. Assessments of subjective status may provide particularly strong motivations for minority religious groups as well as adherents of religions who feel themselves besieged (Fetzer 1998). Subjective status has been used to explain the liberal social and political positions of American Jews. Despite the fact that by objective standards they comprise one of the highest-status groups in the United States, they maintain a firm commitment to liberal political values—a commitment that seems, contrary to all common sense, to increase with economic success (Maller 1977; Fuchs 1956). As measured by social attitudes, Jewish standing in society has not matched the level of Jewish economic and educational attainment. Because of their history as a diaspora people and a strong collective memory of persecution, it has been claimed that Jews tend to think of themselves not as part of the established elite but rather as a group on the margin of society, defensive and vulnerable to attack by the majority. The social insecurity of American Jews has been said to make them especially wary of any political movements that appear to encourage intolerance and bigotry (Cohn 1957; Liebman 1973; Rothman and Lichter 1982; Forman 1997; Dollinger 2000). Hence, Jews make common cause with other subordinate groups in clear defiance of their immediate economic interests.

Theology

According to the models that emphasize theological or creed-based mobilization, religious groups become politically active because they desire congruence between their religious perspectives and public policies. Tim Goeglien, a former assistant to President George W. Bush and a current vice president for the evangelical group Focus on the Family, put it this way: "Self-described evangelicals are overwhelmingly supportive in presidential elections of the Republican party because, by and large, conservative Christians see the Republican Party as the vehicle for the way that they view public policy."[8] However, the desire to have beliefs and policy correspond is not the exclusive domain of conservatives. The liberal practitioners of the social gospel at the turn of the twentieth century sought to establish the kingdom of God through a whole series of social reforms. They took on everything from child labor to urban squalor in an effort to rectify injustice. A liberal coalition of black preachers, Catholics, Jews, and liberal Protestants were at the forefront of the racial revolution that was the 1960s civil rights movement. Today, a powerful coalition of both conservative and liberal religious interest groups is emerging in the arena of international human rights policies including sex trafficking, slavery, and hunger (Hertzke 2004). Historically, conservatives and liberals have justified their political activities on the basis of their faith.

Research reveals that among faith elites such as members of the clergy, a level of consistency exists between theological beliefs and political outlooks (Crawford and Olson 2001; Guth et al. 1997; Beatty and Walter 1989; Balswick 1970). Although the relationship is not perfect, these studies show that clergy are able to unite their religious beliefs with their political perspectives in a coherent way. Because members of the clergy have more coherent worldviews, they can be particularly effective opinion leaders, framing grievances in a way that makes them politically relevant to parishioners. However, as Campbell and his colleagues (1960) demonstrated in their classic work, *The American Voter*, everyday Americans are nonideological. Most hold only very superficial attitudes (Zaller 1992). How does religion help forge a tight link between religious beliefs and political outlooks among ordinary folk?

Increasingly across denominations, religious elites are trying to link theological positions with public policies. Whether it is Catholics opposing the 2010 Affordable Care Act because of its birth control provisions, Quakers conscientiously objecting to the war in Iraq, Assemblies of God condemning homosexual unions as evil and ungodly, or the National Baptists calling on President Obama to pass gun control legislation, religious groups are trying to rally the faithful to political causes. Even these direct efforts do not always produce results among their followers. For example, despite encyclicals, papal bulls, letters from bishops, condemnations by priests, and the teaching of nuns, American Catholics are notoriously independent of theological input in constructing their political beliefs (Steinfels 2003). For the most part, contemporary research confirms a consistent relationship between conservative theology and conservative political attitudes only in the domains of sexual and social roles, and even in these areas tolerance appears to be growing (Turner et al. 2005; Brewer and Wilcox 2005). It may be that the connection between doctrine and politics draws on theological tradition in subtle ways. Certain common ways of thinking about religion may spill over into politics (Laitin 1978; Parenti 1967). A conservative approach to religion may support a conservative approach to politics. For example, the "image of God" studies have for the most part confirmed that the perception of a stern and vengeful deity is linked to political conservatism, while the view that God is nurturing and loving is associated with political liberalism (Greeley 1988, 1993; Welch and Leege 1988; but see MacIver 1990). How might these dimensions of religious belief take on political significance? Because of their emphasis on faith in fixed authority over the free play of intellect, persons of a conservative orientation are more likely than religious liberals to stress the need for obedience than to encourage skepticism or dissent (Rokeach 1969; Carroll 1995). If redemption is interpreted to mean bringing the kingdom of God to realization on earth, as liberal religions seem to argue, movements for political change are infused with a transcendent purpose. But if, as in conservative religion, life is seen as a mere preparation for the next world or the imminent return of God to earth, then little can be done except to live as righteously as possible and to guard the integrity of one's soul from temptation and corruption (Kleppner 1970). An emphasis on sinfulness as the essential condition of humankind seems quite compatible with a skeptical orientation toward the prospect of improving conditions through political action (Rosenberg 1956). Similarly, if human pleasures are judged inferior to spiritual rewards, there is little urgency about improving material conditions. The liberal belief in "social" sin and the dignity of earthly existence, which contrasts sharply with conservative religious assumptions, spurs efforts to eradicate structural barriers to justice and to improve the material conditions of life. Belief in a warm, caring God who is part of the world tends to enhance commitment to social welfare, whereas the image of a cold and authoritative deity lends support to government's role in securing order and property.

These contrasting modes of thought can be illustrated by the way in which Jews and Lutherans apply their differing religious styles to the political realm. A classic example of a liberal faith, Judaism venerates learning and charity as major virtues and is relatively silent about the origin of sin and the prospect of life after death. That combination of values encourages optimism about the human condition and a sense of urgency about the application of reason to human problems. Implicit in this perspective is a view of law that it is changing and made for man. And especially implicit in such a style is the belief that what happens in this life on this earth is very important, what happens here and now matters very much (Fuchs 1956, 191). As described by some experts, the Jewish outlook seems almost to demand social and political involvement on behalf of liberal causes.

The Jewish stress on human capacity to remake the world through political action finds barely an echo in Lutheran doctrine. Martin Luther taught that salvation would come only to the person who submitted thoroughly and wholeheartedly to the will of an omniscient God. In sharply contrasting the evil of mortals to the perfection of God, Lutheran thought treats humans as creatures of passion and sin who should not interfere with the divine plan for the world. Based on an extensive survey of Lutheran laypersons in the Detroit metropolitan area, Lawrence K. Kersten (1970, 31) found that Luther's spiritual descendants accepted his counsel to take the world as it is: "Lutheran social philosophy suggests that true happiness for man and total release from the bondage of sin are not possible until after death. If earthly conditions are undesirable, man should patiently endure them, for they may actually be a test of his faith. Man must trust that God will change the social structure or social conditions when He sees fit." Such religious beliefs may help account for the Lutherans' pronounced economic, social, racial, and political conservatism (Weber 1983).

Still, the relationship between theology and political attitudes is not simple or straightforward because religious perspectives are rarely fully liberal or conservative in their orientation (Froese and Bader 2007). Most religious traditions are elastic enough to support very different political applications. In his study of Mississippi's Freedom Summer, Charles Marsh (1997) found that the same Christian tradition can inspire very different activities. It strengthened black sharecropper Fannie Lou Hamer to overcome oppression and become a civil rights icon. It motivated Sam Bowers to lead the Klan in a Christian crusade to preserve the traditional South. It reassured Rev. Douglas Hudgins, the leader of the largest Baptist church in Jackson, that he was doing the right thing when he refused to use his influence to speak on behalf of embattled civil rights workers. He insisted that God counseled people to accept their fate and await justice in the afterlife. He sat out the momentous events symbolized by the struggle between Hamer and Bowers. In the case of Freedom Summer, a common tradition understood very differently oriented three believers to take radically different paths. Religious culture structures political action (Wood 1999; DeLeon and Naff 2004). Though sharing the same religious tradition, the specific religious culture of each of these individuals yielded dissimilar results.

Those who would insist on drawing too strong a connection between religious orientations and particular forms of political belief should remember the many exceptions to the rule. Left-wing movements for social reform have frequently been inspired by Christian doctrine (Murchland 1982; Littell 1970). William Jennings Bryan, the defender of religious conservatism par excellence, had no difficulty combining a deep commitment to fundamentalist theology with passionate conviction in international arbitration, the rights of urban workers, women's suffrage, public ownership of utilities, and, in general, support for an extensive government effort to secure social and economic justice. The same Bryan who condemned evolution, in large part for its pernicious social implications, saw his commitments to social reform as the logical outgrowth of Christian morality (Levine 1975). Like Bryan, many African American Protestants, white evangelicals, and Roman Catholics find no contradiction between theological conservatism and political liberalism.

The confluence of liberal theology with conservative politics can also be found in American political life. Despite a traditional commitment to liberalism, some Jews have enlisted on behalf of conservative programs and policies. Milton Friedman, the dean of laissez-faire economists, was Jewish; so is William Kristol (himself the son of noted neoconservative Irving Kristol and historian Gertrude Himmelfarb), a conservative editor of the *Weekly Standard* and key strategist for the Republican Party. Much to the dismay of many liberals in the Jewish community (see Shorris 1982), the principal leadership of the American neoconservative movement comprises Jewish intellectuals disillusioned by the liberalism they championed in the 1960s and 1970s. Indeed, the idea that political values derive easily from the content of the religion has been challenged by the discovery that the most religiously observant Jews, who should have the greatest exposure to the implicit liberal messages of Judaism, in fact constitute the most politically conservative element of the community (Cohen 1983; Liebman 1973, 139–44).

A very compelling study by Alan Hertzke (2004) details how conservative Christians are increasingly partnering with social liberals to engage international humanitarian and human rights causes the world over. For some, the end of the Cold War diminished the salience of human rights as an issue. Hertzke asserts that it was the interest of evangelicals in religious freedom that served to reenergize the human rights movement. In international politics, he documents that conservative theology motivates evangelicals to pursue what are interpreted as very liberal positions on human rights policies worldwide, including support for open immigration to the United States. Working with nonevangelical associates from feminist, Catholic, mainline Protestant, African American, Jewish, and secular groups, evangelicals reframed religious freedom as a human rights issue and have worked to pass major pieces of legislation designed to ensure that a country's record on religious freedom is a major factor in the construction of American foreign policy toward that state. Hertzke's study of evangelical interest groups in international politics challenges simplistic assumptions about the relationship between theology and political activity.

The weakness of a simple theological interpretation is further underscored by the manner in which religious views on political behavior change over time. Consider again the case of evangelical Protestantism. In the nineteenth century, evangelical Protestants provided many of the leaders of progressive causes such as the antislavery movement and populism. They also supported Prohibition, a movement that can now be understood as a sincere attempt to improve social conditions (Clark 1976; T. L. Smith 1965; Hammond 1974). At the turn of the twentieth century, many influential leaders of evangelical Protestantism still read the Bible as a blueprint for the social gospel, the effort to bring justice to social relations. By the 1920s, however, the predominant interpretation shifted to emphasize biblical passages that promoted political withdrawal (Moberg 1977)—the perspective that governed Douglas Hudgins's reaction to white racist violence during the civil rights era in Mississippi. In the 1970s, however, many leading evangelicals found a mandate for political activism in what they regarded as the morally corrupt tone of public life. All three perspectives—social gospel, political quietism, and moral restorationism—are said to rest on an unchanging religious ethic. The bottom line is that the assumption that there will be congruence between religious beliefs, attitudes, ideas, and behavior is fallacious and can lead to a misinterpretation of the role of religion in social and political life (Chaves 2010).

Scholars have also examined how religious orientations motivate political beliefs through orthodoxy and whether a cleavage exists in American politics between individuals who are committed to orthodox beliefs—the religiously observant—and those who have abandoned traditional orthodoxy in favor of more modern views—the religious nonobservant (Fiorina, Abrams, and Pope 2005; Kohut et al. 2000). Hunter (1991) named the politics around this cleavage "the culture war." According to Hunter, the two extreme poles of the modern cultural spectrum are marked by very distinct worldviews. The advocates of traditionalism draw on religious orthodoxy for their understanding of the world and consciously reject many "modern" ideas about human standards. Their opposite number, "progressives," often reject the legitimacy of traditional religious doctrine in favor of moral authority drawn from human reason and experience. In a recent study, Weisberg (2005) found that an important determinant of public opinion was whether a person was inclined to make moral judgments about other people's lifestyle choices. These kinds of moral evaluations are related to moral traditionalism and strongly influence public opinion even after controls for socio-demographic, partisan, and ideological variables.

Distinctions between traditionalists and progressives are manifested in political debates over federal arts funding, Obamacare, abortion, the causes and control of crime, feminism, marriage equality, welfare, and a wide range of other issues. Some advocates of culture war theory contend that it has superseded the old types of religiously based conflicts that once divided Catholics from Protestants or mainline from evangelical Protestants (Layman 2001). The most salient political conflicts, they contend, now divide religious traditionalists in all denominations from religious modernists of whatever tradition. Although there is some evidence that cooperative coalitions are harder to put together on the religious right than the religious left (Evans 2006), collaborations among Orthodox Jews, traditionalist Roman Catholics, and mainline and evangelical Protestants in the pro-life movement have been effective. From the culture war perspective, it is not specific doctrinal content but general adherence to faith that makes a difference in political outlook.

With some success, parties have tried to exploit this cleavage. Since the 1990s the Republican Party has attempted to present itself as the party of traditional values against a Democratic Party that has forgotten God, family, and decency. In recent elections the difference between the voting preferences of religious practitioners and those who are less observant has been called the "God gap" (Green, Rozell, and Wilcox 2006; Smidt et. al 2010). As in other recent elections, this gap was again evident in the 2012 campaign. Nearly 60 percent of voters who said that they attend church every week voted for Mitt Romney. Among those who never attend, over 60 percent voted to reelect President Obama.[9] The culture war thesis continues to be popular among political pundits because it parsimoniously explains the deep societal divisions around culture that exist in American society today. Dividing the nation into red and blue states is a simple way of reducing complex political reality to a manageable dimension.[10] However, as we explore in chapter 7, the relationship between orthodoxy and public opinion is not straightforward. The empirical evidence is much more ambiguous than news stories suggest. Indeed, the culture war analogy inaccurately describes the cleavages surrounding most political issues in the United States.

Worldview

One of the reasons we may not see stronger direct connections between religion and political values may rest in the simplistic measures of religion that we employ.

Brian Kaylor (2010) suggests that religion operates differently in elections than it has historically. Americans insist on a confessional form of politics that integrates religious-political rhetoric. Politicians are expected to talk about their faith. If they do not talk about it, then it will be questioned. According to Kaylor, Americans use this "god-talk" to evaluate sincerity. Since 1976, the presidential candidate who has talked the most about religion has won the election—even if he was not the most religious candidate. Proclaiming a worldview that incorporates faith advantages evangelical Christians, because talking about a personal relationship with God is something that they do, and it disadvantages atheists and others who do not proselytize.

Frequency of worship, denominational affiliation, simple statements of beliefs, and the other basic measures of religion that we utilize may not in the end be sufficient indicators of the deeper content of religious values. They may not capture the "faith" element. In a study of the relationship between religion and civic responsibility, Smidt and his colleagues (2008) emphasize that in measuring religion, it is important to capture how an individual views and expresses his or her religiosity on both public and private dimensions. Several scholars have attempted to uncover the impact of beliefs on political perspective by exploring the "mental maps" of religion that may be held by individuals. These maps reference the different ways that people understand religious truth.

In a strikingly original study of members of Congress, Benson and Williams (1982) found that the voting records of members of Congress varied based on four different aspects of personal religious philosophy. The "agentic-communal" dimension indicated whether religion focused more on personal or social problems. The second dimension concerned religious messages—were they restrictive, setting limits and regulating conduct, or did they offer release through forgiveness? In the third dimension, religion might be perceived as vertical, with the lines of communication flowing down from God, or horizontal, from person to person. In the final dimension, the primary task of religion was either to offer comfort to individuals or, alternatively, to challenge them to rebuild society. The authors discovered that advocates of communal, horizontal, challenging, and release-oriented religions were much more likely to support liberal political causes than their religious opposites. These findings are important given the prevailing tendency to dismiss religious influences on the behavior of elected officials.

This pattern has also been observed among everyday citizens. People with a more communal approach to religion tend to have more liberal political outlooks than those with a more individualist orientation (Leege and Welch 1989). Even more powerfully, those who felt close to God when working for justice and peace were disposed to political liberalism in general and to liberal preferences on issues such as abortion, defense spending, and school busing (Welch and Leege 1988). In another interesting study, those who had more inclusive religious worldviews that reflected knowledge of foreign religious ideas were more liberal than those who had more exclusive religious perspectives (Smith 2007).

Studies of activists also find political relevance to variations in religious worldviews. For example, Green and his colleagues (1994) find that activists on the left side of the political spectrum tend to be communitarians and are defined by belief in the social justice mission of the church, the need to change institutions, the societal origins of poverty, and the inadequacy of personal conversion as a means of solving social problems. Those who instead thought in more individualist terms—seeing the church as concerned principally with individual morality and confident in the power of conversion to solve social problems—were attracted to conservative organizations. Studies like these suggest that more sophisticated measures of religion have a great potential to uncover the full impact of religious belief on political outlooks.

Institutional Interests

Institutional interests provide the final source of motivation for the political engagement of religious faith. Denominations, faith-oriented communions and associations, individual churches and synagogues, interest groups, religious schools, religious broadcasters, religious social service providers, and charitable organizations all have a stake in particular public policies and may attempt to mobilize constituents in support of their causes. While ostensibly acting on behalf of the public good, all are simultaneously institutions with more narrow economic and ideological interests as well.

For example, Catholic hospitals and universities have lobbied aggressively against a decision by the Obama administration to require religiously affiliated employers to offer their employees free access to contraception in the health care plans they provide. Assailing the decision as an assault on religious liberty because contraception is inconsistent with the teachings of the Catholic Church, these organizations have sought a yet un-awarded exemption from this requirement. Institutionally, what is at risk for them is both the church's theological principles and the insurance costs associated with these products and access to multiple millions of dollars in federal funds for health care if they fail to comply with the regulation.

Institutional interests not only are meaningful for the institutions that generate them but also can serve as bases for political support among ordinary people. Religious organizations are often part of broad networks of members and sympathizers that can be marshaled to champion their cause. When this occurs, differences in institutional interests are reflected both among institutions and in the attitudes and loyalties of mass publics. In the United States, we see different institutional interests related to support for public and private schools. In addition to the universal public education system, American churches have supported extensive systems of elementary, secondary, and postsecondary education. These schools provide instruction in basic skills as well as training in religious traditions and practices. According to recent statistics, more than four million school-age children attend church-related elementary and secondary institutions (National Center for Educational Statistics 2002). The Catholic parochial schools provide the best-known example of religious education, accounting for more than half the students in private education, but many denominations have built their own facilities in locations where their members are concentrated. Approximately seven hundred thousand students now attend Christian schools with a conservative or fundamentalist perspective.

The enormous cost of maintaining these institutions and paying for tuition gives churches and families a strong interest in securing government assistance. Under these circumstances, it is hardly surprising that studies of voting on urban bond issues dedicated to financing public education have revealed a high level of opposition from Catholics—who have a financial interest in minimizing the cost of a school system many do not utilize (Cattaro and Cooper 2008; Cataldo and Holm 1983). Other polls have shown very strong support for various forms of state aid among denominations that maintain schools and much more resistance in churches in which the bulk of children attend public institutions (Menendez 1977, chap. 11; Rothenberg and Newport 1984, 58–61). Terry Moe (2001) demonstrated that the strongest supporters of school vouchers are religiously motivated.

Interests do not have to be restricted to the financial sphere or to a single issue. Groups may perceive that their interests will be better regarded—that they will "get a better deal"—with one political party than the other. In part, the emergence of the New Deal Coalition in the 1930s was recognition by Jews and Catholics that the Democrats would better meet their economic needs and protect the rights of immigrants and religious minorities. The close political relationship between evangelicals and Republicans today reflects a similar understanding. Institutional interests and political dynamics can combine to create powerful and persistent incentives for political engagement among religious groups. Through the process of political socialization, group members may even come to regard affiliation with a political party as one element of their religious identity (Irvine 1974). Support for the party can become, in essence, a natural reflex for members of the religious group. Political commitments based initially on common interests may broaden into durable loyalties that outlive their original causes (Leege, Lieske, and Wald 1991).

ESTABLISHING MEANS

The Role of Elites

A religious group's social situation, creedal forces, and institutional interests are potential sources for aggravation and complaint. All can result in discontent on the part of a religious group. However, motive alone does not solve the "mystery" of the participation of religious groups in politics. The mystery is not solved because motive is insufficient without means and opportunity. Discontent does not automatically lead to political participation. Although grievance is an important precondition for political activity, it does not necessitate it. As Snow and his colleagues (1986) explain:

> The most striking shortcoming is the tendency to gloss questions concerning the interpretation of events and experiences relevant to participation in social movement activities and campaigns. This tendency is particularly evident in the treatment of grievances. Too much attention is focused on grievance per se . . . to the neglect of the fact that grievances or discontents are subject to differential interpretation, and the fact that variations in their interpretation across individuals, social movement organizations and time can affect whether and how they are acted upon. (465)

In other words, the discontent must be framed and organized in a manner that supports political activity. It makes sense to think of grievances as latencies, tools that are available for exploitation by strong or aspiring leadership (Wald, Silverman, and Fridy 2005).

Religious appeals can be very effective for political mobilization, and increasingly political elites are using religious themes to mobilize the faithful to act. Simple bits of information such as a candidate's religion can be an important political cue (McDermott 2009). For example, using survey experiments, Campbell, Green, and Layman (2011) found strong evidence that identifying a candidate as evangelical (a group viewed as Republican) increased Republican support for, and Democratic opposition to, the candidate, while identifying the candidate as a Catholic (a group lacking a partisan profile) had no bearing on partisan voting. In addition to recognizably religious communications, candidates and politicians may attempt to "narrowcast" their messages, using coded language and symbols that resonate with the faithful while not alienating less religious voters (Weber and Thornton 2012; Calfano and Djupe 2009; Domke and Coe 2008). What is particularly interesting is that there is evidence these kind of religious messages may influence citizens at both explicit and implicit levels. Because religious attachments are formed early in the lives of many Americans, religious language may influence citizens without their awareness. In an interesting experimental design, Albertson (2011) found that Christian religious appeals impacted the political behavior of people who currently or even previously identified as Christian. Significantly, this affect held even for people who said they wanted less religion in politics, a group who would not be very open to obvious religious influences and messages. Appeals that tap into implicit, symbolic-type interests may be more effective than appeals to material interests to selectively engage targeted groups (Claibourn and Martin 2012).

For religious people, those most adept at identifying the significance of symbolic interests or communicating the political dimensions of religious issues are members of the clergy and leaders of organized interest groups. These elites can serve as political entrepreneurs for religiously based grievances in two ways: they frame the issues, and they bear the costs of facilitating action related to discontent.

Political science models of participation have recognized the importance of these external influences to political participation. Rosenstone and Hanson (1993) and Verba, Schlozman, and Brady (1995) suggest that even if an individual has all the requisite personal traits and attitudes for participation, he or she may not act without additional encouragement. This encouragement may come in the form of ideological or organizational stimuli. Often religious leaders offer both. They provide ideological encouragement through the way they frame issues, and they provide organizational encouragement through the use of their institutions to facilitate action. In this section, we examine how this works by looking at the means that are available to opinion leaders to politicize grievances. What resources do they have at their disposal? We look first at the clergy and then at religious and community-based interest groups.

Clergy as Political Leaders

Studies suggest that it is relatively common for clergy to send political messages (Djupe and Gilbert 1999, 2003, 2008a, 2008b; Smidt 2004; Guth et al. 1997, 2002; Crawford and Olson 2001; Beatty and Walter 1989; Jelen 1993b). The research also indicates that these messages are well received by parishioners (Olson and Crawford 2001; Wald, Owen, and Hill 1988, 1990), especially when they address issues that their congregations already care about (Djupe and Gilbert 2001). Moreover, people may hold their pastor's ideas in particular esteem and give his or her issue positions more credibility than positions they hear through some other medium (Buddenbaum 2001; Welch et al. 1993). Ministers' views not only inform their own activity but also can shape the perspectives of their congregations.

As Smidt (2004) observes, although there is variation in the levels of political engagement among the clergy based on theological (Guth et al. 1997), contextual (Crawford and Olson 2001), and personal factors (Brown and Smidt 2003; Sawyer 2001), clergy are particularly well situated to politicize grievances in a way that facilitates social change. They are by definition opinion leaders. They think ideologically, can communicate their positions through religious culture, have access to institutional resources, and have an audience who voluntarily comes to hear what they have to say.

Their institutions—churches, temples, mosques, and synagogues—are powerful contexts for religious mobilization not only because of the ministers but also because they are rich in resources. Social movement theorists have traditionally emphasized the role of environmental resources in facilitating movement. From this perspective, the central concern of the mobilization model is the link between collective interests and the resources needed for action (Jenkins 1983). Churches are fantastic contexts for mobilization because they combine culture, leadership, money, facilities, infrastructure, an audience, and a communication network. By comparison, secular elites are resource disadvantaged, lacking regular access to such valuable assets.

Although resource mobilization theory has traditionally focused on tangible resources, it is also important to understand that churches are powerful purveyors of religious culture. Ideas and how they are communicated are crucial to united social actions. During the civil rights movement, black religious culture provided such a strong collective action frame because the black church had been a "free space" in the black community for centuries. *Free spaces* are places where politicized grievances can be fostered and developed (Morris 1992). "As a free space, the church offered an environment in which people were able to learn a new self-respect, a deeper and more assertive group identity, public skills, and the value of cooperation and civic virtue" (Evans and Boyte 1986, 17).

All this does not suggest that religious leadership always translates into effective mobilization—even when the minister is attempting to act as a political entrepreneur. Churches are not equally successful in prompting members to perceive connection between religious and political ideas. Richard L. Wood (1999, 2002) has reported on two homogeneous congregations in Oakland, California. Despite similar grievances, the St. Elizabeth congregation mobilized for action, and the Gospel Church did not. Congregational culture is an important determinant of results. The charismatic yet authoritarian leadership style of the Gospel Church pastor was not effective in promoting political participation because, conditioned by that leadership style, its congregation had a hard time challenging authority—even political authority. Moreover, the clarity of the pastor's simple right-versus-wrong, good-versus-evil messages was lost in the ambiguity of the political realm, in which things are rarely so straightforward. At Gospel Church, they were frustrated by an attempt to pursue righteousness through politics. The St. Elizabeth congregation was mobilized because they viewed involvement in the community as a civic and religious virtue.

Although it is important to remember that religious mobilization in churches is not a foregone conclusion, we know that at the congregational level churches have the potential to be powerful political contexts. Because a church is the institutional expression of a system of beliefs about how people are rightly related to God and one another, it by definition will shape people's behavior. This natural capacity is enhanced when participating in the church immerses an individual in a culture in which norms, identity, and boundaries are communicated and maintained. This is especially true of what Iannaccone (1994, 1187) characterizes as "strict" churches that impose significant costs on their members. These churches "penalize or prohibit alternative activities that compete for members' resources." The high price of entry is paid both in moral correctness—no drinking, no smoking, no extramarital sex—and in intense participation with the church. This price weeds out "free-riders" who do not have what it takes to be part of the fellowship. In strict churches, religious, social, and political networks are all focused on the church and thus can be mutually reinforcing. Interestingly, this may not always be politically beneficial. A noteworthy study by David E. Campbell (2004) finds the tight social networks formed through intensive church activity may actually inhibit political engagement with the broader community. He observes that intimate church networks can facilitate rapid episodic mobilization, but intense church participation ordinarily detracts from civic and political participation.

Commitment to and involvement with a religious institution appear to strengthen conformity to the political norm of the religious group and accentuate attitude and behavior differences between persons from other groups (Driskell et al. 2008a, 2008b; Beyerlein and Hipp 2006; Guth and Green 1993; Wald, Leege, and Kellstedt 1993). Hence the discovery, to cite only one of many available from the literature, that religious group differences in party identification and presidential voting are greatest among persons with the strongest involvement in their respective religious families (Anderson 1973; Knoke 1974; Wald 1989; Mockabee, Monson, and Grant 1999). The more a church dominates and circumscribes the life of its members, the greater the political cohesion among congregants (Wald et al. 1990).

Scholars continue to study precisely how churches promote political learning. Wald and his colleagues discovered that the acceptance of conservative or liberal politics depended less on an individual's religious outlook than on the religious values held by a majority of fellow congregants (Wald et al. 1988). Using a similar congregational design, Ted Jelen (1992) found that the impact of the religious environment was strongest precisely when the linkage between religious values and political objects was most difficult for congregants to infer on their own. The relative power of congregational influence as opposed to residential forces or other personal traits has been the focus of important research by Huckfeldt, Plutzer, and Sprague (1993) and Gilbert (1993). Using a unique set of interviews that assessed the views of individuals, their fellow parishioners, and neighbors, these studies found that the opinions of fellow congregants enhanced the underlying attitudes of the denomination. Indeed, it is important to recognize that the experience of religion does not exist solely on the institutional or individual dimension, but also in the collective, public, cultural dynamic (Besecke 2005). There are a myriad of ways beyond the Sunday sermon that ideas and perspectives about the cultural relevance of the religious tradition can be conveyed. Noninstitutionalized religious communication may be a particularly important part of the political socialization that takes place in churches. Interesting studies have focused on the role the informal communication that takes place in small groups can play in this process (Bloom and Levitan 2011; Neiheisel, Djupe, and Sokhey 2009; Djupe and Gilbert 2006; McKenzie 2004; Harris-Lacewell 2004). Research by Djupe and Gilbert (2009) suggests that it is very important to remember the entire congregational context when thinking about the political influence of clergy and churches. In a study of two mainline denominations, the Episcopal Church and the Evangelical Church in America, they found direct clergy influence on politics to be relatively limited while social networks effects such as participating at church in a small group environment could affect political perceptions. They caution that churches are "complex organizations, encompassing multiple points of contact with their members that may bear on individual decisions to participate in politics" (184). The political implications of variations in the types of communication people hear at church as well as the sociodemographic characteristics of clergy and congregants may be particularly consequential because of the uniqueness of every congregation (Neiheisel and Djupe 2008; Djupe and Olson 2006).

Religious Activists

Another major set of opinion leaders in the religious community are activists in religiously based organizations and interest groups. While clergy may episodically focus on politics, their essential responsibility is to meet and care for the spiritual needs of their congregations. However, the primary orientation of religiously based activists is centered on public policy.

Like other interest groups, religious advocacy organizations have proliferated in the past forty years, and their theological, ideological, organizational, structural, and agenda-based diversity is notable (Weber 1982). The Pew Research Center for Religion and Public Life reports that the number of organizations that engage in religious lobbying has increased roughly fivefold in the past four decades, from fewer than forty in 1970 to more than two hundred today. These groups spend at least $350 million a year on efforts to influence national public policy.[11] Any basic American government textbook will teach that these types of groups are organized to influence both their members and the government. Their ability to mobilize can be formidable. For example, a coalition of progressive religious groups, including Sojouners, Catholics in Alliance for the Common Good, and People Improving Communities through Organizing (PICO), sponsored "40 Days of Health Reform" in 2009 as a way to increase awareness about what was at risk in the debate. The campaign included national television ads, prayer vigils, and weekend sermons among the thirty denominations that participated in the group. The coalition reported that on a single "conference call" with President Obama they had more than 140,000 participants and this was a way for the religious left to counter the intense opposition to the bill that members of Congress were facing in local town hall meetings on the issue during the August recess of 2009. Many attributed this level of opposition to the mobilization that the religious right had launched through volunteer phone banks and e-mail messages earlier in that year. In his 1994 study, Robert Zwier divided religious organizations into two broad categories: church-based groups that usually represent denominations and individual membership groups that are not directly affiliated with any particular church. The church-based groups primarily represent the institutional interests of their parent denomination. As we have discussed earlier, denominations own property, have employees, operate schools, run publishing houses, produce radio and television broadcasts, and have many other initiatives that cause them to interact with and care about public policies. Individual membership organizations were founded primarily to address public policy concerns. Examples of individual membership groups include the American Jewish Committee, Interfaith Alliance, and Bread for the World. In some respects, church-based interest groups have an advantage over the individual membership groups because church-based groups can use their member clergy and member churches for mobilization purposes. For example, the Baptist Joint Committee potentially has millions of constituents who can be activated through thousands of churches for a particular political cause. While individual membership organizations can perhaps make appeals through sympathetic churches, they do not have the automatic access to the base that denominational organizations possess. Moreover, the survival and success of membership groups is more directly tied to the victories they achieve in the policy realm. Without public victories, their membership may withdraw its support and leave the interest group without the resources to fight another day.

Lacking institutional resources, membership groups have had to develop additional means to reach their audience and provide cues about the political relevance of religious issues. Both church-based and membership-based interest groups have become masters in the utilization of communication technology. Although the empirical evidence is ambiguous (Kerr 2003; but see Silk 1995; Schmalzbauer 2003), religious organizations often allege that they are portrayed negatively in the press. Still, they are adept at mounting public relations campaigns using the media to articulate their political views. The Church of Scientology has advertised regularly in the pages of the *Washington Post*, seeking public support as it contests several indictments by the federal government. Subscribers to national newspapers and magazines should be familiar with other religiously sponsored advertisements, addressing issues such as abortion, school prayer, and foreign policy. Borrowing a page from family planning groups, the Roman Catholic bishops have spent millions of dollars in public relations offensives against abortion.[12] The Catholic Church uses public opinion studies and marketing research to develop public education campaigns. For groups without the resources to mount such expensive public relations exercises, free publicity can be obtained by having interesting website and blogs, writing letters to the editor, press releases, and making guest appearances on local talk shows or news broadcasts. In this way, religious groups can frame their issues in an attempt to create a favorable climate for their causes.

In addition to the use of the secular media, religious activists have long used religiously oriented media to communicate their perspective and to differentiate themselves from other subcultures in society. Studying the impact of the religious press, Quentin Schultze (2003, 95) notes, "The rise of powerful, general interest mass media in America seems to elicit the development of more specialized, countervailing media aimed at particular speech communities, including religious groups." For example, in the early 1800s, the advent of the penny press corresponded to an increase in the number of religious periodicals. By 1850, there were 181, at least half of which were newspapers; many viewed themselves as competing with secular outlets. Assessing the value of these periodicals to faith traditions (which Schultze refers to as tribes), he continues:

Religious journals of comment and opinion provide both priestly and prophetic ways of imaging the religious tribe. As priestly media they help the
tribe recognize what it believes as well as confirm those beliefs in the midst
of a wider culture that might dismiss such beliefs or even attack them. The
journal as priest says to the speech community: This is who we are and what
we believe. . . . As prophetic media, however, these journals apply their own
faith traditions to an ongoing critique of the life of the church and the wider
society; they provide a forum for the faithful members of the tribe to discuss
the implications of the tribe's faith commitments for its understanding of human culture . . . but also politics, economics and the sciences. (99)

Said simply, religious media outlets, and perhaps even more religious
websites, listserves, twitter accounts, and blogs, offer group identity and
frame issues in a way that is meaningful to the faith community. In so
doing, they reach an audience far beyond the parish doors and forge
linkages across geographic space and strict theological tradition. Today
some of the more notable religious periodicals include *Commonweal* and
America (Catholic), *Christian Century* (mainline Protestant), and *Christianity Today* (evangelical Protestant). Each has a website that allows the organization to reach many more than just its subscription holders.

Religious broadcast was hugely important in the politicization of conservative Christians during the 1980s (Hadden 1987a; Frankl 1987). Jerry
Falwell founded his now-defunct Moral Majority in part on the basis of
the appeal of his television program *The Old Time Gospel Hour*. Though
now an independent organization, the Family Research Council and
its agenda were initially supported by James Dobson and his popular
evangelical radio program *Focus on the Family*. Pat Robertson utilized his
Christian Broadcasting Network and its flagship program *The 700 Club* as
resources in his 1988 bid for the Republican presidential nomination and
later to back his grassroots political organization, the Christian Coalition.

Jelen and Wilcox's (1993) analysis of election-year data show that televangelism has had a modest impact on the politicization of evangelicals.
Religious television had its strongest effects on issues of personal and social morality. Additionally, they found that the combination of church attendance and watching religious television increased feelings of personal
political efficacy and voter turnout.

Contemporary religious organizations have incorporated all forms of
traditional and information age communication technology to increase
their reach and their effectiveness. They use direct mail, telegrams, tele-
phones, fax machines, e-mail, websites, blogs, twitter, texts and other
forms of instant communication to get their message out. One commentator has coined the term *technopopulism* to reference the ability of interest groups to reach people directly using technology (Reed 1994, 159).
Reaching people directly can be very effective at contributing to political

participation. A study by Wilcox and Sigelman (2001) that probed the impact of voter contacts by religious groups found that in some elections, voters were contacted almost as often by religious groups as they were by political parties. Moreover, they found that political contacts by religious organizations have the potential to be even more effective than contacts by political parties because religious messages can be more narrowly targeted.

Community Activists

There is one additional group of elites that utilize religious culture as a means to organize and encourage people to address their political and social grievances. Increasingly, community activists at the local level are harnessing the potential of religious faith to organize people to address the material realities of their lives. Community activists—who may not themselves be religious—recognize how helpful faith-based organizing can be. Working through congregations, these organizers use religious practices, worldview, and culture to empower people to address the concerns of their communities. Though linked to religious congregations, these institutions are usually tax-exempt entities that operate and are incorporated independently of any specific congregation or denomination. Their work focuses primarily on lower-income, often minority, Americans, revealing an interesting liberal intersection for religion, politics, and social issues.

The research in this area is unique because most religion and politics studies examine national-level mobilization, leaving local-level stories untold. Most social science work has focused on broad social movements. However, there is no reason to believe that the power of religious belief, identity, culture, community, and leadership may not operate more effectively at the neighborhood level, where both religion and grievance may be more proximate and real to individuals. It is one thing for the radio preacher you like to tell you to e-mail your congressperson about a piece of legislation designed to bring religious freedom to the people of Sudan. It is quite another to have the preacher who baptized you as a child encourage you to boycott the convenience store at the corner because its owner refuses to hire people like you from the community.

Indeed, this model of organizing appears to be growing (Swarts 2008; Wood 2002; Warren 2001; Hart 2001). A recent study showed that this kind of religious mobilization has grown 42 percent (fifty-six new federations) since 1999 (Wood et al. 2012). The four major faith-based organizing networks—PICO National Network (PICO), Gamaliel, Industrial Areas Foundation (IAF), and Direct Action, Research, and Training (DART)—link more than thirty-five hundred congregations and incorporate more than two million people. A recent study demonstrated that the faith-based organizing is "second only to the labor movement among drives for social justice among low-income Americans" (Wood 2002). These organizations are explicitly political, although nonpartisan, will partner with secular, civic, and union organizations, and are often willing to use types of aggressive tactics learned from 1940s Chicago organizer Saul Alinsky in pursuit of their goals.

Generally, faith-based organizing begins with a local organizing committee that is affiliated with a specific congregation. Through their work with the congregation, the committee helps identify issues about which the community is concerned. The congregation then sponsors a political action to address this concern. The organizing committee facilitates and supports the action by helping with strategy, training leaders, building networks with other congregations and community groups, and linking their efforts to broader citywide organizing projects. Eventually a local federation includes ten to sixty institutions, usually congregations from different faiths. Institutions, not individuals, are the members of the federation. In this way, the resources of organized religion—cultural, institutional, and human—are marshaled to produce policy change. These faith-based organizations have dual structures, with the congregations handling the religious and moral aspects of an issue and the federation handling the politics.

Richard L. Wood's *Faith in Action* (2002) and Stephen Hart's (2001) *Cultural Dilemmas of Progressive Politics* examine how faith-based organizing works at the community level. Comparing a PICO organization to two other nonreligious multiracial coalitions, Wood finds that there is something to the faith factor. PICO projects were more successful than the projects of the other organizations because religion created a ready sense of community, provided an effective ideological context for political action, and sustained hope even in the face of defeat. Moreover, because they organized through congregations, they were able to draw on all the advantages that clergy and institutional church resources offer to mobilization discussed earlier. Having a "shared membership in a moral community" (140) not only increases social capital but also serves as an effective institutional culture on which to build a movement. Examples of PICO's successful organizing are detailed in chapter 6.

Hart (2001) observes that political progressives have not done a good job linking their politics to culture and argues that conservative groups have been more effective mobilizers because they better integrate values, morality, and politics. Thus, conservative politics resonates in civil society in a way progressive political causes do not. Studying a congregation-based community organization in Milwaukee, Hart concludes that it is possible through culturally expansive discourse for people to make progressive politics religiously, morally, and ethically salient. In his estimation, too often progressive organizations unnecessarily operate like the local chapter of Amnesty International examined in the study, constraining the political discourse by divorcing it from a more expansive moral and political vision.

Together these studies highlight religious culture as a powerful vehicle for politicizing grievances—even grievances that may not have originated as moral or religious concerns. More recent research by Heidi Swarts on "congregation-based community organizations" explains that when the cultural elements of collective action are embedded in religious ideology, a "culture of commitment" is developed in adherents. Swarts observes that compared to secular organizing models, the faith-based approach "combines the expressive and the instrumental, the moral and the virtuous, with the strategic pursuit of power" (2008, 45). The faith-based organizing model assumes grievance. Poverty is a given, and the poor will have problems related to it. Elites then use religious culture to frame and contextualize those grievances and employ religious resources to organize and strengthen individual resolve to do something about them.

The success of organizations such as PICO at the local level are increasingly giving them a platform to operate nationally and attempt to influence legislation at the federal level. For example, PICO was very involved in the effort to pass the recent Affordable Health Care Act. Working at all levels of its network, the group utilized social media, call-in campaigns, and traditional on-the-ground organizing to push for the policy. PICOs ability to vertically integrate their campaign and mobilize large numbers of people gives them the potential to influence both local legislation and federal policy. It is important to remember that grassroots resources are not solely local in orientation or influence.

The Question of Representation

Clergy, religious activists, and community activists play a major role in framing political discourse and supporting political engagement. Their political intervention has often been condemned (Atkins and McConnell 1986). Although some of these complaints probably represent dissatisfaction with the positions taken rather than with the act of advocacy itself, many critics have argued that churches and religious groups are prone to misrepresent the views of their members (Reichley 1985; Hallum 1989). In formulating church statements on public policy, it is charged, religious elites take advantage of their power to foist their own views on denominations, speaking in the name of the church when its members are divided on or even opposed to the church's official stance. For example, a recent study of the political agendas of fifteen prominent religious offices in Washington finds that the laity play almost no role in the agenda-setting process, although offices do consider their theological tradition and the institutional politics of their sponsoring religious bodies in adopting policy positions (Kraus 2007). This charge, long made against the liberal Washington representatives of the mainline Protestant churches, was also lodged against the Roman Catholic bishops in the 1980s for their public opposition to support for the Nicaraguan Contras, abortion, nuclear weapons, and "supply-side" economic policy. Despite its constituency's deep support for human rights, some Jewish organizations have appeared to lend uncritical support to Israeli actions against Palestinians on the West Bank. Likewise, the conservatives who claim to speak for the white evangelical Protestants have also been charged with misrepresenting the more moderate views of their members on several issues.

The charge of misrepresentation is doubly serious. First, it impugns the religious organizations by suggesting they are out of touch with their members. "Correct" public policy positions may be chosen at the expense of alienating congregants and weakening the church. Second, such charges undermine the effectiveness of church representatives. An advocate who confronts a public official without membership support will have little credibility. In response, religious elites often claim they play a prophetic role. In this view, churches are not democracies that determine policy on the basis of majority votes but proclaimers of the truth that must follow the dictates of conscience and educate their members. If the price of prophecy is dissension in the ranks, they reply, so be it. This response does not deny that official positions may differ from the preferences of the laity; it justifies such deviation in terms of moral imperatives.

American religious elites certainly appear to differ from the citizenry. Leaders of Catholicism and mainline Protestantism are much more likely than their parishioners to identify with liberalism, support Democratic candidates for president, and hold liberal views across a range of political and social issues (Lerner, Rothman, and Lichter 1989). But do the church advocacy groups accurately represent their congregants' policy views when they lobby the government? Allen Hertzke's (1989, 134; see also 1988, chap. 5) answer, based on comparing lobbying positions with poll data, is mostly yes. Mainline Protestant lobbies diverged from member preferences on social issues, but they agreed with their members on other controversial issues—from environmental protection to food stamps. Almost a mirror image of mainline lobbying, evangelical lobbyists reflect member concerns about social policy while taking a more conservative line on several domestic and foreign policy issues. Both Catholic and Jewish lobbyists were close to member opinion on most issues.

Interesting research by Brian Calfano reveals that clergy, unlike activists, are reluctant to advocate for issues that they fear may not be popular with their parishioners. Clergy generally defer to their reference groups and avoid activism that they suspect will elicit a negative or nonsupportive reaction (2009, 2010). Studying mainline denominations, however,

Djupe and Gilbert (2008b) found that if clergy members are perceived to be satisfying and caring for the spiritual needs of their congregants, congregational opposition to clergy political activity is likely to be muted. These studies suggest that religious elites blend a concern for rank-and-file opinion with a prophetic orientation. If not perfectly representative of mass opinion, neither are they consistently out of step.

The net effect of this activity may contribute an important balance to the political system. As decades of research have demonstrated convincingly, the voice transmitted by the public to elected officials does not accurately represent the views of a diverse citizenry. In particular, the concerns of working-class and poorer Americans simply are not expressed with the same weight as the interests of more affluent citizens. Whether the venue is voting, lobbying, campaigning, or other forms of political participation, the skew is constant. Under these circumstances, the involvement of religious groups may be one of the few effective ways that the needs of the poor are represented. Consider the work of the Joint Religious Legislative Coalition, an organization of Catholics, Protestants, Jews, and Muslims that has lobbied the Minnesota legislature for thirty years.[13] The JRLC speaks for the needs of welfare recipients, immigrants, victims of hate crimes and racial violence, gambling addicts, and those without health care and decent housing. In a political system that favors majorities, the religious sector often gives voice to minorities that are otherwise underrepresented.

CONCLUSION

This chapter has examined the motives and means for religious mobilization. Whether religious groups enter the political arena because of their group identity, concern over their group's status, theology, orthodoxy, worldview, or institutional interests—whatever the initial source of motivating grievance, religious culture is important to politicizing the discontent. The language, symbols, rituals, relationships, values, and discourse of faith help make the grievance both corporately relevant and actionable. The means to politicize motives are provided by religious elites and the institutions they represent.

Elites contribute to the participation process by first framing the issue and then bearing the cost of mobilization by facilitating action related to discontent. They facilitate action through the institutional resources of their churches and organizations, even directing people toward specific ways to respond politically to the issues that concern them.

Based on the topics discussed in this chapter, it is clear that religious people do have interests in the public square and much latent capacity to act on them. They have "motive" and "means," but the mystery is solved only with opportunity. We turn to political opportunity in the next chapter.

6

Religion and Political Action

I prayed for twenty years but received no answer until I prayed with
my legs.

—Frederick Douglass

In 2012 the former leader of the Christian Coalition, Ralph Reed, returned from the political wilderness. Once hailed as the "right hand
of God" because of his effectiveness at mobilizing religious voters for
Republican causes, Reed fell from grace, diminished by his relationship
with convicted lobbyist Jack Abramoff and embarrassed by an election
night trouncing in a bid to become lieutenant governor of Georgia in
2006. But in 2012 he was back as founder of the Faith and Freedom Coalition, leading another get-out-the-evangelical-vote operation in an effort
to secure the victory of Republican presidential candidate Mitt Romney.
Reed's efforts were valiant, contacting seventeen million voters in fifteen
states—a notable undertaking, considering that many evangelicals do not
consider Mormons to be Christians at all. In the end, evangelicals turned
out in record numbers and voted as heavily for Mitt Romney as they did
for a victorious George Bush in 2004 and more heavily than they did in
the losing effort of John McCain in 2008.

But Romney lost and with his defeat the legislative hopes of social conservatives were dashed. They failed to regain Republican control of the
Senate, witnessed the election of more abortion rights legislators, were
defeated in fights against same-sex marriage in all four states where the
issue was on the ballot, and watched two states vote to legalize marijuana
for recreational use. Albert Mohler, president of the Southern Baptist

Theological Center, called the election "an evangelical disaster."[1] Facing stark realities, another evangelical leader confessed that "we [Christians] must face the reality that we may be on the losing side of the culture war."[2] This is probably an overstatement. It would be premature to declare the defeat of religious conservatism. However, there was a sense of loss after the election for many evangelicals because without a win they could expect no policy change. At the launch of Faith and Freedom's 2012 campaign, Reed had said the mission was to "take back our country and end the Obama agenda forever."[3] Without winning, this mission had failed. Reed and other evangelical leaders recognize that elections matter because of the policy implications related to being on the winning side or on the losing side.

Changes in the electoral environment reflect shifts in political opportunity structure, a variable that strongly conditions the success or failure of religiously based political action. *Political opportunity structure* can be defined as the "consistent—but not necessarily formal or permanent—dimensions of the political environment that provide incentives for people to undertake collective action by affecting their expectations for success or failure" (Tarrow 1998, 85). As we learned in chapter 5, religion can be a powerful source of motivation in politics. Beliefs, social status, group identity, and institutional interests all can provide reasons to enter the political arena. Moreover, the resources that religious groups have significantly affect their ability to mobilize and their effectiveness in doing so. Still, social movement theory holds that the structure of political opportunities, not grievances or resources, is the main determinant of when, where, and how religious mobilizing efforts develop (Tarrow 2011; McAdam 1984; McAdam, McCarthy, and Zald 1996). Political opportunity structures change over time as governments, political parties, public opinion, and other socioeconomic and political conditions respond to movement activity (Tarrow 2012; Tilly and Tarrow 2007). Political opportunity structures influence not only a religious group's ability to aggregate and articulate interests—to mobilize for a cause—but also the way it formulates strategies to attain public policy goals. While groups are free to define their own interests and choose how to advance them, implementation requires success in a political process involving elections, legislation, and regulations. Expressed formally, exogenous factors enhance or inhibit prospects for mobilization. Stated plainly, context matters. However intense the grievances or bountiful the resources of the Faith and Freedom Coalition's political supporters, after the election of 2012 they face a diminished political opportunity structure for their ambitions.

Although scholars disagree about which aspects of the political environment are central to political opportunity (Meyer 2004), they focus on factors that affect "the costs, possibilities and likely payoffs" of collective action (134). Drawing on general political opportunity research and studies of public policies in which religion is particularly salient (Meier 1994; Tarrow 1998), five important considerations help structure opportunities for religious interests: (1) the religious cultural environment, (2) institutional context, (3) partisan political alignments, (4) the existence of influential allies within or outside the political system, and (5) the domain of the public policy proposal.

RELIGIOUS CULTURAL ENVIRONMENT

Several studies have found that issues involving "morality politics" have a distinct set of explanatory variables (Mooney and Lee 1995; Sharp 2005; Meier and McFarlane 1993; Norrander and Wilcox 1999; Mooney 2008). *Morality policies* involve cases in which "one segment of society attempts by governmental fiat to impose their values on the rest of society" (Meier 1994, 4). Public policies such as abortion, pornography, drug and alcohol regulation, lotteries, gay rights, and the like are morality issues. Unlike most public policies, which are driven principally by socioeconomic factors, morality policies reflect a state's cultural values more than the material interest of political actors and their constituents. Opinions about morality issues require very little information because they are based on deeply held values. They also tend to be highly salient because "everyone is an expert on morality" (Haider-Markel and Meier 1996, 333). Although it is not entirely clear that morality politics constitutes a wholly different policy dimension (Mucciaroni 2011; Wald, Button, and Rienzo 2001), it is obvious that the distribution of values in a community is an important determinant of political outcomes.

The morality politics research clarifies that religious adherence affects not only political attitudes but also political outcomes. Studies have consistently shown that cultural environments with higher concentrations of evangelical Christians have more conservative public policies on morality politics issues. For example, Gibson (2004) evaluated the impact of evangelical adherence on whether a state had evolution-friendly science standards. The teaching of evolution in public schools has been a major problem for religious conservatives since the Scopes Monkey Trial in the 1920s. Their belief in the inerrancy of the Bible leads them to reject any theory that denies God the primary role in creation. Moreover, they abhor the idea that human beings, "created in the image of God," might have somehow evolved from lower life-forms. Gibson found that states with sizable evangelical populations adopted standards more hostile to evolution. The nature of the religious cultural environment was a better predictor of science standards than socioeconomic factors or the state's ideological context.

Similarly, Jacobs and Carmichael's (2004) research on the death penalty indicates that the number of death sentences in a state is dependent on the level of membership in conservative churches. They explain that "because conservatives stress deterrence and retribution, successful demands for death sentences ought to be likely where conservative values are the strongest" (251; see also Curry 1996). Conservatives see crime as the result of wrong choices; liberals see crime as the result of inequality and other unjust social arrangements. Jacobs and Carmichael found that contextual variation mattered at the state level. Where liberal values and liberal religion were strong, prosecutors, judges, and juries had less incentive to pursue the ultimate penalty, and the death sentence was given fewer times. Similar patterns have been detected in policies involving gambling (Pierce and Miller 1999), abortion (Calfano 2006), gay rights (Oldmixon and Calfano 2007; Haider-Markel 2000), pornography (K. Smith 1999), statutory rape (Cocca 2002), liquor consumption (Satterthwaite 2005), and funding for the arts (Lewis 2006).

Given that churches have often spoken out forcefully on matters of personal conduct, it should not be surprising to discover a correlation between legal restrictions on unorthodox activities and religious geography. But studies of the American states have supplied much evidence that religious composition is related to policy patterns that do not have such an obvious link to theological values. Most such studies have built on the hypothesis that religion contributes in a major degree to the assumptions, values, and habits that may define policy preferences over a wide range of public issues.

In the area of race relations, for example, Fenton and Vines (1967) argued that the level of voter registration of Louisiana blacks depended largely on the religious values of the politically dominant whites in the community. More than a decade after the Supreme Court struck down state laws excluding African Americans from voting in public elections, local communities had found ways to keep more than two-thirds of black adults off the electoral registers. As a rule, the level of African American registration in Louisiana was much higher in the predominantly Catholic parishes (counties) of the southern area of the state than in the northern area, where Protestant groups predominated. Finding that this difference held up in the face of checks for the influence of various nonreligious social, political, and cultural factors, the investigators pointed to differences in social attitudes between Catholics and Protestants:

Permissive attitudes toward Negro registration in French-Catholic parishes seem expressive of the basic value that the Negro is spiritually equal in a Catholic society. Such a view of man's relation to man, a scheme of elementary justice implicit in a Catholic society, some Catholics maintain, is sustained by traditional Catholic theology and actively promoted by the Church in Louisiana. There is little evidence in the Protestant parishes of cultural values assigning the Negro a spiritually equal place in the community or of activity by the church itself toward these values. (176)

In addition to possessing a doctrinal basis for racial tolerance, the Catholic Church also had institutional and social reasons to discourage ill treatment of African Americans. As a universal church that crosses racial and ethnic boundaries, Catholicism itself would be threatened if all the faithful were not treated on equal terms. Moreover, because the Catholic Church was one of the few integrated institutions in the South, its members were given the opportunity to dispel their prejudices. In contrast, the segregated white Protestant churches of northern Louisiana catered to the segregationist values of their members and did little to promote the contact between races that might have fostered mutual tolerance.

Religion may affect an even broader range of policies through its influence on attitudes toward the role of government in society. In chapter 3, we noted that religion shapes American political behavior by its general effect on the national political culture. Along the same lines, a leading authority on American federalism has suggested that the religious and ethnic groups that settled the various American states were the carriers of particular cultural values that have left a mark on contemporary state politics and policy. According to Daniel Elazar, migrating groups subscribed to different views about the nature and purpose of government, the role of politics in society, and other politically relevant beliefs. For example, he noted the emphasis in Puritan thought on using the power of the state to create a holy commonwealth on earth. In the parts of the country settled by Puritans, their successors, and immigrants with similar religious traditions, this conception of politics as a calling has survived in a highly moralistic approach to politics:

> Politics, to the moralistic political culture, is considered one of the great activities of humanity in its search for the good society—a struggle for power, it is true, but also an effort to exercise power for the betterment of the commonwealth. Consequently, in the moralistic political culture both the general public and politicians conceive of politics as a public activity centered on some notion of the public good and properly devoted to the advancement of the public interest. Good government, then, is measured by the degree to which it promotes the public good and in terms of the honesty, selflessness, and commitment to the public welfare of those who govern. (Elazar 1984, 117)

Research by Barker and Carmen (2009) finds that elected officials who live in moralistic states are more likely to hold "trustee"-oriented representational preferences compared to people in individualistic states who were more likely to see themselves as delegates. Delegates see themselves as advocates for their constituents' positions; trustees act in what they believe to be the best interest of their constituents. Indeed, one recent article suggests that more conservative religious values in a community are actually detrimental to the responsiveness of community leaders to the general public (Hill and Matsubayashi 2008). This moralistic orientation, like those of the individualistic and traditionalistic cultures elsewhere, dictates a particular configuration of values that affect the scope, nature, and style of political practice. Noting that religious groups with such distinctive political conceptions clustered in different parts of the country, Elazar predicted a correlation between state policy orientations and ethno-religious settlement patterns.

Although it was developed principally to account for contemporary policy differences, Elazar's theory has been strikingly confirmed by studies of political conflict in the nineteenth-century United States (Hammond 1979; Kleppner 1979). Abolition, prohibition, and a host of other social reforms were fired by the enthusiasm and crusading mentality of a moralistic culture and resisted on the basis of values that sound remarkably like Elazar's description of the traditionalist culture. What is more, according to the influential ethnocultural school of American history, the basic groupings of voters were defined largely by the type of religious values that Elazar identified as the core of differing political cultures. Whatever its historical value, Elazar's assertion about the policy impact of religiously based value systems has inspired several research projects on contemporary state-level variations in public policy. Although the specific predictions have not always been confirmed, several scholars have detected affinities between the concentration of certain religious groups and particular sets of policies enacted by the states, including levels of taxation (Hutcheson and Taylor 1973), spending on social welfare (Johnson 1976), use of government to help disadvantaged groups, and anticorruption measures (Johnston 1983).

The religious context structures political opportunities by offering advantages to interests advocating policies consistent with the cultural environment. Political culture often plays a role in the vote choice of a region. Fischer (2010) found that even though during the 2008 presidential primaries Hillary Clinton and Barack Obama were ideologically similar, states with moralistic political cultures were more likely to give Obama a greater share of the primary vote than states with more traditional or individualistic ones. Cahn and Carbone (2010) conclude that much of the contemporary "red" state–"blue" state polarization in American politics can be attributed to the geographically based cultural divisions and the different types of laws that are passed in the two areas. Their work details how in red states cultural beliefs influence legal regulations by controlling sexuality and blue states' beliefs are more oriented to promoting equality. None of this is deterministic. Policies inconsistent with the religious cultural environment can emerge. Several factors influence a state's policy positions, including its budget, level of economic development, level of government capacity, previous programs, and partisanship. But the point is clear. It was much easier for gay rights advocates to gain marriage rights in the New England states, where evangelical Protestants constitute no more than 15 percent of the electorate, than it will be in states like Oklahoma or Alabama, where evangelicals comprise 53 percent and 49 percent, respectively.[4] The political opportunities are not the same. No matter the resources, regardless of the grievance, Oklahoma and Alabama have so many evangelicals that the possibility of obtaining same-sex marriage rights by electoral action is nearly precluded.

INSTITUTIONAL CONTEXTS

When seeking favorable public policies, all institutional environments are not created equal. Organizations may try to pursue political goals through statutes, administrative procedures, and/or court cases. They can focus on elected and government officials or choose to apply pressure through nongovernmental organizations. The options for involvement also extend to the various stages of the policy process: churches and religious groups can specialize in raising awareness of problems, shaping policy alternatives, trying to influence the content of policies, or monitoring the implementation of government action. Decisions about what to pursue and how to pursue it are not neutral but significantly influence the political opportunity structures that groups face relative to a political issue.

Institutional context is one of the reasons that the abortion issue has been much less divisive in Canada than it has been in the United States, despite the fact that the combined number of Catholics and evangelical Christians in both countries is similar and that each state liberalized its abortion policies about the same time in the 1960s and early 1970s. Examining the abortion issue in the United States, Canada, and Great Britain, Halfmann (2011) explains how the nature of political institutions structured the opportunities that citizens opposed to abortion in each of these countries had. According to Halfmann, the reason anti-abortion activists in the United States have been much more successful restricting abortion rights is not because of greater political opposition. Indeed, public opinion on the abortion issue looks similar in each country. A majority of people were inclined to support abortion to protect the health of the mother and in the case of fetal abnormalities and oppose it for "softer" reasons such as economic hardship, family limitation, or for "own reason." The primary reason for the difference is that the more disciplined, centralized party systems of Canada and Britain kept the issue from becoming overly politicized. While in the United States, the decentralized, grassroots nature of political parties, coupled with the multiplicity of political arenas that separating powers (among the legislative, judicial, and executive branches of government) and dividing powers (among the national, state, and local governments) provides, encouraged the parties to stake out polarized positions and allowed anti-abortion activists to have influence disproportionate to their numbers in the many low-turnout, candidate-centered elections that are held in the United States. On the abortion issue, the structure of the American political system created greater opportunities for successful opposition to abortion rights policies in America than were available in Canada or Great Britain.

The importance of institutional context is also evident in the politics of gay marriage. Gay rights advocates have historically preferred the relative quiet of legislative or even judicial politics to the high-profile nature of the electoral arena that has traditionally favored the policy aspirations of religious conservatives. Haider-Markel and Meier explain why this is the case. "If the scope of the conflict can be kept narrow, then interest group pressures can prevail if elite attitudes are supportive" (1996, 346). This is particularly important for gay rights supporters because they do not have the same resources as their detractors. Simply recall from the previous chapter the means available to politically mobilized religious groups to appreciate the resource deficit faced by gay rights advocates. As a result of this dynamic, until 2012, no state had ever voted to legalize gay marriage at the ballot box. Among the sixteen states where gay marriage is legal, only four have extended the right to marry to same-sex couples through the electoral process. More dramatically, more than thirty states have voted to deny this right by adding language to their state constitutions that defines constitutional amendments defining marriage as the union between a man and a woman.[5] These kinds of restrictions have been passed either as an initiative, a citizen-created amendment placed on the ballot for public review, or as a referendum, a statewide vote on a law passed by the legislature. Both forms of "direct democracy" tip the power balance in favor of ordinary citizens.[6] Policies in states with initiatives are more likely to be consistent with the majority opinion in the state than policies in states without the initiative process (Matsusaka 2004). However, most public policies are not the result of direct democracy but are established by elites, either elected or appointed. Given general public indifference to most government action, interest groups with specialized knowledge and more constant access to public officials are better equipped to influence the policies that emerge from less open processes. This style of policymaking advantages smaller minority groups and interests.

This does not mean that religious interests will always be successful, of course, only that the electoral arena offers them an advantage due to religion and party competition. Recent research on gay rights issues reveals that for the most part public policy is responsive to public opinion at the state level even after controlling for ideology, interest group pressure, and other factors. However, as we explore in chapter 11, in instances in which gay rights policies are not congruent with the will of the majority, policies tend to favor conservative interests (Lax and Phillips 2009). To give a sense of the magnitude of advantage that religious conservatives enjoy relative to gay rights advocates in the electoral arena, consider California's Proposition 8. In the eyes of many who do not live on the West Coast, the state of California is synonymous with liberal, Hollywood, celebrity-type lifestyles. It would seem an unlikely place for a successful anti-gay crusade. Yet in November 2008 religious interests managed not only to get the initiative on the ballot but also to persuade the citizens of the state to amend the California constitution to eliminate the rights of same-sex couples to marry. All five of California's most populous counties—Los Angeles, Orange, Riverside, San Bernadino, and San Diego—voted in favor of Proposition 8.[7] The intended effect was to overturn a ruling by the California Supreme Court earlier in the year that had found that same-sex couples had the right to marry under the state's constitution. Nearly eighteen thousand same-sex couples had done so in the months before the practice was halted as a result of the amendment's passage. Conservative Christian organizations, the Catholic Church, African American churches, and the Latter-Day Saints utilized their existing grassroots networks as well as their resources to gather the signatures necessary to place the measure on the ballot. Protect Marriage, the official proponent of Proposition 8, was able to frame the issue successfully and raise concerns about whether allowing same-sex couples to marry would undermine the fabric of society by altering the traditional definition of marriage. Although some liberal clergy denounced the measure, more clergy members spoke out in favor of it or were at least ambivalent. Public opinion favored conservative religious interests, and they were able to use the ballot box to restrict those rights.

However, when the constitutionality of Proposition 8 was tried in the courts, the institutional advantage that religious interests enjoyed in the electoral arena was lost. Both U.S. District Court Judge Vaughn Walker and the U.S. Court of Appeals for the Ninth Circuit have held the initiative unconstitutional. In court, neither the California governor, attorney general, nor other state and local officials who would implement and enforce Proposition 8 have opted to defend its constitutionality. Despite the lack of elite support for the amendment, Proposition 8 precluded legislative activity in support of gay marital rights.

Today, marriage laws vary by state. In most of New England, Iowa, Illinois, Maryland, Minnesota, New Mexico, California, Washington State, and the District of Columbia, gay marriage is legal; in more than 60 percent of the country it is prohibited by constitutional amendments and other laws. Because the "full faith and credit" clause of the U.S. Constitution requires states to recognize and enforce other states' actions, opponents fear that same-sex marriages originating in states that allow them will have to be accepted as legal in other states. The state constitutional amendments are an attempt to preempt this by removing the policy from both the legislative and the judicial arenas. It is unclear whether this strategy will be successful. In spring 2013, the Supreme Court remanded the appeal of Proposition 8 back to a lower court on a technicality and did not rule on the matter of whether states would indeed have to recognize gay marriages legalized in other states. Ultimately, the Court will have to decide what the full faith and credit clause means in the case of same-sex marriage. Whatever the final outcome, moving the issue from the realm of electoral politics to the courts shifts the opportunity structure for conservative religious and gay rights supporters alike. The advantage that conservatives enjoy is lost because the courts regard legal, not moral, arguments.

Mucciaroni (2011) suggests that what is unique about morality politics is the moral frame that is used to present it. As social conservatives are compelled more and more to talk about rights, the passion, energy, and momentum that come from religious arguments based on the morality of the matter dissipate. As we explore in chapter 7, increasingly Americans regard same-sex marriage as an equality, not a morality, issue. As public opinion continues to move in favor of gay rights and gay marriage, the electoral advantage that conservative groups have traditionally enjoyed in the electoral arena will be diminished.

Though religious organizations have been more successful with policies that emerge out of the electoral political context than with those that come out of the legislative and bureaucratic arena, like all interest groups, they utilize strategies designed to affect politics in these areas as well. *Lobbying* is an attempt to bring pressure on the political system in an attempt to influence public policy. Broadly, there are two types: insider and outsider lobbying. When an issue is dealt with outside the electoral arena, inside lobbying is the normal way to influence the policymaking process. Inside lobbying occurs at the elite level and consists of activities like monitoring government actions, assembling facts and figures, making public presentations, visiting offices, and negotiating the details of legislative and governmental regulation. It advantages small groups because access to government officials provides a direct channel to influence public policy. The inside lobbying of most religious organizations is not unlike that of secular advocacy groups (Hertzke 1988). In a study of religious organizations at the state level, Micon (2008) found that a good inside lobbyist was "an organization's single most important asset" and a major determinant in whether the group was able to wield influence in the state legislative arena.

However, when an issue is debated and salient beyond the halls of the legislature, outside lobbying strategies can be brought to bear. Indeed, Hofrenning (1995) observes that religious lobbies use outside strategies to a much greater extent than secular interests. Ideally outside and inside strategies are mutually supporting and together provide a group with maximum leverage. Still, religious organizations are more likely to rely on outside strategies in part because they tend to play a very different role than advocates of secular causes. Unlike secular lobbyists, who typically focus on a narrow range of issues and seek only incremental changes, religious lobbyists often take on the mantle of biblical prophets, challenging the political system in the name of sacred values such as justice, freedom, and decency. Through outsider tactics, religious groups try to convey the impression that their constituencies stand ready to support officials who go along and to penalize legislators who do not. Because Americans belong to more religious organizations than to any other voluntary association, religious groups are advantaged in outside lobbying, and public officials are disposed to listen. This gives them a greater political opportunity when an issue is salient to the public. Religious organizations have broad church networks that they can tap into to barrage public officials with direct communications from their constituents. Contacting public officials by letters, postcards, telegrams, faxes, e-mails, and personal visits is a tried-and-true strategy of many political organizations. Often portrayed as spontaneous outbursts by concerned congregants, mass mobilization usually results from campaigns that are meticulously planned by the Washington office of the religious groups or by media-based ministries.

Beyond directly contacting public officials, religious organizations also can engage in the lobbying strategies of direct action and political campaigning to raise the profile of the issue they are advocating. The strategy of direct action may entail activities as diverse as peaceful demonstrations, marches, public relations campaigns, civil disobedience, and, in extreme cases, violence. These techniques have been widely adopted by various religious groups.

Peaceful demonstrations have been particularly attractive to groups motivated by intense and deeply felt commitments but lacking in other resources such as money, political experience, and permanent organizations. For example, by holding prayer services in public, religiously motivated demonstrators have tried to add moral weight to their position. Religious organizations have also organized boycotts, conducted marches, and mounted public relations campaigns to advance their objectives.

Sometimes, however, frustrated by the failure of more conventional efforts to influence policy, religiously oriented persons have purposely taken actions that violated the law. Religion has inspired many campaigns of civil disobedience, in which protesters have intentionally challenged laws in the name of higher laws. In July 2012, Sister Megan Rice, an eighty-two-year-old nun, with two others aged fifty-seven and sixty-three, managed to breach security at the Oak Ridge nuclear reservation in Tennessee, where the United States keeps materials to create thousands of nuclear weapons. Inside they splashed blood and hung pacifist banners on the walls of the highly enriched uranium materials facility. Charged with trespassing and felony destruction and depredation, Sister Rice is part of a long tradition of religiously inspired activists who have challenged the government by violating the law.[8] Despite the alleged illegality of the actions, throughout American history, religious individuals and organizations have used civil disobedience to highlight injustice in nearly every area of public life. The most extreme forms of public action, calculated acts of violence, have occasionally been undertaken by people who claimed to hear God's command. No modern moral issue can match abortion as a focus of religiously connected violent protest in the United States (Silverman 2002). Abortion service providers continue to be violently targeted by extremist anti-abortion activists. In May 2009, a clinic operator from Wichita, Kansas, Dr. George Tiller, was shot dead as he served as an usher at his church. Dr. Tiller was one of the few doctors in the nation who performed abortion late in pregnancy. Although violence has been denounced by virtually all leaders of the anti-abortion movement, most of the persons convicted of major assaults have cited religious convictions in their defense (Blanchard and Prewitt 1993). (They also claim that attacks on abortion facilities represent a measured response to the much greater violence used against the fetus.) When four young people were accused of bombing two facilities in a Florida city, one Baptist minister even hailed them as "heroes."[9]

Citizens who regard the Golden Rule as the essence of all religious teachings may be shocked to learn the degree to which the most violent and bigoted social movements in the United States claim a religious justification for their actions (Dobratz 2002). The trial of Timothy McVeigh, the Oklahoma City bomber executed in 2001, exposed links between the so-called patriot movement, a loosely knit network of anti-government activists organized in militias and paramilitary cults, and several extremist religious communities. Groups such as Christian Identity justify anti-Semitism, racism, and hatred of immigrants from a very peculiar religious perspective (Dobratz 2002). Several adherents of these groups have gone on killing sprees aimed at racial and religious minorities. In the wake of the September 11 terrorism that killed thousands in New York, Washington, D.C., and rural Pennsylvania, researchers have documented the links of support and fellowship between the patriot movement and virulent Muslim extremists around the world (Lee 2002).

The final way that religious organization can lobby in the electoral political arena is through political campaigning. Issue appeals may be more common than communication about candidates for public office because of the restrictions on churches and religious organizations in the campaigning arena. Unlike secular interest groups, religiously based movements cannot make financial contributions to candidates or openly campaign on their behalf. However, churches have been allowed to host political speakers and voter registration drives, lobby for and against referenda, and issue voter guides that provide virtual recommendations to members. The extent of campaigning is limited by federal tax regulations. Under the Internal Revenue Service (IRS) Code, charitable organizations such as churches are exempt from taxation and may receive tax-exempt contributions only if they refrain from excessive direct involvement in political campaigns (Davis 1991). Despite its broad powers, the IRS has generally refrained from invoking this law.

For example, in 2012, the group Alliance Defending Freedom sponsored "Pulpit Freedom Sunday," encouraging more than fifteen hundred pastors to stand before their congregations and publically endorse the Republican presidential candidate. Their aim was to provoke a challenge from the IRS in order to have standing to file a lawsuit that would assert that the restriction on congregational endorsements is a violation of freedom of speech. To date, no such challenge has come. Indeed, since 1954 when the IRS restriction was written into the tax code, there have been many investigations, but the exempt status of only one church has been revoked and the Supreme Court has never ruled on the constitutionality of this matter. In an age of weak political parties and generally low rates of political participation, the support of religious groups—even without formal endorsement—is usually seen as a valuable asset in a political campaign. By extolling the moral virtues of one candidate and pointedly refraining from comment about the competition, a minister can clearly indicate a preference without actually recommending a vote from the pulpit. The electoral environment is so potent for religious groups because religiously involved people can supply resources to help favored candidates or, conversely, to defeat unacceptable ones.

PARTISAN POLITICAL ALIGNMENTS

The political opportunity literature specifies that disarray in traditional political alignments offers enhanced opportunities for political mobilization by social movements (Steigenga and Coleman 1995). When interests, religious or otherwise, are able to gain leverage in a political party, it becomes easier for them and the policies they favor to find institutional expression. In the period following the upheaval of the civil rights movement in the 1960s, conservative religious interests were able to parlay their concerns onto the national political agenda of the Republican Party. As we examine in considerable detail in chapter 8, the same process allowed religious conservatives to penetrate the Republican Party in the 1980s. Eager to expand its base among religious conservatives, the GOP embraced the cause of the Christian Right, and the movement, in turn, worked to impose its agenda on the party.

Religious conservatives have become such a part of the Republican Party that some assert that there has been a Republican realignment based on religious differences. The relationship between religious conservatives and the Republican Party has become so conventional that simple characterizations (though exaggerated) of regular churchgoers as Republican are commonplace.

These divisions are even reflected in the familiar red-state–blue-state maps used to describe electoral support for the two candidates. As one observer put it, "Red folks are NASCAR-lovin', gun-ownin', God-fearin' Republicans who mostly inhabit the rural, suburban, and small-town heartland stretching from the Deep South through the Great Plains and into the mountain states. Blue types, by contrast, are highly secular, latte-sipping, diversity-embracing Democrats concentrated in the urban areas on the two coasts and around the Great Lakes."[10] As overstated as this portrait is, the perception that the values religious people care about will be treated better by Republicans has been validated by subsequent Democratic efforts to correct it. Speaking at the 2004 Democratic National Convention, then senator Barack Obama sincerely declared, "We worship an awesome God in the blue states too."[11]

It is important to remember that disarray in the traditional political alignments improves the political opportunity structure. Religious conservatives are increasingly viewed as part of the Republican base. The Republican Party must work to add to this base in order to form a winning coalition. Much like African American voters in the Democratic Party, religious conservatives have lost some degree of policy leverage because there is little possibility that they will act differently or change their partisan affiliation and alignment if the party does not actively work to advance their agenda.

The extent of the attachment of religious conservatives to the Republican Party is revealed by how completely ineffective President Obama has been at attracting them despite efforts in both 2008 and 2012. Obama, unlike many traditional Democratic politicians, seemed comfortable talking about the relevance of his faith to public life. He explained his approach in a 2006 speech to Sojourners, a respected Christian progressive organization headed by Jim Wallis. Wallis had recently written the book *God's Politics: Why the Right Gets It Wrong and the Left Doesn't Get It.*

> If we truly hope to speak to people where they're at—to communicate our hopes and values in a way that's relevant to their own—then as progressives, we cannot abandon the field of religious discourse. . . . [S]ecularists are wrong when they ask believers to leave their religion at the door before entering into the public square. The majority of great reformers in American history were not only motivated by faith, but repeatedly used religious language to argue for their cause.[12]

Few presidents have spoken about their faith as often or as eloquently as Obama as he explained the religious basis for his liberal, social justice orientation. In the 2008 campaign Obama reached out to the Christian community in a knowledgeable and credible manner by fully prioritizing religious outreach to voters in the campaign, meeting with evangelical leaders and working with religious grassroots organizations interested in common social justice concerns. In 2012, Obama and the Democratic National Committee continued the somewhat unusual practice for Democratic campaigns of hiring faith outreach staffers. Obama continued to talk about the importance of faith. But some of his policy positions since becoming president, including his endorsement of same-sex marriage, the requirement that religious groups provide insurance that covers birth control, and a fractious relationship with Israeli prime minister Benjamin Netanyahu, may have limited the appeal he had to some conservative religious groups in ways that were not as apparent when he was running on the inclusive themes of hope and change in 2008. In 2012, compared with his 2008 electoral performance, Barack Obama lost ground among white evangelicals, white Catholics, and Jewish voters. However, despite these incremental losses, the underlying structure of the American political landscape did not change, and partisan political alignment remained largely polarized. As we saw in chapter 2, there is a correlation between religious tradition and political party affiliation. There is also a correlation between religious tradition and presidential vote choice (Green et al. 2005). Obama continued to be the favored choice of black Protestants, Hispanic Catholics and Protestants, Jews, atheists and agnostics, unaffiliated believers, non-Christian faith traditions, less observant Catholics, and seculars. Romney, like McCain in 2008, was preferred by evangelicals, mainline Protestants, observant Catholics, and smaller traditions such as the Mormons and the Eastern Orthodox. These divisions are closely tied to not only religious tradition but also differences in church attendance and orthodoxy. Among whites in every Christian religious tradition, the most observant voted for Romney.[13] This kind of polarization between religious constituencies underscores the recognition by religious leaders and activists that political alignments influence the political opportunity structures that are available for each type of religious group.

INFLUENTIAL ALLIES

Religious groups have traditionally been viewed as supplicants to power, outsiders trying to influence the policy process. But in fact, religion may influence policy more directly, through the religious views and preferences of policymakers. A well-placed and sympathetic ally can contribute to an organization's ability not only to mobilize but also to formulate and implement favorable public policies. Most laws are enacted not by a public vote but by the concerted action of elected officials. Religion can play a role in this process by influencing the values of officeholders. Particularly when they are chosen by public election, government officials are likely to share the dominant religious values of their community. Even if the officials come from another religious tradition, a dependence on public approval for reelection should motivate them to express the preferences of their constituents. In either case, government officials can play a crucial role in translating religious sentiment into public law.

It is important to recognize the limits of the hypothesis that the behavior of political elites can be shaped by their personal religious orientations. Political scientists continue to debate the relative weight to assign the many factors that influence the behavior of public officials. In deciding how to cast a roll call vote, for example, members of Congress are subject to the pull of party loyalty, regional culture, judgments about constituency preferences, the influence of the president, the flow of national public opinion, staff recommendations, the lobbying efforts of myriad groups, and other personality characteristics. For instance, a recent study of Mormon legislators found that they were no more unified in their voting behavior than a randomly selected set of legislators (Cann 2009). Religion is just one of the factors that might account for an official's decision to favor or oppose a particular course of action on a public problem. Although the sources of influence might be different, officials in the executive and judicial spheres are similarly buffeted by forces that could override any single personal characteristic.

Until quite recently, political scientists had paid little attention to the study of the religious factor in congressional behavior. Most early research in this genre simply attempted to establish whether Protestants and Catholics voted as religious blocs in general or on specific issues (Fenton 1960). In recent work, scholars have distinguished more carefully among religious traditions, separating the large "Protestant" category into more meaningful subdivisions, and have also controlled for a variety of background factors that might influence the relationship. Two studies (Green and Guth 1991; Fastnow, Grant, and Rudolph 1999) in this genre have attempted to determine the factors that influenced the score of each member of Congress on a widely used index composed by the Americans for Democratic Action (ADA), a liberal interest group. After controlling for partisanship, the authors reported that ADA scores varied significantly with the personal religious identity of the representative and the religious composition of the congressional district. As expected, the greater the concentration of theologically conservative religious groups, the more conservative the voting habits of the district's representative in Congress. This research suggests a significant religious impact on the legislative process.

Denominational affiliation can affect legislative voting as well— especially—when the issue under consideration has been the subject of intense religious controversy. For instance, research in a variety of legislative settings finds Catholic, Mormon, and evangelical Protestant legislators more likely to support restrictive abortion legislation after taking account of personal qualities such as party and ideology and the influence of the legislators' district (Page et al. 1984; Day 1994; Fastnow et al. 1999; Oldmixon 2002).

For elites just as the masses, studies using denominational affiliation alone may underestimate the connection between religious values and legislative behavior. Other, more nuanced measures of religion in the lives of legislators, including orthodoxy (Green and Guth 1991) and salience (Yamane and Oldmixon 2006), confirm that religion influences legislator policy preference and decision-making. Elizabeth Oldmixon's (2005) study of Congress details that this effect is particularly acute on moral issues. Most lawmakers view moral issues as a distinctive policy domain and that in areas such as reproductive policy, gay rights, and school prayer, background factors including religion and ideology take on greater importance in relation to foreground goals such as reelection, policy implementation, and institutional power.

As valuable as they are, these statistical investigations of denominational differences in legislative behavior only scratch the surface of possible religious effects on political elites. Much additional light has been shed by a pair of studies that transcended simple denominational classification by interviewing legislators to learn their religious values. Based on her interviews with twenty-five Catholics serving in the U.S. Congress in the period 1973–1974, in a classic study, Mary Hanna (1979) concluded that Catholics did not form a separate bloc and, with a few exceptions on issues such as abortion, were not strongly influenced by their Catholic constituents or the lobbying efforts of the church. Rather, Hanna found, the principal contribution of faith to Catholic legislators' political identity was its influence on their basic political attitudes. Two different streams of Catholicism guided their values, one "that emphasized strict codes of conduct, rules, and guidelines, a rather rigid, puritanical devotion to duty and order; and one which stressed Christian love, compassion, and concern for one's fellow man, especially the poor, the helpless, and the unfortunate" (99). Not surprisingly, adherents of the first tradition were conservative Republicans, and legislators who drew from the social reform stream were liberal Democrats.

A similar distinction between religious types was noted by Peter L. Benson and Dorothy L. Williams (1982), who interviewed eighty members of the House of Representatives from a wide range of denominations. Politically conservative and liberal representatives were found in each major American denomination, but members of the two camps tended to stress different aspects of belief. The conservatives conceived of religion as something for the individual, a force that gave them comfort in times of distress, strength of conviction, self-discipline, and the promise of eternal reward. In contrast, political liberals put a great deal of emphasis on the communal aspect of religion. Where conservatives saw religion as a one-to-one relationship between individuals and God, the theology of liberalism stressed the oneness of humanity and the need for social transformation on earth if God's will is to be recognized adequately. These differences showed up in voting on specific types of legislation. "Individualism preserving" religion was correlated with support for free enterprise, private ownership, and military expenditures and with opposition to government spending on social programs. Its opposite, what Benson and Williams labeled "community building" religion, encouraged support for programs of foreign aid, hunger relief, civil liberties, and liberalized abortion rights. These differences in religious style appeared much stronger than the group differences normally observed when legislators are divided into broad families, such as Protestant, Catholic, and Jew, or classified according to denominations.

The Judiciary

If legislators may be influenced by religious backgrounds, the same force could in principle affect the decisions of judges. Some scholars have argued that in the American political system, which gives judges broad discretion to interpret the laws, a complete understanding of judicial decisions requires the use of information about personal and social background. Although this point has by no means been universally accepted by judicial scholars, it has inspired several careful studies that have traced patterns of judicial behavior to the traits of individual judges. The need to be cautious in ascribing religious motives to public acts must once again be recognized. A judge's decision is likely to reflect certain norms of the legal profession—a respect for precedent, the quality of advocacy, views about the proper scope for judicial discretion, and, of course, the facts surrounding any particular case. If religion fits into the equation, it does so merely as one factor among many.

Systematic analysis of religion has been as scarce in research on judicial behavior as in studies of legislative behavior. Probably the best evidence for a religious effect can be found in Sorauf's (1976, chap. 9) analysis of denominational differences in voting on church-state issues by judges on high appellate courts. In analyzing non-unanimous decisions during the 1950s and 1960s, he found that more than 80 percent of Jewish judges favored a strict "separationist" policy that limited government's ability to recognize religion, whereas Roman Catholic judges, by an equally lop-sided margin, voted to endorse policies and practices that accommodated religious interests. Protestants, who made up by far the bulk of the judges hearing the church-state issues, split roughly in half between the separationist and accommodationist camps. The historic tension between Protestants and Catholics in the United States was apparent in the tendency of Protestant judges to become more accommodationist when Catholics were not a party to a lawsuit and for Catholics to become decidedly more separationist when non-Catholic groups were involved in the case (Sorauf 1976, 225). As Sorauf realized, this set of cases was particularly conducive to the operation of a denominational effect because "the religious affiliation of the judge relates in the judicial decision to the direct and immediate interests of his religious group as well as to the social values derived from the religious tradition and its belief system" (222). Perhaps for that same reason, Yarnold (2000) found that Catholic and Baptist judges on the federal circuit courts of appeals were more likely to rule in favor of religious plaintiffs in cases under the religion clauses. When the interests of specific denominations are not so self-evident, religious affiliation should play a lesser role.

The existing research supports the foregoing conclusion. Although scholars have found some differences between Protestant and Catholic judges in various judicial environments, most differences are due to partisanship or regional factors rather than religion (Nagel 1961, 1962; Goldman 1966; Ulmer 1973). However, these studies may have understated religious differences because they lumped all Protestants into a single group. A more recent study of state supreme court judges distinguished between Protestant judges belonging to mainline denominations—the traditional high-status groups such as Episcopalians, Methodists, and Presbyterians—and judges who came from evangelical denominations, principally Baptists (Songer and Tabrizi 1999). The authors found that evangelical judges were indeed more conservative than Catholics, mainline Protestants, and Jews on cases about obscenity, the death penalty, and gender discrimination. Similarly, a study of federal district court decision-making in religious speech cases found that mainline Protestants were significantly less likely to support religious speech in public forums than non-mainline Protestant judges (Blakeman and Greco 2004). These differences on public policy and the role of religion in society are consistent with religious group patterns from public opinion studies, suggesting that the judges largely reflect the social values of their religious group.

If analysis of religion in Congress were similarly dependent solely on statistical studies, negative conclusions about religious effects in that branch might also have been reached. A fuller understanding of the legislative arena was possible because members of Congress were available for interviews that could elicit religious beliefs beyond mere denominational affiliation. Because judges rarely submit to such interviews, it has been difficult to find out whether more sensitive measures of religious values might account for behavioral differences. Nonetheless, some judicial biographies have speculated about possible religious influences on particular decisions or even judicial style (Przybyszewski 2000).

The President's Religion

Because laws are not self-executing, the administrative agencies of government play an important part in public policymaking. Yet, despite how little is known about religion in the legislative and judicial branches, even less seems clear about the executive wing. For the political appointees and career civil servants who staff the executive branch and its agencies, only fragmentary evidence about religious values is available. A recent study by Davidson, Kraus, and Morrissey (2005) reports that although the colonial "Protestant Establishment" denominations—Anglicans, Congregationalists, and Presbyterians—have less access to political power than they once did, they are still disproportionately found in positions of governmental influence compared to other Protestants and people of different faith traditions. This may be significant because there is at least anecdotal evidence that religion may influence the execution of duties. Since the reawakening of faith-based politics during the Carter presidency in the 1970s (Flint and Porter 2005), the religious underpinnings of presidential politics have been particularly engaging for politics and policy.

As the official head of the executive branch and the principal focus of American government, the president has a unique opportunity to affect both the substance and tone of public policy in the area of religion (Treene 2001). The president's actions may well shape and guide public opinion on controversial moral questions. President Bush's understanding of the moral imperative in stem cell research led him to forbid a federally funded medical researcher from conducting stem cell research on tissue recovered from discarded embryos. President Obama, embracing moral arguments about aiding the sick and infirmed, reversed President Bush's policy on this issue just a few months after taking office. Apart from contributions to legislative debate and public opinion, the president has direct responsibility for departments and agencies that come into direct contact with religious organizations.

Additionally, the president's authority over the Department of Justice determines which side the government takes in critical issues before the courts and, perhaps most important, who will sit on the federal courts to hear disputes involving religion. Scholars have disagreed about the importance of social background factors relative to the many competing influences brought to bear on presidential decision-making in this realm. The specific influence of religion has been even harder to assess because all presidents but one have come from Protestant backgrounds, usually the so-called mainline Protestant tradition of Methodists, Episcopalians, and Presbyterians (see table 6.1). This is significant because there is at least suggestive evidence that religious background may affect a president's approach to politics, if not the specific policies of a chief executive. This can best be demonstrated by examining the most recent occupants of the White House.

Table 6.1. Religious Affiliation of U.S. Presidents

Affiliation	Number	Percentage
Episcopalian	11	26
Presbyterian	6	14
Methodist	5	12
Baptist	4	9.5
Unitarian	4	9.5
Disciples of Christ	3	7
Dutch Reformed	2	5
Quaker	2	5
Catholic	1	2
Congregationalist	1	2
No specific denomination[a]	(3)	
Totals	39	102[b]

Source: Adherents.com (www.adherents.com/adh–presidents.html) cites Jonathan Kane and Joseph Nathan, *Facts about the Presidents*, 4th ed. (New York: Wilson, 1981), 360; and William A. DeGregorio, *The Complete Book of U.S. Presidents*, 2nd ed. (New York: December, 1989).
[a]The three presidents in this category—Jefferson, Lincoln, and Andrew Johnson—are not included in the totals or percentages.
[b]Total exceeds 100 percent due to rounding error.

Superficially, George W. Bush and Barack Obama were heirs of the same Protestant tradition. Their paths to this tradition differed markedly. Bush grew up a Presbyterian but experienced an evangelical-style conversion at the age of forty. For Bush, who disclosed a struggle with alcohol abuse that included a drunk-driving conviction, the epiphany, or moment of insight, came when his wife confronted him with a choice between Jim Beam (a popular brand of bourbon) and his family. He thereafter joined his wife's Methodist congregation. Obama was raised in a religiously open environment. He described his mother as an "agnostic" and his Muslim-raised father (who left the family when Obama was two) as "a confirmed atheist." As a child Obama had Christian, Catholic, Muslim, Hindu, and animist religious experiences.[14] It was not until after law school, as a community organizer on the South Side of Chicago, that Obama became a Christian. He recognized the linkages between faith and social action and acknowledged the power of Christ's death on the cross as relevant to his own life and work. Both men have talked freely about the difference that religion has made in their lives. Bush described himself as somebody who was saved from dissolution by the power of God and has volunteered that Jesus changed his heart. In explaining the significance and meaning of "Christianity" in his life, Obama clearly stated that "the source of strength and sustenance on a daily basis" was that "Jesus Christ died for my sins, and that I am redeemed through him."[15] Both have talked about how they continue to seek the Lord's guidance through prayer.

Where the two have diverged sharply is not in issues of style but rather those of substance. Bush's religion focused on the transformative personal nature of a relationship with Christ. In policy terms, Bush embraced the social traditionalism of conservative Protestantism, opposing abortion wholeheartedly, promoting his faith-based initiatives, and supporting school vouchers. In the application of religion Obama has identified with the social justice tradition of liberal Protestants in general and African American Protestants in particular (Copeland 2009). From that perspective, Obama has said that he has a "belief in the redemptive power of Jesus Christ and that through him we [can] achieve eternal life—but also that, through good works we find order and meaning here on Earth and transcend our limits and our flaws and our foibles."[16] Obama has not been a proponent of traditional values, but has pursued a legislative agenda that embraced social justice and equality concerns. In the national policy arena he has championed and passed national health care reform, ended the "don't ask, don't tell" policy that affected gays in the military, came out in favor of gay marriage, and has been critical of state laws that restrict abortion access. Recent research details that linkages between religious perspectives and presidential policy positions are the norm in

American politics. Whether it's Washington trying to guarantee liberty, Lincoln opposing slavery, Franklin Roosevelt trying to address the ills of the Great Depression, Truman fighting Communism, or Kennedy engaging the civil rights of African Americans, presidents tend to bring their religious understandings to bear on some defining aspect of their administration (Rozell and Whitney 2007; G. S. Smith 2006). The manner in which they do this might take several different forms. Domke and Coe (2008) argue that American presidents from Ronald Reagan onward have used four types of signals in their "God strategy" of connecting with the public. First, presidents have acted as "political priests" by invoking God and faith in their addresses to the public. Second, they have used such addresses to link God and country through "prophetic" language. Third, they have appealed more narrowly to the faithful through religious pilgrimages, proclamations, and rituals. Finally, they have used party platforms to address "morality" issues such as school prayer, abortion, and stem cell research. Questions surrounding the appropriate role of religion in American politics continue to be at the forefront of American national elections, because candidates offer significantly different visions of this relationship, and these visions inform their policy positions. As DiSalvo and Copulsky (2009) explain in their article that examines faith in the 2008 primaries, the ways in which faith was incorporated by Barack Obama, Mitt Romney, former Arkansas governor and evangelical pastor Mike Huckabee, and Christian libertarian Ron Paul differ substantially and make up a good portion of the range of ways that religion can be treated in a liberal democracy like the United States.

POLICY DOMAIN

Another important consideration relevant to the political opportunity structure faced by religious interests is whether the general public interprets the issue as a moral one. If an issue is not perceived by the broader community to be one of morality but of sectarianism, civil rights, economics, national security, or simple partisan preference, then religious interests will find more limited public support for their efforts and have a harder time creating a coalition that favors its policy perspective. A self-evidently "moral" issue to one religious group may strike another as something wholly unrelated to religious values.

In the following sections, we examine the policy domains in which religious interests are active—social regulation, social justice, and faith-based initiatives—to demonstrate how religious political opportunities are structured by public perceptions of religious relevance. We also look at the influence of religious interests on foreign policy. These examples of different political opportunity structures demonstrate that religion can influence political decision-making but is rarely decisive once other considerations enter the mix.

Social Regulation

Issues of social regulation are particularly well suited to the moralistic style of American politics because they involve the use of the state to restrict individual behaviors thought to threaten public health, safety, welfare, or well-being. Most policies normally associated with morality politics are issues of social regulation, including abortion, prostitution, gambling, liquor consumption, pornography, and the like. These issues are more easily portrayed as matters of right and wrong, and advocacy organizations often engage moral arguments grounded in religion to support their policy positions (Sabatier 1988). Religious conservatives tend to be most active in this policy area as they seek to ensure society remains committed to a traditional way of life that does not provide too many opportunities for poor choices. Still, despite the ease with which these issues can be framed as right or wrong, they are not always straightforwardly interpreted as matters of morality. Each issue contains moral facets, but these are balanced against other considerations, including personal liberties and rights. To the extent that the public understands the issue in terms of morality, opportunities for religious interests are enhanced.

The abortion issue provides a simple illustration. Most Americans do not endorse an absolute stance on abortion but instead vary their position based on the circumstances of the case—specifically, whether the woman can't afford more children, does not want a larger family, is concerned about her health or a birth defect in the child, or became pregnant as a result of rape or incest (Cook, Jelen, and Wilcox 1992; Zucker 1999). Americans are much more likely to support abortion for medical reasons (meaning birth defects), the mother's health, or rape than for what they consider "social" reasons, such as affordability or not wanting a child (Gillespie, Vergert, and Kingma 1988). This helps explain why the current legal landscape that favors abortion rights has been challenged by a cascade of successful abortion restrictions, including waiting periods, parental notification requirements, mandatory counseling, and other provisions.

Congressional passage of the 2003 Partial Birth Abortion Act illustrates the political dynamic. The pursuit of a legal ban on what was called "partial birth abortion" had been one of the defining issues of the pro-life movement. It was strongly opposed by pro-choice forces who believed it to be an attempt to overturn *Roe v. Wade*. Usually used for second- and third-trimester abortions and medically known as *intact dilation and extraction*, it involves a series of steps that sound gruesome to the layperson. Although the procedure is used relatively rarely and almost always for reasons involving the health of the mother or in instances of severe fetal defects, reaction to details of the procedure captured the American imagination. Concerns about the appropriateness of this policy—about whether a fetus can feel pain and whether this procedure was barbaric and inhumane—dominated public discourse. More than 70 percent of Americans approved of the ban on the procedure, including many who supported abortion rights in principle.[17] A bill was twice passed by Congress but vetoed by President Clinton because it lacked an exception for the health of the mother. George Bush signed the legislation in 2003, and its constitutionality was upheld by the Supreme Court in the case *Gonzales v. Carhart*.[18]

This pattern of opportunities for religious input is also seen in lottery politics. Pierce and Miller (1999) describe how different types of lotteries generate different types of politics and provide distinct opportunity structures for the social regulation of gambling. Lotteries that are intended to raise general revenue are not as attractive as those dedicated to funding education. When the goal is merely to fund the normal operations of government, lottery proposals encourage opponents to attack gambling as sinful. Lotteries for education, however, equip advocates with a powerful symbol—"the education of our children"—to counter moral arguments. Consider South Carolina's experience with an education lottery referendum in 2000 (Olson, Guth, and Guth 2003). Despite vociferous opposition by the state's strong evangelical community, clear clergy cues, and the salience of religion in South Carolina, the state's lottery referendum passed. Although the clergy were "nearly unanimously opposed" to the lottery, their rationales differed appreciably. Evangelicals framed gambling as a personal moral failing. Catholics, mainline Protestants, African Americans, and others suggested that the lottery would prey on the poor and undermine public morality. This confusing welter of arguments made it hard for voters to see the issue in terms of right and wrong, depriving religious interests of a major advantage. Recent research by Ferraiolo (2013) reveals that increasingly critics of state gambling policies are unsuccessful in framing state-sponsored lotteries as a morality issue. Counterarguments about the educational benefits of these programs are forcing religious conservatives to make other rational-instrumental arguments about the regressive nature of these policies and the revenue inefficiencies of raising state funds in this way. However, these kinds of arguments lack a moral imperative and fundamentally diminish the political opportunity structure for those who oppose these policies in the states.

A similar dynamic is at work in the politics of stem-cell research. If the moral imperative of stem cell research is the protection of human embryos and life from conception, then religious conservatives will have a political advantage. If, on the other hand, the morality of stem cell research involves using every available resource to aid the sick and infirm, the ideas of religious moderates, religious liberals, and seculars will be advantaged over those of conservatives (Patel 2011)—as they were when President Obama reversed President Bush's policy prohibitions in this area not long after taking office in 2009.

The politics around teaching creationism in public schools provides a final example of how whether a policy is perceived to be moral impacts the political opportunity structures that religious groups face (Lugg and Robinson 2009). Ironically, because of the restrictions of the establishment clause, if the public perceives an issue as purely moral or religious in the policy arena of church-state relations, religious groups are disadvantaged. The very purpose of the establishment clause is to ensure that religion does not unduly define or influence state activities. In accordance with the establishment clause, in *Edwards v. Aguillard* (1987) the Supreme Court found that teaching creation lacked a secular purpose and ruled it unconstitutional. After this ruling some proponents of creationism began to argue for the teaching of intelligent design (ID). ID is the proposition that biological life is too complex to have evolved randomly. Instead of God creating the heavens and the earth, intelligent design holds that some intelligent force—God, an alien species from far, far away, something—must have had a hand in the process. However, in 2005 a federal court ruled that teaching ID was also unconstitutional because it "cannot uncouple itself from its creationist, and thus religious antecedents."[19]

Rebuffed, proponents are trying a different tack. Though it is not possible at the state level to legislate in favor of creationism or ID, it is possible to pass laws that support "academic freedom." Framed as a way to "assist teachers, principals, and other school administrators to create and foster an environment within public elementary and secondary schools that promotes critical thinking and logical analysis," in 2008 Louisiana passed the Science Education Act. The bill cited the subjects that might need more critical thinking, such as evolution, the origins of life, global warming, and human cloning. While the constitutionality of this strategy is yet to be proven, the fact that advocates were able to build public support and get such a bill through the legislature indicates the political appeal of religiously based arguments in this policy area.

Social Justice

Social justice also draws the active participation of religious organizations and clergy. Social justice is fundamentally about societal equality, the idea that every person has the same basic rights, opportunities, and social benefits. Poverty, hunger, homelessness, affordable housing, civil rights, criminal justice, education, racism, immigration, the environment, and related issues all involve questions of social justice because they invoke concern about whether a society's resources are being distributed fairly. As we argued earlier, in most cases, the more an issue is perceived to involve morality, the greater the influence of religious organizations. When the distribution of a societal resource is thought to be both inefficient and unjust, the moral authority of religion can be used by religious interests to shape public policies.

Religious organizations have long been involved in the domain of social justice. The social gospel tradition of liberal and mainline Protestantism, the imperative to expand the kingdom of God by eradicating societal injustice, fueled Progressive Era reforms in the early decades of the 1900s. As Walter Rauschenbusch (1917, 53) explained, the kingdom of God "is not a matter of getting individuals to heaven, but of transforming the life on earth into the harmony of heaven." Today, many Methodist, Lutheran, Presbyterian, Episcopalian, and Congregationalist denominations continue to preach a gospel less focused on individual sin than on transforming society through the power of God's love. Improving the material circumstances of people's lives is also a recognized priority for African Americans and for Jews because of the disadvantages and oppression that they have faced historically. Expressed in their support of liberal political positions, Jews have a commitment to social justice that is unrivaled by any other religious group. African Americans also have a liberal social outlook, but it is very different from the mainline or Jewish perspective concerning personal salvation. Though supportive of making life better here, the hereafter is still of major concern. African American churches continue to preach strongly the need to be "born again" to avoid the "hellfire and brimstone" that is to come.

Catholic social teaching has also been instrumental in providing religious justification for activism in support of social justice. Catholic social teaching emphasizes that there is a right not only to life but also to all that sustains life. From this perspective, human beings are entitled to human rights that encompass the right to decent housing, food, health care, work for a living wage, and life in a healthy and protected environment. Catholic social teaching dictates that society must have compassion for the poor and that the state has a responsibility to ensure that all of its citizens— especially the poor and vulnerable—are provided with human rights. To prevent the unnecessary loss of life, the Catholic Church also has rules for when war is just and military intervention permissible. These efforts were invigorated in the mid-twentieth century by the Vatican II conclave in Rome, the elaboration of liberation theology, and other developments that we will detail in chapter 9.

The social justice tradition clearly influenced the growth of the civil rights and anti–Vietnam War movements as well as other social reforms in the 1960s (Friedland 1998; Hall 1990; Polner 1998). It is not too much to say that mainline Protestant, Jewish, African American, and Catholic clergy and their supporters changed society motivated by the power of their religious beliefs. The Civil Rights Act of 1964, the Voting Rights Act of 1965, the War on Poverty (including the Job Corps program, Head Start, and the Social Security Act of 1965, which established both Medicare and Medicaid), the Fair Housing Act of 1968, the Twenty-Sixth Amendment (giving eighteen-year-olds the right to vote), and the War Powers Resolution of 1973, among many other pieces of legislation, were significantly affected by the public activism and lobbying of religious groups.

More recently liberal religious groups in the social justice tradition were active in the passage of the controversial Patient Protection and Affordable Care Act, commonly called Obamacare, in March 2010. More than sixty faith groups filed amicus briefs with the Supreme Court supporting the constitutionality of the act when the Supreme Court heard a challenge to it in 2012.[20] For these groups obtaining national health care was a proper expression of faith. As a spokesperson for the National Council of Churches explained, "Christians believe that human beings—all of them—are infinitely-valued children of God, created In God's image. Adequate healthcare, therefore is a matter of preserving what our gracious God has made. . . . Healthcare is not a privilege, reserved for those who can afford it, but a right that should be available, at high quality to all."[21]Although social conservatives receive the lion's share of popular attention nationally, religious groups that support social justice have remained engaged in the political sphere, particularly at the elite level (Wuthnow and Evans 2002). Liberal organizations such as a Call to Renewal, the National Council of Churches, the United States Conference of Catholic Bishops, Sojourners, Evangelicals for Social Action, the Salvation Army, and the various lobbying arms of the mainline denominations continue to attempt to shape public policy. As Olson (2002, 55) observes, liberal religious organizations "retain an institutional presence on the national political stage."

The visibility and impact of liberal religious groups on federal policy have been limited by the public's perception that matters such as poverty, crime, and homelessness are personal failings more than societal responsibilities. This example highlights the importance of looking below the national level to understand the true impact that religious organizations are having on social justice issues. Although not well publicized in the media and only recently researched by scholars (Swarts 2002; Wood 2002; Warren 2001; Hart 2001), religious organizations and especially faith-based organizing groups at the subnational level are active and successful at shaping the nature of social justice policy in the United States. The strong community linkages that churches and clergy possess make it natural for them to care deeply about the health and well-being of the people who go to the church and who live in the area. Urban areas, especially, maintain a long tradition of church-based leadership on social issues. For example, when African Americans were not permitted to elect officials, clergy and churches often "represented" the interests of the community. Institutionally independent, black clergy and churches were relatively free from the influence of whites. They were thus well positioned to advocate for services and benefits to flow to the black community and to speak prophetically about the injustices that African Americans faced. In a recent book Jeff Stout (2010) argues that religious community organizing is essential to the democratic process because it creates "enduring publics of accountability" that are engaged between elections and able to counter dominant interests that easily find economic and political expression in the media age.

Many clergy members continue to feel a "calling" to local ministry. For most religious types, this calling encompasses helping to meet the physical and emotional needs of parishioners and the community. For some, it incorporates political activism. As the leader of one faith-based community organization noted, "Most congregations have mercy and charity at the center of their ministry, we suggest they add justice."[22] As explored in chapter 5, faith-based community coalitions increasingly use the religious, cultural, physical, financial, and human resources of churches to empower people to address the issues that they care about. Millions of activists based in houses of worship are trained through these organizations to confront the government and produce social change. Unlike government-sponsored faith-based initiatives, which provide social services in lieu of government, faith-based community organizations try to motivate the government to live up to its responsibilities. These networks have been active in setting state and local political agendas and behave as "invisible actors" (Swarts 2008) in state and local politics.

Richard Wood (2002) details how the faith-based organization PICO and its allies dramatically shifted the politics of health policy in California. In 2000, it persuaded the state to give an additional $50 million for community health clinics and ease the eligibility requirements for immigrants. By 2001, it also extracted state funding for a new program to provide health care for working families, despite a "worsening of the state's financial position" (3). The capacity to influence state-level politics came through building on successes at the local level, a hallmark of faith-based organizing. Early efforts focus on winnable issues. For example, the PICO federation in Oakland started by addressing relatively noncontroversial issues such as neighborhood crime and child safety. It then moved on to citywide issues such as employment initiatives and reducing school class sizes. As PICO in Oakland and other cities produced policy change at the local level, it began to focus on statewide initiatives such as health care and public school funding. Doing something about the smaller issues gives people a sense of accomplishment and develops leadership and organizational abilities for addressing more complicated challenges. Success at the state level frees up money to facilitate greater effectiveness through local-level initiatives.

The record of faith-based organizing in promoting social justice policy is noteworthy. Leaders in many cities have been able to secure extensive reforms of public education. Some of the strongest federations (e.g., BUILD in Baltimore, COPS and EPISO in Texas, GBIO in Boston, MICAH in Milwaukee, HOPE in Tampa, All Congregations Together in New Orleans, and East Brooklyn Congregations in New York) are effectively taking on complex social issues. During the economic recession of 2009 these organizations had their work cut out for them. For example, GBIO in Boston undertook an anti-usury campaign that would cap interest at 10 percent in order to protect families from permanent indebtedness. East Brooklyn Congregations continued to work for affordable housing. The East Brooklyn Congregations has built more than four thousand moderately priced homes in one of New York's poorest communities. This project has become a model for what can be done in other states. Called Nehemiah Homes, East Brooklyn Congregations' activity is based on a verse from the Book of Nehemiah: "Come, let us rebuild the walls of Jerusalem, so that we may no longer suffer disgrace." One indication of the group's success is that in an area where foreclosures topped 10 percent, remarkably no more than ten of the properties built by the Nehemiah Homes program suffered such a fate.[23] Today faith-based organizing efforts are beginning to be directed at the national level as well. In 2004, PICO changed its name from the Pacifica Institute for Community Organizing to the PICO (People Improving Communities through Organizing) National Network to reflect the expansion of its focus. Since then it has used its network and partnered with other organizations to challenge predatory lending, home foreclosures, immigration policies, and health care access both locally and at the federal level.

Faith-Based Initiatives

Although it may surprise many readers, religiously affiliated organizations have long been major providers of public services in the United States and have become more active since government cutbacks in the 1980s (Brown and McKeown 1997; Cnaan, Wineburg, and Boddie 1999; Wineburg 2000). In the field of human welfare, for example, major religious charities have received government contracts to help citizens deal with unemployment, hunger, disaster relief, refugee resettlement, low-cost housing, and other social services. Large charities like Lutheran Services in America, Catholic Charities, the YMCA (Zald 1970), and the Salvation Army receive sizable portions of their funding from the government (Black, Koopman, and Ryden 2004, 21). The money comes from a number of federal programs that authorize nongovernmental agencies to deliver tax-supported services, with selection determined in a competitive grant process.

Such programs have not been challenged on constitutional grounds because they were run in a nonsectarian manner. That meant, first, that the money or services had to be distributed without regard to the religious affiliation or membership of recipients and, second, that the provision of services could not be used to spread a religious message. In practice, most of the religious groups that competed for federal grants and contracts created separate charitable organizations for that purpose. While affiliated with a parent denomination, these charitable organizations avoided trying to influence the religious values of their clients. These organizations had the capacity to submit applications for federal programs and to account for their spending as required under federal law.

In the 1990s, several public officials called for the expansion of what became known as "faith-based public services." Some public officials wanted the state to retreat from some of its redistributive functions, others argued that religious groups were an important resource that had been blocked due to cumbersome program requirements. Advocates wanted more funds with fewer strings made available to churches and religious groups. In a major departure from the old model of service delivery, these new "faith-based initiatives" made money available to churches and other religious organizations to deliver social services, even in a sectarian manner—as long as the funds were not used to support proselytizing and the organization did not discriminate against participants who did not share the organization's religious beliefs. The effort to expand faith-based public services spread to the federal level when Congress passed federal welfare reform legislation in 1996. The bill's Charitable Choice provision mandated that religious organizations be eligible for contracts in states that used nongovernment providers. When Bush became president in 2000, he attempted to pass comprehensive legislation to expand these programs. However, this agenda met with considerable resistance because some supporters of the faith-based movement and many other citizens reacted negatively when they learned government funds would be available to any religious group, even unpopular "cults" or sects. Efforts to loosen the restrictions on proselytizing galvanized separationists into equally intense opposition. This criticism significantly compromised the application of Charitable Choice. As scholars have documented (Formicola, Segers, and Weber 2003; Black, Koopman, and Ryden 2004), constitutional, administrative, legal, and fiscal questions impeded the success of this noteworthy component of "compassionate conservatism." In the absence of new legislative authority, the Bush administration moved aggressively to advance faith-based initiatives through executive orders, rules changes, managerial realignment in federal agencies, and other innovative uses of the prerogatives of his office. This included setting up the White House Office of Faith-Based and Community Initiatives in the White House offices and eleven government agencies. These moves were designed to "level the playing field" between secular and religious organizations. One analyst concluded that the changes that Bush was able to implement "really don't have a parallel in contemporary administrative law." One measure of their success is that the faith-based office model has spread to the states (Sager 2010). Another indicator is that President Obama has continued them. He too is supportive of religious organizations competing for government contracts, although he rejects that those who take government money can discriminate on the basis of faith in employment decisions. With his Office of Faith Based and Community Partnerships he has set up a structure very similar to the Bush administration's to deal with these issues.[24] Biebricher (2011) suggests that this administrative apparatus is necessary because moving from public to private faith-based community service provisions introduces significant challenges for governance. He explains:

> States and governments cannot simply unburden themselves of tasks and delegate them to civil society actors. This transition has to be organized in meticulous ways and it presupposes, for example, an intricate knowledge of the existing state of affairs in local service delivery, accurate conceptions about the needs and concerns of faith-based organizations and, more generally, the skills to craft a functioning public-private partnership. (1008)

Nevertheless, this new environment has encouraged a broader range of religious organizations to vie for government dollars (Wuthnow 2004). Commentators distinguish between the older, nonsectarian social service agencies and the new faith-based providers (Jeavons 1998; Ebaugh et al. 2003). The basic characteristics of faith-based agencies include an organization that self-identifies as religious, has participants (staff and clients) that are religious, obtains physical and financial support primarily from religious people or congregations, delivers a variety of religious services as part of its social service delivery, and relies on both spiritual and secular expertise in making decisions. Finally, some congregations also engage in the delivery of social services, although this is not their primary function.

Congregations can formally sponsor service organizations or just act as "caring communities" (Wuthnow 2004). Either way, they are best known for offering ways to help the poor and needy, including "ministries" such as food pantries, clothing closets, soup kitchens, educational programs, and programs for the elderly. One estimate suggests that the typical congregation contributes more than $184,000 per year to the local community (Cnaan et al. 2002). Chaves (2004) concludes that congregations with more middle-class members are more likely to support service activities than ones made up of wealthy or low-income people. Being geographically located in a poor neighborhood is also conducive to such activity.

There is mixed evidence concerning which types of congregations are most likely to engage in service delivery. Cnaan et al. (2002) do not find any statistically significant difference between conservative and other churches in the types of things they offer. However, several studies (Ebaugh et al. 2006; Chaves 2004; Wuthnow 2004) report that evangelical or theologically conservative congregations are less likely to sponsor social service programs outside of the "caring community" model. Owens (2007) finds that fear of government entanglement with religion and a positive attitude toward partnerships between congregations and secular groups are major determinants of whether a congregation will take advantage of charitable choice. Although Chaves (2004) reports that 57 percent of congregations have a social service program of some kind, it is important to recognize there is a significant difference between the personal forms of support that churches provide to their members and the surrounding community as caring communities and the more systematic approach that faith-based and nonsectarian organizations offer—an approach that does not differ dramatically in scope or quality from that of secular organizations (Wuthnow 2004). There is considerable diversity in the kinds of faith-based organizations and the ways that they attempt to do their work (Adkins et al. 2010).

Advocates of faith-based initiatives in general and charitable choice in particular claim that religious groups have greater effectiveness in the delivery of social services. The greater effectiveness of religious groups in service delivery is an article of faith among advocates of faith-based public services. Because they are small and community based, advocates believe, churches can deal with clients on a personal level. Moreover, churches can provide powerful incentives for personal change that are unavailable to secular groups. For a person struggling with alcoholism or drug addiction, it is asserted, surrendering to God is a much more effective way to kick a habit than any other form of counseling. Still, like many articles of faith, the belief that religious groups run the most effective programs persists despite a stunning lack of evidence. While advocates can offer anecdotes, there is remarkably little creditable scientific evidence to sustain the belief that churches or religious groups do a better job of service provision than state or secular organizations. Scholars are just beginning to conduct the kinds of careful, systematic program evaluations that would permit objective observers to weigh the effectiveness of faith-based social services against secular counterparts. It is difficult to do. Defining and measuring effectiveness and controlling for all relevant factors are complicated tasks. Ironically, the scholar whose work has been cited as proof of the superiority of religious programs in drug addiction and crime control was one of the first to admit that no such conclusion can legitimately be drawn from his own research.[25] Recent research has focused on perceptions of those utilizing service agencies. It reveals that faith-based organizations help a very diverse constituency and garner higher mean effectiveness and trustworthiness scores from clients than public welfare departments (Wuthnow, Hackett, and Hsu 2004; Wuthnow 2004). Nonetheless, this research shows little evidence that faith-based organizations are in fact more effective than secular or nonreligious organizations in the actual delivery of services. Examining secular and faith-based welfare-to-work programs in Los Angeles, Monsma and Soper (2006) find that different types of programs have different effects on different types of clients and that "effectiveness" is contingent on the outcome being measured. It is interesting that for all the focus on government funding of faith-based initiatives, only one-third of congregations seemed open to the idea of contracting these services to the state and that the most theologically conservative congregations, who were expected to most welcome the opportunity, were least likely to embrace the concept (Chaves 1999). Moreover, it is not entirely clear that faith-based initiatives are any more successful at overcoming systems of racial and class-based stratification to meet the needs of the community (Bartkowski and Regis 2003). For example, looking at the delivery of housing-related services in Michigan, Jackson-Elmore and her colleagues (2011) find major regional differences in the configuration of housing-related service networks. Politically active African American churches in Detroit affected the delivery of housing-related services in Michigan. However, beyond the city, there was considerable regional variation and ultimately few substantive differences between faith-based organizations and their secular counterparts in delivering services in these issue areas.

Foreign Policy

Because religion is usually measured as a distinct dimension, the impact it has on mobilization in global society may be underappreciated (Bush 2008). Particularly in the area of foreign policy, religious organizations must compete with many other factors in decision-making. The influence of a particular religious group in a policy area represents only one force in the struggle to shape government action. These political opportunity structures are particularly complex. Through them we can appreciate how religion and moral influences compete with other factors for an impact on decisions. The need for a balanced appraisal can best be conveyed through a case study of American policy in the Middle East. Though frequently cited to illustrate the potential impact of religious considerations, this case also points to conditions that limit religious influence on public policy.

Since the state of Israel was founded in 1948, the United States has supported it with vigorous diplomatic action, military aid, and significant amounts of economic assistance. That support has frequently been attributed to a pair of religious factors—namely, the Jewish lobby in the United States and the moralistic strain in U.S. foreign policy. American Jews have used their considerable political resources—voting strength, organizational ties, campaign contributions, access to decision-makers, and media influence—to mount an energetic campaign on behalf of Israeli interests. The campaign has succeeded because a pro-Israel position suits the moralistic style of American foreign policy. Formed in the shadow of the Holocaust, besieged by hostile neighbors, and holding steadfastly to the same democratic political values as the United States, the new state drew on a powerful current of goodwill in postwar American opinion. Zionism appealed especially strongly to American Christians. Liberal Protestants admired Israel for its social and ethical values; conservative Protestants were heartened by Israeli military successes that seemed to confirm biblical prophecies.[26] Today, religious beliefs continue to predict public opinion on foreign policy in the Middle East, with evangelicals being the strongest supporters of Israel and also having the most negative views of Islam (Baumgartner et al. 2008). A recent study of support for the state of Israel in the House of Representatives from 1997 to 2002 found that on bills that substantively engaged the Palestinian issue, religious, ideological conservatives and Republicans had very different attitudes from Democrats, liberals, and African Americans, suggesting that ethnoreligious forces continue to be relevant in this policy arena (Oldmixon et al. 2005). It is crucial to put U.S. policy toward Israel into a broader context. In a survey of religious influences on U.S. foreign policy, Leo Ribuffo (2001) emphasizes that ethnic groups that tried to influence foreign policy succeeded only to the extent that they had allies outside their own communities; could frame their policy in terms that resonated with American values; and, perhaps most important, offered plans consistent with American national interest as perceived by the president and public opinion. That latter factor seems to have been the secret to Israeli success in maintaining an alliance with the United States. Reviewing President

Harry S. Truman's initial commitment to Israel, Ganin (1979) concludes that the chief motivations were fear of disorder and bloodshed in Palestine, competition with the Soviet Union for Middle East influence, and Truman's desire to assert his primacy over the U.S. State Department. Successive administrations maintained and expanded the U.S. commitment to Israel because it served their overriding foreign policy objectives (Spiegel 1985). The Carter administration, preoccupied with maintaining American access to Middle East oil supplies, valued Israel because it was located near the crucial transportation lanes for petroleum exports. Concerned above all else with containing the Soviets, the Reagan administration saw great benefits in cooperating with Israel, which had the military might to deter Soviet proxies in the region. With the end of the Cold War, the first Bush administration appeared to assign lower priority to the U.S.-Israeli alliance, refusing to underwrite loans to Israel in protest against Israeli settlements on land claimed by Palestinians. The Clinton administration subsequently threw its weight behind a treaty returning some of those lands to the Arab inhabitants. The Bush administration continued to endorse many aspects of this plan, even during the Palestinian uprising in the West Bank and Gaza in 2002 and the democratic election of radical Islamist group Hamas to a majority in the Palestinian Parliament in 2006. Although there has been some heightened tension between Israel and the Obama administration over the expansion of Israeli settlements, Obama has been a strong supporter of Israel and has not pursued policies that were dramatically different from his predecessors. The Israeli lobby in Washington has been effective because its objectives have largely lined up with perceptions about the United States' overriding strategic objectives for the Middle East. Certainly, religious factors undergird this dynamic. However, they are in no way determinative. When the Israeli lobby's policies conflict with the wishes of the chief executive, the lobby loses three-fourths of the time (Bard 1991; Goldberg 1990).

The Israeli case, usually cited to illustrate domestic influence on U.S. foreign policy, shows how many forces have to fall into place to produce a religious impact. Consider as a more typical case the conspicuous failure of Irish Catholics in the United States to build similar levels of American support for a united Ireland (Healy 1989). No doubt, this failure reflects the complex issues at stake in the conflict between the Protestants and Catholics of Northern Ireland. These conditions make it harder to claim that unswerving support for the Catholic minority is consistent with American national interest or the moralistic strain in U.S. foreign policy. Even if that case could be made to the American public, the potency of lobbying by Irish Catholics would be diminished because Irish nationalism is much less salient for American Catholics than is the cause of Israel for American Jews. Moreover, were American Catholics to mobilize aggressively on behalf of their brethren in Northern Ireland, they would face intense opposition from American Protestants who are equally committed to the cause of their coreligionists in Ulster. Religious influence on foreign policy is far from straightforward, particularly in heterogeneous religious societies like the United States. Differences in mobilization are usually attributed to the behavior and resources of elites with the key question being how well they are able to get their group together. However, a recent study demonstrated that variation in the readiness of ethnic diasporas to mobilize for their homelands can be attributed to differences in "politicized ethnic identity" measured by the strength of individual ties to their ethnic group and the social conditions that accompanied their emigration and reception in the new country (Wald 2008). This research underscores the need to take both mass and elite attitudes into account when examining religiously based mobilization.

Increasing scholarly attention is being given to how transnational mobilization influences international politics. For example, Susanne Hoeber Rudolph and James Piscatori (1997) argue that religion and ethnicity have replaced ideology as a major source of intra- and international conflict. Hill (2000) explains the significance of beginning to think about the world in this way:

> Conceptualizing a transnational civil society constituted by nongovernmental organizations and communities of activists working on a variety of global issues as well as religious communities and movements represents an important theoretical advance over current paradigms of sovereign states acting in anarchic space or in the context of international society constituted through the cooperative actions of states. (637)

While it may be premature to get rid of the state as a critical concept for analysis, there are indications that transnational ethnic and religious movements are playing an increasing role in international politics (T. Smith 2000)—both in conflict and in the process of mediation (Bercovitch and Kadayifici-Orellana 2009). An excellent example of transnational ethnic and religious alliances is the increased engagement of evangelicals in the United States with other evangelical Christians worldwide. Their efforts in trying to stop religious persecution, slavery, and sex trafficking have led many in the Religious Right not only to abandon their traditionally domestic focus but also to align with common domestic "enemies" such as the National Council of Churches, the Democratic Party, African American politicians and black churches, the U.S. Conference of Catholic Bishops, women's rights groups, mainline Protestant lobbying organizations, Jewish political organizations, and other religious minorities to produce policy change in the international arena (Hertkze 2004). These alliances are not easy to develop or maintain. They are often fraught with discord (Buss and Herman 2003). Still, such unusual coalitions have helped pass several major pieces of legislation in the United States designed to support religious freedom and by extension the plight of persecuted evangelical Christians throughout the world. Notable examples include the International Religious Freedom Act of 1998, the Trafficking Victims Protection Act of 2000, Sudan Peace Act of 2002, and the North Korean Human Rights Act of 2004. In 2005, religious groups were also influential in lobbying the International Monetary Fund and the World Bank to cancel the debts of the poorest countries in the world. As one indication of the influence of religion in international politics, the Council on Foreign Relations now hosts an "Evangelicals and Foreign Policy Roundtable" that aims to identify common threads among evangelicals in terms of foreign policy priorities and to explore their practical applications.

We often think about transnational religious immigrant communities (see chapter 10). We are less familiar thinking about transnational religious communities that transcend ethnic or racial groups. Still, we have seen them emerge before. Nepstad (2004) depicts how U.S. Christians were moved by the liberation struggles in Central America in the 1980s. Similar to evangelicals today, Christians in the United States—particularly Catholics, but other denominations as well—came to understand what was going on in Central America through missionaries and aid agencies that were active in those countries. The common cultural resources of Christianity led to solidarity between people separated by ethnicity, class, race, and national boundaries. This solidarity movement made U.S. policy toward Central America one of the most contentious issues of the 1980s.

Transnational mobilizing is not always a positive development. Generally the introduction of allies is regarded as helpful to social movements serving to enhance the political opportunity structures they face (Tarrow 1998). However, research by Maney (2000) qualifies that conclusion. He conducted a study of the transnational network of organizations supporting civil rights demands in Northern Ireland between 1967 and 1972. He found that mobilizing in more than one society complicates the ability of domestic groups to pursue their goals and creates a politics in the society that reflects not only the original disagreement but also the aggregated and multiplied interaction of that disagreement with the politics and cleavages that exist in other societal contexts: "Rather than alleviating tensions, events involving activists from Northern Ireland deepened hostilities by bringing ideologically disparate US support groups into direct contact with one another" (171).

Even with these transnational developments it is important to realize that the religious groups that lobby in Washington have minimal budgets, small staffs, and limited government experience (Hertzke 1988, 70–79;

Zwier 1988). This lack of resources can be offset somewhat by the pursuit of a modest strategy that includes, among other things, attempting to influence the early stages of legislation through contacts with key officials and developing expertise and effective communication skills (Weber and Stanley 1984). Their highly positive images and substantial social prestige have helped religious lobbies enjoy some success, particularly in securing religious liberty or other concerns in which they supported narrow goals. Still, when the pursuit of broad goals such as social justice or world peace puts them in head-to-head competition with entrenched secular lobbies fortified by ample resources, the religious lobbyists seldom win.

Even if they were better endowed with material resources, the religious interest groups would still face the inherent challenge of applying moral standards to items on the public agenda. Foreign policy matters are rarely a simple issue of right and wrong. According to former Illinois Senator Paul Simon (1984), "Practical dilemmas that real-life politicians face do not fit into easily wrapped packages to which moral labels can be attached" (131). As an example, Simon cites a 1977 congressional debate on a bill to renew a federal program that sent American agricultural products to countries facing food shortages (22–23). When a representative introduced an amendment to prohibit the purchase of tobacco for export under the program, Simon faced a moral dilemma. Because tobacco was a significant crop in nearly a hundred House districts, the amendment might endanger support for the program, resulting possibly in the "clearly immoral" denial of food to starving people. Yet without the amendment, the government would spend money that could buy food for nine hundred thousand hungry people on a product with lethal consequences for public health. As Simon asked rhetorically, "What could be a clearer moral issue?" The testimony of other legislators and administrators amplified Simon's conclusion that policymakers normally confront choices between conflicting moral norms, rather than simply between good and evil (Haughey 1979).

CONCLUSION

This chapter has examined the political opportunities that structure and limit religious groups engaged in political activity. Even with the motive and the means to act politically, religious groups face considerable hurdles in their ability to influence public policy. These hurdles may be high or low depending on the religious cultural environment, partisan political alignments, influential allies, and the nature of the policy domain. The decision to enter the political arena, whether taken by a religious group of its own volition or virtually commanded by external authorities, may impose a significant cost. Political conflict is characterized by disagreement, strife, and competition. In associating itself with such a process—or being seen as part of it—the church could lose its reputation as a place apart.

Yet, paradoxically, abstention from politics may also diminish the church's stature. If members of the community perceive religious values as relevant to a political issue or under threat from some external actor, they may lose faith in a church that stands idly by. Because religious values are so all-encompassing and couched in a universal language, indifference is not really an option.

7

Religion and Public Opinion

Political issues reflecting religious values figure prominently on the American agenda. Think of the political debate surrounding issues such as abortion, gay marriage, gay rights, stem cell research, the teaching of creationism, euthanasia, public displays of the Ten Commandments, the words "under God" in the Pledge of Allegiance, and prayer in schools. All these reveal, more or less overtly, the application of religious and moral principles to political life. Beyond these morality issues, we can find strong moral arguments in support of or in opposition to particular policies about war, access to health care, immigration, support for the poor and elderly, gun control, crime and punishment, racial and ethnic matters, the environment, fiscal and economic priorities, and foreign relations. If competition over the moral order brings culture into politics (Leege et al. 2002), then politics takes on a religious dimension whenever morality is defined by religious considerations. Twenty years ago in his speech to the 1992 Republican National Convention, Pat Buchanan famously declared, "There is a religious war going on in our country for the soul of America. It is a cultural war, as critical to the kind of nation we will one day be as was the Cold War itself."[1] Even today, some, like Fox News commentator Bill O'Reilly, continue to define themselves as combatants in the war:

> I have chosen to jump into the fray and become a warrior in the vicious culture war that is currently underway in the United States of America. And war is exactly the right term. On the one side of the battlefield are the armies of the traditionalists like me. . . . On the other are the committed forces of the secular-progressive movement that want to change America dramatically.[2]

While Buchanan and O'Reilly exaggerate in likening American politics to murderous religious wars, bellicose terminology has become the norm in describing the relationship between religion and politics in the United States.

In the past few elections journalists have tried to capture the nature of this dynamic in characterizing America as split between the so-called red and blue states. The red states are full of God-fearing Republicans; the blue states are dominated by somewhat secular Democrats. While this distinction has gotten a lot of traction in the past several years, examining the distribution of public opinion helps to highlight its limits and expose it as a gross oversimplification. Most American states and the political attitudes of the people that live in them are some shade of purple—the combination of blue and red. Looking at the degree of overlap between the political positions of red- and blue-state citizens, there is a good deal of common ground on many issues (Levendusky and Pope 2011).

Moreover, similar percentages of people are very involved in church activities in red and blue states. Similar percentages think churches should stay out of politics. Majorities of people in both red and blue states say that religion is very important in their lives. Similar percentages of evangelical Christians are found in both environments (Fiorina, Abrams, and Pope 2005, 17–21). Governor Romney and President Obama each enjoyed substantial support from religious constituencies. While conservative Protestants and Latter-Day Saints backed Romney, Jews, black Protestants, Muslims, liberal Protestants, and Catholics all favored Obama. Also important, in the last two presidential elections moral-cultural issues have not been particularly salient. Reflecting on the election, *Washington Post* columnist E. J. Dionne observed, "We did not see a sharpening of the battles over religion and culture. . . . The culture wars went into recession along with the economy." It may be premature to announce an end to these conflicts, because differences in moral-cultural politics remain. However, in the 2008 and 2012 presidential elections people voted on classic "guns and butter"–type issues—primarily U.S. foreign policy, especially in the Middle East and the economy.

This chapter examines the extent to which religion divides the nation on political issues. How sharply are religious differences reflected in American public opinion? Our review of public opinion data in chapter 2 demonstrated that there are important differences between religious groups. For example, evangelical Protestants are usually politically conservative; Jews and seculars are more reliably liberal. However, most groups exhibit ideological diversity across the range of political issues. Moreover, the clearest distinctions between religious groups are seen on a relatively limited number of moral-cultural issues—and even on these issues considerable variation of opinion persists within the religious groups. Finally, even when there are differences between religious groups, the degree of separation in their political attitudes is not always so extreme as to be accurately described as polarized. Such polarization, where it exists, has more to do with electoral and party developments at the elite level than with radical religious rifts in American public opinion. To get a better sense of the politics of religious groups, we again use the American National Election Study (ANES) data we first examined in chapter 2 to look at public opinion in four policy domains: economic values, moral-cultural issues, social justice concerns, and foreign policy.[3]

ECONOMIC LIBERALISM

Since the 1930s, the domestic policy debate in the United States has been dominated by disagreement about the role of government. Today, the most salient political conflicts in Washington are between Tea Party congressional representatives and their supporters, who want to increase fiscal responsibility by cutting government programs, and the advocates of an active government, who have traditionally managed to guide public policy. Thus, the question of government's scope and effort is the logical starting place to study religious groups' attitudes on public issues. The ANES inquires directly about this principle through two of its standard questions. The first asks whether the government should see to it "that every person has a job and a good standard of living" or whether "government should just let every person get ahead on their own." The second asks whether "the government should provide fewer services, even in areas such as health and education, in order to reduce spending" or whether "it is important for the government to provide many more services even if it means an increase in spending." Together these questions give a good indication of a respondent's support for economic liberalism and their ideas about the appropriate role of government in society.

Figure 7.1 reports results from the first question about the government's responsibility. In this figure, religious groups are arrayed by the percentage inclined toward the government taking responsibility for jobs and the standard of living. Although too few Muslims are included in the survey to analyze, we find that racial and ethnic minorities are the most supportive of economic liberalism. More than half of all black Protestants reported that the government should do more to ensure jobs and a standard of living. Expressing similar sentiments, although in smaller percentages, were Hispanic Catholics, Hispanic Protestants, Jews, and seculars. Less than 30 percent of respondents who were Catholics, mainline Protestants, Latter-Day Saints, and evangelicals supported increased government responsibility.

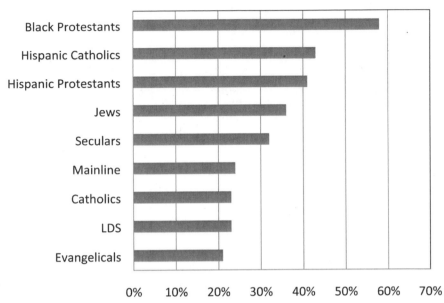

Figure 7.1.   Economic Liberalism by Religious Tradition

Almost an identical pattern emerges on the second indicator of economic liberalism, support for additional government services even if it means an increase in spending. Figure 7.2 reveals minorities were more comfortable with a larger governmental role in society than other groups. What is interesting for every religious group is how much higher support for government services was than the first measure of economic liberalism, the guarantee of a job and standard of living.

In the midst of one of the worst economic recessions in American history, people seemed to reject the idea that the government should guarantee a job and a standard of living, but clearly they wanted the government to do more to help them. Although many commentators believe that moral-cultural values define partisan identity, these data suggest that partisan alignments in contemporary politics are still structured by economic policy differences. Consistent with their views of the appropriate role of government in society, blacks, Hispanics, Jews, and seculars are more likely to support the Democratic Party than evangelical Protestants and Latter-Day Saints, who are more reliably Republican. Catholics and mainline Protestants, who were found in the middle categories on each measure in the past few years, have acted as swing voters, vacillating in their partisan vote choice. Feldman and Zaller (1992) demonstrated that people who opposed a greater role for the government were more likely to justify their positions based on "moral" and individualistic principles.

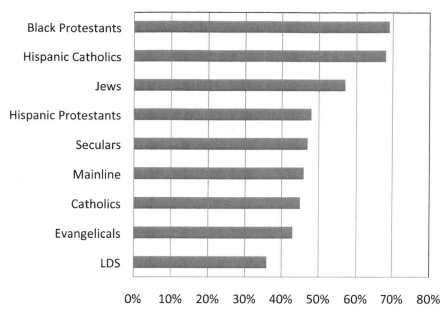

Figure 7.2. Support for Government Services by Religious Tradition

As Barker and Carman (2000) show, conservative Protestant doctrine both directly and indirectly engenders political preferences for individualist economic policies among whites. It is interesting that these same conservative Protestant religious ideas have the opposite effect on black Protestants, in whom biblical literalism is related to greater government support of the poor (McDaniel and Ellison 2008).

Economic policy preferences express status differences between religious groups as well as socioeconomic inequalities. American religion remains socioeconomically stratified and patterned by theology, race, and ethnicity (Smith and Farris 2005). Evangelical Christians, Mormons, established mainline Protestant groups, and Catholics, who have experienced considerable upward mobility in the past forty years (Park and Reimer 2002), are less inclined to support an expansion of the government's role in society. Better-educated conservative Protestants are considerably more conservative economically than their coreligionists without as much education (Felson and Kindell 2007). Despite debates about moral issues in public life, vote choice usually comes down to the New Deal debate about the appropriate role of government in American life. Recent research suggests that the effect of religious identification is structured by race and contingent on location in the stratification order (Hirschl, Booth, and Glenna 2009).

MORAL-CULTURAL ISSUES

When most people think about religion and politics, they think about the whole constellation of moral-cultural issues that have dominated public debate since the 1970s. After the social upheaval of the 1960s, people began to question traditional social and gender roles. At the heart of these issues is whether society is best served by a traditional or by a progressive view of moral and social values in public policy. As we explore in greater detail in chapter 11, supporters of the progressive view believe that morals and truths must be adapted to changing societal circumstances. Supporters of the traditional perspective believe these kinds of moral adjustments undermine the well-being of society, and many contend that they violate the very laws of God. Much of the impetus for the politicization of the Christian Right beginning in the 1980s revolved around the desire to restore and protect "traditional family values." The fact that these new political issues seemed to engage personal morality linked them to religion in novel ways (Shafer and Claggett 1995) and brought religiosity into the public square and into partisan politics to a much greater degree (Layman 1999). Some scholars suggest that promoting traditional public policies on sex and gender issues has become central to certain conservative faith traditions (Smith et al. 1998).

Accordingly, we now examine the relationship between religion and public opinion for the rights of women and the rights of homosexuals. We also examine whether cleavages on women's rights and gay rights are better characterized by divisions between faith traditions or by divisions between more and less religious groups within religious communities, as argued by the "culture war" thesis. As we explained in chapter 5, Hunter (1991) argued that the culture war cuts across religious traditions and divides society into orthodox forces with unyielding principles and progressive supporters with shifting standards. We find here some salient divisions between and within religious groups but nothing of sufficient scope and magnitude to constitute a war.

There is no doubt that the social changes of the latter part of the twentieth century have unnerved Americans. The ANES asks a series of questions about the overall state of the country and what should be done about it. Questions include whether new lifestyles are destroying society, whether society would be better off emphasizing traditional family ties, whether there should be toleration for moral differences, and whether morals should be adjusted to a changing world. Table 7.1 reports these results.

Clear majorities of nearly all the religious traditions agree that newer lifestyles are breaking down society. The notable exceptions to this pattern are Jews and seculars, but even near majorities of these groups agree with

Table 7.1. Societal Attitudes by Religious Tradition (% agreeing)

	New Lifestyles Destroying Society	Better with Traditional Family Ties	Tolerate Morals of Others	Adjust Morals
Evangelical Protestants	74	86	52	35
Mainline Protestants	65	78	58	39
Black Protestants	65	76	69	59
Hispanic Protestants	73	77	61	50
Catholics	61	73	64	48
Hispanic Catholics	62	72	68	68
Jews	40	54	85	61
Latter-Day Saints	75	80	60	25
Seculars	46	50	73	73

the statement. There is also broad support for the idea that the country would have fewer problems if there were more emphasis on traditional family ties. Overwhelming numbers of all religious groups and half of all seculars said that this would be helpful. What constitutes a traditional family tie is not defined by the ANES, so there is broad latitude in the interpretation of this question. Still, people also report that they are willing to be tolerant of those who live according to moral values that differ from their own. Seculars and Jews are most enthusiastic about the need to tolerate different standards of morality. The lowest level of agreement was found among evangelicals, but even half of them agree that it is important. On these questions, there is more unanimity of opinion in some traditions than others, but in almost every instance, the majority opinion about the threat from new lifestyles, the propriety of emphasizing traditional ties, and toleration for different moral standards was the same.

Religious groups are most divided about whether views of morality should be adjusted to a changing world. More than 60 percent of Hispanic Catholics, Jews, black Protestants, and seculars agree that morals should be adjusted. This is compared to a little more than a third of evangelical and mainline Protestants and only about a quarter of Latter-Day Saints who hold more conservative views. Hispanic Protestants and Catholics again occupied a midrange position—more supportive than the most conservative groups, less supportive than the most liberal. While in the moderate category on this issue, it is interesting that Hispanic Protestants were much less liberal than Hispanic Catholics. Hispanic Protestants are of higher status than their Catholic counterparts and often more conservative in their approach to political matters (Hunt 2001).

Most Americans are not obsessed with cultural issues. Rather, many people are best described as ambivalent (Craig et al. 2005; Craig and Martinez 2005). We found broad agreement across religious traditions about the moral and cultural challenges faced by the United States. Concerns about "new" lifestyles and the decline of the traditional family are almost universal. Yet people also want to get along with one another, reflected by the stated willingness in all religious traditions to tolerate those who live according to different moral standards even if, in some traditions, it requires adjusting standards of morality to changing times. Because it is possible to tolerate the standards of others without rejecting your own, there is opportunity in American politics for religion to be much less divisive than many expect. Moreover, as we shall see, consensus exists across religious traditions even on some specific moral-cultural issues.

Women's Rights

The politics of women's rights encompasses all the questions about the place of traditional social and moral values in public policy. What does it mean to families and to society if women have equal rights and if the roles of men and women are not differentiated? Shouldn't women have the right to control their destinies? Can women control their destiny without the fullest range of reproductive options? The increasing educational and economic opportunities that women began to experience in the 1970s brought these issues to the fore (see chapter 11). Feminist calls for equality differed sharply from conservative religious teaching about female submission. Outraged by *Roe v. Wade*, religious conservatives effectively stymied the ratification of the equal rights amendment and began to mobilize against abortion rights. Because of the political salience of these issues, parties started using them for partisan advantage, further defining and magnifying cultural conflict.

Yet figure 7.3 demonstrates that respondents overwhelmingly favor equality for women regardless of tradition. The ANES asked whether respondents thought a woman's place was in the home or that men and women should have an equal role in society. The figure reports the percentage of respondents supportive of equal gender roles.[4] Nearly 75 percent of every religious tradition reported that men and women should have an equal role in business, industry, and government, as opposed to a woman's place being in the home. The only exception to this trend was Latter-Day Saints, but even among this group a clear majority supports the principle of gender equality. As the figure shows further, even when we control for the importance of religion, support for the equal rights of women does not decline significantly. Those for whom religion is important are as supportive as the tradition is overall. At the abstract level, which the question emphasizes, there are few distinctions in support for the equal rights of women based on religion or level of religious commitment.

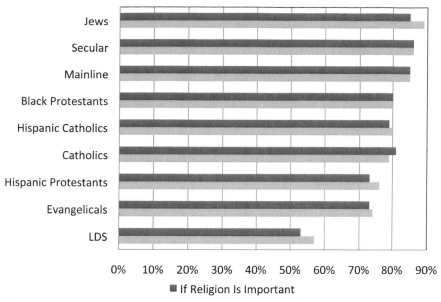

0%   10%   20%   30%   40%   50%   60%   70%   80%   90%

■ If Religion Is Important

Figure 7.3. Support for Gender Equality by Religious Tradition

However, the abortion issue exemplifies the fact that the nature of the relationship between religion and gender equality is complicated. Abortion is the definitive issue for the women's rights movement. Reproductive choices epitomize freedom for women's rights proponents (Mansbridge 1986). It is also substantively and symbolically significant for religious conservatives. In addition to their fundamental concerns about when life begins, abortion represents to them everything that is wrong with contemporary cultural change—excessive individualism and personal liberties taken to unwise, unethical, and immoral extremes.

Table 7.2 shows how the religious traditions differ on the abortion issue.[5] National Election Study participants were given a chance to declare whether and under what circumstances pregnant women should be permitted by law to obtain abortions. The choices range from a complete prohibition of abortion to support for complete discretion by the pregnant woman. There is considerable variation between the religious groups on this issue. Jews and seculars support the unadorned pro-choice position. Eighty percent of Jews and nearly 60 percent of seculars believe that a woman should have the right to choose an abortion if she wants to do so without regard to circumstances. We were surprised to see how few people embraced the other extreme, the belief that abortion should never be permitted. In every religious tradition except for evangelical and Hispanic Protestantism, more people committed to the pro-choice extreme than the pro-life extreme. Even among the two excep-

Table 7.2. Abortion Attitudes by Religious Tradition (%)

	Never	Rape, Incest, or Mother's Health	With Established Need	Always	Total
Evangelical Protestants	20	37	19	24	100
Mainline Protestants	8	24	25	43	100
Black Protestants	13	29	14	44	100
Hispanic Protestants	15	38	23	23	99
Catholics	19	20	24	36	99
Hispanic Catholics	28	26	13	33	100
Seculars	3	23	11	62	99
Jews	0	8	13	79	100
Latter-Day Saints	11	54	9	26	100

Note: Total percentages may be less than 100 due to rounding.

tions, the balance was nearly even. In general, the most pro-life groups have retreated from total prohibition is to a position that accepts abortion under some conditions.

It is notable how much the distribution of these data differ from patterns we observed on the equal role question in figure 7.3. In the minds of most Americans, it seems, the general question of equal rights for women is distinct from abortion as evidenced by their very different support patterns. While most groups were committed to an equal role for women, they differed much more in their views on abortion. When we compare the abortion pattern with the economic liberalism distribution summarized earlier, the complexity of American religious politics begins to emerge. Black Protestants, overwhelmingly liberal on economic policy, were split on the abortion question. The fact that these data reveal them to be more divided on this issue is consistent with other research that shows that they may be moderating somewhat on abortion (Evans 2002; Strickler and Danigelis 2002). Overall they are dramatically less liberal on the abortion question than on economic policy measures. In this regard, many African Americans are conflicted ideologically, as are other groups, including Hispanic Catholics and Hispanic Protestants.

Mainline Protestants provide an example from the other end of the spectrum. They are relatively conservative on matters of economic policy but are not consistently conservative on the abortion issue. In fact, more mainline Protestants support choice than oppose it. These differences across issue areas should prompt us to recognize that religious groups may share a common political space on some questions but part company and find new allies on other issues.

Abortion cleavages are even more clearly seen when we examine the differences of opinion between those most committed to their religious

Table 7.3. Support for Abortion by Religious Tradition and Religious Importance (%)

	Religion Important	Religion Not Important
Evangelical Protestants	18	53
Mainline Protestants	42	52
Black Protestants	42	67
Hispanic Protestants	19	57
Catholics	35	40
Hispanic Catholics	35	60
Seculars	35	74
Jews	73	87
Latter-Day Saints	16	62

faith and those who report it is not important in their lives. Table 7.3 reports these results. It shows that in every religious tradition except Catholics, majorities of those for whom religion is not important support a woman's right to choose. The difference between the involved and the uninvolved members of the same faith tradition often exceed the gap between the various religious groups. For example, Hispanic Protestants who consider religion unimportant in their lives more closely resemble the religiously unaffiliated on this question than the white evangelical Protestants with whom they share a common religious perspective. There is a "values" component to the abortion issue, but we still find wide variations in views about abortion among the religious and nonreligious in many traditions. The "orthodox," applying Hunter's term to those who consider religion important in their lives, hardly form a uniform bloc of pro-life sentiment.

Gay Rights

Along with women's rights, gay rights has dominated contemporary public debate over morality. Gay men and lesbian activists have worked tirelessly for the civil rights of homosexual Americans, achieving notable victories represented by the ending of the military's "don't ask, don't tell" policy, the legalization of gay marriage in sixteen states and the District of Columbia, and the defeat of the Defense of Marriage Act before the U.S. Supreme Court in 2013. Though, nationally, gay Americans are still subject to discrimination, public opinion on these issues suggests a growing tolerance—even among religious people.

The ANES asked respondents, "Should same-sex couples be allowed to marry or do you think they should not be allowed to marry?" The number of respondents who volunteered that same-sex couples should not be allowed to marry but to form civil unions was also recorded. Figure 7.4 displays these results. What is perhaps most striking is that in every

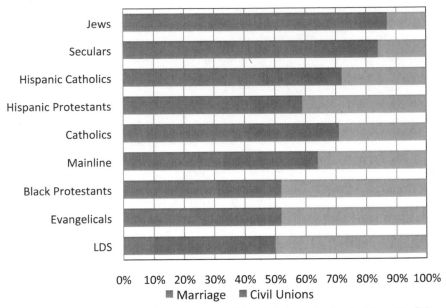

0%   10% 20% 30% 40% 50% 60% 70% 80% 90% 100%
■ Marriage   ■ Civil Unions

Figure 7.4.   Support for Legal Recognition of Gay Relationships by Religious Tradition

religious tradition at least half of the respondents felt that there should be some legal recognition of committed gay relationships. This is an indication of how attitudes toward gay rights have moderated over time. Polls conducted as recently as the 2004 presidential election cycle showed that large majorities of several religious traditions opposed any legal recognition of gay relationships.[6]

Still, even given this general trend, attitudes toward gay marriage remain polarized across religious traditions. Broadly, the religious traditions can be divided into three groups. In the first group, near majorities of evangelicals, Latter-Day Saints, and black Protestants oppose any legal recognition of homosexual relationships. At the other end of the continuum, more than 60 percent of seculars and more than 75 percent of Jews favor legal marriage, and almost 90 percent of both groups favor either marriage or civil unions. The opinions of the other religious traditions are divided more evenly, with sizable portions in each tradition favoring marriage, opposing marriage, and supporting civil unions. Mainline Protestants and Catholics are split about evenly among the three categories. Equal numbers of Hispanic Protestants oppose gay marriage as favor it, with only about 20 percent supporting civil unions. Among Hispanic Protestants a plurality favor marriage, but more than half either oppose it or only support civil unions.

Table 7.4. Opposition to Gay Rights by Religious Tradition (%)

	Gay Adoption	Anti-Job Discrimination	Military Service
Evangelical Protestants	59	34	29
Mainline Protestants	54	24	18
Black Protestants	58	35	23
Hispanic Protestants	50	32	27
Catholics	44	22	21
Hispanic Catholics	42	26	20
Seculars	29	20	16
Jews	13	13	10
Latter-Day Saints	58	44	30

Table 7.4 records levels of opposition to gay rights on several other issues. Respondents were asked whether they thought homosexual couples should be legally permitted to adopt children, whether they favored or opposed laws to protect homosexuals against job discrimination, and whether they thought homosexuals should be allowed to serve in the United States Armed Forces.

The table indicates American public opinion is most divided on the issue of adoption by gay people. With the exception of Jews and seculars, who are clearly supportive, the other religious traditions are split on the subject. Evangelical Protestants, black Protestants, Latter-Day Saints, and mainline Protestants are inclined to oppose it, but large minorities in each tradition are supportive. Similarly, a majority of Hispanic Catholics and other Catholics are inclined to support gay adoption, but large minorities in each tradition oppose it. Hispanic Protestants are evenly divided for and against.

The country is not hopelessly divided along religious lines on matters of gay rights. As table 7.4 records, with the exception of marriage and adoption, there is a growing consensus on gay rights issues. Only minorities of each religious tradition—including vehement opponents of gay marriage such as evangelical Protestants and Mormons—claim to oppose laws that protect homosexuals against discrimination. It is also interesting that many black and Hispanic Protestants who are very opposed to gay marriage and adoption are significantly less opposed to antidiscrimination legislation. The minority experiences of these groups may mediate their religious perspectives on the question of job discrimination and make them much more likely to support the protection of rights.

Even more support across religious traditions is observed for permitting homosexuals to serve in the military. No more than a third of the groups most strongly against gays in the military (Latter-Day-Saints, evangelical Protestants, and Hispanic Protestants) indicated opposition. In the other traditions, only about one in five adherents opposed gay service in the military, and the proportion was lower still among American Jews and seculars. When one divides survey respondents according to the importance of religion in their lives, as we did for abortion attitudes in table 7.3, no significant differences are seen (not shown). Faithful adherents are more opposed than those who are less committed, but not dramatically so. Based on public opinion data it was not politically risky for President Obama to end the controversial "don't ask, don't tell" policy because most people indicate they do not have a problem with gay troops. Though his position in support of gay marriage is a little more contentious and there are significant divisions based on religious affiliations, several recent studies report that overall, American attitudes on gay rights issues are moderating (Fiorina, Abrams, and Pope 2005; Loftus 2001). There is no evidence that Americans cannot come to consensus even on these kinds of highly charged religious and cultural matters. Even on highly symbolic issues like gay rights, the empirical data for deep and abiding religious cleavages is at best mixed.

SOCIAL JUSTICE

While moral-cultural issues focus on the regulation of personal behavior, social justice issues emphasize whether a society distributes its benefits fairly and equitably. Social justice incorporates important democratic principles such as equal rights and equal opportunity as well as practical considerations about the availability of food and affordable shelter. Such issues have to do with ensuring that there is indeed "freedom and justice for all." As we detailed in chapter 6, churches have long been concerned with issues of social justice, primarily through the provision of material resources but also through lobbying efforts to encourage the government to take greater responsibility for the welfare of citizens. However, while clear patterns of religious interaction are evident at the elite level in the area of social justice, identifying the effects of religion on public opinion has been much more elusive. How religion shapes attitudes about equality, individual responsibility, justice, and race is complicated and still not well understood. In this chapter, we explore two issues to get a feel for the relationship between religion and social justice. We first examine support for equal opportunity and then for regulations to protect the environment.

There is broad support for egalitarian principles of equal opportunity. The American National Election Study asked respondents whether "our society should do whatever is necessary to make sure that everyone has an equal opportunity to succeed."[7] Nearly 90 percent of people in every religious tradition agreed with the importance of ensuring equal opportunity for all (not shown). However, when asked to respond to the statement "the country would be better off if we worried less about how equal people are" a different pattern emerges.[8] Figure 7.5 indicates that for the most part, the religious traditions of racial minorities and Jews are less likely to agree with the statement that America would be better off if it worried less about equality than the traditions of racial majorities in the United States, mainline Protestants, Catholics, evangelical Protestants, and Latter-Day Saints. That the majority religious traditions support the importance of ensuring equal opportunity but are more likely to reflect a belief that the country would be better off if we worried less about it is consistent with a paradox about equality more generally in the United States. White Americans believe in the principle of equality, yet they are consistently opposed to government programs designed to produce it (Sears, Sidanious, and Bobo 2000). White evangelical Protestants are more likely to hold individualistic explanations for racial inequality than other Americans (Emerson, Smith, and Sikkink 1999; Emerson and Smith 2000). Logically, if one believes that structural causes are not the reason for inequality, it follows that structural solutions such as government programs are not required.

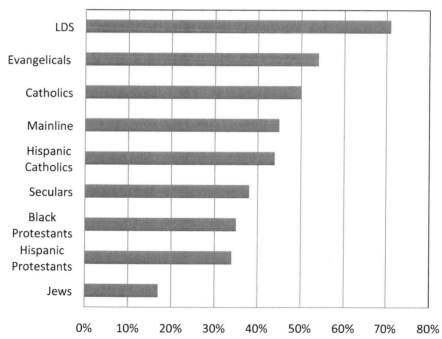

Figure 7.5. Believe Country Would Be Better Off If Worried Less about Equality by Religious Tradition

Still, opposition to structural remedies extends far beyond just white conservative Protestants. Previous polls indicated that 80 percent of evangelicals, mainline Protestants, Catholics, Latter-Day Saints, and the liberal stalwart, American Jews, opposed affirmative action.[9] Moreover, research indicates that blacks who are members of white religious traditions are consistently more likely to affirm structural causes for racial inequality even though whites in the tradition do not (Hinojosa and Park 2004; Cavendish, Welch, and Leege 1998). This observation suggests that the differences among religious traditions that we notice reflect racial and socioeconomic differences more than true religious distinctions. As Hinojosa and Park (2004, 235) and others have observed, "religion as structured in America does little to alter racial subgroups and may in fact enforce racial divides."

A recent poll by the Public Religion Research Institute asked respondents whether when Jesus and the prophets were talking about helping the poor, they were talking primarily about our obligation to create a just society or charitable acts by individuals. A majority of white Catholics and white mainline Protestants, and nearly two-thirds of white evangelicals said charitable acts by individuals. A majority of black Protestants and Hispanic Catholics said Jesus meant we had an obligation to create a just society. Individuals who were part of the same faith tradition, but different races, held very different opinions about the religious imperative inherent in social justice.

Social justice also encompasses concern for the environment. Although politics still primarily revolve around socioeconomic issues, there is today a greater concern with what social analysts call "postmaterial" values. Unlike concerns for economic security, postmaterialism focuses on quality-of-life issues such as freedom, creativity, individual autonomy, and self-expression. Interestingly, this increase in concern with postmaterial values has coincided with increases in the politicization of religion. The two impulses come head to head over the issue of the environment. For the most part, the conventional wisdom is that Christianity, and particularly orthodox Christianity, leads people to be opposed to environmental regulation. Apparently the biblical mandate to "be fruitful and multiply, replenish the Earth, subdue it and have dominion" serves to justify environmental degradation. In an influential essay published in 1967, Lynn White argued that the Christian belief in dominion over nature was a major factor in the ecological crisis of the West. According to this logic, Christians should show no interest in environmental protection and those most involved in churches should be the least environmentally conscious of all.

The ANES allows for a test of this hypothesis. Respondents were asked to indicate their position on a seven-point scale ranging from 1 ("Protect the environment even if it costs jobs and the standard of living") to 7

("Jobs and the standard of living are more important than the environment"). Examining the average position of each of the religious groups on the scale, only evangelical Protestants, Latter-Day Saints, and Jews emerged as distinctive from seculars (not shown). As on many other issues, Jews were more liberal. Latter-Day Saints and evangelicals were more conservative. This seems to provide some tentative support for White's thesis. Foltz (2000) found that the teachings of the Latter-Day Saints church may be particularly conducive to the dominion mentality and that people with the dominion preferences are less likely to support environmental programs. Other studies have found that Mormons are less environmentally oriented than other local residents (Brehm and Eisenhauer 2006; Schultz 2000), although disentangling the effects of religion, political identity, and regional culture can be challenging (Peterson and Liu 2008). Still, the differences between the religious groups are not dramatic. The mean for seculars is 3.8; for evangelicals and Latter-Day Saints, it is 4.4. As a practical matter conservative Christians and Mormons demonstrate nearly as much concern for the environment as people who have no religious affiliation at all. When we control for the importance of religion, no significant differences to this pattern emerge. Contrary to White's hypothesis, attitudes toward the environment are not heavily influenced by religious tradition (Hayes and Marangudakis 2000).

More recent research suggests that one of the major reasons Christianity does not lead to more definitive positions on the environment is that the Bible can be used to support both pro-environmental and anti-environmental stances. Although early research on mass environmental attitudes found a greater disposition to assert human dominion among people with a Judeo-Christian background (see Shaiko 1987) and an apparent link between religious involvement and support for environmental exploitation (Eckberg and Blocker 1989; Kanagy and Willits 1993), subsequent research has qualified that conclusion. These more recent studies contend that hostility to environmental protection is concentrated among those Christians who hold specific views about the relationship between humanity and nature (Woodrum and Hoban 1994; Wolkomir et al. 1995) or who perceive the end of the world as imminent (Guth et al. 1993, 1994; Boyd 1999). Many Christians believe that they are "stewards" of the environment and accountable to God for how they care for it (Kearns 1996). Djupe and Hunt's research finds little support for White's position among the mainline congregants they surveyed. To the contrary, members held fairly pronounced pro-environmental views, and the social communication that took place in the church reinforced this position (Djupe and Hunt 2009). The emerging debate among evangelicals about "creation care" has conservative Christians asking what Jesus would do about global warming and whether he would drive an SUV.

These two issues suggest that the influence of religion on public opinion for social justice issues is much more ambiguous than it is for moral-cultural issues. This underscores that significant group differences do not extend to all specific issues and controversies on the American agenda. It is important to remember that religious networks and religious ideas cannot be used to access support for all issues in the same manner. Despite elite mobilization, public opinion in the area of social justice is not straightforwardly influenced by religion.

FOREIGN POLICY

Religious differences in the domain of foreign policy have also proved particularly elusive. To a large degree, foreign policy opinions are typically less stable and informed than attitudes on domestic policy questions, and group differences of any kind are less common. In the 1950s and the 1960s, when the major issue of foreign policy was clearly the Cold War, strong religious differences were apparent. As a rule, evangelical Protestants and Roman Catholics tended to call for a more aggressive military posture against Communism than Jews, seculars, African Americans, and mainline Protestants (Wald 1994). With the end of the Cold War and the collapse of the Soviet bloc, the debate over international policy entered a new era in which opinion seems to crystallize differently based on each particular case or controversy. During the Gulf War, an unlikely alliance of evangelical Protestants and Jews was most inclined to accept the case for American military intervention, while the mainline churches and Roman Catholicism were far more dovish (Jelen 1994). Still, the nature of military intervention has expanded significantly within the past several decades, with America increasingly willing to undertake humanitarian and peacekeeping missions in many places in the world. On a generic question in the ANES about whether this country would be better off if we just stayed home and did not concern ourselves with problems in other parts of the world, roughly 70 percent of each of the religious traditions disagreed with the statement (not shown). These data indicate that there is still strong support for engaging world problems. Which problems to engage and in what manner are highly contingent on the politics around the issue involved.

Thus, in many areas of foreign policy, religious tradition does not differentiate between those in favor of increased activity and those opposed to it. It does not have a significant influence on attitudes toward defense spending. ANES respondents were asked on a seven-point scale whether defense spending should be increased or decreased. The average mean for all respondents was 4.2. Most religious traditions could not be distinguished from one another in a statistically significant way. Evangelical Protestants were a little more likely to support increases (mean of 4.6), and, reflecting their liberalism, Jews (mean of 3.3) and black Protestants (mean of 3.7) were a little less likely to support increases. However, substantively, as one can see from the averages, the differences are not large. Religion has only a marginal effect on whether people would like to see more money go to defense.[10]

On attitudes toward the Iraq War, however, this marginal effect is increased. Although U.S. troop withdrawal from Iraq was completed in December 2011, continued concerns about the region and U.S. involvement in disputes there have structured foreign policy positions. The ANES asked participants whether they approved of the president's handling of the war with Iraq. Figure 7.6 reflects that the war in Iraq was very unpopular among American citizens. Still, amid this reality there are some distinctions based on religious tradition. The largest remaining reservoirs of approval were among evangelicals and Latter-Day Saints. Forty percent of evangelicals and more than 30 percent of Latter-Day Saints still felt positively about the president's war strategy. For mainline Protestants and Catholics, that number dropped to about one-quarter, and for the remaining faith traditions, support fell to less than 20 percent,

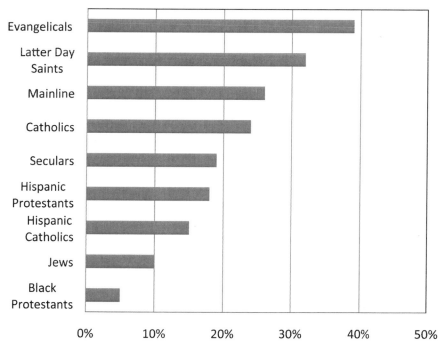

Figure 7.6.   Support President's Handling of War with Iraq by Religious Tradition

with even lower levels of approval coming from Jews at 10 percent and black Protestants at just 5 percent. Other questions in the ANES about whether the United States should have sent troops to fight the war in Iraq in 2003 and whether the war in Iraq decreased the threat of terrorism reveal similar results (not shown). Evangelical protestants and Latter-Day Saints consistently are most supportive of U.S. policy, Jews and black Protestants are least supportive, and the other traditions fall somewhere in the middle, though majorities in these remaining traditions expressed dissatisfaction with the war. This finding of a positive correlation between military engagement in Iraq and evangelical Protestantism has been found in other studies (Smidt 2005) and is consistent with recent research that indicates religious affiliation has a powerful and independent impact on foreign policy attitudes (Taydas, Kentmen, and Olson 2012). There is some evidence this relationship may be explained by the extent to which a respondent wants religion and politics to be comingled. One interesting study found that a Democrat who supports a close relationship between religion and politics is more likely to approve of U.S. foreign policy toward Iraq than a Republican who does not share these views (Froese and Menken 2009).

WHAT CULTURE WAR?

Recently, Pope Francis expressed concern that the Catholic Church had grown obsessed with homosexuality, abortion, and birth control and that the focus on these issues was detracting from the larger mission of the church. The same concern could be expressed when it comes to reporting on politics in the United States. Focusing on a few highly symbolic social issues without understanding the true pattern of public opinion gives the false impression that the United States is under siege in the culture war. For example, when Louie Giglio was forced to decline President Obama's invitation to give the benediction at his second inauguration because of controversial remarks he made about the morality of homosexuality in the 1990s, it looked like Giglio was a typical evangelical combatant in another culture war skirmish. What most missed was that Giglio, an Atlanta pastor, was founder of the Passion Movement, a group that has organized hundreds of thousands of high school and college students and raised millions of dollars to oppose human trafficking and sex slavery. On these issues, he and the Obama administration are aligned. It is easy to miss points of commonality. As for opposition to gay rights, Giglio said it was no longer in "his range of priorities," indicating that even when there are political differences, they are not always especially salient.[11]

The examination of the relationship between religion and politics in this chapter suggests that agreement and consensus is more common in American public opinion than the oft-used culture war analogy might suggest. Americans are universally concerned about the social impact of social and technological changes and "new" lifestyles. There is broad unanimity of opinion about a woman's role in society and high levels of support for gays in the military and laws to protect homosexuals against discrimination. Americans are not significantly divided by religion on social justice, and differences on economic issues reflect socioeconomic realities more than religious distinctions. They also support the United States' engaging world problems, although they differ by degree in their lack of support for the war with Iraq.

Although some studies suggest political alignments are increasingly tied to moral-cultural cleavages (Layman 1997, 1999, 2001; Layman and Carmines 1997; Kohut et al. 2000; Green et al. 1996), culture war theory has fared more poorly in other systematic studies (Layman and Green 2006; Fiorina, Abrams, and Pope 2005; Clydesdale 1997; Hoffmann and Miller 1997; McConkey 2001; Williams 1997). Using surveys of the general public, Nancy Davis and Robert Robinson (1996) have made direct comparisons of people who subscribe to the central tenets of the orthodox and modern worldviews. They find the two groups polarized only on a limited set of social issues involving education, sexuality, abortion, and gender. Those who fit the orthodox profile are indistinguishable from progressives in their racial thinking and often prove more liberal on economic issues (see also Johnson and Tamney 2001). Other observers contend that the emphasis on polarization in culture war theory obscures a growing complexity and ambivalence in the broader culture (Ray 1997). After conducting in-depth interviews with hundreds of religiously diverse Americans in a cross-section of middle-class communities, Alan Wolfe (1998, 279) found many conservatives exhibited substantial tolerance for people whose behavior they disliked and liberals who worried about the loss of moral compass in American society. "It is a basic truth of American society," he writes, "that no one is a traditionalist or a modernist, but that everyone lives with varying degrees of both." Recent research by Putnam and Campbell (2010) suggest that, for the most part, Americans extend grace to one another. A commitment to pluralism keeps insurmountable religious differences from emerging. Americans are so exposed to difference in culture and religion that tolerance is the result. Even if "Aunt Susan" or "Pal Al" don't believe the way they do, most Americans refuse to believe that they are damned and seek to pursue the common good with them. This extends to politics. Fiorina and colleagues (2005) explain that while

elites are polarized on the issues, mass public opinion even on contentious matters like abortion and gay rights is not substantially divided.

Even if we grant that there has been some strengthening of religious-
political ties in recent elections, that should not be taken as undeniable
evidence of the severe political polarization implied by the culture war
hypothesis. Religious groups may have developed certain political tendencies without automatically rejecting those who hold different views.
Looking at the views of both seminary professors and parishioners, so-
ciologists Daniel Olson and Jackson Carroll (1992) report that religious
liberals gave the greatest priority to what have been called "social justice"
questions such as poverty and peace, while religious conservatives were
more concerned with sexual morality questions that fit under the "social
issues" umbrella. Although this finding appears to support a culture war
model, the authors emphasize that the two perspectives were usually not
in direct conflict. That is, religious liberals did not reject the conservative
agenda but simply gave it lower priority, while religious conservatives
took the same stance regarding many liberal values. That finding resonates with the observation of a scholar invited to speak to an audience of
religious liberals in an affluent suburb. Amitai Etzioni (1988) notes that
while they were "quite keen to discuss the plight of the homeless, the
American poor, the starving in Africa," the audience rejected his efforts to
discuss crime, family problems, and drug use because those were "right-
wing issues" (2). Rather than a war, this situation seems to resemble a political division of labor as religious groups assume primary responsibility
for certain issues and consign other questions to another realm.

The limited political polarization evident in these findings has its roots
in the presence of mixed tendencies in most religious groups. It helps to
remember that the labels used in religious classification, terms like *evangelical* and *mainline* or *liberal* and *conservative* are simplifications, not rigid
distinctions between sworn enemies. Beyond the Protestant heritage that
unites white evangelicals, black evangelicals, and mainline Protestants,
the three groups share a common Christian fellowship with Catholics
and are also part of a larger Judeo-Christian tradition. Because of these
common origins, we should not be surprised to find progressive and traditional factors operating in each religious tradition, preventing the sharp
division into warring camps that would signal the presence of a culture
war (Ammerman 1994). We need to understand the cultural roots of political differences while remembering that they are differences of degree.

So why do so many people believe that American political life is religiously polarized? In part, the mass media embraces simplistic divisions

between red and blue states or between evangelical Christians and other religious traditions because they help to simply communicate complicated political phenomena. As with any generalization, such simplicity overlooks important details and sometimes distorts the nature of the relationship. The media is not entirely to blame. Another perhaps more important reason is that elite-level partisan politics has indeed become increasingly polarized (Fiorina, Abrams, and Pope 2005). Republicans and Democrats have adopted more extreme positions on issues and have become more ideologically consistent. Many fewer conservative Democrats or liberal Republicans exist today than did thirty years ago. This helps explain why religious cleavages seem to be driving partisan realignment (Layman 1999, 2001) and why the parties seem farther apart on the issues than ever. Parties are using cultural and religious differences to mobilize voters, and they are presenting their positions on these issues in stark terms (Leege et al. 2002). For example, a recent study of American public opinion confirmed that ideological conservatism is largely unrelated to beliefs about the origins of life. Yet pundits and activists seeking to make the evolution debate politically relevant often stake out extreme positions on this issue (Freeman and Houston 2009). Looking at mass opinion— even on most moral-cultural issues—polarization is largely an elite-level phenomenon that simply does not exist at the mass level. Religion is not the dominant dividing line in American politics, just one of many cleavages around which politicians attempt to gain partisan advantage.

This point emphasizes a second important observation about the relationship between religion and public opinion. Religious divisions are not consistent across all policy domains. Recall that even the most consistently liberal groups, Jews and seculars, opposed affirmative action. Although only one issue, it is important to many racial minorities and could exacerbate cleavages among otherwise liberal voters. Black Protestants, liberal on questions about the role of government and very opposed to the war, were among the most conservative groups on gay marriage and gay adoption and somewhat inclined to oppose abortion rights. Hispanic Protestants, who are conservative on a range of issues, strongly support increased government services. In sum, religious traditions are crosspressured ideologically. Catholics are presently swing voters because they are split on almost every issue. Partisan politics may be increasingly polarized, but in some ways this makes it more and not less difficult to mobilize people on the basis of their religious identities.

This examination also highlights the differences between elite behavior and mass opinion. Although the data indicate that the vast majority of mainline Protestants oppose policies such as affirmative action, official church positions can differ. For example, the United Methodist Church and other denominations continue to support and officially endorse affirmative action despite its unpopularity among members. Evangelical elites are stridently against gay rights even though only a minority of their members oppose laws to protect homosexuals against discrimination. It is important always to remember religion operates as an institution as well as a creed and culture and that each can influence public opinion, not always in consistent ways.

Although the relationship between religion and public opinion is not always straightforward, the data indicate that there are important political distinctions related to religious traditions. Notably, the differences between Hispanic Catholics and Hispanic Protestants suggest that religious affiliation matters in politics and may mediate ethnic, racial, and socioeconomic identities.

Finally, despite the attention devoted to values, it is important to recognize that partisan cleavages are still primarily based on socioeconomic realities and most clearly reflect New Deal differences about the appropriate role of government more than anything else. Religion influences public opinion within this context, not separate from it. The distinctiveness of black Protestants from other evangelicals is a clear example of this fact. Religion is an important part of the American cultural and political debate, but it does not wholly define it. Religion is a rich source of motivation for political activity, but it must interact with many other factors.

8

The Political Mobilization
of Evangelical Protestants

The advantage we have is that liberals and feminists don't generally go
to church. They don't gather in one place three days before the election.

—Ralph Reed

The chances are very good you would not be reading this book if it
weren't for the social movement known as the Christian Right. Today,
even people who follow politics casually are aware of the important role
evangelical Protestants play in American political life. In the 1970s, when
the senior author was completing a doctoral dissertation about the role of
religion in elections, most scholars of American politics considered religion a quaint subject having more to do with Prohibition and ancient blue
laws than with contemporary political life. But by 1980, he was besieged
with questions about religion and modern politics from scholars, journalists, and students alike. Once a marginal subject, religion and politics had
suddenly become a hot topic.

The explosion of evangelical political activity associated with the 1980
presidential election helped put that topic on the scholarly map in the
United States. Although we now recognize that the movement had developed years before, the phenomenon first captured headlines in 1976, *Time*
magazine's "Year of the Evangelical," when a "born-again" Southern
Baptist Democrat named Jimmy Carter won the presidency. The movement quickly shifted partisan gears as the so-called New Christian Right
became closely allied with the Republican Party. The leaders of the movement and a sizable number of journalists were quick to credit the new political force with responsibility for Republican capture of the White House

and U.S. Senate in 1980. Although the movement has ebbed and flowed over the past thirty-some years, it has remained a significant presence in American public life (Wilcox and Larson 2006).

This chapter explores the political engagement of evangelical Protestants by focusing on the movement that purports to speak in their name. How and why did this movement develop? Has the mobilization of evangelicals altered the pattern of American political life? How has the activism changed over the decades? These questions will guide the analysis of a political force that some observers denounced as dangerous to the political system and others heralded as a movement to revitalize American politics.[1]

THE POLITICAL BACKGROUND

Of all the shifts and surprises in contemporary political life, perhaps none was so wholly unexpected as the political resurgence of evangelical Protestantism in the late 1970s. Under the spell of modernization theory, many observers had treated traditional religion as a spent force in American life and politics (see chapter 1). Like other predictions rooted in secularization theory, this assessment was rudely challenged by evidence that evangelical Christianity had achieved new strength and was ready to assert that power in political activity. The nomination of Jimmy Carter in 1976, the rise to national notice of organizations such as Moral Majority, the restoration of spirited public debate about certain "moral" issues—all these signs of evangelical political awakening marked the return to national prominence of a force that knowledgeable observers had long ago written off.

Until the 1920s, evangelical Protestantism was an animating force in American political life. It had contributed greatly to the growth of anti-slavery sentiment in the Northern states during the period leading up to the Civil War and, paradoxically, reinforced the commitment of Southerners to the maintenance of the slave economy (Carwardine 1993). In the decades following that great conflict, evangelicals led a variety of movements to purify American politics of various corrupting influences. Before World War I, when it was embodied in the national arena by William Jennings Bryan, the evangelical impulse was a driving force behind such disparate movements as currency reform, women's suffrage, regulation of corporate abuses, arbitration of international conflicts, and adoption of "direct democracy" through the initiative, referendum, and recall election (Levine 1975). These reforms of the Progressive Era were advanced as means to defend the economic interests and social values of traditional Protestantism. Their widespread adoption before World War I attested to the central place of evangelicalism in American culture.

In the period following World War I, evangelical Protestantism was displaced from its perch as a major cultural force by a series of major social developments that culminated in a virtual social revolution. It is important to recognize the shattering impact of these trends.

> The disintegration of traditional American values—so sharply recorded by novelists and artists—was reflected in a change in manners and morals that shook American society to its depths. The growing secularization of the country greatly weakened religious sanctions. People lost their fear of Hell and at the same time had less interest in Heaven; they made more demands for material fulfillment on Earth. Most important, the authority of the family, gradually eroded over several centuries, had been sharply lessened by the rise of the city. "Never in recent generations," wrote Freda Kirchwey, "have human beings so floundered about outside the ropes of social and religious sanctions." (Leuchtenburg 1958, 158)

Under the impact of rapid urbanization, the spread of science and technology, and skyrocketing birthrates in the predominantly non-Protestant immigrant communities, the conditions that had once favored traditional Protestant religion began to lose hold. The weakening of the social values associated with evangelicalism was apparent in such disparate trends as the growth in women's employment, the loosening of restraints on sexuality, the rising prestige of science, and a general tendency to exalt hedonism and materialist values. Even many Protestants, later recognized as founders of the "mainline" approach, began to doubt the literal authority of the Bible and its superiority relative to science. Collectively, these trends amounted to a cultural displacement of traditionalist Protestantism, what some have called a "Second Disestablishment."

Whether these developments were ever as widespread as imagined is really beside the point. Accurately or not, evangelicals thought they were confronted with threats to orthodox Christianity, and they reacted with furious defensive activity. One such reaction was the Ku Klux Klan, a massive nationwide social movement that defined itself in the 1920s primarily as a campaign to preserve Christian values. The Klan drew heavily on white evangelical Protestants for its mass membership, and evangelical clergy were prominent among the leadership (Gatewood 1965; Hunt 1999). In places, it actually appealed to African Americans to join in a Christian alliance against the immigrants, Catholics, and Jews who were, the Klan alleged, polluting the moral environment of the United States.

Attempting to resist the encroachments of secularism in the political realm, evangelical Protestants concentrated on a pair of causes: the campaigns to restrict the sale of intoxicating liquor and to prohibit the teaching of evolution in the public schools. Both movements attained temporary success, but in the end, neither could withstand the shift of power to the burgeoning cities, where evangelicalism was weak and a new set of issues commanded public interest. Hence, the fate of evangelicalism was tied to "a receding and beleaguered small-town culture" (Burner 1967, 4).

As many predominantly northern Protestant denominations embraced modernity and expressed a willingness to apply scientific insight to religious belief, the center of gravity in evangelicalism shifted decisively to the South (Heyrman 1997). There were significant political implications in the increasing southern orientation of traditional Protestantism. Unlike northern evangelicals, who had argued that salvation depended on both faith and works, the southern variety of Protestant Christianity stopped short of demanding social transformation as a condition for salvation. To most southern theological conservatives,

> salvation was an act, a transaction between God and the individual that was separable from the life that followed. Those who had been born again were expected to practice Christian morality, to behave rightly in their own lives, and to work and pray for the conversion of others. Yet these expectations were never connected with any imperative to transform their culture in the name of Christ. They did not deprecate the world about them; they simply saw religious life as something to be carried on in a separate compartment. (Kleppner 1979, 187)

From its new southern base, evangelicalism thus chose to remain outside the political arena—a withdrawal broken only by participation in sporadic rearguard actions through fringe movements and extremist crusades. From the 1920s through the 1970s, whether scholars studied the Ku Klux Klan, segregationists, book censors, or virulent anti-Communists, they found evangelical Protestants overrepresented (Grupp and Newman 1973; Ribuffo 1983). These links between evangelicalism and regressive political movements fixed traditional religion with a public image as narrow minded, bigoted, and backward looking—an image that obscured earlier associations between the same religious community and progressive political causes.

Observers relied on social and theological factors to explain the political style of traditional Protestantism during this period. The social and economic deprivation that typified evangelicals denied them the time, energy, or skill to carry on sustained political participation and isolated them from experiences that would have promoted tolerance, compromise, and other democratic values. Lesser educational opportunities were said to afflict evangelicals with cognitive rigidity, an inflexibility of mind that kept them at a disadvantage in genuinely democratic political competition (Lipset 1960, 100). Furthermore, the otherworldly orientation of southern religion, the divorce of religion from social conditions, discouraged participation in the earthly process of political action.

To the extent that evangelicals participated in national political life after Bryan's eclipse, their sympathies remained with the Democratic Party.[2] The alliance can be explained largely in regional and class terms. The force of tradition kept white Southern Baptists, the largest evangelical denomination, firmly attached to the party that had reestablished white political dominance in the late nineteenth century and usually selected its vice presidential nominee from the region. The linkage was further cemented in the 1930s by the popularity of the New Deal social welfare programs that attacked poverty and agricultural distress in the region (Billington and Clark 1991). The first academic studies of public opinion and party allegiance, published in the 1940s and 1950s, confirmed what southern election returns had suggested—that white Southern Baptists were disproportionately attached to the Democratic Party and much more prone than other groups to support government programs of economic security (Allinsmith and Allinsmith 1948). Though the "states' rights" revolt at the 1948 Democratic National Convention had demonstrated the capacity of the civil rights issue to draw southern whites away from a Democratic allegiance, the partisan impact of the controversy was checked by the similarity of the Democratic and Republican positions until the 1960s.

The first stirrings of change in the pattern of evangelical politics were visible in presidential elections of the 1960s. When the Democratic Party nominated a Catholic for president in 1960, large numbers of white, churchgoing southern Protestants defected to the Republican candidate (Converse 1966). Four years later the same parts of the country that had given William Jennings Bryan his greatest margins of support responded favorably to the candidacy of Senator Barry Goldwater (R-Ariz.), who had cultivated their favor by emphasizing conservative social values (Burnham 1968). Goldwater's candidacy appeared to galvanize many evangelicals who had previously stayed outside the political arena. In 1968, George Wallace's independent presidential candidacy showed extraordinary strength among southern whites belonging to theologically conservative denominations (Orum 1970). By the end of the decade, the level of psychological attachment to the Democratic Party and voting support for its presidential candidates had eroded considerably among white southerners (Knoke 1976, 23). Factoring defections and turnout into voting patterns from 1960 to 1996, Leege and colleagues (2002, chap. 10) discovered that white evangelicals last contributed a net partisan advantage to the Democrats in 1964.

These trends did not wholly prepare observers for the subsequent attempts to turn evangelical Protestants to the political right. The changing voting patterns in the South were not interpreted principally in terms of a revolt by theological conservatives but rather in racial and economic terms. The Republican surge in 1960 was attributed directly to anti-Catholic sentiment, but most observers perceived it in the context of a steady postwar erosion of Democratic support in the region, occasioned by the increasing liberalism of the national Democratic Party on race and social welfare issues and the corresponding move to the right by the Republican leadership. Most influential commentators on southern politics did not dwell on the role of religious values in stimulating these voter transitions.

The rise of Jimmy Carter to national power in 1976 focused public attention on the growing political significance of evangelical Protestantism and further undermined the stereotype of rabid extremism. A well-educated and scientifically trained man, comfortable with contemporary culture and modern theology, Carter advocated moderate to liberal policies without the excited appeals to emotion that had been the hallmark of evangelical politics. In the face of publicly expressed doubts by Catholic, Jewish, and black leaders who associated southern evangelicals with religious and racial bigotry, Carter's moderation seemed to promise a welcome break with that unpleasant historical tradition. In the election of 1976, he carried Catholic and Jewish voters by the same or greater margins as had most other postwar Democratic presidential candidates and, like Lyndon Johnson and Hubert Humphrey, received virtually unanimous support from African Americans. That Carter could appeal so strongly to liberal social groups and carry most of the southern states suggested the end of evangelical political distinctiveness. That impression might not have been so widely accepted had more people realized that a majority of white southerners voted for Carter's Republican opponent.

ROOTS OF THE "NEW CHRISTIAN RIGHT"

The return of evangelicals to organized political action, manifested in what was originally labeled the New Christian Right (NCR), was facilitated by a number of local movements that developed during the social ferment and upheaval of the 1970s. Alan Crawford (1980) identified three grassroots campaigns that paved the way for subsequent national organizations: a textbook controversy in West Virginia, a gay rights referendum in Dade County (Miami), Florida, and a campaign in the early 1980s to defeat the proposed equal rights amendment (ERA) to the Constitution. In each case, evangelical Protestants rallied strongly to the defense of traditional cultural and social values.

In the mid-1970s, protesters in a mining valley of West Virginia challenged some English textbooks that the Kanawha County Board of Education had approved for use in public schools. Led by the wife of a fundamentalist minister, who denounced most of the books as "disrespectful of

authority and religion, destructive of social and cultural valu
pornographic, unpatriotic, or in violation of individual and familiar
of privacy" (Jenkinson 1979, 18), the campaign ignited a massive boycott
of the schools by the parents of most students, sympathetic wildcat strikes
by coal miners, mass picketing all across the county, a teachers' strike,
temporary closure of the schools, and several violent assaults on people
and property. Although all the books were eventually approved for
classroom use, the controversy led to the resignation of the school super-
intendent and a new textbook adoption procedure that made it easier for
parents to screen out "offensive" books. The apparent success of the parent groups in the Kanawha County "battle of the books" inspired similar
challenges around the country.

The seeds of the New Christian Right were also planted by the 1977
Dade County, Florida, referendum on a gay rights ordinance. Gay leaders
had persuaded the county commission to pass an ordinance prohibiting
discrimination on the basis of sexual orientation in housing, employment,
and public accommodations. The ordinance prompted formation of a
new organization, Save Our Children, which claimed that the law would
require private and religious schools to employ homosexuals as teachers.
After a petition drive led by the singer Anita Bryant and many religious
leaders, the ordinance was submitted to a popular referendum and voted
down by more than a two-to-one margin. Similar ordinances were subsequently repealed elsewhere around the country.

The potential clout of religious conservatism was also on display in the
remarkable campaign that defeated the proposed equal rights amendment
to the Constitution (Boles 1979). Approved by Congress early in 1972, the
amendment prohibiting sexual discrimination by the states and the federal government quickly sailed through ratification votes in twenty-two
state legislatures, leaving it only sixteen states short of formal adoption.
The seemingly inevitable path to constitutional status was interrupted
by the formation of two powerful organizations: Stop ERA, founded by
Phyllis Schlafly, and Concerned Women for America, the brainchild of
Beverly LaHaye. In the face of determined lobbying by Schlafly's organization and allied groups, the rate of ratification dropped sharply, and the
amendment ultimately died three states short of the thirty-eight needed.
To underline the religious dimension to the conflict, most of the states that
failed to ratify had substantial concentrations of Mormons (Utah, Nevada,
Arizona) or evangelical Protestants (all the southern states except Texas
and Tennessee), and conservative churches supplied the recruitment base
for most of the antiratification leaders and activists (Arrington and Kyle
1978; Brady and Tedin 1976; Mueller and Dimieri 1982; Jones 1983; Tedin
1978; Tedin et al. 1977; Wohlenberg 1980; Mansbridge 1986; Mathews and
De Hart 1990). Among ordinary citizens, both membership in fundamen-

talist churches and high rates of church attendance were associated with opposition to the amendment (Burris 1983).

Although geographically dispersed and motivated by different issues, these three campaigns were tied together by common dissatisfaction with what the participants saw as a godless society that had replaced firm moral standards with a system of relativism. Like their ancestors who had crusaded against alcohol, evolution, and sexual laxity in the 1920s, evangelicals in the 1970s "felt that their country was being taken from them, their children were being turned against them, the Bible was being mocked" (Wills 2007, 486). The campaigns against "obscene" schoolbooks, gay rights ordinances, and the ERA thus appealed most strongly to white evangelical Protestants, who saw each movement as a crusade in defense of traditional Christian values and institutions. The particular value presumed under attack ranged from respect for social conventions in West Virginia to heterosexual marriage in Miami to the maintenance of traditional social roles for women in the struggle over the ERA. Underlying the challenges to orthodox Christian values, some leaders of the movement argued, was a doctrine called "secular humanism" that asserted the supremacy of humanity rather than of God. According to the advocates of traditional social values, the doctrine of secular humanism had become entrenched in the government, schools, media, and other institutions that molded public perceptions. Through state and local campaigns against particular outcroppings of what they saw as a pernicious idea, conservative religious activists began to forge organizational links and a common view about the source of major social problems.

Although traditionalist Protestants often subscribe to a model of gender complementarity, a position that allocates different social roles to men and women, women played a central role in the mobilization of Christian conservatives. They were prominent leaders of all three movements that Crawford identified as pivotal in leading to the New Christian Right and have continued to exercise considerable authority in subsequent campaigns (Ribuffo 2006). In fact, Concerned Women for America remains one of the few organizations to have survived from the early days of the Christian Right. Often recruited from churches and women's groups (Andersen 1988), these traditionalist women stood in opposition to the feminist movement while occupying positions of authority that seem inconsistent with a traditionalist model of gender relations (Schreiber 2008).

These movements represented a sea change in the thinking of evangelical Protestants, a "coming out" almost as dramatic as the political awakenings of feminists and homosexuals that had triggered it. Once ridiculed as being "so heavenly minded they were of no earthly good," evangelicals had been theologically unequipped for regular participation in society. Their ministers had long warned them to steer clear of "secular" politics and focus their energies on their salvation. Even as the black civil rights movement exploded in their midst, the leaders of Southern evangelicalism derided the "marching ministers" who demonstrated for desegregation and reminded their flocks that salvation was more important than social reform (Marsh 1997, chap. 3). But now, in response to the menacing social trends unleashed in the 1960s, they were counseled to "reject the division of human affairs into the 'secular' and 'sacred' and insist, instead, that there is no arena of human activity, including law and politics, which is outside of God's lordship. The task is not to avoid this world, but to declare God's Kingdom in it" (Buzzard 1989, 137). Animated by this ideal, evangelicals began to apply to politics the same missionary zeal they had traditionally shown in converting individuals (Regnerus and Smith 1998; Weeks 1998).

BUILDING A NATIONAL MOVEMENT

The political successes of grassroots evangelicalism did not go unnoticed by "secular" conservative activists. Casting about for a strategy to restore a Republican Party dispirited by consecutive electoral defeats in 1974 and 1976, they attempted to capitalize on the political energy displayed by evangelicals and to transfer it from the local to the national arena. These largely secular activists offered assistance to the emerging leaders of the Christian conservative movement and urged the most vocal leaders of the evangelical community to make common cause with other single-issue groups. The basis for coalition would be a frontal attack on "big government" as a threat to traditional religious and economic values. With that theme, they hoped to harness evangelicals to a comprehensive conservative program, including opposition to liberal policies on gun control, the treaty relinquishing American control over the Panama Canal, nonrestrictive abortion laws, labor unions, public education, and defense cutbacks. Using their contacts and ample political resources—especially the conservatives' demonstrated ability to raise money through direct mail appeals to sympathizers—the secular conservatives helped build up several national organizations designed to appeal to evangelical Protestants and other theological conservatives.

The most prominent of the new organizations, Moral Majority, was founded in 1979 by television evangelist Jerry Falwell, the minister of the nation's largest independent Baptist church, in Lynchburg, Virginia. Concentrated mostly in the southeastern states, Moral Majority drew most of its membership and leadership from other independent Baptist churches. To reach into the Southern Baptist Convention, the single largest evangelical denomination, Ed McAteer started the Religious Roundtable. Christian

Voice, the oldest of these Christian Right groups, grew out of an unsuccessful attempt by California evangelicals to pass a state law limiting the public employment of homosexuals or homosexual advocates. Initially formed to defend the interests of the burgeoning Christian schools movement in 1977, the National Christian Action Coalition (NCAC) was a multipurpose organization (Moen 1989, 71–73) using diverse tactics to defend Christian schools from what it saw as governmental intrusion. All the organizations established at the end of the 1970s also drew on the experience and expertise of earlier movements designed to spur evangelicals into political action, including some with ties to Ronald Reagan's unsuccessful bid for the 1976 Republican presidential nomination (Blumenthal 1984).

These organizations also shared a common agenda (Shriver 1981). Described by the Christian Right as the "pro-family" program, the same specific proposals showed up in the literature of all four organizations. Moral Majority's "Christian Bill of Rights" stressed opposition to abortion, support for voluntary prayer and Bible reading in public schools, the responsibility of government to encourage the "traditional family unit," maintenance of tax exemption for churches, and noninterference by the authorities with Christian schools. Christian Voice expanded the list of social evils to include the teaching of evolution, pornography, the celebration of "immoral" behavior on television, and liquor and drug abuse. True to its roots in the Christian school movement, NCAC pressed relentlessly for income tax credits to offset private school tuition.

Although assigning preeminence to family issues, the leaders of these movements did not ignore the issues that concerned "secular" conservatives, justifying conservative positions on these issues with a religious rationale. Thus, increased defense spending was a way to keep the nation free for the continued preaching of the Gospel, and support for the governments of Taiwan and South Africa was necessary to protect Christian allies from the "Godless forces of anti-Christ Communism." Similarly, Falwell asserted a scriptural basis for low inflation, flat-rate taxation, and a balanced federal budget. In practice, however, conservative social values drove the formation and activity of the New Christian Right.

EVANGELICAL POLITICAL ACTION

The New Christian Right, as it was styled by media and academic observers, coalesced around the candidacy of Ronald Reagan in the 1980 presidential campaign. Divorced, an intermittent churchgoer from a mainline denomination, the father of children who pursued unconventional lives, and a veteran of Hollywood, Reagan seemed a most unlikely object of support for the devout—doubly so in a race with two other evangelical Protestants, Jimmy Carter and John Anderson. But as Reagan alone embraced the political efforts of the conservative evangelical leaders and pledged to work for enactment of their agenda, he increasingly drew the New Christian Right into his camp. All the groups encouraged pastors to sign up evangelicals on the voter rolls and to impress on churchgoers the necessity of expressing their religious convictions in the polling booth. These efforts led to a substantial evangelical presence in Republican Party activities during the 1980 and 1984 campaigns (see Baker, Steed, and Moreland 1983, chaps. 5–7).

For their part, the leaders of the GOP granted considerable symbolic recognition to the emerging leaders of the Christian Right by featuring them at the Republican National Convention and adding to the party's platform calls for a constitutional amendment to restrict abortion, the legalization of prayer and religious meetings in public schools, and opposition to the ERA. In language that spoke directly to the concerns that had prompted formation of the evangelical political movement, the 1984 platform accused the Democrats of "assaulting our basic values." To hammer home the point about the differing stands taken by the two major parties, speakers referred constantly to their opponents as "the San Francisco Democrats," linking the freewheeling city where the Democrats had met for their convention with the policies pursued by the party. And on the morning of his renomination in 1984, President Reagan brought religion even more firmly into the campaign by giving a speech at a prayer breakfast that had been organized by the convention host committee.

Without the unifying presence of Ronald Reagan at the head of the ticket, evangelical leaders split during the 1988 Republican primary campaign. Some supported the campaign of Pat Robertson, an ordained Southern Baptist minister who had built the Christian Broadcasting Network into the nation's largest religious broadcasting empire. But Robertson's hopes of riding to the nomination on the basis of a strong showing in the "Super Tuesday" southern primaries in March were dashed by his poor showing throughout the region. He eventually withdrew, a victim of the strong competition, his own verbal gaffes and limited experience, and strong divisions within the evangelical camp (Wald 1991). In the general election, the evangelical leadership lined up behind Reagan's vice president, George H. W. Bush, who gave some emphasis to conservative cultural themes (White 1990). Facing reelection with a sagging economy, Bush pushed the "pro-family" agenda much more aggressively in 1992. In several well-publicized talks, Vice President Dan Quayle attacked moral relativism, unmarried mothers, and the low moral standards of the mass media. At the Republican convention in Houston, delegates heard prime-time addresses on the same subjects from Pat Buchanan, Pat Robertson, and Marilyn Quayle. Bush himself criticized the Democrats for omitting

God from their platform. When Bush's decisive defeat was attributed in part to the concerns of moderate voters about the Christian Right's "capture" of the party, several moderate Republicans announced plans to challenge the Christian Right influence. By 1996, when Senate leader Robert Dole captured the Republican nomination, the party made virtually no effort to embrace the central themes of the Christian Right.

ORGANIZATIONAL TRANSFORMATION: THE SECOND GENERATION

Their contribution to Republican victories in 1980 had given evangelical leaders a place at the table (Oldfield 1996). But after a decade of work yielded little in the way of concrete policy changes, many activists began a period of soul-searching about their efforts. To some outside observers, this period was tantamount to the death of the Christian Right (Bruce 1988; D'Antonio 1989). In retrospect, it was a prelude to transformation instead. Many politically engaged evangelical Protestants resolved to change the strategy and the tactics pursued by the Christian Right. In particular, they argued, the movement had erred by concentrating on changing national government by capturing the presidency. With its fragmented structure and multiple centers of power, the U.S. political system has long resisted radical attempts to reshape public policy. Hence, the movement might do better if it concentrated energy at the state and local levels, building up an infrastructure of support within the Republican Party and a network of genuine mass-based organizations. After more than twenty years, the New Christian Right was not so new, and the term was usually dropped in favor of Christian Right or Religious Right.

Accordingly, the Christian Right underwent a thorough transformation in the early 1990s (Moen 1997; Rozell and Wilcox 1996). Formerly a collection of "direct mail lobbies, led by prominent fundamentalists who championed a moralistic agenda on Capitol Hill," the Christian Right became "a variety of well-established membership organizations, whose leaders use mainstream language and organize followers in the grassroots" (Moen 1995, 131). (See table 8.1 for information on some of the major groups.) Most of the pioneering organizations folded, replaced by new groups that were genuine mass-membership organizations with stronger local chapters than their predecessors (Berkowitz and Green 1997). For the most part, the leadership passed from media ministers to seasoned political operatives recruited from secular conservative organizations. In style and form, these new activists tried to avoid the divisive moral language and censorious tone that had characterized the first wave of New Christian Right groups. Indeed, borrowing the language from military

Table 8.1. Organizations in the Christian Right

Organization Data	Purpose and Method
Christian Right Groups	
American Family Association Tupelo, Mississippi http://action.afa.net	Has added anti-gay rights platform to traditional focus on obscenity in the mass media
Center for Christian Statesmanship Washington, D.C. www.statesman.org	Assists Christians who work on Capitol Hill
Christian Coalition of America Washington, D.C. www.cc.org	Emphasizes legislative lobbying and mobilizing Christian conservatives
Citizens for Excellence in Education Costa Mesa, California www.nace-cee.org	Devoted to electing fundamentalists to school boards; has fallen on hard times
Concerned Women for America Washington, D.C. www.cwfa.org	Long-time organization emphasizes an array of issues with recent focus on gay rights controversies
Eagle Forum Alton, Illinois www.eagleforum.org	Continues to emphasize Phyllis Schlafly's anti-feminist and gay rights agenda
Family Research Council Washington, D.C. www.frc.org	Arguably the most influential lobbying and research organization with the Christian Right
Focus on the Family Colorado Springs, Colorado www.focusonthefamily.com	Ministry active in a wide range of social issues
Traditional Values Coalition Washington, D.C., and Anaheim, California www.traditionalvalues.org	California-based organization begun to counter gay rights
Groups Opposed to the Christian Right Agenda	
Americans United for Separation of Church and State Silver Springs, Maryland www.au.org	Ecumenical organization devoted to church-state separation
American Civil Liberties Union New York, New York www.aclu.org	Comprehensive First Amendment group covers church-state issues
Faith and Progressive Policy Initiative Washington, D.C. www.americanprogress.org/projects/faith	Promotes discussion of progressive religious values in political debate
Faith in Public Life Washington, D.C. http://faithinpubliclife.org/	Encourages liberal Christians to take part in policy debates
Interfaith Alliance Washington, D.C. www.interfaithalliance.org	Educational and lobbying group founded to counter Christian Right organizations
People for the American Way Washington, D.C. www.pfaw.org	Conducts research and lobbies against Christian Right policies

terminology, social conservatives seeking public office were advised to run "stealth" campaigns that did not mention religious motivations or the full range of policies they wanted to implement. Similarly, candidates were counseled to reach out to voters who were not part of the evangelical tradition and to build strategic alliances with sympathizers from other religious families. The target audience evolved from "Christians" (meaning evangelical Protestants) to "religious conservatives" to "people of faith." Once approached to defend "Christian values" or "Christian America," the new goal became "traditional values" or, even more popular, the "pro-family agenda." That agenda moved beyond moral concerns that generated the New Christian Right to a much broader set of issues that would appeal to secular conservatives.

Among the new groups or groups with renewed influence, scholars called attention to the Family Research Council, the Traditional Values Coalition, Citizens for Excellence in Education, and, for a time, the evangelical men's movement known as Promise Keepers. Pat Robertson founded the most prominent of the new organizations, Christian Coalition, hiring a veteran of conservative campaigns as his executive director. By 1995, under the leadership of Ralph Reed, Christian Coalition claimed 1.6 million members in more than 1,600 local chapters, access to a network of 60,000 churches, and $25 million in funds.

During the 1994 election alone, it distributed thirty-five million voter guides and seventeen million congressional scorecards, and made telephone calls to three million voters. The group's annual conference became a mandatory stop for candidates seeking the Republican presidential nomination. In the pivotal 1994 congressional elections, Christian Coalition lobbied heavily for the "Contract with America," the Republican legislative program emphasizing such "secular" policies as the Balanced Budget Amendment, tax relief for families, welfare reform, and term limits (Christian Coalition 1995). Its own "Contract with the American Family," introduced with great fanfare on the steps of the U.S. Capitol in mid-1995, included traditional calls for restricting abortion, pornography, and obscene art, as well as laws to shield Christian schools and "homeschoolers" from state regulation and to promote school prayer and state funding of religious education. But it gave equal billing to lowering taxes, dismantling welfare programs, and increasing penalties for convicted criminals.

Even when Christian Coalition embraced the same policies as Moral Majority, the differences in language revealed a striking tactical shift. Christian Coalition representatives spoke the liberal language of "rights, equality, and opportunity" (Moen 1995, 130). In this framework, school prayer was defended as the right of religious students to free speech, state subsidies for religious schools became transformed into "school choice," and abortion was denial of the right to life. Similarly, Christian Coalition also worked diligently to appeal to groups outside evangelical Protestantism, disavowing the racism, anti-Semitism, and anti-Catholicism in previous evangelical political movements. Ralph Reed (1996) declared such bigotry unacceptable and assured Jewish audiences that his organization stood for "a nation that is not officially Christian, Jewish, or Muslim. A nation where the separation of church and state is complete and inviolable. Where any person may run for elective office without where they attend church or synagogue ever becoming an issue. A nation where no child of any faith is forced by government to recite a prayer with which they disagree." By turning the language of religious pluralism into a shield, the Christian Right of the 1990s tried to overcome another of the singular weaknesses it displayed in the 1980s.

Many conservative Christians redirected their efforts to the states and localities, working diligently for goals as disparate as banning "obscene" lyrics in popular music, challenging sex education programs, fighting against gay rights legislation, and providing options to abortion. By concentrating on the lower levels of American political life and doing so without emphasizing their religious orientations, these activists represented an important new stage in evangelical political mobilization.

THEORIES OF EVANGELICAL MOBILIZATION

Describing the origins and development of the Christian Right is much easier than explaining it. The emergence of the movement contradicted social science research about the secularization of political conflict and the social and doctrinal bases for evangelical political apathy. Initially caught off guard by the upsurge in evangelical political action, scholars soon began to analyze the new coalition according to theories and concepts that have been applied to similar social movements of the past. Because no single factor is sufficient to explain such an unexpected social development, the responsibility for the social movement must be apportioned among the three facets of religion previously shown to have political relevance: social influences, institutional influences, and values. To return to the crime novel theory first introduced in chapter 5, these factors supply both motive and means for political activity.

Social Influences

Although evangelical Protestants still rate below the national average on factors such as education, income, and occupational status, the group achieved dramatic socioeconomic gains in the last half century (Roof and

McKinney 1987). In terms of educational attainment, younger evangelicals now resemble the American population as a whole (Massengill 2008).
Fueled by these changes, the presence of evangelicals in urban areas,
higher income brackets, and white-collar occupations has grown. This has
been symbolized by the replacement of modest churches with lavish and
well-appointed worship centers.

This objective gain in economic standing undercut evangelical traditions of political apathy and Democratic partisanship. As evangelicals
moved into the middle class, they gained social resources that encouraged political participation—increased free time, organizational skills,
access to social and communication networks, contacts with government
officials, and greater exposure to information (Claassen and Povtak 2010).
With increased economic standing, evangelicals also tended to acquire
more interest in policies of low taxation and limited government advocated by the Republican Party. In migrating to different states, cities and
suburban communities in search of better jobs and opportunities, evangelicals carried their traditionalist religious values with them (Dochuk
2011). Migration to these new environments eventually stimulated political activity by bringing evangelicals face-to-face with direct assaults on
the social values dominant in the rural and small-town strongholds where
they came from (Green, Guth, and Hill 1993; Burris 2001; Regnerus, Sikkink, and Smith 1999).

But to explain why evangelicals were mobilized principally on the basis of traditional moral and social values, rather than economic appeals,
reference to changes in objective economic achievement is not sufficient.
For many observers, the critical factor in preparing the ground for the
New Christian Right was change in subjective social status. According to
the "status politics" model that has been used to explain different types
of right-wing political action, moral crusades such as those mounted by
the Religious Right represent a symbolic response by groups to declines
in their social prestige (Lipset and Raab 1981). Joseph Gusfield (1963) describes "status politics" in the following terms:

> As his own claim to social respect and honor [is] diminished, the . . . citizen
> seeks for public acts through which he may reaffirm the dominance and
> prestige of his style of life. Converting the sinner to virtue is one way; law
> is another. Even if the law is not enforced or enforceable, the symbolic im-
> port of its passage is important to the reformer. It settles the controversies
> between those who represent clashing cultures. The public support of one
> conception of morality at the expense of another enhances the prestige and
> self-esteem of the victors and degrades the culture of the losers. (4–5)

The evangelicals, it has been argued, watched with dismay during the
1960s as society turned away from the values represented by traditional

morality and opinion leaders appeared to give priority to the interests and aspirations of groups, such as African Americans, who had long ranked below them in social esteem. Under this interpretation, resentment about declining social respect paid to devout members of the evangelical community prompted their support for movements pledged "to reestablish, through formal political processes, the social support that the group's values once commanded" (Crawford 1980, 149).

Challenging the assumption that evangelicals were necessarily losing social prestige, some observers have broadened the status politics framework into a "politics of lifestyle concern." In this view, movements such as the Christian Right, rather than trying to recapture lost prestige or social honor, have attempted to defend moral traditionalism, the values, customs, and habits that form the basis of their lifestyle (Brint and Abrutyn 2010; Page and Clelland 1978). Through early training and later participation in group life, evangelicals are exposed to a culture that emphasizes "adherence to traditional norms, respect for family and religious authority, asceticism and control of impulse" (Wood and Hughes 1984, 89). When social policies appeared to challenge this frame of reference by endorsing attacks on religion or encouraging self-indulgence and alternatives to the traditional family, it has been argued, evangelicals fought back by supporting policies more in tune with their cultural values. Although the goals were different, the logic of defending a way of life was common to social movements across the political spectrum.

The concerns of the evangelicals were not entirely symbolic. They criticized the federal government for taking over a number of tasks once reserved for the family (Moen 1989). Medicare was condemned for encouraging people to shirk family obligations, welfare benefits were alleged to encourage promiscuity, and high rates of taxation were blamed for forcing women from the household into the workplace. Of course, the long string of Supreme Court decisions restricting government action in support of religion did hamper the expression of evangelical faith in public schools. Although claims of a conspiracy of "secular humanists" were an effective rhetorical device rather than an empirical reality, there is undeniable evidence of a broadly secular orientation among strategically placed members of the American elite (McCloskey and Zaller 1984, 26). Evangelicals had something to worry about.

Institutional Influences

The role of religious institutions was important in this regard. Even during its supposed period of weakness in the interwar period, fundamentalist evangelicalism built a strong organizational infrastructure that created social networks among believers (Carpenter 1997; Lienesch 1997). The social transformation of evangelicals also produced a major emphasis on what was called "church planting." The so-called megachurches, such as Jerry Falwell's Thomas Road Baptist Church, took on a wide range of functions and developed into religious equivalents of major corporations (Fitzgerald 1981). Evangelical seminaries produced clergy who managed church entry into such fields as education, day care, and counseling. The evolution of the churches from places of worship to social service centers brought them under the authority of government regulations affecting zoning, educational practices (curriculum content, teacher certification, desegregation mandates, tax-exempt status), day care facilities, minimum wage laws, and working conditions. The result was a series of classic confrontations between the state's interest in regulating the private provision of social services and the church's claims of immunity under the free exercise clause. With such substantial investments, the churches could no longer afford a policy of political disengagement.

Whatever their motivation, evangelical clergy gradually took up more active political involvement. In the 1960s, clergy from conservative Protestantism were much less likely than their liberal counterparts to take public stands on political concerns and were themselves less likely to participate in politics (Quinley 1974). The emphasis on converting sinners took precedence over changing laws. By the 1990s, the conservative clergy appeared to have caught up with their mainline counterparts in the degree to which they preached about politics (Beatty and Walter 1989; Guth et al. 1997; Regnerus et al. 1999). As we would expect, the priorities of the communication differ, with conservative clergy stressing the pro-family agenda, while liberal ministers emphasize "peace and justice" issues such as hunger and poverty. The parishioners appeared to be listening. Those from doctrinally conservative Protestant denominations did not report receiving any less political direction than mainline Protestants or Catholics (Welch et al. 1993). The churches of evangelical Protestantism also may provide Christian Right organizations with access to parishioners via mailing lists and supplies of voter guides. Such efforts seem to pay off in encouraging evangelicals to go to the polls and vote for conservative candidates (Wilcox and Sigelman 2001).

The rapid expansion of the "electronic church" was another manifestation of evangelical growth that stimulated political involvement (Hadden and Swann 1981). Dominating religious broadcasting, evangelicals now "control six national broadcasting networks, each reaching tens of millions of homes," as well as more than two thousand radio stations and a satellite network that beams Christian-only programming on both radio and television (Blake 2005). Because the airwaves are regulated by the Federal Communications Commission (FCC), religious broadcasters have a natural interest in government decision-making. When the FCC was rumored (falsely) to be considering regulations that limited the access of religious groups to the public airways in the 1970s or later considered reserving part of the FM spectrum for educational institutions, religious broadcasters mobilized their audiences to act against the proposals. Action by the Carter administration to eliminate the tax exemption for racially segregated religious schools, many of which were religiously affiliated, also generated mass demonstrations and letter-writing campaigns. Although these issues were enough to give religious leaders an incentive to enter the political arena, it was doubtful that mass movements could be founded on matters that concerned a relatively small portion of the evangelical population. Hence the emphasis on the broader "pro-family" agenda, of which religious broadcasting and tax exemption were but two elements.

The growth of evangelical institutions affected not only the interests but also the political capacity of the Christian Right. According to resource mobilization theory, social movements cannot convert grievances into political action unless they have access to potential supporters and other organizational resources that can be pressed into service. Potentially powerful political forces in their own environment, local evangelical churches are also aligned with central organizations that can coordinate nationwide political action. Part of Moral Majority's strength was its direct access to local preachers through the network of churches affiliated with the Baptist Bible Fellowship (Liebman 1983). Television evangelists have direct access to viewers and the capacity to tap into mailing lists with millions of names. Not surprisingly in view of these resources, the major political movements targeting evangelicals were initiated by pastors with access to vast broadcasting empires. Falwell had his *Old Time Gospel Hour*, the Christian Voice was connected to Pat Robertson's Christian Broadcasting Network, and the Roundtable's leading spokesman also had a nationally syndicated program. Of course, reliance on broadcasting and national church alliances cannot guarantee success in political life. As some of the liberal clergy discovered in the 1960s, an evangelist who preaches politics instead of the Gospel may lose those in the audience who want religion to address their spiritual concerns. Moreover, constant demands for funds may produce decreasing returns from a weary audience. Competition among media ministers may undermine the unity required for effective political action. The local churches that serve as the base of operations for the Christian Right, finally, may also fiercely resist attempts at central coordination, fragmenting the energy of the group and giving unwanted publicity to loose cannons such as the Moral Majority chapter head from California who publicly advocated the execution of homosexuals.

Values

The third aspect of religion, comprising theology and values, has also played a part in stimulating the New Christian Right. As we saw in chapters 5 and 6, evangelical Protestants are extremely conservative on virtually every social issue. Yet this was not enough to draw them into national politics before the 1960s because it was offset by an emphasis on other-worldliness and personal salvation. Why did this change in the 1970s?

Robert Wuthnow (1983) suggested that evangelicals were responding to changes in society that encouraged the application of religious values to public policy. Several trends blurred the traditional view of "morality" as a matter largely for individual behavior and thus raised new public concern about the ethical standards of public institutions. As evidence of the growing trend to approach public policy from an ethical viewpoint, Wuthnow cited "criticism of the Vietnam war as an act of public immorality, the various legislative actions taken in the aftermath of Watergate to institutionalize morality as a matter of official concern, and major Supreme Court decisions symbolically linking government with morality" (Wuthnow 1983, 176). Ironically in light of the degree to which he was targeted by the Christian Right, Jimmy Carter helped point the way for evangelicals when he hinged his 1976 campaign on the need to restore trust, honesty, and morality to American public life. All these developments reflected growing recognition that government should not be totally independent of moral considerations and paved the way for morally based criticism of national policy.

Few groups were as receptive to this approach as the evangelicals. They have a long tradition of fighting back against perceived assaults by public authority on their favored social values. In the past, this tendency had surfaced mostly in local and state conflicts over issues such as liquor licensing, sex education, and pornography. In the 1970s, however, the challenge appeared to emanate from a national government that seemingly had loosened restraints in hundreds of ways. Faced with a Supreme Court that reduced limits on public expressions of sexuality to an administration that allowed homosexuals to meet with a presidential assistant, evangelicals felt their values under siege in the national arena.

The actions of secular authority not only offended traditional moral values—reason enough to act—but also seemed to threaten the ability of evangelicals to protect themselves and their families from corrupting influences. Encouraged by the politicizing of morality exhibited in the reaction to the civil rights struggle, Vietnam, and Watergate, theological conservatives sought to draw from the same reservoir of moral outrage to influence social policy. And to prosecute the crusade, they could call on an increasingly affluent constituency through several organizational channels.

THE IMPACT OF THE CHRISTIAN RIGHT

What difference has the Christian Right made in American political life? While acknowledging the movement's electoral clout, the first editions of this book emphasized how little it had changed public policy. But in light of events during the administration of George W. Bush (2001–2009), that judgment surely needs reassessment. During the eight years of the Bush administration, such distinguished observers and Southern Baptists as Bill Moyers and former president Jimmy Carter (2005) wrote in alarmist tones about the Christian Right's "capture" of American public life.[3] Noting that President Bush reported that he regularly talked to God for political guidance and received the adulation of his evangelical supporters,[4] one shrewd reporter argued that the Christian Right had become superfluous because the movement's leader now occupied the White House.[5] We will thus examine the impact of the Christian Right as an electoral movement, for which the evidence is relatively clear, and the more difficult realm of public policy.

Considered as a mass movement, the Christian Right has succeeded in harnessing most white evangelical Protestants to the GOP at election time. As we saw in chapter 2, they have become the most pro-Republican of all the major religious traditions and are considered the base or core of the contemporary party in elections. We would be wise not to attribute this transformation entirely to the Christian Right. Evangelical Protestants had begun to vote more Republican in the 1950s, long before the movement developed (Woodberry and Smith 1998, 42–43; Manza and Brooks 1997; Leege et al. 2002). At best, the Christian Right intensified changes that were already under way by teaching many evangelicals to weigh moral issues heavily in choosing between presidential candidates (Hammond, Shibley, and Solow 1994; Johnson 1994; Layman and Carmines 1997). For most white evangelicals, voting Republican has become second nature.

Because elections depend on voter turnout, Republican candidates have become skilled at raising cultural issues that encourage evangelical Protestants to participate. By blaming liberal programs like welfare spending for breaking down family structure, fueling a rise in crime, and undermining the social order, Republican campaign themes have echoed the language of the Christian Right. In a script designed explicitly to appeal to Christian conservatives, Republican strategists like Lee Atwater and Karl Rove tried to frame campaigns as a battle between "decent, God-fearing people" and an unholy coalition of "gays, radical feminists, and arts people," the latter referring to cultural elites who allegedly favored federal funding for blasphemous and pornographic works of art. To stimulate turnout among evangelicals, Republicans have also employed a tactic used by liberals—encouraging and promoting state-level ballot initiatives likely to draw their base (conservative Christians) to the polls. In 2000, George W. Bush won such a narrow victory in part because evangelical Protestants did not vote at the same levels they had in previous presidential elections, perhaps because of late-breaking news about his drunk-driving conviction in Maine. Determined to avoid a repeat in 2004, the Republicans encouraged state referenda on gambling, gun ownership, and same-sex marriage, red meat issues to many religious conservatives. Bolstered by these tactics (Campbell and Monson 2008; Smith, DeSantis, and Kassel 2006), there was unprecedented religious mobilization on behalf of Bush in 2004, some coordinated by the campaign and some resulting from independent action by evangelical leaders.[6]

THE CONSEQUENCES FOR PUBLIC POLICY

The Christian Right embraced electoral activity as a means to change public policy at the national level. Yet by the end of the twentieth century, the record had been one of failure. To quote David Frum (1994), a conservative journalist, most politicians refused to regard the Christian Right as "anything more than a nuisance to be managed." Despite the prodding of the evangelical groups, lobbying by church members, the vocal support of Presidents Reagan and George H. W. Bush, the presence of important allies in the House and Senate, and fear of electoral retribution, the major programs advocated by Christian Right groups were not enacted into law (Courtwright 2010). The Senate voted down a constitutional amendment permitting organized school prayer and did not enact the tuition tax credit requested by supporters of religious schools. Neither the Reagan nor Bush I White Houses made these policies clear priorities for the Republican Party (McAndrews 2000; Shoon 2007). Another primary objective of the movement, prohibiting abortion, remained elusive. While it accepted some narrowing of reproductive rights, the Supreme Court did not invalidate the *Roe v. Wade* precedent.

The evangelical groups had affected national policies in ways short of changing public policy. As Matthew C. Moen (1989) argues, the Christian Right succeeded in obtaining passage of national legislation offering partial redress of its grievances. As we saw in chapter 4, it obtained "equal access" for religious group meetings in schools, a concession but still short of the goal of restoring organized school prayer. Many states sheltered evangelical Christian schools from educational regulation and permitted parents to teach their own children in "home schools." Abortion was not prohibited, but federal funds no longer supported it, and abortion access was severely curtailed in many places. The equal rights amendment was defeated, and attempts to add sexual orientation to national antidiscrimination policy were similarly doomed. Outraged by federal subsidies to artists who purveyed offensive art, critics managed to instruct the National Endowment for the Arts to consider "decency" as a criterion in making grants. At the state and local levels, some Christian Right organizations carried other proposals into law. Moreover, efforts to challenge national policy on social issues kept those controversies from falling off the national agenda.

These accomplishments may have been important, but they hardly met the rallying cry that first brought evangelical Protestants into the political arena. As the twentieth century neared its end during the late Clinton years, some of the movement's most influential activists began to issue calls for a retreat from politics in favor of cultural change, and organizations such as Christian Coalition and Promise Keepers largely faded from action.

GOOD TIMES? THE CHRISTIAN RIGHT
AND THE BUSH ADMINISTRATION

With the election of George W. Bush in 2000, the Christian Right could claim one of its own in the White House. Unlike his father, who never seemed comfortable with the fervor of religious conservatives and disappointed them repeatedly, the second President Bush was much more a part of the culture that generated the Christian Right. Known for his hard-partying ways as a young man and then as an ambitious business owner, Bush referred repeatedly in 2000 to the adult religious awakening that enabled him to overcome a lifelong drinking problem. Designated as the outreach expert to evangelicals in his father's losing 1992 campaign, Bush discovered that he spoke the language of evangelical Protestants and quickly became a favorite of the Christian Right. The leaders of the movement mobilized wholeheartedly on his behalf in both 2000 and 2004.

The administration repaid the loyalty of its evangelical base with various policy initiatives, most prominently the expansion of faith-based government services detailed in chapter 6. In international affairs, evangelical concerns about the persecution of Christians and opposition to abortion exerted some influence on American foreign policy (Hertzke 2004; Buss and Herman 2003). Despite public rhetoric to the contrary, President Bush made opposition to abortion a litmus test for Supreme Court appointees, signaling to evangelical allies that his candidates belonged to pro-life churches. The president put severe limits on the use of federal funds for stem cell research, publicly advocated teaching "intelligent design" in biology, and came out for a constitutional amendment against gay marriage in 2004. Even the Iraq War, more strongly supported by evangelical Protestants than any other faith community (Froese and Mencken 2009), was sometimes framed as a war against radical Islam. All in all, as Garry Wills noted (2007, 498), President Bush provided his base constituency with "faith-based war, faith-based law enforcement, faith-based education, faith-based medicine, and faith-based science."

During the Bush administration, religious conservatives enjoyed unparalleled access to the levers of power. Bush appointed a large number of evangelical stalwarts and approved their appointments of fellow activists to lower-level positions. The White House appointed a liaison to evangelicals and cooperated with congressional staff members in crafting legislation pleasing to evangelical activists.[7] Unlike the past, when they were outsiders looking in, Christian Right supporters had their hands on the policy process.

Rather surprisingly, the Christian conservatives whom President Bush so eagerly courted were not entirely happy with the results of the prolonged romance. This unhappiness boiled over late in 2005 when the president nominated his personal attorney, Harriet Miers, for a Supreme Court seat. Though Miers was a social conservative, many in the movement were deeply unhappy about the nomination of someone they perceived as a "stealth" moderate.[8] Angry over the "betrayal," conservative Christians generated much of the heat that prompted the nominee to withdraw. Beyond this particular issue, there is strong evidence that President Bush simply did not give the movement's priorities anything like the energy assigned to other causes (Wilcox 2005). On the legislative goals central to the GOP agenda—tax cuts, social security reform, the war in Iraq, oil drilling in the Arctic National Preserve, and so forth—the administration deployed all its ammunition and usually secured legislative approval. By contrast, social conservatives complained, the president's advisers who drove the White House agenda gave only halfhearted efforts to their cherished goals of ending abortion, prohibiting gay marriage, and other such aims. It seemed like a repeat of the Reagan years with their manifold disappointments amid so much hope.

ASSESSING THE CHRISTIAN RIGHT

Over its long history, the Christian Right has achieved more publicity than influence, a seat at the table but never, it seems, the head of the table. In thinking about why the movement has achieved less in the long run than many of its founders expected, we need to consider three significant structural factors: the nature of the American political system, the political culture of the American public, and political diversity among the constituency that the movement has tried to claim.

Clearly, much of the disappointment of the Christian Right was a replay of the experience of other groups dedicated to fundamental political change. The U.S. founders built a political system for the express purpose of making such change very difficult to achieve. More than two centuries later, the constitutional system still works to deflect passion. Even if Republican presidents oppose stem cell research, federalism permits states to develop and fund their own stem cell initiatives. Even if *Roe v. Wade* were overturned, returning the abortion question to the states, many would retain a liberal abortion option. President George W. Bush signed on to a constitutional amendment to ban gay marriage, but it died in Congress and the Supreme Court subsequently mandated federal recognition of same-sex marriages performed in the states. Congressional opposition to the initial Bush legislation on faith-based federal services forced severe compromises in the program. Taken together, these institutional barriers to change have played a role in frustrating the hopes of Christian conservatives.

Beyond the basic inertia of the American political system, the Christian Right also faces a cultural barrier. Americans frequently echo Christian Right rhetoric about the erosion of traditional values and look back wistfully to a kind of moral golden age. Yet at the same time, Americans partake of a culture that celebrates individualism and responds skeptically to government as a moral tutor. For example, Americans worry about the high divorce rate and many disapprove of couples who live together without marriage. Yet when asked whether "the government [should] start up programs that encourage people to get and stay married," a resounding 79 percent want the government out of the picture (Pew Research Center for the People and the Press 2002). As table 8.2 shows, most citizens wish that their fellow Americans would behave more circumspectly but do not see the government as the appropriate agent of that transformation. The first three questions in the survey shown in the table portray a population seemingly hungry for moral leadership and a government inspired by godly values—a population ripe, in other words, for the moral appeals of the Christian Right. Yet responses to the questions in the bottom of the table show a population equally committed to letting individuals chart their own moral paths. Uncertain that God directs the nation, this resilient individualism creates barriers to using the state to enforce traditional morality. The contradiction embodied in these questions, a yearning for authoritative values coupled with a reluctance to impose them by law, creates an opening for moral reform movements such as the Christian Right but also limits their mass appeal. These patterns have changed very little since the emergence of the Christian Right in the early 1980s (Sigelman, Wilcox, and Buell 1987).

Table 8.2.   General Attitudes to Government and Morality

Percentage who agree that . . .

Our government would be better if policies were more directed by moral values.	84%
The president should be a moral and spiritual leader.	78%
God is a heavenly father who can be reached by prayers.	76%
Individual freedom is critical to democracy in this country.	91%
Each individual must determine what is right or wrong.	70%
God is the moral guiding force of American democracy.	55%

Source: U.S. News poll, March 5–7, 1994, cited in Jeffery L. Sheler, "Spiritual America," *U.S. News and World Report,* April 4, 1994, 48–59.

The Christian Right has also been constrained by political diversity among the population it tries to claim as its electoral base. Although professed Christians still make up three-quarters of the adult population, a plethora of evidence shows the Christian Right has struck the most responsive chord among only one segment of this vast population—persons deeply attached to white evangelical Protestant denominations and values (Brudney and Copeland 1984; Hertel and Hughes 1987; Sigelman, Wilcox, and Buell 1987; Tamney and Johnson 1983; Wilcox 1989; Regnerus, Sikkink, and Smith 1999). In fact, even that description may be too generous because of evidence that the movement is anchored by fundamentalists who constitute only one subgroup among evangelicals (Green and Guth 1988; Jelen 1987). The movement has had much less success among the other large religious families within Christianity.

Mainline Protestantism has, on the whole, been cool or hostile, due in part to the negative views of social conservatives held by Republican women in business and professional roles (Regnerus, Sikkink, and Smith 1999; Leege et al. 2002, chap. 10). African American Protestants, despite widespread adherence to the religious doctrines of evangelicalism and its moral conservatism, did not embrace the Christian Right (Calhoun-Brown 1997). Apart from the unsavory racial history of the southern wing of evangelical Protestantism, African Americans tend to value government as an engine to combat discrimination and address economic problems, putting them at odds with the Christian Right's anti-government animus. Many Catholics, too, were suspicious of the movement despite its shared objection to abortion. More liberal than Protestant evangelicals, particularly on questions for which church leaders have transmitted a "peace and justice" orientation (Welch and Leege 1991), they also remembered the history of evangelical anti-Catholic bigotry that dated back to the Protestant Reformation.[9]

Even if we limit the Christian Right's core constituency to white Protestant evangelicals, that base, roughly 20–25 percent of the population, has not enlisted wholeheartedly in the crusade for traditional values (Smidt 1993, 102). This constituency has become a core element of the Republican coalition; in 2012, almost three-quarters of white evangelicals supported Mitt Romney, and they constituted 40 percent of his voters, by far the largest single component (Jones, Cox, and Navarro-Rivera 2012, 4). Yet one should not necessarily assume that their support for Romney was based principally on their religious values. Reviewing a wide range of surveys of evangelicals, Christian Smith (2000) concludes:

> Large majorities of conservative Protestants do not think women belong in the home; do believe that people have the right to live by their own moral-ity, whether Christian or not; do oppose Christian social activism that would cause social conflict; do not believe public schools should teach Christian values and morals, or require spoken Christian prayers in the classroom; do not think there is only one Christian view on most political issues; do not support a constitutional amendment declaring the United States a Christian nation . . . do not believe that America's laws that protect freedom of speech, the welfare of children, or the rights of women, minorities, immigrants, or the disabled go too far; and are not soft on racially, religiously, or ethnically bigoted "hate crimes." (225)

Mobilizing this community is challenging because it is diverse. Among white Protestants in evangelical denominations, there is more "family resemblance" than homogeneity. Consider the three subcategories of fundamentalists, charismatics, and neo-evangelicals (sometimes called *mainstream evangelicals*). Beyond respect for the authority of the Bible, a sense that salvation depends on Jesus, and a commitment to spread the Gospel, these groups often follow different paths. Since the traditionalist/ modernist debate of the late nineteenth century, fundamentalists have rejected much of modern culture, insisted on the importance of maintain-ing purity by separation from other faiths, and tended more than other evangelicals to a literal understanding of the Bible. Charismatics, once found only in Pentecostal churches but now present in many evangelical denominations, emphasize the "baptism of the Holy Spirit," based on events recorded in Acts 2, whereby they are infused with divine power by the Holy Ghost. The "indwelling of the Spirit" enables them to speak in tongues, heal by faith, and utter prophecies based on the Bible. These views are often regarded as heretical and perhaps even satanic by fun-damentalists who assign exclusive religious authority to scripture. Both fundamentalists and charismatics may seem strange or extreme to those evangelicals who maintain the essential theological principles mentioned earlier but find a way to accommodate modern culture, recognize that religious truth is embodied in other faiths, and see the Bible as authorita-tive but not determinative in all matters.

Tension among these groups sometimes leads to political conflict. Some leaders of the fundamentalist wing, believing the only task of the churches is to win souls for Christ, preach against any political involvement, while others, accepting a political role, believe that fundamentalists should not be yoked into unholy alliances with the unsaved. Pat Robertson's involvement in the charismatic renewal movement brought him substantial support from that group of evangelicals (Green and Guth 1988, 156; Penning 1994; Green 1993) but limited his appeal among fundamentalists (Jelen 1993a; Johnson, Tamney, and Burton 1989). From the left wing of evangelical- ism, social gospel advocates such as the Sojourners have protested against an unholy alliance between the "pro-life" forces on abortion and such "antilife" causes as militarism, capital punishment, apartheid, and social inequality. Within the mainstream of evangelicalism, comprising those who accept neither fundamentalism nor the charismatic approach, the New Christian Right received a guarded reception. As Robert Booth Fowler (1982) documented, the leaders of this wing of evangelical Protestantism had been moving toward a more moderate political position throughout the 1960s. The most widely recognized spokesman for this perspective, the Reverend Billy Graham, is a case in point (Pierard 1983). At the beginning of his career, Graham exhibited some of the political and social tendencies that were typical of fundamentalist Protestants. But over the course of the years, he moved toward the center of the political system by integrating his crusades, speaking out in favor of civil rights legislation, and advocating limits on the nuclear arms race. Graham repeatedly warned that any at- tempt to identify a particular political agenda with Christianity is likely to bring discredit on religion and to interfere with evangelization.[10]

That message seems to resonate with the "emerging church" move- ment prominent among young evangelicals today. Increasingly disturbed by what they sometimes call the Republican captivity of their churches, these disaffected Christians have criticized evangelical leaders for what they view as a single-minded focus on a small set of issues to the exclu- sion of broader concerns such as economic justice, environmental stew- ardship, and racial reconciliation. Young evangelicals in particular show signs of much broader political concerns than their elders, leading some important megachurches to withdraw from political activism.[11]

STRATEGIC REALITIES

The political structure of the United States, the attachment to libertarian social values, and the political diversity of American Christians are long- term constraints on the success of the Christian Right. In recent years, the movement has struggled with an additional set of barriers that grow out of strategic considerations by movement activists and the movement's longtime patron, the Republican Party.

As a political party in a system in which it usually takes a majority of votes to win, the Republican Party needs to assemble a coalition of groups to hold public office. When one element of the coalition comes to define the party—particularly in a negative way—the party needs to find a way to avoid taking a hit in public support due to guilt by association. Back in the 1970s, when the Republicans seemed to be a permanent minority party, some Republican activists saw white evangelicals as their best hope of achieving majority status and reached out to the movement and its voters. We have already told that story earlier in this chapter.

Christian conservatives responded by flocking to local and state party caucuses, taking control of the Republican apparatus in at least eighteen states—not only evangelical strongholds in the South but also such apparently unlikely places as Minnesota, Iowa, and Oregon (Persinos 1994; Conger and Green 2002). By conventional wisdom, about one-fourth of the delegates to the Republican national convention are thought to be affiliated with this bloc, giving them substantial platform influence. As one of the largest groups within the GOP, the Christian Right has effectively vetoed the presidential nominations of several pro-choice Republicans and exerted considerable pressure on the choice of potential running mates, Supreme Court appointees, and cabinet-level appointments.[12]

Despite the prospect of attracting new partners to their coalition, longtime Republicans did not always welcome the converts when they first appeared in the 1980s (Hertzke 1993, 158–71). Describing the Pat Robertson forces as something like "the bar scene out of Star Wars" (cited in Hertzke 1989, 6), the Republican state chairman of Michigan articulated the repugnance that many in the GOP establishment felt toward the newcomers. His counterpart in Georgia declared that the Christian Rightists who took over that state's party had the attitudes "that brought you the burning of Joan of Arc, the Salem Witch trials, and the Ayatollah Khomeini" (Gurwitt 1989, 54). The tendency of the evangelicals to portray this conflict as a battle of "Christians versus Republicans" did not smooth over the situation. To some extent, the resentment directed by party regulars against the evangelical newcomers is an inevitable by-product of a struggle for power between passionate newcomers and entrenched interests, an old story in American politics. But it also reflects a cultural conflict—what one participant called "the God Squad versus the Regulars" (Gurwitt 1989, 57). The conservative Christian activists who moved into Republican Party circles brought different values, priorities, and styles. Compared with party regulars, they were decidedly more religious, and religious in a different, more intense manner. Despite sharing the economic conservatism of the regulars, they attached much greater priority to social issues and took an extremely nationalistic line in foreign policy (Knuckey 1999). Although these differences seem to have softened somewhat in recent years, the gap between Christian conservatives and non-evangelical Republicans remains wide (Miller and Schofield 2008).

The entry of the evangelical activists threatened both the internal harmony and larger electoral prospects of the Republican Party. According to Rebecca E. Klatch (1988), social and economic conservatives disagree fundamentally over the individual and society, the role of the state, and the position of women. Unlike economic conservatives, who believe society will thrive when individuals are free to pursue self-interest, social conservatives entertain a model in which "society brings the individual under the moral authority of God, the church, and the family, thereby restraining man's instincts and curbing individual self-interest" (Klatch 1988, 31). It follows that economic conservatives want to limit and dismantle the state while social conservatives want to use the state to achieve a different set of goals from those it has recently pursued under the influence of "secular humanism." Thus, proposals to regulate the entertainment media, set federal standards on sex education, restrict access to birth control, or control the flow of information across computer networks—just some of the legislation implied by the various conservative "contracts"—appeal to social conservatives but conflict with economic conservatives' desire for smaller and less intrusive government.

Finally, according to Klatch, social conservatives assign priority to defending a traditional role for women as housewives and caregivers; they oppose day care, liberalized abortion, and gay rights as threats to traditional sex roles. "Laissez-faire women, on the other hand," writes Klatch (1988, 34), "are pro-choice and support day care, as long as it remains in private hands; they firmly reject any government role in legislating sexuality or moral matters as an intrusion on individual liberty." Although Klatch emphasizes the differences among women, this divide seems to extend to the larger population (Johnson and Tamney 2001). It may prove difficult for the Republicans to contain two such contradictory worldviews within the same party.

The challenge has become greater over time as the appeal of many of the Christian Right's core social issues has waned among the non-evangelical voters who are needed to forge an electoral majority and who respond positively to economic conservatism but take a libertarian line on social issues (Miller and Levitin 1976). To wit, referring to the administration's policy against stem cell research, the son of President Reagan rebuked President Bush for "wearing his faith on his sleeve to gain political advantage."[13] Similarly, the 2005 debate over Terri Schiavo, the brain-dead Florida woman whose husband wanted her feeding tube removed, pitted many women and mainline Protestants within the Republican Party against their evangelical colleagues who tried to force medical authorities to continue her treatment or face legal penalties. Many in the GOP want day care facilities, environmental protection, and greater spending on public education—issues that leave conservative evangelicals either indifferent or alienated (Berke 1995). An emphasis on Christian Right concerns is thus likely to drive non-evangelicals—and moderate evangelicals as well—away from the GOP.

George H. W. Bush lost net electoral support in 1992 because of his commitment to the pro-life cause and public perceptions of his association with the Christian Right (Abramowitz 1995; Alvarez and Nagler 1995; Miller 1993, 205–9). Christian Right activists have sometimes succeeded in obtaining senatorial or gubernatorial nominations for their favored candidates but then witnessed the candidate lose to a coalition of moderate Republicans, Democrats, and Independents (Rozell and Wilcox 1995). Hostility to the Christian Right was a large factor in the Republican presidential defeats of both 1992 and 1996 (Bolce and De Maio 1999). In the past several national elections, House Democrats have picked up seats in suburban districts that had gone heavily Republican in the past but were heavily populated by GOP moderates with a different issue agenda from that of the Christian Right. In 2008, Sarah Palin's strong attachment to evangelical Christianity may have placated the social conservatives who were lukewarm to John McCain, but it appears to have cost him support among other Republican-oriented constituencies.

The public backlash against Christian conservatives has also been evident at the local level. As part of the return to the grass roots, Christian activists have tried to elect conservative Christians to local school boards to cleanse public schools of the "alien philosophy" and "secular humanism" pervading them (Nazario 1992; Simonds 1985; Deckman 2004). In many cases, such candidates ran so-called stealth campaigns in which they disguised their commitment to Christian Right priorities by using broad slogans about maintaining discipline and values. Once in office, they pressed for replacing sex education curricula with abstinence-only policies, mandated the teaching of creationism in biology, encouraged school prayer, and generally tried to implement the social conservatism that resides at the heart of the movement. In places as diverse as Lake County, Florida, and Dover, Pennsylvania, school board majorities associated with the Christian Right were summarily voted out of office as soon as they revealed their true colors.

Concerned about Republican strategic interests in the early 1990s, Christian Right activists tried to "mainstream the message" by downplaying harsh rhetoric and framing their critiques in nonreligious language. As we noted above, the Christian Coalition led the way with "rights-based" rhetoric that it thought would appeal to voters not steeped in evangelical piety. Although there were some successes, this new approach does not seem to have worked much on social issues such as gay marriage. Approaching same-sex marriage from a rights perspective appears to concede the argument to supporters because it draws on notions of human equality. Arguing that extending marriage rights to same-sex couples somehow impinges on the rights of heterosexual couples or children does not seem nearly as persuasive as claims rooted in biblical morality or social tradition. So giving up the morality-based argument to enhance the appeal of the Christian Right's position does not seem to have strengthened the social movement's mass appeal. When candidates affiliated with the movement do make unfettered statements about the real reasons for some of their issue positions, it costs them (and the GOP) serious votes.

The issue came to a head in the aftermath of the 2012 election, the fifth of the last six when the GOP presidential candidate lost the popular vote. Some influential voices in the Republican Party have called on their fellow members to spend less time and energy on social issues like gay marriage or other moral concerns (Barbour et al. 2013). During the long presidential primary season, the relentless culture war rhetoric of candidates Michele Bachmann, Herman Cain, Newt Gingrich, Rick Perry, and Rick Santorum painted the party with an image that hurt it not only among gay voters but also among the young. A postelection study of voters under thirty found that the GOP was seen as close-minded and rigid, whereas young voters found the Democrats to be best described by positively valued terms such as *tolerant, diverse,* and *open-minded* (Anderson 2013, 69). This is particularly worrying to Republican leaders because their party's base is increasingly gray haired. As younger voters are becoming strikingly less religious and more open to accepting gay marriage (even young evangelicals), the Republican future looks less promising (Putnam and Campbell 2010, 120–32; Farrell 2011). It is not surprising that some GOP leaders are losing their ardor for the Christian Right.

Perhaps one symbol of the decline of the social conservatives was the emergence after 2008 of the Tea Party movement. This social movement was focused principally on traditional GOP issues of high taxes and government spending but with a much more disdainful attitude to political negotiation and compromise. Upon closer inspection, however, the Tea Party turns out to be much closer to the Christian Right than the traditional GOP leadership. According to a national survey in 2010 (Jones and Cox 2010), a majority of Tea Party supporters (self-identified) are also Christian conservatives. Accordingly, almost two-thirds would ban abortion in all or most cases and fewer than 20 percent support same-sex marriage. Tea Party identifiers share Christian Right positions on America as a Christian nation and on immigration. Their most favored candidates are, to a person, social conservatives and evangelical Protestants. Rather than an alternative to the Christian Right, it is more accurate to use biblical language likening the Tea Party's mass supporters to old wine in new wineskins or, as Democrats delight in calling them, Teapublicans.

The GOP reformers after 2012 apparently don't see much difference either. Karl Rove, George W. Bush's main political strategist, has created a new Super PAC expressly intended to discourage Republican primary voters from nominating extremist candidates who are likely to lose general elections for what are considered winnable seats.[14] The kind of "unelectable" nominees whom Rove had in mind apparently include an announced 2014 senatorial candidate in Georgia, who recently described evolution, embryology, and the Big Bang theory as "lies straight from the pit of hell," or the party's 2010 senatorial nominee in Missouri, who famously asserted that women have the innate capacity to prevent pregnancy in cases of "legitimate rape." All these candidates, Tea Party favorites, cannot really be distinguished from Christian conservatives and would simply reinforce the strategic challenges facing the GOP.

As the furor that greeted Rove's announcement demonstrates, downplaying the issues of concern to Christian conservatives will not be easy. The Christian Right is now organizationally entrenched in the Republican Party (Conger 2010), supplying its largest group of voters and activists. Watching how the party's internal critics of the Christian Right manage to "tame" the base will be an important political story over the next decade.

CONCLUSION

The Christian Right played an important role in moving evangelical Protestants into the Republican camp, paving the way for its national ascendance in the 1980s and thereafter and generating pressure for policy change. Nonetheless, the movement does not control the party. In some ways, the situation of the Christian Right among Republicans resembles the condition of African Americans among the Democrats. In the latter case, blacks are sometimes described as a "captured" constituency. Because the Democrats embraced the cause of civil rights when the Republicans moved the other way in the 1960s, blacks have essentially no meaningful political alternative besides abstention if they are dissatisfied with Democratic fidelity to their cause. In the same way, it seems, the parties have become so polarized over the Christian Right agenda that conservative Christians must either live with the Republican Party or retire from politics. That is not an idle threat, because evangelicals have built a thriving Christian subculture with its own bookstores, mass media, celebrities, and institutions (Bandow 1995).

The evangelical embrace of politics through the Christian Right is tenuous for another reason. Some thoughtful critics have wondered whether participation in politics, an inherently messy business, may compromise the integrity of people who got involved precisely to secure higher levels of public integrity. Because evangelicals put such high stock in personal morality (as they understand it), they may be less willing to remain politically responsive to leaders who are compromised. That hypothetical scenario became real in the case of Republican lobbyist Jack Abramoff, a longtime friend and associate of many GOP activists. The investigation of Abramoff's activity revealed that he provided funds to a number of high-profile leaders of the Christian Right, men such as the one-time leader of Christian Coalition, Ralph Reed, the Rev. Louis Sheldon of the Traditional Values Coalition, and Rabbi Daniel Lapin of Toward Tradition. Although the men claim to have intended to defeat a bill that liberalized gambling, they accepted money from a lottery company to help kill a bill that would actually have banned online gambling.[15] Despite claiming they didn't know the source of the money or realize the ultimate purpose of the funds, the leaders of traditionalist groups have opened themselves up to severe criticism from a movement that considers gambling a source of moral decay. Ordinary lobbyists may claim to be amoral about their clients and causes, but self-described advocates of moral regeneration cannot take that tack without losing their credibility. The imperatives of politics and religious norms may come into conflict in ways that discourage continued evangelical political involvement. As if more examples were needed, the highly publicized marital infidelities of several evangelical elected officials—Governor Mark Sanford of South Carolina and Senator John Ensign of Nevada, among others—added fuel to the fire.

We have considered the Christian Right from a number of angles. In concluding the chapter, it would be useful to remember that the movement is not quite as innovative as it may appear. The Christian Right drew on well-established traditions of American life. Some observers have even interpreted the new Christian conservatism as an attempt to revitalize the civil religion discussed in chapter 3. The idea of the United States as a redeemer nation and its people as "chosen" to lead humankind took a severe beating in the 1960s and 1970s. These developments may have accelerated an ongoing shift in cultural values that undermined the moral consensus in American society. By insisting on official support of traditional moral values and of the view of the United States as a nation under divine judgment, the leaders of the Christian Right have sounded themes with a strong civil religious orientation.

As new players in the game of national politics, the evangelical Protestants have attracted most of the attention of trend spotters. But the evangelicals have not been the only religious group to reassess traditional political loyalties. As the next chapter will make clear, Catholics have also undergone a profound political transition at the same time that mainline Protestant churches have appeared to lose enthusiasm for constant political engagement. Meanwhile, Jews continue to exhibit a type of political behavior that confounds many observers.

9

Continuity and Change in the Religious Center

Catholics, Mainline Protestants, and Jews

The really big story is that amid the clamor of invisible armies and righteous empires, there is a noticeable silence in the way most Americans bring their values and beliefs to bear upon the democratic process.

—Wade Clark Roof

Because of all the attention devoted to the mobilization of evangelical Protestants by the Christian Right, it has been easy to lose sight of the other major religious traditions in the United States. In the next three chapters, we turn our attention to religious communities that also matter in American public life. This chapter examines three of the largest and most politically significant traditions: mainline Protestantism, Roman Catholicism, and Judaism. In chapter 10, we focus on a group of minority religions that either have played or are likely to play an important role in politics. Following that discussion, chapter 11 looks at the role of religion in political mobilization based on gender and sexuality. By studying women and gays, we try to shed light on the capacity of religion to inspire both movements of social change and resistance.

As the epigraph to this chapter attests, scholars and journalists pay little attention to groups that conduct their political activity without a crusading mentality. Because Catholics, mainline Protestants, and Jews have generally avoided the inflamed rhetoric that often characterizes the public discourse of evangelical Protestants, these groups have not been the subject of the same intensive scholarship as the newly mobilized evangelicals. Moreover, to the extent these groups do draw attention, the coverage is more misleading than enlightening. Catholicism attracts political attention mostly because of the church's opposition to abortion, leaving its other political activities largely beneath the radar. By emphasizing decline and apparent political disengagement, discussions of the mainline denominations of American Protestantism overlook a vital political witness that concentrates forcefully on local affairs. Similarly, Jews are hardly the single-issue constituency (Israel) that media accounts suggest.

Beneath the surface, all three traditions have faced pressure to modify their traditional political patterns and involvement in public affairs. They have responded in different ways. After a period of dramatic internal changes in the 1960s, the Catholic Church shed its predictable conservatism, especially on foreign and military policy, to adopt a new role as gadfly and activist on a wide range of issues. Although Catholic thought generally moved to the left for a time, the church hierarchy (a term commonly used for the bishops and other top officials, including the Vatican) has maintained a staunchly conservative outlook on the issue of abortion and appears to have moved to the right on a range of issues (McDonough 2013). The mainline denominations in American Protestantism, once the driving force for many social reform campaigns, seem to have pulled back somewhat from active engagement in the political realm or have at least changed the way they act in public affairs. And Jews, though still a mainstay of the liberal coalition, have had occasion to reassess their traditional alliances. These are the major trends to be discussed here.

In examining the recent political tendencies of American religious groups, we emphasize the role of religious leaders. In many religious communities, the clergy take the lead in defining institutional interests and applying theology to public issues. If social change alters the perspective of church members, the impact will usually register first with the ministry. Hence our discussion of trends in the political behavior of religious groups would be incomplete without close attention to the clergy. At the same time, as we have mentioned throughout the book, it is important to recognize that religious leaders do not control the political perspectives of church members. Rather, in their attempt to shape the political outlook of coreligionists, ministers compete for influence with secular politicians, the media, and many other organized groups. The political attitudes of congregants are also shaped by personal experiences and the perspectives derived from living in a variety of social contexts that cannot be manipulated by the church. In each religious group under study here, even the most centralized and hierarchical, some discrepancy between the attitudes of the religious elite and the views from the pews is inevitable.

CATHOLICISM: CONFLICTING POLITICAL IMPULSES

Once exiled to the margins of American public life, Catholics have become deeply enmeshed in the political system. The largest single religious denomination in the United States, a position first achieved in the mid-nineteenth century, they now have considerable political standing. Roman Catholics currently occupy six of the nine seats on the United States Supreme Court, the vice presidency (Joe Biden), and the speakership of the U.S. House of Representatives (John Boehner). In 2012, both vice presidential candidates were Catholics, a coincidence that virtually nobody mentioned. Some Catholics are already being touted as strong candidates for major presidential nominations in 2016. In a phrase, Catholics have arrived.

For most of the twentieth century, the Catholic Church in the United States was closely associated with conservative political causes. In foreign affairs, the church was synonymous with vigorous opposition to Communism and other perceived threats to the social order. As decades of Catholic (and ex-Catholic) novelists have reported, the church was perceived by its members as an implacable opponent of moral change. It represented discipline, order, hierarchy, and the stifling of sensual urges. This impulse bred a sense that politics was not the solution to social problems. Instead of laws or social programs, William Kerben (cited in Lynd 1968, 300) contended, the Catholic tradition put its faith in "correction of minds by true teaching and reforming hearts by instilling virtue." We hear echoes of this perspective today from Catholic conservatives such as Patrick Buchanan, Phyllis Schlafly, and William Bennett.

In the early twenty-first century, the Catholic Church in the United States has been consumed by scandal over the sexual abuse of children by priests. Beyond the charges of sexual assault, the church is under attack by Catholics who believe the hierarchy looked the other way, responding to charges of misconduct not by disciplining the violators but by reassigning them to other parishes where they were free to prey upon other children. The scandal wreaked havoc on church finances, morale, cohesion, and perceived moral credibility. It may well diminish the public voice of Catholicism for some time to come.

In the time and space between these two eras, the Catholic Church developed and occupied a distinctive centrist position in American political life. Catholicism shed its once predictable moral traditionalism to embrace a number of major social reforms. During the 1980s, the church came to public attention because of its opposition to many of the policies pursued by the Reagan and Bush administrations. The bishops issued critical pastoral letters on nuclear strategy and the economy, priests and nuns participated enthusiastically in mass movements against nuclear weapons, and Catholics spearheaded opposition to U.S. policy in Central America. In the political realm, this perspective was embodied by Catholic liberals such as Senator Edward Kennedy and Mario Cuomo. During the Clinton era of the 1990s, the church leadership spoke out against what it saw as the harsh treatment of helpless people by the program changes called "welfare reform" and the apparent eagerness of politicians to embrace capital punishment. While those themes still sounded during the Bush presidency, the bishops also took a strong stand against going to war with Iraq because they saw the military campaign as preemptive and unilateral, qualities that undermined its moral credibility in Catholic teaching.[1] All the while, the church maintained a strong witness against the death penalty and in favor of humane policies toward immigrants who had entered the United States illegally.

Yet the church did not shed its conservative moral tradition entirely. The leadership of the church remained adamant about the protection of embryonic human life. This took the form of political opposition to legalized abortion and, during the presidency of George W. Bush, to the attempt by scientists to harvest stem cells from discarded embryos. How and why has the church developed and sustained such conflicting political impulses?

THE CONSERVATIVE POLITICAL HERITAGE

The traditional pattern of Catholic politics in the United States was epitomized by the career of Francis Cardinal Spellman, from 1939 to 1967 the archbishop of New York. As head of the major Catholic center in the United States and a person of considerable persuasive ability, he imposed a distinctly conservative tilt to the church's effort to influence the public realm (Cooney 1984). Intensely anti-Communist, suspicious of the civil rights and labor movements, and a strong advocate of government efforts to prohibit public displays of "immorality," Spellman forged strong links between the church and leaders of secular conservative movements. Under his influence, the Catholic hierarchy enthusiastically endorsed the active involvement of the United States in military conflicts wherever Communism was thought to be a threat. From Spain in the 1930s through Vietnam in the 1960s, Spellman consistently favored a policy satirized by the phrase "Pass the Lord and praise the ammunition." A similar emphasis marked the ministry of Archbishop J. Fulton Sheen, the public voice of the church through his weekly radio and television programs (Sherwood 2011).

Spellman's views on world affairs resonated with rank-and-file members of the church (Lipset 1964). Two post–World War II ultranationalistic social movements, McCarthyism and the John Birch Society, drew greater backing from Catholics than from the population at large. This militaristic tendency was also apparent in young Catholics who participated in surveys about the use of force in international politics (Klineberg 1950, 175; Eckert and Mills 1935; Blau 1953; Connors, Leonard, and Burnham 1968).

The strong conservatism evinced by American Catholics during the time of Spellman's reign as the "American pope" has been explained by the familiar forces of group interests, social standing, and creed. Because the Catholic Church was a dominant force in many of the countries where Communism sought power, Communism represented a fundamental threat to Catholic institutions. The outspoken antireligiousness of Communist leaders and the active persecution of the church wherever the Communist Party had come to power further inflamed Catholic opinion. This concern helped build early Catholic support for the U.S. military effort in Vietnam. The dispatches from the National Catholic News Service made it seem "as though the big story in Vietnam is how the war affects Catholic missionaries, Catholic institutions, Catholic programs, Catholic political personalities, Catholic villages, Catholic soldiers, Catholic anything" (Deedy 1968, 126). In domestic politics, too, the church leaders fought innovative national government programs when they threatened Catholic local institutions and authority (Byrnes 1991).

Social factors, principally the insecure social status of Catholic immigrants, also contributed to the tendency of Catholic spokespeople "to identify their Americanism with their Catholicism" (Dohen 1967, 175). Militant native-stock Protestants had long impugned the "Americanism" of Catholics, citing Pope Leo XIII's hostility to church-state separation as proof that "Romanism" threatened American religious liberty. One way to challenge this claim was to "overidentify" with American nationalism (Hofstadter 1965). Hence, Catholic immigrants and their descendants flocked to patriotic societies and veterans' groups, eager to display extreme vigilance through acts of superpatriotism. From the viewpoint of status politics theory, the fervent anti-Communism of Catholics represented an opportunity to assert their oneness with American values.

As noted earlier in this chapter, the conservatism of American Catholics has also been attributed to creedal factors. From the eighteenth-century Enlightenment through the middle of the twentieth century, "Catholicism and liberalism stood in a vigorously adversarial relation to each other" (Hollenbach 1990, 103). Catholic teaching looked askance at liberalism's distrust of tradition and authority, stress on religious freedom and skepticism, and philosophical individualism. Domestic or international movements associated with such values—such as Communism or even milder schemes of social reform—drew opposition from the church. Moreover, the church often considered political issues through the haze of "nostalgia for agrarian, local, organic forms of social life" (103), values rooted in the peasant cultures that Catholic immigrants brought to America from the Italian and Irish countryside. The Catholic emphasis on authority and hierarchy may have further disposed American Catholics to support national leaders who undertook military intervention in the name of national security.

On the basis of such explanations, Catholics acquired a reputation for extreme political conservatism that has been hard to shake—even in the face of polls showing that Catholics now occupy the middle of the American political spectrum (see chapter 2). That reputation was never entirely warranted, even in the heyday of anti-Communism during the 1950s. Catholic politicians such as Alfred E. Smith and Robert F. Wagner, who served as New York's governor and senator, respectively, helped lay the foundations for the welfare system in the United States (O'Brien 1968). During the period that Cardinal Spellman tried to steer Catholics in the New York diocese to conservative causes, Dorothy Day founded the Catholic Worker movement to promote progressive policies on poverty, labor, social justice, civil liberties, and international disarmament (Piehl 1982). Catholic theologians, too, were steadily moving away from traditional beliefs about the rigid separation between heaven and earth, forging a new concern with social ethics (Curran 1982).

Even if they dismissed the signs of liberalization as unrepresentative of mainstream Catholic thought, political analysts could not overlook hard evidence of Catholic support for the Democratic Party. Yet rather than acknowledge that this partisan tradition indicated the potential for Catholic liberalism, most scholars attempted to explain away the Democratic affiliation with the same economic self-interest argument used to account for the Democratic affiliation of southern evangelicals. By addressing the economic problems of the working class, they argued, Franklin D. Roosevelt had safeguarded the immediate interests of most American Catholics. Due to gratitude for his policies and for his appointments of Catholics to public jobs, Roosevelt and his immediate successors enjoyed continuing electoral support from the Catholic voter. But as the memory of the New Deal eroded and issues of foreign policy and civil rights replaced economic security on the Catholic political agenda, the "natural" conservatism of American Catholics once again came into play. During the late 1960s and 1970s, when conservative political activists hoped to replace the New Deal coalition with a right-wing majority more to their liking, Catholics were perceived as the most likely converts and became the target of special appeals (McAndrews 2012). Despite these efforts, the subsequent political movement of Catholics has not been toward a whole-hearted embrace of conservatism but, at least among the clergy, toward a more liberal posture on most major national issues apart from abortion.

THE TRANSFORMATION OF CATHOLIC ATTITUDES

If the conservatism of traditional Catholic politics was due to communal isolation and immigrant culture, the social transformation of Catholic life was bound to produce new departures in political action. Indeed, during the decades after World War II, due in part to the GI Bill that paid for the college education of ex-soldiers, Catholics in America experienced dramatic upward mobility. Even when allowance is given for the enormous variation among individual Catholics, the community as a whole enjoyed substantial increases in economic status, social acceptance, and the acquisition of politically relevant skills and resources.[2] Having "left the ghetto" (Hanna 1979, 22) economically and psychologically, Catholics were primed to assume a larger role in national political life. The direction of that new energy was principally determined by events in Rome.

What changed the Catholic Church in America—or what gave official approval to trends that might have been developing independently—was a 1962 meeting of the world's bishops that became known as Vatican II, or the Ecumenical Council. Under the guidance of Pope John XXIII, this historic meeting of church fathers revolutionized church liturgy and ritual. As part of that reformation, Catholic leaders urged their parishioners to apply their Christian values to the problems of the world. Condemning the sinfulness of poverty, war, injustice, and other social ills, the church put its authority squarely behind the worldwide movement for social change. This profound shift of mood, coinciding with the assumption of the presidency by an energetic and vigorous Catholic, prompted an enthusiastic response from the American Catholic community (Hanna 1979, chap. 2). In developments that did not always meet with the approval of the older and more conservative bishops or of many Catholic laypersons, many young priests and nuns enrolled in the civil rights and antipoverty movements.

The enthusiasm for political change among Catholic leaders might not have survived into the 1980s without a corresponding transformation in the organization of the American church (E. Kennedy 1985). Under the impact of Vatican II, the American bishops established the United States Catholic Conference to speak with one voice about public issues. Absorbing several older institutions, the newly established organization developed departments specializing in domestic antipoverty efforts, campaigns for third-world economic development, and the promotion of world peace and social justice. This action-oriented church bureaucracy was increasingly staffed by professionals with substantial secular training and a commitment to broad-ranging social reforms. A new breed of bishops, large in number because a mandatory retirement age produced more openings than normal in the hierarchy, proved highly receptive to the Vatican II outlook. Although the differences between the current and pre–Vatican II bishops can easily be overstated (see the data in E. Kennedy 1985, chap. 2), the leaders of the post–Vatican II Catholic Church, like the parishioners, experienced a much more cosmopolitan upbringing than their predecessors. Young enough to have absorbed the liberalism of the 1960s and more familiar with secular environments, they imparted a much more liberal cast to Catholic social and political thought.

The movement known as liberation theology, with its "preferential option for the poor," also stimulated a new direction during the 1970s. Responding to the papal call for a renewed emphasis on social justice, some Latin American bishops and many clergy abandoned the traditional alliance between the church and the ruling classes of the region. Instead of defending the status quo, liberation theologians argued, the church should join the poor in resisting large landowners and their allies in military governments. Many priests and lay Catholics acted on this belief by forming a "church of the people" that engaged oppressive regimes in direct political, economic, and military challenges. Liberation theology imparted a willingness to challenge the power of the state in pursuit of the prophetic mission of the church. This model stimulated many American Catholics (and Protestants) similarly to reconsider the role of their church in struggles between rich and poor.

The most dramatic evidence of the new mood came in Catholic reactions to the war in Vietnam. As it did for so many other Americans, the Vietnam War eventually prompted many Catholics to rethink their traditional support for U.S. military involvement around the globe. At the extreme wing of the antiwar movement, a Catholic was the first young man to be imprisoned for publicly destroying his draft card, and a pair of Jesuit priests, Daniel and Phillip Berrigan, became leaders of a campaign of civil disobedience launched to protest U.S. military action in Vietnam (Meconis 1979; Polner 1998). Among the young men who fled to Canada rather than serve as conscientious objectors, Catholics were apparently represented to a disproportionate degree (Surrey 1982). Despite these passionate expressions of antiwar feeling, most Catholics did not abandon their strong support for military action during the early years of the war. In Gallup polls taken between 1965 and 1967, Catholics were more supportive than Protestants of U.S. military participation by about 10 percent (calculated from data in Mueller 1973, 143). Whereas many Protestant and Jewish spokespersons condemned U.S. participation in the war, the

Catholic bishops issued a statement that concluded "it is reasonable to argue that our presence in Vietnam is justified" (reprinted in Drinan 1970, 192). Cardinal Spellman was perhaps the most enthusiastic supporter of military action in American religious circles.

But as the war dragged on into the late 1960s, Catholic support gradually eroded. In 1968, the bishops issued a new pastoral letter that was notably less enthusiastic than its 1966 predecessor (Drinan 1970, 195). While raising more questions than answers, the new statement called on Catholics to judge the legitimacy of U.S. participation in Vietnam by the "just war" principle—a doctrine that deems military action appropriate only if all other methods have failed to achieve an equitable settlement and if the use of force is proportional to the goal of the war. One Catholic clergyman who decided that Vietnam violated the standard set by the just war doctrine, Father Robert Drinan of Boston, ran for a seat in the U.S. Congress on an antiwar platform and became the first priest elected to the House in many years. The bishops eventually moved wholeheartedly into the antiwar camp, passing a resolution calling for an immediate halt to U.S. military participation in Southeast Asia, taking a strong position in favor of amnesty for draft evaders and war resisters, and opposing military conscription outside the context of a genuine national emergency. As the hierarchy moved, so in time did the laity (Mueller 1973, 143).

Since those watershed years, the American bishops have consistently called for conciliation and negotiation in preference to military action in world affairs. In Latin America, for example, the Catholic Church spearheaded opposition to U.S. financial and military assistance for dictatorial governments that hewed to an anti-Communist line. Catholics played a key role in providing illegal sanctuary for refugees from the strife in Central America. Through acts of civil disobedience ranging from nonpayment of income taxes to assaults on military property, individual Catholics, including members of the clergy, protested efforts by the U.S. government to take the side of conservative forces in that region or otherwise to promote violence (Nepstad 2008). In addition, missionaries from the Maryknoll order have worked throughout Latin America to promote social change through programs of land reform, social welfare benefits, and the like. Whenever military action has been contemplated—in the Middle East, southern Europe, the Caribbean—the American bishops have counseled leaders to consider first various nonviolent alternatives. They have also been a leading voice on behalf of humanitarian assistance to nations around the globe.

This evolution was marked dramatically by a well-publicized letter on nuclear weapons, issued by the bishops in 1983. "The Challenge of Peace: God's Promise and Our Response" was intended to educate Catholics about church doctrine on war and violence in world affairs. It urged

Catholics to measure government action against the just war standard and respect persons whose conscience prompted them to refuse to bear arms or to otherwise defend themselves with tools of violence. The bishops declared that the idea of deterring war by matching the weaponry of an opponent—a cornerstone of U.S. nuclear strategy—was an inadequate basis for long-term peace on earth. Indeed, because deterrence rested on a willingness actually to use nuclear weapons, some bishops found the entire concept immoral and called on the government to accelerate efforts to achieve disarmament. The letter, an open challenge to Reagan administration policy on several counts, undercut the notion that world tension was the exclusive responsibility of the "evil empire," holding the United States equally to blame for failing aggressively to address the underlying sources of global instability.

Did the hierarchy carry the parishioners? Although some conservative Catholics denounced the letter as naive or inappropriate, it apparently stimulated the Catholic rank and file to reconsider their positions on questions of peace and war. As Andrew Greeley (1985) pointed out, Catholic opinion on military spending underwent a dramatic shift after the issuance of the pastoral letter in 1983. By comparison with their earlier preferences and Protestant opinions, the Catholic population moved significantly toward the view that the United States was devoting too many resources to military purposes. A study in one midwestern city found that Catholics were substantially more likely than Protestants to know of their church's position on nuclear weapons and that knowledge of the hierarchy's position produced greater approval for a "freeze" on the further construction and deployment of nuclear warheads (Tamney, Burton, and Johnson 1988). Gallup surveys also found sharp growth in Catholic support for the nuclear freeze after "The Challenge of Peace" was issued (Gallup and Castelli 1987, 83).

Although these changes were relatively short lived (Davidson 1989), the magnitude of the change the pastoral letter produced was more impressive than its rapid demise (Wald 1992). The letter eventually stimulated similar reaction among Protestants (Curry 1984) and appeared to promote a change in public opinion that forced the Reagan administration to move to the negotiating table. In these terms, "The Challenge of Peace" stands out as a remarkably effective political intervention by a modern religious group.

The leftward shift on international politics was accompanied by a growing concern among Catholic clergy about questions of economic policy. This was not a break with tradition but a renewal of a traditional theme in Catholic social thought. In various statements on economic questions going back to the nineteenth century, the papacy had criticized the doctrine of capitalism and the market for its undue emphasis on competition and individualism. In this tradition, the American bishops had first called for regulating unrestricted market economies in 1919 and embraced many of the proposals later enacted by Franklin Roosevelt's New Deal (Billington and Clark 1993). In the 1966 statement on Vietnam, the bishops had hinted that the ultimate source of world tension was to be found in social conditions such as hunger, poverty, and unemployment. With each successive statement on national or international conflict, this theme grew stronger. The church became more active in the domestic economic arena as well, concentrating resources to combat poverty and giving strong support to César Chávez, a Catholic activist, first to organize farmworkers and then to boycott corporations that undermined contracts between agricultural producers and the union (Ortiz 1984). From this experience and their own firsthand experience with the poverty in inner-city parishes, the bishops developed a strong interest in economic policy and began preliminary work in 1980 on a pastoral letter.

"Economic Justice for All," issued in 1986, emphasized the prevalence of economic inequality, denounced such suffering in biblical terms, and attributed economic problems to the U.S. economic and political system. Putting the church on the side of the poor and underprivileged, the bishops endorsed proposals for a substantial increase in the minimum wage, statutory limits on personal income and wealth, federally mandated welfare standards, federal support for new job programs, and pay scales that reflected the intrinsic worth of a job as well as market considerations. They called for massive emergency aid to farms and rural banks damaged by defaulted loans. At the same time, the bishops showed considerable sympathy for such capitalist and market-based practices as tax incentives, small business, multinational corporations, and policies designed to promote entrepreneurial activity. Nonetheless, the message was interpreted as a challenge to ongoing efforts by conservatives to reduce governmental involvement in the domestic economy.

The bishops faced considerable difficulty in swinging Catholic opinion to their side on this issue. Indeed, compared with the pastoral letter on nuclear war, the bishops' economic proposals were greeted unenthusiastically by the rank and file (Davidson 1989; Tamney, Burton, and Johnson 1988). The greater impact of the pastoral letter on nuclear war compared with the economic message underscores the importance of process, timing, and content in church political action. The credibility of the nuclear letter was enhanced by the careful and public deliberations that preceded it. The letter on war and peace was framed and issued at a time of grave public concern over the possibility of nuclear war; the economic letter, by contrast, emerged when the economy seemed buoyant and the extent of problems like homelessness and unemployment was not fully recognized. Furthermore, war and peace are among the kinds of issues that more readily lend themselves to sudden shifts of opinion. Calls for reducing military spending can be simple and powerful, appealing to both altruism and self-interest. By contrast, calls by the bishops for higher rates of taxation and redistribution of resources may appear to many rank-and-file Catholics to strike at the very economic system that provides advantages to them. As such, they will inspire greater resistance.

ABORTION: THE CATHOLIC RESPONSE

During the same period that the Catholic religious elite was rethinking traditional positions on a wide range of political issues, the church also gained public attention as the major force resisting the liberalization of abortion laws in the United States.[3] That stance was derived from Catholic doctrine defining the fetus as a form of human life that should enjoy a nearly absolute right to existence. From that perspective, abortion, along with any other deliberate interference with the gestation of a fertilized human egg, constitutes the moral equivalent of murder (Callahan 1970, chap. 12). This position, reiterated in the 1968 papal encyclical *Humanae Vitae*, had undergirded the church's opposition to making birth control devices freely available to the public and motivated subsequent activism against liberalized abortion. Before 1973, when the U.S. Supreme Court struck down most existing state abortion laws, the church was active in fighting state efforts to loosen restrictions on abortion through so-called right-to-life organizations. These activities increased dramatically after the *Roe* decision (Jung and Shannon 1988; Rubin 1994).

In *Roe v. Wade* (1973), the Supreme Court argued that a constitutional right to privacy prohibited states from limiting abortion during the first three months of pregnancy. Concerns for maternal health could justify medical regulations in the second trimester, and the government's interest in encouraging "normal childbirth" permitted restrictive policies in the last three months. The decision wiped out state laws that forbade abortion without regard to circumstance or timing. Armed with a record of public opposition to what the advocates of liberalization called abortion reform and the network to organize parishioners, the Catholic Church was well placed to provide leadership when the *Roe* decision brought the issue to national prominence.

The attack on liberalized abortion laws was waged on several fronts. Shortly after *Roe* was announced, the bishops created the National Committee for a Human Life Amendment, whose goal was to reverse the Supreme Court decision by passage of a constitutional amendment extending legal protection to the fetus. When these efforts failed, Catholic abortion opponents decided to press the attack through a variety of interim measures, focusing on the more immediate goal of limiting the availability of abortion by restricting government funding and using administrative regulations to deter women from using abortion facilities. Like other groups that seek to wield influence in the legislative process, the opponents of abortion have attempted to accumulate power through the development of grassroots electoral organization. Although they have intervened in presidential politics, even to the extent of sponsoring a symbolic campaign for the Democratic presidential nomination, their major focus has been on electing anti-abortion candidates to state and congressional office. The full extent of church involvement in these actions was spelled out in the highly detailed "Pastoral Plan for Pro-Life Activities" issued in 1975 by the bishops. The bishops' plan called for the development in each congressional district of an identifiable, tightly knit, and well-organized "pro-life" unit (Jaffe, Lindheim, and Lee 1981, 75) that would provide financial assistance, campaign workers, and publicity to anti-abortion candidates. The plan envisioned close ties between the secular right-to-life organizations and the Catholic parish. In practice, the church has supplied the movement with physical, financial, and human resources, leading to the perception that the right-to-life movement is largely an expression of the Catholic hierarchy. Although academic researchers were skeptical about the electoral impact of the abortion issue in national elections (Traugott and Vinovskis 1980; Granberg and Burlison 1983; Granberg 1987; Vinovskis 1979; Bolce 1988), the anti-abortion movement gained a reputation for political clout that prompted many lawmakers to pay it careful heed (Margolis and Neary 1980).[4]

As the prospect of amending the Constitution faded, the opponents of abortion confronted the Supreme Court with a variety of laws testing the limits of the *Roe* decision. In several states and localities, legislative bodies tried to qualify the Court's ruling by imposing preconditions on women seeking abortions—permission of the spouse or parents, mandatory waiting periods—or by setting medical requirements intended to make the operation impractical. Some localities adopted zoning regulations to prevent the operation of abortion facilities and required that physicians warn prospective patients to expect serious physical and psychological aftereffects. The Supreme Court struck down most of these restrictive features as religiously motivated laws with no overriding secular purpose (Friedman 1983).

Other laws and regulations received Court approval, however. Most important, the Court upheld the legality of a ban on the use of Medicaid funds for abortion under most circumstances and permitted publicly funded hospitals to refuse to perform elective abortions. Given the green light in the Medicaid decision, Congress put similar anti-abortion restrictions on military benefits, District of Columbia appropriations, federal employee health insurance, and the foreign assistance program. In addition, many states prohibited their health care contributions from being used to support elective abortion. Starting with the Reagan administration, Republican presidents extended these limits to the international sphere, denying funding to agencies that provide abortion options, and imposed a "gag" rule that prohibits federally funded family planning agencies in the United States from even mentioning abortion as an option.

With the gradual replacement of justices from the majority faction in *Roe* by conservative appointees, many observers had expected that decision to be overturned during the 1988–1989 session of the Supreme Court. When it finally issued its ruling in the case known as *Webster v. Reproductive Health Services*, the Court severely qualified the guarantees extended in 1973 but did not invalidate the earlier decision. Specifically, the five justices in the *Webster* majority gave Missouri the right to forbid public employees and facilities from conducting discretionary abortions or counseling in favor of it and to insist the physicians must determine whether the fetus is "viable" outside the womb before performing abortions on women who are twenty or more weeks pregnant. More generally, the decision signaled the Court's willingness to consider new state restrictions on the availability of abortion, and it subsequently upheld parental notification laws for abortion seekers under the age of eighteen, mandatory waiting periods, and other such limits. But despite furious activity by pro-life advocates in state legislatures, the *Roe* principle of liberal access to abortion held steady (Byrnes and Segers 1992). The principle of *Roe* was reaffirmed in convincing fashion by the 1992 decision of the Supreme Court in *Planned Parenthood v. Casey* (Garrow 1999).

The *Casey* decision and the election of a Democratic president in 1992 swung the tide decisively in favor of the pro-choice faction. Among his earliest official acts, Bill Clinton repealed the gag order, authorized the resumption of medical research using fetal tissue, restored the authority of overseas military hospitals to perform abortions, permitted importation of a "morning-after" abortion pill (RU-486), and reinstated foreign aid to groups that advocated abortion. He urged states to fund abortions for poor women who were pregnant as the result of rape or incest. In response to the mounting tide of violence aimed at family planning clinics and abortion providers, Clinton also supported a 1994 law that made it a federal crime to intimidate women seeking abortion or to impede their access to clinics. When the Republicans gained control of Congress following the 1994 election, abortion opponents tried to tie up several foreign policy appropriations by attaching riders demanding reinstatement of the gag order and also rejected a surgeon general nominee who had performed abortions. Their major victory, a bill prohibiting a rare form of abortion used late in pregnancy, was vetoed by Clinton in a decision that drew a sharp rebuke from the nation's Roman Catholic cardinals.

Clinton's successor, George W. Bush, signaled his alliance with the pro-life coalition by restoring the gag rule on his first working day as president in 2001, and he eventually signed the "partial birth abortion" ban that Clinton had vetoed, a law upheld by the Supreme Court in 2007. Although denying that he had a litmus test for Supreme Court nominees, observers argued that Bush's selection of two Catholic lawyers for the Supreme Court was a means to the end of overturning *Roe*. According to the *Washington Post*'s Baghdad bureau chief, applicants for positions with the American occupation authority in Iraq were actually questioned not about their expertise but about their attitude to abortion (Chandrasekaran 2006).

With the return of a Democrat to the White House after the 2012 election, the cycle repeated itself as President Obama repealed the gag order, overturned the ban on federal funding of stem cell research, appointed pro-choice judges to the Supreme Court, and endorsed federal funding of Planned Parenthood services.

Although abortion remains established as a legal right during the first two trimesters of pregnancy, the facts on the ground tell a somewhat different story. Access to abortion facilities has diminished appreciably due to the hostility of some state and local governments, fears of malpractice suits, the murder and assault of several abortion providers, and the harassment of personnel and patients at clinics. In many states, women seeking abortions have no effective access to abortion facilities without traveling great distances and incurring significant financial costs (Gober 1997). The legal right to an abortion, still intact, is constrained in practice by barriers to implementation.

IS ABORTION A CATHOLIC ISSUE?

Can abortion be considered a Catholic issue? To some extent, the answer depends on whether the church—both the hierarchy and the laity—is wholeheartedly united around an anti-abortion stance. At the level of religious elites, there is no question that the Catholic bishops have invested enormous energy and passion in the abortion issue, assigning it priority over many other concerns (Byrnes 1991). Even though the church's position on the issue has not produced the same level of dissent as its policy against artificial contraceptives, visible signs of disagreement within the Catholic community have cropped up. A small group of scholars and members of various religious orders, organized in "Catholics for

Choice," has publicly argued that church teaching is in fact compatible with the public availability of abortion under some circumstances (Segers 1992). Roughly one-third of the parish priests interviewed in a *New York Times*/CBS News poll supported that view, against the remaining two-thirds who endorsed official church teaching against abortion under any circumstances.[5] The two-to-one margin in favor of the bishops' position constitutes a strong consensus but falls short of unanimity.

But do the parishioners accept the guidance of the church on abortion? On matters of moral judgment, Vatican II clearly shifted the balance from the authority of the institutional church toward a more individualistic style of reasoning (Pogorelc and Davidson 2000). On many public questions that impinge on personal behavior, including the use of artificial birth control methods, the Catholic laity clearly does not welcome the counsel of its clergy (Leege 1988; McNamara 1992). In the most active form of disagreement, many Catholic women have utilized the freedom brought by *Roe v. Wade* to obtain legal elective abortions.[6] In fact, Catholic women who conceive a child outside of marriage are just as likely to elect abortion as Jewish or mainline Protestant women in the same situation (Adamczyk and Felson 2008, 34). Less dramatically, Catholics have split over abortion policy, with many favoring a liberalized policy in cases of rape, probable birth defects, or serious threat to maternal health (Sullins 1999). Indeed, it appears that most lay Catholics now favor access to abortion under those conditions, believe that "good Catholics" can reject church teaching on abortion, and strongly disapprove of church efforts to change national abortion policy directly or by pressuring Catholic officials (Moore 1993; Cook, Jelen, and Wilcox 1992). The "blatantly pro-choice tone" of the 1992 Democratic campaign did not prevent Catholics from handily favoring Bill Clinton over George H. W. Bush, nor have Catholics generally shown much willingness to vote against candidates who favor abortion access (Toner 1993). Trend studies suggest that Catholic opinion about abortion has become more polarized over time, attesting to higher levels of diversity that may complicate the task of mobilizing the community on behalf of a pro-life platform (Evans 2002). If defining abortion as a Catholic issue implies unanimity of opinion, then the label does not fit.

Abortion still might be considered a Catholic issue if it is uniquely salient to members of that faith. More so than in other groups, the *Roe* decision stimulated Catholics to adopt anti-abortion positions, and the church unquestionably took the lead in mobilizing opposition and resistance (Franklin and Kosaki 1989; Hofman 1986). Yet even in this sphere, Catholics cannot be depicted accurately as the sole source of opposition to liberalized access, and in fact are not the most intransigent opponents of abortion; that status falls to evangelical Protestants, white and black alike (see table 7.2).[7] The most radical forms of attack on abortion—sit-ins, acts of civil disobedience, clinic bombings, and murders of clinic workers—have primarily been the province of fundamentalist Protestants. The most restrictive state laws, pushing well beyond *Roe* and thus usually struck down by the courts, have typically come from states like North Dakota, where the Catholic population is proportionately quite small. More detailed research indicates that opposition to abortion is primarily a matter of moral traditionalism, gender roles, and sexual relations, not denominational affiliation (Harris and Mills 1985; Emerson 1996; Cook, Jelen, and Wilcox 1992; Jelen 1984; Woodrum and Davison 1992). Liberalized abortion is particularly abhorrent to persons enmeshed in traditional social settings and imbued with conservative norms.

If opposition to abortion is not a Catholic monopoly or a position accepted by all members of the church, neither is support for *Roe v. Wade* a wholly secular phenomenon. While public leadership of the pro-choice movement has been associated with feminist organizations like the National Organization for Women and the family planning advocate, Planned Parenthood, several Protestant and Jewish groups have worked to resist restrictive abortion policy. The Religious Coalition for Reproductive Choice, a Washington-based umbrella group with more than forty institutional members, has gained a reputation for effective lobbying in Congress (Mills 1991). It branched out to monitor abortion-related activity in the administrative agencies and has tried to raise public support for the principle of free choice in reproductive decisions. The group does not take a theological position on the abortion issue but rather emphasizes the diversity among American faiths over the status of the fetus as a human being. With such divergent views, the organization argues, extending legal protection to the fetus amounts to enshrining one theological view— the Catholic doctrine—as law. The alleged Catholic basis for anti-abortion legislation is then cited as a violation of the establishment clause of the First Amendment, and *Roe v. Wade* is portrayed as a contribution to religious freedom in America (Wenz 1992).

Although abortion cannot be reduced to an exclusively Catholic issue, the earliest active opponents of liberalization were recruited from the Catholic community. Several studies of the anti-abortion movement identified the typical activist (outside the South) as a Catholic housewife of limited education, much of it obtained in church-affiliated schools. Deeply devout and a regular churchgoer, she was likely to come from a large family and to be the mother of several children (Granberg 1981a, 1982a, 1982b). According to an insightful study of California right-to-lifers conducted by sociologist Kristin Luker (1984), these women overcame a background of political inactivity out of anger at a Supreme Court decision that seemed to strike directly at their fundamental values about motherhood, the role of women, and the purpose of sex. Assuming that men and women differ in nature, the former best suited for the role of public work and the latter for raising children, the women chose to forgo opportunities for attaining professional skills in favor of stressing their role as caregivers to children and husband. Luker points out that liberalized abortion laws undermine that set of values in three respects:

> First, it is intrinsically wrong because it takes a human life and what makes women special is their ability to nourish life. Second, it is wrong because *by giving women control over their fertility*, it breaks up an intricate set of social relationships between men and women that has traditionally surrounded (and in the ideal case protected) women and children. Third and finally, abortion is wrong because it fosters and supports a worldview that de-emphasizes (and therefore *downgrades*) the traditional role of men and women. Because these roles have been satisfying ones for pro-life people and because they believe this emotional and social division of labor is both "appropriate and natural," the act of abortion is wrong because it plays havoc with this arrangement of the world. (161–62)

The supporters of liberalized abortion have proved to be almost the complete opposite of these traditionalist Catholics in social condition and outlook.

Because abortion touches on such fundamental differences in how some people view the world and their own place in it, it should not be surprising that the debate has unleashed so much passionate energy. The tension has been particularly acute for Catholics holding public office. Traditionalist Catholics, whose views were formed in the pre–Vatican II era, have tended to justify opposition to abortion in terms of a universal doctrine of the sanctity of life that need not be restricted to Catholics. But other Catholic officials, including those sympathetic to liberalized abortion on social grounds or representatives of constituencies with mixed attitudes, have not found it easy to stake out an acceptable position. If they were to honor their Catholic background by opposing the free availability of abortion, they could be criticized for representing Catholic interests—a charge that historically has handicapped Catholics seeking public office in the United States. Yet coming down on the side of liberalized abortion would endanger their ability to draw Catholic electoral support.

The Catholic officials who have supported liberalization have justified their position by claiming that their primary responsibility as public officials is to uphold decisions legitimately promulgated by the Supreme Court. Just how fiercely church officials have reacted to this claim was best illustrated in 1984, when Representative Geraldine Ferraro (D-N.Y.), a devout Catholic, received the Democratic nomination for vice president.

Though personally opposed to abortion, she had voted against curbs on the use of federal funds to prohibit elective abortion and indicated that her votes on abortion policy would not be influenced by her private faith. Among many church officials who castigated her, the archbishop of New York wondered aloud how Catholics could vote in good conscience for a candidate who did not pledge to support restrictive abortion policies. The steady drumbeat of criticism directed at Representative Ferraro and the appearance of several bishops at Reagan campaign rallies amounted to a virtual endorsement of the Republican ticket.

By seeming to endorse a candidate in a partisan election, the church hierarchy came in for its own share of criticism from political leaders. While endorsing the church's right to speak out on issues with a moral dimension, leading Catholic Democrats asserted that the clergy had overstepped the proper "wall of separation" between church and state. Senator Edward Kennedy publicly asserted the impropriety of his church's attempts to impose a restrictive abortion policy on the nation:

> Where decisions are inherently individual ones or in cases where we are deeply divided about whether they are, people of faith should not invoke the power of the state to decide what everyone can believe or think or read or do. In such cases—cases like abortion or prayer or prohibition or sexual identity—the proper role of religion is to appeal to the free conscience of each person, not the coercive rule of secular law.[8]

In his defense of Ferraro and other Catholic politicians who opposed restrictive abortion policies, New York governor Mario Cuomo revived the notion of "civil peace" first enunciated in the 1950s by the Catholic theologian John Courtney Murray. In a religiously diverse society like the United States, Murray had argued, attempts by one religious group to prohibit what it regards as evil practices might endanger the harmony of the social order. Hence, he reasoned, it is better to tolerate such evil rather than undermine a society that has permitted such a wide degree of freedom to Catholics and other religious minorities (Wolf 1968, chap. 1). By insisting on the need for an abortion policy that did not enjoy national consensus, Cuomo argued, the Catholic Church might well encourage other religious groups to press for policies that endangered religious liberty.

> The Catholic public official lives the political truth most Catholics through most of American history have accepted and insisted on: the truth that to assure our freedom we must allow others the same freedom, even if occasionally it produces conduct by them which we would hold to be sinful. We know that the price of seeking to force our beliefs on others is that they might someday force theirs on us.[9]

Thus, according to Cuomo, Catholics should not threaten the peace of society and the freedom accorded to religion by using the state to impose policies deeply offensive to many people. He conceded that the church had every right to condemn abortion and to work for conditions that would eliminate its necessity, but, echoing Senator Kennedy, he believed it should attempt to implement its views by appealing to the consciences of individuals.

A quarter-century later, that conflict over means has yet to run its course, as was apparent in 2004, when John F. Kerry, another Catholic, won the Democratic presidential nomination, and again in 2008, when Rudy Giuliani, former mayor of New York, sought the Republican nomination. Like Ferraro before them, Kerry and Giuliani insisted on the distinction between personal views on abortion and duty to uphold the law, a position that cut no ice with a very critical hierarchy (Formicola 2009).

The church leadership has long been deeply divided over tactics in the anti-abortion campaign. For some bishops, abortion is the paramount moral issue of the day and a candidate's position on that single issue remains a litmus test of acceptability. Accordingly, some bishops have occasionally denied communion to pro-choice Catholics, a tactic that works to mobilize pro-life Catholics against such candidates but actually increases their support among pro-choice Catholics (Hofstetter, Ayers, and Perry 2008). Another camp, stimulated by the late Joseph Cardinal Bernardin of Chicago, has taken the position that abortion should be part of a "seamless garment" of issues—including nuclear war, human rights, capital punishment, doctor-assisted suicide, and poverty—all involving threats to human life. According to this perspective, candidates and officials should be judged on the full range of their beliefs, not just abortion.

Those who subscribe to the "consistent ethic of life" approach face an uphill battle to restructure Catholic opinion along new lines. Rather than apply a consistent principle to all questions involving threats to life, most Catholics (and, indeed, most Americans, according to Unnever, Bartkowski, and Cullen 2010) appear to compartmentalize each issue. Early research revealed that relatively few Catholics combined anti-abortion sentiment with opposition to capital punishment, military spending, and the use of force in world affairs—all positions that the bishops treated as expressions of the pro-life ethic. Despite the common link among the issues, opponents of abortion were no more favorable than supporters of liberalization to increased spending on health, gun control laws, or the mandatory use of seat belts (Granberg 1981b; Granberg and Granberg 1981; Cleghorn 1986; Johnson and Tamney 1988). On the other hand, more recent research suggests that the bishops' preaching about life issues generally may indeed affect regular mass attenders (Bjarnason and Welch 2004; Perl and McClintock 2001). By the same token, Catholics who admired the late Pope John Paul II were more likely to oppose abortion (Mulligan 2006). Nonetheless, what most distinguishes pro-life activists—aside from resistance to abortion, euthanasia, and suicide—is conservative preferences on social issues relating to traditional sex roles.

Standing apart from the traditional lines of political debate, the abortion dispute constitutes an exception to the recent trend of liberalized thinking among the clergy. But because its leaders have been so vocal about the issue, the anti-abortion movement has sometimes obscured the trend in Catholic politics—even from Catholic parishioners themselves. To date, concern over abortion has dominated the church's political action whenever it entered the equation. The church's concern that it might be required to provide abortion services in Catholic hospitals delayed passage of the Civil Rights Restoration Act in 1989. Continuing concern over the implications of feminism on abortion rights prevented the bishops from passing a pastoral letter on the status of women in the church. The church also opposed conservative proposals for welfare reform in 1995, fearing that reductions in aid to single mothers would stimulate pregnant poor women to seek abortions, but it has since joined evangelical Protestant leaders in condemning embryonic stem cell research.

During the 2009 debate over health care reform, the bishops insisted they would not support any proposal that permitted the use of government funds to purchase health plans that provided abortion coverage. The Affordable Care Act was amended to follow the precedent of other federal insurance programs: The insurance provided under the plan would pay for abortion only in cases of rape or incest, or to save the life of the mother. In 2012, when Catholic leaders criticized the plan on the grounds that it provided contraceptive care, another prohibited practice, the White House adopted a compromise it had previously worked out with Catholic dioceses in various U.S. cities. Religious institutions—churches, congregations, and other organizations—would not be required to provide contraceptive coverage to their employees but church-related institutions that provided services to the public and employed non-Catholics would have to insure such coverage. However, the employer would not be charged, leaving insurance companies responsible for artificial contraception out of their own pockets. As we noted in chapter 1, this compromise was denounced as an attack on religious freedom by the Catholic bishops and some Catholic Republican candidates.

The church's official position on abortion has become more difficult because of the increasing polarization of American political life. Specifically, the pro-life movement led by evangelical Protestants takes positions that diametrically oppose the Catholic line on almost all issues. The Catholic Alliance, a Conservative Coalition auxiliary that attempted to attract Catholic support, used a "family-friendly" voting scorecard that celebrated the very policies explicitly condemned by the bishops—cuts in welfare benefits, support for capital punishment, restrictive immigration policy, and so forth. Ironically, Catholic Republicans in Congress have been less likely than Jewish or black representatives to support many of the legislative priorities of the National Conference of Catholic Bishops (Oldmixon and Hudson 2008). Conservative policies may be attractive to a middle-class constituency that is generations removed from immigrant status and imbued with the notion that individual Catholics are free to pick and choose from church teachings. Catholics who identify with the evangelical movement do seem to acquire much of its political conservatism, at least on issues that have not been the subject of pastoral letters (Welch and Leege 1991). But such policies alienate the "other" Catholic Church—the "urban, ethnically diverse and economically precarious" church of recent immigrants (Hampson 1995). To maintain connections with an increasingly Hispanic constituency who will be discussed in more detail in chapter 10, church officials have often embraced liberal social welfare programs and called for generous treatment of immigrants (Rogers 1990). Negotiating a coherent path between these competing agendas remains a vivid challenge for the bishops.

As if to illustrate the conflicting political poles of Catholicism, the two professing Catholics on the national ballot in 2012 diverged sharply on the core issues of the day. The incumbent, Joe Biden, attributed his commitment to social welfare programs to his church's position on social justice, while challenger Paul Ryan, who said Catholicism was only part of his motivation for a pro-life position, echoed the bishops' claim that the contraceptive mandate in the Affordable Care Act violated Catholic religious freedom. In truth, both candidates accurately represented one view of their church but not the other. Like fellow "Kingdom Catholics," Biden came of age in the era of Vatican II and perceives the task of the church as standing with oppressed minorities, while Ryan, typical of "Communion Catholics," saw the need to restore social order after the liberal experiments of the 1960s (Radcliffe 2005).

The challenge of such divergent priorities is even greater owing to long-standing tension between the American Catholic hierarchy and the increasingly conservative Vatican. Pope John Paul II and his successor, Benedict XVI, sought to counter what they saw as a wayward national church, too open to feminism and lay influence, by promoting to bishop men who shared his traditionalist understanding of Catholic doctrine. Despite the more conservative cast to the church leadership, the American hierarchy continues to maneuver between the watchful eye of Rome and parishioners, who in large measure embrace a more individualistic and progressive style of Catholicism.

Although he was thought to be a doctrinal conservative when elected in 2013, Pope Francis has confounded some expectations with his sharp criticism of the course of the Catholic Church (Spadaro 2013). Some comments made early in his papacy suggested a more liberal attitude to gays and a more expansive role for women in the church as well as a strong sympathy for the reforms of Vatican II. While the pope has not instituted any changes in policy, his pointed comments in an interview about six months after his election suggested a very different set of priorities. He opined that the church had become fixated on "small-minded" rules, rather than the cardinal message of God's love for humanity. More explicitly, he asserted, "We cannot insist only on issues related to abortion, gay marriage and the use of contraceptive methods" and "it is not necessary to talk about these issues all the time." As if siding with the late Cardinal Bernadin's "seamless garment," the pope declared that the church should not "be obsessed with the transmission of a disjointed multitude of doctrines to be imposed insistently," but rather find a "new balance" in proclaiming the truth of doctrine without "losing the freshness and fragrance of the Gospel." Reinforcing the message near the end of the interview, he denounced those in the church "who today always look for disciplinarian solutions, those who long for an exaggerated doctrinal 'security,' those who stubbornly try to recover a past that no longer exists," who reduce faith to a mere "ideology among other ideologies." If Francis moves the Catholic Church in that direction, emphasizing social justice and God's love, the church could once again command a central role in progressive politics. The change of emphasis might be welcome among American bishops but not as much among other parts of the global church. Ironically, if he also delivers on his commitment to decentralize the church by granting more power to bishops, that could empower the traditionalists to resist changes.[10]

THE POLITICAL TRADITIONS OF MAINLINE PROTESTANTS

Unlike evangelical Protestants or Roman Catholics, mainline Protestants had established a strong and active presence in American political life well before the 1970s and long occupied a disproportionate share of public offices (Davidson 1994, 431; Duke and Johnson 1992). Most presidents have been members of a mainline Protestant church; especially strongly represented have been Episcopalians and Presbyterians. For most of the twentieth century, Catholics and Protestants from an evangelical background were rarely considered serious candidates for the nation's highest elective position. Times have changed. Numerically, Protestants have apparently become a minority of the total population (T. W. Smith and Kim 2005), and mainline Protestants have been ahead of the trend. As a sign of their diminished political power, Protestants do not hold even one of the nine Supreme Court seats since the retirement of Justice John Paul Stevens. To the extent that Protestants attract political attention, the focus is on the evangelical wing rather than the declining mainline denominations.

The loss of political and social dominance by mainline Protestantism forms the backdrop for a discussion of their changing political orientation. The political predominance of mainline Protestants, largely due to their high socioeconomic status, was usually enlisted during the twentieth century to resist governmental programs of social welfare and economic regulation. As noted in chapter 2, this tradition survives in the high (although, apparently, declining) levels of Republican identification and economic conservatism among rank-and-file members of mainline denominations.

Echoing the tension between the Catholic hierarchy and laity, the membership of mainline Protestant denominations has frequently collided with church leaders. Mainline clergy have periodically given birth to movements that cast a skeptical eye on prevailing social and economic arrangements. In this "social gospel" tradition, the distinctive feature of reform sentiment has been a belief that God's spirit pervades the world. Rather than seeing God as aloof to human social patterns, the liberal theological tradition has insisted that God is immanent, or present, in human life. Consequently, love of one's neighbor, not personal holiness, should be the principal ethical concern of Christianity (Gilkey 1968). According to this perspective, the will of God is associated with social reform, so it falls to the Christian, as a religious duty, to strive to bring about change in human social conditions. The clergy have usually been the most active carriers of this particular vision (Garrett 1973), abetted by the lobbying efforts of their denominations' Washington offices.

This rise of the social gospel movement in the early twentieth century contributed to the split in American Protestant Christianity between the mainline denominations and their evangelical and fundamentalist adversaries. Although the conflict was rooted in a number of sources, the traditionalists who appropriated the evangelical label objected to the tendency among modernist theologians to equate Christianity with support for social reform. Though the evangelicals were not indifferent to social problems, they emphasized the priority of spiritual communion between God and individuals. Hence, they interpreted social problems as the outgrowth of individual moral failings and supported solutions such as conversion or spiritual rebirth. As pointed out in the previous chapter, the evangelical wing eventually found itself cast in the role of defending traditional social values against the onslaught of modern

forces and largely retreated from the national political arena after repeated defeats during the 1920s.

Even though members of what became known as the mainline wing
were divided internally over the proper definition of Christianity, much
of the clergy moved into the social gospel camp. Their enthusiasm for
social reform waxed and waned with national political circumstances
(Carter 1954; Meyer 1961). Enthusiasm was high in the period before
World War I, low in the decade after, and high again during the presidency of Franklin D. Roosevelt. Interest in social problems dropped to
the bottom of the church agenda during the prosperous years of the post–
World War II era, when many churches concentrated their energies on
building new facilities for their suburban congregants. By the late 1950s,
the Protestant churches from the mainline denominations were the targets of strong attacks for their supposed indifference to social problems.

Few of the critics could have imagined just how sharply the situation
would change in a short time. During the 1960s, social reform moved
back to the top of the Protestant agenda. In the churches, a "new breed"
of social-action-oriented clergy jumped enthusiastically into a variety of
progressive causes (Cox 1968). Members of the new breed led rent strikes,
organized pickets around city hall, served in community action organizations, financed low-cost housing projects, and helped welfare recipients
form unions to better press their claims on reluctant government bureaucracies. At the same time that such action flourished in isolated communities, national attention was drawn to the Protestant clergy's participation
in civil rights demonstrations and their leadership role in organizations
that opposed U.S. involvement in the Vietnam War (Hall 1990).

In a 1968 survey of parish ministers in California, taken when political
activism was at its height, political scientist Harold Quinley (1974) reported on the extent of clergy involvement in three social movements—
campaigns to defend California's "fair housing" ordinance from a repeal
effort, to unionize migrant farmworkers, and to oppose the Vietnam War.
Among the 1,580 clergy who responded to Quinley's survey, the rate
of activism was pronounced—though uneven—across the three issue
areas. On the fair housing campaign, a civil rights issue that attracted
the highest level of activism, a clear majority of the Protestant ministers
took public action in the form of sermons, petitions, or other public statements conveying support for maintenance of the ordinance. For Methodist, Congregationalist, Episcopalian, and Presbyterian clergy, who most
enthusiastically endorsed the social reform ministry, antirepeal activity
also included prayers about the issue, organization of study or advocacy
groups in the church, service on public committees, and the writing of
letters to public officials. Roughly one-fourth of the ministers took similar
high-profile stances on the Vietnam War, including a substantial number

who attended protest meetings, belonged to antiwar organizations, or participated in public marches. The plight of farmworkers drew somewhat lower rates of involvement but still gained attention and support from a sizable share of the sample.

The impression of a united bloc of liberal clergy was further reinforced by their high visibility in some of the most dramatic protests of the era. In a number of southern communities where conflict over desegregation of public schools raised social tension to a fever pitch, clergymen played a key role on the front lines, frequently exposing themselves to intimidation and violent assaults from segregationists (Campbell and Pettigrew 1959, 3–4; Friedland 1998). Shortly before the 1965 Selma-to-Montgomery march to secure voting rights, the civil rights movement gained another martyr in the Rev. James Reeb of Boston. A Unitarian minister who had answered the call of Martin Luther King Jr. for ministerial involvement, Reeb died from a savage beating inflicted by opponents of the planned march. Other ministers similarly risked their lives in boarding buses bound for the South during the "Freedom Summer" campaigns. In expressing their opposition to racial segregation and, later, to U.S. policy in Vietnam, some clergy departed from conventional political activity to perform acts of civil disobedience or even violence. The nation grew accustomed to pictures of clergymen being led off to jail for participation in illegal sit-ins or other such activities.

It is important to keep in mind, however, that a great many ministers did not conform to this description of social action. In their study of the Little Rock (Arkansas) school desegregation crisis of 1957–1958, Campbell and Pettigrew (1959) stressed that most ministers from the mainline churches, while not supporting school segregation, kept their distance from the controversy engulfing their community. Similarly, if Quinley's study of California ministers held true nationwide, many clergy apparently kept their Sunday sermons free of any sustained commentary on the divisive political and social issues of the 1960s (Stark et al. 1971, chap. 5). Nor would it be accurate to conclude that the politically active mainline clergy uniformly supported the liberal side on these issues; some members of Quinley's sample reported undertaking activities in favor of repealing the housing ordinance, defending U.S. military involvement in Southeast Asia, or resisting the unionization campaign on the farms. Similarly, several community surveys revealed that substantial numbers of mainline ministers continued to preach the traditional Protestant perspective, emphasizing personal piety as the best response to social problems (Koller and Retzer 1980; Nelsen 1975). Such conservative activism was much less common than liberal mobilization (Tygart 1977).

In attempting to account for the level of political activism among mainline clergy, scholars have stressed both individual and structural factors. As individuals, the activist clergy were more likely than their inactive counterparts to have received advanced education from secular institutions and to have been raised in urban areas (Ammerman 1981). These traits reflect exposure to agents of modernization that probably undermined a traditional conception of religion and encouraged clergy to view their task in much broader terms. Indeed, according to the research of sociologist Hart Nelsen (1975), activists and nonactivists exhibited very different understandings about the role of religion in society and adjusted their ministerial priorities accordingly. Nelsen discovered that clergymen who regarded themselves principally as spiritual leaders, personal counselors, church administrators, or educators tended to embrace conservative political ideas and to preach the traditional moral concerns about individual rectitude. The activists were recruited from the ranks of clergy who defined their principal responsibility as community problem solving. Believing they were meant to address a wide range of problems that could not necessarily be solved by personal piety, these clergy were more likely to sermonize on social problems and to favor direct political involvement as a solution.

These differences in role orientation were reinforced by participation in supportive social networks. Protestant parish ministers were more likely to engage in civil rights activity—even in the face of congregational resistance—when they belonged to national denominations that issued clear directives in support of the civil rights movement (Wood 1981). It was equally important for activists to find a local haven to sustain their liberal activities. In her study of civil rights involvement among Protestant ministers in Tuscaloosa, Alabama, Nancy Ammerman (1981) found that geographic proximity to a university campus and a perception of pro–civil rights attitudes in the local community were important factors drawing clergymen into public activism.

MAINLINE ACTIVISM: SOURCES AND REACTIONS

The political issues that engaged clergy during the activist era—civil rights, Vietnam, social justice—touched on profound moral values at the core of Christian thought. As Quinley (1974, 3) put it, "The churches could hardly preach Christian brotherhood and love for one's fellow man and at the same time remain silent on such issues as civil rights and the war in Vietnam." Yet many congregants, who considered churches places primarily for fellowship and personal spiritual growth, did not welcome what they saw as unwarranted political intrusions by their clergy (Hadden 1969). Faced with this resistance from congregations who gave priority to worship and spirituality, many clergy sought safe havens in

appointments outside the local parish, in campus ministries, denominational "social action" bureaucracies, the seminaries, and other environments that were more supportive of political activity by church leaders.
Freed from accountability to a conservative constituency, ministers in
these positions supplied a disproportionate share of the activist clergy
(Hadden and Rymph 1971). Other reform-minded members of the clergy
and seminary students, weary of the constant battles within the church,
simply opted to leave the ministry for opportunities in secular agencies.

Does this mean that mainline traditions have retreated from politics?
The answer is not simple. On the one hand, evidence suggests continuity
in political orientations among the religious leaders of mainline Protestantism. Those who remain in the pulpit have, for the most part, continued to press for a liberal and activist social agenda. Although there are
differences among mainline denominations, most clergy continue to affirm social justice as the core of the gospel (Smidt et al. 2003). Nationwide
surveys show that clergy from mainline denominations still give greater
emphasis than their evangelical counterparts to the social reform mission
of the church—particularly antipoverty initiatives—and assign less importance than evangelicals to missionary activities (Guth et al. 1997). They
remain the leaders and base constituency of many of the anti–Christian
Right organizations identified in table 8.1.

Yet, on the other hand, recent research on congregational activities
suggests that these progressive sentiments are being translated into different idioms than were common during the era of activism. Rather than
political withdrawal and retrenchment, the terms once used to describe
what happened in this tradition since the 1970s, it is more accurate
to describe a *transformation* of mainline Protestant civic engagement.
Mainline Protestants now devote fewer resources to political action and
are less likely to call for major structural changes at the national level.
Rather than disappear, however, mainline Protestants are socially engaged in a different way. Much of their political witness is directed toward the local arena and is conducted in partnership with both religious
and secular organizations (Ammerman 2002). Mainline congregations
have become important components of ecumenical community organizing coalitions (Hart 1996), and mainline churches stand out from other
religious traditions in their focus on poverty relief, environmental justice, and other community problems (Chaves, Giesel, and Tsitsos 2002).
Across the country, these religiously based movements have become
key advocates of social reform and economic development, providing
direct services to the poor and prodding governments to become more
involved in the fight against homelessness, addiction, hunger, and other
social problems. Most of these activities are likely to be acceptable to

congregants if only because they are the province of a relatively small proportion of the membership (Ammerman 2002).

If there has been any kind of mainline withdrawal from civic involvement, that has been principally a consequence of declining membership and, consequently, fewer financial resources. Since the mid-1960s, the major mainline denominations have lost a significant proportion of membership. Some observers interpreted the erosion of mainline membership in terms of parishioner resistance to the social activism characteristic of liberal Protestantism (Reeves 1996; Kelley 1977). According to one reading, members in search of spiritual sustenance and meaning deserted the mainline in favor of evangelical churches that spoke more forcefully to their personal needs and fears. The mainline could not compete effectively, suggested religious historian Randall Balmer (1996, 148), because "mainline Protestants have been so intent on blurring theological and denominational distinctiveness that they stand for nothing at all, aside from some vague (albeit noble) pieties like peace, justice, and inclusiveness." The mainline clergy seem to have ended up with the worst of both worlds: too action oriented to suit the preferences of many congregants, and too conventional to maintain the faith of their young, affluent, well-educated constituents (Hoge, Johnson, and Luidens 1994).

Although scholars now tend to see the mainline decline as more a consequence of demography than politically inspired desertion (Hout, Greeley, and Wilde 2001), the fact of fewer members has meant that mainline churches now give more attention to problems of church vitality and fewer resources to political action (Woodward 1993). The eroding membership base seriously diminished the funds available for the "peace and justice" ministries of national church offices and ecumenical organizations. The National Council of Churches (NCC), an ecumenical organization of mainline denominations that spearheaded church social action during the 1960s, did not abandon its political role but has since given more attention to traditional religious issues such as the extent of sex and violence in popular media.

The public debate over homosexuality has replaced the concerns of the 1960s as the principal political divide within the mainline tradition (Olson and Cadge 2002). Gays and lesbians have increasingly sought sanctuary and recognition from their churches, asking for churches to perform gay unions, sponsor gay support groups, admit gays to the ministry, and otherwise incorporate homosexuals in congregational life. Because of traditional Christian understandings of homosexuality as sinful, this campaign has bitterly divided many mainline Protestant congregations. When mainline ministers have supported gay rights, they have roiled congregations across the country with the same or even greater intensity than elicited by the black civil rights movement of the 1960s (Hartman 1996). By installing an openly gay man as a bishop in New Hampshire, for example, the Episcopal Church prompted the secession of entire congregations from the authority of the church and threats by the international Anglican Communion to disaffiliate the American church entirely.

As a recent study of mainline political engagement reminds us, it would be foolhardy to write off the mainline Protestant tradition as a spent force (Wuthnow and Evans 2002). Despite the decline in membership and division over homosexuality, this religious family still constitutes a formidable social force with thousands of clergy and congregations, substantial economic resources, and a population of well-educated and affluent parishioners. Its penchant for quieter political activity should not prompt us to assume that it has withdrawn from politics. The impulse that powered the social gospel movement has changed form and expression but has hardly been extinguished.

AMERICAN JEWS

Given their relatively small numbers, Jews might not seem to warrant special attention in a general volume about religion in U.S. politics. But several aspects of Jewish political behavior have prompted scholars to pay close attention to this particular community. To begin with, Jews are extremely active in American political life. They are represented well beyond their numerical share of the population as candidates and officials, campaign activists, political contributors, members of interest groups, and—not least—regular voters in primary and general elections. Their high rate of voting, coupled with geographic concentration in large states, makes them especially important in presidential elections. The nature, as well as the amount, of Jewish activism also stands out. Collectively an affluent religious group, Jews nonetheless hold liberal political views that seem contrary to their economic self-interest. In fact, unlike non-Jews, who typically become much more Republican as their income increases, Jewish voters do not "vote their pocketbooks" to the same degree (Sigelman 1991; Fisher 1989, 43). Although most religious groups define themselves in terms of theological beliefs or prescribed codes of behavior, many Jews actually regard liberalism as the essence of Judaism itself (Sklare and Greenblum 1967, chap. 10; Liebman and Cohen 1990, 97). For many Jews, liberalism is not just the product of a secularized prophetic tradition but also a means to protect and maintain ethnic identity while fully incorporating into mainstream American politics (Dollinger 2000; Svonkin 1997).

Where does this liberalism come from? The once-popular theory that liberalism was somehow implicit in Jewish theology has been undercut by repeated findings that the most religiously observant Jews, presumably those most familiar with religious texts, are also the most politically conservative (Cohen 1983, 143–53; Lazerwitz, Winter, and Dashefsky 1988).[11] If their liberalism is not mandated by creed and seems counter to group interest, then social standing probably supplies the best explanation. Scholars generally attribute Jewish political preferences to the community's sense of itself as a potential target of hostility from the non-Jewish majority. Despite attaining objective levels of prominence undreamed of by earlier generations, American Jews still feel vulnerable to persecution and anti-Semitism (Cohen 2010).

Why should a sense of social marginality attract American Jews to the left side of the political spectrum? From history, Jews learned that the left historically favored the cause of minorities, and liberalism is still seen as more sympathetic to minority groups than the political alternatives. Even if they do not benefit directly from the social programs sponsored by liberals, Jews regard such programs as a safeguard against the social tensions that breed religious bigotry (Fein 1988). In essence, this position suggests, Jews consider liberalism in their interest. As long as the left is associated in the Jewish mind with the maintenance of the separation of religion and state, the quality of the political system that contributed to unparalleled Jewish success in the United States, Jews are likely to remain part of the Democratic and liberal coalition.

Back in the 1960s, some observers predicted that urban unrest, affirmative action, and concern for the fate of Israel would eventually drive Jews out of the Democratic coalition and into alliance with conservative forces. One powerful impetus to political change was the upsurge in conflict between Jews and African Americans. Before the "black power" movement, when the civil rights campaign concentrated principally on attacking formal barriers to equality, Jews were the single most ardent supporters of the movement in the white community. Aside from membership and leadership roles in interracial civil rights organizations, Jews made up a massively disproportionate share of the young white students who went south as volunteers for desegregation (Friedman 1995, chaps. 6–8). White politicians who developed a reputation as civil rights activists enjoyed nearly unanimous electoral support from Jewish voters; those who became symbols of white resistance, such as George Wallace of Alabama, looked elsewhere.

Although the civil rights movement represented a strong alliance between blacks and Jews, the relationship between the two groups was not as close as that might suggest. Many southern Jews were reluctant to support civil rights for blacks because of the risks that such support might entail for a southern Jewish community precariously placed between the white and black communities (Webb 2001; Forman 1997). Outside the

South, relations between blacks and Jews were also complex. In the 1800s, black migrants from the South first began interacting with northern Jewish shopkeepers in urban communities. While Jews may have recognized and empathized with the oppression of blacks as a minority, this recognition did not bridge the differences of race, class, religion, and culture between the two groups (Adams and Bracey 1999; Salzman 1992).

These cleavages emerged clearly once the civil rights movement moved to northern cities and came to focus on de facto expressions of racism. The functioning alliance began to break down. Tensions arose over demands by the advocates of black power for "community control" of ghetto life. As the immigrant group that had preceded African Americans to the city, Jews still occupied an important place in private businesses and public institutions in the central city. Hence, though directed at whites in general, demands for black ownership of businesses, black-only leadership in civil rights groups, and increased African American representation in public employment challenged Jews in particular. The bitter expressions of hostility from some protagonists on both sides conveyed the impression of a fundamental estrangement rooted in a rising tide of black anti-Semitism and Jewish racism.

In New York, the city with the largest concentration of Jews, these clashes became particularly intense. Attacks on Jewish-owned businesses during ghetto riots and conflicts between African Americans and Jews in the public schools brought national publicity. Relationships eventually deteriorated to the point that a Brooklyn-born rabbi, Meier Kahane, formed the Jewish Defense League (JDL) to patrol inner-city neighborhoods with sizable concentrations of Jews. By offering armed protection to Jews who felt threatened by crime and anti-Semitic attacks, the JDL bore a strong resemblance to the most militant black organizations in the ghetto. Condemned by many Jewish leaders as a thinly disguised appeal to racist sentiment, the JDL nonetheless played on fears of racial violence widespread in the Jewish community (Dolgin 1977).

On a more general level, tensions arose over the development of affirmative action programs in public employment, graduate and professional school admission, and other important sectors. The principle of affirmative action is that past discrimination against African Americans or any other group can most effectively and justly be overcome by giving temporary preference to African American applicants in competition for channels to upward mobility. The legitimacy of the principle and its application to concrete situations have generated considerable conflict within the liberal community. The doctrine goes well beyond the traditional understanding of "equality" into realms that have been described by unfriendly observers as "reverse discrimination" or "affirmative discrimination." Some of the most trenchant criticisms of the new policy came from Jews who regarded the programs as tantamount to setting up governmentally approved "quotas" for access to social advancement. Because such quotas had once been used to exclude Jews from careers in prestigious and remunerative occupations, their proposed introduction for purposes of spurring African American advancement called forth strong opposition from much of the Jewish community. When the Supreme Court considered cases about the constitutionality of specific affirmative action programs, the major Jewish organizations that had once joined African American plaintiffs in discrimination cases usually weighed in on the side challenging the new schemes.

Once the closest of allies, the two groups began to trade charges of racism and anti-Semitism. Blacks attributed the deteriorating relationship to Jewish unwillingness to admit their legitimate claims for jobs, housing, and political power, whereas Jews tended to blame racial agitation and envy. In retrospect, the clash seems to have been a predictable outcome of the process of ethnic succession in American cities, the process by which each newly arrived ethnic group stakes its claim to power at the expense of its predecessors. Even at the height of the conflict in New York, a specially commissioned public opinion poll revealed an underlying harmony between African Americans and Jews (Harris and Swanson 1970, chap. 2). According to the poll, Jews were more likely than white Catholics and no less likely than white Protestants to acknowledge that blacks suffered discrimination, and only African Americans shared the Jewish perception that the latter were still victims of discrimination in the city.

The Jewish commitment to liberalism was thought to have been further undermined by the issue of Israel. The Jewish community was galvanized by the outbreak of the Six-Day War in 1967 between Israel and its Arab neighbors, which immeasurably strengthened the commitment of American Jews to the Zionist cause. As American Jews increased their support for the Jewish homeland in the Middle East, many self-identified liberals moved the other way by showing greater sympathy for the claims of Palestinian nationalists. Jews who had once championed the United Nations and given verbal support to some national liberation movements watched with dismay as the 1975 General Assembly declared Zionism to be a form of racism and equated Israelis with white South Africans as colonial oppressors.

During the administration of President Jimmy Carter, the Israeli issue fused with concern over African American attitudes toward the Jewish community (Feuerlicht 1983, chap. 6; for an earlier tie, see Carson 1984). At the United Nations, U.S. Ambassador Andrew Young had forged strong ties with some of the third-world representatives who had been the most vociferous critics of U.S. support for Israel. In August 1979 it was revealed that Ambassador Young had held a meeting with a representative of the Palestine Liberation Organization (PLO), the umbrella group of Palestinian nationalism. Since the United States then had an official policy to boycott the PLO until it granted recognition to Israel, Young's meeting was condemned by Israel and by leaders of American Jewish organizations. Under pressure from the State Department, Young eventually resigned. Blacks were angry about the apparent Jewish attack on their most influential advocate in the administration and felt that Young had been singled out for retribution. Jews were outraged at the sympathy that African Americans had shown to an organization that advocated violence in order to achieve Palestinian aims.[12]

In 1980, Jewish voters appeared to repay the Carter administration for its alleged pro-Arab tilt by giving President Carter less than a clear majority of their vote in his reelection bid. Although Israel was not the only reason for the decline in Jewish support for the Democratic ticket, it surely contributed in a major way. For Jews religiosity is associated with conservative ideological positions, particularly on issues like the Middle East peace process and Palestinian affect. Interestingly, this relationship holds cross-nationally with religious commitment affecting Jews in Israel and the United States in similar ways (Wald and Martinez 2001). In very different political contexts, religious cleavages are a significant factor in producing political divisions among Jews (Kotler-Berkowitz 2002).

This diversity of perspective is reflected in the suggestion by a small group of Jewish intellectuals that Jews change their political alliance. In journals like *Commentary* and *Public Interest*, neoconservatives such as Irving Kristol urged Jews to reconsider their traditional attachment to liberalism. Jewish interests, it was argued, were most likely to be served by the conservative policies of the Republican administration that took office in 1981. In national defense, for example, Jews were told that Israel would benefit from the massive rearmament undertaken by the Defense Department. The administration's hostility to affirmative action programs fell well within the Jewish opposition to the use of quotas to increase African American representation in the public sector and other places. Similarly, some of the neoconservatives encouraged Jews to vote their pocketbooks by supporting the anti-inflation and tax-cutting programs launched by the Reagan White House.

The attempt to move Jews out of the Democratic camp received an unexpected push from the presidential campaign of the Rev. Jesse Jackson in 1988. Unlike Martin Luther King Jr., who was revered by Jews (Schneier 1999), King's successor appeared less committed to the black-Jewish coalition. During a public appearance in 1984, Jackson was overheard to refer to Jews as "Hymies" and New York City as "Hymietown." Although Jackson apologized for his offensive language, bad feelings were revived as the public learned more about his ties with Minister Louis Farrakhan, the head of a black Muslim sect known as the Nation of Islam. By meeting with Libyan leader Col. Muammar Qaddafi in 1995 and referring to Judaism as either a "gutter" or a "dirty" religion, Farrakhan revived all the Jewish fears about the growth of black anti-Semitism. Jackson's insistence on condemning Farrakhan's remarks but not the man himself did not placate Jewish anger.[13] Nor were Jews endeared to a candidate so clearly sympathetic to Palestinian nationalism. Though Jackson endorsed the existence of Israel and called for secure borders, Jews were more persuaded by the photograph of him in the physical embrace of PLO leader Yasir Arafat and the candidate's (unsuccessful) efforts to pass a platform plank endorsing an independent Palestinian state. Usually much more supportive of black candidates than other white voters, Jews rejected Jackson because they regarded him as antagonistic. Despite Jackson's lower profile after 1988, black-Jewish tensions remained high (Berman 1994). The increasing prominence of the Nation of Islam, symbolized by Louis Farrakhan's prominence in the Million Man March of 1995, raised concern about the power of anti-Semitic appeals in the African American community. The problem took on concrete form in the Crown Heights section of Brooklyn in 1991. The accidental death of a black child at the hands of a Jewish driver set off several days of anti-Jewish rioting in which a rabbinical student was targeted and killed. The eventual acquittal of his accused murderers angered many in the Jewish community.

The cumulative effect of these developments is apparent in figure 9.1, which shows the presidential vote of self-identified Jews from 1972 to

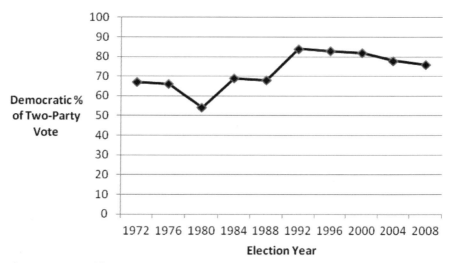

Figure 9.1.   Presidential Vote among Jews, 1972–2008. *Source:* **Mellman, Strauss, and Wald 2012, 5.**

2008, a period in which exit polls produced large samples of Jewish participants. Although we do not have definitive data about Jewish voting before the advent of exit polls in 1972, the best estimates indicate that Jews had given nearly 90 percent of their votes to the Democratic nominee in the three presidential elections of the 1960s (Weisberg 2012, 231). From 1972 to 1988, while Jews remained much more Democratic than Republican, the split was closer to two-to-one, and in 1980, when Carter stood for reelection, he achieved a bare majority of the Jewish two-party vote, as shown in figure 9.1. Starting in 1992, Jews moved back in a pro-Democratic direction, giving Democrats three-fourths of their votes.

Despite predictions that Jewish liberalism would decay under the combined onslaught of all these factors, the voting results and the findings of other studies show Jews still much more likely than others to favor liberal policies on a wide range of public issues (Lerner, Nagai, and Rothman 1989; Glaser 1997). This liberalism has continued to translate into very high levels of Jewish support for Democratic candidates across the board (Greenberg and Wald 2001).

The failure of Jews to respond to Republican overtures throughout the rest of the twentieth century and into the twenty-first evidently meant that Jewish voters were more worried about the post-1980 political prominence of evangelical Protestants in the Republican coalition than about the conflicts with African American leaders. In support of this interpretation, a 1984 *Los Angeles Times* poll revealed that Jewish voters were actually more hostile to Rev. Jerry Falwell, who had courted them on behalf of the Reagan campaign, than to Jesse Jackson (Schneider 1985, 58). The antipathy to evangelical Protestant candidates has persisted. Looking at the 2004 election, Eric Uslaner and Mark Lichbach (2009) found that (largely negative) feelings toward evangelicals had a more powerful influence on Jewish voting than any factor other than partisanship but mattered little among non-Jews. A revealing 2007 Pew Center survey, which found Jews much more likely than the rest of the population to vote for gay, female, black, Hispanic, Mormon, Muslim, and atheist presidential candidates, also disclosed a greater unwillingness by Jews to vote for an evangelical Protestant. In fact, Jews were three times as likely as the population to admit they would be less likely to vote for a candidate who was an evangelical Christian.[14] Why? About 70 percent of Jews (versus 45 percent of the population) said they were uncomfortable when candidates talked about how religious they were, and 87 percent (against just 41 percent of all respondents) agreed that religious conservatives had too much control over the Republican Party.

Why have Jews been so worried about evangelical Protestants who reached out to them? The source of this behavior is not religious bigotry—as evident in Jewish support for evangelical Protestants such as Harry Truman, Lyndon Johnson, Jimmy Carter, Bill Clinton, and Al Gore—but rather hostility to the political values now associated with evangelicalism. Evangelical Protestants are associated in the Jewish mind both with the policies of "Christian government" and with skepticism about the value of government support for welfare. Neither association endears the GOP to Jews. In response to the second rise of the Christian Right in the 1990s, the Anti-Defamation League (ADL), a Jewish human rights agency, issued a stinging critique of the movement for its alleged antidemocratic and antipluralistic orientation (Cantor 1994). Although the Christian Coalition's executive director later addressed the ADL in an attempt to mend fences, the strongly antiseparationist posture of the Christian Right reinforced Jewish doubts about the movement's respect for religious pluralism. The Tea Party, which we suggested might represent yet a new version of the Christian Right, also had a powerful negative effect on Jews in 2012, keeping them firmly in the Democratic camp.

This concern about Jewish identity has kept the large majority of Jews in the Democratic camp despite efforts to pry them away based on Israel. Poll data display American Christian fundamentalists as the strongest supporters of Israel in America after Jews themselves (Mayer 2004). Their distinctive views are shaped by their literal interpretation of the Bible, the belief that U.S. policy can lay a foundation for Christ's return, and their leaders' increased cues on the subject of the Middle East (Gormly 2005). Still, despite their support on this issue, which has become central to the Republican Party, many Jews are more concerned by the prevalence of Jewish stereotypes in evangelical circles and the efforts by evangelical denominations to convert Jews to Christianity (T. Smith 1999). Some Jews took particular offense at what they perceived as the overt sectarianism of George W. Bush's administration reflected in a routine emphasis on the importance of religion, his support of faith-based initiatives, and the growing political influence of evangelical Christians in the Republican Party. These actions raise questions about Jewish membership in the political community (Wald 2003, 2005).

Jews today are cohesive but certainly not unanimous in their preferences for liberal issues and candidates. There are signs of willingness by some members of the community to reconsider their traditional ties. Younger Jews, though still much more Democratic than their non-Jewish counterparts, are more sympathetic to Republican candidates than their grandparents, and a gender gap has developed between males and females within the Jewish community (Fisher 1989). Pro-Israel political action committees donate roughly one-third of their funds to Republican candidates (Malbin 1986). Some Republican candidates have won mayoral elections with substantial Jewish support (Sonenshein and Valentino 2000). But even these changes are tempered by group traditions. The young Jews who identify less with the Democrats are predominantly independent rather than Republican, and the gender gap within Judaism is much less substantial than that recorded for other religious groups. While Jews will support selected Republican candidates, they still remain far more disposed than equivalent Protestants and Catholics to voting for Democrats. Jews remain politically where they have been for more than half a century—well to the left on the American political spectrum.

10

Religion and the Politics of Ethnic and Religious Minorities

Black theology puts black identity in a theological context, showing that black power is not only consistent with the gospel of Jesus Christ: it is the gospel of Jesus Christ.

—James Cone

I don't think I could base my will to struggle on cold economics or some political doctrines. I don't think that there would be enough to sustain me. For me the base must be faith.

—César Chávez

W e have seen throughout the book that religious ideals can be powerful sources of political motivation. For religious groups active in politics, religious culture becomes a significant way to create the joint identity, sense of grievance, and impetus for mobilization required for collective political action. This chapter explores the relationship between religion and politics for religious minorities and for groups whose religious culture is overlaid with racial or ethnic distinctiveness. As we saw with American Jews in the previous chapter, for minority groups, religion may represent not only a belief system and a communion of faithful adherents but also a connection to the broader racial, ethnic, or religious community and to the maintenance of that community's history, identity, institutions, and way of life.

In many minority communities, it is difficult to separate religious culture from the culture of the minority group. Religion is of course a major way that a group communicates its culture. Because places of worship are the most common civic associations to which people belong, minority religious institutions—churches, synagogues, temples, and mosques—can reflect the heartbeat and aspirations of an entire community. When racial, ethnic, or religious cleavages interact with and correspond to differences related to identity, group status, doctrine, or worldview, potential motivations for religiously grounded political engagement are greatly increased.

Although religion in minority communities has the potential to reinforce group identity and important aspects of culture, it is not a foregone conclusion that it will always serve as an effective vehicle for their political aspirations. The relationship between religion and politics among these groups is governed by many of the same dynamics that relate to religion and politics more generally. Those interested in realizing the political potential must begin the policy process with articulation and aggregation. As Snow and his colleagues (1986, 465) remind us, issues must be framed in ways that render events and occurrences as politically meaningful. At times religion is helpful in this effort; at other times it can be a hindrance. Religious traditions have both prophetic and otherworldly components. Most religious traditions can also support both liberal and conservative policy positions. Moreover, grievances alone do not produce political mobilization.

Whether religion becomes a politicized force suggests a lot about the nature of identity, leadership, resources, and culture in minority communities. Regardless of whether their mobilization results in policy responsiveness reveals much about the operation of and challenges to true religious and ethnic pluralism in a democratic society. Reflecting on America's growing diversity in a speech, President Obama has said, "We are no longer just a Christian nation; we are also a Jewish nation, a Muslim nation, a Buddhist nation, a Hindu nation, and a nation of nonbelievers."[1] Increasingly, this may be true, but as we explained in chapter 3, historically American identity is intertwined with a particular European brand of Protestantism. It matters. The considerable media attention given to Mitt Romney's faith and whether Americans would vote for a presidential candidate who was Mormon during the 2012 presidential election campaign reminds us that the political experiences of minorities are distinct and that religious prejudice and inequality persist in the United States.

AFRICAN AMERICAN PROTESTANTS

President Obama's announcement that he would favor gay marriage in the spring of 2012 was not met with enthusiasm in the African American religious community. Though economically liberal, African American Protestants are theologically conservative. Obama's announcements left both the clergy and many of the congregants who weekly look to them for guidance conflicted about "what direction he is taking the nation."[2] Though it would have been overly simplistic to conclude that African American Protestants would not vote for Obama because of this issue, there were serious concerns that it might dampen enthusiasm for his candidacy. One observer summarized the dynamic in this way: "I'm going to vote for him, but I'm not going to talk about him much. It's the difference between voting for him, or voting for him and putting out a street sign and making sure your neighbor gets to the poll."[3] The reaction of many in the black church to Obama's gay marriage announcement reveals much about the complexity of the relationship between race, religion, equality, and politics in the African American community. Historically a standard bearer for equal rights, and politically supporters of Democratic candidates in general (and Obama in particular), the vision for how to establish justice in America in a way that reflects their religious and ideological principles is not always straightforward to members of this group.

This was dramatically illustrated during the 2008 presidential election campaign. Many Americans were shocked when they heard the provocative preaching of Barack Obama's pastor, Rev. Jeremiah Wright. Instead of the kind of staid message about love of God and love of country that one might expect from the minister of a man who would be president, like some kind of Old Testament character, Wright boldly proclaimed:

> Not "God Bless America." God damn America—that's in the Bible—for killing innocent people. God damn America for treating her citizens as less than human. God damn America as long as she keeps trying to act like she is God and she is supreme! (Ross and El-Buri 2008)

Obama had been a member of Wright's Trinity United Church of Christ for twenty years. Rev. Wright had presided at his marriage and baptized both of his children. People did not understand how Obama's "spiritual mentor" could be filled with such vitriol when Obama himself seemed to symbolize the unity and hope of a country that would no longer be fettered by its ugly racial past. The United States got an introduction to the complexity of the African American community that the black church represents. In studying the relationship between religion and politics among African American Protestants, we must start with the awareness "that there is no disjunction between the black church and the black community" (Lincoln 1982, 115). Trying to contextualize his relationship with Wright and his membership at Trinity, Obama explained:

> Like other predominantly black churches across the country, Trinity embodies the black community in its entirety. . . . The church contains in full the kindness and cruelty, the fierce intelligence and the shocking ignorance, the

struggles and successes, the love and yes, the bitterness and bias that make up the black experience in America.[4]

Data reveal that Wright's remarks were viewed very differently by whites than by African Americans. Wright's comments had no effect on black opinions. However, whites who were disturbed by the statements were more likely to express negative sentiments about Obama, even though Obama disavowed the remarks and ultimately repudiated the man (McKenzie 2011). Reflecting on the media storm that the Jeremiah Wright controversy produced, Blum explains that for the African American community this kind of disagreement about the "person, place and meaning of Jesus" that this episode revealed is central to the social development, political thinking, and civil rights activism of African Americans as a group (2011). For blacks, Wright's brand of defiance preaching reflects the social, theological and political discourse of the African American community (Clardy 2011; Marshall 2011; Grant and Grant 2012). As Blum notes and we have seen throughout this book, religious discussions and political cultures are always intertwined (2011).

Primarily because of racism and discrimination in the United States, black churches and denominations were established separately from their white counterparts. The reasons for division were rarely theological. Instead, black religion developed as a response and expression of a people oppressed on the basis of race. The very existence of black churches is in part a testament and a response to societal inequality. Gayraud Wilmore (1983, 78) has described the movement to establish independent black churches as "the first black freedom movement." Churches in the African American community provided more than just a separate place for blacks to worship. They became the medium for all of civil society. In the absence of other viable institutions, the church became the focus of not only spiritual but also secular pursuits. Religion became a basis for cultural cohesion among blacks. Eddie Glaude (2000) recounts how black leaders took Bible stories such as the Exodus and used them to create a sense of community and nationhood among African Americans even in the early nineteenth century. Today, the fact that thousands of disparate groups can be referenced with meaning as "the black church" is a testament to the centrality of churches to African American culture and community and the degree to which these congregations have been separate and distinct from mainstream religious organizations as well as white society.

Dr. Martin Luther King and the civil rights movement were able to draw on this common religious culture to effectively mobilize the black community for protest and change (Williams 2002; Chappel 2003, 2004). Even today black congregations tend to be more politically active than the congregations of other ethnic groups because of their orientation toward equality and social justice (Brown 2009).

Interestingly, throughout much of African American history, both Christianity and black churches were criticized as being contrary to African American political advancement. Lincoln and Mamiya's (1990, chap. 1) review of the literature on black churches reveals that several of the earlier theoretical models used to describe the black church's relationship to politics characterize churches as anti-intellectual, antidemocratic, apolitical, and otherworldly. People writing from this so-called opiate perspective insist that religion has primarily been a conservative force, its otherworldly nature helping blacks to cope by encouraging them to wait for justice in heaven rather than pursue it here on earth (for examples of this perspective, see Marx 1967; Myrdal 1944; Frazier 1964; Reed 1986). To be sure, African American Christianity has not always been associated with progressive political activism. Savage (2008) chronicles that throughout history most black activists and scholars have lamented the failure of the black church to produce (or even support) social and political change.

This kind of duality is inherent in most religious traditions. Fred Harris (1999) references it in describing how African American churches produce "oppositional group consciousness." According to Harris, churches "provide African Americans with material resources and oppositional dispositions to challenge their marginality," and at the same time help members "to develop positive orientations toward the civic order" (40). Viewed from this perspective, the black church can be seen to have engendered in members an oppositional consciousness that predisposed them to challenge society and, concurrently, served to reinforce their attachment and loyalty to the principles of American government and politics. This duality is reflected in Rev. Wright, his prophetic style of preaching, and his enlistment of the Lord in the cause of justice. It may also be reflected in President Obama. In an interpretive exposition of Obama's major writings and speeches through 2010, Rogers Smith (2012) concludes that Obama's ideas stress deliberative democratic processes but also show a commitment to the black church's social justice values.

Since the inclusion of blacks in the electorate as a result of the civil rights movement, the close relationship between religion and politics among African American Protestants has continued to develop and expand into the arena of voting behavior. Blacks who are active in African American churches are more likely to vote even when taking into account their socioeconomic status and other related factors (Harris 1994). Attending black churches enhances group identification, and this sense of group solidarity, in turn, encourages blacks to pursue collective political remedies for the challenges they face (Allen, Dawson, and Brown 1989;

Brown and Wolford 1993; Wilcox and Gomez 1990; Dawson, Brown, and Allen 1990; Calhoun-Brown 1996, 1998).

Several reasons explain why black churches have been effective in stimulating African American political action. First, the church environment provides a platform for political learning. In a racially nonsupportive world, churches constituted what Evans and Boyte (1986, 17) call a "free space," an "environment in which people are able to learn a new self respect, a deeper and more assertive group identity, public skills and the values of cooperation and civic virtue." How does this happen? Sometimes it occurs through the communication of overt political messages. Several scholars have found that hearing political messages in church significantly increases political engagement (McClerking and McDaniel 2005; Reese and Brown 1995; Calhoun-Brown 1996). Verba and colleagues (1995, 384) find African Americans are "more politicized, where they are exposed to political stimuli, requests for political participation, and messages from the pulpit about political matters." Other research recognizes that both direct and indirect communication in church can increase political involvement (Huckfeldt, Plutzer, and Sprague 1993). Brian McKenzie's (2004) work suggests that the informal political communication that occurs through congregant social networks is an even more effective stimulus for political involvement than hearing clergy messages. Melissa Harris-Lacewell (2004, chap. 3) also cautions against employing a purely elite model of the political and ideological development that occurs in African American churches. She found that church-based political activity has no statistically significant effect on many African American political ideas once other forms of communal church-based political discussions are taken into account.

Black churches also empower their members politically by increasing social capital (Calhoun-Brown 2003; Wood 2002; Harris 1999). Some evidence indicates that simply attending an African American church is not enough to produce voting or other nonpolitical activities (Brown and Brown 2003). By participating in church through activities such as coordinating a meeting, committee work, or volunteering, individuals develop certain psychological dispositions that enhance their stock of what is known as "social capital"—interpersonal trust, access to networks, and beliefs about responsibility to the community (Putnam 2000). With these mental resources, black churchgoers learn "to act together more effectively to pursue shared objectives" (Greenberg 2000, 377). Recent research suggests that the bonding social capital that church attendance generates may be particularly important to the political participation of African Americans (Liu et al. 2009). Although social capital may be acquired in the workplace or other voluntary organizations, the centrality of religious congregations in African American life makes them critical environments for generating African American participation.

Finally, African American church culture itself communicates powerful messages about the relevance of religion to civic life. Through prayer, song, dialogue, rituals, and Christian imagery, congregants are taught about their obligation to the larger community and to their own people (Patillo-McCoy 1998; Harris 1999). The cumulative result of these influences makes African Americans much more likely than other population groups to attend church meetings about politics and to hear discussions of political issues from the pulpit (Verba et al. 1993). This does not mean that every African American church is a hotbed of political activity. Significant variation exists based on the pastor's level of activism, the church's resources, and the attitudes of the members (McDaniel 2003, 2008). Nonetheless, taken together the transmission of organizational skills, platform for political learning, and participatory political culture provided by black churches make them important to the ability of African Americans to overcome the resources shortages that might otherwise hinder their political involvement.

Another interesting characteristic of the relationship between religion and politics among African American Protestants is its consistent support of political liberalism. African Americans are overwhelmingly evangelical in theological orientation. They are substantially more likely than whites to say that they believe in the inerrancy of the scripture, the divinity of Christ, his physical resurrection from the dead, and the necessity of a "born again" experience in order to receive salvation (Wilcox 1992). However, unlike that among white evangelicals, the religious conservatism of African Americans is not usually associated with conservative political activism. To be sure, black evangelicals, as we have seen (chapter 7), tend toward conservatism on moral-cultural issues. The data indicate and several studies have confirmed that black Protestants are very likely to believe homosexuality is wrong, to believe prayer in schools is right, and to believe the government should do more to protect morality in society (Lewis 2003; Smith and Seltzer 1992; Secret, Johnson, and Welch 1986).

However, even on some moral-cultural issues, conservative religion does not predict conservative policy positions for blacks. Public opinion shows a liberalizing of black evangelical attitudes with regard to abortion. Several studies appear to demonstrate that since the 1970s, African American Protestants have gone from being the most conservative group on the pro-life side to actually being supportive of pro-choice positions (Evans 2002; Strickler and Danigelis 2002; Gay and Lynxwiler 1999). Conservative religion also does not appear to affect African Americans' views on many other women's rights issues. For example, Susan Marshall (1990) found that church attendance correlated strongly with opposition to the Equal Rights Amendment among white women but had no impact on the attitudes of black women toward the amendment. Another study reports that the political messages conveyed in black churches actually enhance concerns about gender equity among parishioners despite the patriarchal culture that dominates many of them (Calhoun-Brown 1999).

Both liberal and conservative perspectives can be supported through African American Protestantism. One component of black evangelical theology emphasizes the innate sinfulness of humankind and the consequent importance of family values in restraining immorality. The other, more prophetic component, a response to centuries of oppression, sees Jesus as a liberator establishing a system based on justice.

Republicans have desired to mobilize black Protestants on the basis of their zeal for family values, and there is evidence that some aspects of personal religiosity can promote Republican identification. However, the socialization that takes place in African American churches supports Democratic partisanship (Mangum 2007, 2008). Black partisanship is not principally a function of moral-cultural issues but rather of stark economic realities. As an identifiable minority group, the object of continuing discrimination, subject to the highest rates of unemployment and the lowest levels of economic security, the African American community has remained overwhelmingly in favor of an activist government. The partisan implications of conservative religious worldviews are conditioned by race and culture. White people who take the Bible seriously tend to be concerned about personal piety, while in minority communities biblical literalists are concerned about personal piety in addition to social justice (McDaniel and Ellison 2008). Due to the salience of social justice issues, blacks (and other minorities) choose the Democratic Party, while their white co-believers favor the Republicans based on concerns about piety and tend to eschew the very social justice issues that minorities embrace. A recent study of black Republican Alan Keyes's gubernatorial race in Pennsylvania reveals the extent of these attachments. Party identification and ideology were stronger influences on voter behavior than social group loyalties. The fact that Keyes was both religious and black did nothing to upend this dynamic. Despite the racial factor, black (and white) evangelicals chose candidates on the basis of their (divergent) policy preferences (Calfano and Paolino 2010). Black evangelicals were cool to Keyes. The Keyes campaign demonstrates that although African American religion is conservative on many moral-cultural issues, politically it serves as a greater resource for the Democrats. Today, many black churches and preachers continue to be integral parts of the Democratic Party's nationwide get-out-the-vote network.

Still, for all the strength of the relationship between religion and political participation in the African American community, there are some significant challenges and limitations to the connection. First, because of the continuing support of black churches for electoral activity to address the needs of the black community, they have suffered some spillover from disappointments with the limited progress produced by electoral politics. This dissatisfaction has contributed to some losses of the church's hegemony in social and political affairs. This dynamic was first seen during the later years of the civil rights movement when some of the younger activists from outside the churches called on blacks to pursue more aggressive action to achieve social, economic, and political progress. They often denounced the clergy of the major black denominations for a supposed unwillingness to challenge the white power structure. To the extent that the black power movement was church related, its center of gravity was located in the group most critical of Christianity, black Muslims.

A second potential challenge to the continued influence of religion in the African American community is the secular leadership class that has developed since the end of the civil rights movement. With the more equal opportunities that followed the civil rights movement, black people were able to move into and develop expertise in areas where they had been excluded. With professional training, administrative skills, and political sophistication, these experts assumed some of the political and social responsibilities previously monopolized by ministers (Wilson 1965, 297–300).

Contrast the presidential campaigns of Jesse Jackson in the 1980s with the campaign of Barack Obama two decades later. Jackson's campaigns were deeply rooted in black churches (Hertzke 1993; Wald 1991). Having never held elective office, Jackson's legitimacy as a candidate came in part from his status as a minister and leader of the civil rights movement. He portrayed political action in messianic terms, constantly invoking biblical metaphors and utilizing the social gospel and tenets of liberation theology to give his campaigns the aura of a great religious crusade. Obama, on the other hand, talked about faith but made his appeals as a professional politician on the basis of policies and positions. He tried to deracialize his campaigns, not earn civil victories. Jackson revealed the tension between these two approaches in an embarrassing moment in summer 2008. He spoke candidly during a television appearance when he thought the microphones had been turned off. Instead of celebrating the "rainbow coalition" Obama had been able to put together, Jackson assailed Obama for "talking down to black people" and made a crude comment about wanting "to cut his nuts off."[5]

Still, most African American leaders remain closely tied to black churches utilizing church networks to mobilize participation for their

candidacy and causes (Fenno 1978, 113–24; Salamon 1973, 628–29). Usually, black ministers and black politicians have congruent views. However,
there are instances in which ministers and black politicians part company
on the interest of the black community (Cohen 2004). School vouchers and
state bans on gay marriage are two recent examples.[6] As African American
candidates run more deracialized campaigns and represent constituencies
comprised of more than just the African American community, the differences between religious and secular leaders in the African American community may be expected to continue. Such divergences indicate that there
is viable political leadership in the black community that does not draw
on religious authority and that the political perspectives of ministers are
no longer the de facto representation of what the black community wants.
In many ways the election of an African American president is a prime example of this issue. Though black, President Obama represents the entire
country and does not articulate the interests of the black community the
way activist clergy do. As one scholar opined, "One day the question will
be asked . . . whether the sacrifices of previous generations were worth the
rise of a race-neutral black president, whose ascendancy was made possible by their efforts" (Harris 2012, 192).

A final limitation on the relationship between religion and politics in
the African American community is the difficulty that black churches
and black religion have in more fully engaging the policymaking process
outside of electoral politics. While there is much research on the relationship between African American religion and voting behavior since the
civil rights movement, recent research suggests that religiosity may work
to suppress nonelectoral political involvement (Swain 2010). As Smith
(2004, 1) observes, "There are very few assurances, in fact, that citizen
power to elect government officials will necessarily carry over into citizen
influence on the political priorities, interests and actions of the government." Democrats have often failed to deliver fully on the commitments
made to black voters. Some blacks accuse the party of taking their votes
for granted, not linking African American political support with policy
outcomes favorable to the black community.

However, tensions between religious and political imperatives, the
decentralized nature of black religion, and a lack of policy consensus on
key issues all contribute to the difficulties of making black churches more
politically responsive to the real-life social urgencies that affect people in
the post–civil rights era (Owens 2003). Barnes (2004) found that churches
were more inclined to sponsor programs that were economic or youth
oriented rather than political or civic. Certainly black churches continue
to engage in charitable works and provide many social services to those
in need (Billingsley 1999; Tsitsos 2003). However, these activities are often directed more toward enhancing the church's own ability to address

the needs of its communities through "ministries" than toward helping develop or advocate government policies and programs that would address these needs. In a study of housing redevelopment in New York, Owens (2007) finds that partnerships with the government through faith-based initiatives or community development corporations yield mixed results. Ministers choose to collaborate in order to better address the needs of the community and to enhance their own credibility as effective leaders. However, the inherent risk in this is cooptation by the government and the depoliticization of the community. In many ways recent faith-based initiatives exacerbate this dynamic because churches partner with the government to provide services instead of encouraging the government to increase its own capacity and take more responsibility for social problems (Roberts 2003).

Many hold out hope that black churches will be able to "save" problem-plagued inner-city neighborhoods. Often they are the only viable institutions that remain there. They maintain a prophetic role in the African American community (Swain 2008). There is no doubt that religion can influence how people view problems. Matthew Hunt's (2002) research reveals that religious factors can shape beliefs about poverty. For instance, because of the communal nature of African American (and Hispanic) Protestantism, African Americans were more likely to see structural causes for poverty than their Catholic counterparts, who were more fatalistic in orientation. Moreover, there is evidence that local communities can be empowered through churches (Wood 2002; Day 2002). This is the basis of faith-based organizing that we review in chapter 6. Interesting recent research by Melissa Snarr describes how African American religious organizations are active and effective in helping to build progressive partnerships and living wage coalitions to address issues of economic justice in low-income communities. While praising these efforts, her work highlights the ethical challenges that underlie these relationships, including the sexism that has historically plagued both religion and social movements (2011a, 2011b, 2009). While religion serves as a resource for black women, some contend that it does not lead to increased support for a gender-equitable political agenda or improve the sense of satisfaction they have with their lives (Harris-Perry, 2011).

Despite the obvious potential, McRoberts (2003) suggests other significant challenges to churches in poor communities as agents of political and social transformation. He and others have found that churches in low-income neighborhoods are often primarily commuter congregations who generally serve their own parishioners, not members of the broader neighborhood community (Alex-Assensoh 1996; Alex-Assensoh and Assensoh 2001; Laudarji and Livezey 2000). Being located in the neighborhood does not mean actively working with or for the neighborhood. In a study of three low-income housing complexes in Indianapolis, Indiana, R. Drew Smith (2001) found little church-initiated contact with its low-income neighbors and relatively few area residents belonging to a community church. Even so-called mega-churches engage activism in very uneven ways. Tucker-Worgs's research on their community development organizations suggest that the degree of engagement for these resource-rich institutions is highly contingent on having a color-blind theology and not being supportive of the prosperity gospel (2011). As theological ideas about health and wealth spread in the African American community there is a need to more fully understand what these interpretive frames mean for the black church's tradition of civic action (Barnes 2012). While African American religion and African American churches can serve as important resources for political, social, and civic activism, other significant factors related to theology, class, social distance, and geography may mitigate their impact.

While the vast majority of research on the relationship between religion and politics in the African American community has looked at blacks who are a part of black Protestant denominations, it is important to remember that as many as 15 to 20 percent of blacks belong to white Protestant congregations or to other faith traditions (Lincoln and Mamiya 1990, xii). For instance, the association of some black Americans with Roman Catholicism predates even slavery (Davis 1990). Today, there are as many black Catholics as there are African Americans in historically black Methodist denominations (Kosmin and Lachman 1993). Overtly, the religious cultural environment in nonblack religious institutions differs from traditionally black denominations. Challenging racism and discrimination is not the primary objective of nonblack religious institutions in America. After the civil rights movement had improved the social status of blacks, some scholars believed that African Americans would seek to become a part of white churches that were not so racialized, perhaps diminishing their own sense of racial identity (Glenn 1964; Frazier 1964). Although there are better explanations for patterns of religious mobility among blacks (Ellison and Sherkat 1993), whether one attends a black or a white church may be consequential for important political constructs such as racial identification (Ellison 1991).

Still, the relationships among race, religion, and politics are not fully understood, and they are complicated by the fact that many blacks who are affiliated with white denominations still attend congregations that are predominantly black. Moreover, blacks in white denominations are politically much more like other blacks than they are like whites in those denominations. This suggests religion in the African American community is a significant cultural resource for racial mobilization and that white or interracial religious contexts will not fully mediate the powerful effects of race.

LATINO CATHOLICS AND PROTESTANTS

Compared with African Americans, not as much scholarly attention has been given to the relationship between religion and politics in the Latino community. Critical of this oversight, Espinosa, Elizondo, and Miranda (2005, 3) explain there is a "long-standing perception that religion has not had an important role in Latino political, civic, and social action." They observe that many books on Latino history and political movements make religion and faith-informed activism "almost appear to be irrelevant" or incompatible (4). Their volume, *Latino Religions and Civic Activism in the United States*, was one of the first books to challenge this perception by detailing how religious ideologies, institutions, leaders, and symbols have influenced the lives of prominent Latino movements and leaders.

This relationship has not been examined more thoroughly, in part, because of the dominance of Catholicism among Latino Americans. Without religious variation, there is no tangible effect of religion on partisanship or other political attitudes or behavior. The content of Catholicism has also been assumed to inhibit political mobilization. Catholicism as an institution was complicit in the conquest and colonization of Latino people. The history of the Southwest, the names of cities and towns from Texas to California, remind us how thoroughly Catholicism and colonization were bound together. Far from being an instrument of change, as Rodolfo Acuna (1972, 148) writes, "the Catholic Church refused to promote social action and limited itself to meeting the minimal spiritual needs of the people. . . . [It] was a missionary group that, by its silence, tacitly supported the oppressive conditions under which Chicanos had to live and work." While local priests and parishes occasionally used religion to support faith-based action and to oppose oppression, the institutional Catholic Church was a nonindigenous institution whose leaders and resources could not be easily marshaled for the political goals of the minority group.

Nonetheless, today, it is increasingly clear that religion is relevant to the structuring of contemporary political attitudes in the Latino community. For instance, religion has helped construct a Hispanic ethnic identification in the United States. Hispanic group identification is in part a creation of "situational ethnicity" by Latino activists (Garcia 2003). They have worked to mobilize the Latino community by highlighting similarities in the disparate experiences of Spanish-speaking immigrant subgroups. Instead of the subgroups being politically influential only where they live in concentrated numbers (i.e., Cubans in Florida, Puerto Ricans in New York, Mexicans in the Southwest), Hispanics are a force to be reckoned with nationwide. Research indicates that religiously based organizations facilitate both conventional and unconventional protest politics as well. Although Latinos are less likely to protest than non-Latinos, concerted elite mobilization and the religious politicization of identity makes a significant difference in the political behavior of this ethnic group (Martinez 2005).

Latino religious leaders, churches, and faith-based organizations have been integral to the promotion of Latino identities (Wilson 2008). From religious involvement in high-profile efforts like the sanctuary movement of the 1980s (Garcia 2005) to more recent battles over immigration reform, religious leaders have helped create around immigrant experiences a common desire for self-determination that seems to unite all Latinos (Barreto, Manzano, Ramirez, and Rim 2009; Benjamin-Alvarado, DeSipio, and Montoya 2009). This dynamic has been operative not only at the national level but also, and perhaps as important, in organizing and mobilizing communities at the local and regional levels. In many urban areas, faith-based organizations are a critical material resource, and they also provide the "context and content of the religious beliefs, values and culture that inform social action" (Wilson 2008, 68). Probably the most famous example of religion and community organizing among Latinos is César Chávez's unionization of farmworkers in California in the late 1960s and 1970s (Dalton 2003). His incorporation of religious themes elevated this movement from a simple strike over grapes to La Causa—the cause of dignity and a better life for all marginalized people. As Wood (2005) notes, religiously based organization and mobilization may be particularly important in the Latino community because of the large number of people who are not citizens and the number of citizens who do not engage in electoral politics.

The previous lack of a common identification is one of the reasons that the relationship between religion and politics for Latinos was not more apparent. The importance of religion is to some degree contextual, existing in a particular time and place and contingent on the traditions, beliefs, and meaning that people ascribe to it. The religious expression of each of the twenty-two Latino nationality groups has operated in a different regional, economic, cultural, political, and social context. Moreover, each of these groups came to the United States under different conditions. Some Mexican American families have been in America longer than the United States has been a country. Some Latinos have come to escape political oppression; others have come in search of economic gain. The dynamic between religion and politics is somewhat different for people of Puerto Rican, Mexican, Cuban, or Central American descent. In some ways, only recently has the relationship between Latinos and politics been substantively meaningful, because the term *Latino* itself has only recently come to have political and social import.

But today Latinos are a very critical sociopolitical and electoral grouping. The number of Hispanics in the United States rose from 14 million in 1990 to more than 50.5 million in 2010 comprising about 16 percent of the U.S. population. According to the latest census data, Latinos have surpassed African Americans as the nation's largest minority group.[7] Their political influence is increasing (Kelly and Kelly 2005; Jones-Correa and Leal 2001; Hritzuk and Park 2000; Garcia 1997; Arvizu and Garcia 1996; DeSipio 1996; Hero and Campbell 1996; de la Garza et al. 1992; Verba et al. 1993; Calvo and Rosenstone 1989). At 43 percent, the Hispanic population's growth rate is more than four times the 10 percent growth rate of the total population, ensuring that Latinos are well positioned to influence elections for years to come.[8]

Because of their growing electoral significance, both politicians and political scientists are paying close attention to the factors that influence Latino voting behavior, including how religion affects the attitudes and behavior of this group.

Contrary to common perception, Latinos are religiously diverse, a condition that significantly affects political engagement and participation. While a majority identify as Catholic, the percentage has dropped from the 80 percent figure registered in 1950 (Greeley 1994) to below 60 percent in 2013.[9] Highlighting the trend, in April 2013 a *Time* magazine cover article titled "The Latino Reformation" describes how newly converted "evangelicos" are changing the nature of Latino Christianity and infusing it with Protestant flavor.[10] In a recent survey of those who were not Catholic, 15 percent categorized themselves as evangelical Christians, 8 percent said they were mainline Protestants or some other type of Christian, and about 8 percent cited no religious affiliation. This kind of religious change is likely to continue among Latinos because those born and raised in the United States are less Catholic (58 percent) than those who immigrated more recently (74 percent).[11] As second- and third-generation Latinos are assimilated into American culture, they may feel less tied to traditional cultural markers, including Catholic religiosity (Hunt 2000). Furthermore, the United States has a much more competitive religious market than the mostly Catholic countries of origin from which immigrants arrived (Finke and Stark 2000). After being in the United States for a while, Latinos may feel free to choose other religious options. Consider the marked rise in the number of Latino Pentecostals. Whether they are attracted to the more expressive worship style, to social outreach, to a more personal relationship with God, to the strict code of moral conduct, or to the signs and wonders of the Pentecostal church, estimates are today that more than three-quarters of Hispanic Protestants are Pentecostal in orientation (Walsh 2003).

Hispanic defections may also reflect ethnic and racial tensions within the Catholic Church. Today Hispanics constitute the fastest-growing ethnic bloc in Catholicism, comprising about a third of the Catholic Church. Some have been critical that the growing diversity is not adequately reflected in the church. As a reporter recently observed, "Euro-American

Catholics have tended to give the most attention to the internal dynamics of the church: liturgical reform, the voice and role of the laity, dissent or obedience to sexual ethics and other church teachings, the proper exercise of authority, the question of who is called to ordination." He continues, "[Hispanics] have been much more inclined to accentuate the mission of the church, frequently calling for more Hispanic ministry offices, youth initiatives, outreach efforts, and leadership training programs, as well as an increase in Spanish Masses, Hispanic bishops, celebration of feast days that are part of their Hispanic traditions and culturally sensitive formation programs for seminarians and other Hispanic leaders."[12] Hispanics want the Catholic Church to become more inclusive, representative, and committed to its social mission. In 2013, the historic election of Jorge Mario Bergoglio of Argentina as Francis, Bishop of Rome, was in part recognition of this demographic reality. Francis is the 266th pope, but the first non-European to ever lead the Catholic Church. While much of the discussion of Catholicism in America focuses on the divide between conservatives and liberals, issues related to ethnicity and class constitute another salient break. It is a source of continuing frustration and division that Hispanics are socioeconomically disadvantaged in a wealthy church. Whatever the cause of the defections from the Catholic Church, such moves have led to a much more religiously heterogeneous Latino population, with consequences for civic participation, partisanship, vote choice, and public opinion. Some scholars suggest that Catholicism contributes to lower participation rates among Latinos (Verba, Schlozman, and Brady 1995; Hritzuk and Park 2000). Compared with Protestantism, the more hierarchical organizational style of Catholicism may impede opportunities to develop civic skills (Djupe and Neiheisel 2012). Recent research by Espinosa (2005) also identifies Catholicism as a challenge to Latino political action but explains the challenge is not found in Catholicism itself but in the fact that Catholics are more likely to be immigrants, live in poverty, have lower levels of elementary education, and have lower levels of religious activity than Protestants. Using data from the Hispanic Churches in American Public Life survey, Espinosa finds that different types of Protestant churches are associated with differing levels of political engagement. For instance, mainline Protestants were more likely than evangelical, Pentecostal, or "other" Christians to indicate that their churches engaged in political action.

Thus, church variation is particularly relevant because Latinos consistently vote at lower rates than Anglos, which depresses their potential electoral influence (DeSipio 1996; Michelson 2003). As it does among African Americans, community church involvement may increase civic skills and help compensate for the shortages in resources that otherwise might impede Latino political engagement (Verba, Schlozman, and Brady 1995).

Jones-Correa and Leal (2001, 753) explain that, for Latinos, "participation in church activity is an important corrective to the uneven benefits of education and income, which give an advantage to some political actors at the expense of others." Because Latinos as a group are continually incorporating new immigrants who are unfamiliar with the American system, the political socialization role that churches play may be enhanced even more (de la Garza 2004). "Unless [new immigrants] are mobilized, the new electorate will not be socialized into the political system and are condemned to political limbo" (DeSipio and de la Garza 1994, 112). This kind of mobilization does not happen uniformly. In an interesting study of this kind of variation, Martini (2012) finds that in the Latino community, evangelical Protestants are much more supportive of religious involvement in politics than mainline Protestants or Catholics.

Religious variation also has significant effects on partisanship. Although most Latinos (excepting Cuban Americans) identify as Democrats, the magnitude of that preference differs substantially. Surveys indicate that more than 70 percent of Latino Catholics see themselves as Democrats compared to about half of Latino Protestants.[13] Kelly and Kelly (2005) report not only that Catholics are more Democratic but also that the effect of affiliation with a non-Catholic tradition varies depending on the specific non-Catholic affiliation. Hispanic evangelicals and mainline Protestants are much less Democratic in their partisan identification.

In the last several election cycles, Republicans have desired to mobilize these voters to their candidates. Among Latinos, religion seems to contribute to conservative positions on morality issues including abortion, homosexuality, and societal gender roles. For example, two-thirds of Latino evangelicals oppose same-sex marriage, compared to 44 percent of the U.S. general public, and Latino Protestants are more opposed to abortion than even Latino Catholics (Bartkowski, Ramos-Wada, Ellison, and Acevedo 2012).[14] Republicans have sought to find common ground on the basis of these issues. The problem for Republicans (and the good news for Democrats) is that religiosity does not translate neatly to partisanship or presidential vote choice in the Latino community. The effect of religious traditionalism on political attitudes and behavior varies between Anglos and Latinos. Among Latinos religious conservatism encourages conservative attitudes primarily in the domain of moral issues and general ideological orientations (Kelly and Morgan 2008).

By comparison with Anglos, Latinos are less likely to agree that the government has gone too far in promoting equal rights and more likely to want the government to increase spending on social services (Claassen 2004). Indeed, there is some evidence among Latinos that taking the Bible literally liberalizes attitudes on social welfare and crime issues (McDaniel and Ellison 2008). This is not the pattern among Anglos. De la Garza and Cortina (2007) demonstrate that even though a majority of Latino evangelicals voted for the Republican candidate George W. Bush in 2004, they did so because they liked Bush personally and approved of his performance as president. Their evaluation was substantially independent of partisan ideologies. Other research indicates that conservative religiosity may loosen traditional Democratic loyalties, but this does not lead to a "groundswell" of support for the GOP (McDaniel and Ellison 2008). It is unclear that conservative religiosity has been permanently politicized in a conservative direction for this group (Lee and Pachon 2007).

Further complicating the appeal of the Republican Party in the Latino community is the Republican refusal to seriously engage the nation on the matter of comprehensive immigration reform. In a recent poll, 26 percent of Obama voters and 35 percent of independents indicated that they would consider voting Republican if the party helped to pass immigration reform.[15] Clarrisa Martinez-DeCastro from the National Council of La Raza, the nation's largest Hispanic civil rights and advocacy organization, explained potential long-term costs of anti-immigration positions for Republicans: "The toxic rhetoric has affected all of us regardless of immigration status. It is undeniable that because of the multidimensional impact that this is having on our community, it stands to shape the views of the nearly 900,000 Latino citizens who will turn eighteen each year between now and 2028."[16] Religion is often central to calls for immigration reform. As Rev. Samuel Rodriguez, the leader of the National Hispanic Christian Leadership Conference, a group encompassing more than 40,000 Latino evangelicals, said recently, "It is very difficult to argue theologically that Jesus would be opposed to immigration reform. Beyond the issue of the public policy, the heart of God is for those that are suffering and for the oppressed and the marginalized."[17]

During the presidential primaries, Mitt Romney took a hard line on the issue, endorsing an immigration crackdown that would result in "self-deportation" of the undocumented in the United States. His position alienated many in the Latino community. Meanwhile, President Obama was advocating a path to citizenship and implementing provisions of the DREAM Act by executive order. In the end, Obama won 73 percent of Latino Catholics, more than 50 percent of Latino Protestants, and a majority of Latino voters in Nevada, Colorado, New Mexico, and Florida, critical swing states that contributed to the Obama reelection victory.[18] Thus, although some attributed President Bush's victory in 2004 to successfully targeting Latino evangelicals in several Latino-rich western states, conservative religiosity has not been determinant in vote choice. Barack Obama's victories in 2008 and 2012 with both Latino Catholics and Latino Protestants belie that conclusion.

Disentangling what structures Latino vote choices and how much these are the result of immigrant and minority experiences, socioeconomic status, the social justice and liberationist teachings of Catholicism, the social gospel influence of Protestantism, or the moral teachings of conservative religiosity is difficult to do, and not much research has yet been dedicated to it. It is clear that among Latinos religiosity influences politics, but stable trends are yet to emerge in the ideological and partisan implications of their faith.

MUSLIM AMERICANS

The horrors of September 11, 2001, dramatically focused American attention on the relationship between Islam and politics. These atrocities were committed in the name of God. However, the fundamentalist and radical Islam of the terrorists is very different from the Islam practiced daily by millions of Americans. In the words of Sheik Hamza Yusef, one of the nation's most influential imams, "Islam was hijacked on September 11, 2001, on that plane as an innocent victim."[19] As a result of those horrible events, there has been considerable recent interest in the size and nature of the Muslim population in the United States and the relationship between religion and politics among the members of this community.

The Muslim population in the United States has been estimated to be between three and nine million. However, the best and most reliable estimate using adjusted survey data suggests that the Muslim population in the United States is closer to 1 percent of the population, about 2.8 million people.[20] The majority of Muslims in the United States are of the Sunni tradition, but every Islamic sect is represented in the United States, including Shi'ites, Sufis, and the Druze.

The American Muslim community is strikingly diverse, representing a mosaic of ethnic, racial, linguistic, and national identities. As one scholar observes, "If one wants to see the wide interplay and dizzying range of Muslim cultures [there are] two places. One is the holy city of Mecca, where Muslims gather from every corner of the globe to fulfill a sacred duty. The other is the United States" (Afridi 2001, 1). Muslims in the United States are drawn from more than fifty nations stretching from Africa to Southeast Asia. Sixty-five percent of Muslims in the United States are foreign born, and 35 percent are natives of the United States. The three largest American Muslim groups—African Americans, Arabs, and South Asians—are very different from one another. African Americans make up an estimated 20 percent, South Asians another 18 percent, and Arab Americans about 32 percent of the Muslim population in the United

States. The remainder of the Muslim population in the United States comprises people from Europe, Africa, and South America.[21] In examining the three major groups, we can see how issues of race, ethnicity, national origin, and immigration affect the construction of a Muslim political identity and structure the relationship between religion and politics.

African American Muslims in the United States are as old as the institution of slavery. Austin (1984) estimates that Muslims constituted as much as 20 percent of the slave population on some large southern plantations. However, because American slavery denied slaves the ability to worship freely, Islam was basically lost to black people in the United States until the early twentieth century. It reemerged in 1913 with the founding of the Moorish Science Temple by Noble Drew Ali and later during the 1930s through Master Wali Fard and the Honorable Elijah Muhammad of the Nation of Islam. Both movements were racially separatist in nature, presenting Islam as an alternative to Christianity, the "white man's religion" that had been used to justify racism and the oppression of black people (Mamiya and Lincoln 1988; Lincoln 1982). In the northern cities where it flourished, the early appeal of Islam for African Americans was its black nationalist orientation. Liberated from the constraints of "false beliefs," black people would be free to create new societies for themselves through the power of Islam. For many African Americans, Islam represented a way to achieve racial equality and justice (Curtis 2002; Allen 1998; McCloud 1995).

This point is most clearly demonstrated through the history of Nation of Islam, led for more than forty years by Elijah Muhammad. The Nation made its biggest inroads into the African American community during the 1960s, when Malcolm X was Muhammad's national representative. As Lincoln and Mamiya (1990, 389) observe, "Malcolm X and the Nation are credited with the primary ideological foundations that led to the development of the concepts of 'black power,' 'black pride' and 'black consciousness.'" However, the doctrines of black nationalism, espoused so powerfully by Malcolm X and the Nation of Islam, contradicted some of the traditional practices and beliefs of orthodox Islam. These contradictions were illuminated when Malcolm X renounced the ideas of the Nation after his pilgrimage to Mecca in 1964, where he met "blonde haired, blue-eyed men I could call my brothers" (Haley 1966).

After the death of Elijah Muhammad in 1975, the Nation of Islam split into two factions. Most black Muslims followed Elijah's son Imam Warith Deen Mohammed to orthodox Sunni Islam in the American Society of Muslims. Throughout his lifetime, Imam Mohammed continued to speak out forcefully on issues of concern to the African American community, and his more mainstream Islamic doctrine led to his recognition as an Islamic leader worldwide. The other smaller—though higher-profile—

faction of the Nation of Islam is led by Minister Louis Farrakhan and continues to adhere to the original racialized theology of Elijah Muhammad. For many blacks today, Farrakhan symbolizes black nationalist politics. Among the lower-socioeconomic-status African American urban males to which Islam in general (and the Nation of Islam in particular) most appeals, Islam is a way to overcome racism and reconstitute a community based on alternative values.

The South Asian immigrant community in the United States comes from countries such as India, Pakistan, and Bangladesh. Most have come to the United States since the 1960s. Although these immigrants have different and sometimes conflictual political histories, they constitute one diasporic group in the United States because of such commonalities as memories of British colonialism and the establishment of Pakistan and later Bangladesh (Leonard 2003). In the United States, Islam can provide a point of reconnection for them to a time when the culturally artificial boundaries of contemporary South Asian nation-states did not exist. Today South Asians are often the leaders of major American Muslim organizations (see Leonard 2003, app. 2, for a list of these groups).

The largest group of immigrant Muslims in America are of Arab descent. While some arrived in the late 1800s, most came to the United States after the liberalization of immigration law in the mid-1960s and the development of Arab nationalism in their countries of origin. This was a geographically diverse, politicized, Muslim group whose members tend to feel that they have suffered ethnic and religious discrimination in the United States and throughout the world (Suleiman 1994). Haddad (1994) finds that Arab self-identification is influenced by the waves of immigration and by the ideologies and commitments new immigrants bring with them.

Still, these immigrants are often separated by the histories that divide them. For example, the politics of Iranians and Iraqis, Kuwaitis and Iraqis, and Saudis and other non-Gulf Arabs are not always mediated in the United States by common linkages of ethnicity or religion. Moreover, recent immigrants are often ideologically different from third- and fourth-generation immigrants, who are more likely to see themselves as Americans of ethnic descent rather than as hyphenated Americans who give greater significance to the identity of their nation of origin (Suleiman 1994).

Apart from nationality and generation, the cohesion of the Muslim community in the United States is further challenged by differences regarding the appropriate role of Islam in public life. One of the major issues for Muslims is how Islam, which defines a comprehensive way of life, can function in a secular context (see Saeed 2002; Nimer 2002; Voll 1991; J. Smith 1999). Perhaps every faith tradition faces this challenge in a nonreligious state, but the problem is particularly acute for those religions not tied to the dominant Judeo-Christian worldview of the United States.

This issue is at the heart of the debate between Muslims and Islamists. Islamists see no redeeming quality in secular democracy, finding it diametrically opposed to the basic teachings of Islam. Thus, Islamists seek no incorporation in American society but rather strive to turn the United States into a strictly Muslim country. Muslims, in contrast, believe that Islam is fulfilled in American values and that the religious, political, and social freedom that America offers is actually beneficial to the faith (Khan 1998). They desire a greater level of integration in American society.

But defining the proper role of Islam in society is still no easy task. Should Islam be the basis for political identity? How does it mediate nationalist orientations? What is the relevance of Islam for politics? Who are appropriate partners? What are appropriate goals? Many of the issues that are most salient to separate groups of Muslims—the Palestinian conflict for Arab Americans; Kashmir for South Asians; democratization in Egypt, Syria, Bosnia, Iraq, Iran, Afghanistan, Israel, and so on—are foreign policy questions with the capacity to undermine transnational Islamic unity (Khan 2000, 2002). This tension is manifested in intergenerational differences between American-born Muslims and their parents (Suleiman 1994). Reflecting on this kind of tension, Muqtedar Khan observes, "It boils down to the difference in which the new generation of Muslims is constructing their Islamic identity as opposed to the manner in which their parents have constructed their Islamic identity. And the significant difference is that the new generation is struggling to accommodate their American-ness (saying): I am a Muslim. I am also an American" (quoted in Afridi 2001, 6).

A Muslim American political identity is beginning to emerge. A recent poll indicated that 70 percent of Muslim voters consider their religion important to their voting decisions.[22] American foreign policy in the Middle East and the United States' relations with Muslim countries have been extremely influential in this process (Haddad 1994). U.S. foreign policy coupled with perceived violation of civil liberties related to the war on terror in the United States have served to increase Muslim identification and led to the maturation of American Islam in terms of structural organization as well (Saeed 2002).

One indication of this increased organizational capacity is the recent attempt to coordinate bloc voting among Muslims in presidential elections. The 1996 presidential election was the first in which Muslims as a group were politically engaged (Durán 1997). Perhaps owing to some of the Islamic political identity issues discussed earlier or to the fact that that many first-generation Muslim Americans came from contexts of political repression that left them reluctant to participate, Muslims have not historically been a factor in electoral politics at the national level. However, their concentration in traditionally important battleground states like Michigan, California, Illinois, Ohio, and Texas suggests they could be. Harnessing institutional resources, major Muslim political organizations—including the Islamic Society of North America (ISNA), the American Muslim Council (AMC), the American Muslim Alliance (AMA), the Council on American Islamic Relations (CAIR), the Muslim Public Affairs Council (MPAC), and others—have overcome factionalism and concerns about the appropriateness of Islamic participation in elections to establish coordinating committees and work collaboratively to increase the Muslim vote.

However, challenges to the political inclusion of Muslim Americans were on dramatic display during President Obama's first presidential election campaign in 2008. This election should have been a breakthrough electoral moment for the Muslim American community. The Democratic Party nominated Barack Obama—a thoroughly unique candidate whose father and stepfather were Muslim, who lived for a time in a Muslim country, and whose middle name, Hussein, is distinctly Muslim as well. Obama himself is Christian, not Muslim. Still, having a candidate with this kind of background should have been the best of political times for Muslim Americans. Muslims clearly favored Obama. The American Muslim Taskforce's political scorecard gave Obama 981 points to McCain's 291.[23] However, instead of campaigning vigorously for Obama, the Muslim community was trying to avoid negative reprisals toward both the candidate and the community. Even Obama's loose connections to Islam were used to denigrate his campaign and in the process exposed how ugly religious fears and prejudice undermine the promise of religious equality and freedom for Muslims in the United States. Although both major parties spoke of inclusiveness and tolerance, neither campaign was overly anxious to court the Muslim vote. Despite multiple trips to churches and synagogues, neither candidate visited a mosque to try to speak directly to the Muslim community. Throughout the campaign, Obama's opponents assailed him through viral e-mails that alleged he was a "secret Muslim" who had only embraced Christianity for political reasons.[24]

Moreover, a survey by the Pew Forum on Religion and Public Life conducted in March 2008 reported that 45 percent of respondents said they would have reservations about voting for a presidential candidate who is Muslim, compared with 25 percent for a Mormon candidate and 11 percent for a Jewish candidate. Research indicates that conservative Christian religiosity is a major predictor of negative feeling toward Muslims and a propensity to see them as a religious and cultural group outside the mainstream of American society (Penning 2009; Johnson 2006; Rowatt et al. 2005). In an interesting article, Kalkan and his colleagues (2009) found that antipathy toward Muslims predated the tragedy of September 11,

2001. In each time period feelings were driven primarily by affect toward Muslims as both a cultural and a religious minority group. The good news is with increasing contact and familiarity, opinions toward religious minorities tend to moderate over time. The bad news is that Muslims are not seen exclusively as a religious but also as a cultural minority. Attitudes toward cultural minorities tend to be less changeable because these groups are defined as those whose behaviors or values many in society find unusual or offensive.

For his part, Obama disappointed many Muslim voters with how vigorously he denied claims that he was Muslim—as if there were something inherently wrong with belonging to that tradition. Obama tried to counter such "smears" on his campaign website by stating the fact that he was a committed Christian and had never been Muslim. Many Muslim Americans were incredulous at the idea that being called a Muslim constituted some kind of "smear." Moreover, instead of speaking out against anti-Muslim bigotry, the Obama campaign tried to minimize the issue. Volunteer campaign workers even asked two hijab-wearing women to move to seats off camera at a June 2008 campaign event to avoid the perception of too much Muslim support.[26]

The dynamic in the 2012 election was different, but no less troubling for the political interests of the Muslim American religious community. During the Republican primaries candidates did nothing to endear themselves to Muslims, as many stumbled facing hysteria over the debate on the Ground Zero Mosque, questions about whether the U.S. court system was in danger of being taking over by sharia (Islamic law), if they would appoint Muslims to their cabinet—even whether Muslims were diminishing French culture in France. By the time Romney emerged as the candidate in late spring 2012, the tone of the campaign was negative, with some even condemning Romney and the Republican Party for failing to fight Islamophobia.[27]

President Obama was not accused of Islamophobia but was impugned for failure to deliver on promises that he had made during the 2008 campaign that were particularly meaningful to Muslim voters. After four years as president, Guantanamo Bay remained open, the administration continued PATRIOT Act policies that allowed enhanced surveillance of Muslims, and Obama supported drone strikes in Pakistan and reportedly kept a secret "kill list" of terrorist targets. Though he gave an address in Cairo not long after he took office, calling for an end to the marginalization of Muslims while fighting the war on terror, his weak record led many Muslims to question his commitment to these matters. Neither Romney nor Obama made a concerted effort to attract Muslim voters or strongly pursued their votes in 2012.

In the end, according to a poll released by the Council on American-Islamic Relations, 85 percent of Muslims cast their ballot to reelect President Obama, only slightly fewer than the 89 percent that voted for him in 2008. But high levels of support did not signal enthusiasm. It is often hard for minorities to leverage their voting power in national elections. As Representative Keith Ellison, the first Muslim congressman, explained, "The Muslim community doesn't have a real choice in this election. . . . If there's anything about Obama you don't like, triple it when it comes to Romney."[28]

There is some evidence that antipathy toward Republicans is translating to not only Democratic vote choice but also Democratic Party affiliation. According to a 2011 Pew Forum for Religion and Public Life, nearly 70 percent of American Muslims identified as Democratic (46 percent) or leaned Democratic (24 percent), compared to only 11 percent who identified or leaned Republican.[29] Given these numbers, it is perhaps surprising to learn that in 1988 Muslim Americans voted two to one for George H. W. Bush and, although they supported Democrat Bill Clinton in 1992 and 1996, the majority voted for the Republican George W. Bush in 2000, believing he would pursue a more evenhanded policy in the Middle East than his Democratic opponent, Al Gore.[30] Of course, Bush administration policies after September 11, 2001, estranged many Muslim voters from the Republican Party, and they have voted for Democrats since that time. Recent research of mosque-attending Muslims indicates that socially conservative, negative perceptions about the treatment of Muslims living in America in response to wars in the Middle East have prompted many to switch their partisan loyalties (Patterson, Gasim, and Choi 2011). Muslims of Southeast Asian and Arab descent have been particularly sensitive to these concerns (Jalalzai 2009). For now, Muslim Americans seem to be inclined toward the Democrats, but the pattern of their vote choice indicates a willingness to evaluate candidates and to change their vote choice based on who they perceive will best represent their interest as Muslim American citizens.

Though in the last several years neither political party has been a strong advocate of antidiscrimination measures for Muslim Americans, there is no evidence that as a group they are disconnected or disaffected with the American political system. On the contrary, Jalalzai (2011) finds that in a post-9/11 world, Muslims who are concerned about discrimination or who know someone who has been a victim of discrimination are more likely to be politically engaged. Religion is a major factor in this political participation. Jamal (2005) finds that mosques, similar to other religious institutions, are effective vehicles for mobilization and foster higher levels of Muslim consciousness in some groups. In 2007 the Pew Forum on Religion in Public Life conducted the first nation-wide, random sample of Muslim Americans. The study revealed the importance of the political socialization that takes place in religious institutions. Personal religiosity—being a devout Muslim—was actually negatively associated with political participation (Ayers and Hofstetter 2008). Indeed, there is some evidence that gender differences in Arab Muslim political engagement can be explained by the higher levels of political religiosity among men (Read 2007).

However, though Muslims are engaged at the national level, their political representation lags far below the 1–2 percent that they make up in the U.S. population. The first Muslim American representative to Congress was elected in 2006, with a second elected in 2008.[31] There are no Muslim members of the Senate. Latter-Day Saints, a group of similar size, hold seven times the seats. In an experiment with undergraduate college students, Braman and Sinno (2009) found encouraging evidence that students evaluated Muslim and Christian candidates similarly. Nonetheless, the students were less likely to say that a candidate shared their values if they were Muslim. Given how Islam has been treated politically in the United States and the role that values assessments play in voting, it would be interesting to see whether the general population also evaluated Muslim candidates similarly.

At the local level there are places were Muslim Americans are well incorporated in the American political system. For example, throughout Michigan and in specific cities such as Detroit and Dearborn, Muslims are a major factor in the local political dynamic (Abraham and Shryock 2000; Terry 1999). Congresspersons with Muslim Americans in their districts are more sympathetic to Muslim American preferences than those who do not represent them, even on domestic security votes (Martin 2009). Still, given the way Islam developed as a political issue in the 2008 election and the way that Muslims have been treated in the war on terror, there is some question about whether the interest of Muslims as a religious minority will be effectively represented in the American democratic system. They are participating, but many questions remain about the nature of religion and politics among Muslim Americans. Can a Muslim political agenda be advanced in a party system not inclined to accommodate it? What are the limits of religion and politics, both for the Muslim American community and for an American society that increasingly is dealing with the political implications of religious pluralism in a democratic state? These implications are particularly important for Muslim Americans, whose race, ethnicity, and religious affiliation are all interconnected and for whom each demographic characteristic represents a minority experience in the United States. Much interesting research remains to be done in this emerging area.

CHURCH OF JESUS CHRIST OF LATTER-DAY SAINTS

In spring 2012, *Time* magazine ran an article asking if the 2012 presidential election campaign of Mitt Romney represented a "Mormon moment" for the United States.[32] Certainly it looked like the potential was there to elect him as president. His church had mounted a nationwide public relations campaign, *The Book of Mormon* was a Broadway sensation, and major television networks were broadcasting shows that made the faith the subject of cultural entertainment. In many ways the time seemed right and the former Massachusetts governor seemed like a Republican dream come true—"a social conservative from the most cerulean of blue states who could please the base while not scaring off moderates."[33] In a weak economy, he had strong business credentials. And if credentials weren't enough, he had the benefit that good looks produce in a media age. Both he and his family look like they came out of central casting. But still there was the issue of what Romney's 2008 team had called "TMT"— that Mormon thing—that might undermine the support of the American people for his candidacy.

The Church of Jesus Christ of Latter-Day Saints (LDS) has had very interesting experiences at the intersection of religion and politics. The early history of the Mormon Church was shaped significantly through political conflicts with non-Mormons. Ideologically cohesive and geographically concentrated, the LDS continue to have considerable potential political influence. In Utah, which is about 70 percent Mormon, one of the major state newspapers (the *Deseret News*) as well as radio and television stations are church affiliated. One scholar estimates that 80 percent of legislators in Utah are likely to be church members. Because of the large number of church members working in government, he observes, "it may not be necessary for church authorities to proclaim what they want, much less to lobby members of the legislature" (Sharkansky 1997). The LDS church has access to political power. However, the Mormon experience also reveals the limits and challenges of minority religious influence in a secular state.

The LDS church was established in 1830 by Joseph Smith in western New York. From its inception, it was politically controversial. Mormons are Christians in that they claim salvation through Jesus Christ. But the faith introduced several new doctrines that conflicted substantially with the fundamentals of both Protestantism and Roman Catholicism. The tenets of Mormon faith differ from other Christians in important ways, including the origin of God, the doctrine of the Trinity, the role of works in salvation, the nature of man, original sin, baptism of the dead, sacred temple rights, and the long-repudiated practice of polygamy. Latter-Day Saints believe that there were ancient Israelite prophets in the Americas who foretold the coming of the Messiah and that Christ himself came to minister to those who were waiting for him in the New World after his resurrection and ascension. The Book of Mormon, embraced as scripture on a par with the Bible, records these events. Mormon doctrine also asserts that prophetic revelation did not end with the Bible but continues to this day through the president of the LDS church. Hierarchically organized and led by revelation, Mormons believe the LDS church embodies true Christian faith, restoring to the world what had been lost through apostasy.

The Mormons further strayed from what was considered mainstream Christianity in their emphasis on creating Zion, a just society within America's borders. They developed unified communities that followed the revelations of their spiritual leader on economic, social, and political matters. They sought to establish a theodemocracy, and for them, "building the kingdom of God literally meant building a godly society" (Mason 2011, 373). Their increasing numbers and their willingness to vote as a bloc made them a political threat. Perceived as heretics who did not respect the boundaries of church and state, they were driven from their homes and violently persecuted in several states. Seeking safety after Joseph Smith was killed in 1844, most Mormons followed their new leader, Brigham Young, west to Utah Territory.

Even as the majority in the Utah Territory, the Mormons had a difficult relationship with the federal government. These difficulties were exacerbated in the mid-1850s when the church revealed its support for polygamy—the marriage of one man to multiple wives. The Republican Party used the polygamy issue to highlight the danger of unrestrained popular sovereignty. The Democratic-supported Kansas-Nebraska Act of 1854 had given the people the right to choose whether their states would be slave or free. The Republicans asserted that if this kind of choice were lawful, then the people of Utah would be able to vote in polygamy as lawful in their area. For the next forty years, the federal government and the LDS church were in constant political conflict. Several congressional acts were passed that effectively disenfranchised Mormons and restricted their political freedoms. The constitutionality of these acts was consistently upheld by the Supreme Court.[34] The Court even upheld a congressional act to dissolve the LDS church as a legal and economic corporation and dispose of its assets because of its position on polygamy.

Facing these realities and the limits of free exercise of religion, the LDS president ended the practice of polygamy in 1890. Furthermore, the church disbanded its People's Political Party that had dominated state politics for many years, and it encouraged church members to affiliate with the national parties. With these and other concessions, Utah was admitted as the forty-fifth state to the Union in 1896. The LDS church traded its overt political power for more subtle and traditional forms of political influence.

Today, the Mormon hierarchy is officially neutral politically. Like most religious organizations, the LDS church and its general leadership do not endorse parties, candidates, or political platforms. Nor does it use church facilities for political purposes. In spite of these formal rules, the political potential of Mormonism remains formidable. At approximately 5.5 million members in the United States, it is the nation's sixth-largest and fastest-growing religious group. Although Mormons account for just 1.6 percent of the population, in the 113th Congress (2013–2014) there were fifteen Mormon members of Congress, eight in the House and seven in the Senate. Interestingly, though most Mormons are conservative, these leaders represent a variety of political perspectives and are both Democrats and Republicans, including Senate majority leader Harry Reid (D-N.V.). Notably, Mormon representatives are no more unified in their voting behavior than randomly selected sets of legislators (Cann 2009).

Despite the political diversity of the Mormon congressional leadership, as a lay group Latter-Day Saints are ideologically cohesive, measuring to the right of all major religious traditions in ideology and partisanship alike. Only one in ten identify as liberal.[35] Moreover, because they are geographically concentrated in many of the western states, they are well positioned to affect politics in Utah, Idaho, Washington, Wyoming, Nevada, Arizona, and other states.

Campbell and Monson (2002) describe the potential Mormons have to mobilize as the political equivalent of "dry kindling." The high expectations for church participation in Mormon culture help increase social capital and civic skills and render church members unusually politically active. LDS members are expected to attend three hours of meetings on Sunday; periodically travel to regional temples for special services; fulfill congregational assignments; spend up to two years as full-time missionaries when young or retired; refrain from pre- and extramarital sex, tobacco, coffee, tea, and alcoholic beverages; and give at least 10 percent of their income to the church. Mormons are a classic example of a "strict church" that places so many demands on its members that it naturally weeds out those inclined to be less than fully committed (Finke and Stark 1992; Iannaccone 1992, 1994, 1995). Their geographic concentration in the West may enhance this dynamic. Although some theories of religious participation hold that a lack of diversity in the religious marketplace retards activity, Phillips (1969) observes that Mormon concentration strengthens participation. He notes that consolidation of church and social ties "makes deviance from the former a breach of decorum in the latter" (127). Even educational attainment, which usually has a secularizing influence on most religious groups, does not undermine the religiosity of LDS members (Merrill, Lyon, and Jensen 2003). With this extensive political history and latent political potential, why are Mormons just characterized as dry kindling? What can impact their ability to catch fire?

First, intensive church involvement builds political capacity, but it is only activated when Mormon leaders give clear instructions on political matters (Campbell and Monson 2002). They are reluctant to do this and prefer to work behind the scenes to mobilize support through congregations. However, they have taken positions on equal rights, gambling, and gay marriage (Mansbridge 1986). When there is agreement among LDS leaders on an issue and an official pronouncement is made, Mormons become politically activated based on their religious beliefs (Campbell and Monson 2003). Obeying the prophet is a sign of being a good Mormon. There are strong linkages between Mormon theology and these moral-cultural type issues (Alexander 1995; Richards 1995; Magleby 1992; Campbell and Monson 2002). Although it does not happen often, when the LDS church asks for the support of its members in pursuit of a "moral" political goal, it can be a very powerful thing.

This is what happened in the ballot battle to ban gay marriage in the state of California in 2008. The California Supreme Court ruled in the spring of 2008 that it was unconstitutional to treat people differently on the basis of sexual orientation, including denying them the right to marry. In response to this decision, opponents put a proposition on the November 2008 ballot to amend the state constitution to say that "only marriage between a man and a woman is valid in California." Though Mormons constitute only 2 percent of the state's population, LDS spokesman Michael Otterson called this "a moment of emergence."[36] In June, a letter from Prophet Thomas Monson and the leadership of the church called on believers to "do all you can to support the proposed constitutional amendment by donating of your means and of your time."[37] This was a strong endorsement; Mormons are likely to both give money and campaign for the positions they support (Campbell and Monson 2003). Although they did not hold meetings on LDS property, "good" Mormons individually became the feet and the finances of the Protect Marriage movement. They volunteered and contributed more than $20 million to the proposition's campaign fund. When the measure passed by less than 5 percent of the vote, Mormons were credited (or condemned) as a major cause for gay rights defeat.

They were also attacked on the basis of their religious identity for engaging the political process. The episode reveals the challenges minority faiths can experience when engaging in politics. Mormon participation in Proposition 8 resulted in a backlash against the church for mobilizing religious citizens based on the convictions of their faith. One TV ad opposing Proposition 8 showed two Mormon missionaries visiting a lesbian couple. When the couple opens the door, the missionaries say, "Hi, we're from the Church of Jesus Christ of Latter-Day Saints! We're here to take away your rights." The missionaries then proceed to terrorize them by ransacking their house, removing their wedding rings, and tearing up their marriage certificate. Against these disturbing images the narrator says, "Say no to a church taking over your government!"[38] At pro-gay marriage rallies there were chants of "Mormon scum."[39] Mormon temples were vandalized, and lists of Mormon businesses to boycott were distributed on the Internet. It is hard to conceive that this kind of attack would have gone unaddressed had the missionaries been Jewish rabbis, black preachers, or Catholic nuns.

Officially the LDS church remains nonpartisan. This reveals a second reason Mormons must be considered "dry kindling"—despite their demonstrated political capacity. Under most circumstances, the political force the LDS church exerts does not come from formal alignments with parties, candidates, or platforms. Even for native son Mitt Romney, they offered no official pronouncements. Mormons, however, vote overwhelmingly Republican, largely on the basis of cultural conservatism. Mormons can be expected to be attracted to the Republican Party as long as the political environment is characterized by conflict over cultural issues. However, religious influence rarely extends to other issue areas (Jelen 1998). Indeed, the first book-length treatment of Mormon political ideology challenges the conventional wisdom that Mormon theology unavoidably results in conservative political ideas. Jeffrey Fox (2006) finds some Mormon teachings can be used to support thoroughly unconservative ideas like radical economic redistribution and liberal immigration reform policies (Hunter and Toney 2005). Additionally, as the Mormon Church in the United States becomes more geographically, culturally, and racially diverse, it may not remain as politically cohesive. For instance, many more African Americans have joined since the church lifted its ban on blacks entering the priesthood in 1978.[40] Interestingly, today fewer than half of the church's twelve million members even live in the United States. Some of the conservative tendencies identified with Mormonism may be a function of studies that have focused on white westerners (Fox 2003). "Members of the church who are socialized in other political milieus will certainly have systematically different political outlooks that reflect indigenous cultural preferences" (286).

Finally, while Mormons are politically influential where they are geographically concentrated, their nationwide influence is constrained by the difficulties they face forming political coalitions with what would appear to be their natural political allies in the Christian Right. Although Mormons identify themselves as Christians and are conservative on social issues, doctrinal differences with evangelicals hinder political relationships. Many in the Christian Right do not acknowledge Mormonism as part of the Christian faith tradition, often even identifying it as a cult. For example, as late as October 2012, the Billy Graham Evangelistic Association had the Mormon faith listed as a cult on its website.[41] A lack of evangelical enthusiasm for Mormonism is one of the primary reasons Romney was not able to secure the Republican presidential nomination until nearly six months after the contest began. Despite the down economy and Romney's business expertise, evangelicals rallied to support other candidates with strong religious credentials, including Congresswoman Michele Bachmann, Senator Rick Santorum, Minnesota governor Tim Pawlenty, Texas governor Rick Perry, and Godfather's Pizza magnate Herman Cain, before at last turning their attention to Romney. Romney ultimately won the Republican nomination, but he did so without the strong support of the evangelical community. Of course, given a choice between Obama and Romney, evangelicals chose Romney. Significantly, they voted for him as heavily in the general election as they had for GOP candidates in 2008 and 2004. Indeed, in the end, the election was dominated by the economy, and Mitt Romney's Mormon background remained mostly a nonissue. For his part, Romney seemed uncomfortable talking about religious matters. When he did mention them, he spoke "Christianese," preferring to focus on the ethical commonalities that people of faith share and to minimize the theological differences that exist. It was a good strategy to break the "stained glass ceiling," the barrier that religious affiliation presents to the presidency (Campbell, Green, and Monson 2012). To some extent, it worked. Republican partisans and conservatives across most faith traditions supported Romney. For many people the real substance of religion is morality, and the standard by which they judge a candidate is whether he or she shares values that are consistent with their own (Prothero 2010). In some ways this is in keeping with the U.S. Constitution, which explicitly states that "no religious test shall ever be required as a qualification to any Office or public trust under the United States."

However, while Romney's nomination and support in the 2012 election reflects a level of religious tolerance, public opinion data suggest that there is a long way to go before religious skepticism about the Mormon faith is abated. In a recent poll, only about 50 percent of Americans say that Mormonism is a Christian religion, more than 60 percent say Mormonism is very different from their own beliefs, and nearly 70 percent of respondents do not see Mormonism as mainstream. Even more telling, 50 percent of Mormons say that there is *a lot* of anti-Mormon discrimination.[42] In their book *American Grace*, Bob Putnam and David Campbell (2010) examine religious diversity in the United States and explain that the overriding commitment to pluralism and interaction in assorted social networks keeps insurmountable religious differences from emerging.

They also explain that although most Americans are quite comfortable with people of other religions, faith traditions that are not as familiar—Mormons, Muslims, and other non-Christian faiths like Buddhism and Sikhism—are notable exceptions to the rule. In the end, the Romney campaign did little to familiarize America with the Mormon faith. Eight in ten Americans reported that they learned little or nothing about the Mormon religion during the presidential campaign. Even after the election, when asked in an open-ended question to offer one word that best describes the Mormon religion, 70 percent of Americans said "cult."[43] It is a double standard. In the world of faith Mormonism is no more ridiculous than anything else. As one blogger wrote:

> Religions are inherently unable to withstand rational scrutiny from without. This is the real Mystery of Faith; that people are able to accept and believe ideas both supernatural (the Resurrection) and social (love thy enemy, turn the other check) that make no logical sense. It's no different if you're Christian or Muslim or Scientologist. There's an inherent hypocrisy to the debate circling Romney—as if believing that Jesus appeared in the Americas is somehow more implausible than believing he appeared, resurrected from the dead, to that doubtful fellow Thomas.[44]

In a book that explores the role of Mormonism in American culture, Trepanier and Newswander (2012) explain that "By challenging the accepted parameters of what it means to be Christian in America . . . Mormons indirectly question the religio-cultural foundation of America." It is significant that a Mormon secured the nomination of a major political party and that millions of Americans voted for him. In the end, however, as one observer noted, Romney is more likely a catalyst for religio-political acceptance than the culmination of it. He is more like Al Smith, the first Catholic to run for president in 1929, than John Kennedy, the first Catholic elected president in 1960.[45] It took decades for Catholicism to become part of the American mainstream. The Romney campaign and the religious conservatives who backed him demonstrate that religion matters politically and can overcome creedal differences. But the skepticism that Mormons continue to face in public life is a testament to the fact that politicized religious perspectives do not fully compensate for old loyalties, identities, and stereotypes. As a country we have removed some barriers, but significant inequalities based on religion persist.

OTHER FAITH TRADITIONS

Religious diversity is increasing in America. Non-Judeo-Christian religions make up a small but growing share of America's religious marketplace. From the 1970s to the early 2000s, the proportion of these religions more than tripled. Followers of nontraditional American religions now constitute approximately 5 percent of the U.S. population.[46] In 2012 the first Buddhist was elected to the Senate and the first Hindu was elected to the House of Representatives.[47] These two join four others in the House but no others in the Senate to comprise the members of "other" faith traditions in the 113th Congress. Immigrants bringing their faith to American shores as well as converts adopting alternative spiritual paths are increasing the ranks of these faith traditions. Not much political science research has yet been devoted to the way religions like Hinduism, Buddhism, Jainism, Sikhism, Wicca, Taoism, and others influence political attitudes and behavior in the United States. Admittedly, the number of people in these traditions is relatively small, and it is difficult to get reliable quantitative data about them. Still, in a chapter on religion and politics for minorities in the United States, it is important to acknowledge that these groups exist and that religion's impact in the United States stretches far beyond the Christian Right and other "mainstream" American faiths.

There are several important reasons to keep these groups in mind. First, the influence of these faith traditions may affect more than the "true believers." Buddhism, for example, is not an exclusive religion like Christianity, Judaism, or Islam. As Wuthnow and Cadge (2004, 364) observe, "The number of 'nightstand Buddhists' . . . who keep a book of Buddhist sayings on their nightstand or who practice a little Zen meditation when they get out of bed in the morning is often thought to be larger than the number of people who actually call themselves Buddhist" (also see Tweed 1999). Their research indicates that as many as one person in eight believes that Buddhist teachings or practices have had an important influence on their own religion or spirituality. Native American spirituality has also been warmly embraced by Americans. Once derided as "devil worship," it has evolved into a well-regarded religious tradition, and many elements of "new age" religion reflect its philosophies (Jenkins 2004). The Buddhist and Native American experience may highlight an understudied area of religion and politics. It is true that much of religion's impact comes out of the communal experience of worshipping—of being a part of a religious community. Still, the power of religious ideas should not be discounted. Traditions may have political impacts that go well beyond the number of their faithful adherents.

Second, we have seen that religion is often an integral part of ethnic identity and that it can be a principal factor in the construction of group consciousness among minorities in the United States. Evidence from the National Asian American Political Survey suggests that religions such as Hinduism and Buddhism are significant variables in the political adaptation of Asian Americans (Lien 2004). A growing body of research examines how non-Christian immigrants use religious institutions to negotiate the new realities of their lives (Stepick et al. 2009; Hagan 2008; Foley and Hoge 2007; Kniss and Numrich 2007; Ecklund and Park 2005; Guest 2003). These studies reveal that after arriving in the United States many immigrants increase their religious participation; participation has a positive impact on civic and political involvement (Akresh 2011). They also demonstrate how religious preferences help shape ethnic identity preferences for immigrant groups and thus influence the nature and character of ethnic pluralism in the United States (Chen 2008). Moreover, it is worth remembering that this occurs in the context of a globalized transnational politics in which ethnic pluralism in the United States has the potential to affect politics in other countries as well (Levitt 2007). Kurien (2001, 264) describes how "nationalist movements are frequently initiated and orchestrated by immigrant communities living thousands of miles from the homeland" (see also Kurien 2007). Min (2002) explains how states such as India and Korea have established places of worship in the United States in an effort to maintain the link between religion and certain forms of nationalism in the expatriate community.

Scholars are beginning to examine this link between religiosity and nationalism in nontraditional American faith communities such as the Hindu (Sriram 2005). It is interesting that historically Hinduism on the Indian subcontinent has varied widely by region and practice. It is being "standardized" in the United States by Hindu organizations trying to conform to the requirements of American governmental policies that reflect acceptable (largely Christian, particularly Protestant) ways of practicing religion in order to receive the benefits and recognition of being classified as a tax-exempt "religious group." The creation of "American Hinduism" and its link to American ethnic Indian identity has had a major effect on the development of Hindu nationalist politics in India as American conceptions of what it means to be Hindu and what it means to be Indian are communicated transnationally and impact politics on the subcontinent (Kurien 2006, 2007).

Finally, although the number of participants in other faith traditions in the United States is small, numbers are not the only way to influence politics. Interest group activities by religious minorities in legislatures and especially in courts have long helped define the limits of establishment and free exercise for all in the United States. For instance, organizations such as the Hindu American Foundation were active in the recent Ten Commandments cases.[48] Their argument was that some of the commandments were irreconcilable with their beliefs. While the commandments prohibit the making of graven images to represent God, idol worship is basic Hindu practice. Although the Supreme Court nonetheless supported the constitutionality of a Ten Commandments display in the 2005 case of *Van Orden v. Perry*, small religious groups have been central to cases clarifying the protections of the First Amendment. The experience of minorities in the United States and particularly religious communions outside the Judeo-Christian tradition helps us explore the boundaries of religious establishment in a country that is increasingly diverse and that can no longer be linked neatly to the norm of Christianity or Anglo-European ethnic and racial identity.

CONCLUSION

This brief review of religion and politics among racial, ethnic, and religious minorities in the United States helps us better understand the communal nature of religion and how participation in a religious community can increase identity, consciousness, and political engagement. This is particularly true when religion is more than just a faith tradition, becoming a means to convey minority culture as well. In these instances, religion often meaningfully interacts with ideology, partisanship, and policy positions. Although religion has the potential to be a source of mobilization for religious groups, cross-cutting cleavages of ethnicity, race, class, and creed remain salient. Religion does not always mediate them. Indeed, in some cases it may exacerbate them as it does in many ways for homosexuals and women, the two groups we examine in the next chapter.

11

The Other Minorities

Women and Gay People

But I would have you know that the head of every man is Christ; and the head of the woman is the man; and the head of Christ is God.

—Apostle Paul (I Corinthians 11:3)

They exchanged the truth of God for a lie. . . . Because of this God gave them over to shameful lusts. Even their women exchanged natural relations for unnatural ones. In the same way the men also abandoned natural relations with women and were inflamed with lusts for one another. Men committed indecent acts with other men, and received in themselves the due penalty for their perversion.

—Apostle Paul (Romans 1:25–28)

The writings of Paul, like our state constitutions, are susceptible of various interpretations. But when the human soul is roused with holy indignation against injustice and oppression, it stops not to translate human parchments, but follows out the law of its inner being written by the finger of God in the first hour of creation.

—Elizabeth Cady Stanton, 1854

In June 2013 the Supreme Court ruled the federal Defense of Marriage Act (DOMA) unconstitutional and again laid bare how definitions of marriage and gender roles in society remain highly contested religio-cultural and political territory. At the federal level, DOMA had been a triumph for advocates of "family values." Passed in 1996 by veto-proof majorities in both the House and the Senate, DOMA codified nonrecognition of same-sex marriage at the federal level by defining marriage as the legal union between one man and one woman, and as a result, all federal benefits were denied to legally married same-sex couples. For some, DOMA represented a bulwark against forces that were attempting to change the nature of family in opposition to the laws of God. For them, declaring DOMA unconstitutional represented a "profound injustice."[1] In a statement condemning the ruling, Cardinal Timothy Dolan, president of the United States Conference of Catholic Bishops, opined that "our culture has taken for granted for far too long what human nature, experience, common sense and God's wise design all confirm: the difference between a man and a woman matters, and the difference between a mom and a dad matters. The preservation of liberty and justice requires that all laws, federal and state, respect the truth, including the truth about marriage."[2]

For others, DOMA represented an active symbol of the ways that the legal system propagates injustice and unfairness toward gay people in the United States. In the landmark 5–4 decision the Supreme Court agreed with this interpretation by ruling that DOMA violated the Fifth Amendment's guarantee of equal liberty. A majority of the justices unequivocally declared that "the principal purpose and necessary effects of the law are to demean those persons who are in lawful same-sex marriage." In strong language, the decision clarified that, in the opinion of the Court, DOMA "imposes disadvantages," creates a "stigma," enshrines a "separate status," "humiliates," and "burdens" citizens of the United States who enter into these lawful relationships.[3] Ironically, despite the gross unfairness and inequality that the Court said it recognized when same-sex couples are discriminated against at the federal level, it refused to take the opportunity to make such distinctions about marriage unlawful at the state level. The Court deferred the broader issue of the constitutionality of gay marriage for another day, guaranteeing that traditionalists desiring consistency between their values and the law will continue to be in conflict with the civil rights efforts of homosexuals trying to affirm their worth and contest for respect and recognition in the public square.

As we saw in chapter 7, the religious sensibilities of the American people have helped shape and justify discrimination toward women and homosexuals. For many religious people, the norms and laws are morally correct and changes are morally wrong. For more than forty years now, religious traditionalists seeking "righteousness in the culture" have collided with those calling for reform, and in the process they have fused religion, politics, gender, and homosexuality. This conflict has helped redefine partisan politics in the United States.

There are several reasons to examine issues involving homosexuals and women in an effort to better understand the nature of the relationship between religion and politics in American society. First, women and homosexuals are "the other minorities." Gender and sexual orientation are cross-cutting cleavages that affect every race, ethnicity, and religious tradition. However, the struggles of women and gays are unique among minorities in the United States because their subordinate positions in society are still justified by religious faith long after theological arguments for racial discrimination have been repudiated. While we can point to cases in which religion provided the motivation and means to oppose oppression based on gender or sexual orientation, the research in this area clearly shows that greater religiosity is associated with greater moral traditionalism (Sears and Huddy 1990; Himmelstein 1986; Kellstedt et al. 1996; Leege and Kellstedt 1993; Layman 2001). At the nexus of religion, politics, gender, and sexual orientation, we learn how religion in a postmodern secular society still shapes political culture and influences both perceptions of inequality as well as support for and opposition to the rights and policies designed to address it.

The second reason for studying this conflict and these groups is simply that these issues are a "big deal" in American politics today. Examining the politics around issues of gender and sexual orientation gives us insight into the very nature of the "culture war," defined by James Davison Hunter (1991, 41) as "political and social hostility rooted in different systems of moral understanding." Of course, religion is a major basis for moral understandings, and these issues are framed as religious controversies when elites mobilize supporters on the basis of appeals to cultural differences (Leege et al. 2002). The politics surrounding religion, gender, and sexual orientation remind us of the importance of incorporating cultural politics in the study of mass political behavior. Most models attribute political and voting behavior either to partisan-oriented sociodemographic cleavages (Campbell et al. 1960) or to rational social choices based on utilitarian preferences (Downs 1957). Culture—grounded in and communicated through faith traditions—helps us understand how cleavages are politicized as well as the origin of social preferences. Cultural politics is not new, and American political history is replete with moral controversies and cultural debates (Noll 1990). Contemporary politics also can be more fully understood through a cultural connection. By examining the relationship between religion and the politics of women and homosexuals, we see how cultural politics is just the politics of group conflict. Like politics in general, it is about who gets to "authoritatively allocate" what society values. Leege and his colleagues (2002) detail how the passions of cultural politics and the intensity generated by contemporary issues such as gay marriage and abortion are part and parcel of this dynamic:

> People who identify with different social groups often have different, deeply held perspectives not only on how they should live but also on the scope of the political community and its purposes. They have a sense of legitimate moral order, and they expect other citizens and the government to further

that design. They often dislike and distrust groups with rival perspectives and they even feel that some groups have no right to participate in democratic politics, much less to have their rival's perspective become binding on society. Parties become anchored in social groups, and political leaders fashion value and interest coalitions for electoral advantage. (5–6)

Third, looking at the relationship between religion and the politics of women and homosexuals gives insight into the reciprocal nature of the interaction between religion and politics. This book is about the myriad ways that religion influences politics. It is important to recognize that religion and religious interpretations are not static but are affected by the societies in which they operate. As we saw in chapter 7, a significant increase in support for equal rights for women and homosexuals over time—even among religious individuals—demonstrates that religious interpretations are impacted by the context in which they operate. Moreover, religio-political identities are in part forged by societal experiences. These identities provide powerful sources of political motivations that can be marshaled to mobilize individual and institutional resources. African American Christians hold beliefs that are theologically similar to most conservative Protestants. However, their unique experiences in the United States have helped to create a religious and political subculture that is very different from their coreligionists. Similarly for conservative Protestants, the discourse around sex and gender issues has served to construct their contemporary group identity and to distinguish their religious subculture from alternatives. Smith and colleagues (1998) assert that the very vitality of evangelical Protestantism is attributable to the strength of the subcultural identity they have engendered around these matters. Still, thirty years ago it was unthinkable that religious conservatives would be supportive of equal rights for women or gay people. Today, in part because of the cultural politics around these issues, traditionalists are not as traditional as they used to be. They, too, are framing and coming to understand these issues in new and different ways. This chapter focuses first on women and then on homosexuals. We examine how cleavages of sex and gender orientation influence political mobilization and continue to affect the nature of politics and religion in the United States.

WOMEN, RELIGION, AND POLITICS

Religion and Social Reform Movements

Women were influential in politics long before they gained the right to vote in 1920. Indeed, such major movements as the abolition of slavery, temperance, the Progressive Movement, and of course voting rights were heavily influenced and shaped by the political participation of women (Edwards and Gifford 2003; Giele 1995; Battle 1989). Religion played a major role in empowering these women to participate politically. In many ways, both reform movements and the participation of women in them were outgrowths of the religious revivalism of the Second Great Awakening (1820s–1830s). Some credit American feminism itself to ideas associated with religious revivalism (Rossi 1973, 241–81). The Second Great Awakening introduced a radical egalitarianism into Christianity by moderating the message of Calvinism. Salvation was not something bestowed on the elect because of the arbitrary and predestined will of a severe God, but was available to all—rich and poor, men and women, whites and blacks, slave and free—through individual expressions of faith and trust. Christianity was democratized, open and equal to all.

This perspective, powerfully communicated by revival preachers such as Charles Finney, Lyman Beecher, and Francis Asbury, was novel in its evangelical sense that salvation could be obtained through personal choice. People were free moral agents. They were in control of their eternal destinies, and if they controlled their eternal destinies, how much more the material circumstances of their natural lives? Religiously based social optimism as well as postmillennial doctrines of the reign of Christ infused secular reform movements and provided justification for the political involvement of many religious women in these activities. Chicago settlement house worker Mary Eliza McDowell spoke of the necessary blending of Christianity and democracy and saw the state as the principal instrument of morality (Thuesen 2002). Christians in reform movements thought they were merely acting to help usher in the kingdom of God by infusing public policy with a moral outlook.

Participation in presuffrage reform movements contributed to the link between religion and politics among women in several ways. First, it enabled women to recognize their common oppression. In contemporary political science parlance, we might say it helped develop a political identity. Women increasingly recognized themselves as a deprived political group. Through abolitionism, for example, women perceived similarities between their status and those of the slave. As women's rights advocate Elizabeth Cady Stanton reflected, "Humiliations of the spirit are as real and as visible as badges of servitude."[4] Many of the biblical arguments against slavery were seen as equally applicable to women. Female abolitionists such as former slave Sojourner Truth rejected on the basis of religion the inequality of women as vigorously as the inequality of blacks. Her feminism comes through in her response to a comment by a man at a women's rights convention in 1851: "Dat little man in black dar, he say women can't have as much rights as men, 'cause Christ wan't a woman!

Whar did your Christ come from? Whar did your Christ come from? From God and a woman! Man had nothin' to do wid Him."[5]

It is important to recognize that the different needs and realities of white and black women were not well appreciated by early feminists. Still, the similarities in their struggle were clearly apparent. As one observer remarked, "The prejudice against color of which we hear so much, is not stronger than that against sex. It is produced by the same cause and manifested very much in the same way."[6]

Second, religion provided a rationale for sociopolitical activism. The role of activism as hastening the dominion of Christ is very clearly seen in the activities of the Woman's Christian Temperance Union (WCTU). From the beginning, temperance was perceived to be a women's issue because alcohol posed a direct threat to the home and family—institutions that women were expected to protect (Blocker 1989). The perils of what Susan B. Anthony called "the virtuous woman in legal subjection to a drunken husband" were manifest (quoted in Kraditor 1969, 160–61). Temperance became a respectable reason to take a public role. Occupying a saloon for the purpose of prayer was not "political" when understood as a way to fulfill a woman's God-given traditional role. Eventually, for some, the right to vote itself was seen as a way to fulfill this mandate. Many women active in the WCTU and other organizations devoted to improving the lives of women and children "came to see the ballot as a prerequisite for success. They claimed the vote would allow women to reform society, a task that they as women, were particularly well suited to do. . . . [L]eaders of the suffrage movement viewed motherhood and marriage as an important basis for the right to vote" (McGlen et al. 2002, 8). Most sought no overarching change in the status of women.

Of course, there were others who recognized traditional religion and its mandates as impediments to the progress and empowerment of women. These women wanted fundamental social change, not just the right to vote. Stanton, who later in life became a strong critic of traditional Christianity, complained that "woman's religion, instead of making her noble and free, by the wrong application of great principles of right and justice, has made her bondage but more certain and lasting, her degradation more hopeless and complete."[7] She and nearly two dozen collaborators published the *Woman's Bible* in 1895 in response to these concerns. This radical commentary on scripture encouraged a reexamination of the theological and cultural bases of the subordination of women. It began a discussion of the Bible as a man-made expression of patriarchal culture that continues today (Kern 2001; Daly 1973). The commentaries of the *Woman's Bible* emphasized how the holy text supported egalitarianism between the sexes. Because the *Woman's Bible* seemed to undermine the validity of scripture and threatened women's traditional role, it alienated those outside and many inside the women's rights movement. Still, religion provided a reason for the sociopolitical participation of both critics and orthodox Christians in the liberation campaign. For traditionalists, women were fulfilling women's God-given role to protect the family; for radical feminists, the logic came through reconceptualizing scripture.

Third, participation in religiously infused reform movements afforded women opportunities to exercise leadership and develop organizational skills and networks in ways uncommon for the times. For example, women's rights activists such as Sarah and Angelina Grimké, Lucretia Mott, Jane Addams, Lucy Stone, Maria Stewart, Frances Willard, Elizabeth Stanton, and others advocated admirably for an end to slavery in a time when women generally did not even speak in public. Zeal for the impact they were having is conveyed in Angelina Grimké's exclamation that "we abolition women are turning the world upside down" (quoted in Lerner 1967, chap. 1). Still, gender qualified their success. Frustrated, Grimké stated, "Can you not see that women could do a hundred times more for the slave, if she were not fettered?" (quoted in Lerner 1967, chap. 12). However, through conventions, publications, organizations, civic clubs, and friendships that developed around social reform causes, women gained many of the resources and skills to enter the public square and to influence public policies as social reformers in unprecedented ways albeit without the right to vote. They utilized these resources in organizations such as the National American Woman Suffrage Association to champion their own political rights and to demonstrate they had the political capacity to participate effectively.

Women were enfranchised with the passage of the Nineteenth Amendment in 1920. They began to participate in electoral politics but did not pursue a gender-specific agenda because the alliance of interested women's groups that had pushed for suffrage disagreed about what an appropriate postsuffrage goal might be. No clear postsuffrage agenda emerged for nearly forty years until a new women's rights movement began in the 1960s. The momentum and style of women's politics changed in the late 1960s and early 1970s when partisan politics was again animated by gender issues. Interest groups mobilized and responded to the campaign for the equal rights amendment (ERA), Supreme Court rulings such as *Roe v. Wade* (1973), and the extension of affirmative action provisions to women.

Women, Religion, and Women's Rights Issues

In the 1970s, the increasing politicization of women as well as improved educational and economic opportunities for them led to a confrontation between those committed to cultural change and those who believed newer gender roles undermined American society by threatening the traditional family and the institution of marriage. As we explored in chapter 7, feminist calls for equality between the sexes clashed sharply with traditionalist ideas about a God-ordained hierarchy in family life. As Gallagher (2004a, 219–20) describes the idea of "gender complementarity" most closely associated with conservative Protestants, "wives should submit to husbands, children to parents, congregations to church leadership, citizens to the state and all to God." Gender roles for men and women are clearly defined and call for separate spheres. Socialization in such an environment worked against a desire for cultural change (Clark and Clark 1986). Conservative activists were able to frame women's rights issues as threats to the traditional way of life venerated by many women, including fundamentalist and evangelical Protestants, traditionalist Catholics, Mormons, Orthodox Jews, Muslims, and others.

The ERA

In the early 1970s, Congress considered a proposed equal rights amendment (ERA) with simple language:

> Section 1. Equality of rights under the law shall not be denied or abridged by the United States or by any State on account of sex.
>
> Section 2. The Congress shall have the power to enforce, by appropriate legislation, the provisions of this article.

Although the language was simple, it left unclear exactly what kinds of social changes the amendment required. Although proponents emphasized equal access to jobs and equal pay for equal work, opponents capitalized on the vagueness to portray the amendment as mandating unisex toilets, the end of same-sex schools, homosexual adoption, and forcing women into combat (McGlen et al. 2002, 52). Feminists maintained that it was necessary to ensure gender equality, but others saw it as an impediment to the development of legislation and policies needed to protect the health and welfare of women.

After an overwhelmingly favorable Senate vote, the ERA was sent to the states for ratification in 1972. Between March 1972 and January 1973, twenty-two of the thirty-eight states needed to adopt the amendment ratified it, and it appeared inevitable that another sixteen would ratify by the initial deadline in March 1979—more than six years away. The initial success of the ERA was the result of the mobilization of feminist women. Although the amendment was the result of feminist political consciousness, it served to create consciousness among traditionalist women, who mobilized against it. These forces were led by conservative Catholic activist, lawyer, and former Barry Goldwater speechwriter Phyllis Schlafly.

Supporters of the ERA had pursued a national strategy but lacked structure at the state and local levels. Schlafly was able to exploit this weakness through effective grassroots mobilization (Mansbridge 1986; Mathews and De Hart 1990). She and her Eagle Forum, an organization founded to support the ratification fight, built their Stop ERA coalition by activating those concerned about the new lives and values the ERA represented (Wuthnow 1988; Hunter 1991).

One coalition partner, Concerned Women for America (CWA), was established in the late 1970s by Beverly LaHaye. Organized through local prayer circles, CWA and groups like it provided an effective means to oppose the ERA at the state level. CWA was composed of middle- to lower-middle-class evangelical Protestants who very much supported traditional gender roles and conservative Christian values (Guth et al. 1994). These women believed homemaking should be respected and honored but that the ERA diminished their social role. They worked against pro-ERA feminists in a classic counterreform movement to maintain traditional values.

They were successful. The state and local connections of the anti-ERA coalition stopped the progress of the amendment three states short of the thirty-eight needed for ratification. Even with a seven-year extension of the ratification deadline, another three votes could not be obtained. The fifteen states that never ratified the ERA are concentrated in the conservative Protestant South and in western areas with high Mormon populations, environments abounding with traditionalists who likely opposed the ERA on religious grounds.[8] Conservative churches played a key role by providing leaders and activists for the anti-ERA movement at the state and local level—many of whom were women (Conover and Gray 1983; Mansbridge 1986; Mathews and De Hart 1990; Tedin 1977; Mueller and Dimieri 1982).

Abortion

No issue has come to represent the divide between feminists and traditionalists more decisively than abortion. The controversy is emotionally intense because of the symbolic meaning attached to it by both sides. For feminists, greater access to legal abortion is a matter of personal liberty and freedom. The right to make a choice about whether to have a child epitomizes a woman's control over her own body and her own destiny. From this perspective, this most basic and fundamental of choices should certainly be free from undue government restraint. As Justice Ruth Bader Ginsberg said in 1974, long before her appointment to the Supreme Court, "the emphasis must not be on abortion, but the right to privacy and reproductive control."[9] Feminists have seized on the abortion issue as essential to making women equal to men (Mansbridge 1986), and it has become the definitive issue for their movement (Leege et al. 2002, 124).

For traditionalists, however, abortion symbolically represents precisely what is wrong with the values of the feminist movement and the direction in which it would take American society. Liberalized abortion, to these opponents, exalts individualism to an immoral degree by justifying ending the life of a child as a matter of personal choice. Nothing undermines traditional values more than this issue because terminating pregnancy as a legal right negates the most basic gender difference between men and women and in the process redefines ideas about gender, sex, marriage, and the family.

Abortion is also objectionable because of foundational conservative Christian teaching about God as the sole author of life independent of human choices. A fetus—even an embryo, they believe—is God-ordained life. To nullify God's decision is blasphemy, not freedom. Several studies confirm this traditionalist-modernist split based on how religion affects attitudes toward abortion (Evans 2002; Cook, Jelen, and Wilcox 1992; Wilcox and Cook 1989; Emerson 1996). Activists, in particular, tend to hold extreme and uncompromising positions on this issue (Rozell, Wilcox, and Gunn 1996). Chapters 8 and 9 detail the politics that have taken place around this issue for more than thirty years since the historic Supreme Court ruling in *Roe v. Wade* (1973) relaxed abortion restrictions. Immediately, the National Conference of Catholic Bishops as well as the newly independent (but church-sponsored) National Right to Life Committee condemned the decision as "an unspeakable tragedy for the nation" (quoted in Nolan 1984, vol. 2, 366). Others, like Schlafly, herself a Catholic, began to link abortion rights to the ERA, using the decision to illustrate the potential perils of life under a ratified ERA (McGlen et al. 2002, 271).

Since that time, many battles have been fought over abortion rights in the courts, Congress, and state legislatures. Although the constitutional right to an abortion remains the law of the land, the state may regulate abortion as long as such regulations do not constitute an "undue burden."[10] Precisely what that phrase means is the subject of continuing controversy and has generated vigorous and successful countermobilization by those on the Religious Right. In the first half of 2013 alone, twenty-two states adopted restrictions on abortion rights.[11] While implementation of some of the more strident restrictions such as North Dakota's ban on abortion after a fetal heart beat has been detected (about the sixth week of pregnancy) have been blocked by the courts, momentum seems to be growing for some policies including bans on abortions at or after twenty weeks. Such laws have been enacted in ten states, and a bill with this provision passed the U.S. House of Representatives in June 2013. Several other states have returned to the familiar territory of imposing regulations on abortion providers. Targeted regulations of abortion provider (TRAP) laws ostensibly increase the safety of abortion procedures by requiring abortion providers and/or abortion facilities to meet additional medical standards. Critics contend these standards are well beyond what is necessary for safety and the laws are a poorly veiled attempt to limit abortion access. For example, in Texas only five of the forty-two existing abortion clinics in the state met the requirements passed by the state legislature in July 2013.[12]

Questions about the legality of these matters will likely find their ultimate resolution before the Supreme Court. While in many states conservative interests are gaining traction, liberals celebrated recently when a federal court judge ordered the Food and Drug Administration to lift all age restrictions on the over-the-counter sale of the "Morning After Pill" and to make it available to women of any age without a prescription. Though *Roe vs. Wade* was decided forty years ago, the abortion debate and the underlying conflict over values that it exemplifies continues to provide its combatants opportunities to reaffirm the important principles of the feminist or traditionalist position.

Electoral Politics

Because of the cultural salience of women's rights in general and the abortion issue in particular, political parties have attempted to use them for partisan advantage. The Republicans have positioned themselves as the party of traditional values and the Democrats as the party of civil rights. Much of the research on religion and voting behavior reports that the religiously observant who attend worship services regularly support Republicans, while those who are less observant, non-Christian, or not a part of a faith tradition support the Democrats (Hunter 1991; Jelen 1997b; Kellstedt et al. 1996; Kohut et al. 2000; Layman 1997, 2001; Miller and Shanks 1996). Even in the 2012 presidential election, when economic issues were more salient than moral-cultural ones, the religiously observant were more likely to vote for the Republican candidate than those who were less devout.[13] This so-called religion gap was first seen in the 1972 presidential election and has continued over time. Some scholars consider these value differences the source of partisan change in American politics (Carmines and Layman 1997; Edsall 1997; Hunter 1991; Kohut et al. 2000).

However, the attitudes and behavior of women in electoral politics present a paradox for this interpretation (Kaufman 2004). Most studies look at either women and electoral politics or religion and electoral politics. Few examine the intersection of religion, politics, and gender, though it is only in their interaction that the partisan paradox is revealed. In 1980, not long after the contemporary women's movement began, polls registered persistent differences in the voting behavior of men and women, the famous "gender gap." Since that time, women have voted more Democratic and have been more likely to affiliate with the Democratic Party than men (Conover 1988; Kaufmann and Petrocik 1999; Norrander 1999). While much of the religion and politics research and many political pundits insist that religious people are likely to embrace Republicans, women—who are in fact more religious than men on every indicator of devotion and orthodoxy—are considerably more likely to identify with the Democratic Party and Democratic candidates.

Karen Kaufmann (2004) examines three potential explanations for the paradox. According to the first, the influence of religion is only considerable among the most committed. Perhaps religion trumps gender among the faithful. However, she finds that the gender gap does not diminish at higher levels of religious devotion but is greater among the devout and nominally religious than among the secular. If religiosity does not mediate gender effects, perhaps men and women politicize their religious beliefs in different ways. Kaufmann finds little evidence for this plausible hypothesis. The highly committed of both sexes are more politically conservative in their attitudes and orientations than the less religious or the secular. She finds strong support for a third explanation, that gender differences in opinion on nonreligious issues sustain the partisan gap over and above the conservative influence of religiosity. As she summarizes, "the gender gap persists in spite of greater female religiosity, not because of it" (492). If women were less religious, the gap between the sexes would be even wider. Women would be even less likely to identify with the Republican Party. According to Kaufmann's (2002, 2004) research, men are more conservative on social welfare issues than women, and it is social welfare issues—not family values or even race or defense issues—that primarily determine partisan choice, especially for men. Their growing Republicanism may reflect an attempt to protect their status in society by ensuring the government plays a more modest role in society, including the protection of "minority rights." Thomas Edsall put it plainly:

> The past 30 years have produced a revolution in the workplace, at home and in bed. These trends have turned men, particularly white men, into powerful agents of conservatism, mainstays of the rightward movement in American politics. For many—but by no means all—men, the past three decades have been years of lost sexual and gender identity, and lost centrality in the culture. The major rights movements on behalf of women, minorities and gays have often identified a common adversary, the heterosexual white man. (quoted in Kaufmann 2002, 288)

Conversely, the growing Democratic partisanship among women may be a reflection of the appeal and empowerment of cultural change. For women, religious commitment affects partisan choice but does not override the powerful effects of gender.

There are several reasons why gender continues to exert such a powerful influence on political orientations even though religiosity is associated with conservatism on most moral and cultural issues. It is important to remember that dichotomizing gender issues and gender's impact into traditionalist and feminist perspectives does not capture the complicated way that ordinary people negotiate gender roles. While religious elites pay attention to minor distinctions and subtle ideological clues, issues are often much more ambiguous and complicated for the average parishioner (C. Smith 2000).

Still, today the majority of conservative Protestants formally espouse a hierarchically ordered view of family life with the husband as the head of both the wife and the house (Bartkowski 2001, 2004; Gallagher 2003). Several studies suggest that conflict over gender is the defining characteristic of the evangelical subculture and that the very boundaries of evangelicalism are defined by positions on these types of issues (Gallagher 2003, 2004a, 2004b; Brasher 1998). The consistent and resolute opposition to feminist ideas has been explained as a way for them to resist the cultural changes taking place in the larger society (Ammerman 1987; Wilcox 1987; Bendroth 1993), as well as a means to help adherents negotiate the cross-pressures around career and family unleashed by cultural change (Griffith 1997; Pevey, Williams, and Ellison 1996).

However, religious women are not immune to the same social trends that affect the rest of society. Although conservative religious discourse still reflects very traditional gender roles, domestic practice is far more equivocal—even for conservative evangelical Christian women. Gallagher (2004a, 228) describes the approach of everyday evangelicals on questions of gender roles as "pragmatic." While they are significantly more likely to believe the husband should be the head of the household, the vast majority also believe that marriage should be a partnership of equals. Although they are critical of the "excessive individualism" of feminism, they are also cautiously appreciative of the greater opportunities it has secured for women in employment, education, and church leadership. Affected by the societal changes of the past forty years, more than half of evangelical women work outside the home. Far from being doctrinaire in these matters, only a small minority (10 percent) identify themselves as strongly antifeminist (Gallagher 2004b).

Ordinary evangelicals are much more egalitarian in their approach to domestic life than elite rhetoric suggests (Bartkowski 2001, 2004; W. Wilcox 1998, 2002). The idea of a hierarchy with gender-defined roles in the family has been transformed over time through practical application. "Headship" is increasingly framed as "servant leadership," which encompasses nurturing and sensitivity to wives and children and not authoritarian patriarchy (Gallagher 2004a; Bartkowski 2004). This same disconnect between the discourse of elites and the everyday application of gender realities is also seen among Catholics (Dillon 1999). The division between the all-male Catholic leadership and women over their status in the church is a source of continuing controversy (Tentler 2004; Winter, Lummis, and Stokes 1994; Browne and Lukes 1988; Greeley and Durkin 1984). While the Vatican has maintained unyielding opposition to abortion, birth control, and female ordination, many American Catholics have grown apart from the church hierarchy on these issues (D'Antonio 1994; Greeley 1990; Hoge et al. 2001; Dillon 1999). The level of divergence around these issues is dramatic. As D'Antonio (1994, 384) reflects, "The laity are developing an image of a good Catholic very much at variance with the traditional model set forth by the magisterium in Rome."

Similar patterns are found among other conservative religious groups as well. The forces of modernity relative to gender issues may overwhelm religious pronouncements. The understanding that conservative religiosity necessarily translates into conservative political positions is hopelessly simplistic. Women may embrace patriarchal religion but at the same time find ways to empower themselves within traditional religious communities. Studying how Jewish feminists reconcile the patriarchal nature of Judaism with their feminist identity, Dufour (2000) observes that these women take what is useful to them from the religious tradition and "sift out" the offensive aspects. Religious feminists criticize the damage done to women's identity by a masculine image of God and a paternal image of leadership (Daly 1973; Gross 1979; Plaskow 1990; Fiorenza 1984; Ruether 1985). On this basis, some have rejected Christianity and Judaism altogether for religious traditions such as goddess worship, nature religion, or other pagan practices, including Wicca (Christ 1987; Biehl 1991; Heine 1988; Diamond and Orenstein 1990). Still, most women in the United States remain attached to the Judeo-Christian tradition and continue to embrace this religious identification—although they may be uncomfortable with some aspects of their faith and may even struggle to move the tradition toward more egalitarian gender interpretations (Winter, Lummis, and Stokes 1994; Carr 1996; Brasher 1998; Ecklund 2003).

Religiosity does not override the effects of gender among religious women for another reason: the association between religiosity and the subjugation of a woman's identity is not entirely accurate—even in conservative denominations (Griffith 1997). Debra Kaufman's (1991) study of newly Orthodox Jewish women reveals that these women choose orthodoxy as a way to affirm themselves. "Like feminists, these newly orthodox women are women-identified, celebrating the female and her life-cycle experiences; however they eschew feminist politics by choosing to enhance the status of women and protect them as a group within the boundaries of patriarchal religion" (3). According to her research, these women did not find the personal satisfaction and stability that feminism represents through work and career. They turn to Orthodox Judaism as a way to maximize their lives as women. Rather than examining how conservative religiosity frames women, studies like Kaufman's look at how women frame and understand their own religious choices.

Brenda Brasher's (1998) research on the social networks of women within fundamentalist congregations demonstrates that the stark gender divisions in many conservative denominations provide opportunities for women to exercise considerable personal and institutional power. Because men and women are perceived to be distinct from each other, female-only meetings are common in such contexts. Although women in some conservative traditions are not permitted to become members of the clergy, it is common for them to minister to other women. In the fundamentalist congregations Brasher studied, despite the fact men and women have different societal roles, there is no spiritual difference in the relationship they are permitted with Christ. Thus, women can minister to other women (and even sometimes informally to men) in such a compelling manner that they command the respect of both other women and men. In the black church experience, the "Mother's Board," a group of "seasoned" women without formal authority, could often "check" anyone in the church from the pastor and the ministers to the newest member of the congregation. For these women, church represented a means to empowerment, not gender degradation.

Third, gender mediates the effects of religiosity because religion itself is not invariably a conservative force. Especially for women, it can be a powerful force for change in politics and society. The battles over female ordination in many denominations have paralleled the struggle for public gender equity. Symbolically, the meaning of female ordination varies from denomination to denomination. For some, it has no broader meaning at all and is just about trying to fulfill an individual "call" from God. However, for many, it is an expression of gender equality and represents a manifestation of the women's movement in religion—motivated and sustained by their faith (Cott 1987). Interestingly, while conservative theology is related to gender traditionalism in women, it is strength of denominational affiliation that is associated with gender traditionalism in men (Bartkowski and Hempel 2009). The struggle for female ordination in these denominations represents a serious challenge to structural inequality.

The political differences between male and female ministers are striking. Several studies have found that female clergy are more liberal than men on nearly every political issue (Deckman et al. 2003; Olson, Crawford, and Guth 2000; Guth et al. 1997; Carroll, Hargrove, and Lummis 1983; Zikmund, Lummis, and Chang 1998). Unlike laywomen, however, they are also more likely than clergymen to participate in political activities (Deckman et al. 2003). The political issues that matter most to clergywomen focus on social justice causes "to help [the] disadvantaged, marginalized and forgotten members of their communities" (Olson, Crawford, and Deckman 2005, 137).

In an informative study, Chaves (1997) examines why denominations decide to allow the ordination of women when they do. Interestingly he found that formal denominational rules about ordination are only "loosely coupled" and often at odds with internal, pragmatic organizational activity. As an example, the Catholic Church forbids female priests, yet a lack of male clergy has led to hundreds of priestless parishes effectively pastored by women (Wallace 1992). Whether or not women are doing the work of ministry and whether there is a "need" for them to do it are largely irrelevant to whether a denomination will make a decision to ordain them. Chaves (1997) reports that one of the factors that matters to whether a denomination permitted the ordination of women early was the presence within the denomination of an autonomous women's mission society. In the 1800s, many denominations formed women's mission societies, but some lacked real authority as they were organized as auxiliaries to denominational agencies while others were wholly independent and only denominationally affiliated. In the autonomous organizations women were "more likely to develop a consciousness about gender inequality" as well as to have "enhanced power within the denomination" to facilitate their advocacy for women's ordination (143). The secular women's movement provided alternative interpretative frames for understanding women's ordination, and organizational autonomy offered both the means and opportunity to engage in denominational agitation for equality.

This suggests a fourth reason why religious adherence does not always produce traditional values politics in women. Religious organizing can be politically empowering even when not explicitly focused on politics. The ideal of social justice and the opportunity to work for social change are important to many women of faith. Politics is often narrowly defined as electoral activity or participation in a recognized "social movement." However, increasingly scholars are acknowledging that women "participate politically in ways that are rarely recognized or documented as political behavior or social protest—for example, by engaging in action through churches, clubs and other organizations" (West and Blumberg 1990, 9). Faver's (2000) analysis of female Episcopal lay volunteers details how spiritual practices bond coworkers to one another and infuse their activities with a transcendent meaning that helps them relate to God and further ties them together. This "relatedness" itself empowers women in their participation and helps sustain their commitment to caring. This is as true for conservative women's groups like Concerned Women for America as it is for liberal women's organizations.

This point also highlights that there are many different ways that political socialization occurs in churches. Far more than just formal doctrinal positions and messages from the pulpit influences the political socialization of women in a congregation. Indeed, there is a rich and growing literature that documents that participating in religious institutions is a source of political empowerment especially for women (Verba, Schlozman, and Brady 1995; Schlozman, Burns, and Verba 1994; Djupe, Sokhey, and Gilbert 2007). Both the relationships they develop there and the "church work" they do is a significant source of civic skills, partially compensating for the socioeconomic resource deficits that women have relative to men. Women can be significantly affected by relationships with others in the church and the nature of the "church work" they are doing. These, too, are connected to spiritual practice. Research on black churches (Calhoun-Brown 1999) suggests that hearing equality and empowerment messages is associated with liberal racial as well as gender positions despite the patriarchal structure and conservative doctrine of most black churches (Harris 1999, 165–68; Brown-Douglass 1993; Grant 1989; Cannon 1988; Williams 1993). The experience of other women's groups also confirms that church work can lead to political empowerment. Griffith (2002) relates the story of faith-based women's associations that encounter "persistent obstacles to public activism." Yet even without ideal resources they have achieved impressive victories. It is ironic that women are empowered through highly gendered and often patriarchal religious institutions (Calhoun-Brown 2010). Despite the expectation that religion is a conservative force for women, it produces political results that defy a simplistic understanding.

HOMOSEXUALS

The other major group of people for whom religion and politics interact to confound the struggle for political and civil rights is gay men and lesbians. Like every struggle for minority inclusion, the politics surrounding this issue are intense. Few issues produce more passion. Civility breaks down when opponents see public policies protecting "perverts" and supporters see citizens as "bigots" denying gays and lesbians fundamental freedoms and basic rights. It is hard to reconcile the convictions of those who think gay rights are not in the best interest of society with the belief of activists in the homophile movement that the state denies who they are by criminalizing same-sex intimacy and routinely discriminating against lesbian, gay, bisexual, and transgendered people. Even with the decriminalization of sodomy as a result of the 2003 Supreme Court case of *Lawrence v. Texas*, and the end to federal discrimination against legally married gay couples as the result of the recent ruling in *US v. Windsor*, homosexuals still fail to enjoy equal protection of the laws in many states in the country. Routinely, they are not allowed to marry; are denied partner health, tax, and insurance benefits; face increased scrutiny or outright bans on adoption; have ambiguous parental rights as both nonbiological and biological parents; and contend with many other forms of differential treatment based on their sexual orientation. The Supreme Court has not ruled on whether it is lawful to discriminate on the basis of sexual orientation.

Thus, the debate about homosexual rights is about much more than just the politicization of sex. It reveals individual and societal beliefs about fundamental components of democratic governance, including freedom, equality, the appropriate role of government, majority rule, and minority rights. Stated another way, the politics around homosexuality reflects a discussion about the nature of the social order. It reveals basic beliefs about the institutions of government and core assumptions about societal institutions such as marriage and the family. Questions about who can marry, what constitutes a family, who should bear children, how they should be conceived, who should adopt children, who should raise them, and how these decisions should be made define conflict over homosexuality in political life.

Importantly, the struggle for gay rights also demonstrates the reciprocal nature of religion and politics. Just as we have seen that society makes accommodation for religion, religion makes accommodation for changes in society. As we explored in chapter 7, the big story is not how effectively religion continues to oppose homosexuality, but a growing tolerance, even among religious people, for homosexual rights and inclusion.

To be sure, there remains significant opposition to gay rights, and this opposition is primarily rooted in moral and social traditionalism (Campbell and Robinson 2007; Olson, Cadge, and Harrison 2006; Button, Rienzo, and Wald 1997). Religion is a major source of this traditionalism. Although American denominations hold a great variety of positions on homosexuality, most religious traditions formally assert that homosexuality is morally wrong, even when they support the civil and political rights of homosexual persons. These views are usually based on traditional interpretations of biblical passages (such as the story of Sodom and Gomorrah) that appear to condemn homosexuality as a "very grievous" sin.[14] Particularly strident on this issue are conservative communions who support a more literal reading of the holy scriptures. For most Protestant fundamentalists, Pentecostals, charismatics, Latter-Day Saints, Orthodox

Jews, and Muslims, homosexuality is what the Catholic Church has called "disordered," undermining the structure and function that God intended for males, females, marriage, children, families, and society.[15]

Religious opposition to homosexual rights may also be grounded in civil religion and in the sense that there is a public morality that must be maintained. Examining why conservative Protestants are less tolerant toward homosexuals, Burdette, Ellison, and Hill (2005) explain that many conservative Protestants believe that embracing homosexuality violates America's covenant with God. As we saw in the discussion of civil religion in chapter 4, there is a strong tradition going back to the Puritans that believes the United States will enjoy God's blessing only if it remains faithful to its Christian heritage (Bellah 1975; Wuthnow 1988). From this perspective, what one does in the privacy of one's own home has a direct bearing on the well-being of the entire country. Still, despite religious traditionalism, it is a mistake to conclude that organized religion is uniformly anti-gay (Wald and Glover 2007). It is not. In fact, as Green (2000, 123) notes, "some of the strongest advocates for the gay community are found among theological liberals." For them, homosexuality is simply another way to express the love that God has entrusted to human beings. In these churches, gays and lesbians are welcome members of the congregation, and their love and lives are celebrated as enthusiastically as those of any church congregant. Even among more moderate communities the tone in this area seems to be changing. As Pope Francis recently said, "If someone is gay and he searches for the Lord, who am I to judge?"[16] In the following discussion, we review the variation that exists in the religious community relative to the issue of homosexuality. It is important to understand this diversity because it helps us better comprehend how religion affects politics. If the politics of the culture war is really about the politics of groups, then it becomes necessary to understand how religious groups use issues such as homosexuality to define and identify themselves in a way that provides the motive, means, and opportunity for their political actions. It will also help to understand how the moderating positions of many religious groups on these issues is creating a more favorable opportunity structure for the those seeking to advance gay civil and political rights in the United States.

RELIGION AND HOMOSEXUALITY

There are three broad classifications of religious perspectives on homosexuality. These classifications are offered based on stated denominational positions and behavior at the elite level. While certainly subcultural differences emerge among religious traditions, it is worth remembering that the practice of individual churches may diverge sharply from the stated position of the denomination (Hartman 1996), and at the individual level, there can be considerable heterogeneity and variance in the opinions and attitudes of church members on issues such as these (Gay 1996; Finlay and Walther 2003). Nonetheless, cultural differences at the institutional level have a significant impact on how people frame and understand the issue of homosexuality. As we will see, the strength of a particular subculture in a city or state and the balance between traditionalists and liberal religious groups are major factors in the nature of political opportunities for these issues and help to determine the kinds of public policies that are adopted toward homosexuals (Wald, Button, and Rienzo 1996; Button, Rienzo, and Wald 1997; Haider-Markel and Meier 1996, 2003; Fleischmann and Moyer 2009).

Religious Liberals

Liberal churches embrace homosexuals and have public positions welcoming gays and lesbians to worship in their congregations. Such churches engage in little discussion of equal rights for gays and lesbians, the blessing or marriage of same-sex couples, the propriety of same-sex families, or the ordination of gay clergy members who are involved in homosexual relationships. In these denominations, the homosexual issue has largely been settled in favor of equality for all.

Liberal churches include the United Church of Christ, Unitarian Universalists, and the Society of Friends.[17] Non-Orthodox Jews, especially those in the Reform and Reconstructionist movements, have also adopted liberal positions on this issue. These churches propose to create a welcoming environment for all in which the nature of one's sexuality is not an issue. In December 2004, the United Church of Christ prepared a television commercial that touted its inclusiveness. The advertisement showed two bouncers at the doors of a church rejecting people who wanted to enter on the basis of their race or sexual orientation. The announcer explained, "Jesus didn't turn people away. Neither do we. No matter who you are, or where you are on life's journey, you are welcome here."[18] Interestingly, at that time, several networks, including NBC and CBS, refused to air the ad, citing the controversial nature of its content.

Liberal churches maintain a very different attitude toward homosexual rights than that most commonly associated with organized religion. Button and colleagues (1997, chap. 3) explain how these denominations confront passages in the scriptures that seem to suggest that God's judgment and wrath are directed at homosexuality. They identify three strategies employed by liberal churches. First, some churches (most notably the Unitarians) simply reject the sole authority of the Bible and identify other sources of moral norms. Other churches reinterpret the passages most commonly associated with antihomosexuality as prohibiting only certain nonconsensual homosexual acts or those that were incorporated in pagan worship practices. Yet others suggest that the scriptures are time and culture bound. Just as we no longer stone disobedient children, our contemporary context calls for different responses to present-day realities such as loving, same-sex relationships.

The liberal positions that many churches adopt on the issue of homosexuality are a way for them to define their subcultural identity and to effectively compete in the religious marketplace at a time when liberal churches have been consistently declining in membership. The positions that they espouse provide moral legitimacy for those in the homophile movement seeking to provide a religious basis of support for their call for civil and political rights. Indeed, the Universal Fellowship of Metropolitan Community Churches is a Christian denomination that has traditionally been made up of gay individuals and their families and supporters. The church utilizes Christian cultural themes to communicate a message of self-acceptance and self-worth (Lukenbill 1998; M. Wilcox 2003). Although many homosexuals embrace religious individualism because they have been alienated from Christian communities (M. Wilcox 2002), liberal Protestant denominations are increasingly supportive of same-sex relationships.

Religious Moderates

Most mainline Protestants, Catholics, and conservative Jews are engaged in a vigorous debate about homosexuality and what it means for religious life. This makes them "moderates" among religious traditions. Reflecting on the mainline debate, Cadge (2002, 265) explains that the issue of homosexuality "is a prism through which all the denominations' central questions and issues can be seen to reflect and refract." The issue of homosexuality causes people to evaluate what they believe about scripture, about creation, about families and reproduction, and about the church—both who can serve in it and how much discretion it should be able to exercise in making that determination. The now-more-than-thirty-year debate in mainline and Catholic churches centers on how to balance the interest of the church in ministering to the needs of every individual with doctrines and policies that emphasize the sinfulness of homosexuality and restrict the full participation of gays in church life. Mainline churches are particularly interesting because they seek to find accommodation between contemporary realities and the traditional dictates of scripture. Whereas most liberal denominations support inclusion and most conservative ones hold a more exclusive position, religious moderates—like most in American society—are trying to chart a course that maintains the integrity of their beliefs while respecting the dignity of every person. Despite this moderate approach, the divisions between liberal and conservative theological responses to the question of homosexuality in general and homosexual ordination in particular have strained several mainline traditions nearly to the point of schism. Several large mainline denominations, including the United Methodist Church (UMC), the Presbyterian Church USA (PCUSA), and the Evangelical Lutheran Church in America (ELCA), have discussed splits over this issue.

For the time being, however, mainline churches continue to seek a way to reconcile the divergent perspectives of liberals and conservatives within their denominations. In general, they have tried to welcome homosexuals and support their civil rights without officially altering doctrinal positions. For example, at the UMC's General Conference in 2012, Methodists voted down a resolution to amend their *Book of Discipline*, which characterizes homosexuality as "incompatible with Christian teaching" and outlaws gay ordination, although at the same time it declares the "sacred worth" of homosexual individuals.[19] Conservative Jews, members of the largest denomination within Judaism, have also adopted a moderate position on the issue of homosexuality. In these matters, Conservative Judaism considers Jewish law (which has historically condemned homosexuality), but at the same time believes that the details of the law can continue to evolve in context. In 2006, their governing body allowed for the ordination of gay and lesbian rabbis, and in 2012, it approved a ceremony to allow same-sex couples to marry. In each case, the ruling acknowledged that "same-sex relationships are comprehensively banned by classical rabbinic law." However the Conservative Jewish Movement elected to allow gay ordination and marriage because "human dignity requires the suspension of rabbinic-level prohibitions." While these practices are now permitted, they are not uniformly endorsed. Indeed, because of continuing theological discord on this issue, each rabbi and synagogue is allowed to decide whether to perform gay marriages and either decision can be justified according to Jewish law. The Roman Catholic Church has also attempted to adopt a midrange position on homosexuality. Theologically, its approach is to differentiate between a homosexual orientation that is not sinful and engaging in homosexual behavior that is. As Button and his colleagues (1997, 182) observe, "This distinction permits the church to take a more nuanced position toward homosexuality." Like heterosexuals, gay priests can be ordained as long as they are celibate. However, by interpreting the child abuse scandal as a problem of homosexuality, the Vatican has put pressure on the American hierarchy to weed out seminarians who show strong homosexual tendencies. For Catholics, marriage remains reserved for the relationship between a man and a woman. Still, despite the theological ambiguity, the Catholic Church, like many of the mainline denominations, enthusiastically offers ministry to homosexuals, and in some urban areas, the concentration of gays in a congregation may be so significant that it can be identified as a gay church. Since his election in 2013, Pope Francis has attempted de-emphasize these issues. Perhaps reflecting fatigue over constant questions about moral-cultural concerns, in a recent interview the pope explained that the church's pastoral ministry cannot be "obsessed" with matters like this and that it must seek to "find a new balance; otherwise even the moral edifice of the church is likely to fall like a house of cards." Over the past decade, though still short of embracing full equality, the trend among moderate churches has been a significant liberalizing of attitudes toward homosexuality in response to tremendous mobilization at the grassroots level. Gay support groups have increasingly moved from providing mutual reinforcement to lobbying national denominations to alter their policies. In 2009, the Evangelical Lutheran Church in America voted to permit gays and lesbians in "life-long monogamous relationships" to become members of its clergy, and in 2013 elected its first openly gay bishop. Previously only celibate gays could occupy such offices.[20] The Presbyterian Church has also voted to allow gay ordination. Similarly, in 2009, delegates to the General Convention of the Episcopal Church also voted to open "any ordained ministry" to gay men and lesbians, and in 2012 they developed a liturgy to solemnize and bless same-sex unions—though the church is clear, the ceremony is not the same as marriage.

However, unlike liberal churches that have a long tradition of inclusion, the decisions of these denominations were far from routine or uncontroversial. Personal attitudes, even congregational positions, can be distinct from the formal doctrines and statutes adopted by denominational institutions (Thumma and Gray 2005). For example, when an openly gay Gene Robinson was confirmed as bishop of New Hampshire in 2003, four other Episcopal bishops—with their dioceses—left the church. The potential for schism is great. The Anglican Church in America, founded in 2009, now claims more than one thousand congregations and provides an alternative for Episcopalians who wish to break with the Episcopal Church over this and other issues. Despite the controversy, the Episcopal Church seems determined to open access and selected its first openly lesbian bishop in 2010. For its part, the worldwide Anglican community continues to attempt the kind of balancing that takes place in moderate denominations. Recently, for example, the archbishop of Canterbury, Justin Welby, gave a speech in which he asked that "stable and faithful same-sex relationships" be "recognized and supported" but simultaneously called on Parliament to reject a bill to allow same-sex marriage for these individuals.[21] The variation in moderate faith traditions is also reflected in the many individual congregations that identify themselves as formally welcoming gay and lesbian people. In different denominations—variously called welcoming, reconciling, or "More Light"—they reject the discriminatory doctrines and duplicity of moderate denominations. From their perspective, if homosexuality is incompatible with Christianity, then homosexuals can never be fully a part of these churches. There are at least eight hundred such congregations in forty-five states and efforts to make the movement ecumenical in nature (Cadge 2002, 274). These networks (and those found in liberal churches) provide a means for homosexuals to organize not only to change denominational policies but also to support secular efforts to gain civic and social rights.

Religious Conservatives

The conservative position is most commonly associated with organized religion. Orthodox Jews, Muslims, Mormons, and conservative Protestants (including fundamentalists, evangelicals, and charismatics) subscribe to the view that homosexual behavior is prohibited. Their strict and literal interpretation of the scriptures leaves little room for compromise on this issue. In each religious tradition, homosexuality is understood as contrary to "natural law" and the order that God has set in the universe. Marriage is between a man and a woman. Children have parents from each of the sexes. Wives are primary nurturers; husbands are primary providers. There are no options to renegotiate that which has been divinely established. Orthodox Jews read the Torah, Muslims read the Qu'ran, and conservative Christians read the Bible as explicitly and specifically forbidding homosexual acts. They understand their religious doctrines as unambiguously in conflict with homosexuality.

The antipathy of many conservative Christians toward homosexuality may be rooted in the tremendous societal upheavals that have occurred in the United States since the 1960s. Conservative Christians are concerned that changes associated with minority rights, especially those for women and homosexuals, are destroying the moral fabric of American society. Most conservative religious traditions insist that homosexuality is not an immutable characteristic but a choice. The official position of the Southern Baptist Convention is that "homosexuality is not a valid alternative lifestyle." The very term *lifestyle* suggests a deliberate choice or sexual "preference" rather than an innate human quality. Many conservative denominations, as well as Catholics and mainline Protestants, have established ministries to get gays to "convert" to heterosexuality. In some faith traditions, converting to heterosexuality may even require divine deliverance. Pentecostal and charismatic denominations commonly attribute homosexuality to an indwelling demonic spirit that can only be cast out by exorcism. While official positions remain strident, at a practical level, the possibility and propriety of trying to "convert" homosexuals is increasingly open for debate. Even some conservative Christians are questioning whether being homosexual is something people control. In June 2013, Exodus International, an organization that had offered "freedom from homosexuality through the power of Jesus Christ," closed its doors and apologized to the gay community "for years of undue judgment," explaining that they had been "imprisoned by a worldview that's neither honoring toward our fellow human beings, nor biblical."[22] Recently, Albert Mohler, president of the Southern Baptist Theological Seminary, admitted that his denomination "needs to repent from homophobia" and for "using choice language when it is clear that sexual orientation is a deep inner struggle not merely a matter of choice."[23] Though Mohler went on to maintain that homosexuality is a sin, the suggestion that people do not choose to be homosexual is significant. Traditionally, the Christian Right and the gay movement have been "perfect enemies" because each uses the other as a foil to propel its movement forward by defining and strengthening group identity (Gallagher and Bull 2001). However, as we saw in chapter 7, younger religious conservatives increasingly do not include opposition to homosexuality as part of what defines them as a group. The tremendous change in public opinion among religious people on this issue demonstrates that people in the pews do not always simply accept the stated position of the religious tradition. The differences between official church doctrines and how people interpret and apply them can be striking. Roof (1999) suggests that for the typical person, religion is more than the scripts and practices provided by the faith tradition and is the result of how human beings interact with them, the popular religion we discussed in chapter 1. Increasingly, religion is regarded as a resource, not a rule book (M. Wilcox 2002), and people choose among religious teachings what is and is not helpful to them. Just as conservative religiosity does not translate neatly into conservative political positions on gender issues, at a practical level, conservative religion does not always mean opposition to homosexual rights. In studying homosexuality and everyday theologies Dawne Moon observes that a church member "does not simply absorb what is taught as church doctrines, but engages with those teaching in terms of her or his own social experiences" (2004, 91).

Just as women "sift out" elements of religious gender identity that do not reinforce and empower them, people in conservative religious traditions can adapt and even reorder the negative overt messages that they receive from religious authorities. Conservative biblical ideas such as the value of a human soul, being created in the image of God, and the ability of a person to commune directly with God and to have a personal relationship with the divine can have unanticipated results. These ideas have contributed to adaptations at the individual level that allow gay men, lesbians and their supporters to use religion as a resource to challenge official church positions that undermine the equality and worth of homosexuals in their congregations and society.

Research on the intersection of sexuality and religion reminds us that neither personal nor political identity is imposed from without. The terms and conditions of one's identity are not set by religious institutions. Several recent studies productively examine how individuals adapt when sexual identity and religious identity are seen by society as incompatible (M. Wilcox 2003; Moon 2004; Thumma and Gray 2005; Schnoor 2006; McQueeney 2009). Although many religious institutions continue to be hostile to lesbian and gay people, individuals use their own understanding of religion to find self-acceptance and strength (Mahaffy 1996; Thumma 1991).

Religion, Homosexuality, and Politics

For the past three decades, the politics around gay rights has been at the epicenter of the American culture war. Republicans and Democrats alike have tried to use this issue for their political advantage. Republicans have used it as a plank in their family values platform; Democrats to demonstrate their commitment to equality for all. Taking a hard line, in 2012 the Republican Party reaffirmed its "support for a constitutional amendment defining marriage as the union of one man and one woman" and applauded the states that had "enshrined in their constitutions, the traditional concept of marriage."[24] For a time, these kinds of state initiatives seemed to be an effective way to both hinder the advancement of policies sympathetic to gays and lesbians and elect Republican candidates opposed to gay rights. For example, in 2004, many attributed President Bush's reelection to the mobilization of conservative voters who voted for Bush and helped to pass laws banning same-sex marriage in each of the thirteen states where the measures were on the ballot (Campbell and Monson 2008). However, the strategy failed Republicans in 2008 and completely collapsed in 2012. In 2008, despite the passage of ballot initiatives to ban gay marriage in electorally important states like Florida and California, the Democratic candidate Barack Obama won a majority of votes in both states. In the 2012 election, not only did Obama win, but for the first time, anti-gay ballot measures were rejected by voters at the polls in the four states where the issue was on the ballot.

Indeed, after the 2012 elections, politically the landscape around gay rights was forever changed. Republicans, who had reliably mobilized voters through clarion pro-family-values calls, were left in a state of disarray. On this and other issues, they had misjudged the country. The "autopsy" the party undertook to diagnose how it could have been so wrong about the election indicted the party for "marginalizing itself" and asserted that it must "be inclusive and welcoming" to attract young, minority, and female voters to its rolls. By 2013, members of the GOP were trying to figure out how they could appear more tolerant on LGBT issues while not alienating religious conservatives who still comprise the Republican Party base and are active in its primaries. For their part, Democrats, who at times had been rather tentative advocates of pro-gay policies, were also moving quickly to liberalize their positions. President Obama, who had previously characterized himself as "struggling" with the civil rights of gay Americans, by 2012 was announcing his support for same-sex marriage, and the Democratic Party's platform called for equal treatment under the law for gays and lesbians.[25]

It is really difficult to describe the magnitude and rapidity of the political and cultural shift that took place in the first decade of this century on the issue of gay rights. The Pew Research Center reports that the share of Americans who say that homosexuality should be accepted by society has increased from 46 percent to 60 percent over the past ten years alone.[26] The most interesting thing about the gay rights agenda over the past three decades is not the level of opposition to it but the support that has developed for many antidiscrimination initiatives. Although tolerance has grown for other historically unpopular groups as well, the acceptance of gay and lesbian people has outpaced other levels of support (Schafer and Shaw 2009). Several studies indicate that the willingness of respondents to restrict the civil liberties of homosexuals is declining (T. Smith 1992; Yang 1997; Peterson and Donnenwerth 1998; Loftus 2001). Even among Christians who accept the teaching that homosexuality is immoral, the internalization of Christian beliefs serves as a basis for more positive attitudes toward homosexuals as individuals and as a group (Ford et al. 2009). A sizable body of research has shown that attitudes toward homosexuals affect issue positions regarding gay rights (Henry and Reyna 2007; Brewer 2003; Wilcox and Wolpert 2000). At one time many Americans held very negative opinions about gays and lesbians. However, opinions have moderated (Wilcox et al. 2007). More homosexuals are living free and openly in society. Knowing people that are gay predicts support for equal rights—even after demographic, religious, and political variables are taken into account (Lewis 2011). Having gay friends or family members may be particularly influential in the attitudes of young people because they are much less likely to rely on predispositions based on religion or ideology in constructing their opinions about homosexuality than older Americans (Becker and Scheufele 2011). Even though the conservative doctrinal religious position is that homosexuality is a sinful lifestyle choice, science and public opinion on the matter are much more ambiguous (S. Wilcox 2003). Research indicates that believing there is a biological cause of homosexuality is the strongest predictor of attitudes toward gay rights (Lewis 2009; Haider-Markel and Joslyn 2008). As a result, people are increasingly more hesitant to support state-sanctioned discrimination against homosexuals (Barth and Parry 2009).

Changes in public opinion have led to a political environment that is much more favorable to gay rights. Moderating religious interpretations among the major faith traditions on the issue of homosexuality have contributed to this dynamic. The influence of religious conservatives in this issue area has waned significantly in a short period of time.

In terms of the opportunity structure, a concept we discussed in chapter 6, the impact of religious groups on public policies is contingent on several factors, including their ability to frame a political message, their numbers in the community, the scope of the conflict, and the arena of political activity. Today, with the recent Supreme Court ruling that the federal government cannot discriminate against legally married gay couples, the United States appears to be on the verge of a revolution that will bring greater equality to homosexuals in the United States and runs counter to the political preferences of religious conservatives.

The first reason that the political opportunity structure for religious conservatives has significantly diminished is that they are losing the ability to frame gay rights as a morality issue. Traditional—often religious—frames about morality have been juxtaposed against American norms of freedom, equality, and the right of citizens to live their lives without undue government interference (Wilcox and Norrander 2002). The morality politics framework works to the advantage of religious conservatives because conservative religionists have well-developed doctrines and ideologies on the wrongness of homosexuality. When supporters of homosexual rights try to justify or defend the morality of homosexuality, they find themselves in a weaker debating position. If, on the other hand, religious liberals and those working for gay rights are successful at framing these issues as a matter of equal citizenship, and activists can appeal to government officials based on standards of freedom and equality, the more controversial moral dimensions of gay rights become largely irrelevant.

For most of the past thirty years, some of the most interesting and significant battles in the politics of gay rights have taken place not on the national stage but at the state and local levels in this more understated manner. Indeed, many of the issues that have historically been central to the gay civil rights agenda, including domestic partner benefits, hate crime legislation, the repeal of sodomy laws, adoption guidelines, the utilization of "inclusive" public school curriculum, and other antidiscrimination policies, have been engaged with some degree of success at the local and state levels based on the interest group model of politics (Haider-Markel

2000). In these areas Haider-Markel and Meier (1996) found that for the most part, gay and lesbian politics is not very different from the politics of other issue areas. Interest groups interact with sympathetic political elites in pursuit of favorable public policies. This is regular politics, in which interest group resources, elite values, and the nature of preexisting policies are significant determinants of policy outcomes (Haider-Markel 2000). In gay rights, most antidiscrimination measures for housing, employment, insurance benefits, and so on have historically been treated this way and have had a much greater probability of success than when issues are framed as matters of morality (Mucciaroni 2008).

The moral overtones of the gay marriage debate have historically made the politics in this area different from the politics of other antidiscrimination measures. Gay marriage is the consummate morality politics issue. It is easy to politicize because it is highly salient; requires little additional information; taps into deeply held values; and, as a result, mobilizes preexisting social groups. It is also unique from other antidiscrimination measures because it is directly related to religion. In addition to being a legal contract, from a religious perspective marriage is a spiritual commitment. As Wilcox and his colleagues explain, Americans "are torn between a desire to treat gay men and lesbians with equality and respect on the one hand, and core beliefs that marriage is a sacred institution designed by God, on the other" (2007, 239).

Still, what most powerfully reflects the diminished political opportunity structure for religious conservatives today is how quickly morality is disappearing from the frame for most gay rights issues, including the issue of marriage. One recent poll revealed that most Americans no longer define homosexual behavior as sinful. This decline is particularly powerful among moderate religious denominations. For example, the number of Catholics who say that it is a sin to engage in homosexual behavior has dropped by sixteen points in ten years. Today, only about a third of Catholics hold this view.[27] The change in public opinion, in part precipitated by more liberal ideas and accommodations for homosexuality among religious denominations, has helped gay rights advocates successfully reframe their struggle as not a struggle for "gay marriage" but as a struggle for "equal marriage." Equal marriage does not have the same religious overtones that gay marriage suggests, and it is much harder in the United States to mobilize against equality than it is to mobilize against sin.

The opportunities that religious people have to influence gay rights is also contingent on community characteristics. Button and colleagues (1997) examined the gay and lesbian movement's struggle for protective legislation at the local level from the 1970s to 1993. Their analysis focused on the addition of sexual orientation as a protected class to ordinances designed to stop discrimination in government employment, housing, and public accommodations. They found that the communities that adopted antidiscrimination ordinances were more diverse, more urban, more affluent, younger, and better educated. Notably for the study of the relationship between religion and politics, they further observed that the overall level of church affiliation as well as the concentration of conservative Protestants in an area depressed the likelihood that a community would have an antidiscrimination ordinance. Recent research on how evangelical Protestantism influences a state's sexual orientation policies shows that much of the impact occurs through mediating institutions such as interest groups, issue salience, the political composition of state government, and popular opinion (Scheitle and Hahn 2011). On balance in this area, policies tend to reflect public opinion. Conservative states get conservative policies and liberal states adopt liberal ones. That public policies reflect majoritarian interest in a state is reflected in the geography of where gay marriage is legal. In 2013, gay marriage was not lawful in any red state; it was not permitted in any state that had supported the Republican nominee for president in 2012. Conservative and religious values in red states influence legal regulations. These kinds of regional differences suggest that at the electoral level gay rights has the potential to remain controversial and polarizing for some time to come (Cahn and Carbone 2010).

The scope of the political conflict is another key determinant of the political opportunity structure for gay rights. Until recently, whenever those opposed to homosexual rights were able to expand the scope of the conflict through procedures such as ballot initiatives, the likelihood that a measure would be defeated increased significantly. For example, in 2009, the Maine legislature voted to legalize gay marriage, equalizing the treatment of all couples under the state's civil marriage laws. However, gay marriage opponents were able to place a referendum on the November ballot asking voters to approve or reject the action of the legislature. Because of the libertarian leanings of the state, gay rights activists had hoped that voters in Maine would be the first in the country to extend the right to marry at the ballot box. Instead of confirming the expansion of these rights, at that time Maine became the thirty-first state to block gay marriage through referendum. With shifts in public opinion, expanding the scope of the issue no longer reliably predicts the defeat of such proposals—especially in more liberal-leaning states and localities. Back in Maine, in 2012 proponents of gay marriage were able to again place the measure on the ballot. This time it passed easily, making Maine, along with Washington and Maryland, the first states in the country to approve gay marriage through popular vote. By July 2013, five other states plus the District of Columbia had legalized gay marriage through this kind of electoral process.

The expanded opportunity structure for gay rights and the diminished opportunity structure for conservative religious influence is reflected not only at the state level but also on the national political agenda. Under the Obama administration, gays and lesbians are finally beginning to realize their political aspirations and hopes. Though Democrats began to campaign for their support in the 1990s, it has only been of late that President Obama has begun to unravel the legislation passed in the 1990s that denied homosexual rights. Less than two decades ago, the political opportunity was such that even with a sympathetic president in office, almost no momentum could be gained for gay rights.

For example, when Bill Clinton was elected, gay rights advocates hoped there would be a sea change in support for their issues. They had experienced very chilly relations with the Republican administrations of Ronald Reagan and George H. W. Bush. Everything from the kind of art supported by the National Endowment for the Arts to funding for AIDS research and prevention had been a point of contention (Gallagher and Bull 2001; Rom 2000). Clinton had made promises to end formal discrimination on the basis of sexual orientation, starting with lifting the ban on gay and lesbian service personnel in the military. Since 1943, when the ban was imposed, thousands had been expelled from the military for being homosexual. As commander in chief, Clinton thought he could rescind the anti-gay policy by executive order, the same tool used to desegregate the military decades before. However, although Clinton had used the issue effectively to pursue gay votes, he and gay rights advocates had failed to build political support for the proposal in Washington or beyond activist ranks. As Clinton prepared to take office, religious conservatives expanded the scope of the conflict by mobilizing effectively at both the grassroots and the elite levels. In the end, Clinton had to settle for a compromise "don't ask, don't tell" policy that officially dictated that the armed forces not ask recruits about their sexual orientation and not investigate allegations about a soldier's sexual orientation without solid evidence. It further stipulated that homosexual troops not engage in homosexual acts or do anything that would suggest that they are homosexual, such as make public statements or participate in a same-sex marriage. Critics contend that the number of gays dismissed under the new policy actually exceeded the total of terminations under the old ban.

Even worse, Clinton signed DOMA into law. DOMA had been the federal government's response to court decisions that legalized same-sex marriage in Hawaii, Alaska, and Vermont.[28] It defined marriage within the federal law as meaning "only a legal union between one man and one woman as husband and wife." The act also excused each state from having to follow the "full faith and credit" clause of the U.S. Constitution, thereby permitting states to refuse to recognize same-sex marriages made in states that allow them. President Clinton, bowing to political pressure, signed it during the 1996 presidential election year even while assailing it as "unnecessary and divisive."

Like Clinton, during his 2008 election campaign, President Obama invoked the importance of winning equality, dignity, and respect for gays and lesbians; however, unlike Clinton, he signed the repeal of "don't ask, don't tell," ending a policy that brought nearly two decades of secrets and shame to service members because of their sexual orientation. Perhaps, even more importantly, in 2011 the Obama administration declared that it would no longer defend the Defense of Marriage Act (DOMA) in Court because it believed it to be unconstitutional and in 2012 announced that it would support same-sex marriages throughout the United States.

In 2013, the politics of gay rights in the electoral and legislative arena met the politics of gay rights before the Supreme Court on the DOMA issue. As we described in chapter 6, the Court in unambiguous language ruled that DOMA was indeed unconstitutional. Though somewhat controversial, the decision was not unanticipated. If the political opportunity structure for religious conservatives has diminished because of growing tolerance in the United States, the mobilizing capacity is further attenuated in judicial institutions. Courts do not respond to public opinion and electoral politics in the same direct way as elected officials respond. Certainly religious interest groups argue aggressively for their political positions, with conservatives opposing and liberal and mainline organizations contending for the extension of homosexual rights. However, their influence is indirect because decisions are left to judges and legal, not moral, arguments are supposed to be decisive.

However, the courts have a mixed record. In *Bowers v. Hardwick* (1986), the first major contemporary Supreme Court ruling concerning gay and lesbian rights, a 5–4 decision upheld the constitutionality of laws prohibiting sodomy. After his roommate let the police into their apartment, they found Hardwick engaged in oral sex with another man. This violated a Georgia law prohibiting oral or anal sex for both heterosexuals and homosexuals. Hardwick was arrested and charged but not indicted by the prosecutor. Nevertheless, he challenged the constitutionality of the law on privacy grounds, maintaining that government lacked authority to regulate private sexual acts between consenting adults. While seldom enforced, these laws were sometimes used to deny homosexuals adoption rights because they defined homosexual intimacy as illegal on its face. Writing for the Court, Justice Byron White ridiculed Hardwick's arguments that he had a fundamental right to engage in sodomy. On this logic, the courts subsequently refused to support antidiscrimination policies (Brewer, Kaib, and O'Connor 2000). In *United States v. Meinhold* (1993), the Court refused to interfere with the implementation of the "don't ask, don't tell" policy. In a 1995 case, *Hurley v. Irish Gay, Lesbian and Bisexual Group of Boston (GLIB)*, they declined to recognize the right of homosexuals to march in a privately organized Veterans' Day parade despite a state law against such discrimination. The Court ruled that the parade itself was an expression of the organizer's constitutionally protected speech and not subject to the public accommodation provisions of the State of Massachusetts.

Then came *Romer v. Evans* in 1996. Romer challenged the constitutionality of the 1992 Colorado initiative that had explicitly made it illegal to pass laws to protect homosexuals. The Colorado initiative had been a triumph for the Christian Right. Under the slogan "No Special Rights," conservative religious groups worked diligently for the legislation. The U.S. Supreme Court declared 5–4 that the Colorado initiative was unconstitutional. Rejecting the state's argument that the initiative merely blocked gays from receiving "special rights," Justice Kennedy wrote that "the amendment imposes a special disability upon those persons alone. Homosexuals are forbidden the safeguards that others enjoy or may seek without constraint." He continued, "Its sheer breadth is so discontinuous with the reasons offered for it that the amendment seems inexplicable by anything but animus toward the class that it affects; it lacks a rational relationship to legitimate state interests."

If *Romer* did not signal that the Supreme Court was taking a very different approach to homosexual rights, *Lawrence v. Texas* (2003) certainly did. The circumstances were very similar to those around *Bowers*. After entering an apartment through an unlocked door to investigate a report of a weapons disturbance, police observed Lawrence engaged in intimate sexual conduct with another man, Tyrone Garner. After Lawrence and Garner were both arrested and charged, they decided to challenge the constitutionality of the law. The decision in their case explicitly overruled *Bowers* by holding that intimate consensual sexual conduct was indeed part of the liberty protected by the Fourteenth Amendment. The case invalidated sodomy laws throughout the country. Writing for the majority, Justice Kennedy concluded that "the Texas statute furthers no legitimate state interest which can justify its intrusion into the personal and private life of the individual." *Lawrence v. Texas* was a major defeat for religious conservatives. In the decision quoting Justice John Paul Stevens, Justice Kennedy related, "The fact that the governing majority in a State has traditionally viewed a particular practice as immoral is not a sufficient reason for upholding a law prohibiting the practice."[29] The logic of the decision seemed to suggest the Court would be less willing to entertain morality arguments in the future and more willing to accept antidiscrimination measures in other areas of interest to homosexuals, including marriage and military service.

That proved to be the case in the historic *U.S. v. Windsor* decision. Edith Windsor and Thea Spyer married in Toronto in 2007. At the time of Spyer's death, same-sex marriage was legal in New York, where they lived. However, the IRS denied Windsor the spousal estate tax exception under DOMA. The Supreme Court ruled that DOMA violated the due process clause of the Fifth Amendment and declared that its "principal purpose is to impose inequality." Based on the ruling, the federal government is obliged to recognize the same-sex-marriages that are approved by states. The judgment affirmed several lower-court rulings that had been supportive of gay rights in general, and gay marriage in particular.

However, the Supreme Court declined to establish that same-sex marriage is the right of all citizens of the United States. *Hollingsworth v. Perry*, a case heard during the same session as *Windsor*, provided an opportunity for them to do so. In 2008, the California Supreme Court issued a ruling permitting gay marriage in the state. In November of the same year, led by religious conservatives, voters passed Proposition 8, a ballot initiative that amended the California state constitution to read that "only marriage between a man and a woman is valid and recognized" in the state (Gordon and Gillespie 2012). Same-sex couples filed suit challenging the legality of the amendment. State officials refused to defend it in court, so proponents of the amendment became party to the lawsuit and its defender in the courts. In the end, the Supreme Court ruled that these proponents did not have standing to sue and dismissed the case, leaving the federal district court ruling against Proposition 8 as the final outcome and effectively reinstituting gay marriage in the state of California. Importantly, however, the Court declined to take the chance to settle the broader issue of whether gay marriage should be legal in every state and sidestepped the larger matter of whether state constitutional amendments that define marriage for heterosexuals only are themselves lawful.

Some are concerned that the politics related to gay rights issues produces antidemocratic results. Religious conservatives claim that interest-group politics thwarts the will of the majority, while gay rights advocates claim that voters are violating their rights. In an interesting study of public opinion and policy responsiveness at the state level, Lax and Phillips (2009) found no evidence that anti-gay majorities tyrannize the rights of minorities or that pro-gay elites trump the will of the majority. What they did find was that policies based on both kinds of politics were responsive (although not always congruent) with public opinion and that responsiveness and congruence were contingent on the salience of the issue. Ambivalence can be a challenge to issue salience. As Craig and his colleagues observe, "While some citizens undoubtedly have become more tolerant of homosexuals, others may have made that journey only part of the way—by adopting positive orientations without necessarily abandoning all of the negative ones previously held" (2005, 5). It is unfortunate that progress is slow and that for some issues, even with the support of supermajorities of American citizens (hate crimes, marketplace equality, housing protections), a lack of issue salience often undermines more equal policy outcomes supportive of gay rights.

CONCLUSION

This chapter has examined the relationship between religion and the politics of sex and gender. The patterns of relationship reveal the complicated way that religion interacts with society, often simultaneously producing empowerment and oppression—a reason to mobilize for equality and a major rationale for working against it. Religion can serve as a resource for all sides. It is part of the cultural tool kit regularly incorporated in politics whenever the moral order is thought to be at stake. Studying these "other minorities" also reveals both the heart and the limits of the cultural war. Women's rights, abortion, and gay rights have been at the forefront and have fueled the battle between traditionalists and progressives. However, as the chapter reveals, even in these highly symbolic political areas, moderation increasingly is characterizing both the religion and the politics.

12

Religion and
American Political Life

The challenge of practical politics is to combine the passion of religion
with the civil tolerance of democratic pluralism.

—Clarke E. Cochran

Like other scholars who specialized in religion and politics, our tele-
phones rang off the hook after September 11, 2001. With different
words but in one voice, reporters asked about the religious motivations
of the airplane hijackers. Was this really a religious act, as the terrorists
insisted, or was that just a cover for grievances against American foreign
policy and the behavior of Arab governments? The reporters struggled
with the very idea that somebody could believe murdering thousands
of innocent civilians was a way to pay homage to God. It was easier to
dismiss the terrorists as insane or demon possessed than to assess their
claims about the divine nature of the "mission." The events of that day
force us to confront the potential dangers when religion enters the public
square—or when it is kept out.

Accordingly, this chapter examines the effect of religious activism
on the general tenor of political life in the United States. Specifically,
we assess the benefits and costs to democracy and the functioning of
the political system of the religious presence in public life.[1] Our conclusion, that religion in politics is neither an unvarying source of good nor
a consistent evil influence, is unlikely to please either the most ardent
advocates of a "Christian America" or secularists who want to keep religion safely outside the public square. It is consistent, however, with the

351

historical record, which has shown that religion has the capacity both to ennoble and to corrupt political life.

THE CASE AGAINST RELIGIOUS INFLUENCE IN POLITICS

Even if they were to lower their profile, religious groups would still be important actors in American political life. Does this bode good or ill for the future of politics in the United States? The question is not merely academic. Although certain forms of religious influence cannot be controlled, the government has some limited power to encourage or discourage organized political involvement by the churches (Kelley 1982, 64–83, 111–28, 151–64). To cite one important example, the regulations governing the tax-free status of churches are generally interpreted to give churches substantial leeway for public involvement but could be tightened to make it more difficult for clergy to engage in political action. However, debate about the proper role of religion in public life is not primarily a legal question but a philosophical inquiry. Individuals have the authority to decide for themselves how much they combine or segregate their roles as congregants and citizens, a decision that no government can influence. That makes it even more important to assess the pros and cons of active political involvement by churches and religiously inspired activists.

The rise of religious activism in American politics has been a source of concern and apprehension for many observers. They fear that religious controversy in politics will lead to extremism and polarization, infecting the body politic with unhealthy doses of fanaticism and ill will. Carried to extremes, critics have contended, the entry of religious issues into the public agenda may produce violence, undermining the very foundations of democratic politics. History provides substantial evidence to sustain that assumption, and it seems even more plausible after September 11.

Why should religion have such dire consequences for the stability of government? How can a force intended to make humans better constitute a danger to life and limb? Many commentators have insisted that democratic government depends on a willingness to bargain and negotiate, to approach politics in the spirit of compromise. Some issues naturally lend themselves to this type of treatment. Conflicts over money—demands for pay raises, proposals to increase taxes, competition for federal funding—are inherently subject to bargaining, because financial benefits are divisible in dollars. Hence, economic conflicts can usually be managed within the framework of a stable political system. But when conflicts take on an either/or dimension, the impediments to compromise can prompt antagonists to subvert the political system. "Charged with symbolic freight," Peter McDonough (1994, 124) says of these conflicts, "some issues have the capacity to threaten identities, jeopardize worldviews, and galvanize intense minorities." Issues that involve fundamental social and moral values "are intrinsically harder to be reasonable about than others" (124).

Because they do not lend themselves so readily to compromise solutions, religious issues may challenge the normal system of governance. If you regard abortion as murder, and your friend sees it as a medical procedure, it will be hard to find a middle ground that either one of you will accept as legitimate. The same kind of problem may arise in the context of debates over prayer in public schools, the rights of homosexuals, traditional sex roles, and other policy areas in which religious groups have been active. Without realistic hope for a compromise solution that is minimally acceptable to all sides, such issues are likely to fester and breed support for extremist action.

A related problem raised by critics of church activism involves the potential impact of religious values on the style of political activists. As religious issues do not easily permit compromise solutions, so, too, religious values may produce rigidity, dogmatism, and contempt for alternative points of view. Such destructive traits, far from being accidental, may actually be the consequence of strong religious commitment (Liebman 1988, chap. 3).

One aspect of religious faith that encourages extremism, its claim to possess the truth, may imbue believers with unshakable confidence in the rightness and inevitability of their efforts. As an example, G. Elijah Dann (2010, xi) cited the leader of an anti–gay marriage rally in Washington, D.C., who justified his opposition to same-sex marriage with a simple claim: "When God says you shouldn't do something, it's a no-brainer. You don't do it." Of course, it's not that simple. As Dann notes, the bald-faced claim rests on a string of assumptions about the existence of God, the interpretation of scripture (which says nothing explicit about same-sex marriage), whether citizens of secular states are bound by a claim in the Bible, whether sins (as the speaker considered same-sex marriage) should be prohibited by law, and many others. A thoughtful citizen would ask these questions instead of trying to foreclose the debate before it begins.

Finally, because "religious adherence becomes a criteria by which other people can be evaluated" (Liebman 1988, 40), people of strong faith may not respect the motives and values of their political opponents. A person who believes that he or she is acting under God's direct command may be prone to perceive opponents as not merely misguided or confused but as evil and malevolent. In the prophetic words of the philosopher Martin Buber (1937), religious faith may drive a person to treat an opponent as an "it" rather than a "thou."

While this discussion considers "religion" as a general problem for politics, it seems more accurate to identify the source of difficulty as a particular style of religion that incorporates the dangers we have just described—fundamentalism. Unfortunately, the term *fundamentalism* is often used to identify those evangelical Protestants committed to a literal interpretation of the Bible. When scholars write about the problem fundamentalism poses for democracy, they have in mind something much broader than a particular subgroup within one religious tradition (Marty and Appleby 1992). The "fundamentalism" that worries us is a disposition "characterized by a quest for certainty, exclusiveness, and unambiguous boundaries" regardless of religious tradition (Nagata 2001, 481). Driven by an uncompromising mentality, fundamentalists attempt "to chart a morally black and white path out of the gray zones of intimidating cultural and religious complexity" (481). When they draw boundaries between true believers and those outside the charmed circle, fundamentalists treat the latter as "the Other," a dangerous and threatening enemy.

This disposition or set of traits is not limited to any single religion but can be found in some degree among virtually every major religious tradition (Van der Vyver 1996). While the term may conjure up images of Islamic extremists who carry out acts of terror around the globe, it applies as well to the dominant religious tradition in the United States. As the distinguished philosopher John Rawls observed (cited in Riordan 2004, 178), "a persecuting zeal has been the great curse of the Christian religion. It was shared by Luther and Calvin and the Protestant Reformers, and it was not radically changed in the Catholic Church until Vatican II." This chapter uses fundamentalism to refer to this syndrome without regard to religious tradition, and Protestant fundamentalism to identify a specific religious family.

The dangers posed by fundamentalist involvement in politics can be arranged in a hierarchy. At the lowest level, religious passions may inspire displays of individual intolerance and uncivil behavior. Though troubling, such incidents probably do not threaten the social order. The danger escalates greatly when religious commitment is expressed in violent acts such as property crimes, assaults, terrorist attacks, and killings. As repugnant as they are, such crimes still stop short of the next level of danger—organized, systematic violence against people or nations stimulated by conflicting religious identities. At that level, religious passion can truly overwhelm the political system and destroy social order.

We do not have to look hard to find all three types of domestic, religiously inspired hostility in American political life. As we saw in chapter 8, many observers of the Christian Right were troubled by the religious bigotry and narrow-mindedness among some movement supporters— such as the demonstrator at the 1988 Republican convention whose placard boasted that "Bush Will Win Because God Is a Republican," or the 1992 flier warning Christians that "To Vote for Bill Clinton Is to Sin

against God."[2] As noted, fundamentalism entails demonizing political opponents. A New York homemaker told pollsters she was attracted to the
Religious Right because it "still stands for morals, and the liberal people,
the Democrats, don't have any morals" (quoted in Berke 1994). Another
poll participant, a self-described Republican, did not want her party to
admit people who were tolerant of homosexuality or abortion "because
they don't have moral values." Escalating the rhetoric a notch, the leader
of a militant anti-abortion movement ascribed to feminists a "very anti-
male, lesbian-oriented, Marxist-oriented, put-your-kids-in-day-care-and-
go-out-and-pursue-a-career, proabortion mentality" that was nothing less
than "Satan's agenda" (quoted in Lacayo 1991).

In a troubling sign of religiously based intolerance, the "Christian
Reconstructionist" movement has exerted some influence on leaders of
the Christian Right. Leaders of this fringe movement within Protestant
fundamentalism propose a radical reconstruction of American society
on the basis of their reading of Old Testament law (Hedges 2006).[3]
The blueprint includes severe punishment for assorted "deviants"—
"homosexuals, incorrigible children, adulterers, blasphemers, astrolo-
gers," as well as Sabbath breakers and practitioners of witchcraft. Advocates call for the reimposition of slavery and the abolition of democracy.
Under this regime, religious pluralism would be redefined as heresy,
a crime punishable by death. The assurances by activists that these
changes will be introduced by popular consensus hardly make Recon-
structionism a democratic movement.

What of the next level of threat, the use of violence to further religious
ends? Though we associate religious terrorism with third-world "holy
wars," the United States has not escaped homegrown religious violence.
Since the 1990s, the abortion issue alone has produced twenty-five murders
and attempted murders of abortion providers, over two hundred bomb
and arson attacks, and more than two thousand other acts of violence
against medical facilities offering reproductive health care. Many of these
actions were the result of individual extremists or amateurish conspiracies
(Blanchard and Prewitt 1993). With much less fanfare but a much more
systematic campaign, so-called Christian patriots have since the late 1970s
been engaged in a murderous war against what they call the "Zionist
Occupation Government" (Aho 1990; Barkun 1994). Participants in this
extremist movement perceive the government as the tool of a satanic conspiracy that is devoted to subverting the word of God by promoting racial
equality, multiculturalism, and gun control. As "true" Christians, they see
themselves obligated to resist with whatever means are necessary the authority of this illegitimate occupying power. More than fifty people have
died in violent collisions with this movement, and at least one sympathizer,
Louisiana's David Duke, attained a state legislative seat and ran a strong

gubernatorial campaign. The Oklahoma City bomber, Timothy McVeigh, was a member in good standing (Wright 2007).

Fortunately, the United States has been spared the most intense type of religious-political conflict, the organization of political conflict on strictly religious lines evident in places like Northern Ireland, Lebanon, Burundi, Rwanda, Somalia, India, and Bosnia. A systematic study of seventeen Western nations with strong electoral traditions confirmed the dangers of a strong religious presence in national party politics (Rose and Urwin 1969). In approximately half the countries, the principal line of electoral conflict was defined by religious affiliation or practice; the remaining nine nations lacked a strong religious dimension to party competition. According to Rose and Urwin, the countries with the strongest religious divisions had experienced much more strain, violence, and political instability than those whose politics were largely free of religious controversy. In some cases, religious conflict in the former group had even contributed to the collapse of governmental systems and the emergence of antidemocratic politics.

Does the entry of religious groups in the political arena threaten the stability of the American political system, perhaps leading to the levels of systematic breakdown evident in other nations? Do the instances of individual intolerance and the sporadic cases of violence mentioned here point to a larger and more pervasive climate of hostility? These are not easy questions to answer, and we shall start by looking for evidence relevant to the core assumption that strong religious convictions (of whatever kind) promote an antidemocratic outlook. Many social scientists have interpreted the weight of evidence to support a link between the intensity of religious belief and various indicators of an antidemocratic orientation (Cigler and Joslyn 2002; Kim 2004). That conclusion has been based on comparisons of the expressed political and social attitudes of people with different reported levels of exposure to religious influence.

The link between religious attachment and political intolerance was supported by one of the first major academic surveys of American attitudes toward civil liberties (Stouffer 1966). Using a format that would be widely imitated in subsequent research, the investigator gauged tolerance in 1954 by asking members of a national sample whether they would support various forms of freedom for unpopular groups—socialists, Communists, and atheists. The results indicated that general attachment to religion was associated with low levels of support for basic civil liberties. Specifically, a high level of tolerance characterized 28 percent of respondents who had attended church in the month before the survey but a substantially higher 36 percent of the people who were not churchgoers (Stouffer 1966, 142). The difference held up with controls for social factors related to religion that might independently reduce political tolerance. Stouffer also discovered that some kinds of religion were less conducive to tolerance than others (143–44). At one extreme, only 21 percent of southern Protestants fell into the "most tolerant" category, whereas 73 percent of Jewish respondents were so classified. Northern Catholics and Protestants, who scored about the same on the tolerance scale, held a position midway between the extremes.

In the four decades since Stouffer's findings were first published, they have been repeatedly confirmed by other researchers (Hunsberger 1996). In periodic national surveys about willingness to extend civil liberties to unpopular groups, major religious groups differ roughly the same way they did in 1954. The nonaffiliated are substantially more likely than persons attached to religion to score high on a scale of support for civil liberties. Among American religious groups, the same ordering reported by Stouffer has been in evidence: low tolerance among evangelical Protestants (black and white alike), intermediate support for civil liberties by Catholics and mainline Protestants, and the highest commitment to democratic norms among Jews (Taylor and Merino 2011). In studies that looked at religious beliefs rather than affiliation, scholars have routinely found that the traditionalist orientations associated most closely with fundamentalist Protestantism strongly predict intolerant political views (Gibson 2010). The more tightly an evangelical Protestant is embedded in a congregation, one study reports (Rhodes 2012), the higher that person's level of intolerance.

These findings have also been extended to other antidemocratic orientations. Thus, researchers have found that hostility to blacks, Jews, homosexuals, and other minority groups has most often been expressed by adherents of theological traditionalism and has been least common in persons outside the churches (Byrnes and Kiger 1992; Gibson and Tedin 1988; Scheepers, Gijsberts, and Hello 2002; Finlay and Walther 2003; Rowatt et al. 2009). Evangelical Protestants are similarly more likely to regard the United States as a "Christian Nation," endowing citizenship with a religious definition it does not possess in law (Straughn and Feld 2010). Belief in the United States as a Christian Nation contributes to negative views of religious diversity and to immigrants (McDaniel, Nooruddin, and Shortle, 2011).

What is the source of these apparently antidemocratic orientations among Protestant fundamentalists? Although both intolerance and fundamentalism are often related to limited education, residence in rural and small town areas, and other indicators of minimal exposure to modernity, subsequent research has found that fundamentalist intolerance persists above and beyond social background and demographic factors. Stouffer attributed the connection to the religiously threatening nature of nonconformity—that is, the direct challenge that atheism and Communism posed to religious belief. Jackson and Hunsberger (1999) broadened this argument, suggesting that hostility to other religious groups by fundamentalists reflects genuine competition for resources, social respect, and adherents. Some recent experimental work raises another possibility, that Protestant fundamentalists express more intolerant views because those views are communicated to them in religious messages from the pulpit (Djupe and Calfano 2013).

But other scholars have suggested the more ominous possibility that intolerance might be built into the type of religious commitment that sustains fundamentalism.

Some investigators hypothesized that fundamentalist religion attracts people who cannot accept doubt, ambiguity, or challenges to their belief systems and who are prone to reject people who do not share their attitudes or outlooks (Budner 1962, 38–40; Raschke 1973). Perhaps that is why advocates of biblical literalism, who deny the possibility of any cultural influences on the Bible, tend to be more highly prejudiced than others (Burdette, Ellison, and Hill 2005; Tuntiya 2005; Burge 2013). Finding that the intolerance of fundamentalist Protestants could not be explained wholly by hostility to specific groups, Wilcox and Jelen (1990) attributed narrow-mindedness primarily to doctrine.[4] Persuaded they already have the truth, true believers see nothing valuable about hearing dissenting views (see Kirkpatrick 1993; B. Smith 2007). That could explain why a scholar found that donors to Republican presidential campaigns who were affiliated with a Christian Right organization were appreciably less likely than other Republican donors to embrace the "civic norms" that underlie democratic government—interpersonal trust, respect for intellectual differences, and the value of compromise (Wilcox 2010). Some researchers emphasize the tendency of fundamentalist Protestants to draw sharp boundaries between themselves and the unsaved and to avoid contact with persons from outside their church world (Reimer and Park 2001; Schwadel 2005). Other scholars believe the causal factor is the Protestant fundamentalist insistence that human beings should not be allowed to behave contrary to God's will (Tamney and Johnson 1997; Froese, Bader, and Smith 2008). Putnam and Campbell (2010, 488–89) suspect that fundamentalists are more willing to limit political freedom because of their concern to protect authority. Whatever the origin of the pattern, it raises concern about the attitudes that may accompany the political mobilization of persons with fundamentalist religious orientations.

ASSESSING THE EVIDENCE

These results paint a disturbing portrait of the capacity for democratic thinking and action among deeply religious people and lead to concern about the implications of their increasing involvement in political life. Dogmatism, closed-mindedness, and intolerance are not traits that promote civility or the free exchange of ideas. If such fundamentalist traits are pronounced among religious activists and their opponents, there is a solid basis for concern about the increasing politicization of religious issues. In our view, however, the evidence supporting a link between religiosity and the propensity to intolerance is not strong enough to warrant alarm.

One problem has been the reliance of all such studies on attitudes rather than on behavior. People do not always act consistently with their expressed beliefs. The crisis that enveloped the American Civil Liberties Union (ACLU) over the Skokie case in 1977 showed that the attitude-behavior gap can be especially large in the realm of civil liberties. In Skokie, a Chicago suburb with a high concentration of Jewish refugees from the Nazi Holocaust, local authorities tried to block a planned march by members of a Nazi organization. When the ACLU provided support for the Nazis' legal challenge to the Skokie ordinance—an action for which there was ample precedent in its history—the organization lost thousands of members and a vital proportion of financial resources. Even for supporters of an organization whose sole purpose was the defense of civil liberties, it was easier to express tolerance in the abstract than in practice (Gibson and Anderson 1985). The higher levels of tolerance expressed by the nonreligious might erode under similar pressure.

Moreover, those who have viewed religious commitment as a source of antidemocratic sentiment have not always distinguished among different types of commitment. Most studies have simply examined the attitude differences between church members and nonaffiliates, or between different denominations, or, in a few cases, between churchgoers of varying frequency. These are poor approximations of what might well turn out to be the real source of variation in the linkage between religious commitment and tolerance—the manner in which people absorb religious values. In a pioneering survey of democratic attitudes in the United States, researchers from the University of California stressed that people hold their religious values in different ways (Adorno et al. 1950, chap. 18). For example, some attend church only out of a sense of duty to parental expectations or because it conforms to social practice in their community. They find in religion support for their way of life and sanctification of the social order—but nothing of a prophetic vision that might challenge them to change their behavior or act more sensitively to others. What is missing from such conventional or nominal religiosity is deeply rooted acceptance of the nobler values associated with major religious traditions—love, charity, compassion, and forgiveness. Some adherents do not hear these messages either because they do not attend often enough or, more likely, because "while hearing they do not hear, nor do they understand" (Matt.

13:13). But other persons who take religion seriously—meaning that they embrace the ethical messages transmitted by a religious tradition—internalize that tradition and assign the highest priority to acting righteously. Before condemning individuals for falling short of biblical standards, they are likely to recall the admonition to hate the sin but love the sinner. Hence, the authors predicted, "The more 'human' and concrete a person's relation to religion, the more human his approach to those who 'do not belong': their sufferings remind the religious subjectivist of the idea of martyrdom inseparably bound up with his thinking about Christ" (731).

In a moving illustration of precisely that style of deep commitment, the psychiatrist Robert Coles (1985) reported about six-year-old Ruby. The first black child to integrate a New Orleans school in 1960, she had to march every day past a howling and vicious mob threatening her life: "As she walked by the mob, sometimes a hundred or so strong, protected by federal marshals on her way to a sadly deserted classroom, she said, 'Please, dear God, forgive those folks, because they don't know what they're doing.' She'd heard in Sunday school that Jesus had once reached out similarly and she was trying to follow suit." That type of religious commitment—which is precisely what is meant by "taking religion seriously"—could very likely militate against the arrogance that threatens democratic interchange.

This argument about a link between "genuine" religious commitment and thoughtful, reasoned behavior has attracted some research support. Gordon Allport (1958, 421–22) reported an intriguing study in which standard prejudice scales were administered to Catholic and Baptist laymen. The process of selecting respondents was designed to produce persons who exhibited diverse styles of religiosity—commitment to the essence of the faith versus commitment for social or professional reasons. These different styles of commitment were labeled, respectively, as "intrinsic" and "extrinsic" orientations to religion. The Catholic participants were selected by a knowledgeable parishioner who was asked to recommend some church members who were deeply influenced by faith and others who participated for secular advantages. In an attempt to match this distinction between "devout" and "institutional" church members, the Protestant participants were recruited from regular and irregular attendees at Bible class. In both cases, "the most devout, more personally absorbed in the religion, were far less prejudiced than the others."

The negative association between "intrinsic" religious commitment and prejudice has been found to hold in larger and more systematic studies (Gorsuch and Aleshire 1974; Wilson and Bagley 1973). The findings point to a curvilinear pattern: broad-mindedness is endorsed by people on the extremes of religious commitment—those outside the churches and those most deeply involved in religious groups—and the association between religion and various forms of prejudice is highest among people who are only moderately involved with churches. H. Wesley Perkins (1983, 1985, 1992) has further rehabilitated strong religious commitment by linking it empirically to social compassion and concern for inequality, as well as to lower levels of racial prejudice. When intrinsic religious commitment is coupled with an open and tolerant religious environment, the probability of prejudice is reduced. But if the religious environment sends a narrow and particularistic message, the intrinsically committed may also absorb that perspective (Griffin, Gorsuch, and Davis 1987; Fisher, Derison, and Polley 1994).

C. Daniel Batson has refined Allport's "intrinsic" category by introducing a third form of religious commitment, the "quest" dimension. In this "mature" form of religiosity, faith encourages believers to accept complexity, criticize and doubt their own motivations, and keep an open mind as they search for truth (Batson et al. 1986). This third style of attachment is designed to distinguish between fundamentalists (of all faiths) whose commitment to orthodoxy makes them intolerant and highly committed persons who do not demand from their faith "black and white" answers to all of life's dilemmas. Persons with high scores on the "quest" scale generally turn out to be less prejudiced (Batson et al. 1986; Fisher, Derison, and Polley 1994; Leak and Randall 1995) and to employ more sophisticated standards of moral judgment (Sapp and Jones 1986). Similarly, when religion is interpreted symbolically rather than literally, the link to prejudice largely disappears (Duriez 2004; Leiber, Woodrick, and Roudebush 1995).

Hence, it seems reasonable to maintain that religion versus irreligion is not the crucial dimension underlying political attitudes but that religious people differ politically based on the nature and motivation of their religiosity and the political norms transmitted in their religious communities. Specifically, some forms of religious commitment, far from threatening democracy, may reinforce constructive tendencies in public life. Unfortunately, we have not yet found any studies that examine directly the relationship between democratic attitudes and styles of religious commitment in the United States. In the closest such research project, support for unquestioning loyalty to the president was positively related to religious orthodoxy, high levels of ritual involvement, and strong belief in God but was negatively associated with the incidence of private prayer (Schoenfeld 1985). The author interpreted the findings in a manner consistent with the hypothesis suggested here, finding the more "priestly" aspects of religion conducive to support for political authority, but the spontaneous, unstructured, and unmediated act of prayer imparting a healthy sense of skepticism about public officials. Until more direct studies become available, it will remain arguable that intense religious commitment—measured in qualitative rather than quantitative terms—actually promotes healthy democratic orientations.

Finally, we are comforted by the belief that political participation may actually teach religious activists to moderate their style and tame their expectations. Using the intriguing example of nineteenth-century Belgium, Stathis Kalyvas (1998) demonstrated how Catholicism, a movement that at the time rejected democracy and toleration in principle, paradoxically ended up reinforcing Belgium's democratic political system. There were ample opportunities to destroy democratic institutions during the thirty years that a Catholic party governed Belgium. But, Kalyvas argues, the church made a strategic judgment that participating in a liberal system it rejected on principle would nonetheless further its "one overriding concern, its influence in society," more effectively than destroying the political system (312). Ironically, the hierarchical nature of Roman Catholicism, its most strikingly undemocratic feature, permitted the leadership to swing the Catholic party behind its decision. As this case suggests, institutional self-interest may prove more powerful than theology in determining how religious groups interact with democratic political systems.

There is fairly consistent evidence from the contemporary United States that political activists are more tolerant than nonparticipants. Although it has not yet been shown that political participation actually causes more tolerant outlooks, a logical case can be made for such a relationship. From the perspective of social learning theory, political participation should bring the individual into contact with others who value the opportunity to influence policy through democratic means. This experience might enhance the individual's respect for a system that facilitates such opportunities (Sullivan et al. 1993). Based on interviews with longtime Christian Right activists and analysis of party elites over time, some scholars contend that such elites have indeed become more respectful of democratic norms (Conger and McGraw 2008; Shields 2007; Layman 2010). Given growing experimental evidence of the power of religious messages about tolerance to produce more favorable attitudes, such communication may counteract tendencies to ethnocentrism and hyper-patriotism (Robinson 2010, Nteta and Wallsten 2012).

Hence, some observers have retreated from earlier predictions about the baleful effect of religious activism on the political system. Of course, people tend to find what they are looking for, so we want to point with caution at some signs that the American political system can indeed accommodate religiously inspired campaigns for candidates or issues. The essence of the argument is that while such issues may strain the system by making compromise difficult and attracting the attention of persons with passionate commitments, the system can cope with this situation. To some extent, such activity may even enhance the vitality of political life.

The abortion issue provides perhaps the best illustration of how the political system adapts to the pressure applied by deeply committed activists. When advocates throw phrases like "baby killer" and "Nazi" at one another, the rhetoric does not elevate the tone of political discourse. In Congress and other governmental arenas, the issue has from time to time undermined a civil decision-making process. The fear about abortion's disruptive potential has certainly been intensified by the alarming outbreaks of murderous violence on the fringes of the anti-abortion movement. Taken together, those trends have persuaded some observers that the abortion debate might actually threaten the American form of government.

Despite such fears, careful study suggests that most of the abortion-related activity has stayed well within the bounds of democratic norms (Steiner 1983). Despite its bitterly divisive nature, the abortion issue has engendered willingness to compromise. The advocates of restriction by constitutional amendment have seemingly withdrawn from a position of favoring only an absolute prohibition on abortion to one that would permit abortion under certain conditions. Supporters of liberalized policies might not appreciate the magnitude of these compromises nor their divisive impact on pro-life activists, but they do in fact constitute a significant revision of earlier positions, indicating the willingness of anti-abortion forces to adapt to political realities.

The search for compromise is also apparent in the courts and the legislative branch. Ever since *Roe v. Wade*, the Supreme Court has steered a middle course by rejecting the extreme options of allowing abortion on demand or returning to the pre-1973 situation. Instead, the Court has granted its approval to some limitations on access to abortion while continuing to uphold the principle of abortion as a constitutionally protected right of privacy. Similarly, Congress has moved the issue to the familiar terrain of the budgetary process, debating whether federal funds should be used to pay for abortion (Oldmixon 2005). This conflict follows a well-established precedent of using control over appropriations as a means for settling policy debates. In both the legislative and the judicial arenas, the debate has focused on bargainable questions of implementation of the law.

To go one step further, it can be argued that the abortion debate has actually invigorated public life in the United States. This argument challenges the standards of democracy used by critics of religiously inspired political activism. Those who have criticized the place of such passionate issues on the public agenda have sometimes argued from a conception of democracy that treats mass involvement in policymaking as suspect or potentially dangerous to governmental stability. These critics contend that high-energy issues such as abortion may promote an excess of public excitement and involvement, inhibiting the possibility of rational policymaking or intelligent compromise. Rather than treating active citizen participation as a requirement of the democratic process, these "revisionist" democrats have tended to approach it as a threat to the stability of democratic governance and look benignly on apathy as a useful way of managing intense political conflict.

But this particular view of democracy is not the only model available. Another view defines the continuous and active involvement of the people in public decision-making as the key characteristic of a democratic system (Pateman 1970; Tesh 1984). In this view, issues like abortion enhance democracy by forcing ordinary men and women to take a stand on issues of public significance and by encouraging them to act on their beliefs in the public realm. The rise of the abortion issue challenges not democracy per se, but rather a particular conception of democracy that keeps important issues off the agenda, limits their focus, or leaves decision-making to political elites (Casanova 1994, 102ff.). When religious convictions propel groups to enter the political process, they add a new voice to the public debate on issues such as abortion. These new activists "try to politicize that which had been private, to broaden that which had been narrow, and to bring ordinary citizens into that which had been the province of professionals" (Tesh 1984, 44). That may not be orderly—but perhaps orderliness is not an appropriate standard for democratic politics.

THE CASE FOR RELIGION IN POLITICS

In the previous section, we evaluated the case against religious activism in politics and found it wanting. Though the rise of religiously based political issues may present challenges to the capacity of a democratic political system, the American political process seems adequate to the task. Now it is time to consider the positive claims for religion in politics.

In chapter 3, we noted that some scholars believe that religion contributed to the development of democratic values and the acceptance of democratic practices in the United States. Some observers have gone well beyond that statement, debatable as it is, to make an even larger claim for religion. They argue that religion is an essential support for a democratic political orientation and warn that the decay of religious values or their exclusion from policy debate will weaken the health of the American political system (Maddox 1996). While acknowledging that problems accompany political debate over moral values, they have asserted that the departure of faith from the political realm is far more dangerous to democracy than is an excess of passion.

Whatever its role in the past, how might religion today be expected to sustain democratic political institutions? According to some advocates, the dominant religions in the United States uphold beliefs that are essential to the maintenance of democratic values. Consider the notion of "human rights," a fundamental element of American political culture. On what basis can we assert that human beings, simply because they are human beings, are entitled to the various liberties spelled out in the U.S. Constitution? Although the idea of human rights is so deeply embedded in American thought that it almost seems natural, it has usually been justified in religious terms, specifically as mandated by the equality of human beings before God. By virtue of humankind's common link to God, it is declared, all people deserve to be treated with a minimum of decency and respect.

Other elements in the American creed have been said to originate in some conception of a divine presence. The political scientist Ernest Griffith and his coauthors, John Plamenatz and J. Roland Pennock (1956), once attempted to list the beliefs essential to the survival of democracy and to show how each one depended on the Judeo-Christian heritage:

1. Love for and belief in freedom: best based upon belief in the sacredness of the individual as a child of God.
2. Active and constructive participation in community life: best based upon the obligation of the Christian, the Jew, and other believers to accept responsibilities, cooperating with and working for their brother men.
3. Integrity in discussion: best based upon the inner light of truth being primary in a world God meant to be righteous.
4. The freely assumed obligation of economic groups to serve society: best based upon the Christian insight into the nature of society as set forth, for example, by the parable of the body and its members.
5. Leadership and office holding regarded as public trusts: best based upon or inspired by the example and teachings of religious prophets, such as Jesus, who accepted such a service "to the death."
6. Attitudes assuring that passion will be channeled into constructive ends: best based upon religious faiths that unite an obligation to love and serve with a recognition of the primacy of individual personality.
7. Friendliness and cooperation among nations: best based upon the vision of world brotherhood derived from a faith that we are all children of a common Heavenly Father. (113)

In this view, religion provides the standards for judgment that are necessary to give meaning to concepts such as fairness, justice, goodness, and dignity.

The bald claim that religion is essential to maintain democratic values immediately inspires two critical questions. First, is religion the only basis for supporting the democratic outlook, or are other secular systems of belief capable of performing the same task? If alternatives are available, then religion can hardly be treated as essential to the survival of democratic government. But even if religious values do undergird freedom, that does not necessarily suggest that religious groups should enter the political arena. Hence the second question: Should religion fulfill its public function only by speaking to the consciences of individuals or by entering the political arena more directly?

To maintain that religion is the only basis for morality is to ignore the existence of secular philosophies that also support respect for human rights and liberties. In fact, the research of many political scientists has suggested that the health of democracy depends less on public opinion of any sort than on favorable social and economic conditions (Lipset 1960, chap. 2). Nonetheless, advocates of religion have argued that it supplies a more powerful rationale for democracy than does any competing system of thought. In particular, they have claimed, religion—and religion alone—has the capacity to impart a sacred character to democratic values, to make them objects of faith that can resist all threats. By grounding a respect for human dignity in a force beyond human comprehension, like a transcendent God, the values rise above debate and are protected from the whims of public opinion or the challenges of competing philosophies. Only religion can provide a standard of judgment that transcends human authority (Bird 1990). In the United States, the major religious groups thus contribute to the preservation of a democratic order by making support for political liberty an article of faith.

But does this necessarily mean that religious groups should enter the political order? Can they contribute to the defense of democratic values without becoming embroiled in political activity and partisan debate? The advocates of a strong religious presence have answered these questions by pointing to the danger of a rigid separation between private conscience and public activity. When religious groups refrain from taking stands on controversial public issues, they may give the impression that religion speaks only to the concerns of private life. If religion is rigidly confined to the sphere of private morality, it has been argued, society runs the risk of enacting public policy without regard for moral consequences. It is important that religious claims enjoy a legitimate status in political debate, if only to guard against the danger of amoral government actions. This argument recalls the emphasis on the prophetic role of the churches, a familiar theme in the American civil religion discussed in chapter 3.

Religious groups thus perform the important task of reminding us that public decisions inescapably involve and reflect values. Without such reminders, political conservatives have warned us, society might be willing to sacrifice the aged and the ill in the name of "efficiency" or some other standard.[5] Liberals have relied just as much on transcendent values when they have demanded protection for the poor and oppressed, even at the cost of economic growth. The values operating in these examples—respect for life and compassion—will carry greater force in public consciousness when they are defended with the same resources as are competing secular values. The political activity of religious groups can thus be seen as necessary for the defense of moral judgment in public policymaking. Even in a society in which religious commitment is widespread, the churches have a duty to insist on its application to the problems of the day. Contentious though that might be, the alternative is even less satisfactory for the health of society.

In the modern world, Richard J. Neuhaus has argued, religion supplies a counterweight to the greatest threat faced by democracy—a slide into totalitarianism. In a passage worth quoting at length, Neuhaus (1984) summarized the importance of religion in keeping government under popular control:

> Once religion is reduced to nothing more than privatized conscience, the public square has only two actors in it—the state and the individual. Religion as a mediating structure—a community that generates and transmits moral values—is no longer available. Whether in Hitler's Third Reich or in today's sundry states professing Marxist-Leninism, the chief attack is not upon individual religious belief. Individual religious belief can be dismissed scornfully as superstition, for it finally poses little threat to the power of the state. No, the chief attack is upon the institutions that bear and promulgate belief in a transcendent reality by which the state can be called to judgment. Such institutions threaten the totalitarian proposition that everything is to be within the state, nothing is to be outside the state. (82)

If that analysis is correct, the church alone stands between the individual and the government, preventing the latter from swallowing up the former.

In truth, world history has supplied notable examples of religious values inspiring stubborn resistance to governments that demand complete obedience. Although the German churches as a group did not cover themselves with glory during the rise of Nazism, some of the most courageous resisters to Hitler were motivated by belief in divinely inspired values transcending the norms of national loyalty. In the 1980s, the Catholic Church preached on behalf of the autonomy of individuals against both leftist governments—as in Poland and Nicaragua—and right-wing regimes in countries such as El Salvador and the Philippines. Some progressive social movements mentioned previously in this book—sanctuary, the nuclear freeze, antidraft activity, refusal to pay taxes for military programs—seem to draw disproportionately from Catholics attuned to the message that emanated from the Second Vatican Council. In all such cases, religion can provide a sense of perspective that may prompt the individual to challenge the authority of the state. By forcefully reminding individuals that their behavior must conform to higher standards, a religious tradition can promote disobedience to the excessive demands of government or other authority figures.

Religious values may guard against totalitarian sympathies in yet another manner. One great source of evil behavior is certainty, the unshakable conviction that the individual possesses some higher truth. Armed with certainty about the "one true master race" or the "inevitable destiny" of Communism, human beings have committed some of the greatest crimes in history. Doubt is a potential antidote to such monstrousness because it activates the conscience. A person who is not wholly certain may question the rightness of a particular behavior—including his or her own actions.

Christianity in particular may engender doubt by its insistence on the fallenness of humankind. The doctrine of original sin teaches that humans are depraved and cannot be certain even of the righteousness of their own behavior. Sustained by this assumption, as we saw in chapter 3, the Founders devised a governmental system that would make it difficult for would-be tyrants to accumulate enough power to overwhelm democratic institutions. One who assumes that humans are imperfect may counsel against the type of utopianism that has occasionally disfigured the world. While doubt can lead to confusion and paralysis, it may also prompt a pause that enables people to rethink the possible consequences of a particular course of action. In that way, the doctrine of original sin may serve as a hedge against extremism (Niebuhr 1944).

Apart from its effects on democracy through values and institutions, religion may also promote democratic orientations in its communal incarnation. Robert Putnam (2000) has argued that religious communities are important incubators of social capital, the habits of mind that promote social trust and thus encourage collective action. This shows up in the tendency of religiously engaged people (more so than the less religious) to participate in community organizations, donate to charities of all kinds, and engage in a wide variety of civic enterprises (Putnam and Campbell 2010, chap. 13). This outcome is something of an accident because most religious traditions do not exist primarily for the purpose of encouraging their members to develop attitudes that promote social action. Nonetheless, because individuals who are deeply attached to communities of any kind generally prove more resistant to recruitment by political causes that threaten human rights (Kornhauser 1959), churches contribute significantly to the stock of "social capital" in American society. Taking their lead from Putnam, other scholars have examined in great detail how democratic norms and values may be generated in a religious context (Smidt 2003).

The foregoing argument provides the strongest case for an active religious presence in all aspects of society, including the political arena. Like the case against religious activism in politics, it is best treated as a hypothesis. Note that we described religion's impact on democracy in terms that emphasized potential—can, may, might, and could. Those conditional verbs were used because they convey the conditional impact of religion. According to one eminent historian (Muller 1963), the record of religion with regard to human freedom is remarkably mixed. As we have just pointed out, religious values have in some instances supported the spirit and practice of democratic government. Yet the concept of democracy arose with the Greeks, well before the beginning of the Judeo-Christian era, and the church has often been a bulwark of resistance to the spread of democratic values. In a conclusion that dramatically calls attention to the coexistence of democratic and antidemocratic impulses in Western religion, Muller states that "Christianity did more to promote the growth of freedom than did any other of the higher religions . . . while it also opposed freedom of thought, speech, and conscience more fiercely than did any other religion except Mohammedanism" (3).

If religion is to fulfill its promise as a bulwark against tyranny, it must encourage its followers to resist rulers who demand actions that are inconsistent with religious values. The evidence on that point does not suggest that religious commitment necessarily works that way. The ambivalent relationship between religion and support for constituted authority was revealed in a disturbing study conducted by two psychologists (Bock and Warren 1972). They built on the famous experiments devised by another psychologist, Stanley Milgram (1974), who put laboratory subjects in a situation in which an authority figure encouraged them to help with an experiment that involved inflicting pain on other subjects. Specifically, the participants were ordered to administer what they thought were electrical shocks to fellow subjects who had been unsuccessful in what was portrayed as a learning experiment. Milgram's finding that most persons obeyed the commands—even in the face of loud protests from the purported victim of the shocks—raised fundamental questions about which human qualities accounted for refusal to go along with destructive behavior.

The scenario devised by Milgram seemed an excellent opportunity to investigate one issue not carefully considered in his original experiments, the role of religious values in producing compliance or resistance. The psychologists thus recruited thirty college students, measured their religious values and commitment, and then put them through what amounted to a facsimile of the original Milgram experiments. In findings that will recall the studies of prejudice described earlier in the chapter, Bock and Warren (1972) discovered a strong but nonlinear relationship between religious commitment and willingness to inflict pain on others. Those with low or high levels of attachment to religion were substantially more likely than persons of moderate attachment to resist the instructions to administer shocks. To explain this finding, the investigators suggested that the nature of religious commitment—rather than its amount—was a critical factor in the subjects' decision to comply or refuse:

> In the Judeo-Christian tradition, a high value is placed on a strong, well-defined response to "the will of God." In fact, a decisive response even if negative is to be preferred over neutrality. The biblical position is that the man who is undecided about basic religious issues is unable to be decisive when confronted by an ethical dilemma. His tendency is to forfeit his choice to any impinging power. On the other hand, having taken a definite religious stance, one is in a position to act in accord with conscience. (190)

Bushman et al. (2007) also used an experiment to explore the possibility that religion encourages divinely sanctioned violence. College students in the United States and Holland read a violent biblical passage. Half were told the true source of the passage (the Bible), and half read a version indicating that God called for retribution against the sinners. Students were then asked to complete a competitive reaction time test in which the winner could direct bursts of loud noise against the loser, a common laboratory measure of aggression. Students who were told that the passage was biblical and those who had read that God punished the sinners were in fact more aggressive on the laboratory task. The effect was stronger yet among participants who believed in God and the Bible.

If the findings of these studies can be assumed to hold for the general population in real-world settings—an untested assumption—then they should diminish our confidence that religious commitment will automatically inspire resistance to tyranny or discourage violence. Once again, it depends on the quality of religious commitment that brings people into the public sphere. People who appear to have internalized the ethical principles of religion—along with those who have minimal contact with religious institutions—will probably prove most likely to resist orders that conflict with widely accepted ethical principles. Based on the limited experimental data, those with moderate religious commitment do not seem endowed with a tendency to challenge rulers who demand that citizens abdicate conscience.

According to various attitude surveys, the disposition to challenge authority appears quite weak among the white fundamentalist Protestants who have greatly increased their political involvement since the 1980s (Altemeyer 1988; Altemeyer and Hunsberger 1992). There seems to be little room for open political debate within the Christian Right. When two pioneers of the movement wrote a book about misplaced faith in politics as an agent of moral regeneration, they found themselves under incredible attack from their erstwhile allies. They reported pressure on the publisher not to print or distribute the book, campaigns to encourage bookstores to boycott it, and a smear campaign by televangelists to systematically misrepresent the arguments. Sadly, they concluded, "many of those who most need to hear this message are the least interested in listening" (Thomas and Dobson 1999, 7). When another well-placed Christian Right pioneer broke ranks by endorsing the presidential candidacy of John McCain early in 2000, offering a principled justification, he, too, was ostracized by the very people with whom he had long labored (Rosin and Milbank 2000).

This authoritarian tendency may offset the capacity of religious communities to generate the kind of democratic attitudes and dispositions that Putnam (2000) links to social capital. While he portrays social capital as a potential positive influence on democratic orientations, Putnam recognizes that this syndrome can encourage group members to look outward to the community (bridging) or inward to themselves (bonding). Only the former may encourage political activity and promote respect for democratic norms, while the latter might well promote insulation from the world and permit the kind of horrors associated with what critics denounce as religious cults (Gismondi 2005; Festinger 1956).

The veneration for authority said to characterize Protestant fundamentalism (Wald, Owen, and Hill 1989) seems to pervade many of the institutions that compose the subculture. Thus, the dynamic evangelical churches that have provided leadership for the Christian Right conform to fairly rigid and hierarchical authority patterns that give members very little experience of democratic decision-making (Fitzgerald 1981). The textbooks used in some Christian schools are lukewarm in their support of democracy and respect for people outside the faith tradition (Menendez 1993), although it is not clear that these traits translate into less respect for democratic norms (Godwin, Godwin, and Martinez-Ebers 2004). The law school founded and led by Pat Robertson has been sued by students and faculty alleging a lack of academic freedom (Myers 1994). At the Christian university he founded, the Rev. Jerry Falwell provided a code of conduct that that forbade students at Liberty University from participating in unauthorized demonstrations, obliged them to attend church, and potentially expelled them for mounting petition drives not approved by university authorities. Students were asked to waive a number of rights guaranteed under the Constitution, including protection against warrantless searches of their rooms (Baker 1985). Similarly, the law schools at both universities express what Hanson (2009, 286) calls an "absolutist" ethos that calls for "a pervasive theocracy consisting of a wholly God-centered society, encompassing both church and state."

These rules may reflect a generalized emphasis on obedience in the worldview of fundamentalist Protestantism (Ellison and Sherkat 1993; Danso, Hunsberger, and Pratt 1997; Starks and Robinson 2005). Again, we cannot know for certain whether these practices are widespread in evangelical Protestantism or common among all types of religions; nor is it guaranteed that adherents of such churches draw lessons about governance from religious institutions or that such lessons would carry over to the behavior of church members in other settings. Nonetheless, these tendencies should dissuade observers from asserting too confidently that religious commitment in politics necessarily acts as a brake on totalitarian tendencies.

What, then, can we finally conclude about the impact of religion on democracy in the contemporary situation? There is little alternative but to conclude that religion may sometimes sustain democratic values and sometimes undermine them. The source of the paradox is simply that religious values are ambiguous with regard to politics. They contain messages that can lead persons of common faith in different directions. The multiple political uses of religious ideas have been demonstrated repeatedly throughout history. In the period leading up to the Civil War, Northerners and Southerners alike found ample justification for slavery and abolition in the same religious document. During the Prohibition Era in the 1920s to 1930s, learned clergymen argued earnestly about the message of the scriptures with regard to intoxicating beverages. The problem arises today even in the unlikely context of environmental policy, a subject of conflicting biblical images. Just as some interpret God's intention that people have dominion "over all the earth" (Gen. 1:26) as license to exploit the environment in the interests of human happiness, others cite the twenty-fourth psalm, "The Earth is the Lord's," to promote reverence for the natural environment and to support a preservationist ethic. The problem is no less vexing at the general level of democracy. Jesus's call in Matthew 22:21 to "render therefore unto Caesar the things which are Caesar's; and unto God the things that are God's" does not define precisely what it is that humanity owes to state and to church. Depending on how responsibility is allocated between God and Caesar, that biblical injunction may be interpreted as a call to revolution or, at the other extreme, as a plea for servility.

The problem of limited guidance even extends to such fundamental questions as the best form of human government. The doctrine of original sin is interpreted by some theologians as a call to caution, an injunction against committing evil in the name of higher values. As such, it may promote a belief in the wisdom of limited government. Yet it has also been used as an argument against the human capacity for self-government. If mortals are prone to greed, jealousy, rapaciousness, envy, pride, and other expressions of sinfulness, then they are simply not worthy of basic rights or opportunities to exercise their free will in politics. Even today, people of faith continue to argue whether the Bible is capitalistic or socialistic, supportive of abortion or not, militaristic or pacifistic. The most careful students of religious thought simply cannot agree on the precise relevance of Christian doctrine to specific issues or whether Christianity is inherently conducive to democracy or dictatorship (Wolin 1956). The obstacle is not deficient understanding but the mixed political messages contained in the major religious creeds.

Given the ambiguity of religious texts and teachings, the mixed historical record, and the empirical evidence cited earlier in the chapter, it would be foolhardy to assert that religious faith necessarily upholds democratic values. In some contexts and for some types of people, it may enhance freedom. Or it may encourage particular types of freedom while enforcing conformity in other realms of human endeavor. It seems to matter less whether people are religious than how they hold their religious values and attempt to apply them in concrete situations. An upsurge in religiously based political activity is to be neither welcomed uncritically nor condemned out of hand.

The richness and complexity of religious thought should also moderate how individuals carry their religious faith into the public square. When it is difficult to discern with confidence what a religious tradition actually says about a moral issue—and the very brevity, intricacy, and abstractness of religious creeds often make it so—individuals should be reluctant to assert with confidence that they and they alone possess unique insight. But even if the individual can be confident about the relevant moral judgment, it is still a large step from philosophical principle to public policy. As Kent Greenawalt (1994, 155) reminds us, "There is a difference between telling people that an active homosexual life is sinful and telling them that they should support criminal sanctions for that behavior."

RELIGION IN PUBLIC CONVERSATION

If we are unsure what religion may contribute substantively to political life, there is equally vibrant disagreement over the value of religious language and arguments in political debate (Carter 1993; Riordan 2004). From a legal perspective, of course, people in democracies have the right to say pretty much whatever they like in whatever language they may choose. But not every statement about public policy is taken seriously or treated equally. In a democratic state where religion is a private matter under the law, what status should be accorded to claims based on religious faith? The question is important because the goal of politics in a democracy is control over public policy—the decisions of government—through persuasion rather than coercion. Because the decisions made by governments are both public (they affect all of us) and authoritative (enforced by the power of the state), it is important that justifications for them "be located in a shared set of premises or assumptions" (Jelen 1997a, 251). Otherwise, the policies will lack any semblance of legitimacy.

To ensure a search for common ground in our debates, theorists have offered several standards to judge the persuasive value of statements made in service of policy goals. The key criterion is accessibility. For debate to be fruitful, we need to utilize language that enables us to converse with one another rather than talk past one another. Intelligent conversation is impossible if the concepts used by one speaker are unintelligible to the other. That is why religiously based statements are troubling. A claim that a certain public policy should be adopted because God supported it as revealed in the Bible will only have a chance of persuading people who accept the authority of God as revealed in the Bible. The same is true for appeals to church teaching, tradition, religious leaders, and personal revelation (e.g., "God told me so"). Offering a policy because it emanates from a divine authority—particularly in the form of a personal message from God—ends the debate because the person making the claim cannot be challenged or persuaded that he or she is wrong. The person making such a claim will dismiss an opponent as inherently wrong by a standard that the other person does not accept. If successful in implementing what he or she considers a divine mandate, the religious advocate will have imposed a policy that derives from a particular religious perspective. Those outside the perspective may not consider the policy legitimate.

Hence, many scholars argue, religious claims need to be "translated" into a language accessible to people from outside any single faith tradition. That way, it is claimed, we can argue about the wisdom of particular policies in language that we both understand. We may well disagree about who has the more persuasive evidence, but that is a more productive and satisfying debate than rejecting the other person out of hand. The best example of such translation was the civil rights rhetoric of Martin Luther King Jr. Although steeped in Christianity, based in the church, and a master of using religious metaphors to mobilize his flock, King's public appeal for equality tapped into core American values—what Thomas Jefferson called self-evident truths—that were familiar to all Americans, religious or not. To some critics, this preference for "secular" language amounts to forcing religious people to deny who they are, to "bracket" their religious convictions from their public language and argument (S. D. Smith 2010). That may be the price for political coexistence in a nation so religiously and morally pluralistic.

Some evidence indicates that religious groups do in fact utilize secular arguments in public debate. When testifying before Wisconsin legislative committees about capital punishment and welfare reform, advocates from faith-based organizations employed nonreligious arguments to justify their recommended policies roughly three-fifths of the time (Yamane 2000). Rather than argue from scripture, church tradition, or religious leaders, they appealed to law and morality, science, legal authority, or socioeconomic analysis. The pattern was not uniform, as groups wholly based in a single religious denomination were more likely to use religious justifications than representatives from organizations that spanned several religious traditions. Among the denominational groups, conservative religious traditions used religious language in every single justification they offered. While there is thus some reason to think that religious groups may try to reach out with arguments that are accessible to people outside their tradition, the habit is not yet fully developed.

As we noted in chapter 8, the Christian Right organizations that emerged in the second wave did often attempt to appeal to the mainstream by couching their policy proposals in broad, accessible language. Yet even as they projected an inclusive faith when speaking in public, as Nathan Klemp (2012) has documented, they continued to convey harsh and explicitly sectarian messages when communicating privately to their base of evangelical Protestants. This often entailed demonizing their opponents and using methods of mobilization that betray a fundamental lack of respect for organizations with opposing views. Focus on the Family, which emerged as one of the most influential Christian Right organizations in the 1990s, often uses a technique known as "info-blasting," in which it tries to overwhelm opposing organizations with a flood of e-mails, letters, phone messages, and other persuasive communication. This entails a cost to the targeted organization in terms of the time and energy it must devote to this information flood, but also a psychological cost in that some supporters, egged on by the extreme claims made by Focus via its internal communication, make direct threats to the safety of the recipients of an info blast. These are not the tools of democratic deliberation.

Science cannot establish whether religious claims are true or false. But science, especially social science, can attempt to discover the consequences of religious values, institutions, and communities for the political system. This book has attempted to describe how religion interacts with the political system in one country. Because of the limitations of previous research and the inherent tentativeness of science, we have emphasized the provisional status of our conclusions. More and better research might clarify the patterns of religious influence in politics and might even provide a basis on which to offer confident predictions about the future of the relationship between the two domains. The impact of religion on American political life is surely important enough to warrant the effort.

Notes

CHAPTER 1

* Ronald Reagan's quotation is taken from page 9 of his article "Religion and Politics Are Necessarily Related," which appeared in *Church and State* 37 (October 1984): 9–11.

1. C. Welton Gaddy, "Public Expressions of Religion Related to Public Policy and Elections," address to the Anti-Defamation League's National Executive Committee Meeting, February 8, 2008, Palm Beach, FL, www.adl.org/religious_freedom/speech_welton_gaddy.asp.

2. While Mitt Romney was definitely a member of the Church of Jesus Christ of Latter-Day Saints, President Obama was not a Muslim.

3. Family Research Council, "Pastor Giglio Disinvitation Signals Inauguration of a New Era of Religious Intolerance," January 10, 2013, available at www.frc .org/newsroom/the-inauguration-of-a-new-era-of-religious-intolerance.

4. Elizabeth Tenety, "State Department Seeks to Broaden Religious Reach," *Washington Post,* July 26, 2013, articles.washingtonpost.com/2013-07-26/national/ 40862875_1_religion-part-international-religious-freedom-state-department.

5. Fareed Zacaria, "And He's Head of Intelligence?" *Newsweek,* October 26, 2003, www.newsweek.com/and-hes-head-intelligence-139059.

6. In slighting religion, political science resembles public education (Shriver 1988), psychology (Lehr and Spilka 1989), history (Butler 2004), social theory (Stark 2000), and television (Skill, Robinson, Lyons, and Larson 1994). Ironically, although they are often criticized as the product of a godless Hollywood film industry, secular movies often convey religious messages or themes (Bergesen and Greely 2003).

7. In *Habits of the Heart*, Robert Bellah and his coauthors (1985) demonstrate how the language of contract and the philosophy of individualism have robbed many Americans of the capacity to offer moral justification for even their most intimate ties to other family members.

8. The religious data were obtained from the Pew Global Attitudes Project from 2008 to 2012. These data are available at www.pewglobal.org/category/datasets/. The 2010 per capita GNI was obtained from the World Bank (2012, 392–93) and is available at http://go.worldbank.org/0BP8VT4OE0.

9. For similar findings using other data, see the important work by Norris and Inglehart (2004). They argue that religious sentiments are most likely to develop among people who encounter threats to their security and well-being. Hence, the link between religion and economic development is due to the lower levels of economic and political security in poorer countries. The United States is exceptional, they speculate, because it is the most unequal of the highly developed societies with substantial poverty and insecurity amid affluence.

10. Gallup News Service, "Final Topline," June 9–12, 2011, p. 7, available at www.gallup.com/poll/148178/confidence-institutions-pdf.aspx.

11. "Honesty/Ethics in Professions," November 26–29, 2012, available at www.gallup.com/poll/1654/honesty-ethics-professions.aspx#1.

12. The statistics on Catholic Charities USA are available at www.forbes.com/companies/catholic-charities-usa/.

13. "Mystical Experiences Abound in Culture That Spurns Them, Studies Say," *Tallahassee Democrat*, February 14, 1987, 1-D.

14. For a fascinating account of how religious values may fill a void where science appears to fail, see the *Manchester Guardian* story on a British hospice ("In the Midst of Death We Are in Life," March 4, 1984, 4). It reports, "Religion plays a central part in the life of St. Christopher's. It is not compulsory, nor is it thrust upon patients. 'But I don't think anyone could work here for long without the support of some faith,' she [the founder] says firmly. The pressure and intensity of the work, the great demands of the dying and their relatives means that those who work there need answers, or at least partial answers, in order to sustain themselves."

15. While there is evidence of a growing relationship between religious commitment and (Republican) party choice in American elections (Putnam and Campbell 2010, 374), that relationship should not be overstated. First, two of the most religious groups in the United States, African Americans and Hispanic Catholics, are also two of the most reliably Democratic in electoral behavior. Second, knowing that Americans overstate their degree of religious activity—particularly attendance at worship—many of those who claim to be highly committed may not be. While the United States may be moving toward what is sometimes called a European model, in which secular voters prefer liberal parties and religious voters favor conservatives, the distance between the United States and Europe is still quite marked.

CHAPTER 2

1. For an excellent example of popular as opposed to official Islam, see Aslan's (2005) story of his Iranian family.

2. By focusing on those aspects of religion that are apparent in the form of beliefs, subcultures, and institutions, we have tried to sidestep the perennial debate between substantive and functional definitions of religion. As such, we accept the useful definition of religion as "actions, beliefs, and institutions predicated upon the assumption of the existence of either supernatural entities with powers of agency or impersonal powers or processes possessed of moral purpose, which have the capacity to set the conditions of, or to intervene in, human affairs" (Wallis and Bruce 1992, 10–11).

3. The American National Election Study, a biennial survey of the public, recognizes 135 different denominations (including atheist) in response to its question about religious affiliation.

4. Even though most Americans belong to denominations by virtue of affiliating with a specific congregation, many reject the legitimacy of the word itself and others don't find the denominational label (or even family terms like "Protestant") very meaningful. For example, some Christians dislike giving a denominational identification when asked for it because they think the term suggests there are different ways of being a legitimate Christian when they believe, to the contrary, in only one way to achieve true Christianity. Ironically, many efforts to purify Christianity by defining the essentials of the faith became, in time, particular forms of Christianity, which are called—you guessed it—denominations. The low salience of the term is apparent among American Jews who, when given a choice of denominational labels, generally favor a "just Jewish" label even if most congregations identify with one of several competing denominations available to them.

5. For other recent estimates of the population by religious tradition, see Kosmin and Keysar (2009), Pew Forum (2008), and Baylor Religion Survey (2006). While some of the differences between the estimates from the NES and these other surveys are due to random sampling and the size difference in the samples, much of the variation is a function of different ways of categorizing religious groups.

6. The distinctions between the three categories of Protestants largely followed the procedure outlined by Steensland et al. (2000). A sizable number of Protestants do not identify their denomination clearly and thus may be part of either the mainline or evangelical wing. In this study, Protestants who described themselves as born-again Christians were assigned to the evangelical group, and those who did not accept the label were classified as mainline. For extended general discussion of problems of religious measurement, see the excellent essays by Roof (1979) and J. Wilson (1978, appendix). In practice, apportioning individuals into categories based on religious denomination yields quite different results from classifications based on religious beliefs or orientations (Wald and Smidt 1993). For that reason, it is quite hazardous to compare the results of studies using different types of classification strategies.

7. In 1918, a mainline minister succinctly explained his perspective while taking a swipe at evangelicalism: "The best mark of a 'saved' man is not that he wants to go to heaven, but that he is willing to go to China, or to the battle-field in France, or to the slums of the city, or to the last dollars of his resources, or to the limit of his energy, to set forward the Kingdom of God" (quoted in Gamble 2003, 206).

8. The ANES asks persons who describe themselves as "independent" whether they feel closer to one or other major party. Because of evidence that such "independent leaners" often behave more like partisans than independents who lean toward neither party (Keith et al. 1992), the leaners have been assigned to the partisan group to which they feel closer.

CHAPTER 3

* The chapter epigraph quoting Robert Swierenga is taken from his chapter, "Ethnoreligious Political Behavior in the Mid-Nineteenth Century: Voting, Values, Culture," in *Religion and American Politics*, ed. Mark Noll (New York: Oxford University Press, 1990), 154.

1. The development of contract thought among the colonists has traditionally been credited to the "secular" influence of English philosopher John Locke. But as Winthrop Hudson (1965) argued, Locke drew on the ideas of the Puritans to formulate the doctrine of government by consent of the governed.

2. According to Robert Woodberry (2012, 244), the effect was not limited to the United States. Protestant missionaries sent by American churches to "harvest souls" throughout the world during the early twentieth century were "a crucial catalyst initiating the development and spread of religious liberty, mass education, mass printing, newspapers, voluntary organizations, and colonial reforms, thereby creating the conditions that made stable democracy more likely."

3. In a review of the civil religion concept, Richey and Jones (1974, 14–18) identify five overlapping uses of the term. We have adopted the definition of civil religion as a sense of national transcendence because that is the manner in which the "chosen people" metaphor has entered the political culture.

4. The degree to which this type of civil religion is the unique property of American culture or a more universal phenomenon has yet to be fully addressed. Michael Walzer (1985) has found the Exodus metaphor throughout political history. For some suggestive thoughts on civil religion in comparative perspective, see Coleman (1970) and Bellah and Hammond (1980, chaps. 2–4).

5. The exceptions include Thomas and Flippen (1972), who found few references to any divine plan for the United States in newspaper editorials published during "Honor America" week. In interviews that Benson and Williams (1982) conducted with members of the U.S. Congress, most legislators proved unwilling to endorse statements that interpreted the nation's destiny in transcendent terms.

6. "A Candidate's Morals Matter, and Lying Is the Cardinal Sin," *Atlanta Journal and Constitution*, January 31, 1988.

7. In a similar vein, Fatima Mernissi (1992, 102) reported Arab outrage at President George H. W. Bush's frequent use of religious language during the Gulf War. Invoking God on behalf of American troops created the impression "that the satellites themselves were the objects of spiritual machinations," and that liberating Kuwait from Iraq was merely a pretext to cloak "a religious war, a global conspiracy to destroy Islam and win victory for another religion, the religion of arrogant, capitalist America." Language intended to reassure Americans of the moral worth of a military campaign may inspire quite the opposite reaction among others.

8. There has been growing interest in religious influences on American foreign policy. For a comprehensive overview, see Preston (2012) and Inboden (2008).

9. The detailed differences among religious traditions are reported at Christopher Chapp, "Religious Rhetoric and American Politics: The Endurance of Civil Religion in Electoral Campaigns," retrieved September 6, 2013, from http://blogs .uww.edu/chappc/files/2012/06/appendix_ch61.pdf.

10. Because the Christianity of the Protestant Reformation was skeptical about the capacity for human regeneration and emphasized revelation as the key to understanding, it may be tempting to portray religion and rationalist thought as incompatible. In practice, the two traditions at times found common ground and at times competed for influence—often within the mind of the same individual.

11. Noll, Hatch, and Marsden (1983) make a strong case that a "Christian culture" is generally unlikely and that colonial America was a considerable distance away from a scripturally based commonwealth. They also raise doubts that the Christian influence in early America was uniformly positive.

CHAPTER 4

* Alexander Solzhenitsyn's quotation in the chapter epigraph is taken from "As Breathing and Consciousness Return," in Michael Scammell, compiler, *From under the Rubble* (Boston: Little Brown, 1975), 24–25. James Madison's quotation in the chapter epigraph is taken from Norman Cousins, ed., *In God We Trust: The Religious Beliefs and Ideas of the American Founders* (New York: Harper, 1958), 324.

1. These words, spoken on April 6, 1994, during a floor debate in the Florida House of Representatives, were supplied by Rep. Steven A. Geller.

2. The 2008 "State of the First Amendment Survey" by the First Amendment Center indicated that a large majority of Americans believe that the Founders intended the United States to be a Christian nation and that the Constitution was intended to establish such a state (First Amendment Center 2008). For an interesting assessment of this claim, see Heclo (2007).

3. The "wall of separation" phrase, first used by Roger Williams, is from Jefferson's 1802 letter to a congregation of Connecticut Baptists. Neither this phrase nor "church and state" appears in the Constitution, persuading some critics that the Supreme Court has read something alien into the national charter. Of course, these same critics have no trouble describing the Constitution as a document based on God and religious values even though there is no mention of God or religious heritage in the document. If Jefferson's words do not appear, it is arguable nonetheless that the sentiment does.

4. See Paul Edward Parker, "Judge Sends Corneaus Back to Jail for Not Cooperating," *Providence Journal*, February 15, 2002. For background on the organization, see Farah Stockman and Mac Daniel, "The Sect," *Boston Globe*, November 26, 2000.

5. Associated Press, "Court Upholds Ruling against Attleboro Sect," *Providence Journal Bulletin*, November 22, 2002, B-03.

6. Jeremy Leaning, "N.J. School Sued after Barring Student from Handing Out Religious Gifts," *Freedom Forum* Online, May 18, 2000, downloaded from www .freedomforum.org on February 20, 2002.

7. The full text of the Supreme Court decisions referred to in this chapter can be found in either the *United States Reports* or the privately published *Digest of U.S. Supreme Court Reports*. The major decisions are compiled and updated periodically in the casebook edited by Miller and Flowers (1996). For an inexpensive edited collection of decisions, consult Eastland (1993). Flowers (2005) has written the single most useful overview for general readers, although critics of the separationist orientation might prefer Adams and Emmerich (1990). The quarterly *Journal of Church and State* publishes a valuable preview of court cases as well as the full decisions in important cases.

8. When the question about heritage vs. separation was asked again in 2012 (Kaiser Family Foundation/Washington Post), 40 percent opted to protect religious heritage, 55 percent to support the wall of separation, and 4 percent were undecided or volunteered neither.

9. Craig Timberg, "Bible's Second Coming," *Washington Post*, June 4, 2000, 1A.

10. A similar set of guidelines for federal workers was issued in 1997 (White House Office of the Press Secretary 1997).

11. That bias against minority religions was also evident in a Pew Center (Pew Forum on Religion and Public Life 2001, 13) poll about attitudes toward "faith-based" social services. While roughly three-fifths of adults support giving government funds to Catholic, Protestant, and Jewish organizations, support dropped by more than half when Muslims, Buddhists, and Scientologists are made eligible for participation.

12. Nonetheless, as Robbins (2001) reminds us, constitutional law still provides such religions with much more freedom and protection in the United States than in Western Europe.

13. For a spirited defense of Smith, see Hamilton (2005).

14. On the extent of noncompliance, see "Prayer in Many Schoolrooms Continues Despite '62 Ruling," *New York Times*, March 11, 1984. For a more recent case in which federal courts have stopped school district practices, consult Peter Applebome, "Court Restricts Religious Activity at Mississippi School," *New York Times*, June 4, 1996.

15. Neil A. Lewish, "Justice Department Reshapes Its Civil Rights Mission," *New York Times*, June 14, 2007; Diane Henriques and Andrew W. Lehren, "Religious Groups Reap Federal Aid for Pet Projects," *New York Times*, May 13, 2007.

16. In 1995, the Salt Lake City school board banned all extracurricular student organizations solely to prevent the formation of a gay-lesbian alliance at a local high school. There is no doubt that the board majority was motivated by the anti-gay attitudes of the Mormon church in Utah, yet the decision would also prevent Mormon students from exercising their religious rights while at school. A federal court overturned the ban in 2001, citing the Equal Access Act, which, ironically, was passed as an alternative to the school prayers struck down in the 1960s.

17. There is a parallel case already in the federal courts regarding claims by pharmacists who are licensed by the state that they cannot be required to prescribe certain medications—the "morning after" pill in particular—if they have religious objections to it.

CHAPTER 5

1. For a video clip of this exchange, please see http://nation.foxnews.com/democratic-national-platform/2012/09/05/durbin-dodges-questions-no-god-jerusalem-democratic-party-platform (accessed April 2013).

2. Quote by Ed Stetzer, vice president of research and ministry development for Lifeway Christian Resources. Quoted in *Washington Post*, November 12, 2012.

3. Thomas McKenny, "Hallelujah! Election Did Answer Prayers," letter to the Editor, *JD News*, November 8, 2012, http://www.jdnews.com/opinion/letters/hallelujah-election-did-answer-prayers-1.46604.

4. Research conducted by Pew Forum for Religion and Public Life, "Americans Wary of Church Involvement in Partisan Politics," October 1, 2008.

5. Jesse McKinley and Kirk Johnson, "Mormons Tipped Scale in Ban on Gay Marriage," *New York Times*, November 14, 2008.

6. For more information on the educational attainment of evangelicals, see Beyerlein (2004) and Sherkat and Darnell (1999). It should be emphasized that we are reporting group averages and that many individuals acquire more or less education than is typical of their religious group as a whole. Moreover, there are striking differences among the denominations that compose our broad religious traditions. We know from other studies that some of the very small groups that we discarded from the analysis for lack of cases have some of the most impressive educational credentials (Kosmin and Lachman 1993).

7. Weber's thesis about the relationship between Protestantism and capitalism has also been criticized and rejected by many because of its faulty time order. Economic historians have demonstrated that capitalism abounded in Europe long before the Reformation. For a good critique, see Stark (2004).

8. Huma Khan, "Religion Powerful Force in 2012 Race," ABC News, December 6, 2011, http://abcnews.go.com/blogs/politics/2011/12/religion-powerful-force-in-2012-elections/ (accessed April 2013).

9. Based on exit polls done by the Voter News Service and National Election Pools. Reported in Pew Research Center for Religion and Public Life, "How the Faithful Voted: 2012 Preliminary Analysis," November 7, 2012.

10. For an excellent discussion of cultural politics and the American party system, see Leege et al. (2002).

11. Report by the Pew Research Center for Religion and Public Life, *Lobbying the Faithful*, May 15, 2012.

12. "Catholic Bishops Hire Firm to Market Abortion Attack," *New York Times*, April 6, 1990, 10A.

13. See the Joint Religious Legislative Coalition's website at www.jrlc.org/jrlc/background/ for details about the organization's membership and policy positions.

CHAPTER 6

1. Barbara Bradley Hagerty, "For Religious Conservatives, Election was a Disaster," National Public Radio, November 8, 2012.

2. Quote by Ed Stetzer, vice president of research and ministry development for Lifeway Christian Resources. Quoted in *Washington Post*, November 12, 2012.

3. Video clip of this speech is available at http://mysticpolitics.com/video-ralph-reed-and-the-resurrection-of-the-religious-right (accessed June 2013).

4. To view maps of estimated size of religious group by state, see http://religions.pewforum.org/maps.

5. For a map that details where gay marriage is legal, see Human Rights Campaign: local section, available at www.hrc.org/files/assets/resources/US_Marriage_Prohibition2013.pdf (accessed May 2013).

6. These forms of direct democracy are themselves ideologically neutral. They were first used by Progressives to bypass legislatures in order to implement liberal social reforms such as welfare, old-age pensions, and women's suffrage. Today, however, they are favored by conservatives as a way to slash taxes, prevent antidiscrimination measures for homosexuals, and restrict abortion rights through provisions such as parental notification.

7. Chris Cillizza and Sean Sullivan, "How Proposition 8 Passed in California," *Washington Post*, March 26, 2012.

8. Erik Schelzig, "Sister Megan Rice, 83-Year-Old Nun, Convicted after Nuclear Protest," *Christian Science Monitor*, May 10, 2013.

9. "Defense Fund Set Up for Bombing Suspects," *Gainesville Sun*, March 19, 1985, 11A.

10. Jay Tolson, "How Deep the Divide?" *U.S. News & World Report*, October 24, 2004, 42–50.

11. Mitchell Landsberg, "Obama Praised—and Pummeled—on Matters of Faith," *Los Angeles Times*, April 7, 2012.

12. Full text of Obama's 2006 speech to Sojourners available at www.sojo.net/index.cfm?action=magazine.article&issue=soj0611&article=061110 (accessed January 2010).

13. Pew Research Center, "A Look at Religious Votes in the 2008 Election," February 10, 2009, www.pewtrusts.org/news_room_detail.aspx?id=48870.

14. Obama described these experiences in his books *The Audacity of Hope* and *Dreams of My Father*.

15. Full text of the interview at the Saddleback church available at http://transcripts.cnn.com/TRANSCRIPTS/0808/17/se.01.html (accessed December 2009).

16. Lisa Miller and Richard Wolfe, "Finding His Faith," *Newsweek*, July 12, 2008.

17. The data come from a *USA Today*/CNN/Gallup Poll in September 2003 as reported by Kathy Kiely, "Partial Birth Abortion Ban Nearly Law after an 8 Year Effort," *USA Today*, October 22, 2003, 1A.

18. *Gonzales v. Carhart* (US 124 2007).

19. *Tammy Kitzmiller et al. v. Dover Area School District et al.* 400 F. Supp. 2d 707, Docket no. 4cv2688 (2005).

20. For a list of groups that filed briefs, see www.faithfulreform.org/storage/frhc/AmicusBrief/signers.pdf.

21. Statement of the National Council of Churches quoted in Mark Tooley, "Religiously Celebrating Obamacare," *American Spectator*, June 29, 2012.

22. Quote by Stephanie Gut, the lead organizer of the faith-based community organization the San Diego Organizing Project, in a brochure by Mark Warren

for Interfaith Funders, "Faith Based Community Organizing and the Renewal of Congregations," November 2003, www.unm.edu/percent7Ereligion/new/GoodforSoul.pdf.

23. Jim Zarroli, "Low Cost Brooklyn Housing Sees Few Foreclosures," www.npr.org/templates/story/story.php?storyID=113931948 (accessed December 2009).

24. Robert Tuttle, "Taking Stock: The Bush Faith Based Initiative and What Lies Ahead," available at www.religionandsocialpolicy.org/final_report (accessed December 2009).

25. Laura Goodstein, "Church Based Projects Lack Data on Results," *New York Times*, April 24, 2001.

26. For those Christians who were not moved by either appeal, it might not have escaped notice that the probable alternative to a Jewish state was increased migration of Jewish refugees to the United States.

CHAPTER 7

1. A video transcript of the Buchanan speech is available at http://www.youtube.com/watch?v=W9gSWZxtN1g (accessed May 2013).

2. Bill O'Reilly, *Culture Warrior* (New York: Broadway Books, 2006), 1–2.

3. The data from this chapter are taken from the 2008 American National Election Study. This study is part of the American National Election Study (ANES), a time-series collection of national surveys fielded continuously since 1952. The American National Election Studies are designed to present data on Americans' social backgrounds, enduring political predispositions, social and political values, perceptions and evaluations of groups and candidates, opinions on questions of public policy, and participation in political life. Information presented in the chapter for Jews, Latter-Day Saints, and Hispanic Protestants represents data pooled from 2000, 2004, and 2008 ANES unless the question was not available in each of the years. The cumulative percentages are better indicators of public opinions. The small number of respondents in these traditions in any individual study year may not be representative of members of that tradition. ANES data are available at www.electionstudies.org.

4. Respondents were coded as supportive of equal rights if they were a 1, 2, or 3 on the seven-point scale.

5. The response categories for the abortion questions were (a) "By law, abortion should never be permitted"; (b) "The law should permit abortion only in case of rape, incest, or when the woman's life is in danger"; (c) "The law should permit abortion for reasons other than rape, incest, or danger to the woman's life, but only after the need for the abortion has been clearly established"; and (d) "By law, a woman should always be able to obtain an abortion as a matter of personal choice."

6. In the 2004 National Election Poll large majorities of evangelical Protestants, Latter-Day Saints, black Protestants, and Hispanic Protestants opposed any legal recognition of marriage. National Election Poll data is available at www.icpsr.umich.edu.

7. The ANES question asked respondents whether they strongly agree, agree, neither agree nor disagree, disagree, or strongly disagree that U.S. society should do whatever is necessary to make sure that everyone has an equal opportunity to succeed. A respondent was coded as supporting equal rights if he or she agreed or strongly agreed.

8. The ANES question asked respondents whether they strongly agree, agree, neither agree nor disagree, disagree, or strongly disagree that "this country would be better off if we worried less about how equal people are." Respondents were coded as believing the country would be better off if we worried less about equality if they agreed or strongly agreed with this statement.

9. No questions about affirmative action were included in the 2008 ANES. Cumulative data from earlier studies indicate that a majority of white Americans—regardless of religious tradition—oppose the policy. For a detailed discussion of religion and attitudes toward inequality, see Hinojosa and Park (2004).

10. As we will see in chapter 9, when we review the Catholic bishops' pastoral letter on war in 1986, church elites may alter this pattern when they communicate a clear message.

11. Elizabeth Tenety, "Louie Giglio Backs Out of Inaugural Benediction over Comments on Homosexuality," *Washington Post*, January 10, 2013.

CHAPTER 8

* The chapter epigraph is taken from E. J. Dionne Jr., "Ralph Reed's Balancing Act," *Washington Post National Weekly Edition*, May 5, 1997, 27.

1. For a recent overview of American evangelical Protestants, we highly recommend Smidt (2013).

2. It is very difficult to find information about the political behavior of northern evangelicals after the 1920s. John Hammond's (1974) study of the revivalist ethos in Ohio and New York suggests that northern evangelicals strongly supported both restrictive social policies and the Republican Party.

3. Bill Moyers, "There Is No Tomorrow," *Minneapolis Star-Tribune*, January 30, 2005.

4. The clearest example is the DVD *George W. Bush: Faith in the White House*, which was widely circulated among evangelicals before the 2004 election. A *New York Times* critic mocked it as "The Passion of the Bush."

5. Dana Milbank, "Religious Right Finds Its Center in Oval Office; Bush Emerges as Movement's Leader after Robertson Leaves Christian Coalition," *Washington Post*, December 24, 2001.

6. See Alan Cooperman and Thomas B. Edsall, "Evangelicals Say They Led Charge for the GOP," *Washington Post*, November 8, 2004, and Dana Milbank, "For the President: A Vote of Full Faith and Credit," *Washington Post*, November 7, 2004.

7. David D. Kirkpatrick, "Aide Is Bush's Eyes and Ears on the Right," *New York Times*, June 28, 2004; Hanna Rosin, "Right with God: Evangelical Conservatives Find a Spiritual Home on the Hill," *Washington Post*, March 6, 2005.

8. Jonathan Chait, "Crash Test," *New Republic,* October 24, 2005. The use of Christian Right leaders to try to legitimize Miers is described in Peter Baker and Charles Babington, "Role of Religion Emerges as Issue," *Washington Post,* October 13, 2005, A-8.

9. Some Catholic Republicans have been willing to work with evangelical Protestants. During the 2012 Republican presidential nomination campaign, Rick Santorum became the favorite candidate of leading evangelical activists despite his Catholicism.

10. His son and heir, Franklin, has gone the other direction, enlisting whole-heartedly in the Republican cause and trumpeting his opposition to Islam as a challenge to American values.

11. David D. Kirkpatrick, "The Evangelical Crackup," *New York Times Magazine,* October 28, 2007, 38.

12. For example, see Mike Allen, "Montana Governor Didn't Have Right Stuff," *Washington Post,* January 2, 2001, 1A.

13. Sheryl Gay Stolberg, "Reagans Not Embracing Bush," *International Herald Tribune,* June 16, 2004, 6.

14. Jeff Zeleny, "New Rove Effort Has G.O.P. Aflame," *New York Times,* February 6, 2013, http://www.nytimes.com/2013/02/07/us/politics/new-rove-effort-has-gop-aflame.html (accessed May 29, 2013).

15. The tangled tale is well told in Susan Schmidt and James V. Grimaldi, "How a Lobbyist Stacked the Deck," *Washington Post,* October 16, 2005, A1, A10–A11. See also David D. Kirkpatrick and Philip Shenon, "Ralph Reed's Zeal for Lobbying Is Shaking His Political Faithful," *New York Times,* April 18, 2005.

CHAPTER 9

* The epigraph for this chapter is taken from the *Wall Street Journal,* February 24, 1988.

1. United States Conference of Catholic Bishops, *Statement on Iraq,* November 13, 2002, www.usccb.org/bishops/iraq.shtml.

2. This upward mobility was true mostly for Catholic natives who were at least the third generation of their family in America. For more recent immigrants, especially Hispanic Catholics from Mexico and Puerto Rico, economic conditions and social integration were much less advanced.

3. The terms *liberal* and *conservative* refer to liberal or conservative access to abortion.

4. In the 1990s, it appears that abortion became an issue with more electoral clout, dividing Democrats from Republicans but also strongly affecting pro-choice Republicans (Abramowitz and Saunders 2005).

5. "Poll Shows Most Priests Want the Right to Marry," *New York Times,* September 11, 1987, 1.

6. Catholics constitute about 30 percent of the women receiving abortions, roughly the same proportion as their population share, but the rate varies ap-

preciably by ethnic and racial groups within the church (Henshaw and Silverman 1988; Jones, Finer, and Singh 2010, 6).

7. In their comprehensive study of abortion attitudes, Cook, Jelen, and Wilcox (1992, 122–24) found that Roman Catholicism had a stronger impact on opposition than membership in an evangelical denomination after taking account of a wide range of demographic, attitudinal, and religious factors.

8. "Excerpts from Speech by Kennedy," *New York Times*, September 11, 1984, 10.

9. "Excerpts from Cuomo Talk on Religion and Public Morality," *New York Times*, September 14, 1984, 13.

10. Ken Wald wants to thank his colleague, Michael Martinez, for reviewing this paragraph and adding some nuance to the argument.

11. Jerome Legge (1995) argues that Jewish religious involvement—not orthodoxy per se but religious attachment—does correlate with liberal political outlooks.

12. Whatever the views of African American leaders toward Israel, black Americans remain favorably disposed to that country and prefer it to its Arab enemies (Gilboa 1987, 275–77). The Congressional Black Caucus has also been a consistent supporter of aid to Israel.

13. For black reaction to the Farrakhan movement, see the Simon Wiesenthal Center (1986).

14. See "Religion in Campaign '08," Pew Research Center for the People and the Press, www.people-press.org/report/353.

CHAPTER 10

* The epigraph for James Cone is from Basil Robert, ed., *The Challenge of Black Theology in South Africa* (Atlanta, GA: John Knox Press, 1974), 48. The quotation from César Chávez was recorded in *César Chávez: Autobiography of La Causa* by Jacques Levy (New York: Norton, 1975).

1. Barack Obama, "Call to Renewal" (keynote address, Sojourners/Call to Renewal Conference, Washington, DC, June 28, 2006), http://obama.senate.gov/speech/060628-call_to_renewal (accessed January–February 2008). This speech was expanded in a chapter of Obama's book *The Audacity of Hope: Thoughts on Reclaiming the American Dream* (New York: Vintage, 2006), 195–226.

2. Rachel Zoll, "African-American Christians Waver Over This Year's Election," http://www.huffingtonpost.com/2012/09/16/african-american-christians-voting-election_n_1887956.html (accessed June 2013).

3. John Blake, "Complexity in Black Church Reactions to Obama's Gay Marriage Announcement," http://religion.blogs.cnn.com/2012/05/11/complexity-in-black-church-reactions-to-obamas-gay-marriage-announcement-reveal/ (accessed June 2013).

4. From Obama's speech, "A More Perfect Union." *Vital Speeches of the Day*, May 2008, 194–99.

5. A video clip of his comments can be seen at www.youtube.com/watch?v=zS883xWTKOg (accessed September 2009).

6. For a discussion of this political dynamic in Georgia see Jim Tharpe, "Pastors Send 'Clear' Message: Gay Marriage Weighs on Black Legislators," *Atlanta Journal Constitution*, March 2, 2004, 1B. Also see Elisabeth Beardsley, "Gay/Civil Rights Debate Splits Black Leaders," *Boston Herald*, March 10, 2004, 6.

7. http://www.census.gov/population/pop-profile/2000/chap02.pdf (accessed September 2013).

8. http://www.census.gov/prod/cen2010/briefs/c2010br-04.pdf (accessed September 2013).

9. Frank Newport, "US Catholic Hispanic Population Less Religious, Shrinking," February 25, 2013, http://www.gallup.com/poll/160691/catholic-hispanic -population-less-religious-shrinking.aspx (accessed June 2013).

10. Elizabeth Dias, "The Latino Reformation," April 15, 2013, http://content .time.com/time/covers/0,16641,20130415,00.html

11. These data were compiled in a recent report by the Pew Forum for Religion in Public Life, http://pewforum.org/newassets/surveys/hispanic/hispanics -religion-07-final-mar08.pdf#page=8 (accessed September 2009).

12. Quotation from Timothy Matovina, "A Fundamental Gal," *America*, March 17, 2003, 6.

13. These data were compiled by the Pew Hispanic Center 2012 National Survey of Latinos, September 12–16, 2012, http://www.pewforum.org/2012/10/18/ latinos-religion-and-campaign-2012 (accessed July 2013).

14. "Latinos, Religion and Campaign 2012," Pew Research Religion and Public Life Project, October 18, 2013, http://www.pewforum.org/2012/10/18/latinos -religion-and-campaign-2012/ (accessed June 2013).

15. Poll conducted by Latino Decisions Group reported in Albert Sabate, "More Latinos Likely to Vote Republican If Immigration Reform Passes," ABC News, March 18, 2013, http://abcnews.go.com/ABC_Univision/News/latinos-vote -republican-immigration-reform-passes-poll-finds/story?id=18759902 (accessed June 2013).

16. Ibid.

17. Quoted in Carrie Dann, "From Politics to the Pulpit, Faith Groups See the Hand of God in Immigration Reform," http://nbcpolitics.nbcnews.com/_news/ 2013/08/03/19819640-from-politics-to-the-pulpit-faith-groups-see-the-hand-of -god-in-immigration-reform?lite (accessed August 2013).

18. "Latinos, Voters in the 2012 Election," Pew Research Hispanic Trends Project, November 7, 2012, http://www.pewhispanic.org/2012/11/07/latino-voters -in-the-2012-election/ (accessed June 2013).

19. Hanna Rosin and John Mintz, "Muslim Leaders Struggle with Mixed Messages," *Washington Post*, October 2, 2001, A16.

20. These data are taken from a report by the Pew Forum on Religion and Public Life, "Muslim Americans, Middle Class and Mostly Mainstream." The report can be found at http://pewforum.org/surveys/muslim-american (accessed September 2009). Although not Arab, people of Iranian descent are included in the Arab American numbers reported here.

21. Ibid.

22. Executive summary for the Muslim in the American Public Square/ Zogby Poll conducted October 2004, www.projectmaps.com/AMP2004report.pdf (accessed October 15, 2005).

23. Tahir Ali, "Indirect Endorsement from Muslim Americans," www.pakistan link.com/Community/2008/Oct08/31/02.HTMcite.

24. See, for example, Jerome Corsi's *The Obama Nation: Leftist Politics and the Cult of Personality* (New York: Threshold Editions, 2008).

25. Poll results of Prospects for March 2007 survey, "Inter-religious Understanding," are available at http://pewforum.org/publications/surveys/Inter-Religious-Understanding.pdf (accessed September 2009).

26. Reported in James Zogby, "Arab and Muslim Bashing Failed in '08," *Washington Report on Middle East Affairs* 28 (January/February 2009): 25.

27. Allegation made by Deepa Kumar, author of *Islamophobia and the Politics of Empire*, quoted in Alex Kane, "Romney Campaign's Ugly Anti-Muslim Strategy to Win Cash and Votes," http://www.alternet.org/election-2012/romney -campaigns-ugly-anti-muslim-strategy-win-cash-and-votes (accessed July 2013).

28. Sabrina Siddiqui, "Muslims Say They Can't Guarantee Obama Their 2012 Election Vote," June 11, 2012, http://www.huffingtonpost.com/2012/06/11/ muslims-obama-2012-election_n_1584108.html (accessed June 2013).

29. These data are taken from a report by the Pew Center for People and the Press, "Muslim Americans: No Signs of Growth in Alienation or Support for Extremism," August 30, 2011. The report can be found at http://www.people -press.org/2011/08/30/muslim-americans-no-signs-of-growth-in-alienation-or -support-for-extremism/.

30. For an excellent summary of how Middle East foreign policy affected the Muslim vote in 2000, see Alexander Rose, "How Did Muslims Vote in 2000?" *Middle East Quarterly* 8 (Summer 2001): 13–27.

31. The Muslim members of Congress are Representatives Keith Ellison (D-Minn.) and Andre Carson (D-Ill.). They were first elected in 2008.

32. Jon Meacham, "The Mormon in Mitt," *Time*, October 8, 2012.

33. Reported in Amy Sullivan, "Mitt Romney's Evangelical Problem," *Washington Monthly* (September 2005), 13–16.

34. See *Reynolds v. United States* (1879), *Davis v. Beason* (1890), and *Latter-Day Saints, Church of Jesus Christ v. United States* (1890).

35. "Portrait of Mormons in the US," Pew Forum on Religion and Public Life, July 24, 2009, available at http://pewfoum.org/docs?DOCID=429.

36. David Biema, "The Church and Gay Marriage: Are Mormons Misunderstood?" *Time*, June 22, 2009.

37. Ibid.

38. Mormon missionary ad can be viewed at www.youtube.com/watch?v= q28UwAyzYKE (accessed September 2009).

39. Jonah Goldberg, "An Ugly Attack on Mormons," *Los Angeles Times*, December 2, 2008.

40. See Andy Newman, "For Mormons in Harlem a Bigger Space Beckons," *New York Times*, October 2, 2005, 37.

41. Siobhan Hughes, "Mormonism as 'Cult' Removed from Billy Graham Site," *Washington Wire*, October 18, 2012. *Wall Street Journal*, http://blogs.wsj.com/

washwire/2012/10/18/mormonism-as-cult-removed-from-billy-graham-site/ (accessed June 2013).

42. Data from Pew Research Center non-Mormon survey conducted June 28–July 9, 2012; Mormon survey conducted October 25–November 16, 2011. Results available at http://projects.pewforum.org/2012/08/30/mormon/pf_12-08 -30_mormons-2012election_1-title-slide/in the United States (accessed July 2013).

43. Poll conducted by Pew Research Center, December 5–9, 2012. Results are available at http://www.pewforum.org/2012/12/14/attitudes-toward-mormon -faith/#knowledge (accessed July 2013).

44. This comment was originally posted on a blog by Jarrett Kobek, June 13, 2007, and later printed in the *Chronicle of Higher Education*, September 7, 2007. The blog post can be read at http://blog.kobek.com/2007/06/ (accessed August 2009).

45. Matthew Bowman, "Is This the Mormon Moment?" *Time*, September 27, 2012.

46. Estimated based on data from Pew Center's Religious Landscape Survey, May 8–August 2007. Review summary report of survey at http://www.pew forum.org/files/2008/06/report2-religious-landscape-study-full.pdf.

47. The first Hindu American in Congress is Tulsi Gabbard (D-Hawaii). The first Buddhist elected to the Senate is Mazie Hirono (D-Hawaii).

48. Reported in "American United Files Brief in Commandments Case at the Supreme Court," *Church and State* (February 2005), 28–19.

CHAPTER 11

1. U.S. Conference of Catholic Bishops, "Supreme Court Decisions on Marriage: Tragic Day for Marriage and Our Nation, State Bishops," news release, June 26, 2013, http://www.usccb.org/news/2013/13-126.cfm (accessed June 2013).

2. Ibid.

3. *US v. Windsor*, decided June 26, 2013.

4. Speech before a convention of the International Council of Women in Washington, D.C., March 25–April 1888.

5. Remarks made on the second day of the Woman's Rights Convention held in Akron, Ohio, May 28–29, 1851, represented by Frances D. Gage and printed in Elizabeth Cady Stanton, *The History of Woman Suffrage* (New York: Fowler & Wells, 1881), vol. 1, chap. 6.

6. Quoted in Philip Rubio, *A History of Affirmative Action 1619–2000* (Vicksburg: University of Mississippi Press, 2001), 37.

7. Quote from a letter dated September 8, 1852, sent to the Woman's Rights Convention in Syracuse, New York, cited in Harper 1969, vol. 1, chap. 5.

8. The states that never ratified the ERA include Alabama, Arizona, Arkansas, Florida, Georgia, Illinois, Louisiana, Mississippi, Missouri, Nevada, North Carolina, Oklahoma, South Carolina, Utah, and Virginia.

9. Quoted in *Ms.* magazine, April 1974.

10. This was the major ruling in *Planned Parenthood of Southeastern Pennsylvania v. Casey*, 112 S. Ct. 2791, 120 L. Ed. 2d 674 (1992).

11. Linda Feldmann, "As Abortion Limits Sweep US, Even 'Purple' States Join the Crackdown," *Christian Science Monitor*, July 30, 2013, www.csmonitor.com/USA/DC-Decoder/2013/0730/As-abortion-limits-sweep-US-even-purple-states-join-the-crackdown (accessed June 2013).

12. "Perry Signs Texas Abortion Restrictions into Law," NBC News, July 18, 2013. Story can be viewed at http://usnews.nbcnews.com/_news/2013/07/18/19543555-perry-signs-texas-abortion-restrictions-into-law?lite.

13. "A Look at Religious Voters in the 2008 Election," a transcript of the Pew Research Center's Forum on Religion and Public Life's Faith Angle Conference, http://pewresearch.org/pubs/1112/religion-vote-2008-election (accessed August 2009).

14. The Bible describes the sin of Sodom and Gomorrah as "very grievous" in Genesis 18:30. The story of their destruction is related in Genesis chapters 18 and 19.

15. Homosexuality was referenced as an "objective disorder" by Cardinal Joseph Ratzinger when he was prefect of the Congregation for the Doctrine of Faith in the statement "Notification Regarding Sister Jeannine Gramick SSND and Father Robert Nugent SDS," which prohibited them from pastoral work involving homosexual persons. Gramick and Nugent had been critical of the church's position on homosexuality and had founded a support group for homosexuals within the Catholic Church. Cardinal Joseph Ratzinger was elected Pope Benedict XVI on April 1, 2005.

16. Reported by Rachel Donadio, "On Gay Priests Pope Francis Asks, 'Who Am I to Judge?'" *New York Times*, July 29, 2013.

17. The Society of Friends (Quakers) have no central authority that makes definitive policy statements. Congregations are completely autonomous. Most affirm homosexuals and homosexuality as a lifestyle. Still, there may be some congregations who maintain conservative positions on this issue.

18. The text of the commercial is recorded at www.religioustolerance.org/hom_ucca3htm (accessed November 30, 2005).

19. United Methodist Church *Book of Discipline*, paragraph 304.3; "The Nurturing Community," a section of the church's social principles, paragraph 65G. For a good discussion about gay inclusion in the United Methodist Church, see Amanda Udis-Kessler, *Queer Inclusion in the United Methodist Church* (2008).

20. "Monogamous Gays Can Serve in the ELCA," *Washington Post*, August 22, 2009.

21. Justin Welby, Archbishop of Canterbury, speech before the House of Lords in England, June 3, 2013.

22. The text of the press release concerning the closure of Exodus International is at http://wespeaklove.org/exodus/ (accessed June 2013).

23. "Stances of Faiths on LGBT Issues: Southern Baptist Convention, Human Rights Campaign," http://www.hrc.org/resources/entry/stances-of-faiths-on-lgbt-issues-southern-baptist-convention (accessed June 2013).

24. The 2012 Republican Party platform can be found at www.gop.com/wp-content/uploads/2012/08/2012GOPPlatform.pdf.

25. The 2012 Democratic Party platform can be found at http://www.democrats.org/democratic-national-platform.

26. Pew Center for People and the Press, "In Gay Marriage Debate, Both Supporters and Opponents See Legal Recognition as Inevitable," June 6, 2013, www.people-press.org/2013/06/06/in-gay-marriage-debate-both-supporters-and-opponents-see-legal-recognition-as-inevitable/.

27. Ibid.

28. The court decisions in Alaska and Hawaii were overturned by state constitutional amendments.

29. *Lawrence v. Texas*, 539 U.S. 558 (2003).

CHAPTER 12

* The epigraph for this chapter was taken from Clarke E. Cochran, *Religion in Public and Private Life* (New York: Routledge, 1990), 168.

1. Recognizing the importance of this topic, the American Political Science Association convened a special task force on Religion and Democracy that has studied the subject in considerable detail (Katznelson and Wolfe 2010). For another recent book on the topic with a special focus on evangelical Protestants, see Brint and Schroedel (2009).

2. "Fliers Denounce Clinton," *Gainesville Sun*, October 15, 1992, 17A. To reiterate that such arrogance is not restricted to one side of the political spectrum, a former American hostage in the Middle East reported that the "smug self-righteousness" of nuclear freeze advocates in the United States reminded him of his Iranian captors (M. Kennedy 1985).

3. Like most fundamentalists, Christian Reconstructionists claim merely to be following an age-old religious tradition. In fact, fundamentalists typically distort the past and "invent" traditions that never existed. The portrait of life under the Hebrew Bible as deployed by Reconstructionists bears no discernible resemblance to the reality discovered by archaeologists, historians, and theologians. It also ignores the social, economic, and political context of the times in which the Bible was composed.

4. Wade Clark Roof (1974) has suggested that the apparent prejudice of churchgoers is principally an outgrowth of their localistic orientation, a consequence of their limited exposure to agents of modernity.

5. Opponents of liberalized abortion make just such an argument when they contend that the pro-choice position is grounded in values that lead to disrespect for human life and dignity. Supporters of liberalized abortion would respond that forcing women to bear unwanted children is a greater denial of respect for human life and dignity. Hence, the abortion debate is a conflict between different interpretations of what is right rather than a clash between advocates of morality versus amorality.

References

Abraham, Henry J. 1987. "Religion, the Constitution, the Court and Society: Some Contemporary Reflections on Mandates, Words, Human Beings, and the Art of the Possible." In *How Does the Constitution Protect Religious Freedom?*, ed. Robert A. Goldwin, 15–42. Washington, DC: American Enterprise Institute.

Abraham, Nabeel, and Andrew Shryock. 2000. *Arab Detroit: From Margin to Mainstream.* Detroit: Wayne State University Press.

Abramowitz, Alan I. 1995. "It's Abortion Stupid: Policy Voting in the 1992 Presidential Election." *Journal of Politics* 57: 176–86.

Abramowitz, Alan, and Kyle Saunders. 2005. "Why Can't We All Just Get Along? The Reality of a Polarized America." *The Forum* 3.

Abrams, Paula. 2009. *Cross Purposes: Pierce v. Society of Sisters and the Struggle over Compulsory Public Education.* Ann Arbor: University of Michigan Press.

Acuna, Rodolfo. 1972. *Occupied America: A History of Chicanos.* San Francisco: Canfield Press.

Adamczyk, Amy, and Jacob Felson. 2008. "Fetal Positions: Unraveling the Influence of Religion on Premarital Pregnancy Resolution." *Social Science Quarterly* 89: 17–38.

Adamczyk, Amy, John Wybraniec, and Roger Finke. 2004. "Religious Regulation and the Courts: Documenting the Effects of *Smith* and RFRA." *Journal of Church and State* 46: 237–62.

Adams, Arlin. 1986. "Is the Supreme Court Making a Significant Shift in Church-State Jurisprudence?" In *Government Intervention in Religious Affairs II*, ed. Dean M. Kelley, 69–78. New York: Pilgrim.

Adams, Arlin M., and Charles J. Emmerich. 1990. *A Nation Dedicated to Religious Liberty: The Constitutional Heritage of the Religion Clauses.* Philadelphia: University of Pennsylvania Press.

Adams, Maurianne, and John Bracey, eds. 1999. *Strangers and Neighbors: Relations between Blacks and Jews in the United States*. Amherst: University of Massachusetts Press.

Adkins, Julie, Laurie Occhipinti, and Tafa Hefferan, eds. 2010. *Not by Faith Alone: Social Services, Social Justice and Faith Based Organizations in the United States*. Lanham, MD: Lexington Books.

Adorno, T. W., Else Frenkel-Brunswik, Daniel J. Levinson, and R. Nevitt Sanford. 1950. *The Authoritarian Personality*. New York: Harper.

Afridi, Sam. 2001. *Muslims in America: Identity, Diversity and the Challenge of Understanding*. New York: Carnegie Corporation.

Ahlstrom, Sydney. 1965. "The Puritan Ethic and the Spirit of American Democracy." In *Calvinism and the Political Order*, ed. George L. Hunt, 88–107. Philadelphia: Westminster.

———. 1975. *A Religious History of the American People*. New York: Image.

Aho, James A. 1990. *The Politics of Righteousness: Idaho Christian Patriotism*. Seattle: University of Washington Press.

Akresh, Ilana Redstone. 2011. Immigrants' Religious Participation in the United States. *Ethnic and Racial Studies* 34: 643–61.

Alexander, T. G. 1995. "The Emergence of a Republican Majority in Utah, 1970–1992." In *Politics in the Postwar American West*, ed. R. Lowitt. Norman: University of Oklahoma Press.

Alex-Assensoh, Yvette. 1996. "Race, Concentrated Poverty, Social Isolation and Political Behavior." *Urban Affairs Review* 33: 209–27.

Alex-Assensoh, Yvette, and A. B. Assensoh. 2001. "Inner City Contexts, Church Attendance and African American Participation." *Journal of Politics* 63: 886–901.

Allen, Ernest, Jr. 1998. "Identity and Destiny: The Formative Views of the Moorish Science Temple and the Nation of Islam." In *Islam on the Americanization Path?*, ed. John Esposito and Yvonne Hadded. Atlanta, GA: Scholars.

Allen, Richard, Michael Dawson, and Ronald Brown. 1989. "A Schema Based Approach to Modeling an African American Racial Belief System." *American Political Science Review* 83: 421–22.

Allinsmith, Wesley, and Beverly Allinsmith. 1948. "Religious Affiliation and Politico-Economic Attitudes: A Study of Eight Major U.S. Religious Groups." *Public Opinion Quarterly* 12: 377–89.

Allport, Gordon W. 1958. *The Nature of Prejudice*. Garden City, NY: Doubleday-Anchor.

Almond, Gabriel, Bingham Powell Jr., Kaare Strom, and Russell Dalton. 2004. *Comparative Politics Today: A World View*. 8th ed. New York: Pearson-Longman.

Altemeyer, Bob. 1988. *Enemies of Freedom: Understanding Right-Wing Authoritarianism*. San Francisco: Jossey-Bass.

Altemeyer, B., and B. Hunsberger. 1992. "Authoritarianism, Religious Fundamentalism, Quest and Prejudice." *International Journal for the Psychology of Religion* 2: 113–33.

Alvarez, R. Michael, and Jonathan Nagler. 1995. "Economics, Issues and the Perot Candidacy: Voter Choice in the 1992 Presidential Election." *American Journal of Political Science* 39: 714–45.

Alwin, Duane F., Jacob L. Felson, Edward T. Walker, and Paula A. Tufis. 2006. "Measuring Religious Identities in Surveys." *Public Opinion Quarterly* 70: 530–64.

American Association of Fund-Raising Counsel. 2011. *Giving USA: The Annual Report on Philanthropy for the Year 2010*. New York: AAFRC Trust for Philanthropy.

Ammerman, Nancy T. 1981. "The Civil Rights Movement and the Clergy in a Southern Community." *Sociological Analysis* 41: 339–50.

———. 1987. *Bible Believers: Fundamentalists in the Modern World*. New Brunswick, NJ: Rutgers University Press.

———. 1994. "Telling Congregational Stories." *Review of Religious Research* 35: 289–301.

———. 2002. "Connecting Mainline Protestant Churches with Public Life." In *The Quiet Hand of God: Faith-Based Activism and the Public Role of Mainline Protestantism*, ed. Robert Wuthnow and John H. Evans, 129–58. Berkeley: University of California Press.

Andersen, Kristi. 1988. "Sources of Pro-Family Belief." *Political Psychology* 9: 229–43.

Anderson, Charles. 1973. "Religious Communality and Party Preference." In *Research in Religious Behavior*, ed. Benjamin Beit-Hallahmi, 336–52. Monterey, CA: Brooks-Cole.

Anderson, Kristen Soltis. 2013. *Grand Old Party for a Brand New Generation*. Washington, DC: College Republican National Committee.

Aptheker, Herbert. 1968. *Marxism and Christianity*. New York: Humanities.

Armstrong, Karen. 1996. *Jerusalem: One City, Three Faiths*. New York: Knopf.

Arrington, Theodore S., and Patricia A. Kyle. 1978. "Equal Rights Amendment Activists in North Carolina." *Signs* 3: 666–80.

Arvizu, John, and Chris Garcia. 1996. "Latino Voting Participation: Explaining and Differentiating Latino Voting Turnout." *Hispanic Journal of Behavioral Sciences* 18: 104–29.

Aslan, Reza. 2005. "Aunt Kobra's Islamic Democracy." *Boston Globe*, April 17, 1C.

Asmussen, Nicole. 2011. "Polarized Protestants: A Confessional Explanation of Party Polarization." Paper presented to the annual meeting of the American Political Science Association, Seattle, WA.

Asser, S. M., and R. Swan. 1998. "Child Fatalities from Religion-Motivated Medical Neglect." *Pediatrics* 101: 625–29.

Atkins, Rt. Rev. Stabley, and Rev. Theodore McConnell, eds. 1986. *Churches on the Wrong Road*. Chicago: Regnery Gateway.

Austin, Allan. 1984. *African Muslims in the Antebellum America: A Sourcebook*. New York: Garland.

Ayers, John, and C. Richard Hofstetter. 2008. "American Muslims and Political Participation Following 9-11: Religious Belief, Political Resources, Social Structures and Political Awareness." *Politics and Religion* 1: 3–26.

Baggaley, Andrew. 1962. "Religious Influence on Wisconsin Voting." *American Political Science Review* 56: 66–70.

Baker, Donald. 1985. "It's Not Exactly 'Animal House.'" *Washington Post Weekly Edition*, May 27, 7–8.

Baker, Joseph O'Brian, and Buster Smith. 2009. "None Too Simple: Examining Issues of Religious Nonbelief and Nonbelonging in the United States." *Journal for the Scientific Study of Religion* 48: 719–33.

Baker, Tod A., Robert P. Steed, and Laurence W. Moreland, eds. 1983. *Religion and Politics in the South: Mass and Elite Perspectives*. New York: Praeger.

Balizet, Carol. 1999. *Egypt or Zion? Exposing the Devil's Counterfeits*. 2nd ed. Jacksonville, FL: Home in Zion Ministries.

Balmer, Randall. 1996. *Grant Us Courage: Travels along the Mainline of American Protestantism*. New York: Oxford University Press.

Balswick, Jack. 1970. "Theology and Political Attitudes among Clergymen." *Sociological Quarterly* 11: 393–404.

Bandow, Doug. 1995. "The Parallel Universe." *American Enterprise* 6: 58–61.

Barbour, Henry, et al. 2013. *Growth and Opportunity Project*. Washington, DC: Republican National Committee.

Bard, Mitchell. 1991. *The Water's Edge and Beyond: Defining the Limits to Domestic Influence upon United States Middle East Policy*. New Brunswick, NJ: Transaction.

Barker, David, and Christopher Jan Carman. 2000. "The Spirit of Capitalism? Religious Doctrine, Values and Economic Attitude Constructs." *Political Behavior* 22: 1–27.

———. 2009. "Political Geography, Church Attendance and Mass Preferences Regarding Democratic Representation." *Journal of Elections, Public Opinion and Parties* 19: 125–45.

Barkun, Michael. 1994. *Religion and the Racist Right*. Chapel Hill: University of North Carolina Press.

Barnes, Fred. 1992. "The New Covenant." *New Republic* 207: 32–34.

Barnes, Sandra. 2004. "Priestly and Prophetic Influences on Black Church Social Services." *Social Problems* 51: 202–21.

———. 2012. *Live Long and Prosper: How Black Megachurches Address HIV/Aids and Poverty in the Age of Prosperity Theology*. New York: Fordham University Press.

Barreto, M. A., S. Manzano, R. Ramirez, and K. Rim. 2009. "Mobilization, Participation and Solidaridad: Latino Participation in the 2006 Immigration Protest Rallies." *Urban Affairs Review* 44: 736–64.

Barrett, Justin L. 2004. *Why Would Anyone Believe in God?* Lanham, MD: AltaMira.

Barth, Jay, and Janine Parry. 2009. "Political Culture, Public Opinion and Policy Non-Diffusion: The Case of Gay and Lesbian Related Issues in Arkansas." *Social Science Quarterly* 90: 309–25.

Bartkowski, John. 2001. *Remaking the Godly Marriage: Gender Negotiation in Evangelical Families*. New Brunswick, NJ: Rutgers University Press.

———. 2004. *The Promise Keepers: Servants, Soldiers and Godly Men*. New Brunswick, NJ: Rutgers University Press.

Bartowski, John, and Lynn Hempel. 2009. "Sex and Gender Traditionalism among Conservative Protestants: Does the Difference Make a Difference?" *Journal for the Scientific Study of Religion* 48: 805–16.

Bartkoswki, John, Aida Ramos-Wada, Chris Ellison, and Gabriel Acevedo. 2012. "Faith, Race-Ethnicity and Public Policy Preferences: Religious Schemas and Abortion Attitudes among U.S. Latinos." *Journal for the Scientific Study of Religion* 51: 343–58.

Bartkowski, John, and Helen Regis. 2003. *Charitable Choices: Religion, Race and Poverty in the Post Welfare Era*. New York: New York University Press.

Batson, C. Daniel, Cheryl H. Flink, Patricia A. Schoenrade, Jim Fultz, and Virginia Pych. 1986. "Religious Orientation and Overt versus Covert Racial Prejudice." *Journal of Personality and Social Psychology* 50: 175–81.

Battle, Elizabeth Clark. 1989. "The Politics of God and the Woman's Vote: Religion in the American Suffrage Movement, 1848–1895." PhD diss., Princeton University, Princeton, NJ

Baumgartner, Frank, and Frank Leech. 1998. *Basic Interests*. Princeton, NJ: Princeton University Press.

Baumgartner, Jody, Peter Francia, and Jonathan Morris. 2008. "A Clash of Civilizations? The Influence of Religion on Public Opinion on U.S. Foreign Policy in the Middle East." *Political Research Quarterly* 61: 171–79.

Baylor Religion Survey. 2006. *American Piety in the 21st Century: New Insights to the Depth and Complexity of Religion in the U.S.* Waco, TX: Baylor Institute for Studies of Religion.

Beatty, Kathleen Murphy, and Oliver Walter. 1989. "A Group Theory of Religion and Politics: The Clergy as Group Leaders." *Western Political Quarterly* 42: 129–46.

Becker, Amy, and Dietram Scheufele. 2011. "New Voters, New Outlook? Predispositions, Social Networks and the Changing Politics of Gay Civil Rights." *Social Science Quarterly* 92: 324–45.

Bellah, Robert N. 1966. "Civil Religion in America." *Daedalus* 134: 40–55.

———. 1975. *The Broken Covenant: American Civil Religion in a Time of Trial*. New York: Seabury.

Bellah, Robert N., and Phillip E. Hammond, eds. 1980. *Varieties of Civil Religion*. New York: Harper & Row.

Bellah, Robert, Richard Madsen, William M. Sullivan, Steven M. Tipton, and Anne Swidler. 1985. *Habits of the Heart*. Berkeley: University of California Press.

Bendroth, Margaret Lamberts. 1993. *Fundamentalism and Gender, 1875 to the Present*. New Haven, CT: Yale University Press.

Benjamin-Alvarado, J. L. DeSipio, and C. Montoya. 2009. "Latino Mobilization in New Immigrant Destinations: The Anti HR 4437 Protest in Nebraska's Cities." *Urban Affairs Review* 44: 718–35.

Benson, Peter, and Dorothy Williams. 1982. *Religion on Capitol Hill: Myths and Realities*. San Francisco: Harper & Row.

Bercovitch, Jacob, and Ayse Kadayifici-Orellana. 2009. "Religion and Mediation: The Role of Faith-Based Actors in International Conflict Resolution." *International Negotiation* 14: 175–204.

Bercovitch, Sacvan. 1975. *The Puritan Origin of the American Self*. New Haven, CT: Yale University Press.

Berelson, Bernard, Paul Lazarsfeld, and William McPhee. 1954. *Voting: A Study of Opinion Formation in a Presidential Campaign*. Chicago: University of Chicago Press.

Bergesen, Albert J., and Andrew M. Greeley. 2003. *God in the Movies*. Somerset, NJ: Transaction.

Berke, Richard L. 1994. "Christian Right Defies Categories." *New York Times*, July 22, 1A.

———. 1995. "Poll Finds G.O.P. Primary Voters Are Hardly Monolithic." *New York Times*, October 30, 10A.

Berkowitz, Laura, and John C. Green. 1997. "Charting the Coalition: The Local Chapters of the Ohio Christian Coalition." In *Sojourners in the Wilderness: The Christian Right in Comparative Perspective*, ed. Corwin D. Smidt and James M. Penning, 57–72. Lanham, MD: Rowman & Littlefield.

Berman, Paul. 1994. *Blacks and Jews: Alliances and Arguments*. New York: Delacorte.

Besecke, Kelly. 2005. "Seeing Invisible Religion: Religion as a Societal Conversation about Transcendent Meaning." *Sociological Theory* 23: 179–96.

Beyerlein, Kraig. 2004. "Specifying the Impact of Conservative Protestantism on Educational Attainment." *Journal for the Scientific Study of Religion* 43: 505–18.

Beyerlein, Kraig, and John Hipp. 2006. "From Pews to Participation: The Effect of Congregation Activity and Context on Bridging Civic Engagement." *Social Problems* 53: 97–117.

Biebricher, Thomas. 2011. "Faith Based Initiatives and the Challenge of Governance." *Public Administration* 89: 1001–12.

Biehl, Janet. 1991. *Rethinking Ecofeminist Politics*. Boston: South End.

Billingsley, Andrew. 1999. *Mighty Like a River: The Black Church and Social Reform*. New York: Oxford University Press.

Billington, Monroe, and Cal Clark. 1991. "Baptist Preachers and the New Deal." *Journal of Church and State* 33: 255–70.

———. 1993. "Catholic Clergymen, Franklin D. Roosevelt, and the New Deal." *Catholic Historical Review* 79: 65–82.

Bird, Frederick B. 1990. "How Do Religions Affect Moralities? A Comparative Analysis." *Social Compass* 37: 291–314.

Birkby, Robert H. 1966. "The Supreme Court and the Bible Belt: Tennessee Reactions to the *Schempp* Decision." *Midwest Journal of Political Science* 10: 304–19.

Bjarnason, Thoroddur, and Michael R. Welch. 2004. "Father Knows Best: Parishes, Priests, and American Catholic Parishioners' Attitudes toward Capital Punishment." *Journal for the Scientific Study of Religion* 43: 103–18.

Black, Amy, Douglas Koopman, and David Ryden. 2004. *Of Little Faith: The Politics of George W. Bush's Faith-Based Initiatives*. Washington, DC: Georgetown University Press.

Blake, Mariah. 2005. "Stations of the Cross." *Columbia Journalism Review* 41: 32–39.

Blake, William D. 2013. "Pyrrhic Victories: How the Secularization Doctrine Undermines the Sanctity of Religion." *Journal of Church and State* 55: 1–22.

Blakeley, William Addison, comp. 1970. *American State Papers Bearing on Sunday Religion*. New York: DaCapo.

Blakeman, John, and Donald Greco. 2004. "Federal District Court Decision Making in Public Forum and Religious Speech Cases, 1983–2001." *Journal for the Scientific Study of Religion* 43: 439–49.

Blanchard, Dallas A., and Terry J. Prewitt. 1993. *Religious Violence and Abortion: The Gideon Project*. Gainesville: University Press of Florida.

Blau, Peter M. 1953. "Orientation of College Students toward International Relations." *American Journal of Sociology* 59: 205–14.

Bloch, Ruth H. 1990. "Religion and Ideological Change in the American Revolution." In *Religion and American Politics*, ed. Mark A. Noll, 44–61. New York: Oxford University Press.

Blocker, Jack. 1989. *American Temperance Movements: Cycles of Reform.* Boston: Twayne.

Bloom, Pazit Ben-Nun, and Lindsey Levitan. 2011. "We're Closer Than I Thought: Social Network Heterogeneity, Morality and Political Persuasion." *Political Psychology* 32: 643–65.

Blum, Edward. 2011. "Look Baby, We Got Jesus on our Flag: Robust Democracy and Religious Debate from the Era of Slavery to the Age of Obama." *The Annals of the American Academy of Social Science* 637: 17–37.

Blumenthal, Sidney. 1984. "The Righteous Empire." *New Republic* 191: 18–24.

Bock, David C., and Neil Clark Warren. 1972. "Religious Belief as a Factor in Obedience to Destructive Commands." *Review of Religious Research* 13: 185–91.

Bolce, Louis. 1988. "Abortion and Presidential Elections: The Impact of Public Perceptions of Party and Candidate Positions." *Presidential Studies Quarterly* 28: 815–29.

Bolce, Louis, and Gerald De Maio. 1999. "The Anti-Christian Fundamentalist Factor in Contemporary Politics." *Public Opinion Quarterly* 63: 508–42.

Boles, Janet K. 1979. *The Politics of the Equal Rights Amendment.* New York: Longman.

Bonomi, Patricia U. 1994. "Religious Dissent and the Case for American Exceptionalism." In *Religion in a Revolutionary Age*, ed. Ronald Hoffman, 31–51. Charlottesville: University Press of Virginia.

Boothby, Lee. 1986. "Government as an Instrument of Retribution for Private Resentments." In *Government Intervention in Religious Affairs II*, ed. Dean M. Kelley, 79–106. New York: Pilgrim.

Bostdorff, Denise M. 2003. "George W. Bush's Post–September 11 Rhetoric of Covenant Renewal: Upholding the Faith of the Greatest Generation." *Quarterly Journal of Speech* 89: 293–319.

Bowlby, David Dean. 2011. *The Garden and the Wilderness: Church and State in America to 1789.* Lanham, MD: Lexington Books.

Boyd, Heather Hartwig. 1999. "Christianity and the Environment in the American Public." *Journal for the Scientific Study of Religion* 38: 36–44.

Brady, David W., and Kent L. Tedin. 1976. "Ladies in Pink: Religious and Political Ideology in the Anti-ERA Movement." *Social Science Quarterly* 56: 564–75.

Braman, Eileen, and Abdulkader Sinno. 2009. "An Experimental Investigation of Causal Attributions for the Political Behavior of Muslim Candidates: Can a Muslim Represent You?" *Politics and Religion* 2: 247–76.

Brasher, Brenda. 1998. *Godly Women: Fundamentalism and Female Power.* New Brunswick, NJ: Rutgers University Press.

Brehm, Joan, and Brian Eisenhauer. 2006. "Environmental Concern in the Mormon Culture Region." *Society and Natural Resources* 19: 393–410.

Brenner, Philip S. 2011. "Identity Importance and the Overreporting of Religious Service Attendance: Multiple Imputation of Religious Attendance Using the American Time Use Study and the General Social Survey." *Journal for the Scientific Study of Religion* 50: 103–15.

Brewer, Paul. 2003. "The Shifting Foundation of Public Opinion about Gay Rights." *Journal of Politics* 65: 1208–20.

Brewer, Paul, and Clyde Wilcox. 2005. "Same Sex Marriage and Civil Unions." In *International Handbook of Catholic Education*, ed. G. Grace and J. O'Keefe, 45–69. London: Springer.

Brewer, Sarah, David Kaib, and Karen O'Connor. 2000. "Sex and the Supreme Court." In *The Politics of Gay Rights*, ed. Craig Rimmerman, Kenneth D. Wald, and Clyde Wilcox, 377–408. Chicago: University of Chicago Press.

Bridenbaugh, Carl. 1962. *Mitre and Sceptre: Transatlantic Faiths, Ideas, Personalities, and Politics, 1689–1775*. New York: Oxford University Press.

Brint, Steven, and Seth Abrutyn. 2010. "Who's Right about the Right? Comparing Competing Explanations of the Link between White Evangelicals and Conservative Politics in the United States." *Journal for the Scientific Study of Religion* 49: 328–50.

Brint, Steven, and Jean Reith Schroedel, eds. 2009. *Evangelicals and Democracy in America*. 2 vols. New York: Russell Sage Foundation.

Brown, Brian Edward. 1999. *Religion, Law, and the Land: Native Americans and the Judicial Interpretation of Sacred Land*. Westport, CT: Greenwood.

Brown, D., and Corwin Smidt. 2003. "Media and Clergy: Influencing the Influential?" *Journal of Media and Religion* 2: 75–92.

Brown, Dorothy, and Elizabeth McKeown. 1997. *The Poor Belong to Us: Catholic Charities and American Welfare*. Cambridge, MA: Harvard University Press.

Brown, Khari. 2009. "Racial and Ethnic Differences in the Political Behavior of American Religious Congregations." *Sociological Spectrum* 29: 227–48.

Brown, Khari, and Ronald E. Brown. 2003. "Faith and Works: Church-Based Social Capital Resources and African American Political Activism." *Social Forces* 82: 617–41.

Brown, Ronald, and Monica Wolford. 1993. "Religious Resources and African American Political Action." *National Political Science Review* 4: 30–48.

Brown, Steven P. 2002. *Trumping Religion: The New Christian Right, the Free Speech Clause, and the Courts*. Tuscaloosa: University of Alabama Press.

Brown, Steven P., and Cynthia J. Bowling. 2003. "Public Schools and Religious Expression: The Diversity of School Districts' Policies Regarding Religious Expression." *Journal of Church and State* 45: 259–82.

Brown-Douglass, Kelly Delaine. 1993. "Womanist Theology: What Is Its Relationship to Black Theology?" In *Black Theology: A Documentary History*, ed. James H. Cone and Gayraud S. Wilmore. 2nd ed. Vol. 2. Maryknoll, NY: Orbis.

Browne, Patrick, and Timothy Lukes. 1988. "Women Called Catholics: The Sources of Dissatisfaction within the Church, Santa Clara County, California." *Journal for the Scientific Study of Religion* 27: 284–90.

Bruce, Steve. 1988. *The Rise and Fall of the New Christian Right: Conservative Protestant Politics in America, 1978–1988*. New York: Oxford University Press.

Brudney, Jeffrey L., and Gary W. Copeland. 1984. "Evangelicals as a Political Force: Reagan and the 1980 Religious Vote." *Social Science Quarterly* 65: 1072–79.

Bryant, Clell. 2005. "Tocqueville's America." *Smithsonian*, July, 104–7.

Buber, Martin. 1937. *I and Thou*. Edinburgh: Clark.

Buddenbaum, Judith. 2001. "The Media, Religion and Public Opinion: Toward a Unified Theory of Cultural Influence." In *Religion and Popular Culture: Studies at the Intersection of Worldviews*, ed. D. Stout and J. Buddenbaum. Ames: Iowa State University Press.

Budner, Stanley. 1962. "Intolerance of Ambiguity as a Personality Variable." *Journal of Personality* 30: 29–50.

Bullis, Ronald K. 1991. "The Spiritual Healing 'Defense' in Criminal Prosecutions for Crimes against Children." *Child Welfare* 70: 541–55.

Burdette, Amy M., Christopher G. Ellison, and Terrence D. Hill. 2005. "Conservative Protestantism and Tolerance toward Homosexuals: An Examination of Potential Mechanisms." *Sociological Inquiry* 75: 177–96.

Burge, Ryan. 2013. "Using Matching to Investigate the Relationship between Religion and Tolerance." *Politics and Religion* 6: 264–81.

Burner, David. 1967. *The Politics of Provincialism: The Democratic Party in Transition, 1918–1932.* New York: W. W. Norton.

Burnham, Walter Dean. 1968. "American Voting Behavior and the 1964 Election." *Midwest Journal of Political Science* 12: 1–40.

Burris, Val. 1983. "Who Opposed the ERA? An Analysis of the Social Bases of Antifeminism." *Social Science Quarterly* 64: 305–17.

———. 2001. "Small Business, Status Politics, and the Social Base of New Christian Right Activism." *Critical Sociology* 27: 29–55.

Bush, Evelyn. 2008. "Measuring Religion in Global Civil Society." *Social Forces* 85: 1645–55.

Bushman, Brad J., Robert D. Ridge, Enny Das, Colin W. Key, and Gregory L. Busath. 2007. "When God Sanctions Killing: Effect of Scriptural Violence on Aggression." *Psychological Science* 18: 204–7.

Buss, Doris, and Didi Herman. 2003. *Globalizing Family Values: The Christian Right in International Politics.* Minneapolis: University of Minnesota Press.

Butler, Jon. 1990. *Awash in a Sea of Faith: Christianizing the American People.* Cambridge, MA: Harvard University Press.

———. 2004. "Jack-in-the-Box Faith: The Religion Problem in Modern American History." *Journal of American History* 90: 1357–78.

Button, James W., Barbara Rienzo, and Kenneth D. Wald. 1997. *Private Lives, Public Conflicts: Battles over Gay Rights in American Communities.* Washington, DC: CQ Press.

Buzzard, Lynn. 1989. "The 'Coming-Out' of Evangelicals." In *Contemporary Evangelical Political Involvement: An Analysis and Assessment,* ed. Corwin E. Smidt, 133–46. Lanham, MD: University Press of America.

Byrnes, Deborah A., and Gary Kiger. 1992. "Social Factors and Responses to Racial Discrimination." *Journal of Psychology* 126: 631–38.

Byrnes, Timothy A. 1991. *Catholic Bishops in American Politics.* Princeton, NJ: Princeton University Press.

Byrnes, Timothy, and Mary C. Segers, eds. 1992. *The Catholic Church and the Politics of Abortion.* Boulder, CO: Westview.

Cadge, Wendy. 2002. "Vital Conflict: The Mainline Denominations Debate Homosexuality." In *The Quiet Hand of God: Faith-Based Activism and the Public Role of Mainline Protestantism,* ed. Robert Wuthnow and John H. Evans. Berkeley: University of California Press.

Cahn, Naomi, and June Carbone. 2010. *Red Families v. Blue Families: Legal Polarization and the Creation of Culture.* New York: Oxford University Press.

Caldeira, Gregory A., and James L. Gibson. 1992. "The Etiology of Public Support for the Supreme Court." *American Journal of Political Science* 36: 635–64.

Calfano, Brian. 2006. "Of Denominations and Districts: Examining the Influence of 'Pro-Life' Denominational Communities on State Representatives." *Journal of Church and State* 48: 83–126.

———. 2009. "Choosing Constituent Cues: Reference Group Influence on Clergy Political Speech." *Social Science Quarterly* 90: 88–102.

———. 2010. "Prophetic at Any Price? Clergy Political Behavior and Utility Maximization." *Social Science Quarterly* 91: 649–68.

Calfano, Brian, and Paul Djupe. 2009. *God Talk: Experimenting with the Religious Causes of Public Opinion*. Philadelphia: Temple University Press.

Calfano, Brian, and Philip Paolino. 2010. "An Alan Keyes Effect? Examining Anti-Black Sentiment among White Evangelicals." *Political Behavior* 32: 133–56.

Calhoon, Robert M. 1994. "The Evangelical Persuasion." In *Religion in a Revolutionary Age*, ed. Ronald Hoffman, 156–83. Charlottesville: University Press of Virginia.

Calhoun-Brown, Allison. 1996. "African American Churches and Political Mobilization: The Psychological Impact of Organizational Resources." *Journal of Politics* 58: 935–53.

———. 1997. "Still Seeing in Black and White: Racial Challenges for the Christian Right." In *Sojourners in the Wilderness: The Christian Right in Comparative Perspective*, ed. Corwin D. Smidt and James M. Penning, 93–114. Lanham, MD: Rowman & Littlefield.

———. 1998. "While Marching to Zion: Otherworldliness and Racial Empowerment in the African American Community." *Journal for the Scientific Study of Religion* 37: 427–39.

———. 1999. "No Respecter of Persons: Religion, Churches and Gender Issues in the African American Community." *Women and Politics* 20: 27–45.

———. 2003. "What a Fellowship: Civil Society, African American Churches and Public Life." In *New Day Begun: African American Churches and Civic Culture in Post–Civil Rights America*, ed. R. Drew Smith. Durham, NC: Duke University Press.

———. 2010. "This Far by Faith? Religion, Gender and Efficacy." In *Religion and Democracy in America*, ed. Alan Wolfe and Ira Katznelson. Princeton, NJ: Princeton University Press.

Callahan, Daniel. 1970. *Abortion: Law, Choice and Morality*. New York: Macmillan.

Calvo, Maria, and Steven Rosenstone. 1989. *Hispanic Political Participation*. Latino Electorate Series. San Antonio, TX: Southwest Voter Research Institute.

Campbell, Angus, Philip Converse, Warren Miller, and Donald Stokes. 1960. *The American Voter*. New York: Wiley.

Campbell, David E. 2004. "Acts of Faith: Churches and Political Engagement." *Political Behavior* 26: 155–80.

Campbell, David, John Green, and Geoffrey Layman. 2011. "The Party Faithful: Partisan Images, Candidate Religion and the Electoral Impact of Party Identification." *American Journal of Political Science* 55: 42–58.

Campbell, David, John Green, and Quin Monson. 2008. "The Stained Glass Ceiling: Social Contact and Mitt Romney's 'Religion Problem.'" *Political Behavior* 34: 277–99.

———. 2012. "The Stained Glass Ceiling: Social Contact and Mitt Romney's 'Religion Problem.'" *Political Behavior* 34: 277–300.

Campbell, David E., and Quin Monson. 2002. "Dry Kindling: A Political Profile of American Mormons." Paper presented at the Conference on Religion and American Political Behavior, Southern Methodist University, Dallas, TX.

———. 2003. "Following the Leader? Mormon Voting on Ballot Propositions." *Journal for the Scientific Study of Religion* 42: 605–19.

———. 2007. "The Case of Bush's Reelection: Did Gay Marriage Do It?" In *A Matter of Faith: Religion in the 2004 Presidential Election*, ed. David E. Campbell, 120–41. Washington, DC: Brookings Institution Press.

———. 2008. "The Religion Card." *Public Opinion Quarterly* 72: 399–419.

Campbell, David, and Carin Robinson. 2007. "Religious Coalitions for and against Gay Marriage: The Culture War Rages On." In *The Politics of Same Sex Marriage*, ed. Craig Rimmerman and Clyde Wilcox, 141–54. Chicago: University of Chicago Press.

Campbell, Ernest Q., and Thomas F. Pettigrew. 1959. *Christians in Racial Crisis.* Washington, DC: Public Affairs.

Cann, Damon. 2009. "Religious Identification and Legislative Voting: The Mormon Case." *Political Research Quarterly* 62: 110–19.

Cannon, Katie. 1988. *Black Womanist Ethics.* Atlanta, GA: Scholars.

Cantor, David. 1994. *The Religious Right: The Assault on Tolerance and Pluralism in America.* New York: Anti-Defamation League.

Caplow, Theodore. 1985. "Contrasting Trends in European and American Religion." *Sociological Analysis* 46: 101–8.

Caplow, Theodore, Howard M. Bahr, and Bruce A. Chadwick. 1983. *All Faithful People: Change and Continuity in Middletown's Religion.* Minneapolis: University of Minnesota Press.

Capps, Walter H., ed. 1972. *Ways of Understanding Religion.* New York: Macmillan.

Carey, George W. 1982. "Religion and American Government Textbooks." *Teaching Political Science* 10: 7–19.

Carmines, Edward, and Geoffrey Layman. 1997. "Issue Evolution in Postwar American Politics: Old Certainties and Fresh Tensions." In *Present Discontents*, ed. Byron E. Shafer, 89–134. Chatham, NJ: Chatham House.

Carpenter, Joel A. 1997. *Revive Us Again: The Reawakening of American Fundamentalism.* New York: Oxford University Press.

Carr, Anne. 1996. *Transforming Grace: Christian Tradition and Women's Experience.* New York: Continuum.

Carroll, Jackson. 1995. "Culture Wars? Insights from Ethnographies of Two Protestant Seminaries." *Sociology of Religion* 56: 1–19.

Carroll, Jackson, Barbara Hargrove, and Adair Lummis. 1983. *Women of the Cloth: A New Opportunity for Churches.* San Francisco: Harper & Row.

Carson, Claybourne, Jr. 1984. "Blacks and Jews in the Civil Rights Movement." In *Jews in Black Perspectives: A Dialogue*, ed. Joseph Washington, 113–31. Rutherford, NJ: Farleigh Dickinson University Press.

Carter, Jimmy. 2005. *Our Endangered Values.* New York: Simon & Schuster.

Carter, Paul A. 1954. *The Decline and Revival of the Social Gospel.* Ithaca, NY: Cornell University Press.

Carter, Stephen L. 1993. *The Culture of Disbelief: How American Law and Politics Trivialize Religious Devotion.* New York: Basic Books.

Carwardine, Richard. 1993. *Evangelicals and Politics in Antebellum America*. New Haven, CT: Yale University Press.

Casanova, Jose. 1994. *Public Religions in the Modern World*. Chicago: University of Chicago Press.

Cataldo, Everett, and John Holm. 1983. "Voting on School Finances: A Test of Competing Theories." *Western Political Quarterly* 36: 619–31.

Cattaro, G., and B. S. Cooper. 2008. "Developments in Catholic Schools in the USA: Politics, Policy and Prophesy." In *International Handbook of Catholic Education—Challenges for School Systems in the 21st Century*, eds. G. R. Grace and J. O'Keefe, 61–83. London: Springer.

Cavendish, James, Michael Welch, and David Leege. 1998. "Social Network Theory and Predictors of Religiosity for Black and White Catholic Congregations." *Journal for the Scientific Study of Religion* 37: 397–410.

Chandrasekaran, Rajiv. 2006. *Imperial Life in the Emerald City: Inside Iraq's Green Zone*. New York: Knopf.

Chapp, Christopher B. 2012. *Religious Rhetoric and American Politics: The Endurance of Civil Religion in Electoral Campaigns*. Ithaca, NY: Cornell University Press.

Chappell, David. 2003. "Stone of Hope: Prophetic Faith, Liberalism and the Death of Jim Crow." *Journal of the Historical Society* 3: 129–62.

———. 2004. *A Stone of Hope: Prophetic Religion and the Death of Jim Crow*. Chapel Hill: University of North Carolina Press.

Chaves, Mark. 1997. *Ordaining Women: Culture and Conflict in Religious Organization*. Cambridge, MA: Harvard University Press.

———. 1999. "Religious Congregations and Welfare Reform: Who Will Take Advantage of Charitable Choice?" *American Sociological Review* 64: 836–46.

———. 2004. *Congregations in America*. Cambridge, MA: Harvard University Press.

———. 2010. "SSSR Presidential Address. Rain Dances in the Dry Season: Overcoming the Religious Congruence Fallacy." *Journal for the Scientific Study of Religion* 49: 1–14.

Chaves, Mark, Helen M. Giesel, and William Tsitsos. 2002. "Religious Variations in Public Presence: Evidence from the National Congregations Study." In *The Quiet Hand of God: Faith-Based Activism and the Public Role of Mainline Protestantism*, ed. Robert Wuthnow and John H. Evans, 108–28. Berkeley: University of California Press.

Chen, Carolyn. 2008. *Getting Saved in America: Taiwanese Immigration and Religious Experience*. Princeton, NJ: Princeton University Press.

Cherry, Conrad, ed. 1972. *God's New Israel: Religious Interpretations of American Destiny*. Englewood Cliffs, NJ: Prentice Hall.

Chesterton, G. K. 1922. *What I Saw in America*. London: Hodder & Stoughton.

Christ, Carol. 1987. *Laughter of Aphrodite: Reflections on a Journey to the Goddess*. San Francisco: Harper.

Christenson, James, and Ronald C. Wimberly. 1978. "Who Is Civil Religious?" *Sociological Analysis* 39: 77–83.

Christian Coalition. 1995. *Contract with the American Family*. Nashville, TN: Moorings.

Cigler, Allen, and Mark R. Joslyn. 2002. "The Extensiveness of Group Membership and Social Capital: The Impact of Political Tolerance Attitudes." *Political Research Quarterly* 55: 7–26.

Claassen, Ryan. 2004. "Political Opinion and Distinctiveness: The Case of Hispanic Ethnicity." *Political Research Quarterly* 57: 609–20.

Claassen, Ryan L., and Andrew Povtak. 2010. "The Christian Right Thesis: Explaining Longitudinal Change in Participation among Evangelical Christians." *Journal of Politics* 72: 2–15.

Claibourn, Michele, and Paul Martin. 2012. "Creating Constituencies: Presidential Campaigns, the Scope of Conflict and Selective Mobilization." *Political Behavior* 34: 27–56.

Clardy, Brian. 2011. "Deconstructing a Theology of Defiance: Black Preaching and the Politics of Racial Identity." *Journal of Church and State* 53: 302–21.

Clark, Cal, and Janet Clark. 1986. "Models of Gender Participation in the United States." *Women and Politics* 6: 5–25.

Clark, Norman H. 1976. *Deliver Us from Evil: An Interpretation of American Prohibition.* New York: W. W. Norton.

Cleague, Albert. 1971. "Black Messiah and Black Revolution." In *Quest for Black Theology*, ed. J. G. Gardiner and J. D. Roberts. Philadelphia: Pilgrim.

Cleghorn, J. Stephen. 1986. "Respect for Life: Research Notes on Cardinal Bernardin's 'Seamless Garment.'" *Review of Religious Research* 28: 129–41.

Clinton, Bill. 1992. "Acceptance Address." *Vital Speeches* 58: 642–45.

Clydesdale, Timothy. 1997. "Family Behaviors among Early US Baby Boomers: Exploring the Effect of Religion and Income Change 1965–1982." *Social Forces* 76: 605–35.

Cnaan, Ram, Stephanie Boddie, Femida Handy, Gaynor Yancey, and Richard Schneider. 2002. *The Invisible Caring Hand: American Congregations and the Provision of Welfare.* New York: New York University Press.

Cnaan, Ram, Robert Wineburg, and Stephanie Boddie. 1999. *The Newer Deal: Social Work and Religion in Partnership.* New York: Columbia University Press.

Cobb, William W., Jr. 1998. *The American Foundation Myth in Vietnam: Reigning Paradigms and Raining Bombs.* Lanham, MD: University Press of America.

Cocca, Carolyn. 2002. "The Politics of Statutory Rape Laws: Adoption and Reinvention of Morality Policy in the States, 1971–1999." *Polity* 35: 51–73.

Cohen, Cathy. 2004. "Service Provider or Policy Maker? Black Churches and the Health of African Americans." In *Long March Ahead: African America Churches and Public Policy in Civil Rights America*, ed. R. Drew Smith. Durham, NC: Duke University Press.

Cohen, Jeffrey E. 2010. "Perceptions of Anti-Semitism among American Jews, 2000–05, a Survey Analysis." *Political Psychology* 31: 85–107.

Cohen, Steven. 1983. *American Modernity and Jewish Identity.* New York: Tavistock.

Cohen, Steven, and Robert Kapsis. 1977. "Religion, Ethnicity and Party Affiliation in the United States: Evidence from Pooled Election Surveys, 1968–1972." *Social Forces* 56: 637–53.

Cohn, Werner. 1957. "The Politics of American Jews." In *The Jews*, ed. Marshall Sklare, 614–26. New York: Free Press.

Coleman, John A. 1970. "Civil Religion." *Sociological Analysis* 31: 67–77.

Coles, Robert. 1985. "Out of the Mouths of Babes: When Ethics and Reality Collide." *Washington Post Weekly Edition*, September 2, 24.

Coles, Roberta L. 2002. "Manifest Destiny Adapted for 1990s War Discourse: Mission and Destiny Intertwined." *Sociology of Religion* 63: 403–26.

Committee on Post Offices and Post Roads. 1830. *Report No. 271*. Washington, DC: U.S. House of Representatives.

Conger, Kimberly H. 2010. "A Matter of Context: Christian Right Influence in U.S. State Republican Politics." *State Politics and Policy Quarterly* 10: 248–69.

Conger, Kimberly H., and John C. Green. 2002. "Spreading Out and Digging In: Christian Conservatives and State Republican Parties." *Campaigns & Elections* 23: 58–65.

Conger, Kimberly H., and Bryan T. McGraw. 2008. "Religious Conservatives and the Requirements of Citizenship: Political Autonomy." *Perspectives on Politics* 6: 253–66.

Connors, John F., Richard C. Leonard, and Kenneth E. Burnham. 1968. "Religion, Church Attitudes, Religious Education, and Student Attitudes to War." *Sociological Analysis* 29: 211–19.

Conover, Pamela Johnson. 1984. "The Influence of Group Identification on Political Perception and Evaluation." *Journal of Politics* 46: 760–85.

———. 1988. "Feminists and the Gender Gap." *Journal of Politics* 50: 985–1010.

Conover, Pamela Johnston, and Virginia Gray. 1983. *Feminism and the New Right*. New York: Praeger.

Converse, Philip E. 1966. "Religion and Politics: The 1960 Election." In *Elections and the Political Order*, ed. Angus Campbell, 96–124. New York: Wiley.

———. 1974. "Some Priority Variables in Comparative Electoral Research." In *Electoral Behavior*, ed. Richard Rose, 727–45. New York: Free Press.

Cook, Elizabeth Adell, Ted G. Jelen, and Clyde Wilcox. 1992. *Between Two Absolutes: American Public Opinion and the Politics of Abortion*. Boulder, CO: Westview.

Cookson, Catharine. 1997. "Reports from the Trenches: A Case Study of Religious Freedom Issues Faced by Wiccans Practicing in the United States." *Journal of Church and State* 39: 723–48.

———. 2001. *Regulating Religion: The Courts and the Free Exercise Clause*. New York: Oxford University Press.

Cooney, John. 1984. *The American Pope*. New York: Times Books.

Copeland, Charlton. 2009. "God Talk in the Age of Obama: Theology and Religious Political Engagement." *Denver University Law Review* 86: 663–91.

Cord, Robert L. 1982. *Separation of Church and State: Historical Fact and Current Fiction*. New York: Lambeth.

Coreno, Thaddeus. 2002. "Fundamentalism as a Class Culture." *Sociology of Religion* 63: 335–61.

Cott, Nancy. 1987. *The Grounding of Modern Feminism*. New Haven, CT: Yale University Press.

Courtwright, David T. 2010. *No Right Turn: Conservative Politics in a Liberal America*. Cambridge, MA: Harvard University Press.

Cousins, Norman, comp. 1958. *In God We Trust: The Religious Beliefs and Ideas of the American Founders*. New York: Harper.

Cox, Harvey. 1968. "The 'New Breed' in American Churches: Sources of Social Activism in American Religion." In *Religion in America*, ed. William G. McLaughlin, 368–83. Boston: Beacon.

Craig, Stephen, and Michael Martinez, eds. 2005. *Ambivalence and the Structure of Public Opinion*. New York: Palgrave Macmillan.

Craig, Stephen, Michael Martinez, James Kane, and Jason Gainous. 2005. "Core Values, Value Conflict and Citizens' Ambivalence about Gay Rights." *Political Research Quarterly* 58: 5–17.

Crawford, Alan. 1980. *Thunder on the Right*. New York: Pantheon.

Crawford, Sue E. S., and Laura Olson, eds. 2001. *Christian Clergy in American Politics*. Baltimore, MD: Johns Hopkins University Press.

Crile, Charles. 2003. *Charlie Wilson's War*. New York: Atlantic Monthly Press.

Curran, Charles E. 1982. *American Catholic Social Ethics: Twentieth Century Approaches*. Notre Dame, IN: University of Notre Dame Press.

Curry, Dean C., ed. 1984. *Evangelicals and the Bishops' Pastoral Letter*. Grand Rapids, MI: Eerdmans.

Curry, Theodore. 1996. "Conservative Protestantism and the Perceived Wrongfulness of Crimes: A Research Note." *Criminology* 34: 453–64.

Curtis, Edward, IV. 2002. *Islam in Black America: Identity, Liberation and Difference in African American Islamic Thought*. Albany: State University of New York Press.

Dalton, John. 2003. *The Moral Vision of César Chávez*. Maryknoll, NY: Orbis.

Daly, Mary. 1973. *Beyond God the Father: Toward a Philosophy of Women's Liberation*. Boston: Beacon.

Dann, G. Elijah. 2010. *God and the Public Square*. Lanham, MD: Lexington Books.

Danso, Henry, Bruce Hunsberger, and Michael Pratt. 1997. "The Role of Parental Religious Fundamentalism and Right-Wing Authoritarianism in Child-Rearing Goals and Practices." *Journal for the Scientific Study of Religion* 36: 496–511.

D'Antonio, Michael. 1989. *Fall from Grace: The Failed Crusade of the Christian Right*. New York: Farrar, Straus and Giroux.

D'Antonio, William. 1994. "Autonomy and Democracy in an Autocratic Organization: The Case of the Roman Catholic Church." *Sociology of Religion* 55: 370–96.

D'Antonio, William, and Dean R. Hoge. 2006. "The American Experience of Religious Disestablishment and Pluralism." *Social Compass* 53: 345–56.

Davidson, James D. 1989. "The Pastoral Letters on Peace and the Economy: A New Approach to Church Teachings." In *Catholic Laity in a Changing Church*, ed. Dean Hoge, 121–31. Kansas City, MO: Sheed & Ward.

———. 1994. "Religion among America's Elite: Persistence and Change in the Protestant Establishment." *Sociology of Religion* 55: 419–40.

Davidson, James, Rachel Kraus, and Scott Morrissey. 2005. "Presidential Appointments and Religious Stratification in the United States, 1789–2003." *Journal for the Scientific Study of Religion* 44: 485–95.

Davie, Grace. 1994. *Religion in Britain since 1945: Believing without Belonging*. Cambridge, MA: Blackwell.

Davis, Cyprian. 1990. *The History of Black Catholics in the United States*. New York: Crossroads.

Davis, Derek H. 1991. "The Supreme Court, Public Policy and the Advocacy Rights of Churches." In *The Role of Religion in the Making of Public Policy*, ed. James Wood Jr., 101–26. Waco, TX: Baylor University Press, J. M. Dawson Institute of Church-State Studies.

———. 2000. *Religion and the Continental Congress, 1774–1789: Contributions to Original Intent*. New York: Oxford University Press.

———. 2004. "A Commentary on the Supreme Court's 'Equal Treatment' Doctrine as the New Paradigm for Protecting Religious Liberty." *Journal of Church and State* 46: 717–38.

Davis, Nancy, and Robert Robinson. 1996. "Religious Orthodoxy in American Society: The Myth of the Monolithic Camp." *Journal for the Scientific Study of Religion* 35: 229–45.

Dawson, Michael, Ronald Brown, and Richard Allen. 1990. "Racial Belief Systems, Religious Guidance, and African American Political Participation." *National Political Science Review* 2: 22–44.

Day, Christine. 1994. "State Legislative Voting Patterns on Abortion Restrictions in Louisiana." *Women and Politics* 14: 45–63.

Day, Katie. 2002. *Prelude to Struggle: African American Clergy and Community Organizing for Economic Development in the 1990s.* New York: University Press of America.

Deckman, Melissa. 2004. *School Board Battles: The Christian Right in Local Politics.* Washington, DC: Georgetown University Press.

Deckman, Melissa, Sue E. S. Crawford, Laura Olson, and John Green. 2003. "Clergy and the Politics of Gender." *Journal for the Scientific Study of Religion* 42: 621–31.

Deedy, John G., Jr. 1968. "The Catholic Press and Vietnam." In *American Catholics and Vietnam*, ed. Thomas E. Quigley. Grand Rapids, MI: Eerdmans.

De la Garza, Rodolfo. 2004. "Latino Politics." *Annual Review of Political Science* 7: 91–123.

De la Garza, Rodolfo, and Jeronimo Cortina. 2007. "Are Latinos Republican but Just Don't Know It? The Latino Votes in 2000 and 2004 Presidential Elections." *American Politics Research* 35: 202–23.

De la Garza, Rodolfo, Louis DeSipio, F. Chris Garcia, and Angelo Falcon. 1992. *Latino Voices: Mexican, Puerto Rican and Cuban Perspectives in American Politics.* Boulder, CO: Westview.

DeLeon, Richard, and Katherine Naff. 2004. "Identity Politics and Local Political Culture." *Urban Affairs Review* 39: 689–719.

Deloria, Vine, Jr. 1992. "Secularism, Civil Religion, and the Religious Freedom of American Indians." *American Indian Culture and Research Journal* 16: 9–20.

DeSipio, Louis. 1996. *Counting on the Latino Vote: Latinos as a New Electorate.* Charlottesville: University of Virginia Press.

DeSipio, Louis, and Rodolfo de la Garza. 1994. "Overview: The Link between Individuals and Electoral Institutions in Five Latino Neighborhoods." In *Barrio Ballots: Latino Politics in the 1990 Elections*, ed. Rodolfo de la Garza, Martha Menchaca, and Louis DeSipio. Boulder, CO: Westview.

Diamond, Irene, and Gloria Feman Orenstein, eds. 1990. *Reweaving the World: The Emergence of Ecofeminism.* San Francisco: Sierra Club.

Diamond, Martin. 1977. "Ethics and Politics: The American Way." In *The Moral Foundations of the American Republic*, ed. Robert Horwitz, 39–72. Charlottesville: University Press of Virginia.

Dierenfield, Bruce J. 1997. "'Somebody Is Tampering with America's Soul': Congress and the School Prayer Debate." *Congress & the Presidency* 24: 167–204.

———. 2007. "'The Most Hated Woman in America': Madalyn Murray and the Crusade against School Prayer." *Journal of Supreme Court History* 32: 62–84.

Dierenfeld, R. B. 1967. "The Impact of the Supreme Court Decisions on Religion in the Public Schools." *Religious Education* 62: 445–51.

Diggins, John P. 1984. *The Lost Soul of American Politics: Virtue, Self-Interest, and the Foundations of Liberalism.* New York: Basic Books.

Dillon, Michelle. 1999. "The Catholic Church and Possible Organizational Selves: The Implications for Institutional Change." *Journal for the Scientific Study of Religion* 38: 386–98.

DiSalvo, Danile, and Jerome Copulsky. 2009. "Faith in the Primaries." *Perspectives on Political Science* 3: 99–106.

Djupe, Paul A., and Brian R. Calfano. 2013. "Religious Value Priming, Threat, and Political Tolerance." *Political Research Quarterly* 66: 768–80.

Djupe, Paul, and Chris Gilbert. 1999. "The Political Voice of Clergy." Paper presented to the annual meeting of the American Political Science Association.

———. 2001. "Are the Sheep Hearing the Shepherd? An Evaluation of Church Members' Perceptions of Clergy Political Speech." Paper presented to the annual meeting of the Society for the Scientific Study of Religion, Columbus, Ohio.

———. 2003. *The Prophetic Pulpit: Clergy, Churches and Communities in American Politics.* Lanham, MD: Rowman & Littlefield.

———. 2006. "The Resourceful Believer: Generating Civic Skills in Church." *The Journal of Politics* 68: 116–27.

———. 2008a. *The Political Influence of Churches.* New York: Cambridge University Press.

———. 2008b. "Politics and Church: Byproduct or Central Mission?" *Journal for the Scientific Study of Religion.* 47: 45–62.

———. 2009. *The Political Influence of Churches.* New York: Cambridge University Press.

Djupe, Paul, and Patrick Kiernan Hunt. 2009. "Beyond the Lynn White Thesis: Congregational Effects on Emvironmental Concern." *Journal for the Scientific Study of Religion* 48: 670–86.

Djupe, Paul, and Jacob Neiheisel. 2012. "How Religious Communities Affect Political Participation among Latinos." *Social Science Quarterly* 93: 333–55.

Djupe, Paul, and Laura Olson. 2006. "Preaching in a Different Voice? Gendered Clergy Effects on Public Opinion." Paper presented at annual meeting of Society for the Scientific Study of Religion, Portland, Oregon.

Djupe, Paul, Anand Sokhey, and Christopher Gilbert. 2007. "Gender Differences in Civic Resource Acquisition." *American Journal of Political Science* 51: 906–20.

Dobratz, Betty. 2002. "The Role of Religion in the Collective Identity of the White Racialist Movement." *Journal for the Scientific Study of Religion* 40: 287–302.

Dochuk, Darren. 2011. *From Bible Belt to Sunbelt: Plain-Folk Religion, Grassroots Politics, and the Rise of Evangelical Conservatism.* New York: W. W. Norton.

Dohen, Dorothy. 1967. *Nationalism and American Catholicism.* New York: Sheed & Ward.

Dolbeare, Kenneth. 1967. "The Public Views the Supreme Court." In *Law, Politics, and the Federal Courts,* ed. Herbert Jacob, 194–212. Boston: Little, Brown.

Dolbeare, Kenneth, and Phillip Hammond. 1977. *The School Prayer Decisions: From Court Policy to Local Practices*. Chicago: University of Chicago Press.

Dolgin, Janet. 1977. *Jewish Identity and the JDL*. Princeton, NJ: Princeton University Press.

Dollinger, Marc. 2000. *Quest for Inclusion: Jews and Liberalism in Modern America*. Princeton, NJ: Princeton University Press.

Domke, David, and Kevin Coe. 2008. *The God Strategy: How Religion Became a Political Weapon in America*. New York: Oxford University Press.

Dougherty, Kevin D., Byron R. Johnson, and Edward C. Polson. 2007. "Recovering the Lost: Remeasuring U.S. Religious Affiliation." *Journal for the Scientific Study of Religion* 46: 483–99.

Downs, Anthony. 1957. *An Economic Theory of Democracy*. New York: Harper.

Drakeman, Donald L. 2009. *Church, State and Original Intent*. New York: Cambridge University Press.

Dreisbach, Daniel L. 2011. "The Bible in the Political Rhetoric of the American Founding." *Politics and Religion* 4: 401–27.

Drinan, Robert F. 1970. *Vietnam and Armageddon*. New York: Sheed & Ward.

Driskell, Robyn, Elizabeth Embry, and Larry Lyon. 2008a. "Faith and Politics: The Influence of Religion on Political Participation." *Social Science Quarterly* 89: 294–314.

———. 2008b. "Civic Engagement and Religious Activities: Examining the Influence of Tradition and Participation." *Sociological Spectrum* 28: 578–601.

Drobac, Jennifer Ann. 1998. "For the Sake of the Children: Court Consideration of Religion in Child Custody Cases." *Stanford Law Review* 50: 1609–70.

Dufour, Lyn Resnick. 2000. "Sifting through Tradition: The Creation of Jewish Feminist Identities." *Journal for the Scientific Study of Religion* 39: 90–107.

Duke, James T., and Barry L. Johnson. 1992. "Religious Affiliation and Congressional Representation." *Journal for the Scientific Study of Religion* 31: 324–29.

Dunn, Charles W., ed. 1984. *American Political Theology*. New York: Praeger.

Durán, Khalid. 1997. "Muslims and the US Election of '96." *Middle East Quarterly* 4: 3–13.

Duriez, Bart. 2004. "A Research Note on the Relation between Religiosity and Racism: The Importance of the Way in Which Religious Contents Are Being Processed." *International Journal for the Psychology of Religion* 14: 177–91.

Eastland, Terry, ed. 1993. *Religious Liberty in the Supreme Court: The Cases That Define the Debate over Church and State*. Washington, DC: Ethics and Public Policy Center.

Ebaugh, Helen, Paula Pipes, Janet Saltzman Chafetz, and Martha Daniels. 2003. "Where's the Religion? Distinguishing Faith-Based from Secular Social Service Agencies." *Journal for the Scientific Study of Religion* 42: 411–26.

Ebaugh, Helen, Janet Saltzman, and Paula Pipes. 2006. "The Influence of Evangelicalism on Government Funding of Faith-Based Social Service Organization." *Review of Religious Research* 47: 380–92.

Eck, Diana L. 2001. *A New Religious America: How a "Christian Country" Has Now Become the World's Most Religiously Diverse Nation*. San Francisco: Harper.

Eckberg, Douglas, and T. Jean Blocker. 1989. "Varieties of Religious Involvement and Environmental Concern: Testing the Lynn White Thesis." *Journal for the Scientific Study of Religion* 28: 509–17.

Eckert, Ruth E., and Henry C. Mills. 1935. "International Attitudes and Related Academic and Social Factors." *Journal of Educational Sociology* 9: 142–53.

Ecklund, Elaine Howard. 2003. "Catholic Women Negotiate Feminism: A Research Note." *Sociology of Religion* 54: 515–24.

Ecklund, Elaine, and Howard Park. 2007. "Asian American Community Participation and Religion: Civic Model Minorities?" *Journal of Asian American Studies* 6: 1–22.

Edmondson, Brad. 1995. "Unclaimed by God." *American Demographics* 17: 60.

Edsall, Thomas. 1997. "The Cultural Revolution of 1994: Newt Gingrich, the Republican Party, and the Third Great Awakening." In *Present Discontents*, ed. Byron E. Shafer, 135–45. Chatham, NJ: Chatham House.

Edwards, Wendy, and Carolyn Gifford. 2003. *Gender and the Social Gospel.* Urbana: University of Illinois Press.

Elazar, Daniel J. 1980. "The Political Theory of Covenant: Biblical Origins and Modern Developments." *Publius* 10: 3–30.

———. 1984. *American Federalism: A View from the States.* 3rd ed. New York: Harper & Row.

Elifson, Kirk W., and C. Kirk Hadaway. 1985. "Prayer in Public Schools: When Church and State Collide." *Public Opinion Quarterly* 49: 317–29.

Ellison, Christopher G. 1991. "Identification and Separatism: Religious Involvement and Racial Orientations among Black Americans." *Sociological Quarterly* 32: 477–94.

Ellison, Christopher G., and Darren E. Sherkat. 1993. "Obedience and Authority: Religion and Parental Values Reconsidered." *Journal for the Scientific Study of Religion* 32: 313–29.

Emerson, Michael. 1996. "Through Tinted Glasses: Religion, Worldviews, and Abortion Attitudes." *Journal for the Scientific Study of Religion* 35: 41–55.

Emerson, Michael, and Christian Smith. 2000. *Divided by Faith: Evangelical Religion and the Problem of Race in America.* New York: Oxford University Press.

Emerson, Michael, Christian Smith, and D. Sikkink. 1999. "Equal in Christ, but Not in the World: White Conservative Protestants and Explanations of Black-White Inequality." *Social Problems* 46: 398–41.

Epstein, Leon D. 1967. *Political Parties in Western Democracies.* New York: Praeger.

Espinosa, Gastón. 2005. "Latino Clergy and Churches in Faith-Based Political and Social Action in the United States." In *Latino Religions and Civic Activism in the United States*, ed. Gastón Espinosa, Virgilio Elizonda, and Jesse Miranda. New York: Oxford University Press.

Espinosa, Gaston, Virgilio Elizonda, and Jesse Miranda. 2005. *Latino Religions and Civic Activism in the United States.* New York: Oxford University Press.

Etzioni, Amitai. 1988. "Evading the Issues: Progressives' Political Taboos." *Public Opinion* (March–April), 2–4.

Evans, Bette Novit. 1998. *Interpreting the Free Exercise of Religion: The Constitution and American Pluralism.* Chapel Hill: University of North Carolina Press.

Evans, John H. 2002. "Polarization in Abortion Attitudes in U.S. Religious Traditions, 1972–1998." *Sociological Forum* 17: 397–422.

———. 2006. "Cooperative Coalitions on the Religious Right and Left: Considering the Resilience of Sectarianism." *Journal for the Scientific Study of Religion* 35: 195–215.

Evans, Sara, and Harry Boyte. 1986. *Free Spaces: The Sources of Democratic Change in America.* New York: Harper & Row.

Fairbanks, James David. 1981. "The Priestly Function of the Presidency: A Discussion of the Literature on Civil Religion and Its Implications for the Study of Presidential Leadership." *Presidential Studies Quarterly* 11: 214–32.

Farrell, Justin. 2011. "The Young and the Restless? The Liberalization of Young Evangelicals." *Journal for the Scientific Study of Religion* 50: 517–32.

Fastnow, Chris, J. Tobin Grant, and Thomas Rudolph. 1999. "Holy Roll Calls: Religious Tradition and Voting Behavior in the US House." *Social Science Quarterly* 80: 687–701.

Faver, Catherine. 2000. "To Run and Not Be Weary: Spirituality and Women's Activism." *Review of Religious Research* 42: 61–78.

Fein, Leonard. 1988. *Where Are We? The Inner Life of America's Jews.* New York: Harper & Row.

Feldman, Stanley, and John Zaller. 1992. "Economic Individualism in American Public Opinion." *American Politics Quarterly* 11: 3–29.

Felson, Jacob, and Heather Kindell. 2007. "The Elusive Link between Conservative Protestantism and Conservative Economics." *Social Science Research* 26: 673–87.

Fenno, Richard. 1978. *Homestyle: House Members and Their Districts.* Boston: Little, Brown.

Fenton, John. 1960. *The Catholic Vote.* New Orleans: Hauser.

Fenton, John, and Kenneth Vines. 1967. "Negro Registration in Louisiana." In *Negro Politics in America*, ed. Harry Bailey, 166–77. Columbus, Ohio: Merrill.

Ferraiolo, Kathleen. 2013. "Is State Gambling Policy 'Morality Policy'? Framing Debates over State Lotteries." *The Policy Studies Journal* 41: 217–42.

Festinger, Leon. 1956. *When Prophecy Fails.* Minneapolis: University of Minnesota Press.

Fetzer, Joel. 1998. "Religious Minorities and Support for Immigrant Rights in the United States, France and Germany." *Journal for the Scientific Study of Religion* 37: 41–49.

Feuerlicht, Roberta Strauss. 1983. *The Fate of the Jews: A People Torn between Israeli Power and Jewish Ethics.* New York: Times Books.

Finke, Roger, and Rodney Stark. 1992. *The Churching of America, 1776–1990: Winners and Losers in Our Religious Economy.* New Brunswick, NJ: Rutgers University Press.

———. 2000. *Acts of Faith: Understanding the Human Side of Religion.* Berkeley: University of California Press.

Finlay, Barbara, and Carol S. Walther. 2003. "The Relation of Religious Affiliation, Service Attendance, and Other Factors to Homophobic Attitudes among University Students." *Review of Religious Research* 44: 370–93.

Fiorenza, Elisabeth Schüssler. 1984. *In Memory of Her: A Feminist Theological Reconstruction of Christian Origins.* New York: Crossroads.

Fiorina, Morris, Samuel Abrams, and Jeremy Pope. 2005. *Culture War? The Myth of a Polarized America.* New York: Pearson Longman.

First Amendment Center. 1999. *The Bible and Public Schools: A First Amendment Guide.* Nashville, TN: First Amendment Center. www.firstamendmentcenter.org/PDF/bible_guide_graphics.pdf.

———. 2008. *State of the First Amendment 2008*. Nashville, TN: First Amendment Center. www.fac.org/about.aspx?item=state_first_amendment_2008.

Fischer, Patrick. 2010. "State Political Culture and Support for Obama in the 2008 Democratic Presidential Primaries." *Social Science Journal* 47: 699–709.

Fisher, Alan M. 1989. "Where the Jewish Vote Is Going." *Moment* 14: 41–43.

Fisher, Randy D., Donna Derison, and Chester F. Polley III. 1994. "Religiousness, Religious Orientation, and Attitudes towards Gays and Lesbians." *Journal of Applied Social Psychology* 24: 614–30.

Fitzgerald, Frances. 1981. "A Disciplined, Charging Army." *New Yorker* 57: 53–141.

Fleischmann, Arnold, and Laura Moyer. 2009. "Competing Social Movements and Local Political Culture: Voting on Ballot Propositions to Ban Same-Sex Marriage." *Social Science Quarterly* 90: 134–49.

Flint, Andrew, and Joy Porter. 2005. "Jimmy Carter: The Reemergence of Faith-Based Politics and the Abortion Rights Issue." *Presidential Studies Quarterly* 35: 28–51.

Flowers, Ronald B. 2005. *That Godless Court? Supreme Court Decisions on Church-State Relationships*. 2nd ed. Louisville, KY: Westminster John Knox.

Fogel, Robert W. 1999. *The Fourth Great Awakening and the Future of Egalitarianism*. Chicago: University of Chicago Press.

Foley, Michael, and Dean Hoge. 2007. *Religion and the New Immigrants: How Faith Communities Form Our Newest Citizens*. New York: Oxford University Press.

Foltz, R. C. 2000. "Mormon Values and the Utah Environment." *Worldviews: Environment, Culture and Religion* 4: 1–19.

Ford, Thomas E., Thomas Bignall, Thomas Van Valley, and Michael Macaluso. 2009. "The Unmaking of Prejudice: How Christian Beliefs Relate to Attitudes toward Homosexuals." *Journal for the Scientific Study of Religion* 48: 146–60.

Forman, Seth. 1997. "The Unbearable Whiteness of Being Jewish: Desegregation in the South and the Crisis of Jewish Liberalism." *American Jewish History* 85: 121–42.

Formicola, Jo Renee. 1997. "Catholic Jurisprudence on Education." In *Everson Revisited: Religion, Education and Law at the Crossroads*, eds. Hubert Morken and Jo Renee Formicola. Lanham, MD: Rowman & Littlefield.

———. 2009. "Catholic Moral Demands in American Politics: A New Paradigm." *Journal of Church & State* 51: 4–23.

Formicola, Jo, Mary Segers, and Paul Weber. 2003. *Faith-Based Initiatives and the Bush Administration*. New York: Rowman & Littlefield.

Fowler, Robert Booth. 1982. *A New Engagement: Evangelical Political Thought, 1966–1976*. Grand Rapids, MI: Eerdmans.

———. 1989. *Unconventional Partners: Religion and Liberal Culture in the United States*. Grand Rapids, MI: Eerdmans.

Fox, Jeffrey. 2003. "A Typology of LDS Sociopolitical Worldviews." *Journal for the Scientific Study of Religion* 42: 279–89.

———. 2006. *Latter Day Political Views*. Lanham, MD: Lexington.

Francis, John G. 1992. "The Evolving Regulatory Structure of European Church-State Relationships." *Journal of Church and State* 34: 775–804.

Frankel, Carl. 1984. "A Legacy." *American Scholar* 52: 159–66.

Frankl, Razelle. 1987. *Televangelism: The Marketing of Popular Religion*. Carbondale: Southern Illinois University Press.

Franklin, Charles E., and Liane C. Kosaki. 1989. "Republican Schoolmaster: The U.S. Supreme Court, Public Opinion, and Abortion." *American Political Science Review* 83: 751–77.

Frazer, Gregg L. 2012. *The Religious Beliefs of America's Founders: Reason, Revelation, and Revolution.* Lawrence: University Press of Kansas.

Frazier, E. Franklin. 1964. *The Negro Church in America.* New York: Schocken.

Freeman, Patricia, and David Houston. 2009. "The Biology Battle: Public Opinion and the Origins of Life." *Politics and Religion* 2: 54–75.

Friedland, Michael B. 1998. *Lift Up Your Voice Like a Trumpet: White Clergy and the Civil Rights and Antiwar Movements, 1954–1973.* Chapel Hill: University of North Carolina Press.

Friedman, Lawrence M. 1983. "The Conflict over Constitutional Legitimacy." In *The Abortion Dispute and the American System,* ed. Gilbert Y. Steiner, 13–29. Washington, DC: Brookings Institution.

Friedman, Murray. 1995. *What Went Wrong? The Creation and Collapse of the Black-Jewish Alliance.* New York: Free Press.

Froese, Paul, and Christopher Bader. 2007. "God in America: Why Theology Is Not Simply the Concern of Philosophers." *Journal for the Scientific Study of Religion* 46: 465–81.

Froese, Paul, Christopher Bader, and Buster Smith. 2008. "Political Tolerance and God's Wrath in the United States." *Sociology of Religion* 69: 29–44.

Froese, Paul, and F. Carson Mencken. 2009. "A U.S. Holy War? The Effects of Religion on Iraq War Policy Attitudes." *Social Science Quarterly* 90: 103–16.

Frum, David. 1994. "Dead Wrong: Christian Conservatism's Losing Record." *New Republic* (September): 17–20.

Fuchs, Lawrence H. 1956. *The Political Behavior of American Jews.* Glencoe, IL: Free Press.

Funderburk, Charles. 1986. "Religion, Political Legitimacy and Civil Violence: A Survey of Children and Adolescents." *Sociological Focus* 19: 289–98.

Gallagher, John, and Chris Bull. 2001. *Perfect Enemies: The Battle between the Religious Right and the Gay Movement.* Lanham, MD: Madison.

Gallagher, Sally. 2003. *Evangelical Identity and Gendered Family Life.* New Brunswick, NJ: Rutgers University Press.

———. 2004a. "The Marginalization of Evangelical Feminism." *Sociology of Religion* 65: 215–37.

———. 2004b. "Where Are the Antifeminist Evangelicals? Evangelical Identity, Subcultural Location, and Attitudes toward Feminism." *Gender & Society* 18: 451–72.

Gallup, George, Jr., and Jim Castelli. 1987. *The American Catholic People.* Garden City, NY: Doubleday.

———. 1989. *The People's Religion.* New York: Macmillan.

Gamble, Richard. 2003. *The War for Righteousness: Progressive Christianity, the Great War, and the Rise of the Messianic Nation.* Wilmington, DE: ISI.

Gamoran, Adam. 1990. "Civil Religion in American Schools." *Sociological Analysis* 51: 235–56.

Ganin, Zvi. 1979. *Truman, American Jewry and Israel, 1945–1948.* New York: Holmes & Meier.

Garcia, John. 1997. "Hispanic Political Participation and Demographic Correlates." In *Pursuing Political Power: Latinos and the Political System*, ed. F. Chris Garcia, 187–99. Notre Dame, IN: University of Notre Dame Press.

———. 2003. *Latino Politics in America: Community, Culture and Interests*. Lanham, MD: Rowman & Littlefield.

Garcia, Maria C. 2005. "Dangerous Times Call for Risky Responses: Latino Immigration and Sanctuary, 1981–2001." In *Latino Religions and Civic Activism in the United States*, ed. Gastón Espinosa, Virgilio Elizondo, and Jesse Miranda. New York: Oxford University Press.

Garrett, William R. 1973. "Politicized Clergy: A Sociological Interpretation of the 'New Breed.'" *Journal for the Scientific Study of Religion* 12: 383–97.

Garrow, David J. 1999. "Abortion before and after *Roe v. Wade*: An Historical Perspective." *Albany Law Review* 62: 833–52.

Gatewood, Willard. 1965. "Politics and Piety in North Carolina: The Fundamentalist Crusade at High Tide, 1925–1927." *North Carolina Historical Review* 42: 275–90.

Gauchet, Marcel. 1997. *The Disenchantment of the World: A Political History of Religion*. Princeton, NJ: Princeton University Press.

Gay, David. 1996. "In Search of Denominational Subcultures: Religious Affiliation and 'Pro-Family' Issues Revisited." *Review of Religious Research* 38: 3–17.

Gay, David, and John Lynxwiler. 1999. "The Impact of Religiosity on Race Variation in Abortion Attitudes." *Sociological Spectrum* 19: 359–77.

Geertz, Clifford. 1973. *The Interpretation of Cultures: Selected Essays*. New York: Basic Books.

Gehrig, Gail. 1979. *American Civil Religion: An Assessment*. Storrs, CT: Society for the Scientific Study of Religion.

Gibson, James L. 2010. "The Political Consequences of Religiosity: Does Religion Always Cause Political Intolerance." In *Religion and Democracy in the United States: Danger or Opportunity?*, ed. Alan Wolfe and Ira Katznelson, 147–75. Princeton, NJ: Princeton University Press.

Gibson, James L., and Arthur J. Anderson. 1985. "The Political Implications of Elite and Mass Tolerance." *Political Behavior* 7: 118–46.

Gibson, James L., Gregory A. Caldeira, and Lester Kenyatta Spence. 2003. "Measuring Attitudes toward the United States Supreme Court." *American Journal of Political Science* 47: 354–67.

Gibson, James L., and Kent L. Tedin. 1988. "Etiology of Intolerance of Homosexual Politics." *Social Science Quarterly* 69: 587–604.

Gibson, M. Troy. 2004. "Culture Wars in State Education Policy: A Look at the Relative Treatment of Evolutionary Theory in State Science Standards." *Social Science Quarterly* 85: 1129–49.

Giele, Janet Zollinger. 1995. *Two Paths to Women's Equality: Temperance, Suffrage and the Origins of Modern Feminism*. Old Tappan, NJ: Twayne.

Gilbert, Christopher. 1993. *The Impact of Churches on Political Behavior: An Empirical Study*. Westport, CT: Greenwood.

Gilboa, Eytan. 1987. *American Public Opinion toward Israel and the Arab-Israeli Conflict*. Lexington, MA: Heath.

Gilkey, Langdon. 1968. "Social and Intellectual Sources of Contemporary Protestant Theology in America." In *Religion in America*, ed. William G. McLoughlin, 137–66. Boston: Beacon.

Gillespie, Michael, Elisabeth Vergert, and Johannes Kingma. 1988. "Secular Trends in Abortion Attitudes." *Journal of Psychology* 122: 323–52.

Gismondi, Mark. 2005. "Bridging, Bonding, and Civic Engagement: The Nuances of Tocqueville's Art of Association." Paper presented to the annual meeting of the Midwest Political Science Association, Chicago.

Glaser, James M. 1997. "Toward an Explanation of the Racial Liberalism of American Jews." *Political Research Quarterly* 50: 437–58.

Glaude, Eddie, Jr. 2000. *Religion, Race and Nation in Early 19th Century Black America*. Chicago: University of Chicago Press.

Glenn, Norval. 1964. "Negro Politics and Negro Status in the United States." In *Religion, Culture and Society*, ed. Louis Schneider, 623–39. New York: Wiley.

Gober, Patricia. 1997. "The Role of Access in Explaining State Abortion Rates." *Social Science and Medicine* 44: 1003–16.

Godwin, R. Kenneth, Jennifer W. Godwin, and Valerie Martinez-Ebers. 2004. "Civic Socialization in Public and Fundamentalist Schools." *Social Science Quarterly* 85: 1097–1111.

Goldberg, David. 1990. *Foreign Policy and Ethnic Interest Groups: American and Canadian Jews Lobby for Israel*. New York: Greenwood.

Goldberg, Steven. 2008. *Bleached Faith: The Tragic Cost When Religion Is Forced into the Public Square*. Stanford, CA: Stanford University Press.

Goldman, Sheldon. 1966. "Voting Behavior on the US Court of Appeals, 1961–64." *American Political Science Review* 60: 374–83.

Goodenough, Erwin R. 1972. "Religion as Man's Adjustment to the *Tremendum*." In *Ways of Understanding Religion*, ed. Walter H. Capps, 45–48. New York: Macmillan.

Gordon, Elizabeth, and William Gillespie. 2012. "The Culture of Obedience and the Politics of Stealth: Mormon Mobilization Against ERA and Same-Sex Marriage." *Politics and Religion* 5: 343–66.

Gormly, Eric. 2005. "Evangelical Solidarity with the Jews: A Veiled Agenda? A Qualitative Analysis of Pat Robertson's *700 Club* Program." *Review of Religious Research* 46: 255–68.

Gorski, Philip S., and Ates Altinordu. 2008. "After Secularization?" *Annual Review of Sociology* 34: 55–85.

Gorski, Philip S., and William McMillan. 2012. "Barack Obama and American Exceptionalisms." *Review of Faith & International Affairs* 10: 41–50.

Gorsuch, Richard L., and Daniel Aleshire. 1974. "Christian Faith and Ethnic Prejudice: A Review and Interpretation of Research." *Journal for the Scientific Study of Religion* 13: 281–307.

Grammich, Clifford. 2012. *2010 U.S. Religion Census: Religious Congregations and Membership*. Lenexa, KS: Association of Statisticians of American Religious Bodies.

Granberg, Donald. 1981a. "The Abortion Activists." *Family Planning Perspectives* 13: 157–63.

———. 1981b. "Comparison of Members of Pro- and Anti-Abortion Organizations in Missouri." *Social Biology* 28: 239–52.

———. 1982a. "Comparison of Pro-Choice and Pro-Life Activists: Their Values, Attitudes, and Beliefs." *Population and Environment* 5: 75–94.

———. 1982b. "Family Size Preferences and Sexual Permissiveness as Factors Differentiating Abortion Activists." *Social Psychology Quarterly* 45: 15–23.

———. 1987. "The Abortion Issue in the 1984 Elections." *Family Planning Perspectives* 19: 59–62.

Granberg, Donald, and James Burlison. 1983. "The Abortion Issue in the 1980 Elections." *Family Planning Perspectives* 15: 231–38.

Granberg, Donald, and Beth Wellman Granberg. 1981. "Pro-Life versus Pro-Choice: Another Look at the Abortion Controversy in the U.S." *Sociology and Social Research* 65: 424–33.

Grant, Carl, and Shelby Grant. 2012. *The Moment: Barack Obama, Jeremiah Wright and the Firestorm at Trinity United Church of Christ.* Lanham, MD: Rowman & Littlefield.

Grant, Jacquelyn. 1989. *White Women's Christ and Black Women's Jesus: Feminist Christology and Womanist Response.* Atlanta, GA: Scholars.

Greeley, Andrew M. 1985. *American Catholics since the Council: An Unauthorized Report.* Chicago: More.

———. 1988. "Evidence That a Maternal Image of God Correlates with Liberal Politics." *Sociology and Social Research* 72: 150–54.

———. 1989. *Religious Change in America.* Cambridge, MA: Harvard University Press.

———. 1990. *The Catholic Myth: The Behavior and Beliefs of American Catholics.* New York: Macmillan.

———. 1993. "Religion and Attitudes toward the Environment." *Journal for the Scientific Study of Religion* 32: 19–28.

———. 1994. "The Demography of American Catholics 1965–1990." In *The Sociology of Andrew Greeley*, ed. Andrew Greeley. Atlanta, GA: Scholars.

Greeley, Andrew, and Mary Durkin. 1984. *Angry Catholic Women.* Chicago: More.

Green, John. 1993. "Pat Robertson and the Latest Crusade: Religious Resources and the 1988 Presidential Campaign." *Social Science Quarterly* 74: 157–68.

———. 2000. "Antigay: Varieties of Opposition to Gay Rights." In *The Politics of Gay Rights*, ed. Craig Rimmerman, Kenneth D. Wald, and Clyde Wilcox, 121–38. Chicago: University of Chicago Press.

Green, John C., and James L. Guth. 1988. "The Christian Right in the Republican Party: The Case of Pat Robertson's Supporters." *Journal of Politics* 50: 150–68.

———. 1991. "The Bible and the Ballot Box: The Shape of Things to Come." In *The Bible and the Ballot Box*, ed. James Guth, 207–25. Boulder, CO: Westview.

Green, John C., James L. Guth, and Kevin Hill. 1993. "Faith and Election: The Christian Right in Congressional Campaigns, 1978–1988." *Journal of Politics* 55: 80–91.

Green, John, James Guth, Lyman Kellstedt, and Corwin Smidt. 1994. "The Characteristics of Christian Political Activists: An Interest Group Analysis." In *Christian Political Activism at the Crossroads*, ed. William R. Stevenson, 133–72. Lanham, MD: University Press of America.

———. 1996. *Religion and the Culture Wars: Dispatches from the Front*. Lanham, MD: Rowman & Littlefield.

Green, John, Mark Rozell, and Clyde Wilcox, eds. 2006. *The Values Campaign: The Christian Right and the 2004 Elections*. Washington, DC: Georgetown University Press.

Green, John, Corwin Smidt, James Guth, and Lyman Kellstedt. 2005. *The American Religious Landscape and the 2004 Presidential Vote: Increased Polarization*. Washington, DC: Pew Forum on Religion and Public Life.

Greenawalt, Kent. 1994. "The Participation of Religious Groups in Political Advocacy." *Journal of Church and State* 36: 143–60.

Greenberg, Anna. 2000. "The Church and the Revitalization of Politics and Community." *Political Studies Quarterly* 115: 377–94.

Greenberg, Anna, and Kenneth D. Wald. 2001. "Still Liberal after All These Years? The Contemporary Political Behavior of American Jewry." In *Jews in American Politics*, ed. Sandy Maisel and Ira N. Forman, 167–99. Lanham, MD: Rowman & Littlefield.

Griffin, G. A., R. L. Gorsuch, and A. L. Davis. 1987. "A Cross-Cultural Investigation of Religious Orientation, Social Norms, and Prejudice." *Journal for the Scientific Study of Religion* 26: 358–65.

Griffith, Ernest S., John Plamenatz, and J. Roland Pennock. 1956. "Cultural Prerequisites to a Successfully Functioning Democracy." *American Political Science Review* 50: 101–37.

Griffith, R. Marie. 1997. *God's Daughters: Evangelical Women and the Power of Submission*. Berkeley: University of California Press.

———. 2002. "The Generous Side of the Christian Faith: The Successes and Challenges of Mainline Women's Groups." In *The Quiet Hand of God: Faith Based Activism and the Public Role of Mainline Protestants*, ed. Robert Wuthnow and John Evans. Berkeley: University of California Press.

Gross, Rita. 1979. "Female God Language in a Jewish Context." In *Womanspirit Rising: Feminist Reader in Religion*, ed. Carol Christ and Judith Plaskow. San Francisco: HarperCollins.

Grupp, Frederick W., and William M. Newman. 1973. "Political Ideology and Religious Preference: The John Birch Society and the Americans for Democratic Action." *Journal for the Scientific Study of Religion* 12: 401–13.

Guest, Kenneth. 2003. *God in Chinatown*. New York: New York University Press.

Gurwitt, Rob. 1989. "The Christian Right Has Gained Political Power. Now What Does It Do?" *Governing*, October, 52–58.

Gusfield, Joseph. 1963. *Symbolic Crusade: Status Politics and the American Temperance Movement*. Urbana: University of Illinois Press.

Guth, James L., and John C. Green. 1993. "Salience: The Core Concept?" In *Rediscovering the Religious Factor in American Politics*, ed. Lyman Kellstedt and David Leege, 157–76. Armonk, NY: Sharpe.

Guth, James, John Green, Lyman Kellstedt, and Corwin Smidt. 1994. "Onward Christian Soldiers: Religious Activists in American Politics." In *Interest Group Politics*, ed. Allan Cigler and Bertram Loomis. Washington, DC: CQ Press.

Guth, James L., John C. Green, Corwin E. Smidt, and Lyman A. Kellstedt. 1997. *The Bully Pulpit: The Politics of Protestant Clergy*. Lawrence: University Press of Kansas.

Guth, James, Lyman Kellstedt, John Green, and Corwin Smidt. 1993. "The Theological Perspective and Environmentalism among Religious Activists." *Journal for the Scientific Study of Religion* 32: 373–82.

———. 2002. "A Distant Thunder? Religious Mobilization in the 2000 Election." In *Interest Group Politics*, 6th ed., ed. Allan Cigler and Burt Loomis. Washington, DC: CQ Press.

Guth, James, Lyman Kellstedt, Corwin Smidt, and John Green. 2006. "Religious Influences in the 2004 Election." *Presidential Studies Quarterly* 36: 223–42.

Hadaway, C. Kirk, and Penny Long Marler. 2005. "How Many Americans Attend Worship Each Week? An Alternative Approach to Measurement." *Journal for the Scientific Study of Religion* 44: 307–22.

Hadaway, C. Kirk, Penny Long Marler, and Mark Chaves. 1993. "What the Polls Don't Show: A Closer Look at U.S. Church Attendance." *American Sociological Review* 58: 741–52.

Haddad, Yvonne Hazbeck. 1994. "Maintaining the Faith of the Fathers: Dilemmas of Religious Identity in Christian and Muslim Arab Communities." In *The Development of Arab American Identity*, ed. Ernest McCarus. Ann Arbor: University of Michigan Press.

Hadden, Jeffrey. 1969. *Gathering Storm in the Churches*. Garden City, NY: Doubleday-Anchor.

———. 1987a. "Religious Broadcasting and the Mobilization of the New Christian Right." *Journal for the Scientific Study of Religion* 26: 1–24.

———. 1987b. "Toward Desacralizing Secularization Theory." *Social Forces* 65: 587–611.

Hadden, Jeffrey K., and Raymond C. Rymph. 1971. "The Marching Ministers." In *Religion in Radical Transition*, ed. Jeffrey K. Hadden, 99–110. New Brunswick, NJ: Transaction.

Hadden, Jeffrey K., and Charles Swann. 1981. *Prime Time Preachers*. Reading, MA: Addison-Wesley.

Hagan, Jacqueline Maria. 2008. *Migration Miracle: Faith, Hope and Meaning on the Undocumented Journey*. Cambridge, MA: Harvard University Press.

Haider-Markel, Donald. 2000. "Lesbian and Gay Politics in the States: Interest Groups, Electoral Politics and Policy." In *The Politics of Gay Rights*, ed. Craig Rimmerman, Kenneth Wald, and Clyde Wilcox, 290–346. Chicago: University of Chicago Press.

Haider-Markel, Donald, and Mark Joslyn. 2008. "Beliefs about the Origins of Homosexuality and Support for Gay Rights." *Public Opinion Quarterly* 72: 291–310.

Haider-Markel, Donald, and Kenneth Meier. 1996. "The Politics of Gay and Lesbian Rights: Expanding the Scope of Conflict." *Journal of Politics* 62: 568–77.

———. 2003. "Legislative Victory, Electoral Uncertainty: Explaining Outcomes in the Battles over Lesbian and Gay Civil Rights." *Review of Policy Research* 20: 671–90.

Haley, Alex. 1966. *Autobiography of Malcom X*. New York: Random House.

Halfmann, Drew. 2011. *Doctors and Demonstrators: How Political Institutions Shape Abortion Law in the United States, Britain and Canada*. Chicago: University of Chicago Press.

Hall, Mitchell K. 1990. *Because of Their Faith: CALCAV and Religious Opposition to the Vietnam War*. New York: Columbia University Press.

Hallum, Anne Motley. 1989. "Presbyterians as Political Amateurs." In *Religion and American Politics*, ed. Charles W. Dunn, 63–74. Washington, DC: CQ Press.

Hamilton, Marci A. 2005. *God vs. the Gavel: Religion and the Rule of Law*. New York: Cambridge University Press.

Hammond, John M. 1974. "Revival Religion and Anti-Slavery Politics." *American Sociological Review* 39: 175–86.

———. 1979. *The Politics of Benevolence: Revival Religion and American Voting Behavior*. Norwood, NJ: Ablex.

Hammond, Phillip E. 2001. "American Church/State Jurisprudence from the Warren Court to the Rehnquist Court." *Journal for the Scientific Study of Religion* 40: 455–64.

Hammond, Phillip E., and Eric M. Mazur. 1995. "Church, State and the Dilemma of Conscience." *Journal of Church and State* 37: 555–72.

Hammond, Phillip E., Mark A. Shibley, and Peter M. Solow. 1994. "Religion and Family Values in Presidential Voting." *Sociology of Religion* 55: 277–90.

Hampson, Rick. 1995. "Immigrants and the Church: Who's Changing Whom?" *Gainesville Sun*, October 11, 1G, 4G.

Hanna, Mary T. 1979. *Catholics and American Politics*. Cambridge, MA: Harvard University Press.

———. 1984. "From Civil Religion to Prophetic Church: The Bishops and the Bomb." In *American Political Theology*, ed. Charles W. Dunn, 144–53. New York: Praeger.

Hanson, F. Allan. 2009. "The Jurisprudence of the Christian Right: Teachings from Regent and Liberty University Law Schools." *Journal of Church & State* 51: 265–88.

Harley, Brian, and Glenn Firebaugh. 1993. "Americans' Belief in an Afterlife: Trends over the Past Two Decades." *Journal for the Scientific Study of Religion* 32: 269–78.

Harper, Ida Husted. 1969. *The Life and Work of Susan B. Anthony*. New York: Arno.

Harris, Fredrick. 1994. "Something Within: Religion as a Mobilizer for Political Activism." *Journal of Politics* 67: 42–58.

———. 1999. *Something Within: Religion in African American Political Activism*. New York: Oxford University Press.

———. 2012. *The Price of the Ticket: Barack Obama and the Rise and Decline of Black Politics*. New York: Oxford University Press.

Harris, Louis, and Bert E. Swanson. 1970. *Black-Jewish Relations in New York City*. New York: Praeger.

Harris, Richard J., and Edward W. Mills. 1985. "Religion, Values and Attitudes to Abortion." *Journal for the Scientific Study of Religion* 24: 137–54.

Harris-Lacewell, Melissa. 2004. *Barbershops, Bibles and BET: Everyday Talk and Black Political Thought*. Princeton, NJ: Princeton University Press.

Harris-Perry, Melissa. 2011. *Sister Citizen: Shame, Stereotypes and Black Women in America*. New Haven, CT: Yale University Press.

Harrison, Lawrence E. 1992. *Who Prospers? How Cultural Values Shape Economic and Political Success*. New York: Basic Books.

Hart, Roderick. 1977. *The Political Pulpit*. West Lafayette, IN: Purdue University Press.

Hart, Stephen. 1996. "The Cultural Dimension of Social Movements: A Theoretical Reassessment and Literature Review." *Sociology of Religion* 57: 87–100.

———. 2001. *Cultural Dilemmas of Progressive Politics: Styles of Engagement among Grassroots Activists.* Chicago: University of Chicago Press.

Hartman, Keith. 1996. *Congregations in Conflict: The Battle over Homosexuality.* New Brunswick, NJ: Rutgers University Press.

Haskell, David M. 2012. "The Theological Meaning of Jesus' Resurrection: A Content Analysis of Mainline and Conservative Protestant Easter Sunday Sermons." *Journal of Empirical Theology* 25: 205–35.

Hastings, Philip K., and Dean R. Hoge. 1986. "Religious and Moral Attitude Trends among College Students, 1948–84." *Social Forces* 65: 370–76.

Hatch, Nathan O. 1990. "The Democratization of Christianity and the Character of American Politics." In *Religion and American Politics,* ed. Mark A. Noll, 92–120. New York: Oxford University Press.

Haughey, John C. 1979. *Personal Values in Public Policy.* New York: Paulist.

Hayes, Bernadette, and Manussos Marangudakis. 2000. "Religion, Politics and Environmental Concern." *Review of Religious Research* 42: 159–75.

Hays, Bradley D. 2012. "The Curious Case of School Prayer: Political Entrepreneurship and the Resilience of Legal Institutions." *Politics and Religion* 5: 394–418.

Healy, James. 1989. *Northern Ireland Dilemma: An American Irish Imperative.* New York: Peter Lang.

Heath, Anthony, Bridget Taylor, and Gavor Toka. 1993. "Religion, Morality and Politics." In *International Social Attitudes: The Tenth BSA Report,* ed. Roger Jowell, Lindsay Brook, and Lizanne Dowds, 49–80. Aldershot, UK: Dartmouth.

Heclo, Hugh. 2007. "Is America a Christian Nation?" *Political Science Quarterly* 122: 59–87.

Hedges, Chris. 2006. *American Fascists: The Christian Right and the War on America.* New York: Free Press.

Heine, Susanne. 1988. *Matriarchs, Goddesses and Images of God.* Minneapolis: Augsburg Press.

Hempel, Lynn M., and John P. Bartkowski. 2008. "Scripture, Sin and Salvation: Theological Conservatism Reconsidered." *Social Forces* 86: 1647–74.

Henderson, Jennifer Jacobs. 2004. "The Jehovah's Witnesses and Their Plan to Expand First Amendment Freedoms." *Journal of Church and State* 46: 811–32.

Henry, P. J., and Christine Reyna. 2007. "Value Judgments: The Impact of Perceived Value Violations on American Political Attitudes." *Political Psychology* 28: 273–98.

Henshaw, Stanley K., and Jane Silverman. 1988. "The Characteristics and Previous Contraceptive Use of U.S. Abortion Patients." *Family Planning Perspectives* 20: 158–68.

Hero, Alfred O., Jr. 1973. *American Religious Groups View Foreign Policy: Trends in Rank-and-File Opinion, 1937–1969.* Durham, NC: Duke University Press.

Hero, Rodney, and Anne Campbell. 1996. "Understanding Latino Political Participation: Exploring Evidence from the Latino National Election Study." *Hispanic Journal of Behavioral Sciences* 18: 129–41.

Hertel, Bradley R., and Michael Hughes. 1987. "Religious Affiliation, Attendance, and Support for 'Pro-Family' Issues in the United States." *Social Forces*
65: 858–82.

Hertzke, Allen. 1988. *Representing God in Washington*. Knoxville: University of
Tennessee Press.

———. 1989. "The Role of Religious Lobbies." In *Religion in American Politics*, ed.
Charles Dunn. Washington, DC: CQ Press.

———. 1991. "An Assessment of the Mainline Churches since 1945." In *The Role of
Religion in the Making of Public Policy*, ed. James E. Wood Jr., 43–80. Waco, TX:
J. M. Dawson Institute of Church-State Studies, Baylor University.

———. 1993. *Echoes of Discontent: Jesse Jackson, Pat Robertson, and the Resurgence of
Populism*. Washington, DC: CQ Press.

———. 2004. *Freeing God's Children*. Lanham, MD: Rowman & Littlefield.

Heyrman, Christine Leigh. 1997. *Southern Cross: The Beginnings of the Bible Belt*.
Chapel Hill: University of North Carolina Press.

Hill, Kim Quaile, and Tetsya Matsubayashi. 2008. "Church Engagement, Religious Values and Mass-Elite Policy Agenda Agreement in Local Communities."
American Journal of Political Science 52: 570–84.

Hill, Patricia. 2000. "Commentary: Religion as a Category of Diplomatic Analysis." *Diplomatic History* 24: 633–40.

Himmelstein, Jerome. 1986. "The Social Bases of Antifeminism: Religious Networks and Culture." *Journal for the Scientific Study of Religion* 25: 1–15.

Hinojosa, Victor, and Jerry Park. 2004. "Religion and the Paradox of Inequality
Attitudes." *Journal for the Scientific Study of Religion* 43: 229–38.

Hirschl, Thomas A., James G. Booth, and Leland L. Glenna. 2009. "The Link between Voter Choice and Religious Identity in Contemporary Society: Bringing
Classical Theory Back In." *Social Science Quarterly* 90: 927.

Hodgkinson, Virginia A., Murray S. Weitzman, and Arthur D. Kirsch. 1988. *From
Belief to Commitment: The Activities and Finances of Religious Congregations in the
United States*. Washington, DC: Independent Sector.

Hoffmann, John, and Alan Miller. 1997. "Social and Political Attitudes among
Religious Groups." *Journal for the Scientific Study of Religion* 36: 52–70.

Hofman, Brenda D. 1986. "Political Theology: The Role of Organized Religion in
the Anti-Abortion Movement." *Journal of Church and State* 28: 225–48.

Hofrenning, Daniel. 1995. *In Washington but Not of It: The Prophetic Politics of Religious Lobbyists*. Philadelphia: Temple University Press.

Hofstadter, Richard. 1965. *The Paranoid Style in American Politics*. New York: Vintage.

Hofstetter, C. Richard, John W. Ayers, and Robert Perry. 2008. "The Bishops and
Their Flock: John Kerry and the Case of Catholic Voters in 2004." *Politics and
Religion* 1: 436–55.

Hoge, Dean, William Dinges, Mary Johnson, S.N.D. de N., and Juan Gonzales
Jr. 2001. *Young Adult Catholics: Religion in a Culture of Choice*. Notre Dame, IN:
University of Notre Dame Press.

Hoge, Dean R., Benton Johnson, and Donald A. Luidens. 1994. *Vanishing Boundaries: The Religion of Mainline Protestant Baby Boomers*. Louisville, KY: Westminster / Knox.

Hollenbach, David. 1990. "Liberalism, Communitarianism, and the Bishops' Pastoral Letter on the Economy." In *Church Polity and American Politics*, ed. Mary C. Segers, 99–118. New York: Garland.

Horwitz, Robert H. 1977. "John Locke and the Preservation of Liberty: A Perennial Problem of Civic Education." In *The Moral Foundations of the American Republic*, ed. Robert Horwitz, 129–56. Charlottesville: University Press of Virginia.

Hout, Michael, Andrew Greeley, and Melissa J. Wilde. 2001. "The Demographic Imperative in Religious Change in the United States." *American Journal of Sociology* 107: 468–500.

Howe, Daniel Walker. 1990. "Religion and Politics in the Antebellum North." In *Religion and American Politics*, ed. Mark A. Noll, 121–45. New York: Oxford University Press.

Hritzuk, Natasha, and David Park. 2000. "The Question of Latino Participation: From SES to a Social Structural Explanation." *Social Science Quarterly* 81: 151–66.

Huckfeldt, Robert, Eric Plutzer, and John Sprague. 1993. "Alternative Contexts of Political Behavior: Churches, Neighborhoods and Individuals." *Journal of Politics* 55: 365–81.

Hudson, Winthrop S. 1965. "John Locke: Heir of Puritan Political Theories." In *Calvinism and the Political Order*, ed. George L. Hunt, 108–29. Philadelphia: Westminster.

Hughes, Richard A. 2004. "The Death of Children by Faith-Based Medical Neglect." *Journal of Law and Religion* 20: 247–65.

Hughes, Richard T. 2009. *Christian America and the Kingdom of God*. Urbana: University of Illinois Press.

Hughey, Michael W. 1984. "The Political Covenant: Protestant Foundations of the American State." *State, Culture and Society* 1: 113–56.

Hunsberger, Bruce. 1996. "Religious Fundamentalism, Right-Wing Authoritarianism, and Hostility toward Homosexuals in Non-Christian Religious Groups." *International Journal for the Psychology of Religion* 6: 39–49.

Hunt, Larry. 2000. "Religion and Secular Status among Hispanics in the United States: Catholicism and Varieties of Hispanic Protestantism." *Social Science Quarterly* 81: 344–62.

———. 2001. "Religion, Gender and the Hispanic Experience in the United States: Catholic-Protestant Differences in Religious Involvement, Social Status and Gender Role Attitudes." *Review of Religious Research* 43: 139–60.

Hunt, Matthew. 2002. "Religion, Race/Ethnicity and Beliefs about Poverty." *Social Science Quarterly* 83: 810–31.

Hunt, Robert V., Jr. 1999. "The Fundamentalist–Ku Klux Klan Alliance: A Colorado Study (1921–1926)." *Journal of the West* 38: 83–90.

Hunter, James Davison. 1983. *American Evangelicalism: Conservative Religion and the Quandary of Modernity*. New Brunswick, NJ: Rutgers University Press.

———. 1991. *Culture Wars: The Struggle to Define America*. New York: Basic Books.

Hunter, Lori, and Michael Toney. 2005. "Religion and Attitudes toward the Environment: A Comparison of Mormons and the General US Population." *Social Science Journal* 42: 25–38.

Huntington, Samuel P. 1996. *The Clash of Civilizations and the Remaking of World Order*. New York: Simon & Schuster.

Hutcheson, John, and George Taylor. 1973. "Religious Variables, Political System Characteristics and Policy Outputs in American States." *American Journal of Political Science* 17: 414–21.

Iannaccone, Laurence. 1992. "Sacrifice and Stigma: Reducing Free Riding in Cults, Communes and Other Collectivities." *Journal of Political Economy* 100: 271–91.

———. 1994. "Why Strict Churches Are Strong." *American Journal of Sociology* 99: 1180–1211.

———. 1995. "Risk, Rationality and Religious Portfolios." *Economic Inquiry* 33: 285–95.

Inboden, William. 2008. *Religion and American Foreign Policy, 1945–1960: The Soul of Containment*. New York: Cambridge University Press.

Inkeles, Alex. 1983. *Exploring Individual Modernity*. Cambridge, MA: Harvard University Press.

Irvine, William. 1974. "Explaining the Religious Basis of the Canadian Partisan Identity: Success on a Third Try." *Canadian Journal of Political Science* 7: 560–63.

Ivers, Gregg. 1995. *To Build a Wall: American Jews and the Separation of Church and State*. Charlottesville: University Press of Virginia.

Jackson, Lynne M., and Bruce Hunsberger. 1999. "An Intergroup Perspective on Religion and Prejudice." *Journal for the Scientific Study of Religion* 38: 509–23.

Jackson-Elmoore, Cynthia, Richard C. Hula, and Laura Reese. 2011. *Reinventing Civil Society: The Emerging Role of Faith-Based Organizations*. Armonk, NY: Sharpe.

Jacobs, David, and Jason Carmichael. 2004. "Ideology, Social Threat and the Death Sentence: Capital Sentences Across Time and Space." *Social Forces* 83: 249–78.

Jaffe, Frederick S., Barbara Lindheim, and Philip R. Lee. 1981. *Abortion Politics: Private Morality and Public Policy*. New York: McGraw Hill.

Jalalzai, Farida. 2009. "The Politics of Muslims in America." *Politics and Religion* 2: 163–95.

———. 2011. "Anxious and Active: Muslim Perception of Discrimination and Treatment and Its Political Consequences in the Post-September 11, 2001 United States." *Politics and Religion* 4: 71–107.

Jamal, Amaney. 2005. "The Political Participation and Engagement of Muslim Americans." *American Politics Research* 33: 521–44.

Jeavons, T. H. 1998. "Identifying Characteristics of Religious Organizations: An Exploratory Proposal." In *Sacred Companies: Organizational Aspects of Religion and Religious Aspects of Organizations*, ed. N. J. Demerath III et al. New York: Oxford University Press.

Jelen, Ted G. 1984. "Respect for Life, Sexual Morality, and Opposition to Abortion." *Review of Religious Research* 25: 220–31.

———. 1987. "The Effects of Religious Separatism on White Protestants in the 1984 Presidential Election." *Sociological Analysis* 48: 30–45.

———. 1992. "Political Christianity: A Contextual Analysis." *American Journal of Political Science* 36: 692–714.

———. 1993a. "The Political Consequences of Religious Group Attitudes." *Journal of Politics* 55: 178–90.

———. 1993b. *The Political World of the Clergy*. Westport, CT: Greenwood.

———. 1994. "Religion and Foreign Policy Attitudes: Exploring the Effects of Denomination and Doctrine." *American Politics Quarterly* 22: 382–400.

———. 1997a. "Citizenship, Discipleship, and Democracy: Evaluating the Impact of the Christian Right." In *Sojourners in the Wilderness: The Christian Right in Comparative Perspective*, ed. Corwin E. Smidt and James Penning, 249–68. Lanham, MD: Rowman & Littlefield.

———. 1997b. "Culture Wars and the Party System: Religion and Realignment, 1972–1993." In *Cultural Wars in American Politics: Critical Reviews of a Popular Myth*, ed. Rhys H. Williams, 145–58. New York: Aldine de Gruyter.

———. 1998. "Research in Religion and Mass Political Behavior in the United States." *American Politics Quarterly* 26: 110–34.

Jelen, Ted, and Clyde Wilcox. 1993. "Preaching to the Converted: The Causes and Consequences of Viewing Religious Television." In *Rediscovering the Religious Factor in American Politics*, ed. David C. Leege and Lyman Kellstedt, 255–69. Armonk, NY: Sharpe.

Jenkins, J. Craig. 1983. "Resource Mobilization: Theory and Study of Social Movements." *Annual Review of Sociology* 49: 421–29.

Jenkins, Philip. 2004. *Dream Catchers: How Mainstream Americans Discovered Native Spirituality*. New York: Oxford University Press.

Jenkinson, Edward B. 1979. *Censors in the Classroom*. New York: Avon.

Jensen, Richard. 1980. "Armies, Admen and Crusaders: Strategies to Win Elections." *Public Opinion* 3: 44–53.

John, Richard R. 1990. "Taking Sabbatarianism Seriously: The Postal System, the Sabbath, and the Transformation of American Political Culture." *Journal of the Early Republic* 10: 517–67.

Johnson, Charles. 1976. "Political Culture in American States: Elazar's Formulations Examined." *American Journal of Political Science* 20: 491–509.

Johnson, Richard M. 1967. *The Dynamics of Compliance: Supreme Court Decision-Making from a New Perspective*. Evanston, IL: Northwestern University Press.

Johnson, Stephen. 1994. "What Relates to Vote for Three Religious Categories?" *Sociology of Religion* 55: 263–75.

———. 2006. "Religion and Anti-Islamic Attitudes." *Review of Religious Research* 68: 5–16.

Johnson, Stephen D., and Joseph B. Tamney. 1988. "Factors Related to Inconsistent Life-Views." *Review of Religious Research* 30: 40–46.

———. 2001. "Social Traditionalism and Economic Conservatism: Two Conservative Political Ideologies in the United States." *Journal of Social Psychology* 141: 233–43.

Johnson, Stephen D., Joseph B. Tamney, and Ronald Burton. 1989. "Pat Robertson: Who Supported His Candidacy for President?" *Journal for the Scientific Study of Religion* 28: 387–99.

Johnston, Douglas, and Cynthia Sampson, eds. 1994. *Religion, the Missing Dimension of Statecraft*. New York: Oxford University Press.

Johnston, Hank, and Bert Klandermans, eds. 1995. *Social Movements and Culture*. Minneapolis: University of Minnesota Press.

Johnston, Michael. 1983. "Corruption and Political Culture in America: An Empirical Perspective." *Publius* 13: 19–39.

Joliceur, Pamela M., and Louis K. Knowles. 1978. "Fraternal Organizations and Civil Religion: Scottish Rite Freemasonry." *Review of Religious Research* 20: 3–22.

Jones, Ethel B. 1983. "ERA Voting: Labor Force Attachment, Marriage and Religion." *Journal of Legal Studies* 12: 157–68.

Jones, Rachel K., Lawrence B. Finer, and Susheela Singh. 2010. *Characteristics of U.S. Abortion Patients, 2008*. New York: Guttmacher Institute.

Jones, Robert P. and Daniel Cox. 2010. *Religion and the Tea Party in the 2010 Election*. Washington, DC: Public Religion Research Institute.

Jones, Robert P., Daniel Cox, and Juhem Navarro-Rivera. 2012. *The 2012 Post-Election American Values Survey*. Washington, DC: Public Religion Research Institute.

Jones-Correa, Michael, and David Leal. 2001. "Political Participation: Does Religion Matter?" *Political Research Quarterly* 54: 751–70.

Jung, Patricia Beattie, and Thomas A. Shannon, eds. 1988. *Abortion and Catholicism: The American Debate*. New York: Crossroads.

Kalkan, Kerem, Geoffrey Layman, and Eric Uslaner. 2009. "Bands of Others? Attitudes toward Muslims in Contemporary American Society." *Journal of Politics* 71: 847–62.

Kalyvas, Stathis N. 1998. "Democracy and Religious Politics: Evidence from Belgium." *Comparative Politics* 31: 292–320.

Kanagy, Conrad, and Fern Willits. 1993. "A Greening of Religion? Some Evidence from a Pennsylvania Sample." *Social Science Quarterly* 74: 674–83.

Katz, Ellis. 1965. "Patterns of Compliance with the *Schempp* Decision." *Journal of Public Law* 14: 396–408.

Katznelson, Ira, and Gareth Stedman Jones, eds. 2010. *Religion and the Political Imagination*. New York: Cambridge University Press.

Katznelson, Ira, and Alan Wolfe, eds. 2010. *Religion and Democracy in the United States: Danger or Opportunity?* Princeton, NJ: Princeton University Press.

Kaufman, Debra. 1991. *Rachel's Daughters: Newly Orthodox Jewish Women*. New Brunswick, NJ: Rutgers University Press.

Kaufmann, Karen. 2002. "Culture Wars, Secular Realignment and the Gender Gap in Party Identification." *Political Behavior* 24: 283–307.

———. 2004. "The Partisan Paradox: Religious Commitment and the Gender Gap in Party Identification." *Public Opinion Quarterly* 68: 491–511.

Kaufmann, Karen, and John Petrocik. 1999. "The Changing Politics of American Men: Understanding Sources of the Gender Gap." *American Journal of Political Science* 43: 864–87.

Kaylor, Brian. 2010. *Presidential Campaign Rhetoric in the Age of Confessional Politics*. New York: Lexington Books.

Kearns, Laurel. 1996. "Saving the Creation: Christian Environmentalism in the United States." *Sociology of Religion* 57: 55–70.

Keith, Bruce E., David Magleby, Candice J. Nelson, Elizabeth Orr, Mark C. Westlye, and Raymond E. Wolfinger. 1992. *The Myth of the Independent Voter*. Berkeley: University of California Press.

Kelley, Dean M. 1977. *Why Conservative Churches Are Growing*. San Francisco: Harper & Row.

———, ed. 1982. *Government Intervention in Religious Affairs*. New York: Pilgrim.

Kellstedt, Lyman A., and John C. Green. 1993. "Knowing God's Many People: Denominational Preferences and Political Behavior." In *Rediscovering the Religious Factor in American Politics,* ed. David C. Leege and Lyman A. Kellstedt, 53–71. Armonk, NY: Sharpe.

Kellstedt, Lyman A., John C. Green, James L. Guth, and Corwin E. Smidt. 1996. "Religious Voting Blocs in the 1992 Election: The Year of the Evangelical?" In *Religion and the Culture Wars: Dispatches from the Front,* ed. John Green, James Guth, Corwin Smidt, and Lyman Kellstedt, 267–90. Lanham, MD: Rowman & Littlefield.

Kelly, Nathan, and Jana Kelly. 2005. "Religion and Latino Partisanship in the United States." *Political Research Quarterly* 58: 87–95.

Kelly, Nathan, and Jana Morgan. 2008. "Religious Traditionalism and Latino Politics in the United States." *American Politics Research* 36: 236–63.

Kennan, George F. 1951. *American Diplomacy, 1900–1950.* Chicago: University of Chicago Press.

Kennedy, Eugene. 1985. *Reimagining American Catholicism.* New York: Vintage.

Kennedy, Morehead. 1985. *The Ayatollah in the Cathedral.* New York: Hill & Wang.

Kenyon, Cecelia. 1955. "Men of Little Faith: The Anti-Federalists on the Nature of Representative Government." *William and Mary Quarterly* 12: 3–43.

Kern, Kathi. 2001. *Mrs. Stanton's Bible.* Ithaca, NY: Cornell University Press.

Kerr, Peter. 2003. "The Framing of Fundamentalist Christians: Network Television News, 1980–2000." *Journal of Media and Religion* 2: 203–35.

Kersten, Lawrence. 1970. *The Lutheran Ethic.* Detroit: Wayne State University Press.

Kessel, John H. 1966. "Public Perceptions of the Supreme Court." *Midwest Journal of Political Science* 10: 167–91.

Kessler, Sanford. 1992. "Tocqueville's Puritans: Christianity and the American Founding." *Journal of Politics* 54: 776–91.

Keysar, Ariela, and Barry Kosmin. 1995. "The Impact of Religious Identification on Differences in Educational Attainment among American Women in 1990." *Journal for the Scientific Study of Religion* 34: 49–62.

Khan, Mohommed A. Muqtedar. 1998. "Muslims and American Politics: Refuting the Isolationist Arguments." *American Muslim Quarterly* 2: 60–69.

———. 2000. "Muslims and Identity Politics in America." In *Muslims on the Americanization Path?,* ed. Yvonne Yazbeck Haddad and John Esposito. New York: Oxford University Press.

———. 2002. *American Muslims: Bridging Faith and Freedom.* Beltsville, MD: Amana.

Kidd, Thomas. 2010. *God of Liberty: A Religious History of the American Revolution.* New York: Basic Books.

Kim, Andrew Eungi. 2005. "Nonofficial Religion in South Korea: Prevalence of Fortune-Telling and Other Forms of Divination." *Review of Religious Research* 46: 284–302.

Kim, P. H. 2004. "Conditional Morality? Attitudes of Religious Individuals toward Racial Profiling." *American Behavioral Scientist* 47: 879–95.

King, Martin Luther, Jr. 1963. *Strength to Love.* New York: Harper & Row.

Kirkpatrick, Lee. 1993. "Fundamentalism, Christian Orthodoxy, and Intrinsic Religious Orientations as Predictors of Discriminatory Attitudes." *Journal for the Scientific Study of Religion* 32: 256–68.

Kirwin, Harry W., ed. 1959. *The Search for Democracy*. Garden City, NY: Double-day-Christendom.

Klatch, Rebecca. 1988. "The New Right and Its Women." *Society*, March–April, 30–38.

Klemp, Nathaniel J. 2012. *The Morality of Spin: Virtue and Vice in Political Rhetoric and the Christian Right*. Lanham, MD: Rowman & Littlefield.

Kleppner, Paul. 1970. *The Cross of Culture*. New York: Free Press.

———. 1979. *The Third Electoral System*. Chapel Hill: University of North Carolina Press.

Klineberg, Otto. 1950. *Tensions Affecting International Understanding: A Survey of Research*. New York: Social Science Research Council.

Kniss, Fred, and Paul Numrich. 2007. *Sacred Assemblies and Civic Engagement: How Religion Matters for America's New Immigrants*. New Brunswick, NJ: Rutgers University Press.

Knoke, David. 1974. "Religion, Stratification and Politics: America in the 1960s." *American Journal of Political Science* 18: 331–46.

———. 1976. *Change and Continuity in American Politics: The Social Bases of Political Parties*. Baltimore, MD: Johns Hopkins University Press.

Knuckey, J. 1999. "Religious Conservatives, the Republican Party and Evolving Party Coalitions in the United States." *Party Politics* 5: 485–96.

Kobylka, Joseph F. 1995. "The Mysterious Case of Establishment Clause Litigation: How Organized Litigants Foiled Legal Change." In *Contemplating Courts*, ed. Lee Epstein, 93–128. Washington, DC: CQ Press.

Koenig, Harold G., Michael E. McCullough, and David B. Larson, eds. 2001. *Handbook of Religion and Health*. New York: Oxford University Press.

Kohut, Andrew, John Green, Scott Keeter, and Robert Toth. 2000. *The Diminishing Divide: Religion's Changing Role in American Politics*. Washington, DC: Brookings Institution.

Koller, Norman B., and Joseph D. Retzer. 1980. "The Sounds of Silence Revisited." *Sociological Analysis* 41: 155–61.

Kornhauser, William. 1959. *The Politics of Mass Society*. Glencoe, IL: Free Press.

Kosmin, Barry, and Ariela Keysar. 2009. "American Religious Identification Study: Summary Report." Hartford, CT: Institute for the Study of Secularism in Society and Culture.

Kosmin, Barry, and Seymour Lachman. 1993. *One Nation under God*. New York: Harmony.

Kotler-Berkowitz, Laurence. 2002. "Social Cleavages and Political Divisions: A Comparative Analysis of British, American and South African Jews in the 1990s." *Journal of Modern Jewish Studies* 1: 204–33.

Kraditor, Aileen. 1969. *Up from the Pedestal: Selected Writing in the History of American Feminism*. Chicago: Quadrangle.

Kraus, Rachel. 2007. "Laity, Institution, Theology or Politics? Protestant, Catholic and Jewish Washington Offices' Agenda Setting." *Sociology of Religion* 78: 67–81.

Kurien, Prema. 2001. "Religion, Ethnicity and Politics: Hindu and Muslim Indian Immigrants in the United States." *Ethnic and Racial Studies* 24: 263–93.

———. 2006. "Multiculturalism and American Religion. The Case of Hindu Indian Americans." *Social Forces* 85: 723–41.

———. 2007. *A Place at the Multicultural Table: The Development of an American Hinduism.* New Brunswick, NJ: Rutgers University Press.

Kuru, Ahmet T. 2007. "Passive and Assertive Secularism." *World Politics* 59: 568–94.

Lacayo, Richard. 1991. "Crusading against the Pro-Choice Movement (Interview of Randall Terry)." *Time* 38 (October 21): 26–27.

Laitin, David. 1978. "Religion, Political Culture and the Weberian Tradition." *World Politics* 30: 563–92.

Lambert, Frank. 2003. *The Founding Fathers and the Place of Religion in America.* Princeton, NJ: Princeton University Press.

Laudarji, I. B., and L. W. Livezey. 2000. "The Churches and the Poor in a 'Ghetto Underclass' Neighborhood." In *Public Religion and Urban Transformation,* ed. L. W. Livezey. New York: New York University Press.

Laumann, Edward, and David Segal. 1971. "Status Inconsistency and Ethnoreligious Membership as Determinants of Social Participation and Attitudes." *American Journal of Sociology* 77: 36–61.

Lax, Jeffrey, and Justin Phillips. 2009. "Gay Rights in the State: Public Opinion and Policy Responsiveness." *American Political Science Review* 103: 367–84.

Laycock, Douglas. 2008. "Why the Supreme Court Changed Its Mind about Government Aid to Religious Institutions: It's a Lot More Than Just Republican Appointments." *Brigham Young University Law Review* 2008: 275–94.

Layman, Geoffrey C. 1997. "Religion and Political Behavior in the United States: The Impact of Beliefs, Affiliations, and Commitment from 1980 to 1994." *Public Opinion Quarterly* 61: 288–316.

———. 1999. "Culture Wars in the American Party System—Religious and Cultural Change among Partisan Activists since 1972." *American Politics Quarterly* 27: 89–121.

———. 2001. *The Great Divide: Religion and Cultural Conflict in American Party Politics.* New York: Columbia University Press.

———. 2010. "Religion and Party Activists: A 'Perfect Storm' of Polarization or a Recipe for Pragmatism?" In *Religion and Democracy in the United States: Danger or Opportunity?,* eds. Alan Wolfe and Ira Katznelson, 212–51. Princeton, NJ: Princeton University Press.

Layman, Geoffrey, and Edward Carmines. 1997. "Cultural Conflict in American Politics: Religious Traditionalism, Postmaterialism and US Political Behavior." *Journal of Politics* 59: 751–77.

Layman, Geoffrey, and John Green. 2006. "Wars and Rumours of Wars: The Context of Cultural Conflict in American Political Behaviour." *British Journal of Political Science* 36: 61–89.

Lazerwitz, Bernard, J. Allen Winter, and Arnold Dashefsky. 1988. "Localism, Religiosity, Orthodoxy and Liberalism: The Case of Jews in the United States." *Social Forces* 67: 229–42.

Leak, Gary K., and Brandy A. Randall. 1995. "Clarification of the Link between Right-Wing Authoritarianism and Religiousness: The Role of Religious Maturity." *Journal for the Scientific Study of Religion* 34: 245–52.

Lee, Jongho, and Harry Pachon. 2007. "Leading the Way: An Analysis of the Effect of Religion on the Latino Vote." *American Politics Research* 35: 252–72.

Lee, Martin. 2002. "The Swastika and the Crescent." *Intelligence Report* 105 (Spring): 18–26.

Leege, David C. 1988. "Catholics and Civic Order: Parish Participation, Politics, and Civic Participation." *Review of Politics* 50: 704–36.

———. 1993. "Religion and Politics in Theoretical Perspective." In *Rediscovering the Religious Factor in American Politics*, ed. David Leege and Lyman Kellstedt, 3–25. Armonk, NY: Sharpe.

———. 1996a. "The Catholic Vote in '96." *Commonweal* 73: 11–18.

———. 1996b. "Religiosity Measures in the National Election Study: A Guide to Their Use, Part I." *Votes and Opinions* (newsletter of the Electoral Behavior Section of the American Political Science Association), 6–9, 27–30.

Leege, David C., and Lyman Kellstedt, eds. 1993. *Rediscovering the Religious Factor in American Politics*. Armonk, NY: Sharpe.

Leege, David, Joel Lieske, and Kenneth Wald. 1991. "Toward Cultural Theories of American Political Behavior: Religion, Ethnicity, Race and Class Outlook." In *Political Science: Looking toward the Future*, ed. William Crotty, 193–238. Evanston, IL: Northwestern University.

Leege, David C., Kenneth D. Wald, Brian S. Krueger, and Paul D. Mueller. 2002. *The Political Mobilization of Cultural Differences: Social Change and Voter Mobilization Strategies in the Post–New Deal Period*. Princeton, NJ: Princeton University Press.

Leege, David C., and Michael Welch. 1989. "Religious Roots of Political Orientations: Variations among American Catholic Parishioners." *Journal of Politics* 50: 137–62.

Legge, Jerome. 1995. "Explaining Jewish Liberalism in the US: An Exploration of Socioeconomic, Religious and Communal Living Variables." *Social Science Quarterly* 76: 366–71.

Lehr, Elizabeth, and Bernard Spilka. 1989. "Religion in the Introductory Psychology Textbook: A Comparison of Three Decades." *Journal for the Scientific Study of Religion* 28: 366–71.

Leiber, Michael J., Anne C. Woodrick, and E. Michele Roudebush. 1995. "Religion, Discriminatory Attitudes and the Orientations of Juvenile Justice Personnel: A Research Note." *Criminology* 33: 431–49.

Leonard, Karen. 2003. *Muslims in the United States: The State of Research*. New York: Russell Sage Foundation.

Lerner, Gerda. 1967. *The Grimké Sisters from South Carolina: Rebels against Slavery*. Boston: Houghton Mifflin.

Lerner, Robert, Althea K. Nagai, and Stanley Rothman. 1989. "Marginality and Liberalism among Jewish Elites." *Public Opinion Quarterly* 53: 330–52.

Lerner, Robert, Stanley Rothman, and Robert Lichter. 1989. "Christian Religious Elites." *Public Opinion*, March/April, 54–58.

Leuchtenburg, William E. 1958. *The Perils of Prosperity, 1914–1932*. Chicago: University of Chicago Press.

Levendusky, Matthew S., and Jeremy C. Pope. 2011. "Red States vs. Blue States: Going Beyond the Mean." *Public Opinion Quarterly* 75: 227–48.

Levine, Lawrence W. 1975. *Defender of the Faith: William Jennings Bryan, the Last Decade, 1915–1925*. New York: Oxford University Press.

Levinson, Sanford. 1988. *Constitutional Faith*. Princeton, NJ: Princeton University Press.

Levitt, Peggy. 2007. *God Needs No Passport: Immigrants and the Changing American Religious Landscape*. New York: New Press.

Levy, Leonard W. 1989. *The Establishment Clause: Religion and the First Amendment*. New York: Macmillan.

Lewis, Gregory. 2003. "Black-White Differences in Attitudes toward Homosexuality and Gay Rights." *Public Opinion Quarterly* 67: 59–78.

———. 2006. "Public Spending on the Arts as Morality Policy: The Structure of Public Attitudes." *Policy Studies Journal* 34: 131–38.

———. 2009. "Does Believing Homosexuality Is Innate Increase Support for Gay Rights?" *Policy Studies Journal* 37: 669–93.

———. 2011. "The Friends and Family Plan: Contact with Gays and Support for Gay Rights." *Policy Studies Journal* 39: 217–38.

Lichbach, Mark Irving. 1996. *The Cooperator's Dilemma*. Ann Arbor: University of Michigan Press.

Liebman, Charles. 1973. *The Ambivalent American Jew*. Philadelphia: Jewish Publication Society.

———. 1988. *Deceptive Images*. New Brunswick, NJ: Transaction.

Liebman, Charles S., and Steven M. Cohen. 1990. *Two Worlds of Judaism: The Israeli and American Experiences*. New Haven, CT: Yale University Press.

Liebman, Robert C. 1983. "Mobilizing the Moral Majority." In *The New Christian Right*, ed. Robert C. Liebman and Robert Wuthnow, 50–73. New York: Aldine.

Lien, Pei-te. 2004. "Religion and Political Adaptation among Asian Americans: An Empirical Assessment from the National Asian American Political Survey 2004." In *Asian American Religions: The Making and Remaking of Borders and Boundaries*, ed. Tony Carnes and Fenggang Yang. New York: New York University Press.

Lienesch, Michael. 1997. "The Origins of the Christian Right: Early Fundamentalism as a Political Movement." In *Sojourners in the Wilderness: The Christian Right in Comparative Perspective*, ed. Corwin Smidt and James M. Penning, 3–20. Lanham, MD: Rowman & Littlefield.

Lincoln, C. Eric. 1982. "The American Muslim Mission in the Context of American Social History." In *The Muslim Community in North America*, ed. Earle H. Waugh, Baha Anu-Laban, and Regula Qureshi. Edmonton: University of Alberta Press.

Lincoln, C. Eric, and Lawrence Mamiya. 1990. *The Black Church in the African American Experience*. Durham, NC: Duke University Press.

Lindsay, D. Michael. 2007. *Faith in the Halls of Power: How Evangelicals Joined the American Elite*. New York: Oxford University Press.

Lippy, Charles H. 1994. *Being Religious, American Style: A History of Popular Religiosity in the United States*. Westport, CT: Greenwood.

Lipset, Seymour Martin. 1960. *Political Man*. Garden City, NY: Doubleday-Anchor.

———. 1964. "Three Decades of the Radical Right: Coughlinites, McCarthyites, and Birchers." In *The Radical Right*, ed. Daniel Bell, 373–446. Garden City, NY: Doubleday-Anchor.

———. 1967. *The First New Nation*. Garden City, NY: Doubleday-Anchor.

Lipset, Seymour Martin, and Earl Raab. 1981. "The Election and the Evangelicals." *Commentary* 71: 25–31.

Lipsitz, Lewis. 1964. "Work Life and Political Attitudes: A Study of Manual Workers." *American Political Science Review* 58: 951–62.

———. 1968. "If, as Verba Says, the State Functions as a Religion, What Are We to Do Then to Save Our Souls?" *American Political Science Review* 62: 527–35.

Littell, Franklin. 1970. "The Radical Reformation and Revolution." In *Marxism and Radical Religion*, ed. John Raines, 81–100. Philadelphia: Temple University Press.

Liu, Baodong, Sharon Wright-Austin, and Byron D'Andra Orey. 2009. "Church Attendance, Social Capital and Black Voting Participation." *Social Science Quarterly* 90: 576–92.

Loconte, J. 2003. "Faith and the Founding: The Influence of Religion on the Politics of James Madison." *Journal of Church and State* 45: 699–715.

Loftus, Jeni. 2001. "America's Liberalization in Attitudes toward Homosexuality, 1973–1998." *American Sociological Review* 66: 762–82.

Long, Carolyn N. 2000. *Religious Freedom and Indian Rights: The Case of Oregon v. Smith*. Lawrence: University Press of Kansas.

Lugg, Catherine, and Malila Robinson. 2009. "Religion, Advocacy Coalitions and the Politics of US Public Schooling." *Educational Policy* 23: 242–66.

Lukenbill, Bernard. 1998. "Observations on the Corporate Culture of a Gay and Lesbian Congregation." *Journal for the Scientific Study of Religion* 37: 440–52.

Luker, Kristin. 1984. *Abortion and the Politics of Motherhood*. Berkeley: University of California Press.

Lupu, Ira C., and Robert W. Tuttle. 2008. "Ball on a Needle: *Hein v. Freedom from Religion Foundation, Inc.*, and the Future of Establishment Clause Adjudication." *Brigham Young University Law Review* 2008: 115–68.

Lutz, Donald S. 1984. "The Relative Influence of European Writers upon Late 18th-Century American Political Thought." *American Political Science Review* 78: 189–97.

———. 1994. "The Evolution of Covenant Form and Content as the Basis for Early American Political Culture." In *Covenant in the Nineteenth Century*, ed. Daniel J. Elazar, 31–48. Lanham, MD: Rowman & Littlefield.

Lynd, Helen Merrell. 1968 [1945]. *England in the Eighteen-Eighties*. London: Oxford University Press.

Lynd, Robert S., and Helen Merrell Lynd. 1929. *Middletown: A Study in Contemporary American Culture*. New York: Harcourt, Brace.

MacIver, Martha Abele. 1990. "Mirror Images? Conceptions of God and Political Duty on the Left and Right of the Evangelical Spectrum." *Sociological Analysis* 51: 287–95.

Maddox, Graham. 1996. *Religion and the Rise of Democracy*. London: Routledge.

Maddox, William. 1979. "Changing Electoral Coalitions from 1952–1976." *Social Science Quarterly* 60: 309–13.

Magleby, David. B. 1992. "Political Behavior." In *Encyclopedia of Mormonism*, ed. D. Ludlow. New York: Macmillan.

Mahaffy, K. A. 1996. "Cognitive Dissonance and Its Resolution: A Study of Lesbian Christians." *Journal for the Scientific Study of Religion* 35: 392–402.

Malbin, Michael. 1986. "Jewish PACs: A New Force in Jewish Political Action." *Jerusalem Newsletter* 90.

Maller, Allen. 1977. "Class Factors in the Jewish Vote." *Jewish Social Studies* 39: 159–62.

Mamiya, Lawrence, and C. Eric Lincoln. 1988. "Black Militant and Separatist Movements." In *Encyclopedia of American Religious Experience*, ed. Charles Lippy and Peter Williams. New York: Scribner's.

Maney, Gregory. 2000. "Transnational Mobilization and Civil Rights in Northern Ireland." *Social Problems* 47: 153–79.

Mangum, Maurice. 2007. "The Ties That Unbind: Exploring the Contradictory Effects of Religious Guidance and Church Attendance on Black Partisanship." *Journal of Black Studies* 4: 1–16.

———. 2008. "Examining the Association between Church and the Party Identification of Black Americans." *Politics and Religion* 1: 200–215.

Mansbridge, Jane A. 1986. *Why We Lost the ERA*. Chicago: University of Chicago Press.

Manwaring, David R. 1962. *Render unto Caesar: The Flag Salute Controversy*. Chicago: University of Chicago Press.

Manza, Jeff, and Clem Brooks. 1997. "The Religious Factor in U.S. Presidential Elections, 1960–1992." *American Journal of Sociology* 103: 38–81.

Margolis, Michael, and Kevin Neary. 1980. "Pressure Politics Revisited: The Anti-Abortion Campaign." *Policy Studies Journal* 8: 698–716.

Marsh, Charles. 1997. *God's Long Summer: Stories of Faith and Civil Rights*. Princeton, NJ: Princeton University Press.

Marshall, Stephen H. 2011. *The City on the Hill from Below: The Crisis of Prophetic Black Politics*. Philadelphia: Temple University Press.

Marshall, Susan E. 1990. "Equity Issues and Black-White Differences in Women's ERA Support." *Social Science Quarterly* 71: 299–314.

Martin, Shane. 2009. "Congressional Representation of Muslim American Constituents." *Politics and Religion* 2: 230–46.

Martinez, Lisa. 2005. "Yes We Can: Latino Participation in Unconventional Politics." *Social Forces* 84: 135–55.

Martini, Nicholas. 2012. "La Iglesia in Politics." *Social Science Quarterly* 93: 988–1004.

Marty, Martin E. 1974. "Two Kinds of Civil Religion." In *American Civil Religion*, ed. Russell E. Richey and D. G. Jones, 139–57. New York: Harper & Row.

———. 1984. *Pilgrims in Their Own Land*. Boston: Little, Brown.

Marty, Martin E., and R. Scott Appleby. 1992. *The Glory and the Power: The Fundamentalist Challenge to the Modern World*. Boston: Beacon.

Marx, Gary. 1967. "Religion: Opiate or Inspiration for Civil Rights Militancy among Negroes." *American Sociological Review* 34: 64–72.

Mason, Patrick. 2011. "God and the People: Theodemocracy in the 19th Century." *Journal of Church and State* 53: 359–75.

Massengill, Rebekah P. 2008. "Educational Attainment and Cohort Change among Conservative Protestants, 1972–2004." *Journal for the Scientific Study of Religion* 47: 545–62.

Mathews, Donald G., and Jane S. De Hart. 1990. *Sex, Gender, and the Politics of ERA*. New York: Oxford University Press.

Matsusaka, John. 2004. *For the Many of the Few: The Initiative Process, Public Policy and American Democracy*. Chicago: University of Chicago Press.

May, Henry. 1976. *The Enlightenment in America*. New York: Oxford University Press.

Mayer, Jeremy. 2004. "Christian Fundamentalist and Public Opinion toward the Middle East: Israel's New Best Friends?" *Social Science Quarterly* 85: 695–712.

Mazur, Eric Michael. 1999. *The Americanization of Religious Minorities: Confronting the Constitutional Order*. Baltimore: Johns Hopkins University Press.

McAdam, Doug. 1984. *Political Process and the Development of Black Insurgency 1930–1970*. Chicago: University of Chicago Press.

McAdam, Doug, John McCarthy, and Mayer Zald, eds. 1996. *Comparative Perspectives on Social Movements*. Cambridge: Cambridge University Press.

McAndrews, Lawrence J. 2000. "Late and Never: Ronald Reagan and Tuition Tax Credits." *Journal of Church and State* 42: 467–83.

———. 2012. "Catholic Cacophony: Richard Nixon, the Church, and Welfare Reform." *Catholic Historical Review* 98: 41–66.

McCartney, Paul T. 2012. "Religion, the Spanish-American War, and the Idea of American Mission." *Journal of Church and State* 54: 257–78.

McClay, Wilfred M. 2004. "The Soul of a Nation." *Public Interest* 155: 4–19.

McClerking, Harwood, and Eric McDaniel. 2005. "Belonging and Doing: Political Churches and Black Political Participation." *Political Psychology* 26: 721–33.

McClosky, Herbert, and John Zaller. 1984. *The American Ethos: Public Attitudes toward Capitalism and Democracy*. Cambridge, MA: Harvard University Press.

McCloud, Aminah Beverly. 1995. *African American Islam*. New York: Routledge.

McCloud, Sean. 2007. *Divine Hierarchies: Class in American Religion and Religious Studies*. Chapel Hill: University of North Carolina Press.

McConkey, D. 2001. "Whither Hunter's Culture War? Shifts in Evangelical Morality 1988–98." *Sociology for Religion* 62: 149–74.

McDaniel, Eric. 2003. "Black Clergy in the 2000 Elections." *Journal for the Scientific Study of Religion* 43: 533–46.

———. 2008. *Politics in the Pews: The Political Mobilization of Black Churches*. Ann Arbor: University of Michigan Press.

McDaniel, Eric, and Christopher Ellison. 2008. "God's Party: Race, Religion and Partisanship Over Time." *Political Research Quarterly* 61: 180–91.

McDaniel, Eric, Irfan Nooruddin, and Allyson Faith Shortle. 2011. "Divine Boundaries: How Religion Shapes Citizens' Attitudes toward Immigrants." *American Politics Research* 39: 205–33.

McDaniel, Stephen W. 1989. "The Use of Marketing Techniques by Churches: A National Survey." *Review of Religious Research* 31: 175–82.

McDermott, Monika. 2009. "Religious Stereotyping and Voter Support for Evangelical Candidates." *Political Research Quarterly* 62: 340–54.

McDonough, Peter. 1994. "On Hierarchies of Conflict and the Possibility of Civil Discourse: Variations on a Theme by John Courtney Murray." *Journal of Church and State* 36: 115–42.

———. 2013. *The Catholic Labyrinth: Power, Apathy, and a Passion for Reform in the American Church*. New York: Oxford University Press.

McDonough, Peter, Samuel H. Barnes, and Antonio Lopez Pina. 1984. "Authority and Association: Spanish Democracy in Comparative Perspective." *Journal of Politics* 46: 652–88.

McGarvie, Mark Douglas. 2004. *One Nation under Law? America's Early National Struggles to Separate Church and State*. DeKalb: Northern Illinois University Press.

McGlen, Nancy, Karen O'Connor, Laura van Assendelft, and Wendy Gunther-Canada. 2002. *Women, Politics and American Society*. 3rd ed. New York: Longman.

McGuire, Kevin. 2009. "Public Schools, Religious Establishments and the U.S. Supreme Court: An Examination of Policy Compliance." *American Politics Research* 37: 50–74.

McKenzie, Brian. 2004. "Religious Social Networks, Indirect Mobilization and African American Political Participation." *Political Research Quarterly* 57: 621–32.

———. 2011. "Barack Obama, Jeremiah Wright and Public Opinion in the 2008 Presidential Primaries." *Political Psychology* 32: 943–61.

McLaren, John, and Harold Coward. 1998. *Religious Conscience, the State, and the Law: Historical Contexts and Contemporary Significance*. Albany: State University of New York Press.

McNamara, Patrick H. 1992. *Conscience First, Tradition Second: A Study of Young American Catholics*. Albany: State University of New York Press.

McQueeney, Krista. 2009. "We Are All God's Children Y'all. Race, Gender and Sexuality in Lesbian and Gay Affirming Congregations." *Social Problems* 56: 151–73.

McRoberts, Omar. 2003. *Streets of Glory: Church and Community in a Black Urban Neighborhood*. Chicago: University of Chicago Press.

McTague, John, and Shanna Pearson-Merkowitz. 2013. "Voting from the Pew: The Effect of Senators' Religious Identities on Partisan Polarization in the U.S. Senate." *Legislative Studies Quarterly* 38: 405–30.

Mead, Sidney E. 1974. "The Nation with the Soul of a Church." In *American Civil Religion*, ed. Russell Richey, 45–75. New York: Harper & Row.

———. 1976. *The Lively Experiment: The Shaping of Christianity in America*. New York: Harper & Row.

Meconis, Charles A. 1979. *With Clumsy Grace: The American Catholic Left, 1961–1975*. New York: Seabury.

Meier, Ken. 1994. *The Politics of Sin: Drugs, Alcohol and Public Policy*. Armonk, NY: Sharpe.

Meier, Ken, and Deborah McFarlane. 1993. "The Politics of Funding Abortion: State Responses to the Political Environment." *American Politics Quarterly* 21: 81–101.

Mellman, Mark S., Aaron Strauss, and Kenneth D. Wald. 2012 "Jewish American Voting Behavior 1972–2008: Just the Facts." Washington, DC: Solomon Foundation.

Menendez, Albert. 1977. *Religion at the Polls*. Philadelphia: Westminster.

———. 1993. *Visions of Reality: What Fundamentalist Schools Teach*. Buffalo, NY: Prometheus.

Mernissi, Fatima. 1992. *Islam and Democracy: Fear of the Modern World*. Reading, MA: Addison-Wesley.

Merrill, Ray, Joseph Lyon, and William Jensen. 2003. "Lack of a Secularizing Influence of Education on Religious Activity and Parity among Mormons." *Journal for the Scientific Study of Religion* 42: 113–24.

Meyer, David. 2004. "Protest and Political Opportunities." *Annual Review of Sociology* 30: 125–45.

Meyer, Donald B. 1961. *The Protestant Search for Political Realism, 1919–1941*. Berkeley: University of California Press.

Meyerson, Michael. 2012. *Endowed by Our Creator: The Birth of Religious Freedom in America*. New Haven, CT: Yale University Press.

Michelson, M. R. 2003. "Getting Out the Latino Vote: How Door-to-Door Canvassing Influences Voter Turnout in Rural California." *Political Behavior* 25: 247–63.

Micon, Joe. 2008. "Limestone Prophets: Gauging the Effectiveness of Religious Political Action Organizations That Lobby State Legislatures." *Sociology of Religion* 69: 397–413.

Milgram, Stanley. 1974. *Obedience to Authority*. New York: Harper & Row.

Millar, Ronald B. 2008. "Strategy Trumps Precedent: Separationist Litigants on the Losing Side of Legal Change." *Journal of Church and State* 50: 299–329.

Miller, Abraham. 1974. "Ethnicity and Party Identification: Continuation of a Theoretical Dialogue." *Western Political Quarterly* 27: 470–90.

Miller, Arthur H. 1993. "Economic, Character, and Social Issues in the 1992 Presidential Election." *American Behavioral Scientist* 37: 315–27.

Miller, Gary, and Norman Schofield. 2008. "The Transformation of the Republican and Democratic Party Coalitions in the U.S." *Perspectives on Politics* 6: 433–50.

Miller, Perry. 1956. *Errand into the Wilderness*. Cambridge, MA: Harvard University Press.

———. 1967. *Nature's Nation*. Cambridge, MA: Harvard University Press.

Miller, Robert T., and Ronald B. Flowers, comp. 1996. *Toward Benevolent Neutrality: Church, State, and the Supreme Court*. 5th ed. Waco, TX: Baylor University Press.

Miller, Warren E., and Teresa E. Levitin. 1976. *Leadership and Change: Presidential Elections from 1952–1976*. Cambridge, MA: Winthrop.

Miller, Warren, and Merrill Shanks. 1996. *The New American Voter*. Cambridge, MA: Harvard University Press.

Miller, William Lee. 1961. "American Religion and American Political Attitudes." In *Religious Perspectives in American Culture*, ed. James Ward Smith, 81–118. Princeton, NJ: Princeton University Press.

Mills, Samuel A. 1991. "Abortion and Religious Freedom: The Religious Coalition for Abortion Rights (RCAR) and the Pro-Choice Movement, 1973–1989." *Journal of Church and State* 33: 569–94.

Min, Pyong Gap. 2002. "A Literature Review with a Focus on Major Themes." In *Religions in Asian America*, ed. Pyong Gap Min and Jung Ha Kim. Lanham, MD: AltaMira.

Mitchell, Joshua. 2007. "Religion Is Not a Preference." *Journal of Politics* 69: 351–62.

Moberg, David O. 1977. *The Great Reversal: Evangelicalism and Social Reform*. Philadelphia: Lippincott.

Mockabee, Steve, Quin Monson, and John Grant. 1999. "Measuring the Impact of Religion in Multivariate Models of Political Behavior and Attitudes." Paper presented to the annual meeting of the American Political Science Association.

Moe, Terry. 2001. *Schools, Vouchers and the American Public*. Washington, DC: Brookings Institution.

Moen, Matthew C. 1989. *The Christian Right and Congress*. Tuscaloosa: University of Alabama Press.

———. 1995. "From Revolution to Evolution: The Changing Nature of the Christian Right." In *The Rapture of Politics*, ed. Steve Bruce, Peter Kivisto, and William Swatos, 123–36. New Brunswick, NJ: Transaction.

———. 1997. "The Changing Nature of Christian Right Activism: 1970s–1990s." In *Sojourners in the Wilderness: The Christian Right in Comparative Perspective*, ed. Corwin E. Smidt and James M. Penning, 21–40. Lanham, MD: Rowman & Littlefield.

Monsma, Stephen, and J. Christopher Soper. 2006. *Faith, Hope and Jobs: Welfare-to-Work in Los Angeles*. Washington, DC: Georgetown University Press.

Moon, Dawne. 2004. *God, Sex and Politics: Homosexuality and Everyday Theologies*. Chicago: University of Chicago Press.

Mooney, Christopher Z. 2008. "Does Morality Policy Exist? Testing a Basic Assumption." *Policy Studies Journal* 36: 199–218.

Mooney, Christopher, and Mei-Hsein Lee. 1995. "Legislating Morality in the American States: The Case of Pre-*Roe* Abortion Regulation Reform." *American Journal of Political Science* 39: 599–627.

Moore, David W. 1993. "Catholics at Odds with Church Teachings." *Gallup Poll Monthly* 335: 21–40.

Moore, R. Laurence. 1994. *Selling God: Religion in the Marketplace of Culture*. New York: Oxford University Press.

Morgan, Douglas. 2001. *Adventism and the American Republic: The Public Involvement of a Major Apocalyptic Movement*. Knoxville: University of Tennessee Press.

Morgan, Richard E. 1984. *Disabling America*. New York: Basic Books.

Morgenthau, Hans, and David Hein. 1983. *Essays on Lincoln's Faith and Politics*. Lanham, MD: University Press of America.

Morris, Aldon. 1992. "Political Consciousness and Collective Action." In *Frontiers of Social Movement Theory*, ed. Aldon Morris and Carol McClurg Mueller. New Haven, CT: Yale University Press.

Mucciaroni, Gary. 2008. *Same Sex, Different Politics: Success and Failure in the Struggle over Gay Rights*. Chicago: University of Chicago Press.

——— . 2011. "Are Debates about 'Morality Policy' Really about Morality? Framing Opposition to Gay and Lesbian Rights." *Policy Studies Journal* 39:187–216.

Mueller, Carol, and Thomas Dimieri. 1982. "The Structure of Belief Systems among Contending ERA Activists." *Social Forces* 60: 657–75.

Mueller, John E. 1973. *Wars, Presidents, and Public Opinion*. New York: Free Press.

Muir, William K., Jr. 1967. *Prayer in the Public Schools: Law and Attitude Change*. Chicago: University of Chicago Press.

Muller, Herbert J. 1963. *Religion and Freedom in the Modern World*. Chicago: University of Chicago Press.

Mulligan, Kenneth. 2006. "Pope John Paul II and Catholic Opinion toward the Death Penalty and Abortion." *Social Science Quarterly* 87: 739–53.

Munoz, Vincent Phillip. 2003. "James Madison's Principle of Religious Liberty." *American Political Science Review* 97: 17–32.

Murchland, Bernard. 1982. *The Dream of Christian Socialism: An Essay on Its European Origins*. Washington, DC: Enterprise Institute.

Murphy, Andrew R. 2008. "Two American Jeremiads: Traditionalist and Progressive Stories of American Nationhood." *Politics and Religion* 1: 85–112.

Murphy, Walter F., Joseph Tanenhaus, and Daniel L. Kastner. 1973. *Public Evaluations of Constitutional Courts: Alternative Explanations*. Beverly Hills, CA: Sage.

Murrin, John M. 1990. "Religion and Politics in America from the First Settlements to the Civil War." In *Religion and American Politics*, ed. Mark A. Noll, 19–43. New York: Oxford University Press.

Myers, Ken. 1994. "Professors at Evangelist's School Sue over Defamation, Contracts." *National Law Journal* 17: 17A.

Myrdal, Gunnar. 1944. *American Dilemma: The Negro Problem and Modern Democracy*. New York: Harper & Brothers.

Nagata, Judith. 2001. "Beyond Theology: Toward an Anthropology of 'Fundamentalism.'" *American Anthropologist* 103: 481–98.

Nagel, Stuart. 1961. "Political Party Affiliation and Judge's Decisions." *American Political Science Review* 55: 843–50.

———. 1962. "Ethnic Affiliations and Judicial Propensities." *Journal of Politics* 24: 92–110.

National Center for Educational Statistics. 2002. *Digest of Education Statistics 2001*. Washington, DC: U.S. Department of Education.

National Election Studies. 2009. *American National Election Study, 2008: Pre- and Post-Election Survey* [Computer file]. ICPSR25383-v1. Ann Arbor, MI: Inter-university Consortium for Political and Social Research [distributor].

National Opinion Research Center. 2008. *General Social Survey 2008*. Chicago, IL: National Opinion Research Center.

Nazario, Sonia. 1992. "Crusader Vows to Put God Back in Schools Using Local Elections." *Wall Street Journal*, July 15, A1, A10.

Neiheisel, Jacob, and Paul Djupe. 2008. "Intra-Organizational Constraints on Churches' Public Witness." *Journal for the Scientific Study of Religion* 47: 427–41.

Neiheisel, Jacob, Paul Djupe, and Anand Sokhey. 2009. "*Veni, Vidi, Disseri*." *American Politics Research* 37: 614–43.

Nelsen, Hart M. 1975. "Why Do Pastors Preach on Social Issues?" *Theology Today* 32: 56–73.

Nepstad, Sharon Erickson. 2004. *Convictions of the Soul: Religion, Culture and Agency in the Central America Solidarity Movement*. Oxford: Oxford University Press.

———. 2008. *Religion and War Resistance in the Plowshares Movement*. New York: Cambridge University Press.

Neuhaus, Richard John. 1984. *The Naked Public Square*. Grand Rapids, MI: Eerdmans.

Newport, Frank. 1993. "Half of Americans Believe in Creationist Origin of Man." *Gallup Poll Monthly*, 24–28.

Newton, Merlin Owen. 1995. *Armed with the Constitution: Jehovah's Witnesses in Alabama and the U.S. Supreme Court, 1939–1946*. Tuscaloosa: University of Alabama.

Nichols, J. Bruce. 1988. *The Uneasy Alliance: Religion, Refugee Work, and U.S. Foreign Policy*. New York: Oxford University Press.

Niebuhr, H. Richard. 1959. *The Kingdom of God in America*. New York: Harper Torchbooks.

Niebuhr, Reinhold. 1944. *The Children of Light and the Children of Darkness*. New York: Scribner's.

Nimer, Mohamed. 2002. "Muslims in American Public Life." In *Muslims in the West*, ed. Yvonne Yazbeck Haddad. New York: Oxford University Press.

Nolan, Hugh J., ed. 1984. *Pastoral Letters of the United States Catholic Bishops*. Washington, DC: United States Catholic Conference.

Noll, Mark A. 1988. *One Nation under God? Christian Faith and Political Action in America*. San Francisco: Harper & Row.

———, ed. 1990. *Religion and American Politics: From the Colonial Period to the 1980s*. New York: Oxford University Press.

Noll, Mark A., Nathan O. Hatch, and George M. Marsden. 1983. *The Search for Christian America*. Westchester, IL: Crossway.

Norrander, Barbara. 1999. "Evolution of the Gender Gap." *Public Opinion Quarterly* 63: 566–76.

Norrander, Barbara, and Clyde Wilcox. 1999. "Public Opinion and Policymaking in the States: The Case of Post-*Roe* Abortion Policy." *Policy Studies Journal* 27: 702–22.

Norris, Pippa, and Ronald Inglehart. 2004. *Sacred and Secular: Religion and Politics Worldwide*. New York: Cambridge University Press.

North, C. M., and C. R. Gwin. 2004. "Religious Freedom and the Unintended Consequences of State Religion." *Southern Economic Journal* 71: 103–17.

Northcott, Michael. 2004. *An Angel Directs the Storm: Apocalyptic Religion and American Empire*. London: Tauris.

Nteta, Tatishe M., and Kevin J. Wallsten. 2012. "Preaching to the Choir? Religious Leaders and American Opinion on Immigration Reform." *Social Science Quarterly* 93: 891–910.

Oberschall, Anthony. 1992. *Social Movements: Ideologies, Interests and Identities*. New Brunswick, NJ: Transaction.

O'Brien, David J. 1968. *American Catholics and Social Reform: The New Deal Years*. New York: Oxford University Press.

Oldfield, Duane. 1996. *The Right and the Righteous: The Christian Right Confronts the Republican Party*. Lanham, MD: Rowman & Littlefield.

Oldmixon, Elizabeth. 2002. "Culture Wars in the Congressional Theater: How the US House of Representatives Legislates Morality, 1993–1998." *Social Science Quarterly* 83: 775–79.

———. 2005. *Uncompromising Positions: God, Sex and the U.S. House of Representatives*. Washington, DC: Georgetown University Press.

Oldmixon, Elizabeth A., and Brian Calfano. 2007. "The Religious Dynamics of Decision Making on Gay Rights Issues in the U.S. House of Representatives, 1993–2002." *Journal for the Scientific Study of Religion* 46: 55–70.

Oldmixon, Elizabeth A., and William Hudson. 2008. "When Church Teachings and Policy Commitments Collide: Perspectives on Catholics in the U.S. House of Representatives." *Politics and Religion* 1: 113–36.

Oldmixon, Elizabeth, Beth Rosenson, and Kenneth Wald. 2005. "Conflict over Israel: The Role of Religion, Race, Party and Ideology in the U.S. House of Representatives, 1997–2002." *Terrorism and Political Violence* 17: 407–26.

Olson, Daniel, and Jackson Carroll. 1992. "Religiously-Based Politics: Religious Elites and the Public." *Social Forces* 70: 765–78.

Olson, Laura. 2002. "Mainline Protestant Washington Offices and the Political Lives of Clergy." In *The Quiet Hand of God: Faith-Based Activism and the Public Role of Mainline Protestantism*, ed. Robert Wuthnow and John Evans. Berkeley: University of California Press.

———. 2011. "The Essentiality of 'Culture' in the Study of Religion and Politics." *Journal for the Scientific Study of Religion* 50: 539–653.

Olson, Laura R., and Wendy Cadge. 2002. "Talking about Homosexuality: The Views of Mainline Protestant Clergy." *Journal for the Scientific Study of Religion* 41: 153–68.

Olson, Laura, Wendy Cadge, and James Harrison. 2006. "Religion and Public Opinion about Same-Sex Marriage." *Social Science Quarterly* 87: 340–60.

Olson, Laura, and Sue E. S. Crawford. 2001. "Clergy in Politics: Political Choices and Consequences." In *Christian Clergy in American Politics*, ed. Sue E. S. Crawford and Laura Olson. Baltimore: Johns Hopkins University Press.

Olson, Laura, Sue E. S. Crawford, and Melissa Deckman. 2005. *Women with a Mission: Religion, Gender and Politics of Women Clergy*. Tuscaloosa: Alabama University Press.

Olson, Laura, Sue E. S. Crawford, and James Guth. 2000. "Changing Issue Agendas of Women Clergy." *Journal for the Scientific Study of Religion* 39: 140–54.

Olson, Laura, Karen Guth, and James Guth. 2003. "The Lotto and the Lord: Religious Influences on the Adoption of a Lottery in South Carolina." *Sociology of Religion* 64: 87–110.

Olson, Mancur. 1965. *The Logic of Collective Action*. Cambridge, MA: Harvard University Press.

Orsi, Robert. 2004. *Between Heaven and Earth: The Religious Worlds People Make and the Scholars Who Study Them*. Princeton, NJ: Princeton University Press.

Ortiz, Isidro. 1984. "Chicano Urban Politics and the Politics of Reform in the Seventies." *Western Political Quarterly* 37: 564–77.

Orum, Anthony M. 1970. "Religion and the Rise of the Radical White: The Case of Southern Wallace Support in 1968." *Social Science Quarterly* 51: 674–88.

Ostrom, Elinor. 1990. *Governing the Commons: The Evolution of Institutions for Collective Action*. New York: Cambridge University Press.

Owens, Michael Leo. 2003. "Doing Something in Jesus' Name: Black Churches and Community Development Corporations." In *New Day Begun: African American Churches and Civic Culture in Post-Civil Rights America*, ed. R. Drew Smith. Durham, NC: Duke University Press.

———. 2007. *God, Government in the Ghetto: The Power of Church-State Collaboration in Black America*. Chicago: University of Chicago Press.

Page, Ann, and Donald Clelland. 1978. "The Kanawha County Textbook Controversy: A Study in Alienation and Lifestyle Concern." *Social Forces* 57: 265–81.

Page, Benjamin, Robert Sharpiro, Paul Gronke, and Robert Rosenberg. 1984. "Constituency, Party and Representation in Congress." *Public Opinion Quarterly* 48: 741–56.

Parenti, Michael. 1967. "Political Values and Religious Cultures: Jews, Catholics and Protestants." *Journal for the Scientific Study of Religion* 6: 259–69.

Park, Jerry, and Samuel Reimer. 2002. "Revisiting the Social Sources of American Christianity 1972–1988." *Journal for the Scientific Study of Religion* 41: 733–47.

Patel, Kant. 2011. "The Politics of Stem Cell Policy: Ballot Initiative in Missouri." *Social Work in Public Health* 26: 158–75.

Pateman, Carole. 1970. *Participation and Democratic Theory*. Cambridge, England: Cambridge University Press.

Patillo-McCoy, Marty. 1998. "Church Culture as a Strategy of Action in the Black Community." *American Sociological Review* 63: 767–84.

Patric, Gordon. 1957. "The Impact of a Court Decision: Aftermath of the *McCollum* Case." *Journal of Public Law* 6: 455–64.

Patterson, Dennis, Gamal Gasim, and Jangsup Choi. 2011. "Identity, Attitudes and the Voting Behavior of Mosque-Attending Muslim-Americans in the 2000 and 2004 Presidential Election." *Politics and Religion* 4: 289–311.

Penning, James M. 1994. "Pat Robertson and the GOP: 1988 and Beyond." *Sociology of Religion* 55: 327–44.

———. 2009. "American Views of Muslims and Mormons: A Social Identity Theory Approach." *Politics and Religion* 2: 277–302.

Perkins, H. Wesley. 1983. "Organized Religion as Opiate or Prophetic Stimulant: A Study of American and English Assessments of Social Justice in Two Urban Settings." *Review of Religious Research* 24: 206–24.

———. 1985. "A Research Note on Religiosity as Opiate or Prophetic Stimulant among Students in England and the United States." *Review of Religious Research* 26: 269–80.

———. 1992. "Student Religiosity and Social Justice Concerns in England and the U.S.: Are They Still Related?" *Journal for the Scientific Study of Religion* 31: 353–60.

Perl, Paul Michael, and Jamie S. McClintock. 2001. "The Catholic 'Consistent Life Ethic' and Attitudes toward Capital Punishment and Welfare Reform." *Sociology of Religion* 62: 275–99.

Persinos, John F. 1994. "Has the Christian Right Taken over the Republican Party?" *Campaigns & Elections*, September, 20–24.

Peterson, Larry, and Gregory Donnenwerth. 1998. "Religion and Declining Support for Traditional Beliefs and Gender Roles and Homosexual Rights." *Sociology of Religion* 59: 353–65.

Peterson, M. Nils, and Jianguo Liu. 2008. "Impacts of Religion on Environmental Worldviews: The Teton Valley Case." *Society and Natural Resources* 21: 704–18.

Pevey, Carolyn, Christine Williams, and Chris Ellison. 1996. "Male God Imagery and Female Submission: Lessons from a Southern Baptist Ladies' Bible Class." *Qualitative Sociology* 18: 173–93.

Pew Forum on Religion and Public Life. 2001. *American Views on Religion, Politics and Public Policy*. Washington, DC: Pew Forum on Religion and Public Life.

———. 2008. *U.S. Religious Landscape Survey—Religious Affiliation: Diverse and Dynamic*. Washington, DC: Pew Research Center's Forum on Religion and Public Life.

———. 2010. *U.S. Religious Knowledge Survey*. Washington, DC: Pew Research Center's Forum on Religion & Public Life.

Pew Research Center. 2012. "Pew Global Attitudes Project." Retrieved September 29, 2013, from http://www.pewglobal.org/.

Pew Research Center for the People and the Press. 2002. *Americans Struggle with Religion's Role at Home and Abroad.* Washington, DC: Pew Research Center for the People and the Press.

———. 2010. *Religion and Public Life Survey.* Washington, DC: Pew Research Center for the People and the Press.

———. 2012. *Political Survey, March, 2012.* Princeton Survey Research Associates International. Washington, DC: Pew Research Center for the People and the Press.

Phillips, Kevin P. 1969. *The Emerging Republican Majority.* Garden City, NY: Doubleday-Anchor.

Piehl, Mel. 1982. *Breaking Bread: The Catholic Worker and the Origin of Catholic Radicalism in America.* Philadelphia: Temple University Press.

Pierard, Richard V. 1983. "From Evangelical Exclusiveness to Ecumenical Openness: Billy Graham and Socio-Political Issues." *Journal of Ecumenical Studies* 20: 425–46.

Pierce, Patrick, and Donald Miller. 1999. "Variations in the Diffusion of State Lottery Adoptions: How Revenue Dedication Changes Morality Politics." *Policy Studies Journal* 27: 696–706.

Plaskow, Judith. 1990. *Standing Again at Sinai: Judaism from a Feminist Perspective.* San Francisco: Harper & Row.

Pogorelc, Anthony J., and James D. Davidson. 2000. "American Catholics: One Church, Two Cultures?" *Review of Religious Research* 42: 146–58.

Polner, Murray. 1998. *Disarmed and Dangerous: The Racial Life and Times of Daniel and Philip Berrigan, Brothers in Religious Faith and Civil Disobedience.* Boulder, CO: Westview.

Powell, Milton B., ed. 1967. *The Voluntary Church: American Religious Life, 1740–1860, Seen through the Eyes of European Visitors.* New York: Macmillan.

Presser, Stanley, and Linda Stinson. 1998. "Data Collection Mode and Social Desirability Bias in Self-Reported Religious Attendance." *American Sociological Review* 63: 137–45.

Preston, Andrew. 2012. *Sword of the Spirit, Shield of Faith: Religion in American War and Diplomacy.* New York: Alfred A. Knopf.

Prothero, Stephan. 2010. *God Is Not One: The Eight Rival Religions That Run the World—and Why Their Differences Matter.* New York: Harper One Books.

Przybyszewski, Linda. 2000. "The Religion of a Jurist: Justice David Brewer and the Christian Nation." *Supreme Court History* 25: 228–42.

Putnam, Robert D. 2000. *Bowling Alone.* New York: Simon & Schuster.

Putnam, Robert, and David Campbell. 2010. *American Grace.* New York: Simon and Schuster.

Pyle, Ralph. 2006. "Trends in Religious Stratification: Have Religious Group Socioeconomic Distinctions Declined in Recent Decades?" *Sociology of Religion* 67: 61–79.

Quinley, Harold E. 1974. "The Dilemma of an Activist Church: Protestant Religion in the Sixties and Seventies." *Journal for the Scientific Study of Religion* 13: 1–22.

Radcliffe, Timothy. 2005. *What Is the Point of Being a Christian?* New York: Burns & Oates.

Raschke, Vernon. 1973. "Dogmatism and Committed and Consensual Religiosity." *Journal for the Scientific Study of Religion* 12: 339–44.

Rauschenbusch, Walter. 1917. *Theology for the Social Gospel*. New York: Abingdon.

Rawlyk, George A. 1990. "Politics, Religion, and the Canadian Experience: A Preliminary Probe." In *Religion and American Politics*, ed. Mark A. Noll, 253–77. New York: Oxford University Press.

Ray, Paul. 1997. "The Emerging Culture: Marketing to Cultural Creatives, Americans Who Live by a New Set of Values." *American Demographics* 19: 38–24.

Read, Jen'nan Ghazal. 2007. "More a Bridge Than a Gap: Gender Differences in Arab American Political Engagement." *Social Science Quarterly* 88: 1072–91.

Reed, Adolph. 1986. *The Jesse Jackson Phenomenon: The Crisis of Purpose in Afro-American Politics*. New Haven, CT: Yale University Press.

Reed, Ralph, Jr. 1994. *Politically Incorrect: The Emerging Faith Factor in American Politics*. Dallas, TX: Word Publishing.

———. 1996. "Remarks to the Anti-Defamation League of B'nai B'rith." April 3.

Reese, Laura, and Ronald E. Brown. 1995. "The Effects of Racial Messages on Racial Identity and System Blame among African Americans." *Journal of Politics* 57: 24–43.

Reeves, Thomas C. 1996. *The Empty Church: The Suicide of Liberal Christianity*. New York: Free Press.

Regnerus, Mark D., David Sikkink, and Christian Smith. 1999. "Voting with the Christian Right: Contextual and Individual Patterns of Electoral Influence." *Social Forces* 77: 1375–1401.

Regnerus, Mark D., and Christian Smith. 1998. "Selective Deprivatization among American Religious Traditions: The Reversal of the Great Reversal." *Social Forces* 76: 1347–72.

Reichley, A. James. 1985. *Religion in American Public Life*. Washington, DC: Brookings Institution.

Reimer, Samuel H. 1995. "A Look at Cultural Effects on Religiosity: A Comparison between the United States and Canada." *Journal for the Scientific Study of Religion* 34: 445–57.

Reimer, Sam, and Jerry Z. Park. 2001. "Tolerant (in)Civility? A Longitudinal Analysis of White Conservative Protestants' Willingness to Grant Civil Liberties." *Journal for the Scientific Study of Religion* 40: 735–45.

Renshon, Stanley Allen. 1975. "The Role of Personality Development in Political Socialization." In *New Directions in Political Socialization*, ed. David C. Schwartz, 29–68. New York: Free Press.

Rhodes, Jeremy. 2012. "The Ties That Divide: Bonding Social Capital, Religious Friendship Networks, and Political Tolerance among Evangelicals." *Sociological Inquiry* 82: 163–86.

Ribuffo, Leo. 1983. *The Old Christian Right*. Philadelphia: Temple University Press.

———. 2001. "Religion in the History of U.S. Foreign Policy." In *The Influence of Faith: Religious Groups and U.S. Foreign Policy*, ed. Elliot Abrams, 1–27. Lanham, MD: Rowman & Littlefield.

———. 2006. "Family Policy Past as Prologue: Jimmy Carter, the White House Conference on Families, and the Mobilization of the New Christian Right." *The Review of Policy Research* 23: 311–38.

Richards, P. C. 1995. "Satan's Foot in the Door: Democrats at Brigham Young University." *Dialogue: A Journal of Mormon Thought* 28: 1–29.

Richey, Russell E., and Donald G. Jones, eds. 1974. *American Civil Religion*. New York: Harper & Row.

Riley, Richard W. 1995. "Religious Expression in Public Schools." Washington, DC: U.S. Department of Education.

Riordan, Patrick. 2004. "Permission to Speak: Religious Arguments in Public Reason." *Heythrop Journal* 45: 178–96.

Robbins, Thomas. 2001. "Combating 'Cults' and 'Brainwashing' in the United States and Western Europe: A Comment on Richardson and Introvigne's Report." *Journal for the Scientific Study of Religion* 40: 169–76.

Roberts, Samuel. 2003. "On Seducing the Samaritan: The Problematic of Government Aid to Faith-Based Groups." In *New Day Begun: African American Churches and Civic Culture in the Post-Civil Rights Era*, ed. R. Drew Smith. Durham, NC: Duke University Press.

Robinson, Carin. 2010. "Cross-Cutting Messages and Political Tolerance: An Experiment Using Evangelical Protestants." *Political Behavior* 32: 495–15.

Rogers, Mary Beth. 1990. *Cold Anger: A Story of Faith and Power Politics*. Denton, TX: University of North Texas Press.

Rokeach, Milton. 1969. "Religious Values and Social Compassion." *Review of Religious Research* 11: 24–39.

Rom, Mark. 2000. "Gays and AIDS: Democratizing Disease." In *The Politics of Gay Rights*, ed. Craig Rimmerman, Kenneth Wald, and Clyde Wilcox, 217–48. Chicago: University of Chicago Press.

Roof, Wade Clark. 1974. "Religious Orthodoxy and Minority Prejudice: Causal Relationship or Reflection of Localistic World View?" *American Journal of Sociology* 80: 643–64.

———. 1979. "Concepts and Indicators of Religious Commitment: A Critical Review." In *The Religious Dimension: New Directions in Quantitative Research*, ed. Robert Wuthnow, 17–45. New York: Academic Press.

———. 1999. *Spiritual Marketplace: Baby Boomers and the Remaking of American Religion*. Princeton, NJ: Princeton University Press.

———. 2009. "American Presidential Rhetoric from Ronald Reagan to George W. Bush: Another Look at Civil Religion." *Social Compass* 56: 286–301.

Roof, Wade Clark, and William McKinney. 1987. *American Mainline Religion: Its Changing Shape and Future*. New Brunswick, NJ: Rutgers University Press.

Rose, Richard, and Derek Urwin. 1969. "Social Cohesion, Political Parties, and Strains in Regimes." *Comparative Political Studies* 2: 7–67.

Rosenberg, Morris. 1956. "Misanthropy and Political Ideology." *American Sociological Review* 21: 690–95.

Rosenstone, Steven, and John Hanson. 1993. *Mobilization, Participation and Democracy in America*. New York: Macmillan.

Rosin, Hanna, and Dana Milbank, 2000. "A Political 'Heretic' Is Cast Out." *Washington Post*, March 26, A6.

Ross, Brian, and Rehab El-Buri. 2008. "Obama's Pastor: God Damn America, US to Blame for 9/11." http://abcnews.go.com/Blotter/DemocraticDebate/story?id=4443788&page=1.

Rossi, Alice. 1973. "Social Roots of the Woman's Movement in America." In *The Feminist Papers from Adams to de Beauvoir*, ed. Alice Rossi, 241–81. New York: Columbia University Press.

Rossiter, Clinton, ed. 1961. *The Federalist Papers*. New York: New American Library.

Rothenberg, Stuart, and Frank Newport. 1984. *The Evangelical Voter*. Washington, DC: Free Congress Research and Education Foundation.

Rothman, Stanley, and S. Robert Lichter. 1982. *Roots of Radicalism: Jews, Christians and the New Left*. New York: Oxford University Press.

Rountree, William T., Jr. 1990. "Constitutionalism as the American Religion: The Good Portion." *Emory Law Journal* 39: 203–15.

Rowatt, Wade, Lewis Frankin, and Marla Cotton. 2005. "Patterns and Personality Correlates of Implicit and Explicit Attitudes toward Christian and Muslims." *Journal for the Scientific Study of Religion* 44: 29–43.

Rowatt, Wade C., Jordan LaBouff, Megan Johnson, Paul Froese, and Jo-Ann Tsang. 2009. "Associations among Religiousness, Social Attitudes, and Prejudice in a National Random Sample of American Adults." *Psychology of Religion and Spirituality* 1: 14–24.

Rozell, Mark, and Gleaves Whitney, eds. 2007. *Religion and the American Presidency*. New York: Palgrave.

Rozell, Mark J., and Clyde Wilcox. 1995. "Virginia: God, Guns, and Oliver North." In *God at the Grass Roots: The Christian Right in the 1994 Elections*, ed. Mark J. Rozell and Clyde Wilcox, 109–32. Lanham, MD: Rowman & Littlefield.

———. 1996. "Second Coming: The Strategies of the New Christian Right." *Political Science Quarterly* 111: 271–94.

Rozell, Mark, Clyde Wilcox, and Roland Gunn. 1996. "Religious Coalitions in the New Christian Right." *Social Science Quarterly* 77: 543–59.

Rubin, Barry. 1994. "Religion and International Affairs." In *Religion, the Missing Dimension of Statecraft*, ed. Douglas Johnston and Cynthia Sampson, 20–34. New York: Oxford University Press.

Rubin, Eva R., ed. 1994. *The Abortion Controversy: A Documentary History*. Westport, CT: Greenwood.

Rudolph, Susanne Hoeber, and James Piscatori, eds. 1997. *Transnational Religion and Fading States*. Boulder, CO: Westview.

Ruether, Rosemary Radford. 1985. *Women and Church: Theology and Practice of Feminist Liturgical Communities*. San Francisco: Harper & Row.

Sabatier, Paul. 1988. "An Advocacy Coalition Framework of Policy Change and the Role of Policy-Oriented Learning Therein." *Police Sciences* 21: 129–68.

Saeed, Agha. 2002. "The American Muslim Paradox." In *Muslim Minorities in the West: Visible and Invisible*, ed. Yvonne Yazbeck Haddad and Jane Smith. Lanham, MD: AltaMira.

Sager, Rebecca. 2010. *Faith, Politics and Power: The Politics of Faith-Based Initiatives*. New York: Oxford University Press.

Salamon, Lester. 1973. "Leadership and Modernization: The Emerging Black Political Elite in the American South." *Journal of Politics* 35: 615–46.

Salisbury, Robert H., John Sprague, and Gregory Weiher. 1984. "Does Religious Pluralism Make a Difference? Interactions among Context, Attendance, and

Beliefs." Paper delivered to the annual meeting of the American Political Science Association, Washington, DC.

Salzman, Jack, ed. 1992. *Bridges and Boundaries: African Americans and American Jews*. New York: Braziller and Jewish Museum.

Sandoz, Ellis. 1990. *A Government of Laws: Political Theory, Religion, and the American Founding*. Baton Rouge: Louisiana State University Press.

———. 1994. "Philosophical Foundations of Our Democratic Heritage: A Recollection." *Presidential Studies Quarterly* 24: 669–73.

Sapp, Gary L., and Logan Jones. 1986. "Religious Orientation and Moral Judgment." *Journal for the Scientific Study of Religion* 25: 208–14.

Satterthwaite, Shad. 2005. "Faster Horses, Older Whiskey and More Money: An Analysis of Religious Influence on Referenda Voting." *Journal for the Scientific Study of Religion* 44: 105–12.

Savage, Barbara. 2008. *Your Spirit Walks Beside Us: The Politics of Black Religion*. Cambridge, MA: Belknap/Harvard.

Sawyer, Mary. 2001. "Theocratic, Prophetic, and Ecumenical: Political Roles of African American Clergy." In *Christian Clergy in American Politics*, ed. Sue E. S. Crawford and Laura Olson, 3–14. Baltimore: Johns Hopkins University Press.

Schafer, Chelsea, and Greg Shaw. 2009. "Trends: Tolerance in the United States." *Public Opinion Quarterly* 73: 404–31.

Schappes, Morris U., comp. 1971. *A Documentary History of the Jews in the United States*. New York: Schocken.

Scheepers, Peer, Merove Gijsberts, and Evelyn Hello. 2002. "Religiosity and Prejudice against Ethnic Minorities in Europe: Cross-National Tests on a Controversial Relationship." *Review of Religious Research* 43: 242–65.

Scheitle, Christopher, and Bryanna Hahn. 2011. "From the Pews to Policy: Specifying Evangelical Protestantism's Influence on States' Sexual Orientation Politics." *Social Forces* 89: 913–33.

Schlozman, Kay, Nancy Burns, and Sidney Verba. 1994. "Gender and Participation: The Role of Resources." *Journal of Politics* 56: 964–90.

Schmalzbauer, John. 2003. *People of Faith: Religious Conviction in American Journalism and Higher Education*. Ithaca, NY: Cornell University Press.

Schneider, William. 1985. "The Jewish Vote in 1984: Elements in a Controversy." *Public Opinion* 7: 18–19, 58.

Schneier, Marc. 1999. *Shared Dreams: Martin Luther King, Jr. and the Jewish Community*. Woodstock, VT: Jewish Lights.

Schnoor, Randall. 2006. "Being Gay and Jewish: Negotiating Intersecting Identities." *Sociology of Religion* 67: 43–60.

Schoenfeld, Eugene. 1985. "Religion and Loyalty to the Political Elite: The Case of the Presidency." *Review of Religious Research* 27: 178–88.

Schreiber, Ronnee. 2008. *Righting Feminism*. New York: Oxford University Press.

Schultz, P. Wesley. 2000. "A Multinational Perspective on the Relation between Judeo-Christian Religious Beliefs and Attitudes of Environmental Concern." *Environment and Behavior* 32: 576–82.

Schultze, Quentin. 2003. *Christianity and the Mass Media in America*. East Lansing: Michigan State University Press.

Schumer, Franz. 1984. "A Return to Religion." *New York Times Magazine*, April 13, 90.

Schwadel, Philip. 2005. "Individual, Congregational, and Denominational Effects on Church Members' Civic Participation." *Journal for the Scientific Study of Religion* 44: 159–71.

Sears, David, and Leonie Huddy. 1990. "On the Origins of the Political Disunity among Women." In *Women, Politics, and Change*, ed. Louise Tilly and Patricia Gurin. New York: Russell Sage Foundation.

Sears, David, Jim Sidanious, and Lawrence Bobo. 2000. *Racialized Politics: The Debate about Racism in America*. Chicago: University of Chicago Press.

Secret, Philip, James Johnson, and Susan Welch. 1986. "Racial Differences in Attitudes toward the Supreme Court's Decisions on Prayer in the Public Schools." *Social Science Quarterly* 67: 877–86.

Segers, Mary C. 1992. "The Loyal Opposition: Catholics for a Free Choice." In *The Catholic Church and the Politics of Abortion*, ed. Timothy A. Byrnes and Mary Segers, 169–84. Boulder, CO: Westview.

Sehat, David. 2011. *The Myth of American Religious Freedom*. New York: Oxford University Press.

Sennett, Richard. 1987. "A Republic of Souls: Puritanism and the American Presidency." *Harper's Magazine* 287 (July): 41–46.

Sergeant, Kimon Howland. 2000. *Seeker Churches: Promoting Traditional Religion in a Nontraditional Way*. New Brunswick, NJ: Rutgers University Press.

Shafer, Byron, and William Claggett. 1995. *The Two Majorities: The Issue Context of Modern American Politics*. Baltimore: Johns Hopkins University Press.

Shaiko, Ronald. 1987. "Religion, Politics, and Environmental Concern." *Social Science Quarterly* 68: 244–62.

Sharkansky, Ira. 1997. "Religion and Politics in Israel and Utah." *Journal of Church and State* 39: 523–41.

Sharp, Elaine. 2005. *Morality Politics in American Cities*. Lawrence: University of Kansas Press.

Sherkat, Darren, and Alfred Darnell. 1999. "The Effect of Parents' Fundamentalism on Children's Educational Attainment: Examining Differences by Gender and Children's Fundamentalism." *Journal for the Scientific Study of Religion* 38: 1–24.

Sherwood, Timothy H. 2011. *The Preaching of Archbishop Fulton J. Sheen: The Gospel Meets the Cold War*. Lanham, MD: Lexington Books.

Shields, Jon A. 2007. "Between Passion and Deliberation: The Christian Right and Democratic Ideals." *Political Science Quarterly* 122: 89–113.

Shipton, Clifford K. 1947. "Puritanism and Modern Democracy." *New England Historical and Genealogical Register* 101: 181–98.

Shoon, Kathleen Murray. 2007. "Private Polls and Presidential Policymaking: Reagan as a Facilitator of Change." *Public Opinion Quarterly* 70: 477–98.

Shorris, Earl. 1982. *Jews without Mercy: A Lament*. Garden City, NY: Anchor/Doubleday.

Shriver, Peggy L. 1981. *The Bible Vote*. New York: Pilgrim.

———. 1988. "Religion and Public Education: The American Context." *National Forum* 68: 30–33.

Sigelman, Lee. 1991. "If You Prick Us, Do We Not Bleed? If You Tickle Us, Do We Not Laugh?" *Journal of Politics* 53: 977–92.

Sigelman, Lee, Clyde Wilcox, and Emmett H. Buell Jr. 1987. "An Unchanging Minority: Popular Support for the Moral Majority, 1980 and 1984." *Social Science Quarterly* 68: 876–84.

Silk, Mark. 1995. *Unsecular Media: Making News of Religion in America.* Chicago: University of Illinois Press.

Silverman, Adam. 2002. "An Exploratory Analysis of Interdisciplinary Theory of Terrorism." PhD diss., University of Florida.

Simon, Paul. 1984. *The Glass House.* New York: Continuum.

Simon Wiesenthal Center. 1986. "The Farrakhan Phenomenon." *Response* 13: 2–3.

Simonds, Robert. 1985. *How to Elect Christians to Public Office.* Costa Mesa, CA: National Association of Christian Educators/Citizens for Excellence in Education.

Simpson, Alan. 1955. *Puritanism in Old and New England.* Chicago: University of Chicago Press.

Skill, Thomas, James D. Robinson, John S. Lyons, and David Larson. 1994. "The Portrayal of Religion and Spirituality on Fictional Network Television." *Review of Religious Research* 35: 251–67.

Skirbekk, Vegard, Eric Kaufmann, and Anne Goujon. 2010. "Secularism, Fundamentalism, or Catholicism? The Religious Composition of the United States to 2043." *Journal for the Scientific Study of Religion* 49: 293–310.

Sklare, Marshall, and Joseph Greenblum. 1967. *Jewish Identity on the Suburban Frontier.* New York: Basic Books.

Smidt, Corwin. 1980. "Civil Religious Orientation among Elementary School Children." *Sociological Analysis* 41: 25–40.

———. 1982. "Civil Religious Orientations and Children's Perception of Political Authority." *Political Behavior* 4: 147–62.

———. 1993. "Evangelical Voting Patterns: 1976–1988." In *No Longer Exiles: The Religious New Right in American Politics,* ed. Michael Cromartie, 85–117. Washington, DC: Ethics and Public Policy Center.

———, ed. 2003. *Religion as Social Capital: Producing the Common Good.* Waco, TX: Baylor University Press.

———. 2004. "Clergy in American Politics: An Introduction." *Journal for the Scientific Study of Religion* 42: 495–99.

———. 2005. "Religion, Attitudes toward Islam and the Invasion of Iraq." *Sociology of Religion* 66: 243–61.

———. 2013. *American Evangelicals Today.* Lanham, MD: Rowman & Littlefield.

Smidt, Corwin, Sue Crawford, Melissa Deckman, Donald Gray, Dan Hofrenning, Laura Olson, Sherrie Steiner, and Beau Weston. 2003. "The Political Attitudes and Activities of Mainline Protestant Clergy in the Election of 2000: A Study of Six Denominations." *Journal for the Scientific Study of Religion* 42: 515–32.

Smidt, Corwin, Kevin den Dulk, Bryan Froehle, James Penning, Stephen Monsma, and Douglas Koopman. 2010. *The Disappearing God Gap? Religion in the 2008 Election.* New York: Oxford University Press.

Smidt, Corwin, Kevin den Dulk, James Penning, Stephen Monsma, and Douglas Koopman. 2008. *Pews, Prayers and Participation: Religion and Civic Responsibility in America.* Washington, DC: Georgetown University Press.

Smith, Buster G. 2007. "Attitudes towards Religious Pluralism: Measurements and Consequences." *Social Compass* 54: 333–53.

Smith, Christian. 2000. *Christian America? What Evangelicals Really Want*. Berkeley: University of California Press.

———, ed. 2003. *The Secular Revolution: Power, Interests and Conflict in the Secularization of American Public Life*. Berkeley: University of California Press.

Smith, Christian, M. Emerson, S. Gallagher, P. Kennedy, and D. Sikkink. 1998. *American Evangelicals: Embattled and Thriving*. Chicago: University of Chicago Press.

Smith, Christian, and Robert Farris. 2005. "Socioeconomic Inequality in the American Religious System: An Update and Assessment." *Journal for the Scientific Study of Religion* 44: 95–104.

Smith, Dan A., Matthew DeSantis, and Jason Kassel. 2006. "Same-Sex Marriage Ballot Measures and the 2004 Presidential Election." *State and Local Government Review* 38: 79–91.

Smith, Gary Scott. 2006. *Faith and the Presidency: From George Washington to George W. Bush*. New York: Oxford University Press.

Smith, Jane. 1999. *Islam in America*. New York: Columbia University Press.

Smith, Kevin. 1999. "Clean Thoughts and Dirty Minds: The Politics of Porn." *Policy Studies Journal* 27: 723–35.

Smith, R. Drew. 2001. "Churches and the Urban Poor: Interaction and Social Distance." *Sociology of Religion* 62: 301–13.

———, ed. 2004. *Long March Ahead: African American Churches and Public Policy in the Post-Civil Rights Era*. Durham, NC: Duke University Press.

Smith, Robert C., and Robert Seltzer. 1992. *Race, Class and Culture: A Study of African American Mass Opinion*. Albany: State University of New York Press.

Smith, Rogers. 2012. "The Constitutional Philosophy of Barack Obama: Democratic Pragmatism and Religious Commitment." *Social Science Quarterly* 93:1251–71.

Smith, Steven D. 1995. *Foreordained Failure: The Quest for a Constitutional Principle of Religious Freedom*. New York: Oxford University Press.

———. 2010. *Disenchantment of Secular Discourse*. Cambridge, MA: Harvard University Press.

Smith, T. L. 1965. *Revivalism and Social Reform: American Protestantism on the Eve of the Civil War*. New York: Harper & Row.

Smith, Tom. 1992. "Attitudes toward Sexual Permissiveness: Trends, Correlates and Behavioral Connections." In *Sexuality across the Life Course*, ed. Alice S. Rossi. Chicago: University of Chicago Press.

———. 1999. "The Religious Right and Anti-Semitism." *Review of Religious Research* 40: 244–58.

Smith, Tom W., and Seokho Kim. 2005. "The Vanishing Protestant Majority." *Journal for the Scientific Study of Religion* 44: 211–23.

Smith, Tony. 2000. *Foreign Attachments: The Power of Ethnic Groups in the Making of American Foreign Policy*. Cambridge, MA: Harvard University Press.

Snarr, Melissa. 2009. "Religion, Race and Bridge Building in Economic Justice Coalitions." *Working USA* 12: 73–95.

———. 2011a. "Women's Working Poverty: Feminist and Religious Alliances in the Living Wage Movement." *Journal of Feminist Studies in Religion* 27: 75–93.

———. 2011b. *All You That Labor: Religion and Ethics in the Living Wage Movement.* New York: New York University Press.

Snow, David, E. Burke Rochford, Steven Worden, and Robert Benford. 1986. "Frame Alignment Processes, Micromobilization and Movement Participation." *American Sociological Review* 51: 464–81.

Sonenshein, Raphael J., and Nicholas A. Valentino. 2000. "The Distinctiveness of Jewish Voting: A Thing of the Past?" *Urban Affairs Review* 35: 358–89.

Songer, Donald, and Susan Tabrizi. 1999. "The Religious Right in Court: The Decision Making of Christian Evangelicals in State Supreme Courts." *Journal of Politics* 61: 507–26.

Sorauf, Frank J. 1959. "*Zorach v. Clauson*: The Impact of a Supreme Court Decision." *American Political Science Review* 53: 777–91.

———. 1976. *The Wall of Separation: The Constitutional Politics of Church and State.* Princeton, NJ: Princeton University Press.

Spadaro, Antonio. 2013 (September 30). "A Big Heart Open to God." *America,* http://americamagazine.org/pope-interview.

Spiegel, Stephen. 1985. *The Other Arab-Israeli Conflict.* Chicago: University of Chicago Press.

Sriram, Shyam. 2005. "Yankee Hindutva: Hindu Nationalism and Religiosity Measures." Paper presented to the annual meeting of the American Political Science Association, Washington, DC

Stark, Rodney. 2000. "Religious Effects: In Praise of 'Idealistic Humbug.'" *Review of Religious Research* 41: 289–310.

———. 2004. "Putting an End to Ancestor Worship." *Journal for the Scientific Study of Religion* 43: 465–75.

Stark, Rodney, and William Sims Bainbridge. 1985. *The Future of Religion.* Berkeley: University of California Press.

Stark, Rodney, Bruce D. Foster, Charles Y. Glock, and Harold E. Quinley. 1971. *Wayward Shepherds: Prejudice and the Protestant Clergy.* New York: Harper & Row.

Starks, Brian, and Robert V. Robinson. 2005. "Who Values the Obedient Child Now? The Religious Factor in Adult Values for Children, 1986–2002." *Social Forces* 84: 343–59.

Steensland, Brian, Jerry Z. Park, Mark D. Regnerus, L. D. Robinson, W. B. Wilcox, and R. D. Woodberry. 2000. "The Measure of American Religion: Toward Improving the State of the Art." *Social Forces* 79: 291–318.

Steigenga, Timothy J., and Kenneth Coleman. 1995. "Protestant Political Orientations and the Structure of Political Opportunity: Chile, 1972–1991." *Polity* 27: 465–82.

Steiner, Gilbert Y. 1983. *The Abortion Dispute and the American System.* Washington, DC: Brookings Institution.

Steinfels, Peter. 2003. *A People Adrift: The Crisis of the Roman Catholic Church in America.* New York: Simon & Schuster.

Stepick, Alex, Terry Rey, and Sarah Mahler. 2009. *Churches and Charity in the Immigrant City.* New Brunswick, NJ: New Press.

Stern, Mark. 2012. "'Religious Liberty' in Court." *Religion in the News* 14: 18–19, 32.

Stewart, Thomas A. 1989. "Turning around the Lord's Business." *Fortune,* September 25, 78–84.

Stouffer, Samuel. 1966. *Communism, Conformity, and Civil Liberties*. New York: Wiley.

Stout, Jeffrey. 2010. *Blessed Are the Organized: Grassroots Democracy in America*. Princeton, NJ: Princeton University Press.

Straughn, Jeremy Brooke, and Scott L. Feld. 2010. "America as a 'Christian Nation'? Understanding Religious Boundaries of National Identity in the United States." *Sociology of Religion* 71: 280–306.

Strickler, Jennifer, and Nicholas Danigelis. 2002. "Changing Frameworks in Attitudes toward Abortion." *Sociological Forum* 17: 187–201.

Strout, Cushing. 1974. *The New Heavens and the New Earth*. New York: Harper & Row.

Suleiman, Michael. 1994. "Arab Americans and the Political Process." In *The Development of Arab-American Identity*, ed. Ernest McCarus. Ann Arbor: University of Michigan Press.

Sullins, D. Paul. 1999. "Catholic/Protestant Trends on Abortion: Convergence and Polarity." *Journal for the Scientific Study of Religion* 38: 354–69.

Sullivan, John L., Pat Walsh, Michal Shamir, David G. Barnum, and James L. Gibson. 1993. "Why Politicians Are More Tolerant: Selective Recruitment and Socialization among Political Elites in Britain, Israel, New Zealand, and the United States." *British Journal of Political Science* 23: 51–76.

Surrey, David S. 1982. *Choice of Conscience: Vietnam Era Military and Draft Resisters in Canada*. New York: Praeger.

Svonkin, Stuart. 1997. *Jews against Prejudice: American Jews and the Fight for Civil Liberties*. New York: Columbia University Press.

Swain, Randall. 2008. "Standing on the Promises That Cannot Fail: Evaluating the Black Church's Ability to Promote Community Activism among African Americans in the Present Day Context." *Journal of African American Studies* 12: 1559–1646.

———. 2010. "Shall We March On? An Analysis of Non-Electoral Participation in the Black Community in the Post-Civil Rights Era." *Journal of Black Studies* 40: 566–82.

Swanson, Wayne R. 1990. *The Christ Child Goes to Court*. Philadelphia: Temple University Press.

Swarts, Heidi. 2002. "Setting the State's Agenda: Church-Based Community Organizations in American Politics." In *States, Parties and Social Movements*, ed. Jack Goldstone. Cambridge: Cambridge University Press.

———. 2008. *Organizing Urban America: Secular and Faith-Based Progressive Movements*. Minneapolis: University of Minnesota Press.

Sweet, Martin J. 2010. *Merely Judgment: Ignoring, Evading, and Trumping the Supreme Court*. Charlottesville, VA: University Press of Virginia.

Tamney, Joseph B., Ronald Burton, and Stephen D. Johnson. 1988. "Christianity, Social Class, and the Catholic Bishops' Economic Policy." *Sociological Analysis* 49: 78–96.

Tamney, Joseph, and Stephen D. Johnson. 1983. "The Moral Majority in Middletown." *Journal for the Scientific Study of Religion* 22: 145–57.

———. 1997. "Christianity and Public Book Banning." *Review of Religious Research* 38: 263–71.

Tarrow, Sidney. 1998. *Power in Movement*. 2nd ed. New York: Cambridge University Press.

——. 2011. *Power in Movement*. 3rd ed. New York: Cambridge

——. 2012. *Strangers at the Gates*. New York: Cambridge University Press.

Taydas, Zeynep, Cigdem Kentmen, and Laura R. Olson. 2012. "Faith Matters: Religious Affiliation and Public Opinion about Barack Obama's Foreign Policy in the 'Greater' Middle East." *Social Science Quarterly* 93: 1218–42.

Taylor, Marylee C., and Stephen M. Merino. 2011. "Assessing the Racial Views of White Conservative Protestants." *Public Opinion Quarterly* 75: 761–78.

Tedin, Kent L. 1977. "Social Background and Political Differences between Pro- and Anti-ERA Activists." *American Politics Quarterly* 5: 395–408.

——. 1978. "Religious Preference and Pro/Anti-Activism on the Equal Rights Amendment Issue." *Pacific Sociological Review* 21: 55–66.

Tedin, Kent L., David W. Brady, Mary E. Buxton, Barbara W. Gorman, and Judy L. Thompson. 1977. "Social Background and Political Differences between Pro- and Anti-ERA Activists." *American Politics Quarterly* 5: 395–408.

Tentler, Leslie Woodcock. 2004. *Catholics and Contraception: An American History*. Ithaca, NY: Cornell University Press.

Terry, Janice. 1999. "Community and Political Activism among Arab Americans in Detroit." In *Arabs in America: Building a New Future*, ed. Michael Suleiman, 241–54. Philadelphia: Temple University Press.

Tesh, Sylvia. 1984. "In Support of 'Single-Issue' Politics." *Political Science Quarterly* 99: 27–44.

Thomas, Cal, and Ed Dobson. 1999. *Blinded by Might: Why the Religious Right Can't Save America*. Grand Rapids, MI: Zondervan.

Thomas, Michael C., and Charles C. Flippen. 1972. "American Civil Religion: An Empirical Study." *Social Forces* 51: 218–25.

Thuesen, Peter. 2002. "The Logic of Mainline Churchliness." In *The Quiet Hand of God: Faith-Based Activism and the Public Role of Mainline Protestants*, ed. Robert Wuthnow and John Evans. Berkeley: University of California Press.

Thumma, Scott. 1991. "Negotiating a Religious Identity: The Case of the Gay Evangelical." *Sociological Analysis* 52: 333–47.

Thumma, Scott, and Edward Gray, ed. 2005. *Gay Religion*. Walnut Creek, CA: AltaMira.

Tilly, Charles, and Sidney Tarrow. 2007. *Contentious Politics*. Boulder, CO: Paradigm Publishers.

Tiryakian, Edward A. 1982. "Puritan America in the Modern World: Mission Impossible." *Sociological Analysis* 43: 351–68.

Tocqueville, Alexis de. 1945. *Democracy in America*. Vol. 1. New York: Vintage.

Toner, Robin. 1993. "Clinton's Support of Abortion Rights Has Catholic Leaders on a Tightrope." *New York Times*, February 3, 14A.

Tong, Xiaoxi. 1992. "Market and Political Explanations of Religious Vitality: Comments on Chaves and Cann." *Rationality and Society* 4: 474–76.

Toolin, Cynthia. 1983. "American Civil Religion from 1789–1981: A Content Analysis of Presidential Inaugural Addresses." *Review of Religious Research* 25: 39–48.

Tracy, David. 1973. "The Religious Dimension of Science." In *The Persistence of Religion*, ed. Andrew Greeley, 128–35. New York: Herder & Herder.

Traugott, Michael W., and Maris A. Vinovskis. 1980. "Abortion and the 1978 Congressional Elections." *Family Planning Perspectives* 12: 238–46.

Treene, E. W. 2001. "Religion, the Public Square, and the Presidency." *Harvard Journal of Law and Public Policy* 24: 573–621.

Trepanier, Lee, and Lynita Newswander. 2012. *LDS in the USA: Mormonism and the Making of American Culture*. Waco, TX: Baylor University Press.

Tsitsos, William. 2003. "Race Differences in Congregational Social Service Activity." *Journal for the Scientific Study of Religion* 42: 205–15.

Tucker-Worgs, Tamelyn. 2011. *The Black Megachurch: Theology, Gender and the Politics of Public Engagement*. Waco, TX: Baylor University Press.

Tuntiya, Nana. 2005. "Fundamentalist Religious Affiliation and Support for Civil Liberties: A Critical Reexamination." *Sociological Inquiry* 75: 153–76.

Turner, Charles, Maria Viclarroel, James Chromy, Elizabeth Eggleston, and Susan Rogers. 2005. "Same-Sex Gender Roles among US Adults: Trends across the 20th Century and during the 1990s." *Public Opinion Quarterly* 69: 439–62.

Tweed, T. A. 1999. "Nightstand Buddhist and Other Creatures: Sympathizers, Adherents and the Study of Religion." In *American Buddhism: Methods and Findings in Recent Scholarship*, ed. D. R. Williams and C. S. Queen. Surrey, England: Curzon.

Tygart, Clarence E. 1977. "The Role of Theology among Other 'Belief' Variables for Clergy Civil Rights Activism." *Review of Religious Research* 18: 271–78.

Udis-Kessler, Amanda. 2008. *Queer Inclusion in the United Methodist Church*. New York: Routledge.

Ulmer, Sidney. 1973. "Social Background as an Indicator to the Votes of Supreme Court Justices in Criminal Cases: 1947–1956 Terms." *American Journal of Political Science* 17: 622–30.

Unnever, James D., John P. Bartkowski, and Francis T. Cullen. 2010. "God Imagery and Opposition to Abortion and Capital Punishment: A Partial Test of Religious Support for the Consistent Life Ethic." *Sociology of Religion* 71: 307–22.

Uslaner, Eric M., and Mark Lichbach. 2009. "Identity versus Identity: Israel and Evangelicals and the Two-Front War for Jewish Votes." *Politics and Religion* 2: 395–419.

Van der Vyver, Johan D. 1996. "Religious Fundamentalism and Human Rights." *Journal of International Affairs* 50: 21–40.

Verba, Sidney. 1965. "The Kennedy Assassination and the Nature of Political Commitment." In *The Kennedy Assassination and the American Public*, ed. Bradley S. Greenberg, 348–60. Stanford, CA: Stanford University Press.

Verba, Sidney, Kay Schlozman, and Henry Brady. 1995. *Voice and Equality: Civic Voluntarism in American Politics*. Cambridge, MA: Harvard University Press.

Verba, Sidney, Kay Schlozman, Henry Brady, and Norman Nie. 1993. "Race, Ethnicity, and Political Resources: Participation in the United States." *British Journal of Political Science* 23: 453–97.

Verhoeven, Tim. 2013. "The Case for Sunday Mails: Sabbath Laws and the Separation of Church and State in Jacksonian America." *Journal of Church and State* 55: 71–91.

Vinovskis, Maris A. 1979. "Abortion and the Presidential Election of 1976: A Multivariate Analysis of Voting Behavior." *Michigan Law Review* 7: 1750–71.

Voll, John O. 1991. "Islamic Issues for Muslims in the United States." In *The Muslims of America*, ed. Yvonne Yazbeck Haddad. New York: Oxford University Press.

Wald, Kenneth D. 1983. *Crosses on the Ballot: Patterns of British Voter Alignment since 1885*. Princeton, NJ: Princeton University Press.

———. 1989. "Assessing the Religious Factor in Electoral Behavior." In *Religion in American Politics*, ed. Charles W. Dunn, 105–22. Washington, DC: CQ Press.

———. 1991. "Ministering to the Nation: The Campaigns of Jesse Jackson and Pat Robertson." In *Nominating the President*, ed. Emmett Buell Jr. and Lee Sigelman, 119–49. Knoxville: University of Tennessee Press.

———. 1992. "Religious Elites and Public Opinion: The Impact of the Bishops' Peace Pastoral." *Review of Politics* 54: 112–43.

———. 1994. "The Religious Dimension of American Anti-Communism." *Journal of Church and State* 36: 483–507.

———. 2003. "The Probable Persistence of American Jewish Liberalism." In *Religion as a Public Good: Jews and Other Americans on Religion in the Public Square*, ed. Alan L. Mittleman, 65–90. Lanham, MD: Rowman & Littlefield.

———. 2005. "In the Kingdom of Kindness: American Jews and the Public Role of Religion." In *Taking Religious Pluralism Seriously: Spiritual Politics on America's Sacred Ground*, ed. Barbara A. McGraw and Jo Renee Formicola, 27–44. Waco, TX: Baylor University Press.

———. 2008. "Homeland Interests, Hostland Politics: Politicized Ethnic Identity among Middle Eastern Heritage Groups in the United States." *International Migration Review* 42: 273–302.

Wald, Kenneth D., James Button, and Barbara Rienzo. 1996. "The Politics of Gay Rights in American Communities: Explaining Antidiscrimination Ordinances and Policies." *American Journal of Political Science* 40: 1152–78.

———. 2001. "Morality Politics vs. Political Economy: The Case of School-Based Health Centers." *Social Science Quarterly* 82: 221–34.

Wald, Kenneth, and Graham Glover. 2007. "Theological Perspectives on Gay Unions: The Uneasy Marriage of Religion and Politics." In *The Politics of Same Sex Marriage*, ed. Craig Rimmerman and Clyde Wilcox, 105–30. Chicago: University of Chicago Press.

Wald, Kenneth, David Leege, and Lyman Kellstedt. 1993. "Church Involvement and Political Behavior." In *Rediscovering the Religious Factor in American Politics*, ed. Lyman Kellstedt and David Leege. Armonk, NY: Sharpe.

Wald, Kenneth D., and Michael Martinez. 2001. "Jewish Religiosity and Political Attitudes in the United States and Israel." *Political Behavior* 23: 377–97.

Wald, Kenneth D., Dennis E. Owen, and Samuel S. Hill. 1988. "Churches as Political Communities." *American Political Science Review* 82: 531–48.

———. 1989. "Habits of the Mind? The Problem of Authority in the New Christian Right." In *Religion and Political Behavior in the United States*, ed. Ted G. Jelen, 93–108. New York: Greenwood.

———. 1990. "Political Cohesion in Churches." *Journal of Politics* 52: 197–215.

Wald, Kenneth D., Adam Silverman, and Kevin Fridy. 2005. "Making Sense of Religion in Political Life." *Annual Review of Political Science* 8: 121–41.

Wald, Kenneth D., and Corwin E. Smidt. 1993. "Measurement Strategies in the Study of Religion and Politics." In *Rediscovering the Religious Factor in American Politics*, ed. David C. Leege and Lyman A. Kellstedt, 26–49. Armonk, NY: Sharpe.

Waldman, Steven. 2008. *Founding Faith: Providence, Politics, and the Birth of Religious Freedom in America*. New York: Random House.

Walker, Nathan C., and Edwin J. Greenlee, eds. 2011. *Whose God Rules? Is the United States a Secular Nation or a Theolegal Democracy?* New York: Palgrave Macmillan.

Wallace, Ruth. 1992. *They Call Her Pastor: A New Role for Catholic Women*. Albany: State University of New York Press.

Wallis, Jim. 1997. *Who Speaks for God? An Alternative to the Religious Right: A New Politics of Compassion, Community, and Civility*. New York: Delta.

———. 2005. *God's Politics: Why the Right Gets It Wrong and the Left Doesn't Get It*. New York: HarperCollins.

Wallis, Roy, and Steve Bruce. 1992. "Secularization: The Orthodox Model." In *Religion and Modernization*, ed. Steve Bruce, 8–30. Oxford: Oxford University Press.

Walsh, Andrew D. 2000. *Religion, Economics and Public Policy*. Westport, CT: Praeger.

Walsh, Arlene M. Sanchez. 2003. *El Espiritu Santo: Latino Pentecostal Identity: Evangelical Faith, Self and Society*. New York: Columbia University Press.

Waltman, Jerold L. 2011. *Religious Free Exercise and Contemporary American Politics: The Saga of the Religious Land Use and Institutionalized Persons Act of 2000*. New York: Continuum.

Walzer, Michael. 1985. *Exodus and Revolution*. New York: Basic Books.

Warner, R. Stephen. 1988. *New Wine in Old Wineskins: Evangelicals and Liberals in a Small-Town Church*. Berkeley: University of California Press.

Warren, Mark. 2001. *Dry Bones Rattling: Community Building to Revitalize American Democracy*. Princeton, NJ: Princeton University Press.

Watson, Justin. 1997. *Christian Coalition: Dreams of Restoration, Demands for Recognition*. New York: St. Martin's.

Way, H. Frank. 1968. "Survey Research on Judicial Decisions: The Prayer and Bible-Reading Cases." *Western Political Quarterly* 21: 189–205.

Way, Frank, and Barbara J. Burt. 1983. "Religious Marginality and the Free Exercise Clause." *American Political Science Review* 77: 652–65.

Weaver, Jillinda. 2008. "Civil Religion, George W. Bush's Divine Mission, and an Ethics of Mission." *Political Theology* 9: 9–26.

Webb, Clive. 1998. "Closing Ranks: Montgomery Jews and Civil Rights, 1954–1960." *Journal of American Studies* 463.

———. 2001. *Fight against Fear: Southern Jews and Black Civil Rights*. Athens: University of Georgia Press.

Weber, Christopher, and Matthew Thornton. 2012. "Courting Christians: How Political Candidates Prime Religious Consideration in Campaign Ads." *Journal of Politics* 74: 400–413.

Weber, Mary Cahil. 1983. "Religion and Conservative Social Attitudes." In *Views from the Pews: Christian Beliefs and Attitudes*, ed. Roger A. Johnson, 103–22. Philadelphia: Fortress.

Weber, Max. 1958 [1920]. *The Protestant Ethic and the Spirit of Capitalism*. New York: Scribner's.

Weber, Paul. 1982. "Examining the Religious Lobbies." *This World* 1: 97–107.

Weber, Paul, and Landis Jones. 1994. *US Religious Interest Groups: Institutional Profiles*. Westport, CT: Greenwood.

Weber, Paul, and T. L. Stanley. 1984. "The Power and Performance of Religious Interest Groups." *Quarterly Review* 4: 28–50.

Webster, Gerald, and Jonathan Leib. 2002. "Political Culture and the Confederate Battle Flag Debate in Alabama." *Journal of Cultural Geography* 20: 1–25.

Weeks, David L. 1998. "Carl F. H. Henry's Moral Arguments for Evangelical Political Activism." *Journal of Church and State* 40: 83–106.

Weisberg, Herbert. 2005. "The Structure and Effects of Moral Predisposition in American Politics." *Journal of Politics* 67: 646–68.

———. 2012. "Reconsidering Jewish Presidential Voting Statistics." *Contemporary Jewry* 32: 215–36.

Welch, Michael R., and David C. Leege. 1988. "Religious Predictors of Catholic Parishioners' Sociopolitical Attitudes: Devotional Style, Closeness to God, Imagery, and Agentic/Communal Religious Identity." *Journal for the Scientific Study of Religion* 27: 536–53.

———. 1991. "Dual Reference Groups and Political Orientations: An Examination of Evangelically Oriented Catholics." *American Journal of Political Science* 35: 28–56.

Welch, Michael R., David C. Leege, Kenneth D. Wald, and Lyman A. Kellstedt. 1993. "Are the Sheep Hearing the Shepherds? Cue Perceptions, Congregational Responses and Political Communication Processes." In *Rediscovering the Religious Factor in American Politics*, ed. David C. Leege and Lyman A. Kellstedt, 235–54. Armonk, NY: Sharpe.

Wenz, Peter. 1992. *Abortion Rights as Religious Freedom*. Philadelphia: Temple University Press.

West, Ellis M. 2011. *The Religion Clauses of the First Amendment: Guarantees of States' Rights?* Lanham, MD: Lexington Books.

West, Guida, and Rhoda Blumberg. 1990. "Reconstructing Social Protests from a Feminist Perspective." In *Women and Social Protest*, ed. Guida West and Rhoda Blumberg. New York: Oxford University Press.

White House Office of the Press Secretary. 1997. "Guidelines on Religious Exercise and Religious Expression in the Federal Workplace." Issued August 14.

White, John Kenneth. 1990. *The New Politics of Old Values*. Hanover, NH: University Press of New England.

White, Lynn, Jr. 1967. "The Historical Roots of Our Ecological Crisis." *Science* 155: 1203–7.

Wilcox, Clyde. 1987. "Religious Attitudes and Anti-Feminism: An Analysis of the Ohio Moral Majority." *Women and Politics* 7: 59–77.

———. 1989. "Evangelicals and the Moral Majority." *Journal for the Scientific Study of Religion* 28: 400–414.

———. 1992. *God's Warriors: The Christian Right in 20th Century America*. Baltimore: Johns Hopkins University Press.

———. 2005. "The Christian Right in American Politics: Conquering Force or Exploited Faction?" In *Understanding the "God Gap": Religion, Politics, and Policy in the United States and Germany*, 16–21. Washington, DC: American Institute for Contemporary German Studies, Johns Hopkins University Press.

Wilcox, Clyde. 2010. "The Christian Right and Civic Virtue." In *Religion and Democracy in the United States: Danger or Opportunity?*, ed. Alan Wolfe and Ira Katznelson, 176–211. Princeton, NJ: Princeton University Press.

Wilcox, Clyde, Paul Brewer, Shauna Shames, and Celinda Lake. 2007. "If I Bend This Far Will I Break? Public Opinion about Same-Sex Marriage." In *The Politics of Same-Sex Marriage*, ed. Craig Rimmerman and Clyde Wilcox, 215–42. Chicago: University of Chicago Press.

Wilcox, Clyde, and Elizabeth Cook. 1989. "Evangelical Women and Feminism: Some Additional Evidence." *Women and Politics* 9: 27–49.

Wilcox, Clyde, and Leopoldo Gomez. 1990. "Religion, Group Identification and Politics among Blacks." *Sociological Analysis* 51: 271–85.

Wilcox, Clyde, and Ted Jelen. 1990. "Evangelicals and Political Tolerance." *American Politics Quarterly* 18: 25–46.

Wilcox, Clyde, and Carin Larson. 2006. *Onward Christian Soldiers? The Religious Right in American Politics.* 3rd ed. Boulder, CO: Westview.

Wilcox, Clyde, and Barbara Norrander. 2002. "Of Moods and Morals: The Dynamics of Opinion on Abortion and Gay Rights." In *Understanding Public Opinion*, ed. Barbara Norrander and Clyde Wilcox, 121–47. 2nd ed. Washington, DC: CQ Press.

Wilcox, Clyde, and Lee Sigelman. 2001. "Political Mobilization in the Pews: Religious Contacting and Electoral Turnout." *Social Science Quarterly* 82: 524–35.

Wilcox, Clyde, Kenneth D. Wald, and Ted Jelen. 2008. "Religious Preference and Social Science: A Second Look." *Journal of Politics* 70: 874–79.

Wilcox, Clyde, and Robin Wolpert. 2000. "Gay Rights in the Public Sphere: Public Opinion on Gay and Lesbian Equality." In *The Politics of Gay Rights*, ed. Craig Rimmerman, Kenneth Wald, and Clyde Wilcox, 409–32. Chicago: University of Chicago Press.

Wilcox, Melissa. 2002. "When Sheila's a Lesbian: Religious Individualism among Lesbian, Gay, Bisexual and Transgender Christians." *Sociology of Religion* 63: 497–513.

———. 2003. *Coming Out in Christianity: Religion, Identity and Community.* Bloomington: Indiana University Press.

Wilcox, Sarah. 2003. "Cultural Context and Conventions of Science Journalism: Drama and Contractions in Media Coverage of Biological Ideas about Sexuality." *Critical Studies in Media Communication* 20: 225–48.

Wilcox, W. Bradford. 1998. "Conservative Protestant Childrearing: Authoritarian or Authoritative?" *American Sociological Review* 63: 796–809.

———. 2002. "Religion, Convention and Parental Involvement." *Journal of Marriage and Family* 64: 780–92.

Wildavsky, Aaron. 1987. "Choosing Preferences by Constructing Institutions: A Cultural Theory of Preference Formation." *American Political Science Review* 81: 3–21.

Williams, Delores. 1993. *Sisters in the Wilderness: The Challenge of Womanist-God Talk.* Maryknoll, NY: Orbis.

Williams, Johnny. 2002. "Linking Beliefs to Collective Action: Politicized Religious Beliefs and the Civil Rights Movement." *Sociological Forum* 17: 203–22.

Williams, Rhys H., ed. 1997. *Cultural Wars in American Politics: Critical Reviews of a Popular Myth.* New York: Aldine de Gruyter.

Williamsburg Charter Survey on Religion and Public Life. 1988. Washington, DC: The Williamsburg Charter Foundation.

Wills, Garry. 2007. *Head and Heart: A History of Christianity in America*. New York: Penguin Books.

Wilmore, Gayraud. 1983. *Black Religion and Black Radicalism*. Maryknoll, NY: Orbis.

———. 1998. *Black Religion and Black Radicalism: An Interpretation of the Religious History of African Americans*. Maryknoll, NY: Orbis.

Wilson, Bryan. 1966. *Religion in Secular Society*. Baltimore: Penguin.

Wilson, Catherine. 2008. *The Politics of the Latino Faith: Religion, Identity and Urban Community*. New York: New York University Press.

Wilson, Glenn D., and Christopher Bagley. 1973. "Religion, Racism, and Conservatism." In *The Psychology of Conservatism*, ed. Glenn Wilson, 117–28. New York: Academic Press.

Wilson, James Q. 1965. *Negro Politics: The Search for Leadership*. New York: Free Press.

———. 1973. *Political Organizations*. New York: Basic Books.

Wilson, John. 1978. *Religion in American Society: The Effective Presence*. Englewood Cliffs, NJ: Prentice Hall.

Wilson, John F., and Donald L. Drakeman, eds. 1987. *Church and State in American History*. Boston: Beacon.

Wilson, John K. 1990. "Religion under the State Constitutions, 1776–1800." *Journal of Church and State* 32: 753–73.

Wimberly, Ronald C. 1976. "Testing the Civil Religion Hypothesis." *Sociological Analysis* 37: 341–52.

———. 1979. "Continuity in the Measurement of Civil Religion." *Sociological Analysis* 40: 59–62.

Wineburg, Bob. 2000. *A Limited Partnership: The Politics of Religion, Welfare and Social Service*. New York: Columbia University Press.

———. 2007. *Faith-Based Inefficiency*. Santa Barbara, CA: Garland.

Winter, M. T., A. Lummis, and A. Stokes. 1994. *Defecting in Place: Women Claiming Responsibility for Their Own Spiritual Lives*. New York: Crossroads.

Witte, John, Jr. 1990. "How to Govern a City on a Hill: The Early Puritan Contribution to American Constitutionalism." *Emory Law Journal* 39: 41–64.

———. 1991. "The Theology and Politics of the First Amendment Religion Clauses: A Bicentennial Essay." *Emory Law Journal* 40: 489–507.

———. 2000. *Religion and the American Constitutional Experiment: Essential Rights and Liberties*. Boulder, CO: Westview.

Witten, Marsha G. 1993. *All Is Forgiven: The Secular Message in American Protestantism*. Princeton, NJ: Princeton University Press.

Wohlenberg, Ernest H. 1980. "Correlates of Equal Rights Amendment Ratification." *Social Science Quarterly* 60: 676–84.

Wolf, Donald J., ed. 1968. *Toward Consensus: Catholic-Protestant Interpretations of Church and State*. Garden City, NY: Doubleday-Anchor.

Wolfe, Alan. 1998. *One Nation, After All*. New York: Viking.

———. 2003. *The Transformation of American Religion*. New York: Free Press.

Wolin, Sheldon. 1956. "Politics and Religion: Luther's Simplistic Imperative." *American Political Science Review* 50: 24–42.

Wolkomir, Michelle, Michael Futreal, Eric Woodrum, and Thomas Hoban. 1995. "Conceptualizing Substantive Religious Beliefs and Environmentalism." Paper presented to the annual meeting to the Southern Sociological Society, Atlanta.

Wood, James R. 1981. *Leadership in Voluntary Organizations: The Controversy over Social Action in Protestant Churches*. New Brunswick, NJ: Rutgers University Press.

Wood, Michael, and Michael Hughes. 1984. "The Moral Basis of Moral Reform: Status Discontent vs. Cultural Socialization as Explanations of Anti-Pornography Social Movement Adherence." *American Sociological Review* 49: 86–99.

Wood, Richard. 1999. "Religious Culture and Political Action." *Sociological Theory* 17: 307–32.

———. 2002. *Faith in Action: Religion, Race and Democratic Organizing in America*. Chicago: University of Chicago Press.

———. 2005. "Fe y accion social: Hispanic Churches in Faith-Based Community Organizing." In *Latino Religions and Civic Activism in the United States*, ed. Gastón Espinosa, Virgilio Elizondo, and Jesse Miranda. New York: Oxford University Press.

Wood, Richard, Brad Fulton, and Kathryn Partridge. 2012. *Building Bridges, Building Power: Developments in Institution Based Community Organizing*. Denver, CO: Interfaith Funders.

Woodberry, Robert D. 1998. "When Surveys Lie and People Tell the Truth: How Surveys Oversample Church Attenders." *American Sociological Review* 63: 119–22.

———. 2012. "The Missionary Roots of Liberal Democracy." *American Political Science Review* 106: 244–74.

Woodberry, Robert D., and Christian S. Smith. 1998. "Fundamentalism et al.: Conservative Protestants in America." In *Annual Review of Sociology*, ed. John Hagan, 25–56. Palo Alto, CA: Annual Reviews.

Woodrum, Eric, and Beth L. Davison. 1992. "Reexamination of Religious Influences on Abortion Attitudes." *Review of Religious Research* 33: 229–43.

Woodrum, Eric, and Thomas Hoban. 1994. "Theology and Religiosity Effects on Environmentalism." *Review of Religious Research* 35: 193–206.

Woodward, Kenneth L. 1993. "Dead End for the Mainline?" *Newsweek*, August 9, 46–48.

Woodworth, Steven E. 2001. *While God Is Marching On: The Religious World of Civil War Soldiers*. Lawrence: University Press of Kansas.

World Bank. 2012. *World Development Report 2012: Gender Equality and Development*. Washington, DC: World Bank.

Wright, Benjamin F. 1949. "The Federalist on the Nature of Political Man." *Ethics* 59: 1–31.

Wright, Stuart A. 2007. *Patriots, Politics and the Oklahoma City Bombing*. New York: Cambridge University Press.

Wuthnow, Robert. 1983. "The Political Rebirth of American Evangelicals." In *The New Christian Right*, ed. Robert C. Liebman and Robert Wuthnow, 168–87. New York: Aldine.

———. 1987. *Meaning and the Moral Order: Explanations in Cultural Analysis*. Berkeley: University of California Press.

———. 1988. *The Restructuring of American Religion*. Princeton, NJ: Princeton University Press.

———. 1998. *After Heaven: Spirituality in America since the 1950s*. Berkeley: University of California Press.

————. 2004. *Saving America? Faith-Based Services and the Future of Civil Society.* Princeton, NJ: Princeton University Press.

Wuthnow, Robert, and Wendy Cadge. 2004. "Buddhists and Buddhism in the United States: The Scope of Influence." *Journal for the Scientific Study of Religion* 43: 363–80.

Wuthnow, Robert, and John Evans, eds. 2002. *The Quiet Hand of God: Faith-Based Activism and the Public Role of Mainline Protestantism.* Berkeley: University of California Press.

Wuthnow, Robert, Conrad Hackett, and Becky Yang Hsu. 2004. "The Effectiveness and Trustworthiness of Faith-Based and Other Service Organizations: A Study of Recipients' Perceptions." *Journal for the Scientific Study of Religion* 43: 1–17.

Wybraniec, John, and Roger Finke. 2001. "Religious Regulation and the Courts: The Judiciary's Changing Role in Protecting Minority Religions from Majoritarian Rule." *Journal for the Scientific Study of Religion* 40: 427–44.

Yamane, David. 2000. "Naked Public Square or Crumbling Wall of Separation? Evidence from Legislative Hearings in Wisconsin." *Review of Religious Research* 42: 175–92.

Yamane, David, and Elizabeth Oldmixon. 2006. "Religion in the Legislative Arena: Affiliation, Salience, Advocacy and Public Policy Making." *Legislative Studies Quarterly* 31: 433–60.

Yang, Alan. 1997. "The Polls: Attitudes toward Homosexuality." *Public Opinion Quarterly* 61: 477–507.

Yarnold, Barbara. 2000. "Did Circuit Court of Appeals Judges Overcome Their Own Religions in Cases Involving Religious Liberties? 1970–1990." *Review of Religious Research* 42: 79–86.

Zald, Mayer. 1970. *Organizational Change: The Political Economy of the YMCA.* Chicago: University of Chicago Press.

Zald, Mayer N., and John McCarthy. 1979. *Dynamics of Social Movements.* Cambridge, MA: Winthrop.

————, eds. 1987. *Social Movements in an Organizational Society.* New Brunswick, NJ: Transaction.

Zaller, John. 1992. *The Nature and Origins of Mass Opinion.* New York: Cambridge University Press.

Zikmund, Barbara Brown, Adair Lummis, and Patricia M. Y. Chang. 1998. *Clergy Women: An Uphill Calling.* Louisville, KY: Westminster/Knox.

Zucker, Gail Sahar. 1999. "Attributional and Symbolic Predictors of Abortion Attitudes." *Journal of Applied Social Psychology* 29: 1218–45.

Zwier, Robert. 1988. "The World and the Worldview of Religious Lobbyists." Paper presented to the annual meeting of the Midwest Political Science Association, Chicago.

————. 1994. "An Organizational Perspective on Religious Interest Groups." In *Christian Political Activism at the Crossroads*, ed. William Stevenson, 95–119. Lanham, MD: University Press of America.

Index

Abington School District v. Schempp, 82t, 89, 102
abortion: African American Protestants and, 285; Catholics and, 244, 252–63; Congress and, 159; evangelical Protestants and, 228; institutional context and, 149–50; Latinos and, 295; and political system, 363–64; protests on, 154; public opinion on, 191–93, 192t, 193t; religious influence on, 166–67; women's rights movement and, 323–25
Abramoff, Jack, 143, 240
abstinence-only curricula, 90
accommodationism, 85, 86, 86t, 87; era of, 95–100
ACLU. See American Civil Liberties Union
activism, 133–39; female clergy and, 330; mainline Protestants and, 267–70; and tolerance, 362; women and, 319–21, 323
Acuna, Rodolfo, 291
Adams, John, 51, 72, 73
Adams, Samuel, 76
ADL. See Anti-Defamation League

adoption, by gay couples, public opinion on, 195, 195f
affirmative action, 205–6; Jews and, 272–73
Affordable Care Act, 2; Catholics and, 261–62; faith-based organizing and, 139; institutional interests and, 127; lobbying and, 134; social justice concerns and, 170; Supreme Court and, 106
African Americans: and Carter, 212; and Israel, 388n12; and Jews, 271–73; women, 289, 320, 329, 331
African American Catholics, 146–47, 290
African American Mormons, 309
African American Muslims, 298
African American Protestants, 280–90; and abortion, 192, 192t–193t; and Christian Right, 232; and economic issues, 186f–187f; educational levels of, 115, 116f; and gay rights, 194f, 195t; and gender issues, 191f, 329; group status and, 115; and Iraq War, 201f; and party identification, 117f, 286; political tendencies of, 33, 35t; prevalence of, 28, 28f; and

463

About the Authors

Allison Calhoun-Brown is associate professor of political science at Georgia State University in Atlanta. Her research focuses on religion and politics in the African American community with a special interest in how religious beliefs and associations affect individual political attitudes and capacity. She has published extensively on these topics. She is currently working on a project that examines the relationship between religion and ideological perspectives among African Americans.

Kenneth D. Wald is distinguished professor of political science at the University of Florida, where he has taught since 1983. In addition to the first four editions of this book and numerous journal articles and book chapters, he is the coauthor of *The Politics of Cultural Differences* and *Private Lives, Public Conflicts: Battles over Gay Rights in American Communities*. Wald coedits a series, "Religion, Politics and Social Theory," for Cambridge University Press. He is currently conducting research on Judaism and politics.